Our Job is to Make Life Worth Living (1949–50)

Eric Arthur Blair – better known as George Orwell – was born on 25 June 1903 in Bengal. He was educated at Eton and then served with the Indian Imperial Police in Burma. He lived in Paris for two years, and then returned to England where he worked as a private tutor, schoolteacher and bookshop assistant. He fought on the Republican side in the Spanish Civil War and was wounded in the throat. During the Second World War he served as Talks Producer for the Indian Service of the BBC and then joined *Tribune* as its literary editor. He died in London in January 1950.

Dr. Peter Davison is Professor of English and Media at De Montfort University, Leicester. He has written and edited fifteen books as well as the Facsimile Edition of the Manuscript of *Nineteen Eighty-Four* and the twenty volumes of Orwell's *Complete Works*. From 1992 to 1994 he was President of the Bibliographical Society, whose journal he edited for twelve years. From 1961 Ian Angus was Deputy Librarian and Keeper of the Orwell Archive at University College, London, and from 1975 Librarian of King's College, London. With Sonia Orwell he co-edited the *Collected Essays, Journalism and Letters of George Orwell* (4 vols., 1986). Since early retirement in 1982 he has divided his time equally between assisting in the editing of this edition and growing olives in Italy.
Sheila Davison was a teacher until she retired, for some time teaching the deaf. She checked and proofread all twenty volumes of the complete edition and assisted with the research and indexing.

Down and Out in Paris and London
Burmese Days
A Clergyman's Daughter
Keep the Aspidistra Flying
The Road to Wigan Pier
Homage to Catalonia
Coming Up for Air
Animal Farm
Nineteen Eighty-Four
A Kind of Compulsion (1903-36)
Facing Unpleasant Facts (1937-39)
A Patriot After All (1940-41)
All Propaganda is Lies (1941-42)
Keeping Our Little Corner Clean (1942-43)
Two Wasted Years (1943)
I Have Tried to Tell the Truth (1943-44)
I Belong to the Left (1945)
Smothered Under Journalism (1946)
It is What I Think (1947-48)
Our Job is to Make Life Worth Living (1949-50)

Also by Peter Davison

Books: *Songs of the British Music Hall: A Critical Study; Popular Appeal in English Drama to 1850; Contemporary Drama and the Popular Dramatic Tradition; Hamlet: Text and Performance; Henry V: Masterguide; Othello: The Critical Debate; Orwell: A Literary Life*

Editions: Anonymous: *The Fair Maid of the Exchange* (with Arthur Brown); Shakespeare: *Richard II;* Shakespeare: *The Merchant of Venice;* Shakespeare: *1 Henry IV;* Shakespeare: *2 Henry IV;* Shakespeare: *The First Quarto of King Richard III;* Marston: *The Dutch Courtesan; Facsimile of the Manuscript of Nineteen Eighty-Four; Sheridan: A Casebook; The Book Encompassed: Studies in Twentieth-Century Bibliography*

Series: *Theatrum Redivivum* 17 Volumes (with James Binns); *Literary Taste, Culture, and Mass Communication* 14 Volumes (with Edward Shils and Rolf Meyersohn)

Academic Journals: *ALTA: University of Birmingham Review,* 1966-70; *The Library: Transactions of the Bibliographical Society,* 1971-82

Publication of *The Complete Works of George Orwell* is a unique
bibliographic event as well as a major step in Orwell
scholarship. Meticulous textual research by
Dr Peter Davison has revealed that all the current editions
of Orwell have been mutilated to a greater or lesser extent.
This authoritative edition incorporates in Volumes 10–20
all Orwell's known essays, poems, plays, letters, journalism,
broadcasts, and diaries, and also letters by his wife, Eileen,
and members of his family. In addition there are very many of
the letters in newspapers and magazines of readers' reactions
to Orwell's articles and reviews. Where the hands of others
have intervened, Orwell's original intentions have been restored.

Our Job is to Make Life Worth Living

1949–50

GEORGE ORWELL

Edited by Peter Davison
Assisted by Ian Angus and Sheila Davison

SECKER & WARBURG

———

LONDON

Revised and updated edition published by Secker & Warburg 2002

2 4 6 8 10 9 7 5 3

First published in Great Britain in 1998 by
Secker & Warburg
Random House, 20 Vauxhall Bridge Road,
London SW1V 2SA

Addresses for companies within The Random House Group Limited
can be found at: www.randomhouse.co.uk/offices.htm

The Random House Group Limited Reg. No. 954009
www.randomhouse.co.uk

A CIP catalogue record for this book
is available from the British Library

ISBN 978 0 436 21009 9

The Random House Group Limited supports The Forest Stewardship
Council (FSC®), the leading international forest certification organisation.
Our books carrying the FSC label are printed on FSC® certified paper.
FSC is the only forest certification scheme endorsed by the leading
environmental organisations, including Greenpeace. Our
paper procurement policy can be found at
www.randomhouse.co.uk/environment

Typeset in Monophoto Bembo by
Deltatype Limited, Birkenhead, Merseyside
Printed and bound in Great Britain by Clays Ltd, St Ives PLC

CONTENTS

Titles may be modified and shortened

Contents

Contents

Contents

INTRODUCTION to VOLUME XX

1949–1950: *Our Job is to Make Life Worth Living*

As from time to time these volumes show, among Orwell's most attractive characteristics were his willingness to admit his mistakes, to apologise, and to modify his opinions in the light of criticism. Although he never found Gandhi wholly convincing, in 'Reflections on Gandhi', published in January 1949 (*3516*), he modified the strictures made in his review of Lionel Fielden's *Beggar My Neighbour* in 1943 (*2257*), partly as a result of its author's response (*2258*), but more especially because of the letters he received from the pacifist, Roy Walker (*2372*). It is ironic, especially in view of Orwell's battle against censorship and 'garbling', as he termed it, that the Government's Central Office of Information published a version of this essay, 'Gandhi: a critical study', in *Mirror*, a periodical it distributed in Asia. The cuts it made, garbling what Orwell actually said, are given in the notes to *3516* (see pp. 10–12). It is in this essay that Orwell wrote, 'our job is to make life worth living on this earth, which is the only earth we have' (p. 7). Another kind of 'garbling' arose in the last letter traced from Orwell's agent, Leonard Moore (22 November 1949, *3710*). With this was a list of cuts proposed for an Argentine edition of *Nineteen Eighty-Four*. Edition Kraft feared that, as it stood, it would be banned and wished to cut about 140 lines thought to represent sexual relationships too realistically. The book had a 'basic philosophy . . . aimed directly against some of the most powerful movements of our time' and it was feared that an excuse might be sought to have the book withdrawn on 'moral' grounds. The cuts required are listed on pp. 180–82.

From 6 January until 3 September Orwell was a patient at the Cotswold Sanatorium, Cranham; from there he was transferred to University College Hospital on 3 September 1949. He took pains to ensure that, were he not well enough, Sir Richard Rees, his literary executor, would read the proofs of *Nineteen Eighty-Four* (*3536*), but he did manage a little work including the reading of the proofs of English and U.S. editions of the novel. He found the strength to instruct Roger Senhouse, a director of Secker & Warburg, in the niceties distinguishing 'on to' from 'onto' (*3557*) and to require the U.S. publishers to restore the metric measurements in the novel (*3566*; the Americans had altered them to feet and inches, etc., assuming that the metric system was already in operation in England); he found considerable energy to demand that the American publishers restore a very large section of Goldstein's book, which they proposed to abridge (*3575*), and to have Warburg issue a clarification of the 'meaning' of *Nineteen Eighty-Four* for the U.S.A., in particular that, 'being after all a parody' it was not a forecast of what would happen, and stressing his socialist credentials (*3646*; this also sets out the different versions of the clarification published in the States).

Orwell wrote five reviews. These included reviews of F. R. Leavis's *The Great Tradition* (*3543*), Winston Churchill's *Their Finest Hour* (*3624*, written for the persistent New York *New Leader*), and of Hesketh Pearson's biography of Dickens (*3625*), his very last review to be published of the 379 (of some seven hundred books) he wrote. He also wrote a plea for clemency for a Spanish Republican prisoner sentenced to death in Spain (*3558*, and see *3685*) and a defence of the award of the Bollingen Prize to Ezra Pound (*3612*). He began, but did not finish, an article on Evelyn Waugh (*3585*), drafted notes for a poem (see pp. 210–11), and sketched out a long short-story, 'A Smoking- room Story' (*3722–23* with conjectural fair copy, *3724*). To the last, he hoped to travel to Switzerland to aid his recovery. And he was still being importuned to write more.

The volume includes Dr Morland's report on Orwell at Cranham (*3635*) and Warburg's telling report on his visit there (*3645*). The letters and reports associated with the Foreign Office's Information Research Department are reproduced with very full annotations and explanations ((*3590A, 3590B,* and *3615*; see *3732* for Orwell's list of crypto-communists and fellow-travellers). There are many previously unpublished letters, some responding to such old friends as Brenda Salkeld, Lydia Jackson, Mamaine Koestler, Julian Symons, Tosco Fyvel, Anthony Powell, and, of course, David Astor, who showed Orwell great kindness over several years. Some brought touching echoes of the past, in particular of his childhood friend, Jacintha Buddicom whom he had not seen since he went to Burma (and, indeed, did not see even in 1949; see *3550, 3551,* and *3631*). Other voices from the past included one of his platoon from Spain, John Braithwaite (*3703*); the West Indian writer, Una Marson, with whom he had worked at the BBC (*3587*); and an especially cheerful letter from Nancy Parratt, one of the BBC secretaries, enclosing a photograph (*3713*). There is also Sonia Orwell's letter to Yvonne Davet explaining that Orwell was too ill to write himself but sending her his hope that her translation of *Homage to Catalonia* 'paraître enfin' (*3716*): it did—five years after Orwell had died. Among many friends who came to visit him were colleagues from his Home Guard platoon (see *3590B*). The letters show an enormous fund of love and friendship for Orwell.

Orwell married Sonia Brownell on 13 October 1949. One of the letters that has very recently been discovered (*3695A*) warmly congratulates Orwell and expresses very great admiration for Sonia. In Appendix 13, 'After Orwell's Death', is included a short memoir on Sonia by Ian Angus (pp. 307–09). Another memoir in the appendixes is that by Mrs. Miranda Wood (*3735*), who stayed in Orwell's flat in Canonbury for two summers whilst he was in Jura and who typed for him there.

The volume concludes with a dozen more appendixes. These print all work in progress; a statement of Orwell's assets (the amounts he had lent friends, given on p. 218, are a good indication of his generous nature, especially when converted into today's values); a list of 144 books he read in 1949; Orwell's will and final instructions for his literary executors; the names in his address book; those he considered cryptos or fellow-travellers; a list of books he owned and another of his pamphlet collection (with a long

xvi

explanatory note); and letters that have been discovered after page-proof correction had been completed.

A full General Introduction will be found in the preliminaries to Volume X

ACKNOWLEDGEMENTS and PROVENANCES

specific to Volume XX

The editor wishes to express his gratitude to the following institutions and libraries, their trustees, curators, and staffs for their co-operation and valuable help, for making copies of Orwell material available, and for allowing it to be reproduced: Collection of American Literature, Beinecke Rare Book and Manuscript Library, Yale University; Henry W. and Albert A. Berg Collection, New York Public Library; Arthur Koestler Archive, Special Collections, Edinburgh University Library; Houghton Library, Harvard University; Elisaveta Fen (Lydia Jackson) papers, Leeds Russian Archive, Brotherton Library, University of Leeds; Jack Common papers, University of Newcastle upon Tyne Library; National Museum of Labour History, Manchester; Public Record Office; Secker & Warburg Archive, Reading University Library; Harry Ransom Humanities Research Center, University of Texas at Austin; Dwight Macdonald papers, Manuscripts and Archives, Yale University Library; and the Library of University College London for material in the Orwell Archive.

Gratitude is expressed to Harcourt, Brace and Company and Martin Secker & Warburg Ltd for making available their material relating to Orwell and for permitting it to be published.

Thanks are due to Rosemary Davidson, Guy Gadney and Steven E. Schier for making available letters by Orwell in their possession. I am also deeply indebted to those whose letters by Orwell are available because they donated them or presented copies of them to the Orwell Archive: the Hon David Astor (Editor of *The Observer*), Jacintha Buddicom, Emilio Cecchi, Charles Curran, Yvonne Davet, Tosco Fyvel, Celia Goodman, Harcourt, Brace and Company, Arthur Koestler and his Literary Executor, Robert L. Morris, Melvin Lasky, S. M. Levitas (Editor of *The New Leader* (New York)); Dwight Macdonald, Michael Meyer, William Phillips and Philip Rahv (Editors of *Partisan Review*), Anthony Powell, Sir Richard Rees, Vernon Richards, Brenda Salkeld, Gleb Struve, Julian Symons, George Woodcock, and Fredrik Wulfsberg; and Herbert Read (through Howard Fink) and Vernon Richards for making available to the Orwell Archive copies of the papers of the Freedom Defence Committee. Thanks must also be expressed to Bernard Crick and Michael Shelden through whom many Orwell letters published in these volumes were made available to the Orwell Archive.

I am grateful to the following publications for permission to reproduce material which first appeared in their pages: *Freedom*, *The New Leader* (New York), *The Observer*, *Partisan Review* and *Tribune*.

I would like to thank the following for granting me permission to use material whose copyright they own: the Hon David Astor to quote from letters by him to Orwell; Guinever Buddicom and Dione Venables to quote from *Eric and Us* by Jacintha Buddicom; Mary Fyvel to quote from a letter by Tosco Fyvel to Miss Goalby; The Controller of Her Majesty's Stationary Office to publish materials in items 3590A and 3590B which are at the Public Record Office; Denzil Jacobs to reprint the letter by him to *The Evening Standard*; Robert L. Morris to quote from letters by Arthur Koestler to Orwell; and Mary Struve to quote from two letters by Gleb Struve to Orwell and one to Fredric Warburg.

For their help and valuable information many thanks are due to Stephen Bird, George and Rita Blocke, Richard D. Davies, Denzil Jacobs, Douglas Moyle and Miranda Wood. My gratitude must also be expressed to the following who provided information about Sonia Orwell: Richard Blair, Sir William Coldstream, Michael Dixon, Anne Dunn, Peter Frank, Celia Goodman, Sir Lawrence Gowing, Vanessa Parker, Janetta Parladé, Lady Antonia Pinter, Sir Stephen and Lady Spender, John and Hilary Spurling, David Sylvester, Lord Weidenfeld, Diana Witherby and Francis Wyndham.

My thanks are also due to Janet Percival, Marina Warner and Ian Willison for their translations.

A number of individual acknowledgements are made in foot and headnotes to those who have provided information in books or verbally that I have quoted or referred to.

The editor and publishers have made every effort to trace copyright holders of the material published in this volume, but in some cases this has not proved possible. The publishers therefore wish to apologise to the authors or copyright holders of any material which has been reproduced without permission and due acknowledgement.

PROVENANCES

The locations of letters and documents printed in this volume are indicated against their item numbers in the list given below. However, letters and documents which are not listed below should be taken as being available for consultation in the Orwell Archive, University College London, either as originals or in the form of copies. Sonia Orwell gave all the Orwell papers then in her possession to the Orwell Archive at its foundation in 1960. Many friends, relations and associates of Orwell have given their Orwell letters or copies of them to the Orwell Archive. Materials in the Orwell Archive are only indicated in the location list where there are letters or documents at an item which come from more than one source, e.g. 3524 OA, Reading.

KEY TO LOCATIONS

Beinecke   Yale Collection of American Literature, Beinecke Rare Book and Manuscript Library, Yale University

Berg   Henry W. and Albert A. Berg Collection, The New York Public Library, Astor, Lenox and Tilden Foundations

Davidson   Rosemary Davidson

Edinburgh   Arthur Koestler Archive, Special Collections, Edinburgh University Library

Gadney   Guy Gadney

Houghton   Houghton Library, Harvard University

Leeds   Elisaveta Fen (Lydia Jackson) papers, Leeds Russian Archive, Brotherton Library, University of Leeds

Newcastle   Jack Common papers, University of Newcastle upon Tyne Library

NMLH   National Museum of Labour History, Manchester

OA   Orwell Archive (including the Freedom Defence Committee papers), University College London Library

PRO   Public Record Office

Reading   Secker & Warburg Archive, Reading University Library

Schier   Steven E. Schier

Texas   Harry Ransom Humanities Research Center, University of Texas at Austin

Yale   Dwight Macdonald papers, Manuscripts and Archives, Yale University Library

3518A Davidson	3602A Davidson	3670 Berg
3524 OA, Reading	3603 Houghton	3671 Berg
3525 Berg	3605 Berg	3673 Yale
3533 Berg	3608 Berg	3675 Berg
3534 Berg	3609 Berg	3676 Berg
3535 Yale	3610 Yale	3677 Berg
3538 Berg	3611 Berg	3683 Berg
3541 Berg	3637 Berg	3689 Berg
3544 Berg	3644A Davidson	3694 Berg
3546 Berg	3647 Berg	3697 Berg
3547 Berg	3648 Berg	3700 Berg
3553 Texas	3650 Gadney	3707 Berg
3556 Berg	3651 Berg	3714 Beinecke
3561 Berg	3652A Davidson	
3566 Berg	3655 Berg	413A NMLH
3571 Berg	3657 Berg	414B NMLH
3572 Berg	3659 Houghton	2305A Leeds
3573 Berg	3662 Berg, OA	2317A Leeds
3575 Berg	3663 Berg	2341A Leeds
3580 Berg	3665 Berg	2349A Leeds
3581 Berg	3666 Newcastle	2470A Edinburgh
3583 OA, Reading	3668 Berg	2502A Edinburgh

Acknowledgements and Provenances

2563A Edinburgh   3288A Edinburgh   3681A Edinburgh
2765A Edinburgh   3590A PRO   3684A Edinburgh
3025A Edinburgh   3590B PRO   3695A Edinburgh
          3696A Schier

Editorial Note

THE CONTENTS are, in the main, arranged in chronological order of Orwell's writing. Letters arising from his articles or reviews are usually grouped immediately after that item and Orwell's replies to those letters follow thereon. If there is a long delay between when it is known an article or essay was completed and its publication, it is printed at the date of completion. If items are printed much earlier in the chronological sequence than their date of publication, a cross-reference is given at the date of publication. All entries, whether written by Orwell or anyone else, including lengthy notes and cross-references, are given an item number. Because the printing of the edition has taken place over seven years, some letters came to light after the initial editing and the numbering of items had been completed. These items (or those that had in consequence to be repositioned) are given a letter after the number: e.g., *335A*. Some items included after printing and page-proofing had been completed are given in a final appendix to Volume XX and two (received by the editor in mid January 1997) in the Introduction to Volume XV. Numbers preceding item titles are in roman; when referred to in notes they are italicised.

The provenance of items is given in the preliminaries to each volume. Every item that requires explanation about its source or date, or about textual problems it may pose, is provided with such an explanation. Some articles and broadcasts exist in more than one version. The basis upon which they have been edited is explained and lists of variant readings provided. No Procrustean bed has been devised into which such items must be constrained; individual circumstances have been taken into account and editorial practice explained.

Although this is not what is called a 'diplomatic edition'—that is, one that represents the original precisely even in all its deformities to the point of reproducing a letter set upside down—the fundamental approach in presenting these texts has been to interfere with them as little as possible consistent with the removal of deformities and typographic errors. Orwell took great pains over the writing of his books: the facsimile edition of *Nineteen Eighty-Four*[1] shows that, but in order to meet the demands of broadcasting and publication schedules he often wrote fast and under great pressure. The speed with which he sometimes wrote meant that what he produced was not always what he would have wished to have published had he had time to revise. And, of course, as with any printing, errors can be introduced by those setting the type. It would be easy in places to surmise what Orwell would have done but I have only made changes where there would otherwise have been confusion. Obvious spelling mistakes, which could well be the compositor's or typist's (and the typist might be Orwell), have been corrected silently, but if there is any doubt, a footnote has drawn attention to the problem.

In brief, therefore, I have tried to present what Orwell wrote in his manuscripts and typescripts, not what I thought he should have written; and what he was represented as having written and not what I think should have been typed or printed on his behalf. This is not a 'warts and all' approach because gross errors are amended, significant changes noted, and textual complexities are discussed in preliminary notes. The aim is to bring Orwell, not the editor's version of Orwell, to the fore. Although textual issues are given due weight, an attempt has been made to produce an attractive, readable text.

The setting of this edition has been directly from xeroxes of original letters (if typed), typed copies of manuscript (prepared by one or other of the editors), surviving scripts for broadcasts, and xeroxes of essays, articles, and reviews as originally published (unless a headnote states otherwise). For *The Collected Essays, Journalism and Letters of George Orwell* a 1968 house style was adopted but for this edition, no attempt has been made to impose a late twentieth-century house style on the very different styles used by journals and editors of fifty to eighty years ago. Texts are therefore reproduced in the style given them in the journals from which they are reprinted. To 'correct' might well cause even more confusion as to what was and was not Orwell's: see below regarding paragraphing. Nevertheless, although it is not possible *to know*, one may sometimes hazard a guess at what underlies a printed text. Thus, I believe that most often when 'address' and 'aggression' are printed, Orwell typed or wrote 'adress' (especially until about the outbreak of World War II) and 'agression.' Although American spellings (such as 'Labor') have been retained in articles published in the United States, on very rare occasions, if I could be certain that a form of a word had been printed that Orwell would not have used—such as the American 'accommodations'—I have changed it to the form he would have used: 'accommodation'. Some variations, especially of proper names, have been accepted even if they look incongruous; so, 'Chiang Kai-Shek' as part of a book title but 'Chiang Kai-shek' throughout the text that follows.

Hyphenation presents tricky problems, especially when the first part of a word appears at the end of a line. Examples can be found in the originals of, for example, 'the middle-class,' 'the middle class', and 'the middleclass.' What should one do when a line ends with 'middle-'? Is it 'fore-deck' or 'foredeck'? If 'fore-' appears at the end of a line of the copy being reproduced, should the word be hyphenated or not? *OED* 1991 still hyphenates; Chambers in 1972 spelt it as one word. Where it would help (and it does not include every problem word), the ninth edition of F. Howard Collins, *Authors' & Printers' Dictionary*, Oxford University Press, 1946 (an edition appropriate to the mature Orwell) has been drawn upon. But Collins does not include fore-deck/foredeck. On a number of occasions Orwell's letters, or the text itself, is either obscure or wrong. In order to avoid the irritating repetition of *sic*, a small degree sign has been placed above the line at the doubtful point (°). It is hoped that this will be clear but inconspicuous. It is not usually repeated to mark a repetition of that characteristic in the same item. Orwell was sparing in his use of the question-mark in his letters; his practice has in the main been followed.

Paragraphing presents intractable problems. Orwell tended to write in long paragraphs. Indeed, it is possible to show from the use of many short paragraphs that News Review scripts so written are not by Orwell. The key example is News Review, 30, 11 July 1942 (1267), for which there is also external evidence that this is not by Orwell. This has twenty-one paragraphs as compared to eight in the script for the following week. It so happens that we know that Orwell was not at the BBC for two weeks before the 11 July nor on that day: he was on holiday, fishing at Callow End, Worcestershire (and on that day caught a single dace). But though paragraph length is helpful in such instances in identifying Orwell's work, that is not always so. It is of no use when considering his articles published in Paris in 1928–29 nor those he wrote for the *Manchester Evening News*. These tend to have extremely short paragraphs—sometimes paragraphs of only a line or two, splitting the sense illogically. A good example is the series of reviews published on 2 November 1944 (2572) where a two-line paragraph about Trollope's *The Small House at Allington* should clearly be part of the preceding four-line paragraph, both relating the books discussed to Barchester; see also 2463, n. 2 and 2608, n. 4. There is no question but that this is the work of sub-editors. It would often be possible to make a reasonable stab at paragraphing more intelligently, but, as with verbal clarification, the result might be the more confusing as to what really was Orwell's work and what this editor's. It has been thought better to leave the house-styles as they are, even if it is plain that it is not Orwell's style, rather than pass off changes as if the edited concoction represented Orwell's work.

Usually it is fairly certain that titles of essays are Orwell's but it is not always possible to know whether titles of articles are his. Reviews were also frequently given titles. Orwell's own typescript for his review of Harold Laski's *Faith, Reason and Civilisation* (2309), which survived because rejected by the *Manchester Evening News*, has neither heading (other than the name of the author and title of the book being reviewed), nor sub-headings. That would seem to be his style. In nearly every case titles of reviews and groups of letters, and cross-heads inserted by sub-editors, have been cut out. Occasionally such a title is kept if it is an aid to clarity but it is never placed within quotation marks. Other than for his BBC broadcasts (where Orwell's authorship is clear unless stated otherwise), titles are placed within single quotation marks if it is fairly certain that they are Orwell's.

Telegrams and cables are printed in small capitals. Quite often articles and reviews have passages in capitals. These look unsightly and, in the main, they have been reduced to small capitals. The exceptions are where the typography makes a point, as in the sound of an explosion: BOOM! Orwell sometimes abbreviated words. He always wrote an ampersand for 'and' and there are various abbreviated forms for such words as 'about'. It is not always plain just what letters make up abbreviations (and this sometimes applies to his signatures) and these have regularly been spelt out with the exception of the ampersand for 'and'. This serves as a reminder that the original is handwritten. Orwell often shortened some words and abbreviations in his own way, e.g., Gov.t, Sup.ts (Superintendents), NB. and N.W (each with a single stop), and ie.; these forms have been retained. In order that the diaries should readily be apparent for what they are, they have been set in sloped roman (rather than italic, long passages of which can be tiring to the eye), with roman for textual variations. Square and half square brackets are used to differentiate sources for the diaries (see, for example, the headnote to War-Time Diary II, *1025*) and for what was written and actually broadcast (see, for example, Orwell's adaptation of Ignazio Silone's *The Fox, 2270*). Particular usages are explained in headnotes to broadcasts etc., and before the first entries of diaries and notebooks.

Orwell usually dated his letters but there are exceptions and sometimes he (and Eileen) give only the day of the week. Where a date has to be guessed it is placed within square brackets and a justification for the dating is given. If Orwell simply signs a letter, the name he used is given without comment. If he signs over a typed version of his name, or initials a copy of a letter, what he signed or initialled is given over the typed version. There has been some slight regularisation of his initialling of letters. If he omitted the final stop after 'E. A. B', no stop is added (and, as here, editorial punctuation *follows* the final quotation mark instead of being inside it). Sometimes Orwell placed the stops midway up the letters: 'E·A·B'; this has been regularised to 'E. A. B'.

Wherever changes are made in a text that can be deemed to be even slightly significant the alteration is either placed within square brackets (for example, an obviously missing word) or the alteration is footnoted. Attention should be drawn to one particular category of change. Orwell had a remarkably good memory. He quoted not only poetry but prose from memory. Mulk Raj Anand has said that, at the BBC, Orwell could, and would, quote lengthy passages from the Book of Common Prayer.[2] As so often with people with this gift, the quotation is not always exact. If what Orwell argues depends precisely upon what he is quoting, the quotation is not corrected if it is inaccurate but a footnote gives the correct reading. If his argument does not depend upon the words actually quoted, the quotation is corrected and a footnote records that.

So far as possible, I have endeavoured to footnote everything that might puzzle a reader at the risk of annoying some readers by seeming to annotate too readily and too frequently what is known to them. I have, therefore, tried to identify all references to people, events, books, and institutions. However, I have not been so presumptuous as to attempt to rewrite the history of this century and, in the main, have relied upon a small number of easily accessible histories. Thus, for the Spanish Civil War I have referred in the main to *The Spanish Civil War* by Hugh Thomas; and for the Second World War, to Winston Churchill's and Liddell Hart's histories. The former has useful and conveniently available documents, and the latter was by a historian with whom Orwell corresponded. They were both his contemporaries and he reviewed the work of both men. These have been checked for factual information from more recent sources, one by Continental historians deliberately chosen as an aid to objectivity in an edition that will have world-wide circulation. It is assumed that readers with a particular interest in World War II will draw on their own knowledge and sources and the annotation is relatively light in providing such background information. Similarly, biographical details are, paradoxically, relatively modest for people as well known as T. S. Eliot and E. M. Forster, but far fuller for those who are significant to Orwell but less well known and about whom information is harder to track down, for example, George(s) Kopp, Joseph Czapski, and Victor Serge. It is tricky judging how often biographical and explicatory information should be reproduced. I have assumed most people will not want more than one volume at a time before them and so have repeated myself (often in shortened form with cross-references to fuller notes) more, perhaps, than is strictly necessary. Whilst I would claim that I have made every attempt not to mislead, it is important that historical and biographical information be checked if a detail is significant to a scholar's argument. History, as Orwell was quick to show, is not a matter of simple, indisputable fact. In annotating I have tried not to be contentious nor to direct the reader unfairly, but annotation cannot be wholly impartial.[3]

Each opening is dated. These dates, though drawn from the printed matter, are not necessarily those of the text reproduced on the page on which a date appears. The dates, known or calculated of letters, articles, broadcasts, diaries, etc., will correspond with the running-head date, but, for example, when correspondence (which may have run on for several weeks) springs from an article and follows directly on that article, the date of the article is continued *within square brackets*. Sometimes an item is printed out of chronological order (the reason for which is always given) and the running-head date will again be set within square brackets. Wherever practicable, the running-head date is that of the first item of the opening; if an opening has no date, the last date of a preceding opening is carried forward. Articles published in journals dated by month are considered for the purpose to be published on the first of the month. Inevitably some dates are more specific than is wholly justified, e.g., that for 'British Cookery' (*2954*). However, it is hoped that if readers always treat dates within square brackets with circumspection, the dates will give a clear indication of 'where they are' in Orwell's life.

Great efforts have been made to ensure the accuracy of these volumes. The three editors and Roberta Leighton (in New York) have read and re-read them a total of six times but it is obvious that errors will, as it used to be put so charmingly in the sixteenth century, have 'escaped in the printing.' I offer one plea for understanding. Much of the copy-preparation and proof-reading has been of type set during and after the war when newsprint was in short supply and mere literary articles would be set in microscopic-sized type. Many of the BBC scripts were blown up from microfilm and extremely difficult to puzzle out. When one proof-reads against xeroxes of dim printing on creased paper, the possibilities for error are increased and the eyes so run with tears that

Editorial Note

vision is impaired. We hope we have corrected most errors, but we know we shall not have caught them all.

P.D.

A slightly fuller version of this note is printed in the preliminaries to Volume X.

1. *George Orwell, Nineteen Eighty-Four: The Facsimile of the Extant Manuscript,* edited by Peter Davison, London, New York, and Weston, Mass., 1984.
2. Information from W. J. West, 22 July 1994.
3. The problems of presenting acceptable history even for the professional historian are well outlined by Norman Davies in *Europe: A History,* Oxford University Press, Oxford and New York, 1996, 2–7. I am obviously attempting nothing so grand, yet even 'simple' historical explication is not always quite so simple.

REFERENCES

References to Orwell's books are to the editions in Vols I to IX of the *Complete Works* (edited P. Davison, published by Secker & Warburg, 1986–87). The pagination is almost always identical with that in the Penguin Twentieth-Century Classics edition, 1989–90. The volumes are numbered in chronological order and references are by volume number (in roman), page, and, if necessary (after a diagonal) line, so: II.37/5 means line five of page 37 of *Burmese Days*. Secker editions have Textual Notes and apparatus. Penguin editions have A Note on the Text; these are not identical with the Secker Textual Notes and Penguin editions do not list variants. There is a 32-page introduction to the Secker *Down and Out in Paris and London*. Items in Volumes X to XX are numbered individually; they (and their notes) are referred to by italicised numerals, e.g. *2736* and *2736 n. 3*.

REFERENCE WORKS: These are the principal reference works frequently consulted:

The Oxford English Dictionary, second edition (Compact Version, Oxford 1991): (OED).
The Dictionary of National Biography (Oxford 1885–1900, with supplements and *The Twentieth-Century*, 1901–   ): (DNB).
Dictionary of American Biography (New York, 1946, with supplements).
Dictionnaire biographique du mouvement ouvrier français, publié sous la direction de Jean Maitron, 4ᵉ ptie 1914–1939: De la Première à la Seconde Guerre mondiale (t. 16–43, Paris, Les Éditions Ouvrières, 1981–93).
Who's Who; Who Was Who; Who's Who in the Theatre; Who Was Who in Literature 1906–1934 (2 vols., Detroit, 1979); *Who Was Who Among English and European Authors 1931–1949* (3 vols., Detroit 1978); *Contemporary Authors* and its *Cumulative Index* (Detroit, 1993); *Who's Who In Filmland*, edited and compiled by Langford Reed and Hetty Spiers (1928); Roy Busby, *British Music Hall: An Illustrated Who's Who from 1850 to the Present Day* (London and New Hampshire, USA, 1976).
The Feminist Companion to Literature in English, edited by Virginia Blain, Patricia Clements, and Isobel Grundy, Batsford 1990.
The New Cambridge Bibliography of English Literature, edited by George Watson and Ian Willison, 4 vols., Cambridge, 1974–79.
Martin Seymour-Smith, *Guide to Modern World Literature*, 3rd revised edition, Macmillan 1985.
The War Papers, co-ordinating editor, Richard Widdows, 75 Parts, Marshall Cavendish, 1976–78.

The following are referred to by abbreviations:

CEJL: *The Collected Essays, Journalism and Letters of George Orwell*, ed. Sonia Orwell

References

and Ian Angus, 4 volumes, Secker & Warburg 1968; Penguin Books, 1970; references are by volume and page number of the more conveniently available Penguin edition.

Crick: Bernard Crick, *George Orwell: A Life*, 1980; 3rd edition, Penguin Books, Harmondsworth, 1992 edition. References are to the 1992 edition.

Eric & Us: Jacintha Buddicom, *Eric and Us: A Remembrance of George Orwell*, Leslie Frewin, 1974.

Lewis: Peter Lewis, *George Orwell: The Road to 1984*, Heinemann, 1981.

Liddell Hart: B. H. Liddell Hart, *History of the Second World War*, Cassell, 1970; 8th Printing, Pan, 1983.

Orwell Remembered: Audrey Coppard and Bernard Crick, eds., *Orwell Remembered*, Ariel Books, BBC, 1984.

Remembering Orwell: Stephen Wadhams, *Remembering Orwell*, Penguin Books Canada, Markham, Ontario; Penguin Books, Harmondsworth, 1984.

Shelden: Michael Shelden, *Orwell: The Authorised Biography*, Heinemann, London; Harper Collins, New York; 1991. The American pagination differs from that of the English edition; both are given in references, the English first.

Stansky and Abrahams I: Peter Stansky and William Abrahams, *The Unknown Orwell*, Constable 1972; edition referred to here, Granada, St Albans, 1981.

Stansky and Abrahams II: Peter Stansky and William Abrahams, *The Transformation*, Constable 1979; edition referred to here, Granada, St Albans, 1981.

Thomas: Hugh Thomas, *The Spanish Civil War*, 3rd edition; Hamish Hamilton and Penguin Books, Harmondsworth, 1977.

Thompson: John Thompson, *Orwell's London*, Fourth Estate 1984.

West: *Broadcasts*: W. J. West, *Orwell: The War Broadcasts*, Duckworth/BBC 1985.

West: *Commentaries*: W. J. West, *Orwell: The War Commentaries*, Duckworth/BBC, 1985.

Willison: I. R. Willison, 'George Orwell: Some Materials for a Bibliography,' Librarianship Diploma Thesis, University College London, 1953. A copy is held by the Orwell Archive, UCL.

2194 Days of War: *2194 Days of War*, compiled by Cesare Salmaggi and Alfredo Pallavisini, translated by Hugh Young, Arnoldo Mondadori, Milan 1977; rev. edn Galley Press, Leicester 1988.

A Bibliography of works, books, memoirs and essays found helpful in preparing Volumes X to XX of *The Complete Works of George Orwell* will be found in the preliminaries to Volume X.

CHRONOLOGY

In the main, Orwell's publications, except books, are not listed

25 June 1903 Eric Arthur Blair born in Motihari, Bengal, India.

---

4 Dec 1948 Completes typing fair copy of *Nineteen Eighty-Four* and posts copies to Moore and Warburg. Has serious relapse.

c 2 Jan 1949 Leaves Jura.

6 January–3 Sep 1949 Patient in Cotswold Sanatorium, Cranham, Gloucestershire, seriously ill with tuberculosis.

January 1949 *Burmese Days* published as second volume in Uniform Edition.

Mid-Feb 1949 Starts but never completes article on Evelyn Waugh for *Partisan Review*.

Mar 1949 Corrects proofs of *Nineteen Eighty-Four*.

9 April 1949 Sends off his last completed review: of Winston Churchill's *Their Finest Hour*, for *The New Leader*, New York.

April 1949 onwards Plans a novel set in 1945 (not written). Writes synopsis and four pages of long short-story, 'A Smoking-room Story'. Makes notes for an essay on Joseph Conrad.

8 June 1949 *Nineteen Eighty-Four* published by Secker & Warburg. Published by Harcourt, Brace, New York, 13 June 1949; American Book of the Month Club selection, July 1949. By the end of 1950 it had been published in Danish, Japanese, Swedish, German, Dutch, French, Norwegian, Finnish, Italian, and Hebrew.

Post-June 1949 Signs second instructions for his Literary Executor.

August 1949 Plans a book of reprinted essays.

3 Sep 1949 Transferred to University College Hospital, London.

13 Oct 1949 Marries Sonia Brownell.

18 Jan 1950 Signs his will on eve of proposed journey to Switzerland, recommended for his health's sake.

21 Jan 1950 Dies of pulmonary tuberculosis, aged 46.

26 Jan 1950 Buried, as Eric Arthur Blair, All Saints, Sutton Courtenay, Berkshire.

THE COMPLETE WORKS OF
GEORGE ORWELL · TWENTY

OUR JOB IS TO
MAKE LIFE WORTH LIVING

1949

3516. 'Reflections on Gandhi'[1]

Partisan Review, January 1949

Saints should always be judged guilty until they are proved innocent, but the tests that have to be applied to them are not, of course, the same in all cases. In Gandhi's case the questions one feels inclined to ask are: to what extent was Gandhi moved by vanity—by the consciousness of himself as a humble, naked old man, sitting on a praying-mat and shaking empires by sheer spiritual power—and to what extent did he compromise his own principles by entering into politics, which of their nature are inseparable from coercion and fraud? To give a definite answer one would have to study Gandhi's acts and writings in immense detail, for his whole life was a sort of pilgrimage in which every act was significant. But this partial autobiography,* which ends in the nineteen-twenties, is strong evidence in his favor, all the more because it covers what he would have called the unregenerate part of his life and reminds one that inside the saint, or near-saint, there was a very shrewd, able person who could, if he had chosen, have been a brilliant success as a lawyer, an[1] administrator or perhaps even a business man.

At about the time when the autobiography first appeared I remember reading its opening chapters in the ill-printed pages of some Indian newspaper. They made a good impression on me, which Gandhi himself, at that time, did not. The things that one associated with him—homespun cloth, "soul forces" and vegetarianism—were unappealing, and his medievalist program was obviously not viable in a backward, starving, over-populated country. It was also apparent that the British were making use of him, or thought they were making use of him. Strictly speaking, as a Nationalist, he was an enemy, but since in every crisis he would exert himself to prevent violence—which, from the British point of view, meant preventing any effective action whatever—he could be regarded as "our man." In private this was sometimes cynically admitted. The attitude of the Indian millionaires was similar. Gandhi called upon them to repent, and naturally they preferred him to the Socialists and Communists who, given the chance, would actually have taken their money away. How reliable such calculations are in the long run is doubtful; as Gandhi himself says, "in the end deceivers deceive only themselves"; but at any rate the gentleness with which he was nearly always handled was due partly to the feeling that he was useful. The British Conservatives only became really angry with him when,

* *The Story of my Experiments with Truth*, by M. K. Gandhi. Translated from the Gujarati by Mahadev Desai. Public Affairs Press, $5.00.

as in 1942, he was in effect turning his non-violence against a different conqueror.

But I could see even then that the British officials who spoke of him with a mixture of amusement and disapproval also genuinely liked and admired him, after a fashion. Nobody ever suggested that he was corrupt, or ambitious in any vulgar way, or that anything he did was actuated by fear or malice.[2] In judging a man like Gandhi one seems instinctively to apply high standards, so that some of his virtues have passed almost unnoticed. For instance, it is clear even from the autobiography that his natural physical courage was quite outstanding: the manner of his death was a later illustration of this,[3] for a public man who attached any value to his own skin would have been more adequately guarded. Again, he seems to have been quite free from that maniacal[4] suspiciousness which, as E. M. Forster rightly says in *A Passage to India*, is the besetting Indian vice, as hypocrisy is the British vice.[5] Although no doubt he was shrewd enough in detecting dishonesty, he[6] seems wherever possible to have believed that other people were acting in good faith and had a better nature through which they could be approached. And though he came of a poor middle-class family, started life rather unfavorably, and was probably of unimpressive physical appearance, he was not afflicted by envy or by the feeling of inferiority. Color feeling, when he first met it in its worst form in South Africa, seems rather to have astonished him. Even when he was fighting what was in effect a color war, he did not think of people in terms of race or status. The governor of a province, a cotton millionaire, a half-starved Dravidian cooly,[7] a British private soldier, were all equally human beings, to be approached in much the same way. It is noticeable that even in the worst possible circumstances, as in South Africa when he was making himself unpopular as the champion of the Indian community, he did not lack European friends.

Written in short lengths for newspaper serialization, the autobiography is not a literary masterpiece, but it is the more impressive because of the commonplaceness of much of its material.[8] It is well to be reminded that Gandhi started out with the normal ambitions of a young Indian student and only adopted his extremist opinions by degrees and, in some cases, rather unwillingly. There was a time, it is interesting to learn, when he wore a top hat, took dancing lessons, studied French and Latin, went up the Eiffel Tower and even tried to learn the violin—all this with the idea of assimilating European civilization as thoroughly as possible. He was not one of those saints who are marked out by their phenomenal piety from childhood onwards, nor one of the other kind who forsake the world after sensational debaucheries. He makes full confession of the misdeeds of his youth, but in fact there is not much to confess. As a frontispiece to the book there is a photograph of Gandhi's possessions at the time of his death. The whole outfit could be purchased for about £5, and Gandhi's sins, at least his fleshly sins, would make the same sort of appearance if placed all in one heap. A few cigarettes, a few mouthfuls of meat, a few annas pilfered in childhood from the maidservant, two visits to a brothel (on each occasion he got away without "doing anything"), one narrowly escaped lapse with his landlady in

Plymouth, one outburst of temper—that is about the whole collection.[9] Almost from childhood onwards he had a deep earnestness, an attitude ethical rather than religious, but, until he was about thirty, no very definite sense of direction. His first entry into anything describable as public life was made by way of vegetarianism. Underneath his less ordinary qualities one feels all the time the solid middle-class business men who were his ancestors. One feels that even after he had abandoned personal ambition he must have been a resourceful, energetic lawyer and a hardheaded political organizer, careful in keeping down expenses, an adroit handler of committees and an indefatigable chaser of subscriptions.[10] His character was an extraordinarily mixed one, but there was almost[11] nothing in it that you can put your finger on and call bad, and I believe that even Gandhi's worst enemies would admit that he was an interesting and unusual man who enriched the world simply by being alive. Whether he was also a lovable man, and whether his teachings can have much value for those who do not accept the religious beliefs on which they are founded, I have never felt fully certain.[12]

Of late years it has been the fashion to talk about Gandhi as though he were not only sympathetic to the Western leftwing movement, but were even integrally part of it. Anarchists and pacifists, in particular, have claimed him for their own, noticing only that he was opposed to centralism and State violence and ignoring the otherworldly, anti-humanist tendency of his doctrines. But one should, I think, realize that Gandhi's teachings cannot be squared with the belief that Man is the measure of all things, and that our job is to make life worth living on this earth, which is the only earth we have. They make sense only on the assumption that God exists and that the world of solid objects is an illusion to be escaped from. It is worth considering the disciplines which Gandhi imposed on himself and which—though he might not insist on every one of his followers observing every detail—he considered indispensable if one wanted to serve either God or humanity. First of all, no meat-eating, and if possible no animal food in any form. (Gandhi himself, for the sake of his health, had to compromise on milk, but seems to have felt this to be a backsliding.) No alcohol or tobacco, and no spices or condiments, even of a vegetable kind, since food should be taken not for its own sake but solely in order to preserve one's strength. Secondly, if possible, no sexual intercourse. If sexual intercourse must happen, then it should be for the sole purpose of begetting children and presumably at long intervals. Gandhi himself, in his middle thirties, took the vow of *bramahcharya*, which means not only complete chastity but the elimination of sexual desire. This condition, it seems, is difficult to attain without a special diet and frequent fasting. One of the dangers of milk-drinking is that it is apt to arouse sexual desire. And finally—this is the cardinal point—for the seeker after goodness there must be no close friendships and no exclusive loves whatever.

Close friendships, Gandhi says, are dangerous, because "friends react on one another" and through loyalty to a friend one can be led into wrong-doing. This is unquestionably true. Moreover, if one is to love God, or to love humanity as a whole, one cannot give one's preference to any individual person. This again is true, and it marks the point at which the humanistic and the religious attitude cease to be reconcilable. To an ordinary human being, love means nothing if it does not mean loving some people more than others. The autobiography leaves it uncertain whether Gandhi behaved in an inconsiderate way to his wife and children, but at any rate it makes clear that on three occasions he was willing to let his wife or a child die rather than administer the animal food prescribed by the doctor. It is true that the threatened death never actually occurred, and also that Gandhi—with, one gathers, a good deal of moral pressure in the opposite direction—always gave the patient the choice of staying alive at the price of committing a sin: still, if the decision had been solely his own, he would have forbidden the animal food, whatever the risks might be. There must, he says, be some limit to what we will do in order to remain alive, and the limit is well on this side of chicken broth. This attitude is perhaps a noble one, but, in the sense which—I think—most people would give to the word, it is inhuman. The essence of being human is that one does not seek perfection, that one *is* sometimes willing to commit sins for the sake of loyalty, that one does not push asceticism to the point where it makes friendly intercourse impossible, and that one is prepared in the end to be defeated and broken up by life, which is the inevitable price of fastening one's love upon other human individuals. No doubt alcohol, tobacco and so forth are things that a saint must avoid, but sainthood is also a thing that human beings must avoid. There is an obvious retort to this, but one should be wary about making it. In this yogi-ridden age, it is too readily assumed that "non-attachment" is not only better than a full acceptance of earthly life, but that the ordinary man only rejects it because it is too difficult: in other words, that the average human being is a failed saint. It is doubtful whether this is true. Many people genuinely do not wish to be saints, and it is probable that some who achieve or aspire to sainthood have never felt much temptation to be human beings. If one could follow it to its psychological roots, one would, I believe, find that the main motive for "non-attachment" is a desire to escape from the pain of living, and above all from love, which, sexual or non-sexual, is hard work. But[13] it is not necessary here to argue whether the other-worldly or the humanistic ideal is "higher." The point is that they are incompatible. One must choose between God and Man, and all "radicals" and "progressives," from the mildest Liberal to the most extreme Anarchist,[14] have in effect chosen Man.

However, Gandhi's pacifism can be separated to some extent from his other teachings. Its motive was religious, but he claimed also for it that it was a definite technique, a method, capable of producing desired political results. Gandhi's attitude was not that of most Western pacifists. *Satyagraha*, first evolved in South Africa, was a sort of non-violent warfare, a way of defeating the enemy without hurting him and without feeling or arousing hatred. It entailed such things as civil disobedience, strikes, lying down in front of railway trains, enduring police charges without running away and without hitting back, and the like. Gandhi objected to "passive resistance" as a translation of *Satyagraha*: in Gujarati, it seems, the word means "firmness in the truth." In his early days Gandhi served as a stretcher-bearer on the British side in the Boer War, and he was prepared to do the same again in the war of

1914–18. Even after he had completely abjured violence he was honest enough to see that in war it is usually necessary to take sides. He did not—indeed, since his whole political life centered round a struggle for national independence, he could not—take the sterile and dishonest line of pretending that in every war both sides are exactly the same and it makes no difference who wins. Nor did he, like most Western pacifists, specialize in avoiding awkward questions. In relation to the late war, one question that every pacifist had a clear obligation to answer was: "What about the Jews? Are you prepared to see them exterminated? If not, how do you propose to save them without resorting to war?" I must say that[15] I have never heard, from any Western pacifist, an honest answer to this question, though I have heard plenty of evasions, usually of the "you're another" type.[16] But it so happens that Gandhi was asked a somewhat similar question in 1938 and that his answer is on record in Mr. Louis Fischer's *Gandhi and Stalin*. According to Mr. Fischer, Gandhi's view was that the German Jews ought to commit collective suicide, which "would have aroused the world and the people of Germany to Hitler's violence." After the war he justified himself: the Jews had been killed anyway, and might as well have died significantly. One has the impression that this attitude staggered even so warm an admirer as Mr. Fischer, but[17] Gandhi was merely being honest. If you are not prepared to take life, you must often be prepared for lives to be lost in some other way. When, in 1942, he urged non-violent resistance against a Japanese invasion, he was ready to admit that it might cost several million deaths.

At the same time there is reason to think that Gandhi, who after all was born in 1869, did not understand the nature of totalitarianism and saw everything in terms of his own struggle against the British government. The important point here is not so much that the British treated him forbearingly as that he was always able to command publicity.[18] As can be seen from the phrase quoted above, he believed in "arousing the world," which is only possible if the world gets a chance to hear what you are doing. It is difficult to see how Gandhi's methods could be applied in a country where opponents of the regime disappear in the middle of the night and are never heard of again. Without a free press and the right of assembly, it is impossible not merely to appeal to outside opinion, but to bring a mass movement into being, or even to make your intentions known to your adversary. Is there a Gandhi in Russia at this moment? And if there is, what is he accomplishing? The Russian masses could only practice civil disobedience if the same idea happened to occur to all of them simultaneously, and even then, to judge by the history of the Ukraine famine, it would make no difference.[19] But let it be granted that non-violent resistance can be effective against one's own government, or against an occupying power: even so, how does one put it into practice internationally? Gandhi's various conflicting[20] statements on the late war seem to show that he felt the difficulty of this. Applied to foreign politics, pacifism either stops being pacifist or becomes appeasement. Moreover the assumption, which served Gandhi so well in dealing with individuals, that all human beings are more or less approachable and will respond to a generous gesture, needs to be seriously questioned. It is not necessarily true, for

9

example, when you are dealing with lunatics. Then the question becomes: Who is sane? Was Hitler sane? And is it not possible for one whole culture to be insane by the standards of another? And, so far as one can gauge the feelings of whole nations, is there any apparent connection between a generous deed and a friendly response? Is gratitude a factor in international politics?

These and kindred questions need discussion, and need it urgently, in the few years left to us before somebody presses the button and the rockets begin to fly. It seems doubtful whether civilization can stand another major war, and it is at least thinkable that the way out lies through non-violence. It is Gandhi's virtue that he would have been ready to give honest consideration to the kind of question that I have raised above; and, indeed, he probably did discuss most of these questions somewhere or other in his innumerable newspaper articles. One feels of him that there was[21] much that he did not understand, but not that there was anything that he was frightened of saying or thinking.[22] I have never been able to feel much liking for Gandhi, but I do not feel sure that as a political thinker he was wrong in the main,[23] nor do I believe that his life was a failure. It is curious that when he was assassinated, many of his warmest admirers exclaimed sorrowfully that he had lived just long enough to see his life work in ruins, because India was engaged in a civil war which had always been foreseen as one of the by-products of the transfer of power.[24] But it was not in trying to smoothe down Hindu-Moslem rivalry that Gandhi had[25] spent his life. His main political objective, the peaceful ending of British rule, had after all[26] been attained. As usual, the relevant facts cut across one another. On the one hand,[27] the British did get out of India without fighting, an event which very few observers indeed would have predicted until about a year before it happened. On the other hand, this was done by a Labor government, and it is certain that a Conservative government, especially a government headed by Churchill, would have acted differently. But[28] if, by 1945, there had grown up in Britain[29] a large body of opinion sympathetic to Indian independence, how far was this due to Gandhi's personal influence? And if, as may happen,[30] India and Britain finally[31] settle down into a decent and friendly relationship, will this[32] be partly because Gandhi, by keeping up his struggle obstinately and without hatred, disinfected the political air? That one even thinks of asking[33] such questions indicates his stature. One may feel, as I do, a sort of aesthetic distaste for Gandhi, one may reject the claims of sainthood made on his behalf (he never made any such claim himself, by the way), one may also reject sainthood as an ideal and therefore feel that Gandhi's basic aims were anti-human and reactionary: but regarded simply as a politician, and compared with the other leading political figures of our time, how clean a smell he has managed to leave behind![34]

This article was abridged and modified in *Mirror*, 16, as 'Gandhi: a critical study.' *Mirror: Monthly International Review* was published by the Central Office of Information, London. The journal described itself as 'Presenting to readers in Asia illustrated articles, literary features, book extracts, and essays reflecting the best in current Western thought on important political, scientific, social and economic problems.' The date of the article's publication has been back-calculated from Vol. 3, No. 25, dated July 1950; it was printed in June 1949, and the British Library's copy is date-stamped 27 October 1949. The article is one of three picked for special mention on the page facing the list of contents.

It is possible that one or two changes might have had Orwell's approval (for example, *ns. 15* and *26*), but many of the changes are intended to address Indian and British sensibilities (for example, *ns. 4* and *5*). Rather more serious is the way that the article has been made overtly propagandist in favour of Gandhi. Where Orwell hedges, *Mirror* is quite positive. See, for example, *ns. 11; 12*, especially the cutting of the final sentence; *20; 21; 23*, the omission of Orwell's statement that he had never been able to feel much liking for Gandhi; *30*, where Orwell's 'as may happen' becomes 'as now promises'—very much the kind of propagandist change that the COI might be expected to make; and *33*, omitting Orwell's acknowledgment that he had 'a sort of aesthetic distaste for Gandhi.' There is no way of knowing whether or not Orwell agreed to these changes, still less made them, but the probability is that the essay was 'used' to bolster Anglo-Indian relations and that Orwell was thought particularly appropriate for this because, as a preliminary note states, this 'new evaluation' had been made by 'an English writer and critic well known for the independence and originality of his views.' To put it crudely, it looks as if Orwell's independence was hijacked by the Central Office of Information. It is remarkable that Orwell should have written this article for *Partisan Review* (and reviews for *The Observer*) at the very time he was desperately exhausting himself completing the revision and final typing of *Nineteen Eighty-Four*. In his letter to S. M. Levitas, 3 March 1949 (see *3559*), he says the article was written before the beginning of December 1948.

1. an] *Partisan Review* has 'and'
2. *Mirror* cuts from the start of the essay to 'fear and malice.' Hereafter these notes give the reading of Orwell's essay as printed in *Partisan Review* first; after the square bracket is the change made in *Mirror*. Changes in punctuation, spelling, and paragraphing are not noted.
3. of this] *omitted*
4. maniacal] *omitted*
5. as hypocrisy is the British vice] *omitted*
6. he] Gandhi
7. cooly] labourer
8. beings, to be approached . . . material] *omitted*
9. There was a time . . . whole collection.] *omitted*
10. an adroit . . . subscriptions] adroit at handling committees
11. almost] *omitted*
12. and I believe . . . felt fully certain.] *omitted*
13. It is worth considering . . . is hard work. But] *omitted*
14. the most extreme Anarchist] an extreme Anarchist
15. I must say that] *omitted*
16. usually . . . type.] *omitted*
17. After the war . . . Mr. Fischer, but] *omitted*
18. The important point . . . to command publicity.] *omitted*
19. Is there a Gandhi . . . make no difference.] *omitted*
20. conflicting] *omitted*
21. in his innumerable . . . that there was] There may have been
22. not that there was . . . or thinking] nothing that he was frightened of saying or doing
23. I have never . . . in the main] I do not feel as a political thinker he was wrong.
24. because India . . . transfer of power.] *omitted*
25. had] *omitted*

26. after all] *omitted*
27. As usual . . . the one hand,] *omitted*
28. On the other hand . . . differently. But] *omitted*
29. in Britain] *omitted*
30. as may happen] as now promises
31. finally] *omitted*
32. will this] will not this. *This is not a direct negative, but a rhetorical figure of speech, and could have been intended by Orwell.*
33. That one even thinks of asking] That one asks
34. One may feel . . . to leave behind!] *omitted*

3517. Review of *The English Comic Album*, compiled by
Leonard Russell and Nicolas Bentley

The Observer, 2 January 1949

It is generally admitted that the standard of English comic draughtsmanship deteriorated after 1850, but the collection of drawings now published shows, at any rate, that the standard has risen sharply during the past 15 years. Even if there is no Rowlandson or Cruikshank alive to-day, a period in which Low, Giles, Nicolas Bentley, Ronald Searle, and Osbert Lancaster are all at work simultaneously is not doing so badly.

The collection starts about a century ago, when the self-contained "joke picture," was just coming into being. Unfortunately this was also the period at which English humour was being "purified" for the benefit of a new, largely feminine, public. It is painful to compare, for instance, Tenniel and Charles Keene, or even Edward Lear, with "Phiz" and Cruikshank. Indeed, the funniest pictures that Messrs. Russell and Bentley have been able to find in the late middle of the century are some satires on drunkenness by an anonymous postcard artist.

The eighties and nineties were dominated by George du Maurier and others of the same school, who simply drew naturalistic sketches to go with jokes which, when they were funny, could have got along equally well with no picture. There was also Phil May, Sir Max Beerbohm (who, however, did his best work about 20 years later), and two gifted Frenchmen, Caran d'Ache and Godefroy, apparently included here because of their influence on English draughtsmanship.

The whole period between roughly 1900 and 1930 is a very bad one. Its redeeming features were Sir Max Beerbohm's caricatures, and George Belcher, a social historian rather than a comic draughtsman. Otherwise, nearly all the so-called comic drawings of that time are either weakly naturalistic or display the kind of silly facetiousness that can be seen in, for instance, the Shell advertisements.[1]

This type of drawing still predominates, but since the nineteen-thirties the "American joke" has naturalised itself. It is no longer assumed that every magazine-reader is a member of the upper-middle classes, whose one great terror in life is of being made to think, and, above all, it has come to be accepted that a comic drawing ought to be funny in itself and ought to convey a meaning without further explanation. Mr. Bentley's lumbering Amazon of the hockey field hardly needs the "Pass, Gwyneth!" printed beneath her, and Mr. Lancaster's diptych on the march of progress has no caption and needs none. It is true, however, that the long Victorian caption had its charm. In the hands of a writer like Thackeray it was sometimes a small work of art in itself, and it could be made so again, as Mr. D. B. Wyndham Lewis showed some years ago in a book produced in collaboration with Mr. Topolski.[2]

It is difficult to review an anthology without raising a few complaints. Low is not represented by his best work, and neither is Sir Max Beerbohm. Thackeray does not get a fair showing, and Leech would have been better represented by some of his illustrations to Surtees than by his contributions to "Punch." And since both advertisements and comic strips are included, might there not have been at any rate one seaside post-card? But this is a well-balanced collection, and the most jaded reader can hardly glance through it without laughing several times.

1. Orwell possibly has in mind the 'two-headed man' who featured in advertisements for Shell petrol with the slogan 'That's Shell—that was!' as a car flashed past.
2. *The London Spectacle* (1935) was illustrated by Feliks Topolski, and had an introduction and notes by D. B. Wyndham Lewis.

3518. Dr. Bruce Dick to David Astor

5 January 1949   Handwritten

as from The Peel,
Busby.[1]

Dear Mr David,[2]
I am sorry for the delay in reply° to your letter.

I was for a time in correspondence with Eric Blair. It was obvious° a relapse story, presumably of fairly acute onset. When we saw him in Sept. we thought he was as good as when he left us.

I had offered to take him into our hospital[3] or this one. However he had a hankering for the less rigorous south. He had decided on Mundesley.[4] I expect the delay in getting fixed up made him decide on the Cotswold Sanatorium.[5] I have not been in touch with the Superintendent personally, but one of my assistants sent a detailed history.

I believe the disease will respond again to a course of streptomycin. It can now be procured more easily at home. Certainly no other form of treatment is available.

It is all bad luck for such a fine character & gifted man. I know he gets great heart from your continued comradeship & kindness.

I hope the poor fellow will do well. It is now obvious that he will need to live a most sheltered life in a sanatorium environment. I fear the dream of Jura must fade out.

13

If I can be of the least help, I will. If he was to come north later we would give[6] him refuge.

With kind regards.
Yours sincerely,
Bruce Dick

1. Dr. Dick wrote on paper headed 'Board of Management for Glasgow Victoria Hospitals, Mearnskirk Hospital, Newton Mearns, Renfrewshire.' He wrote over that heading, 'as from The Peel, Busby.' This Busby (there are two in Scotland) is within a mile or two of Newton Mearns, south of Glasgow.
2. David Astor.
3. Presumably Hairmyres Hospital, where Orwell had spent several months in 1948. It was at East Kilbride, about eight miles due east of Newton Mearns. Dr. Dick had treated Orwell at Hairmyres. See 3324, n. 2.
4. On the east coast of England about 20 to 22 miles northeast of Norwich. In his letter to Gwen O'Shaughnessy, 28 November 1948 (see 3499), Orwell said he was hoping to get into the Grampian Sanatorium, Kingussie, 'the only private sanatorium in Scotland.' That had no vacancies, and it seems that, in Orwell's 'hankering for the less rigorous south,' as Dr. Dick puts it, he had decided on Mundesley initially. It is not known why he did not go there. Gwen O'Shaughnessy helped him find a place at Cranham; see n. 5 and also Shelden, 466; U.S.: 426.
5. Orwell was admitted to The Cotswold Sanatorium, Cranham, Gloucester, on 6 January 1949. Richard Rees drove Orwell on the first stage of the long journey from Barnhill to Cranham, 'over the terrible moorland road' (George Orwell: Fugitive from the Camp of Victory, 150). He notes that at Barnhill, Orwell 'was certainly happy. . . . He felt that he was at last putting down roots. But in reality it was obvious that he had chosen a too rocky soil' (149). Orwell completed the journey by train.
6. Written as 'hive.'

3518A. To Lydia Jackson

9 January 1949   Handwritten

The Cotswold Sanatorium
CRANHAM
Gloucestershire

Dear Lydia,

Thank you for your letter, & thank you also ever so much for sending the story of the Three Bears to Richard. (Avril says by the way that the bears in it are so well-behaved that she thinks it must be disguised Soviet propaganda). I can't write much of a letter, because as you see by the above address I am ill again, & have been for some time. I was very well when I left the hospital in July, ie. very weak but with apparently no TB. left, but I began to relapse about the end of September. I could have done something about it then, but I had to finish that wretched book, which, thanks to illness, I had been messing about with 18 months & which the publishers were harrying me for. In the event I didn't finish it till the beginning of December, & then it took some time to make arrangements with a sanatorium. I expect to be here at any rate two months, more I dare say. I can't do any work at present & am trying not to, as I must try & get rid of this beastly disease. Possibly when I'm a bit stronger & can get about a bit you'd like to come & see me some time. I've no doubt I could arrange for you to stay in the neighbourhood for a few days. It's probably very pretty country round here—I don't know this actual part, but it can't be very different from Oxfordshire, where I spent part of my childhood. Please give my love to Pat.[1]

With love
Eric

1. Pat Donahue; see *3354A, n. 3.*

3519. To David Astor

12 January 1949

Witcombe[1]

THANKS VERY MUCH DONT WORRY NOT BEING TREATED WITH STREPTOMY-
CIN THIS TIME WRITING = GEORGE +

1. A village close by Cranham Sanatorium and near Gloucester.

3520. To David Astor

12 January 1949   Handwritten

The Cotswold Sanatorium[1]
Cranham
Glos.

Dear David,
Thanks so much for your two wires & the offer about the streptomycin. But at present they aren't treating me with strepto, & in any case it appears that it is now easier to get & comparatively cheap. They are giving me something called P.A.S.[2] which I gather stands for para–amino–salicylic acid. This sounds rather as if it was just aspirin in disguise, but I assume it isn't. We will give it a trial any way. If it doesn't work I can always have another go of strepto. This seems quite a nice place & comfortable. If you can come any time I should love it, though of course don't put yourself out. I can even arrange meals for you if I get notice. I have felt better the last week or so but I am not going to attempt any work for at least a month.

Yours
George

[Written at the head of page:]
P.S. Looking at the map this isn't so very far from your Abingdon place by road. I've never been in Glos. before but I think it must be rather like the Oxfordshire country I knew as a little boy.

1. 'Cranham was a private sanatorium 900 feet up, almost the highest the south of England can manage, in the Cotswold hills between Stroud and Gloucester with views right across the Bristol Channel to the mountains of Wales. The patients were in individual chalets with central heating; for rest, altitude and fresh air, cold air indeed, were then generally believed to be relevant treatments for tuberculosis' (Crick, 553). The resident physicians were Geoffrey A. Hoffman, BA, MB, TC, Dublin, and Margaret A. Kirkman, MB, BS, London. See *endnote* to *3530*, for the Warburgs' reaction to his treatment.
2. P.A.S. was a chemotherapeutic drug introduced in 1946 for the treatment of tuberculosis. It was only slightly effective used alone and was usually combined with isoniazid or streptomycin. Such a combination delayed the development of the disease. Shelden notes that these drugs were so new that no doctors 'had enough experience with them to understand the best way to use them in treating advanced cases such as Orwell's. He might have benefited from smaller doses or from a combination of drugs and other forms of treatment. Unfortunately, the most potent drug—isoniazid—was not developed for use in tuberculosis cases until 1952. . . . But the fact that he was given PAS at the sanatorium in Cranham shows that he was receiving the latest treatment for the disease. The doctors there seem to have made every effort to achieve an improvement in his condition' (466–67; U.S.: 427).

3521. To George Woodcock

12 January 1949   Handwritten

The Cotswold Sanatorium
Cranham
Glos.

Dear George,
It is ages ago that I received from you a letter with a cyclostyled circular relating to the F.D.C.[1] which I didn't comment on or in fact even read. I have been for some time past & still am seriously ill, & have been almost unequal to answering more than the unavoidable minimum of letters. I was much better when I left the hospital last July, but I began to relapse in September & during the last two months was in a ghastly state. I would have gone for treatment earlier, but I simply had to finish a book which, thanks to illness, I had been messing about with for 18 months, & which the publishers were chasing me for. In the event I didn't finish it till early in December, & of course the effort of doing so didn't make me any better. I came here only recently. It seems a nice place, very comfortable, & I can at any rate completely relax here. They are giving me something called P.A.S. which I suspect of being a high-sounding name for aspirins, but they say it is the latest thing & gives good results. If necessary I can have another go of streptomycin, which certainly seemed to improve me last time, but the secondary effects are so unpleasant that it's a bit like sinking the ship to drown the rats. I hope you & Inge are going on all right. Can you write again giving me the dope about the F.D.C. I am a bit less distraught now & can deal with things a little. About money, beyond very small sums, I don't know. You can imagine that this disease is an expensive hobby, & I have earned very little money since 1947. I hope the book just finished may recoup me a bit, but in my experience one is lucky if

one makes £500 out of a book. Richard is tremendously well & becoming quite a farmer. Please remember me to Inge.

Yours
George

1. Freedom Defence Committee.

3522. To Brenda Salkeld

   13 January 1949 Handwritten

The Cotswold Sanatorium
Cranham
Glos.

Dear Brenda,[1]
How are things going with you? It seems ages since I have heard from you. I suppose you know I have been very ill (TB) during most of the past year. I left hospital in July very much better, but got worse again in September. I couldn't do anything about it then as I had to finish a book I was battling with. I only came to the above recently, & expect to stay here 2 or 3 months. It's a nice place & I have quite a comfortable "chalet"[2] as they are called. I don't suppose your travels take you to this side of England, but if they do, look in on me. Richard is very well & growing enormous.

Yours
Eric

1. A friend of Orwell's from his Southwold days; see *107, n. 1.* He last wrote to her on 1 September 1947; see *3262.*
2. For Orwell's description of his chalet, see Diary entry for 21.3.49, *3579.*

3523. To Fredrik Wulfsberg[1]

   15 January 1949 Handwritten

The Cotswold Sanatorium
Cranham
Glos.

Dear Sir,
I am sorry I have not answered earlier your letter of December 23rd, but I have been seriously ill & have had to cut my correspondence down to a minimum. I am very flattered that you should have done a broadcast on my work, but I should in any case have been unable to give any sort of interview, even if I had been in an accessible place.[2]

Yours truly
Geo Orwell

1. Fredrik Wulfsberg, a Norwegian academic, published an article, 'George Orwell', in *Norseman*, March–April 1950, and a book, also *George Orwell*, in Norwegian (1968).
2. Annotated: 'F. Does this call for a reply? Would be the polite thing I think. T.'

3524. To Fredric Warburg

17 January 1949   Handwritten

> The Cotswold Sanatorium
> Cranham
> Glos.

Dear Fred,

I'd be delighted to see you on Friday, but can you please wire telling me what station you will arrive at, & at what time. I presume you will come to Stroud, & I think there is a train that gets in at 12.5. I have to know because of arranging for the car to meet you. If you come on the 12.5 you will be here about 12.30 & in time for lunch. I can give you lunch here (quite eatable), also tea. Any way let me know.

I was glad to get your letter, as I find that for some days they were sending back letters addressed to "Orwell", not knowing this was me & I was afraid something from you might have gone astray. This seems a nice place & quite comfortable. I am trying to do no work whatever, which I think is the wisest thing at present. They are giving me something called P.A.S. (para-aminosalicylic acid, I believe). I don't know whether it is doing me any good, but I feel better & my appetite has improved. I've just heard from Gleb Struve about "We",[1] also from Moore about the American edition of "1984". But I'll talk to you about that on Friday— Love to everyone.

> Yours
> George

1. The novel by Yevgeny Zamyatin that Struve and Orwell wanted to have published in England; see Orwell's letters to Warburg and Struve, 22 November 1948, *3495* and *3496*. Struve wrote to Orwell on 1 January 1949; for later developments, see *3583, n. 1*. In his letter of 1 January, Struve had sent Orwell reports on articles in recent Soviet periodicals. Two articles 'by a certain Ivan Anisimov' were devoted to Orwell and Arthur Koestler, both of whom are 'taken to pieces. As you may not have heard of this attack, I am enclosing extracts from those articles in translation: they are typical of the literary xenophobia now raging in the Soviet Union.' Struve and Mikhail Zoshchenko (1885–1956; see *3146, n. 3*) and indirectly Zamyatin, had also been attacked by Aleksandr Anikst in an English-language Soviet magazine, *Soviet Literature* ('Slander in the Guise of Scholarship'). Ivan Ivanovich Anisimov (1894–1966) was an academic specialising in literary history and criticism; he became Director of the Gorky Institute of World Literature. Aleksandr Abramovich Anikst (1910–) wrote on a range of English and American literature from the 1930s but later specialised in Shakespeare; several of his books were published in English in the 1960s.

3525. To Leonard Moore
17 January 1949   Handwritten

The Cotswold Sanatorium
Cranham
Glos.

Dear Moore,

I enclose the 6 contracts,[1] duly signed. Thanks also for sending the copies of "Burmese Days," & the magazine with that cartoon.

I am glad the new book is fixed up for the USA. I assume it does no harm for it to have a different title here & there.[2] Warburg seems to prefer the title "1984", & I think I prefer it slightly myself.[3] But I think it would be better to write it "Nineteen Eighty-four,"[4] but I expect to see Warburg shortly & I'll talk to him about that. It's possible that the American publishers will want to cut out the Appendix,[5] which of course is not a usual thing to have in something purporting to be a novel, but I would like to retain it if possible.

The above address will, I am afraid, find me for the next 2 or 3 months. It is a nice place & I am quite comfortable. I am trying to do no work whatever, which I think is the wisest thing at the moment. So, with reference to your other letter, could you tell Harper's Bazaar that I would have liked to do the article, but have been seriously ill & cannot undertake anything. I dare say in a month or so I shall be fit to begin working again, but for the moment I do not want to make any commitments.

Yours sincerely
Eric Blair

1. Unidentified. They could be for *Nineteen Eighty-Four* (English and American editions), volumes in the Uniform Edition, or U.S. reprints; see *3529*.
2. The same title was used, and written out: *Nineteen Eighty-Four*.
3. Robert Giroux (who saw *Nineteen Eighty-Four* through the press for the U.S. edition) gave a paper to The Grolier Club Centennial Convocation, 26–28 April 1984 (and published in that year in New York), entitled 'The Future of the Book.' On page 55 he referred to *Nineteen Eighty-Four* as 'one of the most interesting and famous books I've ever worked on as an editor.' He recalled how he had exchanged letters with Orwell and Warburg and then referred to all that was written and said about the novel in 1984: 'With two notable exceptions— Anthony Burgess and Mary Lee Settle—no writer seems to have perceived that Orwell's book was dealing not with the Future but the Present.' He then explains that the title was obtained by reversing the digits of the year in which Orwell wrote the book—1948 becoming 1984. No letter has been traced to show that Orwell intended this, though it might have struck him as an amusing by-effect. The facsimile of the draft shows clearly that the novel was first set in 1980; then, as time passed in the writing of the book, 1982, and finally 1984. This is particularly plain on page 23 of the facsimile, but the consequential changes occur at various points. It is arguable that, whether the novel is or is not prophetic, in setting the novel in 1980, 1982, and 1984, Orwell was projecting forward his own age, 36, when World War II started, from the time when he was planning or actually writing the novel. Thus, 1944 + 36 = 1980; 1946 + 36 = 1982; 1948 + 36 = 1984. It is not, perhaps, a coincidence that in 1944, when the idea for the novel might reasonably be said to be taking shape, Richard was adopted. It would be natural for Orwell to wonder at that time (as many people did) what prospects there would be for war or peace when their children grew up. The first year chosen for the novel, 1980, was the year Richard would have been the same age as was Orwell in 1939. By choosing *Nineteen Eighty-Four*, Orwell set his novel in both present *and* future. Had Orwell only been

19

writing about the present, there would have been no need for him to have advanced the year beyond 1980, and preserving the interval he did—of 36 years—must have had significance for him. Inverting the final digits of 1980 and 1982 would have been meaningless; the inversion of those for 1984 was, therefore, probably coincidental. 'As I Please,' 57, 2 February 1945 (*2613*) has several ideas which were developed in *Nineteen Eighty-Four*. It also refers to Richard, then a baby, being awakened by a V–2 exploding – a 'Steamer' (*CW*, IX, 87). Orwell refers to Richard as the 'Class of 1964', so looking forward to the age at which he might be expected to graduate. Richard's future was thus in his mind when he was planning the novel.

4. Translations, that in Italian, for example, sometimes used the numerical date.

5. The appendix, 'The Principles of Newspeak,' was included in English and U.S. editions.

3526. To Reginald Reynolds

17 January 1949   Handwritten

The Cotswold Sanatorium
Cranham
Glos.

Dear Reg,[1]

Re. pamphlets.[2] I've just been reading the Hammonds' book "The English Labourer."[3] Don't you think there's sure to be some good inflammatory pamphlet, round about 1800, about either enclosure of the commons, or the workhouses, or the game laws?[4] I'd never realised before that the game laws by which poachers were transported to Australia etc. were new about that date, or at least were tightened up then. I thought they were a Norman survival. The innumerable footnotes etc. in the Hammonds' book might put you on to something.

As to modern ones. One I imagine we might include is Keynes's "Economic Consequences of the Peace"?[5] In a way it's well-known, but I've never seen a copy of it myself. Lawrence's "Pornography & Obscenity" I have already suggested.[6] There's also an attack on Lawrence by Norman Douglas (re. their mutual friend Magnus) that might be worth looking at.[7]

Don't worry about Laski.[8] In the second introduction[9] I'll pick out one of his choicer bits of writing & use it as an example of what political writing in our time has sunk to.

The above address will find me for some months, I fear.[10]

Yours
George

1. Reginald Reynolds (1905–1958), journalist and author. Though a pacifist—he was a Quaker—he and Orwell were good friends: see *1060, n. 1* and *2728*.
2. The second volume of *British Pamphleteers*, edited by Reynolds. The first volume was published on 15 November 1948; see *3487*. For Orwell's introduction to Vol. 1, see *3206*.
3. In his Reading List for 1949 (see *3727*), Orwell included *The Town Labourer* by 'J. L. and B. Hammond' for January with the note, 'Skimmed only.' This refers to *The Town Labourer 1760–1832: The New Civilization* (1917) by John Lawrence le Breton and Lucy Barbara Hammond. *The Village Labourer 1760–1832: A Study in the Government of England before the Reform Bill* was published in 1911.
4. Orwell's letter has been marked, presumably by Reynolds, underlining '1800,' 'enclosure,' 'workhouses,' and 'game laws.'

5. John Maynard Keynes (1883–1946) published *The Economic Consequences of the Peace* in 1919; New York, 1920. Orwell's letter is annotated (by Reynolds?): 'Hardly a pamphlet.'
6. Published in 1929 as *Criterion Miscellany*, 5; New York, 1930. Reynolds (?) underlined and added a question mark at 'Pornography & Obscenity.'
7. George Norman Douglas(s) (1868–1952), *D. H. Lawrence and Maurice Magnus: A Plea for Better Manners* (Florence and New York, 1928). Douglas was prompted to write by Lawrence's introduction to Magnus's *Memoirs of the Foreign Legion* (1924). Orwell's letter is annotated: 'Too personal & not sufficiently political.'
8. Harold Joseph Laski (1893–1950), from 1926 Professor of Political Science, London School of Economics; see *1241, n. 4*. His books and pamphlets include *Authority in the Modern State* (1919), *Communism* (1927), *The Freedom of the Press in Wartime* (1941), *Russia and the West: A Policy for Britain* (1947). A quotation from his *Freedom of Expression* was used by Orwell in 'Politics and the English Language' to illustrate 'the mental vices from which we now suffer,' in particular, staleness of imagery and lack of precision; see *2815*.
9. Orwell did not live to write the introduction to Volume 2.
10. In addition to the annotations mentioned above, there are notes at the head of the letter instructing that Orwell's address be sent to Miss Athill, of Allan Wingate (publisher of *British Pamphleteers*); noting that an earlier letter had been sent with a covering note 'to the Secretary,' dated '26.1.49'; and saying 'Consult re "That's Sedition," ' Two bold exclamation marks are drawn against Orwell's address. Diana Athill (1917–) was the author of *Instead of a Letter* (1963); she edited Jean Rhys's unfinished autobiography, *Smile Please* (1979).

3527. To Tosco Fyvel

18 January 1949   Handwritten

The Cotswold Sanatorium
Cranham
Glos.

Dear Tosco,
The above address will find me (for 2–3 months, I'm afraid), so do you think they can send me Tribune direct here?

Incidentally I imagine my subscription[1] is due for renewal, & they always send me *two* copies every week, owing I suppose to some overlapping of departments, though I've made several efforts to prevent this, as it simply means waste of one copy.

I've felt a bit better since being here. They are giving me something called P.A.S. But I am very weak & am going to do no work for some time to come, which I think is the wisest thing in the circumstances.

Love to all
George

1. Whereas 'two' appears to have been underlined by Orwell, the underlining of 'subscription' (not here indicated by italic) looks as if it has been done in the *Tribune* office.

3528. To *The New Leader* (New York)

18 January 1949   Handwritten

The Cotswold Sanatorium
CRANHAM
Gloucestershire, England

Dear Sir,
I see that you are still sending the "New Leader" to my old address at 27B
Canonbury Square, London N.1. I should be much obliged if you could alter
the address, as I have now given up my Canonbury Square flat & they may
not continue forwarding letters indefinitely.
The above address will find me for the next 2–3 months, but a more
permanent address is:
Barnhill, Isle of Jura, Argyllshire, Scotland.[1]
Do I not owe you a subscription, by the way? I asked my New York agents
to take out a regular subscription to the "New Leader", but I am not certain
whether this was ever done.

Yours truly
Geo. Orwell

1. The address has been underlined, presumably in the office of *The New Leader*. The journal was
edited by S. M. Levitas, who continually pressed Orwell to write articles for him. See *3410,
n. 1.*

3529. To Sir Richard Rees

18 January 1949   Handwritten

The Cotswold Sanatorium
Cranham
Glos.

Dear Richard,
I hope you got home all right & were not too exhausted by all your
journeyings on my behalf. I am well settled in here & quite comfortable. The
"chalet" isn't as grim as I had feared—quite warm, with central heating & hot
& cold water, & the food is quite good. My appetite has definitely improved.
The Tawneys[1] came in & saw me, but now have left for London. Karl
Schnetzler[2] also came, & Warburg is coming on Friday. I'll send back your
book "In Parenthesis"[3] when I can. I think it's very good in a way, but it's
what I call mannered writing, a thing I don't approve of. I haven't heard from
Barnhill yet, but trust Avril has got properly over her cold. I don't know how
the weather has been there, but here it has been as mild & sunny as early April,
& the birds have even been trying to sing. My book has been accepted for the
USA & they've also agreed to reprint a number of earlier ones on quite good
terms, which is unusual in an American publisher. Actually I'm somewhat

against this, as they're sure to lose money on the reprints & this may sour them on later books.

They are giving me something called P.A.S., which I believe stands for para-amino-salicylic acid. They say it is good. It's very expensive, though not so expensive as streptomycin. You take it by mouth, which I must say I prefer to those endless injections. I have been thinking things over, & have decided that even if I am reasonably well by the summer, I must from now on spend my winters within reach of a doctor—where, I don't know yet, but possibly somewhere like Brighton. If, therefore, it is impossible for me to be at Barnhill in the winter, can we fix things somehow so that Bill is looked after during those months?[4] I don't in the least wish to sever my connection with Barnhill, because it is a marvellous place to be at, & in any case we have now sent down fairly respectable roots there, but I think it would be wiser to do as I first intended, when I took the place in 1946, & use it only for the summers. I must try & stay alive for 5–10 years, which involves having medical attention at hand when necessary, & in addition I am just a nuisance to everybody when I am ill, whereas in a more civilized place this doesn't matter. In the summers no doubt I shall generally be well enough to potter about, provided that this present infection is got under. In more reasonable times we might arrange to live every winter in Sicily or somewhere, but nowadays I suppose it will have to be somewhere in England.[5] In the beginning we took the house on the understanding that we should only stay there April—November, but now there is Bill. It is a question of finding a housekeeper for him. Have you got any ideas about this? I'll also write to Avril setting forth the problem.

Gleb Struve sent me a translation of some remarks about me in a Russian magazine.[6] They're really very annoying, but disquieting in a way because the whole thing is somehow so *illiterate*.

Yours
Eric

1. Professor R. H. Tawney (1888–1962), historian, author of *Religion and the Rise of Capitalism* (1926), *Equality* (1931), and other books, was joint editor of *Economic History Review*, 1926–33, and of *Studies in Economic and Social History* from 1934. He and his wife were very old friends of Richard Rees, who had asked them to visit Orwell at Cranham, since they were on holiday nearby at their country home.
2. For Karl Schnetzler, see *534A* and *2893*.
3. *In Parenthesis* (1937) was by David Jones (1895–1974), poet, novelist, and artist. It combines free verse with an autobiographical novel of Jones's World War I experience. It won the Hawthornden Prize. Orwell does not list it in his reading for 1949. It apparently had still not been returned by 25 April; see *3607, n. 3*.
4. Richard Rees had invested £1,000 in Barnhill and was Orwell's 'sleeping partner' in the venture; see Crick, 527, 531, and 535. Bill was William Dunn, who farmed the Barnhill land; see *3235, n. 2*.
5. Travel abroad was made difficult because the government, owing to the poor state of Britain's international financial position, limited severely the amount of money that could be taken out of the country.
6. With his letter to Orwell of 1 January 1949, Gleb Struve had enclosed two articles by Ivan Anisimov attacking Arthur Koestler and Orwell, 'typical of the literary xenophobia now raging in the Soviet Union;' see *3524, n. 1*.

3530. To Fredric Warburg

18 January 1949

LOOK FORWARD TO SEEING YOU FRIDAY DO BRING PAMELA CAR WILL MEET YOU

GEORGE

The visit was arranged for Friday, 21 January 1949. Warburg went with his wife, Pamela, and in *All Authors are Equal: The Publishing Life of Fredric Warburg 1936–1971* (1973) he gives a vivid account of Cranham (which horrified them) and of Orwell's distressing state. Warburg, confirming the visit in a letter to Orwell of 19 January, asked his permission to have a frank discussion with his doctors: 'Your future is important to more people than yourself.' In reply to their questions, Orwell told Pamela Warburg that 'a woman doctor [presumably Margaret Kirkman] visits me every morning. . . . I think she's thoroughly competent and kind, and asks me how I feel and all that.' However, in response to Mrs. Warburg's questions, it transpired that no chest examination by stethoscope had taken place. 'I expect they're understaffed here, you know,' Orwell told her, 'she probably hasn't got time,' to which Mrs. Warburg angrily replied: 'It's monstrous, absolutely shocking' (109). See, however, Shelden's assessment, *3520, n. 2*. Nevertheless, Orwell thought the doctors knew what they were doing, and Warburg remarks, 'The reply was so typical of him—he couldn't bear to make a fuss—and so heartrending that I could hardly believe my ears, but at least it made it easy for Pamela to beg him to see a London specialist.' She persuaded Orwell to promise to let them know if he would like Dr. Andrew Morland (a leading specialist in the field who had treated D. H. Lawrence) to see him and, if necessary, to get him into University College Hospital, London. Warburg also recounts how at this time, Louis Simmonds, a bookseller with whom Orwell dealt and who was a warm admirer of Orwell, told Warburg that he and one or two friends would raise £500—a very large sum in those days—to enable Orwell to go to Switzerland for treatment because 'he is far too precious to lose' (107–09). In his letter of 19 January, Warburg told Orwell that a number of friends (whom he did not name) wished to subscribe money to send him to Switzerland: 'In other words, you are a much loved writer and your public want you to get well.'

3531. To David Astor

20 January 1949   Handwritten

The Cotswold Sanatorium
Cranham
Glos.

Dear David,

I've just received two tins of butter from your secretary, who tells me she is also arranging to send me eggs. I'm writing to her separately. It's awfully kind, but *honestly* I don't want to be sent food, because I can't make use of it. My sister is already sending me butter from Jura, & as to eggs, I really can only just eat so much food as I am given already. Your secretary said you were also sending me a bed-jacket & an electric blanket, for which, again, very many thanks. I don't know why you should take all this trouble about me. I am quite comfortable here & I think improving a little. My temperature chart is what they call "flattening out" & my appetite has been better since I came here. I am trying not to do any work, which means keeping off various people who have been badgering me about articles etc. It was very nice to see Karl.[1] The Tawneys also came to see me, & Warburg is coming tomorrow. My new book is fixed up for publication in the USA, I am glad to say. I had not been sure about this, as I doubt whether it is very much up their street. Richard loved the Meccano you sent him, though I suppose he will have lost most of the screws by this time. I suppose in about a year he will have to go to school & I shall have to start making arrangements. I have thought things over & decided I shall have to spend my winters somewhere near a doctor, & only go to Scotland in the summer months, which will need some adjustments because of Bill Dunn's position at Barnhill. But at any rate Richard can start going to a day school wherever I am next winter. He hasn't any interest in learning his letters yet, though he loves being read to. I hope I shall see you some time, but I know how busy you are. They seem to think I shall have to stay in bed for at least 2–3 months, & to keep on with this P.A.S. stuff for about that long. Thanks so much again for sending the things.

Yours
George

1. Karl Schnetzler.

3532. To Miss Brockholes

     20 January 1949   Handwritten

The Cotswold Sanatorium
Cranham
Glos.

Dear Miss Brockholes,[1]
Very many thanks for your letter of the 19th, & for sending the two pounds of butter. Quite honestly, though, I would prefer *not* to be sent food, because I cannot make use of it. I get butter sent from Jura in any case, & as for eggs, I can hardly eat all the food I am given as it is. It is very kind to think of me, but it is a pity to waste food. I am writing to Mr Astor separately about this.

Yours sincerely
Eric Blair

1. David Astor's secretary.

3533. To Leonard Moore

20 January 1949   Handwritten

The Cotswold Sanatorium
Cranham
Glos.

Dear Moore,

Many thanks for your last letter, & for sending the other copy of "Burmese Days."

I have had a tiresome letter from André Deutsch ("Allan Wingate") about the second vol. of that wretched pamphlets book. He suddenly says that the MS. has got to be ready by the middle of April. I have nothing to do with the compilation of it. This is being done by Reginald Reynolds. I have made a few suggestions to him, but that is all I can do. As to the introduction, I can only write it after the pamphlets have been compiled & after consultation with R.R., & can't possibly be tied down to a date. Could you please make clear to Deutsch that I am seriously ill & am trying to do no work at present, & that I cannot undertake to produce *anything* as early as mid-April, especially if—as will probably be the case—Reynolds does not produce his collection of pamphlets till just about then. Tell Deutsch that if he is in a hurry he had better get someone else to write the introduction for the second vol., & if you can head him off, don't let him nag me about it further, as I do so want a rest, at any rate from hack work of that sort.

I will consult with Warburg, who is coming here tomorrow, about the title of the book. I don't know how much difference it makes to publish a book under different names in the two countries, but I don't think Harcourt Brace should be forced to use one title if they prefer another. On the other hand the Appendix *must* be retained if possible. It is unusual in a novel, but no one is obliged to read it, & it helps to elucidate at least one passage in the body of the book. So don't on any account *suggest* to them that it should be cut out.

Yours sincerely
Eric Blair

3534. To Leonard Moore

22 January 1949   Typewritten

The Cotswold Sanatorium
Cranham
Glos.

Dear Moore,

Many thanks for your letter of the 21st.

I am glad Harcourt Brace seem to be pleased with "1984." I have had a talk with Warburg, who prefers this title and is inclined to agree with me that it would be better to write the number NINETEEN EIGHTY-FOUR rather than put the figure. As I said before, I doubt whether it hurts a book to be published under different names in Britain and the USA—certainly it is often done— and I would like Harcourt Brace to follow their own wishes in the matter of the title.

I don't want to make any changes in the text of the book, but if they are going ahead and not waiting for proofs from Warburg, can you make sure that I am given the proofs to correct myself. I don't fancy there are many mistakes in the typescript, but it is a difficult script because of the many neologisms, and I am the likeliest person to spot any printer's errors. To send the proofs over here won't impose much delay if they airmail them.

I imagine this address will find me for at any rate two or three months.

Yours sincerely
[Signed] Eric Blair
Eric Blair

3535. To Dwight Macdonald

27 January 1949   Typewritten

The Cotswold Sanatorium
Cranham
Gloucestershire

Dear Dwight,

I dare say you may have read this book[1] before, but I thought you might like a copy. It's the second issue of my uniform edit. As you see by the address I've been ill again. I was much better when I came out of hospital in July last year after the streptomycin, but I began to relapse in September, and I would have gone for treatment then only I had to finish a wretched book which, thanks to illness, I had been messing about with for 18 months. It's supposed to come out in June and I'll see you get a copy. I mucked it up really, partly because I was ill almost throughout the time of writing it, but some of the ideas in it might interest you perhaps. I thought the last number of "Politics" was very good, but it seemed to me that you, ie. you personally, had shifted your position somewhat, and I imagine you got some angry reactions from pacifists. I was very sorry I could not be more helpful about your book on Wallace. I suppose he will have another try, by the way?[2]

I really wanted to ask you two things. First of all, have I a regular subscription to "Politics?" I asked my agent to take one out about a year ago, but she may not have done so as she seemed to think I ought to be on the free list of all New York papers. Secondly, I wonder if it would be possible to buy in New York a copy (secondhand of course) of George Gissing's "New Grub Street?" I don't know how one advertises for books in the USA, but if a copy of the book does exist I can pay for it and for any adverts, as I have some dollars over there I think. I have been trying for some time to induce some publisher to reprint certain of Gissing's books, and that particular one, which used to be about his best-known one, is now so rare that after years of trying I can't get a copy. Even the London Library, which lost some its books in the blitz, hasn't now got one. I wonder if you know Gissing—a minor writer, I suppose, but one of the very few true novelists England has produced.

I am writing this in a "chalet" which sounds pretty grim but is actually quite comfortable. I can't see the country round but it is in the Cotswolds which is supposed to be a beauty spot—it's the Beatrix Potter[3] country if that means anything to you. Professor Tawney ("Religion and the Rise of Capitalism") lives a couple of miles away, but unfortunately he's now in London lecturing to the London School of Economics. He is one of the few major figures in the Labour movement whom one can both respect and like personally. I shall probably be here till some time in the spring or summer, then perhaps I can get to Scotland for a few months, then I shall have to spend the winter somewhere within reach of a doctor, perhaps in Brighton or some such place. I am very much out of touch with the literary world. George Woodcock was talking of emigrating to British Columbia, but I don't know whether he is really doing so.

Yours
George

P.S. I don't believe I ever thanked you for so kindly sending me the Dr Johnson book[4] and "Let us Now Praise Famous Men"—the latter I thought very interesting material, and the photographs of the boys in it just like my idea of Tom Sawyer, but what I call undigested—the way *not* to write a book in my opinion.[5]

1. *Burmese Days* was originally published in 1934. 3,000 copies of the Uniform Edition were printed, of which 2,000 were bound initially; the publication date was January 1949. The last copy was sold in 1950. A second impression of 3,000 copies was published in February 1951. Harcourt, Brace published a photo-litho-offset edition from the first impression on 19 January 1950 of 3,000 copies (Willison).
2. Henry Wallace, who failed in his bid for the Presidency of the United States in 1948. See *3215* and *3215, n. 1.*
3. Helen Beatrix Potter (1866–1943), author of children's books, of which *Pigling Bland* was a favourite of Orwell's. Linking her with Gloucestershire is curious. She was born in London and is particularly associated with the Lake District; she bought a farm there, at Near Sawrey, in 1896. As a child she stayed with her grandmother at Camfield Place near Hatfield—but that is still a long way from Cranham. Orwell did fish on a short holiday at Callow End, Worcestershire, in July 1942 (see *1258*), about 20 to 25 miles from Cranham.
4. Joseph Wood Krutch's *Samuel Johnson* (1944); see *3392, n. 1.*
5. By James Agee and Walker Evans (1941). This moving documentary representation of the sharecroppers during the Depression does not attempt to integrate its text (by Agee) with Evans's photographs. For a considered analysis of *Let Us Now Praise Famous Men*, see W. Stott, *Documentary Expression in Thirties America* (New York, 1973).

3536. To Sir Richard Rees

28 January 1949   Handwritten

Cranham

Dear Richard,

I thought over what you said, & it seems to me that unless Bill definitely wants to, it would be a great pity to sever his connection with Barnhill, into which he has put so much work. To move the stock would also cost a great deal, or on the other hand to sell it & start again would presumably involve a loss. I should have thought the Fletchers,[1] who are interested in keeping the North End under cultivation, might be able to arrange for someone to keep house for Bill during the winter. I suggested to Avril that if she *wants* to, she could stay on there & I would make arrangements for R. & myself during the winter months. So far as I am concerned I should be very sorry not to be able to have Barnhill as a place during the summer. Most of my furniture & books are now there, & the garden is more or less under control & could be re-organised so as not to need much doing to it. On the other hand I have no doubt I shall have to live an invalid life in the winters from now on. In the beginning, of course, we took the place as a summer place, & my idea had been to spend the winters in London. It is very unfortunate that the continued working of the farm more or less depends on our presence, although we are not the farmers, & I feel unhappy that my health should interfere with this. I should think it a possible arrangement that Bill should live in winter with the Rosgas,[2] if he & they agreed & if he took his milch cows over there. It occurs to me that as the Rosgas would have to be paid for his keep, it might sweeten them to the arrangement if they made a bit of profit on the transaction,[3] & I wouldn't mind contributing something a week to this. I am in favour of keeping the establishment going & the North End inhabited. You might tell me what you think of all this.

Don't forget that I owe you various sums of money. For a consignment of drink, for a rug & two cushions, & no doubt for other things I've forgotten. We'd better settle this before it gets too muddled up. I was also to contribute £25 towards the lorry.

The American publishers seem quite excited about my book, so they are going to go ahead without waiting for proofs from Warburg.[4] This will mean 2 sets of proofs to correct. I don't suppose it will arise, but *if* I should feel very poorly & unequal to correcting proofs, do you think you could do them for me? As there are a lot of neologisms there are bound to be many printers' errors of a stupid kind, & American compositors are very tiresome to deal with as they always think they know better than the author. I wouldn't trust publishers or agents to do the job. On the other hand you could trust the MS., in which I don't expect there are more than a very few slips. It is most important that there shouldn't be misprints in a book of this kind. However, as I say, I don't imagine this will arise. I have been feeling better & don't have temperatures now, though I don't exactly know how much progress I am making as I haven't been weighed or X-rayed since the first time. This P.A.S. stuff makes me feel sick but otherwise doesn't seem to have secondary effects. One is very well looked after here but the doctors pay very little attention. The chief doctor, Dr. Hoffmann, I have never seen, & the other, a woman, simply looks in every morning & asks how I feel, & never even uses her stethoscope. However, I suppose they know best. When I am about again, I suppose in the summer, I shall see a London specialist, if possible the man I saw just before the war. They can't do anything for you, but I want an expert opinion on how long I am likely to live, because I must make my plans accordingly.

I enclose the remarks from the Russian magazine which Struve translated.[5] Don't lose them, will you, because I haven't a copy. Even allowing for possible unfairness in translation, doesn't it strike you that there is something queer about the *language* of totalitarian literature—a curious mouthing sort of quality, as of someone who is choking with rage & can never quite hit on the words he wants?

I hope you have been able to read this. The bad handwriting is due to my hands being cold. It's turned colder after being incredibly mild for some days. I'm quite warm in bed, however, as I now have an electric blanket, much better than a hot water bottle.

Yours
George

1. Margaret Fletcher (1917–), the laird (or landowner), and her husband, Robin Fletcher, at one time a master at Eton and a Japanese prisoner of war, were concerned to improve the land and the way it was farmed (see Crick, 510). After Robin Fletcher's death, in 1960, Margaret Fletcher married again; as Margaret Fletcher Nelson she gave accounts of Orwell's time on Jura in *Orwell Remembered*, 225–29 and *Remembering Orwell*, 170–74.
2. Tony Rozga, a Polish ex-serviceman, and his Scottish wife, Jeannie. For their reminiscences, see *Remembering Orwell*, 185–87.
3. transaction] *Orwell originally wrote* 'arrangement'
4. U.S. editions were commonly set from proofs of an English edition or were produced by a process such as photo–litho–offset. Harcourt, Brace was so anxious to publish *Nineteen Eighty-Four* that it was set from a carbon copy of Orwell's typescript. For differences between the U.S. and English editions as a result of this, see *CW*, IX, Textual Note, 327–29.
5. Gleb Struve sent this material on 1 January 1949. Two articles had 'taken to pieces' Orwell and Koestler; another attacked Struve. See *3524, n. 1*.

3537. To Anthony Powell

2 February 1949   Handwritten

The Cotswold Sanatorium
Cranham
Glos.

Dear Tony,

I wonder how you are getting on. If you happen to see Malcolm,[1] will you tell him from me that it was awfully kind to suggest that Sanatorium in Kent, but actually I had already arranged to come to this place. I have been here about a month. It's quite comfortable, & I think I am getting slightly better, at any rate I feel better & have stopped having temperatures, though I haven't gained any weight yet. I imagine I shall be here several months, then be at large for the summer, & then I shall [have] to spend the winter somewhere near a doctor, & perhaps somewhere warm as well. They are giving me something called P.A.S., which is rather nasty but nothing to the treatments I had at the other place.

I had to refuse some books the T.L.S. recently offered me. I am trying to do no work whatever for at least another month or two. My new book is supposed to come out in May or June, which doubtless means July.[2] It's a Utopia written in the form of a novel, & I think the title will be "1984", though we haven't fixed that with complete firmness. Malcolm told me he too had finished a novel.[3] How about you? It's a god-awful job getting back to writing books again after years of time-wasting, but I feel now I've broken the spell & could go on writing if I were well again.

This part of England, which I don't know, is supposed to be a beauty spot. The weather has been quite incredible,[4] more like April than January. I live in a "chalet", which isn't quite as grim as it sounds. Please remember me to Violet.

Yours
George

1. Malcolm Muggeridge (1903–1990), journalist, author, and broadcaster; see *604, n. 2* and *2860, n. 1.*
2. For once Orwell was not to be disappointed by delay in the publication of his work. *Nineteen Eighty-Four* was published by Secker & Warburg on 8 June 1949 and on 13 June by Harcourt, Brace & Company in New York.
3. *Affairs of the Heart* (1949).
4. That winter and spring were so mild and sunny that on only one weekend was there even light snow (5 and 6 March 1949).

3538. To Julian Symons

2 February 1949   Handwritten

The Cotswold Sanatorium
Cranham
Glos.

Dear Julian,

I wonder how you & family are getting on. I have been in this place about a month. I think I told you last time I wrote that I had been feeling very bad again. I should have gone for treatment earlier, but I had to finish off a wretched book which I had been messing about with for 18 months, thanks to illness. At present I am trying not to do any work, & don't expect to start any for another month or two. I shall probably be in here for 2 or 3 months, then perhaps I can get up to London & go back to Scotland for a bit, & then spend the winter in some place near a doctor, perhaps in Torquay or somewhere like that. I might even go abroad for the winter, but I so hate the nuisance of passports, currency etc. They are giving me something called P.A.S. which makes you sick all the time but is less unpleasant than injections. During the last month my weight has only increased 4 ounces, but actually I do feel better & I am well looked after here, though the doctors don't strike me as very brilliant.

, Your baby must be getting quite a size & must be cutting teeth & eating solid food. I wonder if you had the battle over weaning that we had with Richard. It's like Machiavelli says about government, you can't do it except by force or fraud. Richard is getting [on] for 5 now & is enormous & very healthy, though still not interested in learning his letters. He likes to be read to, but doesn't see that as a reason for learning to read himself. I suppose this coming winter he will have to start going to school, which he is certain to enjoy as he is very gregarious.

My new book is supposed to come out in July (Warburg said May or June, which means July in publisher's language) but maybe the American edition will be out first. Any way I'll see you get a copy. I must thank you for some friendly references in the M.E. News., including one to that ghastly book of pamphlets in which I reluctantly collaborated. I am having another try to get Warburg to reprint some of Gissing's books, to which I would write introductions. They reprinted (I forget which publishers) those 3 last year, but of course the wrong ones.[1] Meanwhile I am still trying to get hold of a copy of "New Grub Street", & am now trying in New York. Somewhat to my annoyance that paper "Politics & Letters" got me to write an essay on Gissing & then died, & have never sent my article back or answered my queries about it,[2] though it appears distinctly unlikely that the magazine will re-appear. What a calamity that we can't find a way of financing *one* decent magazine in this country. I suppose it's only a question of losing about £2000 a year. The Partisan Review have either increased their sales or got hold of some money from somewhere, as I notice they now pay one quite decently. For all those articles I did during the war for them I got only 10 dollars a time.[3]

I don't know this part of the country but it's supposed to be a beauty spot. Professor Tawney lives nearby, but unfortunately he's had to go back to London as the L.S.E. term had started. The weather is quite incredible, bright sunshine & birds singing as though it were April. Please remember me to your wife & excuse this bad handwriting.

Yours
George

1. *In the Year of the Jubilee* and *The Whirlpool* were published by Watergate Classics; the former had an introduction by William Plomer, and the latter, one by Myfanwy Evans. See Orwell''s essay 'George Gissing,' *3406*.
2. *Politics and Letters* ceased publication before Orwell's essay could be published, but the typescript was not returned until ten years after Orwell's death. See headnote to *3406*.
3. Approximately £2.50 at the exchange rate then in force.

3539. To Anthony Powell

4 February 1949   Typewritten

> The Cotswold Sanatorium
> Cranham
> Glos.

Dear Tony,

Thanks so much for your letter. Of course if you or Malcolm or both could come and see me I'd love it. This place is about seven miles from Cheltenham, but you get here by coming to Stroud on the GWR.[1] If you do come, let me know in advance so that I can arrange about the car to meet you. I can give you lunch and of course tea. I think there's a train that gets in to Stroud at 12.5. I think somebody else is coming on either the 12th or the 26th Feb., but any other day would suit.

I'll see that you get a proof copy or advance copy of my book.

> Yours
> George

---

1. The Great Western Railway, the only company to keep its identity when Britain's railways were grouped into four units in 1923, before nationalisation and the unification of all four on 1 January 1948. Stroud lies some 102 miles west of London. With the breakup of the nationalised system in the 1990s, the name Great Western has been restored for part of the network.

3540. To Sir Richard Rees

4 February 1949   Typewritten

> The Cotswold Sanatorium
> Cranham
> Glos.

Dear Richard,

I enclose cheque for what I owed you. You will notice I have added £3. Do you think you could be kind enough to get your wine merchant to send me 2 bottles of rum, which I suppose will come to about that. I assume he will know how to pack them so as not to get them broken.

I have heard from Avril who says she and Bill both think it would be better to move to a farm on the mainland. I think they are right, but can't help feeling bad about it as I feel my health is the precipitating factor, though the state of the road is a good second. I think you would be rash to sink more money in any non-removable improvements etc.,[1] because such a place might of its nature become untenable at some time. I trust it will be possible to move without selling off the stock and losing on the transaction. I am afraid the actual move will be a godawful° business from which I shall probably absent myself whenever it happens. I have asked Avril to tell Robin[2] that unless he happens on a tenant who would actually farm the place,

I would like to keep on the lease of the house. I don't see why we shouldn't have it as a summer holiday place, and one could leave camp beds etc. there. Of course I may never be strong enough for that kind of thing again even in the summer, but others may be and the rent is next to nothing.

I am reading B. Russell's latest book, about human knowledge.[3] He quotes Shakespeare, "Doubt that the stars are fire, Doubt that the earth doth move" (it goes on I think, "Doubt truth to be a liar, But never doubt I love.") But he makes it "Doubt that the *sun* doth move," and uses this as an instance of S.'s ignorance. Is that right? I had an idea it was "the earth." But I haven't got Shakespeare here and I can't even remember where the lines come (must be one of the comedies I think.) I wish you'd verify this for me if you can remember where it comes.[4] I see by the way that the Russian press has just described B. R. as a wolf in a dinner jacket and a wild beast in philosopher's robes.

I don't know really that I'd be very interested in that book about the cards etc. I had heard of that chap before,[5] but I can't get very interested in telepathy unless it could be developed into a reliable method.

I've been reading "The First Europe"[6] (history of the Dark Ages), very interesting though written in a rather tiresome way. For the first week or two here I hadn't got my book supply going and had to rely on the library, which meant reading some fearful trash. Among other things I read a Deeping[7] for the first time—actually not so bad as I expected, a sort of natural novelist like A. S. M. Hutchinson.[8] Also a Peter Cheyney.[9] He evidently does well out of his books as I used often to get invites from him for slap-up parties at the Dorchester.[10] I have sent for several of Hardy's novels[11] and am looking at them rather unenthusiastically.

Yours
Eric

1. Rees had invested £1,000 in developing Barnhill.
2. Robin Fletcher; see *3536, n. 1.*
3. *Human Knowledge: Its Scope and Limits* (1948). In his list of what he read in 1949, Orwell wrote against this book, 'Tried & failed.'
4. Russell was almost textually correct. The passage is from *Hamlet*, 2.2.116–19; the first line should read: 'Doubt thou' not 'Doubt that.' Russell takes the meaning at its simple, face value—that the earth does not move. If that is correct, Shakespeare (or Hamlet) cannot be accused of ignorance because, as the cosmos was still almost uniformly then understood, that was correct according to Ptolomaic theory. Copernicus and Galileo were challenging that theory (and Galileo and Shakespeare were born in the same year), and their theory was regarded as heretical, as the Inquisition pointedly explained to Galileo. However, this passage is usually interpreted as hinting that the earth does move; Shakespeare was more subtle than either Russell or Orwell seems to have realised, and Hamlet, perhaps, more devious.
5. Professor J. B. Rhine, Director of the Parapsychology Laboratory at Duke University, in North Carolina.
6. By Cecil Delisle Burns; Orwell lists it under March and annotates it, 'Skimmed.' Writing to Brenda Salkeld, 27 July 1934 (see *202*), Orwell asked her, 'Do you remember that afternoon when we had tea with Delisle Burns . . . ?'. For a note on Burns, see *202, n. 4.*
7. Warwick Deeping (1877–1950), a prolific novelist who trained as a doctor. His most successful book was *Sorrell and Son* (1925), based on his work in the Royal Army Medical Corps during World War I. Orwell does not list which of his almost seventy books he read;

he had from time to time expressed some scorn of 'the Dells and Deepings' of fiction. See, for example, *Keep the Aspidistra Flying, CW*, IV, 7/34: 'Even the Dells and Deepings do at least turn out their yearly acre of print.' See also the footnote thereto, where these authors were originally described as writing 'garbage.' Orwell lists nothing by Deeping among books he read in 1949; see *3727*.

8. Arthur Stuart-Menteth Hutchinson (1879–1971), born in Uttar Pradesh, India; a prolific novelist whose *If Winter Comes* had earlier attracted Orwell's attention; see 'Good Bad Books,' *Tribune*, 2 November 1945, *2780*.
9. Peter Cheyney (1896–1951), prolific author, chiefly of detective stories and thrillers, though he also published poems and lyrics. He served in World War I, rose to the rank of major, and was severely wounded in 1916. He was news editor of the *Sunday Graphic*, 1933–34. The novel was *Dark Hero*; see *3727*.
10. The Dorchester Hotel, Park Lane, London.
11. Orwell's reading list for 1949 shows he read *Jude the Obscure* and *Tess of the D'Urbevilles* in February.

3541. To Julian Symons

4 February 1949   Typewritten

> The Cotswold Sanatorium
> Cranham
> Glos.

Dear Julian,

Thanks so much for your letter. Do send me a copy of your thriller.[1] I'm sure I should enjoy it. I do nothing now except read anyway, and I'm rather an amateur of detective stories, although, as you know, I have old-fashioned tastes in them. I recently by the way read for the first time "The Postman always Rings Twice"[2]—what an awful book.

I'd love it if you could come and see me any time, though of course don't put yourself out. I think someone else is coming on either Feb. 12th or Feb. 26th; but any other date. Tony Powell said he might be able to come and see me—if so perhaps you could come the same day. You get here by coming to Stroud on the GWR, and I think there's a train that gets in at 12.5. But if you do come, let me know in advance so that I can arrange for a car to meet you, and for lunch. I can give you lunch and tea.

My new book is a Utopia in the form of a novel. I ballsed it up rather, partly owing to being so ill while I was writing it, but I think some of the ideas in it might interest you. We haven't definitively fixed the title, but I think it will be called "Nineteen Eighty-four." Tony says Malcolm Muggeridge has a novel coming out about the same time.[3]

Please remember me to the family.

> Yours
> George

1. *Bland Beginning*; read by Orwell in February 1949; see *3727*.
2. By James M. Cain, published in 1934; read by Orwell in January 1949.
3. *Affairs of the Heart* (1949). It was the last book listed by Orwell in the list of books he read in 1949; see December in *3727*.

3542. To Fredric Warburg

5 February 1949   Typewritten

> The Cotswold Sanatorium
> Cranham
> Glos.

Dear Fred,

I think you said you had got some photos from the Richards, but at any rate my sister has sent on three which she found at home, one of which isn't bad. It's one of the Richards' ones, so probably, you've got it, but if you like I'll send it on.

Tony Powell said could I send him a proof of "1984" when it appears for the Times Lit. Supp., so I've added him to the list. I think the people we might profitably send proof copies to are the following, including people in the USA:

Betrand Russell
Lancelot Hogben
Dr C. D. Darlington (The John Innes Horticultural Institute)[1]
Aldous Huxley (in USA?)
Edmund Wilson (USA)
Arthur Koestler (USA?)
Anthony Powell (T.L.S.)

If that isn't too many. I suppose it can be marked on the cover of any sent out that this is an uncorrected proof. I imagine that with an MS of that type even the page proofs will have a lot of mistakes.[2]

It was so nice seeing you both last week. The Azalea is blooming beautifully. Thanks so much for paying the advance on the book so early. Please give everyone my love.

> Yours
> George

1. Dr. Darlington had participated in BBC broadcasts to India organised by Orwell; see *1170* and *1170, n. 1*. The reason for his inclusion in this list is not known. No letter to him from Orwell has survived since that of 13 July 1943. He was one of those who spoke out against the man Stalin appointed to head Soviet biology in July 1948, the geneticist T. D. Lysenko. Lysenko's theories raised storms of protest by scientists and others in the West (and proved a costly failure). Other scientists known to Orwell, including C. H. Waddington, also spoke out, so the inclusion of Darlington's name is mysterious. For Lysenko and opposition to him, see Gary Werskey, *The Visible College*, 293–303. Werskey mentions Darlington and Waddington on 294. Orwell read Darlington's pamphlet *The Conflict of Science and Society* in May 1949; see *3727*.
2. Because Warburg was ill with bronchitis, Jon Pattison replied to Orwell on 7 February, saying they had received an envelope containing four different photographs from Vernon Richards (see *3043, n. 1*), 'which probably includes the one you mention,' and copyright terms had been agreed on for their use. Proof copies were expected in about a week, he reported, and would be sent to those listed by Orwell. He enclosed a copy of a letter to Leonard Moore from Robert Giroux (who was seeing *Nineteen Eighty-Four* through the press for Harcourt, Brace); this letter has not been traced, but see *3544*. On 17 February, Warburg wrote to tell Orwell that proofs were, he imagined, being sent out that day and he specifically mentioned that he would

see that proofs were sent to Dr. Darlington and to Anthony Powell; the others Orwell listed are not mentioned. He had no definite news for Orwell, 'but it is true enough to say that all of us here are extremely optimistic about the book's success, and we still envisage a minimum first printing of 15,000 copies.'

3543. Review of *The Great Tradition* by F. R. Leavis

The Observer, 6 February 1949

A draft manuscript opening for this review has survived on a loose sheet of paper; it is reproduced after the printed text of the review. It is written in ink, and the last word fades badly. *The Observer's* sub-editor headed the review, 'Exclusive Club.'

The subtitle of Dr. Leavis's book is "George Eliot, Henry James, Joseph Conrad," and the bulk of it consists of studies of those three writers. There is also a shorter essay on Dickens's "Hard Times," and an introductory essay in which Dr. Leavis attempts, not altogether convincingly, to fit his chosen authors into a coherent pattern.

There are, it seems, only four "great" English novelists: the three named above, and Jane Austen, who is not here discussed at length. Among modern writers, only D. H. Lawrence can be said to have carried on the tradition. Others who are mentioned with approval are Peacock, Emily Brontë, and T. F. Powys, while Fielding, Hardy and Joyce are admitted to have talent, though of a bad kind. The remaining English novelists are not only inferior but—this at least is the impression one carries away—reprehensible.

The best essay in the book is that on Conrad. This does the thing that criticism can most usefully do—that is, it draws attention to something that is in danger of being neglected. Writing at a time when every novelist was expected to have some kind of regional affiliation, Conrad had the label "the sea" stuck so firmly upon him that the excellence of his political novels has hardly been noticed even to this day. He is remembered as the author of "Lord Jim," and not of "The Secret Agent" and "Under Western Eyes," books which are not only far more grown-up than any that could have been written by an English writer at that date, but also have a structural beauty that Conrad did not often achieve. His best books, largely ignored in his life-time, still need advertising, and Dr. Leavis's essay will assist in the process. The Dickens essay, too, may gain new readers for "Hard Times," a first-rate novel which is often rejected even by the faithful on the ground that it is "not like Dickens."

But just where the "tradition" comes in it is not easy to say. Clearly the four writers whom Dr. Leavis has picked out as "great" do not exhibit any sort of continuity. Two of these "English novelists" are not English, and one of them, Conrad, derives entirely from French and Russian sources. One has the impression that what Dr. Leavis most wants to do is to induce in the reader a feeling of due reverence towards the "great" and of due irreverence towards everybody else.[1] One should read, he seems to imply, with one eye

37

always on the scale of values, like a wine-drinker reminding himself of the price per bottle at every sip.

And he has a magisterial manner of writing which is, if anything, somewhat emphasised by sudden lapses into colloquialism ("Isn't" for "is not," etc.). "Remember, boys," one seems to hear a voice saying intermittently, "I was once a boy myself." But though the boys know that this must be true, they are not altogether reassured. They can still hear the chilly rustle of the gown, and they are aware that there is a cane under the desk which will be produced on not very much provocation. To be caught reading George Moore, for example, would be good for six of the best. So also with Sterne, Trollope, and perhaps Charlotte Brontë. Thackeray is permitted reading so far as "Vanity Fair" is concerned, but not otherwise. Fielding may be read—on half-holidays, say—provided that you remember that he is definitely not "great." On the other hand, in reading Bunyan or Defoe or Dickens (apart from "Hard Times"), the important thing to remember is that they are not novelists.

One would be a little more ready to accept Dr. Leavis's guidance if, for example, he were not an admirer of T. F. Powys. However, his three main essays perform some useful expository work, especially at moments when he is able to forget his quarrels with other critics, Lord David Cecil in particular. But surely a book on the English novel ought at least to mention Smollett, Surtees, Samuel Butler, Mark Rutherford, and George Gissing?

Draft opening of Orwell's review; passages crossed out are set within half-brackets.

The Great Tradition. by F. R. Leavis (Chatto & Windus 12/6)
The subtitle of

Dr Leavis's book is sub-titled "George Eliot, Henry James, Joseph Conrad." & the bulk of it consists of studies of these three writers. There is also a shorter ⌈essay⌉ discussion of² Dickens's Hard Times, &, at the beginning, an essay in which Dr Leavis ⌈attempts³ defines what he means by "greatness" & attempts to establish a continuity between the⌉ attempts, not altogether convincingly, to fit his chosen few into a continuous pattern.

There are, it seems, only four "great" English novelists, Jane Austen (not here discussed at length), George Eliot, James & Conrad. Among modern writers, only D. H. Lawrence

1. Orwell's rejection here of exclusiveness is also to be found in a much earlier review in which he criticises the 'Cambridge school' for taking this attitude; it is a review of Michael Roberts's *Critique of Poetry*, in *The Adelphi*, March 1934; see *194*, especially *n. 1*.
2. of] *overwritten on* 'on'
3. attempts] *originally substituted by* 'attempts' *and crossed out; then whole passage, including* 'attempts' *for the second time, crossed out*

3544. To Leonard Moore

8 February 1949   Typewritten

> The Cotswold Sanatorium
> Cranham
> Glos.

Dear Moore,

About a week ago Harcourt Brace sent me a proof copy of a novel[1] with the suggestion that I might like to write something about it. I wonder if in a delicate sort of way you could choke them off doing that. I don't want to do any avoidable writing at present, and at the best of times I very much object to writing blurbs. At the same time Harcourt Brace have been very nice to me and I am most anxious not to offend them. The best line, I should think, would be to take refuge behind my ill health, which is true enough anyway.

> Yours sincerely
> [Signed] Eric Blair
> Eric Blair

1. Unidentified. Books marked as proof copies in Orwell's reading list for 1949 are: Richard Cargoe, *The Tormentors* (February); Hesketh Pearson, *Dickens* (March); Julian Symons's biography of his brother (September); and L. A. S. Salazar, *Murder in Mexico* (October). Cargoe's book is appropriate for the date, but it was published by Gollancz in 1949 and by Sloane in the United States in 1950; Harcourt, Brace would hardly ask Orwell to write a blurb for a rival publisher's book. For Cargoe, see *3598, n. 3*.

3545. To Anthony Powell

10 February 1949   Typewritten

> The Cotswold Sanatorium
> Cranham
> Glos.

Dear Tony,

Thanks so much for your letter. I'll be delighted to see you on the 19th, and unless I hear to the contrary will make arrangements for that date. It's very tough of you to decide to walk (I suppose you know this place is 900 feet up) and I trust you'll have decent weather. Of course if it rains you can probably get hold of a hired car in Stroud. Anyway I'll arrange for a car to take you back in time to catch the 6.30, which means leaving here at 6. I've no doubt you could get dinner in the train going back, but perhaps it's wise to carry food. In Scotland one gets into the habit of never going anywhere without a "piece"[1] as they call it, and often I've been glad of it. So looking forward to seeing you both.

> Yours
> George

1. Slice(s) of bread, usually buttered (Scots).

3546. To Julian Symons

10 February 1949   Typewritten

Cranham

Dear Julian,
Thanks so much for your letter, and for the book,[1] which I am reading and will tell you about when I come.[2]

I'd be delighted to see you on Wednesday 23rd, and if I don't hear to the contrary will make arrangements for that date. If you reach Stroud by the train that gets there at 12.5 (I don't know what time it leaves Paddington) a car will meet you, and you will be here in time for lunch. There's a return train at 4.30 which you can catch by leaving here at 4. I'll expect you then.

Yours
George

1. Symons's thriller *Bland Beginning*.
2. Orwell meant 'when you come.'

3547. To Leonard Moore

12 February 1949   Handwritten

The Cotswold Sanatorium
Cranham
Glos.

Dear Moore,
Many thanks for your letter of the 9th. It was very clever to get Mondadori to sign up so promptly for "1984."[1] I might as well have my press-cuttings—I like to know what people are saying.

Yours sincerely
Eric Blair

1. Mondadori, who had published translations of *Homage to Catalonia* and *Animal Farm*, issued the Italian version of *Nineteen Eighty-Four* in November 1950.

3548. To Philip Rahv

12 February 1949   Handwritten

The Cotswold Sanatorium,
Cranham
Glos. England

Dear Rahv,
Thanks so much for your letter. Yes, I could do you a piece on Evelyn Waugh, though perhaps not very promptly. I have been seriously ill again

(T.B.) & have done no work since December, but I am hoping to start again in about a month, in which case I should be able to let you have the article within 2–3 months. I note that it should be 3–4 thousand words. The above address will find me until the summer, I am afraid.[1]

Yours sincerely,
Geo. Orwell

1. William Phillips, of *Partisan Review*, replied on 28 February 1949 to say that 2–3 months would be fine and, if need be, the word limit could be stretched to five thousand.

3549. To Celia Kirwan

13 February 1949   Typewritten

The Cotswold Sanatorium
Cranham
Glos.

Dearest Celia,
How delightful to get your letter and know that you are in England again. I have been in this place about six weeks and I imagine shall be here till the summer. I'm quite comfortable and well looked after. I had really been ill since about September of last year, but I could not go for treatment till the end of the year because I had to finish a book I had been messing about with for a long time. At present I am trying not to do any work whatever. Richard is very well and growing enormous. He will be 5 in May, so I suppose he will have to start going to school about the end of this year. He is still rather backward about talking but quite forward in other ways. He loves working on the farm and is really quite useful sometimes. I don't quite know where I shall spend the winter, but it will have to be somewhere get-at-able where there is a doctor handy, and perhaps Richard can start going to school then. I think he will like it, because he loves being with other children, but I can't get him to show much enthusiasm for learning his letters. I think he is going to grow up to be a practical man, an engineer or something like that.

I wonder whether you know who has any back copies of Polemic. Failing that, do you know Humphrey Slater's address? He probably has some copies or knows where some are. There was one number which had an article of mine in it that I want to reprint some time, and of which I haven't a copy.[1]

I will send you a copy of my new book when it comes out (about June I think), but I don't expect you'll like it; it's an awful book really. I hope you'll stay in England and that I'll see you some time, perhaps in the summer. Thanks so much for writing.

With much love
George

1. 'Lear, Tolstoy and the Fool,' March 1947, *3181*.

3550. To Jacintha Buddicom

14 February 1949   Typewritten

In her book *Eric and Us*, Jacintha Buddicom explains that after Orwell—to her then, Eric Blair—'had slipped away without trace' after his visit to Ticklerton Court, near Church Stretton, Shropshire, in 1927, they had no contact. Then, on 8 February 1949, she received a letter from her Aunt Lilian (with whom they had all stayed at Ticklerton) to say that George Orwell was Eric Blair. She telephoned Martin Secker to find where Orwell was and wrote to him on 9 February. The following two letters arrived on 17 February enclosed in the same envelope. See *Eric and Us*, 143–45, for Orwell's 'exile' in Burma and his staying for a fortnight at Ticklerton with Aunt Lilian, Prosper and Guinever Buddicom; and 146–58 for the events of 1949.

The Cotswold Sanatorium
Cranham
Glos.

Dear Jacintha,

How nice to get your letter after all these years. I suppose it really must be 30 years since the winter holidays when I stayed with you at Shiplake, though I saw Prosper and Guinever a good deal later, in 1927, when I stayed with them at Ticklerton after coming back from Burma. After that I was living in various parts of the world and often in great difficulties about making a living, and I rather lost touch with a lot of old friends. I seem to remember Prosper got married about 1930. I am a widower. My wife died suddenly four years ago, leaving me with a little (adopted) son who was then not quite a year old. Most of the time since then Avril has been keeping house for me, and we have been living in Jura, in the Hebrides, or more properly the Western Isles. I think we are going in any case to keep on the house there, but with my health as it now is I imagine I shall have to spend at least the winters in some get-at-able place where there is a doctor. In any case Richard, my little boy, who will be 5 in May, will soon have to start going to school, which he can't satisfactorily do on the island.

I have been having this dreary disease (T.B.) in an acute way since the autumn of 1947, but of course it has been hanging over me all my life, and actually I think I had my first go of it in early childhood. I spent the first half of 1948 in hospital, then went home much better after being treated with streptomycin, then began to feel ill again about September. I couldn't go for treatment then because I had to finish off a beastly book which, owing to illness, I had been messing about with for eighteen months. So I didn't get to this place till about the beginning of the year, by which time I was rather sorry for myself. I am trying now not to do any work at all, and shan't start any for another month or two. All I do is read and do crossword puzzles. I am well looked after here and can keep quiet and warm and not worry about anything, which is about the only treatment that is any good in my opinion. Thank goodness Richard is extremely tough and healthy and is unlikely, I should think, ever to get this disease.

I have never been back to the Henley area, except once passing through the town in a car. I wonder what happened to that property your mother had which we used to hunt all over with those "saloon rifles,"[1] and which seemed so enormous in those days. Do you remember our passion for R. Austin Freeman?[2] I have never really lost it, and I think I must have read his entire works except some of the very last ones. I think he only died quite recently, at a great age.

I hope to get out of here in the spring or summer, and if so I shall be in London or near London for a bit. In that case I'll come and look you up if you would like it. Meanwhile if you'd care to write again and tell me some more news I'd be very pleased. I am afraid this is rather a poor letter, but I can't write long letters at present because it tires me to sit up for long at a time.

Yours
Eric Blair

1. Rifles used in shooting galleries—at fairs, for example.
2. Richard Austin Freeman (1862–1943), author of many novels and short stories, particularly featuring the pathologist-detective John Thorndyke, the first of which, written after his enforced retirement as a physician and surgeon in what is now Ghana, *The Red Thumb Mark* (1907), established Freeman (and Thorndyke). His novels and stories were characterised by their scientific accuracy. In 'Grandeur et décadence du roman policier anglais' ('The Detective Story'), *Fontaine*, 1944 (see *2357*), Orwell referred to his books *The Eye of Osiris* and *The Singing Bone* as 'classics of English detective fiction.'

3551. To Jacintha Buddicom

[15 February] 1949   Typewritten

Cranham
Tuesday[1]

Hail and Fare Well, my dear Jacintha,
You see I haven't forgotten. I wrote to you yesterday but the letter isn't posted yet, so I'll go on to cheer this dismal day. It's been a day when everything's gone wrong. First there was a stupid accident to the book I was reading, which is now unreadable. After that the typewriter stuck & I'm too poorly to fix it. I've managed to borrow a substitute but it's not much better. Ever since I got your letter I've been remembering. I can't stop thinking about the young days with you & Guin & Prosper, & things put out of mind for 20 and 30 years. I am so wanting to see you. We must meet when I get out of this place, but the doctor says I'll have to stay another 3 or 4 months.

I would like you to see Richard. He can't read yet & is rather backward in talking, but he's as keen on fishing as I was & loves working on the farm, where he's really quite helpful. He has an enormous interest in machinery, which may be useful to him later on. When I was not much more than his age I always knew I wanted to write, but for the first ten years it was very hard to make a living. I had to take a lot of beastly jobs to earn enough to keep going & could only write in any spare time that was left, when I was too tired & had

43

to destroy a dozen pages for one that was worth keeping. I tore up a whole novel[2] once & wish now I hadn't been so ruthless. Parts of it might have been worth re-writing, though it's impossible to come back to something written in such a different world. But I am rather sorry now. ("'An w'en I sor wot 'e'd bin an' gorn an' don, I sed coo lor, wot 'ave you bin an' gorn an' done?'"[3]) I think it's rather a good thing Richard is such an entirely practical child.

Are you fond of children? I think you must be. You were such a tender-hearted girl, always full of pity for the creatures we others shot & killed. But you were not so tender-hearted to me when you abandoned me to Burma with all hope denied. We are older now, & with this wretched illness the years will have taken more toll of me than of you. But I am well cared-for here & feel much better than I did when I got here last month. As soon as I can get back to London I do so want us to meet again.

As we always ended so that there should be no ending.

Farewell and Hail
Eric

Jacintha Buddicom did not visit Cranham and she and Orwell did not meet again. She died on 4 November 1993.

1. Posted in same envelope as *3550*; see its headnote.
2. In his Introduction to the French edition of *Down and Out in Paris and London*, Orwell says he wrote two novels when living in Paris but neither was published; see *211*. See also Orwell's letter to Michael Meyer, 12 March 1949, *3570*, in which he says he destroyed his first novel after unsuccessfully submitting it to one publisher.
3. In *Eric and Us*, Jacintha Buddicom refers to this as 'the old favourite joke from *Punch* that we used to quote and re-quote to each other on every possible occasion.' A sailor had knocked over a bucket of tar on a newly scrubbed deck prepared for the admiral's inspection, and another sailor gave this as an explanation to the petty officer in charge. She comments, 'That old joke alone, together with the ever-constant beginning and ending, would hallmark that letter as Eric' (152).

3552. Review of *Scott-King's Modern Europe* by Evelyn Waugh

The New York Times Book Review, 20 February 1949

Mr Evelyn Waugh's recent book, "The Loved One," was an attack, and by no means a good-natured attack, on American civilization, but in "Scott-King's Modern Europe" he shows himself willing to handle his native Continent with at least equal rudeness.[1] America worships corpses but Europe mass-produces them, is what he seems to be saying. The two books are indeed in some sense complementary to one another, though "Scott-King's Modern Europe" is less obviously brilliant than the other.

The book has a general resemblance to "Candide," and is perhaps even intended to be a modern counterpart of "Candide," with the significant difference that the hero is middle-aged at the start. Nowadays, it is implied, only the middle-aged have scruples or ideals: the young are born hard-boiled. Scott-King, age about 43, "slightly bald and slightly corpulent," is senior

classics master at Granchester, a respectable but not fashionable public
school. A dusty, unhonored figure, a praiser of the past, a lover of exact
scholarship, he fights a steadily losing battle against what he regards as the
debasement of modern education.

"Dim," we are told, is the epithet that describes him. His hobby is the
study of a poet even dimmer than himself, a certain Bellorius, who flourished
in the seventeenth century in what was then a province of the Habsburg
Empire and is now the independent republic of Neutralia.

In an evil hour Scott-King receives an invitation to visit Neutralia, which is
celebrating the tercentenary of the death of Bellorius. It is the wet summer of
1946—a summer of austerity—and Scott-King envisions garlicky meals and
flasks of red wine. He succumbs to the invitation, although half aware that it
is probably a swindle of some kind.

At this point any experienced reader of Waugh's works would predict
unpleasant adventures for Scott-King and he would be right. Neutralia, a
compound of Yugoslavia and Greece, is ruled over by a "Marshal," and there
is the usual police espionage, banditry, ceremonial banquets and speeches
about Youth and Progress. The commemoration of Bellorius is in fact an
imposture. Its object is to trap the visitors into endorsing the Marshal's
regime. They fall for the trap and later learn that this stamps them
everywhere as "Fascist Beasts." Thereafter Neutralia's hospitality ends
abruptly.

Some of the visitors are killed and the others stranded, unable to get out of
the country. Airplanes are reserved for VIP's, and to leave Neutralia any
other way entails weeks and months of besieging embassies and consulates.
After adventures which Mr. Waugh suppresses because they are too painful
for a work of light fiction, Scott-King ends up stark naked in a camp for
illegal Jewish immigrants in Palestine.

Back at Granchester, amid the notched desks and the draughty corridors,
the headmaster informs him sadly that the number of classical scholars is
falling off and suggests that he shall combine his teaching of the classics with
something a little more up-to-date:

"Parents are not interested in producing the 'complete man' any more.
They want to qualify their boys for jobs in the modern world. You can hardly
blame them, can you?"

"Oh, yes," said Scott-King, "I can and do."

Later he adds: "I think it would be very wicked indeed to do anything to fit
a boy for the modern world." And when the headmaster objects that this is a
short-sighted view, Scott-King retorts. "I think it the most long-sighted
view it is possible to take."

This last statement, it should be noted, is intended seriously. The book is
very short, hardly longer than a short story, and it is written with the utmost
lightness, but it has a definite political meaning. The modern world, we are
meant to infer, is so unmistakably crazy, so certain to smash itself to pieces in
the near future, that to attempt to understand it or come to terms with it is
simply a purposeless self-corruption. In the chaos that is shortly coming, a
few moral principles that one can cling to, and perhaps even a few half-

remembered odes of Horace or choruses from Euripides, will be more useful than what is now called "enlightenment."

There is something to be said for this point of view, and yet one must always regard with suspicion the claim that ignorance is, or can be, an advantage. In the Europe of the last fifty years the diehard, know-nothing attitude symbolized by Scott-King has helped to bring about the very conditions that Mr. Waugh is satirizing. Revolutions happen in authoritarian countries, not in liberal ones, and Mr. Waugh's failure to see the implications of this fact not only narrows his political vision but also robs his story of part of its point.

His standpoint, or Scott-King's, is that of a Conservative—that is to say, a person who disbelieves in progress and refuses to differentiate between one version of progress and another—and his lack of interest in his opponents induces, unavoidably, a certain perfunctoriness. It was a mistake, for instance, to present Neutralia as a dictatorship of the Right while giving it most of the stigmata of a dictatorship of the Left. "There is nothing to choose between communism and fascism," Mr. Waugh seems to be saying: but these two creeds, though they have much in common, are not the same, and can only be made to appear the same by leaving out a good deal. Again, Mr. Waugh's portraits of scheming Neutralian officials would have been more telling if he were not too contemptuous of the kind of state that calls itself a "people's democracy" to find out in detail how it works.

This is an extremely readable book, but it lacks the touch of affection that political satire ought to have. One can accept Scott-King's estimate of the modern world, and perhaps even agree with him that a classical education is the best prophylactic against insanity, and yet still feel that he could fight the modern world more effectively if he would occasionally turn aside to read a sixpenny pamphlet on Marxism.

Orwell's review was printed with one by Alice S. Morris of Elizabeth Bowen's *The Heat of the Day* on the first page of *The New York Times Book Review* under the main headline 'New Novels from Two British Writers.' The reviews were separated by a reproduction of a detail from Henry Moore's 'The Uprooted' and a box containing an editorial introduction to the two reviews. In this, Orwell was described as 'the British novelist-critic, whose latest book is "Animal Farm." In politics, Mr. Orwell notes, he generally favors the Labor Party and adds that he is "very anti-Communist."' Alice Morris was described as 'a young American editor and writer' who had reviewed frequently for the *Book Review*. Orwell's review was given the heading 'Mr. Waugh Pays a Visit to Perilous Neutralia.'

1. In his diary entry for his forty-fourth birthday, 28 October 1947, Waugh wrote that he had written 'two good stories' during the year, *The Loved One* and *Scott-King's Modern Europe*. The latter was inspired by a visit to Spain with Douglas Woodruff; see *Diaries, 1911–1965*, edited by Michael Davie, entry for 15 June 1946 and n. 1 (1976; Penguin Books, 1979)

3553. To [the Editor], *Wiadomości*

25 February 1949   Typewritten

Wiadomości, the Polish émigré literary weekly published in London, sent a questionnaire on Joseph Conrad to several English writers asking them two questions.

'First, what do you believe to be his permanent place and rank in English letters? When Conrad died, some critics were uncertain of his final position, and Virginia Woolf, in particular, doubted whether any of his later novels would survive. Today, on the occasion of a new edition of his collected writings, Mr Richard Curle wrote in *Time and Tide* that Conrad's works now rank among the great classics of the English novel. Which of these views, in your opinion, is correct?

'The other question to which we would like to have your answer, is whether you detect in Conrad's work any oddity, exoticism and strangeness (of course, against the background of the English literary tradition), and if so, do you attribute it to his Polish origin?'

The replies were published in issues 158 and 171 of 10 April and 10 July 1949 under the heading 'Conrad's Place and Rank in English Letters.' Among those who responded were Walter Allen, Clifford Bax, Gerald Bullett, Phyllis Bottome, Arthur Calder-Marshall, Richard Church, G. D. H. Cole, Robert Graves, Graham Greene, J. B. S. Haldane, Raymond Mortimer, Harold Nicolson, Hermon Ould, Victoria Sackville-West, L. A. G. Strong, Frank Swinnerton, and Martin Turnell. Orwell's response was published in the issue of 10 April. The text reproduced here is that in his letter of 25 February 1949. Orwell intended to write a long essay on Conrad, but only a few notes have survived; see *3725*.

> The Cotswold Sanatorium
> Cranham
> Glos.

Dear Sir,

Many thanks for your letter dated the 22nd February. I cannot answer at great length, as I am ill in bed, but I am happy to give you my opinions for what they are worth.

I regard Conrad as one of the best writers of this century, and—supposing that one can count him as an English writer—one of the very few true novelists that England possesses. His reputation, which was somewhat eclipsed after his death, has risen again during the past ten years, and I have no doubt that the bulk of his work will survive. During his lifetime he suffered by being stamped as a writer of "sea stories," and books like "The Secret Agent" and "Under Western Eyes" went almost unnoticed. Actually Conrad only spent about a third of his life at sea, and he had only a sketchy knowledge of the Asiatic countries of which he wrote in "Lord Jim," "Almayer's Folly," etc. What he did have, however, was a sort of grown-upness and political understanding which would have been almost impossible to a native English writer at that time. I consider that his best work belongs to what might be called his middle period, roughly between 1900 and

1914. This period includes "Nostromo," "Chance," "Victory," the two mentioned above, and several outstanding short stories.

2. Yes, Conrad has definitely a slight exotic flavour to me. That is part of his attraction. In the earlier books, such as "Almayer's Folly," his English is sometimes definitely incorrect, though not in a way that matters. He used I believe to think in Polish and then translate his thought into French and finally into English, and one can sometimes follow the process back at least as far as French, for instance in his tendency to put the adjective after the noun. Conrad was one of those writers who in the present century civilized English literature and brought it back into contact with Europe, from which it had been almost severed for a hundred years. Most of the writers who did this were foreigners, or at any rate not quite English—Eliot and James (Americans), Joyce and Yeats (Irish), and Conrad himself, a transplanted Pole.

Yours truly
Geo. Orwell

3554. To Herbert Read

26 February 1949[1]   Handwritten

The Cotswold Sanatorium
Cranham
Glos.

Dear Read,
With ref. to your letter of the 17th, about the Freedom Defence Committee.

As I dare say you know, I have been & still am seriously ill. I can't of course be present at the meeting, nor be active in any way. If this reaches you before then, will you please convey my good wishes & apologies to the others present. If it is decided to continue the organisation, I am good for £10,[2] not more I am afraid. This disease is an expensive hobby.

Yours
Geo. Orwell

1. The date '26' is unclear.
2. It is very difficult to convey an accurate impression of what £10 signified for Orwell; a simple inflation ratio may give a false impression. Some idea of his generosity in the adverse circumstances in which he found himself may be gained by comparing a relative weekly wage forty years later with one of £10 in 1949. It would not be less than £300 and might be closer to £400.

3555. To Celia Kirwan

Sunday [27 February or 6 March 1949?][1]   Handwritten

Cranham

Dear Celia,

Thanks ever so for sending the photostats, but the article I really wanted was one called "Lear, Tolstoy & the Fool". Why trouble with photostats? Couldn't you give the copy of the magazine to a commercial typist to make a copy for me?[2] (I'll pay for the typing of course.) The reason I want it is simply that sometime I may publish another volume of reprinted essays & I want to get all the possible materials together before they get lost.

I trust poor Mamaine is going on better. I have just got a copy of Arthur's book from America.[3] I feel so lousy I can't write any more.

With love
George

1. This letter follows Orwell's to Celia Kirwan of Sunday, 13 February 1949; see *3549*. It would have taken her a little time to respond, and thus probable dates for this reply are those given here.
2. Although the Photostat (a trade name) had been in existence for nearly forty years by the time Orwell wrote, its use was far less widespread than is that of the Xerox and other photocopiers now. Orwell's proposal that his article should be copy-typed rather than photocopied neatly marks the contrast between secretarial practice and relative costs then and now.
3. Although it is not included in his list of reading for 1949, this was probably *Insight and Outlook: An Inquiry into the Common Foundations of Science, Art and Social Ethics* (New York, 1949). Orwell had a copy among his possessions at his death. He records reading Koestler's *Promise and Fulfilment: Palestine 1947–49* (New York, 1949) in September 1949.

3556. To Leonard Moore

1 March 1949   Typewritten

Cranham

Dear Moore,

I have received the proofs of "1984" from Harcourt Brace and am correcting them. I find that all the way through they have altered all measurements, which I was careful to give in the metric system, into miles, yards etc. It isn't a very important point, but the use of the metric system was part of the buildup and I don't want it changed if avoidable. I have already cabled and written about this, but if they show fight, could you try and make sure that they follow the manuscript in this particular.[1] There are one or two other minor alterations they asked for, chiefly because American grammar is slightly different, but these I don't object to.[2]

Yours sincerely
Eric Blair

1. The metric system was used for the U.S. edition.

2. The U.S. edition shows hundreds of variations in spelling, capitalisation, and punctuation from that published by Secker & Warburg. For example, whereas the English edition uses the form 'towards'—though Orwell's typescript has 'toward' on one occasion (*CW*, IX, 180, line 21)—the U.S. edition always has 'toward.' A selection of U.S. readings is given in *CW*, IX, Textual Note, List 2, 334–36. Eleven readings from the U.S. edition have been admitted into the *CW* edition.

3557. To Roger Senhouse

2 March 1949   Typewritten

The Cotswold Sanatorium
Cranham
Glos.

Dear Roger,

I'm awfully sorry I haven't yet dealt with your queries,[1] but the reason is that I lent my spare copy of proofs to Julian Symons, who was in here last week, and haven't had them back yet. But I've been able (I think) to identify the one you refer to in your letter of the 28th, as I have the American proofs here in galley. The passage runs:

He could feel the short springy turf under his feet and the gentle sunshine on his face. At the edge of the   were the elm trees, faintly stirring, and somewhere beyond that was the stream where the dace lay etc. etc.[2]

It should have been "at the edge of the field." "Trees" was evidently a slip in the MS. I've also altered it to field in the American edition.

As soon as possible I'll deal with the other queries and send them on to you, but I imagine most of these were not very important. As to "onto."[3] I know this is an ugly word, but I consider it to be necessary in certain contexts. If you say "the cat jumped on the table" you may mean that the cat, already on the table, jumped up and down there. On the other hand, "on to" (two words) means something different, as in "we stopped at Barnet and then drove on to Hatfield." In some contexts, therefore, one needs "onto." Fowler, if I remember rightly, doesn't altogether condemn it.

I'm afraid there is going to be a big battle with Harcourt Brace, as they want to alter the metric system measurements all the way through the book to miles, yards etc., and in fact have done so in the proofs. This would be a serious mistake. I've already cabled in strong terms, but I don't like having to fight these battles 3000 miles from my base.

Yours
George

1. Senhouse had sent a list of queries on 22 February 1949. Orwell answered them in two parts; he dealt in this letter with Senhouse's objection to 'onto' (see *n. 3*); the bulk of the queries he answered on 9 March (see *3567* and *3568*). Senhouse's letter of the 28th has not been traced.
2. Orwell's typescript of the novel has 'At the edge of the trees'; the correction he gives here was made in the U.S. and English editions; see *CW*, IX, 292, line 34.
3. Senhouse wrote: 'p 15. l 12 (3rd para 2nd line) ". . . had flashed *onto* the screen". I take it that you are using, as one word "onto" throughout the text (52, 59, 79, 85 etc). I raise the point, as I

have an archaic horror of its use, and I mention this specific case also for the used° of 'had flashed' — Surely "had flashed on the screen" is sufficient in this case, though possibly ambiguous, since a torch is "flashed on".' Orwell was allowed to use 'onto': see *CW*, IX, 13, line 27. He had used the one-word form in earlier novels, although, as the Gollancz editions show, that usage is not always systematic.

3558. To *The News Chronicle*

3 March 1949

I appeal on behalf of Enrique Marco Nadal, a Spanish Republican now under sentence of death in Spain.

He was taken prisoner by the Italians when the Spanish Government collapsed in 1939; then by the Germans in 1944–45 after fighting for the French.

He re-entered Spain clandestinely after the war, and was sentenced to death without trial. He has probably not done anything that would constitute a legal offence in any democratic country.[1]

George Orwell

1. The letter was followed by an editorial note: 'Mr. Clement Davies has telegraphed a protest to the Spanish Minister of Justice on behalf of the British Liberal Party.' Nadal was released from Burgos prison at the end of 1964. Clement Davies (1884–1962) was leader of the Liberal Party in the House of Commons, 1945–56; he continued to sit as a Liberal M.P. until his death.

3559. To S. M. Levitas

3 March 1949   Typewritten

The Cotswold Sanatorium
Cranham
Gloucestershire, England

Dear Mr Levitas,

Many thanks for your letter of February 25th.[1] Yes, I am receiving the "New Leader" regularly. I am afraid that my address is likely to remain the above until June or July. They tell me I shall not be able to get out of bed before about May, and presumably I shall remain here for some time after that.

I have been seriously ill, and apart from that book review you noticed in the New York Times, I have not done any work since the beginning of December. The article on Gandhi was written some time before that. I hope, however, to start doing a little work shortly, and I should be happy to do an occasional book review for you. Could you, perhaps, make a suggestion when some book which appears suitable is coming along?[2] I could sometimes make a suggestion myself, but in general I don't hear about American books early enough.

Yours sincerely
[Signed] Geo. Orwell
George Orwell

1. Levitas wrote: 'We have all read with great pleasure and enthusiasm your piece on Ghandi° in the PARTISAN REVIEW. To be frank, we are extremely jealous that it didn't appear in the NEW LEADER. I noticed too, your review in the recent issue of SATURDAY REVIEW OF LITERATURE [it was actually in *The New York Times Book Review*] which also made me envious.' He said he did not wish to impose regular articles on Orwell, 'but, honestly, three or four pieces a year and two or three book reviews, would help us enormously.' Finally, he sincerely hoped Orwell had completely recovered, was back in harness, and would 'think of us.' For Levitas's importunity when Orwell was ill in 1948, see *3410*.
2. Levitas wrote on 16 March 1949 suggesting that Orwell review either Winston Churchill's *Their Finest Hour* (which he did, 14 May 1949; see *3624*) or *Letters of Marcel Proust*, translated and edited by Mina Curtiss, or both.

3560. To Sir Richard Rees

3 March 1949   Handwritten

Cranham

Dear Richard,

Thanks so much for your letter, with the cuttings, which I thought gave quite a good exposition of C.P. policy. I always disagree, however, when people end by saying that we can only combat Communism, Fascism or what-not if we develop an equal fanaticism. It appears to me that one defeats the fanatic precisely by *not* being a fanatic oneself, but on the contrary by using one's intelligence. In the same way, a man can kill a tiger because he is *not* like a tiger and uses his brain to invent the rifle, which no tiger could ever do.

I looked up the passage in Russell's book.[1] If the antithesis to a "some" statement is always an "all" statement, then it seems to me that the antithesis of "some men are tailless" is not "all men have tails," but "all men are tailless."[2] Russell seems, in that paragraph, to be citing only pairs of statements of which one is untrue, but clearly there must be many cases when both "some" and "all" are true, except that "some" is an understatement. Thus "some men are tailless" is true, unless you are implying by it that some men have tails. But I never can follow that kind of thing. It is the sort of thing that makes me feel that philosophy should be forbidden by law.

I have arranged to write an essay on Evelyn Waugh and have just read his early book on Rossetti and also "Robbery under Law" (about Mexico.)[3] I am now reading a new life of Dickens by Hesketh Pearson, which I have to review.[4] It isn't awfully good. There doesn't seem to be a perfect life of Dickens—perverse and unfair though it is, I really think Kingsmill's book is the best.[5] You were right about Huxley's book[6]—it is awful. And do you notice that the more holy he gets, the more his books stink with sex. He cannot get off the subject of flagellating women. Possibly, if he had the courage to come out and say so, that is the solution to the problem of war. If we took it out in a little private sadism, which after all doesn't do much harm, perhaps we wouldn't want to drop bombs etc. I also re-read, after very many years, "Tess of the D'Urbervilles," and "Jude the Obscure" (for the first time). "Tess" is really better than I had remembered, and incidentally is quite funny in places, which I didn't think Hardy was capable of.

The doctor says I shall have to stay *in bed* for another 2 months, i.e. till about May, so I suppose I shan't actually get out till about July. However I don't know that it matters except for being expensive and not seeing little R. I am so afraid of his growing away from me, or getting to think of me as just a person who is always lying down and can't play. Of course children can't understand illness. He used to come to me and say "Where have you hurt yourself?"—I suppose the only reason he could see for always being in bed.[7] But otherwise I don't mind being here and I am comfortable and well cared-for. I feel much better and my appetite is a lot better. (By the way I never thanked you for sending that rum. Did I pay you enough for it?) I hope to start some serious work in April, and I think I could work fairly well here, as it is quiet and there are not many interruptions. Various people have been to see me, and I manage to keep pretty well supplied with books. Contrary to what people say, time seems to go very fast when you are in bed, and months can whizz by with nothing to show for it.

Yours
Eric

1. *Human Knowledge: Its Scope and Limits*, by Bertrand Russell (1948). Orwell spelt 'Russell' with one 'l' on each occasion.
2. "all men are tailless" is underlined, and, written in the margin by Rees, is 'But this is *not* what Russell says!'
3. Orwell's reading list for 1949 also includes Waugh's *When the Going Was Good* under February and *Work Suspended* under March; see 3727.
4. Orwell's review of *Dickens: His Character, Comedy and Career*, by Hesketh Pearson, appeared in *The New York Times Book Review*, 15 May 1949; see 3625.
5. *The Sentimental Journey: A Life of Charles Dickens*, by Hugh Kingsmill (pseudonym of Hugh Kingsmill Lunn) (1934). It is listed by Orwell under May in his reading for 1949; see 3727. See 3622, n. 5 for Kingsmill.
6. *Ape and Essence* by Aldous Huxley (New York, 1948; London, 1949). Orwell wrote his comment about Huxley's later books stinking with sex in his Last Literary Notebook (see 3725, folio 5).
7. Richard Blair later recalled his relationship with his father: 'He was very concerned about not being able to see me as much as he ought to. His biggest concern was that the relationship wouldn't develop properly between father and son. As far as he was concerned, it was fully developed, but he was more concerned about son-to-father relationships. He'd formed a bond with me, but it wasn't as strong the other way around.' Lettice Cooper described the problems posed for Orwell in establishing this bond when he became severely ill and the effect Orwell's illness and Eileen's early death had had. Orwell 'was terrified to let Richard come near him, and he would hold out his hand and push him away—and George would do it very abruptly because he was abrupt in his manner and movements. And he wouldn't let the child sit on his knee or anything. And I suppose Richard had never asked [if his father loved him]. Children don't, do they? And he said, did they love him? And I said they both did, so much. It was very hard, that, wasn't it?' (*Remembering Orwell*, 196–97).

3561. To Leonard Moore

4 March 1949   Typewritten

Cranham

Dear Moore,
Thanks for your two letters. I am very glad to hear about the serialisation of "Animal Farm" in Germany.[1]

Yours sincerely
[Signed] Eric Blair
Eric Blair

1. Serialised in *Der Monat* (West Berlin; sponsored by the American Military Government) as *Der Hofstaat der Tiere: Eine satirische Fabel*, Nos. 5–7, February, March, April 1949 (Willison). See Orwell's letter to *Der Monat*'s editor, Melvin Lasky, 29 October 1948, *3479*, and for Lasky, see *3446, n. 1*. Orwell's sub-title, 'A Fairy Tale,' was changed significantly for this version; there is no record that Orwell knew in advance or approved this alteration.

3562. To David Astor

5 March 1949   Typewritten

Cranham

Dear David,
Thanks so much for your letter.[1] If you don't mind, I would rather not do the article. I haven't started any work yet, and in addition I did an article of the same nature for the Observer 2 or 3 years ago.[2] If you want an article on the Spanish civil war generally, I consider the person who has written about it most sensibly is Franz Borkenau[3] (Faber's would have his address I think), but he is in Germany, I think in Munich, and you mightn't get an article out of him in time. Ramos Oliveira, Negrin's publicity man,[4] knows a great deal about modern Spanish history, and though, of course, a partisan, would probably be reasonably objective. Arturo Barea,[5] again, is a Spaniard and knows the history of the war intimately, but in my opinion both he and his wife are CP-influenced. Perhaps the best man of all would be Gerald Brenan,[6] whose publishers I think are Faber's. If you want an article about the International Brigade, Tom Wintringham, or Humphrey Slater (Secker & Warburg would have his address), or perhaps Slater's friend Malcolm Dunbar, might do it.[7]

If you had the more general kind of article, I should think not a bad subject would be the question of whether the policy of letting Franco win the war and then stay in power has paid, and whether it is likely to pay in future. Has it occurred to you that ultimately Stalin and Franco might get together? I don't say it will happen, but it doesn't seem to me impossible, as the Russians are seemingly very friendly with the rather similar regime in Argentina.

I am feeling a lot better and am planning to start a little work in April. The weather has suddenly turned horrible, in fact we are having a regular blizzard.[8] Karl and Klöse[9] were supposed to be coming to see me tomorrow, but I shouldn't think they'll get here.

Yours
George

1. David Astor wrote to Orwell on 4 March 1949. For the tenth anniversary of the end of the Spanish civil war, on 29 March, *The Observer* wished to have an article on some aspect of that war for Sunday, 27 March, and would be delighted if Orwell would write one; he could choose whatever aspect he wished. Or, would he suggest who might write one and what aspects should be covered. He had in mind two articles, one for *The Observer* and one to be syndicated through *The Observer*'s Foreign News Service: a general review of that war, and something on the International Brigade. The articles should be partly informative and partly an expression of opinion. 'We can't be sure that either the present day° readers of this paper or a much wider readership of syndicated articles will have a working knowledge of the facts.'

2. Orwell had reviewed *The Clash*, by Arturo Barea, 24 March 1946 (see *2944*); on 10 November 1946 he had reviewed *Politics, Economics and Men of Modern Spain, 1808–1946*, by A. Ramos Oliveira (see *3109*). Almost five years earlier he had contributed a special article on Spain, 'The Eight Years of War: Spanish Memories,' 16 July 1944 (see *2510*). See *3577, n. 1* and *3588, n. 1*.

3. Orwell had reviewed several of Borkenau's books: *The Spanish Cockpit*, 31 July 1937 (see *379*); *The Communist International*, 22 September 1938 (see *485*); and *The Totalitarian Enemy*, 4 May 1940 (see *620*). Orwell's letter was annotated by Astor at this point: 'Authority on Comintern. c/o Marburg University, Germany, U.S. Zone.' Borkenau had been a refugee from Nazi Germany.

4. Dr. Juan Negrín (1889–1956), Socialist finance minister and then Prime Minister of Spain. He resigned in exile in 1945. See *908, n. 3*, and *2852, n. 3*. For Oliveira, see *3109*.

5. Arturo Barea (1897–1957) had been Head of Foreign Press Censorship and Controller for Broadcasts, Madrid, 1937. Orwell knew Barea personally.

6. Gerald Brenan (Edward Fitzgerald Brenan; 1894–1987; CBE, 1982), writer of fiction and nonfiction. His *The Spanish Labyrinth: An Account of the Social and Political Background of the Civil War* was published in 1943; revised in 1950. He wrote a Current Affairs pamphlet, *Spanish Scene* in 1946; and also *The Face of Spain* (1950; New York, 1951) and *The Literature of the Spanish People* (1951; revised, 1953; New York, 1957).

7. Tom Wintringham (1898–1949) commanded the British Battalion of the International Brigade before Madrid in 1937, where he was wounded. Earlier, he had edited *Left Review* and later, with Humphrey Slater, he founded the Osterley Park Training Centre for the Home Guard. See *721, n. 1* and also Orwell's War-time Diary, *677, 23.8.40, n. 4* and *3576, n. 2*. Humphrey (Hugh) Slater (1906–1958) was Chief of Operations in the International Brigade and, for a time, a political commissar; see *731, n. 1*. Orwell's letter is annotated in Astor's hand at this point: 'Rose has his address'; Jim Rose was on *The Observer*'s literary staff. Malcolm Dunbar (1912–1962) was Chief of Staff to the 15th International Brigade. The Brigade was initially made up of Yugoslav, British, American, and French sections (Thomas, 969). Thomas notes that when he was made chief of operations, the Americans resented the appointment of this 'efficient young Englishman who three years before had been "leader of an advanced aesthetic set at Cambridge"' (723, n. 1).

8. This was the only weekend it snowed in England between Christmas 1948 and spring 1949.

9. For Karl Schnetzler, see *2893*. Helmut Klöse, a German anarchist who had served on the same front as Orwell in Spain; see Orwell's letter to Vernon Richards, 10 March 1949, *3569*. Orwell omits the umlaut.

3563. To Brenda Salkeld

5 March 1949   Handwritten

The Cotswold Sanatorium
Cranham
Glos.

Dear Brenda,

I don't suppose you ever pass this way on your travels, but if you do, perhaps you could drop in & see me. I have been here since January & have been really very ill—a little better now, I think. I've no idea when I shall get out, possibly some time in the summer. All seems to be well at home. Richard is getting enormous & very self-reliant, though still a bit backward about talking. Avril says he has now become a radio fan, so perhaps that will bring on his talking. He will be 5 in May. I think this winter he will go to the village school on the island, but next year he will have to go to a proper day school on the mainland somewhere. However I can't make plans till I have a clearer idea about my own health & hence my movements. My new book is coming out in June. I'm not doing any work now, of course, but hope I might start something next month.

With love
Eric

3564. Douglas Moyle to Orwell

7 March 1949

Douglas Moyle fought with Orwell in Spain (see *Homage to Catalonia*, *CW*, VI, 117; also Crick, 327, and Moyle's reminiscences in *Remembering Orwell*, 80–81). He and Orwell were both at the Independent Labour Party Summer School at Letchworth in August 1937, and he was one of the signatories to Orwell's letter to *The New Leader*, 24 September 1937, refuting false charges against the POUM made by F. A. Frankfort; see *399*. Moyle wrote giving news of himself and his family. He described the difficult times in Birmingham, with rising unemployment and redundancy, and the effect of the increased cost of living. A friend in common, G. Barber, a member of the Independent Labour Party, had worked in Johannesburg during the war but had now returned because of the increase in racial trouble. He did not mention Eileen, but sent his regards to Gwen (O'Shaughnessy) and the children. In *Remembering Orwell*, he tells of staying with the Orwells at their cottage in Wallington. He and Orwell took long walks with the Orwell's poodle, 'Marx.' He recalled that Orwell said you could tell something about visitors by whether they associated the dog's name with Marks & Spencer, Karl Marx, or Groucho Marx (100). For Moyle, see also *408, n. 1*.

3565. David Farrer to Orwell
8 March 1949

David Farrer, in charge of publicity for Secker & Warburg, wrote to tell Orwell that the London *Evening Standard* was 'definitely going to make *Nineteen Eighty-Four* their book of the month for June.' He also sent a letter from 'Bertie Russell' (Bertrand Russell) about the book, which would be quoted in publicity for it. 'As for my own reactions to the book,' he wrote, 'though I read it in typescript last December' (see *3506*) 'I still cannot get it out of my mind. It is in every sense a major work of fiction.'

3566. To Leonard Moore
9 March 1949   Handwritten

Cranham

Dear Moore,

Thank you for your letter of the 8th. Yes, they could go ahead with the pages.[1] The correction referred to in their cable is one I had already confirmed by cable. The main corrections were the alterations back into metric system, but they could really do this on their own from the MS. & wouldn't need the galleys, which, however, I have airmailed to them. There were also two slips of my own which I pointed out in my letter to Mr Giroux,[2] but these would not involve over-running. So they could go ahead safely even if the galleys have not yet arrived.

I received 2 copies of the Spanish (Argentine) translation of "Critical Essays", provided by a literary agent named MOHRENWITZ, who said they had been sent to him in error by Editorial Sur, the translators. It might be as well to let Sur know that *you* are my agent.[3]

Yours sincerely
Eric Blair

1. Page proofs of the U.S. edition of *Nineteen Eighty-Four*.
2. Robert Giroux, then of Harcourt, Brace (later of Farrar, Straus & Giroux), who saw the U.S. edition of *Nineteen Eighty-Four* through the press.
3. *Critical Essays* was published as *Ensayos Críticos* by Sur, Buenos Aires, July 1948. The translation was made by B. R. Hopenhaym.

3567. To Roger Senhouse

9 March 1949   Typewritten

Cranham

Dear Roger,

Herewith the confirmations of and answers to your queries.[1] I am sorry about the delay, but, as I told you, I had lent someone the proofs and didn't get them back till today. Actually I imagine there are very few changes here you wouldn't have made on your own initiative.

It has turned foully cold here but I am going along all right.

Love to all
George

1. Senhouse had written on 22 February 1949. Orwell replied initially on 2 March and answered Senhouse's question about 'onto'; see *3557*. Senhouse's other queries, with Orwell's answers, are in *3568*.

3568. Roger Senhouse's Corrections and Queries for *Nineteen Eighty-Four* and Orwell's Answers

Sent 22 February 1949

<u>Corrections</u>

p 23.   2 lines above dropped "t" at end and there is a dropped - (every-one)
24.   5 l from end. 'He' for 'Hat'
26.   l3. [turn] *u*. '*in*' for '*iu*'
83.   chap heading VIIII° w.f. (too large)
65.   l7. 'they'*ve*' for 'they'*re*'
77.   l1. revolutionaries
l2. spacing ', a few'

<u>Queries</u>

p 30.   para 4 l i 'seemed' for 'seeming'
p 74.   Diary quotation (*it ran*)
? better printed in roman.
115   mid-way para after dialogue
? trs sentence. "The girl finished her lunch—" etc to end of para. Time sequence seems odd if this precedes "They did not speak again"
116   l.l., truck-load and truckload
and 2nd line of para sub-machine
121   mid. 'bluebells' for 'blue bells'
127   4l end 'overalls' ·· 'overals'
152   snuffbox or snuff-box ?
wornout or worn out ?
four-and-twenty ?

"*Both of them*" (beginning para 4 ll end) after almost a page of description of Charrington & Winston and *no mention* of Julia — appears ambiguous. May only be due to relative position on page, since in previous para opening "they" is clearly the lovers.

217 l5. ? 'to and fro' for 'to and from' ?
242 l4 from end , for . after "pulse."
250 l10. end of line. ————
295 2nd para. 1st word l5. 'diagram' 'for disgram'.

Orwell's replies (most of which require no editorial comment):

P.15. "Onto." Already answered.[1]
P.23. l. 10 from bottom. "every-" (dropped hyphen.)
P.24. l. 5 from bottom. "That" should be "he."
P.30. Para 4 l. 1. "Seeming" should be "seemed."
P.65. l. 7. "they're" should be "they've."
P.74. Unimportant whether "it ran" is its or roms.
77. l. 1. Revolutionaries."
  l. 2. I don't understand this query.
P.115. "The girl finished her lunch" etc. to end of para. This seems to me all right, as the "again" covers the whole period including *before* the girl left.[2]
P.116. "Truckload." Better keep as single word in both cases.[3]
P.121. "Bluebells." Should be one word.[4]
P.127. L. 4 from bottom. "Overalls."
P.152. Middle of page. "Snuffbox." "Wornout." Better as one word in each case.
  "Four-and-twenty." Better with hyphens.
  L. 4 from bottom. "Both of them." I think this is all right as there can be no doubt who is meant.[5]
  L. 2 from bottom. "Lost" should be "last." (Not sure whether I corrected this before.)[6]
P.217. L.5. "To and from." Should be "to and fro."
P.242. L.4 from bottom. After "pulse" . should be ,
P.250. L.10. End of line. . should be ,
P.295. Para 2, L.5. "Disgram" should be "diagram."

Slip typed and initialled by Orwell attached to proofs of *Nineteen Eighty-Four.*[7]

Corrections on pp.:

End paper, 5, 6, 7, 10, 12, 13, 14, 16, 19, 20, 23, 28, 30, 37, 39, 43, 44, 45, 49, 51, 52, 54, 55, 56, 57, 58, 60, 66, 71, 74, 75, 78, 81, 82, 83, 89, 90, 91, 93, 96, 98, 99, 100, 101, 104, 108, 114, 116, 119, 120, 123, 126, 131, 137, 138, 141, 145, 152, 157, 158, 161, 162, 163, 166, 167, 171, 173, 182, 186, 190, 191, 192, 194, 195, 196, 197, 198, 204, 206, 207, 209, 215, 218, 220, 223, 225, 227, 229,

236, 240, 241, 242, 244, 246, 247, 248, 253, 256, 258, 259, 263, 270, 271, 272, 273, 280, 283, 288, 289, 291, 292, 297, 299, 302, 305, 306.

I am sorry that one or two of these corrections are due to a slip in the MS, and I have had to change something. I do not think that any over-running will be entailed, however.

[Initialled] G. O.

1. See *3557*.
2. The change was accepted; see *CW*, IX, 119.
3. Annotated by Senhouse: 'changed   hyphened'; 'truck-load' is hyphenated on 121 of *CW*, IX.
4. Orwell's answers to queries on pages 121 and 127 have been ticked by Senhouse.
5. This suggestion was not accepted by Orwell, and the passage was allowed to stand as written; see *CW*, IX, 158.
6. The first edition has 'last' (*CW*, IX, 158), so the change was noted.
7. The slip was probably not returned on 9 March; a number of pages for which changes were required in Orwell's replies to Senhouse's queries are not listed.

3569. To Vernon Richards

10 March 1949   Typewritten

The Cotswold Sanatorium
Cranham
Glos.

Dear Vernon,
Thanks so much for your letter. Yes, do keep the typewriter.[1] I will make the Freedom Press a present of it. I had to regard it as a loan before because I had only one rather elderly typewriter and I might have wanted the other one back. Now however I have managed to get hold of another portable.

I'd like a copy of "Russia's Third Revolution"[2] and enclose the form herewith. I am putting my Scottish address on it, but I imagine the above will be my address till June or later. If the Freedom Bookshop happens to have them, I would also like one or two copies of my own book "Homage to Catalonia." The publisher now has none left, and I have only one myself, but there are probably some to be found in shops. It's not likely to be reprinted, and I want to make sure a few copies remain in existence. Nowadays so many books drop out of print and then disappear altogether.

I have been here since the beginning of the year. I was much better when I left hospital last summer, but I began to relapse in the autumn and was really very ill for a while. I hope to get out some time in the summer, perhaps spend August or September in Jura, and spend the winter somewhere like Brighton, at any rate some civilized place near a doctor. If I manage to bring Richard down to London for a short visit, as I want to do if possible, I'll bring him to you for another photograph. He will be five in May and is very big and strong, but rather backward in talking, probably because he has not been with other children enough. He is very self-reliant and is good with machinery and seems interested in farming. If he decides later that he wants to be a farmer when he is grown up, I'd be delighted. I think probably he will start going to school this winter when he will be 5½. For the moment he can go to the village school on the island, but next year I shall have to take him somewhere on the mainland where he can go to a better day-school. Thank goodness his health so far has been excellent. Even when he has the usual measles etc. it seems to make no impression on him.

Helmuth Klöse, the German anarchist who was on the same part of the front as me in Spain and was imprisoned for a long time by the Communists, was here the other day. He knew of you but I am not sure whether he said he knew you personally.

Please remember [me] to Marie Louise.[3]

Yours
[Signed] George
George Orwell

1. Eileen's typewriter.
2. This pamphlet was advertised in *Politics*, Winter 1949 (1948–49). Orwell does not list it in his reading for 1949.
3. Vernon Richards's wife, Marie-Louise Berneri; see *3042, n. 4*; for Richards, see *3042, n. 1*.

3570. To Michael Meyer

12 March 1949   Typewritten

The Cotswold Sanatorium
Cranham
Glos.

Dear Michael,
Thanks ever so much for sending all that food, which arrived a day or two ago, and for your letter. You really shouldn't have sent the food, but I take your word that you could spare it, and of course I am delighted to receive it. As a matter of fact I'm sending most of it on to Jura, where food is always welcome as there's usually someone staying.

I've been here since the beginning of the year. I began to relapse last September and should have gone for treatment earlier, but I had to finish that beastly book which I had been struggling with so long. I am a lot better now, but I don't think they'll let me out of bed, let alone out of the sanatorium, before May. It is a great bore, my health breaking up like this. I cannot resign myself to living a sedentary life, which I suppose I shall have to from now on. I shall at any rate have to spend the winters in some get-atable place near a doctor, perhaps in somewhere like Brighton. Richard is now approaching five and will have to go to school before long. We think of letting him go to the village school on the island this winter, but next year I shall have to remove him to the mainland somewhere where he can go to a better day school. I don't want him to go to a boarding school, if at all, before he is 10. Thank goodness he is tremendously strong and healthy and self-reliant. He is still a bit backward in talking, but I imagine that will improve when he is more with other children.

I always thought Sweden[1] sounded a dull country, much more so than Norway or Finland. I should think there would probably be very good fishing, if you can whack up any interest in that. But I have never been able to like these model countries with everything up to date and hygienic and an enormous suicide rate. I also have a vague feeling that in our century there is some sort of interconnection between the quality of thought and culture in a country, and the *size* of the country. Small countries don't seem to produce interesting writers any longer, though possibly it is merely that one doesn't hear about them. I have ideas about the reason for this, if it is true, but of course only guesswork. I hope your novel gets on.[2] Even if one makes a mess of it the first time, one learns a great deal in making the attempt, also if you once have a draft finished, however discouraging it is, you can generally pull it into shape. I simply destroyed my first novel after unsuccessfully submitting it to one publisher, for which I'm rather sorry now. I think Thomas Hood[3] is a very good subject. He is incidentally no longer as well known as he should be, and very thoroughly out of print. I have only a selection of his poems,[4] and have for a long time been trying in vain to get the rest. I want particularly the one where he is writing a poem on the beauties of childhood but can't get on with it because the children are making such a noise (I remember it has the beautiful line, "Go to your mother, child, and blow your nose."[5]) I don't know whether one could call him a serious poet—he is what I call a good bad poet. I am glad you like Surtees. I think after being so long abandoned to the hunting people, who I don't suppose read him, he is beginning to be appreciated again. I haven't however read much of his works, and am trying to get hold of several now.[6] At present I do nothing except read—I'm not going to try and start any work till some time next month. I have been rereading some of Hardy's novels, after very many years, and was agreeably surprised. There is a new life of Dickens coming out, which I had to review, by Hesketh Pearson.[7] It's a bit more readable than old Pope-Hennessy's book,[8] but not any good really. Huxley's new book, which I expect you have seen, is awful.[9] Koestler's new book I haven't seen yet.[10] I am going to do an essay on Evelyn Waugh for the Partisan Review, and have been reading his early works, including a quite good life of Rossetti.[11] My novel is supposed to come out in June. I don't know whether the American edition may come out before the English, but I should think not. I hope to hear from you again some time. This place will be my address till about July, I'm afraid.

Yours
George

1. Meyer was then a lecturer in English at Uppsala University, 1947–50.
2. *The End of the Corridor*, published in 1951.
3. Thomas Hood (1799–1845), poet and journalist. His comic poetry was marked by gallows humour, and he could write with great bitterness (for example, 'The Song of the Shirt,' 1843, on sweated labour), and splendid wit.
4. No selection of Hood's poetry was amongst Orwell's books at his death.

5. From 'A Parental Ode to My Son, Aged Three Years and Five Months.' Alternate lines express warnings or fears of a very down-to-earth kind—for example, 'I knew so many cakes would make him sick,' and the opening of the final stanza:

> Thou pretty opening rose!
> (Go to your mother, child, and wipe your nose!)
> Balmy and breathing music like the South,
> (He really brings my heart into my mouth!)
> Fresh as the morn, and brilliant as its star, —
> (I wish the window had an iron bar!)
> Bold as the hawk, yet gentle as the dove, —
> (I tell you what, my love,
> I cannot write unless he's sent above!)

At a time when Orwell was evidently recalling the past, as the letters to Brenda Salkeld (see 3522, 3563) and Jacintha Buddicom (see 3550, 3551) indicate, this 'Domestic Poem' by one of Orwell's favourite minor authors may well have had significance for him in the desperate rush to complete *Nineteen Eighty-Four*. The verbal slip—'blow' for 'wipe'— suggests that, as so often, Orwell is quoting from memory. For his sympathy for Julian Symons, who was trying to write under such circumstances, see 3694.

6. Orwell read Surtees's *Mr Sponge's Sporting Tour* in April; see 3727.
7. Orwell's review of Hesketh Pearson's *Dickens: His Character, Comedy and Career* appeared on 15 May 1949; see 3625.
8. *Charles Dickens*, by Dame Una Pope-Hennessy (1945). See also 3572.
9. *Ape & Essence*.
10. *Insight and Outlook*. For its inaccurate listing in Orwell's notes, see 3729.
11. *Rossetti: His Life and Works* (London and New York, 1928). Orwell omitted an 's' from Rossetti.

3571. To Leonard Moore

12 March 1949   Typewritten

Dear Moore,

I see that "Der Monat", the American German-language magazine published in Berlin, are serialising "Animal Farm." Is this the serialisation arranged with the American army about which you wrote to me recently? If not, surely the one will cut across the other?

There was some mix-up about the other thing of mine that "Der Monat" reprinted. I don't remember the facts exactly, but they were something like this. About 3 months ago they reprinted an article of mine from "Commentary," and if I remember rightly were to pay me £25 for it. There then arrived some official papers relating to the payment, which I sent on to you. Shortly after this the editor, Mervyn Lasky,[1] wrote to ask, "had I received their cheque?" I thought these papers were the cheque, and answered "Yes." I then heard from you something to the effect that you could not draw the money for me, as the cheque had to be endorsed by the author personally. There the matter has rested, and it rather looks as if an actual cheque, which should have been the sequel to the papers I sent to you, has gone astray. It's not of enormous importance, but could perhaps be cleared up.[2]

Yours sincerely
[Signed] Eric Blair
Eric Blair

1. The editor of *Der Monat*, sponsored by the American Military Government, was Melvin Lasky; see *3446, n. 1*.
2. 'Armut un Hoffnung Grossbritanniens' ('The Labour Government After Three Years,' *Commentary*, October 1948; see *3462*). The German version slightly reworked the original; see headnote to *3462*.

3572. To Julian Symons
15 March 1949   Typewritten

Cranham

Dear Julian,
As you are doing that life of Dickens I thought you might care to glance at this[1] (I don't want it back.) It hasn't been published in this country yet so far as I know. I don't think there's anything in [it] you wouldn't get out of old Pope-Hennessy,[2] but he raises one or two minor points of interest. He makes out for instance that D.'s acceptance of a baronetcy just before his death was merely a sort of practical joke. P-H in her book seems to suggest that this is not so. I have never followed this up, and I must say I don't regard it as important, since by that time D's mind was probably giving way anyway. He also says, what I didn't know before, that D. was impressed by Edgar Allan Poe, who must then (1842) have been very obscure, and tried unsuccessfully to get his Tales published for him in book form. I have often wondered whether Poe was influenced by the madman's tale in Pickwick.

Yours
George

1. Hesketh Pearson's *Dickens: His Character, Comedy and Career*, which Orwell was reviewing for *The New York Book Review*; see *3625*. Orwell notes in his 1949 list of reading that he read this book in March.
2. Una Pope-Hennessy, *Charles Dickens* (1945).

3573. To Leonard Moore
16 March 1949   Typewritten

The Cotswold Sanatorium
Cranham
Glos.

Dear Moore,
Many thanks for your letter of the 15th. I enclose Mondadori's contract, duly signed.
I should be very pleased for "Inside the Whale" to be translated into Italian[1] and "A Hanging" into Swedish.[2]
With regard to the translation of "1984."[3] I assume that Mondadori has made this agreement "blind" without seeing a proof. The point is that the translation will present some difficulty, because of the made-up words. It

may not be easy to find equivalents for these in a foreign language, but they can't simply be left out, as they are part of the story. I don't know Italian and can't criticise the actual translation, but they will have to decide in what manner they are going to tackle this difficulty, and I should be much obliged if the translator would consult me at some point in the process and let me know what line he is taking. In any case I might sometimes be able to help by explaining what something means.

Yours sincerely
[Signed] Eric Blair
Eric Blair

1. The essay was pubished in Henry Miller, *Domenica dopo la Guerra* [*Sunday After the War*]: *con un Saggio [Nel Ventre della Balena]* di George Orwell by Mondadori (1949). The translation omits 211 lines of the English original.
2. Not traced.
3. Published as *1984* in November 1950; the translation was by Gabriele Baldini.

3574. To Sir Richard Rees

16 March 1949   Typewritten

Cranham

Dear Richard,
I hope all is going well with you. I have heard once or twice from Barnhill and things seem to be fairly prosperous. Avril says Bill is going to plant about an acre of kale. Ian M'Kechnie is there at present, working on the road, and Francis Boyle[1] has done some work in the garden. Bill suggested we should sell off the milch cows, as some of his own cows will be calving and will have surplus milk, and of course it would make more room in the byre. On the other hand there is the question of overlapping, so I suggested keeping one Ayrshire. The boat is apparently in good order and they have been over to Crinan in her. Avril says Richard has found out about money, ie. has grasped that you can buy sweets with it, so I expect I had better start giving him pocket money, though at present he hasn't any opportunity to spend it. Incidentally, getting pocket money would probably teach him the days of the week.
    I have been feeling fairly good, though of course they won't dream of letting me up. Most of the time it has been beautiful spring-like weather. I have been reading Evelyn Waugh's very early books (on Rosetti,° and one or two others) as I undertook to write an essay on him for the Partisan Review. Also a not very good life of Dickens by Hesketh Pearson which I had to review. Also re-reading Israel Zangwill's "Children of the Ghetto," a book I hadn't set eyes on for very many years. I am trying to get hold of the sequel to it, "Grandchildren of the Ghetto,"[2] which I remember as being better than the other. I don't know what else he wrote, but I believe a whole lot. I think he is a very good novelist who hasn't had his due, though I notice now that he has a very strong tinge of Jewish nationalism, of a rather tiresome kind. I sent

65

for Marie Bashkirtseff's diary, which I had never read, and it is now staring me in the face, an enormous and rather intimidating volume.[3] I haven't seen Koestler's new book, which I think has only been published in the USA, but I think I shall send for it. My book is billed to come out on June 15th. It is going to be the Evening Standard book of the month, which I believe doesn't mean anything in particular.

Have you torn up your clothing book?[4] The reaction of everybody here was the same—"it must be a trap." Of course clothes are now sufficiently rationed by price. I think I shall order myself a new jacket all the same.

Yours
Eric

1. Ian M'Kechnie was an estate worker at Ardlussa; Francis Boyle, a roadworker on Jura. Both helped at Barnhill from time to time.
2. Israel Zangwill (1864–1926), English novelist and playwright who was one of the first to present the lives of immigrant Jews in fictional form in English literature. *Children of the Ghetto: A Study of a Peculiar People* (1892) is set in Whitechapel. His play *The Melting Pot* (1908) came to be taken as an image of America because of its capacity to transform and meld immigrants of all races. *Grandchildren of the Ghetto* was published in 1914 by the Wayfarers' Library. His other 'Ghetto' books were *Dreamers of the Ghetto* (1898), essays on distinguished Jews, *Ghetto Tragedies* (1893), *Ghetto Comedies* (1907). He was for a time a Zionist and later served as President of the Jewish Territorial Organization for the Settlement of the Jews within the British Empire, 1905–25.
3. Marie Bashkirtseff (1860–1884), Russian-born diarist and painter. Her *Journal* was published posthumously in 1887 and became very fashionable. It was published in English (translated by Mathilde Blind) in 1890. Orwell had the 1891 printing among his books at his death, but he does not include it in his list of reading for 1949.
4. Clothes were severely rationed during the war; see *3121, n. 1*. Rationing ended on 15 March 1949.

3575. To Leonard Moore

17 March 1949   Typewritten

The Cotswold Sanatorium
Cranham
Glos.

Dear Moore,

You will have had Robert Giroux's letter, of which he sent me a duplicate.

I can't possibly agree to the kind of alteration and abbreviation suggested. It would alter the whole colour of the book and leave out a good deal that is essential. I think it would also—though the judges, having read the parts that it is proposed to cut out, may not appreciate this—make the story unintelligible. There would also be something visibly wrong with the structure of the book if about a fifth or a quarter were cut out and the last chapter then tacked on to the abbreviated trunk. A book is built up as a balanced structure and one cannot simply remove large chunks here and there unless one is ready to recast the whole thing. In any case, merely to cut out the suggested chapters and abridge the passages from the "book within the book" would mean a lot of re-writing which I simply do not feel equal to at present.

The only terms on which I could agree to any such arrangement would be if the book were published definitely as an abridged version and if it were clearly stated that the English edition contained several chapters which had been omitted. But obviously the Book of the Month people couldn't be expected to agree to any such thing. As Robert Giroux says in his letter, they have not promised to select the book in any case, but he evidently hopes they might, and I suppose it will be disappointing to Harcourt & Brace° if I reject the suggestion. I suppose you, too, stand to lose a good deal of commission. But I really cannot allow my work to be mucked about beyond a certain point, and I doubt whether it even pays in the long run. I should be much obliged if you would make my point of view clear to them.[1]

Yours sincerely
[Signed] Eric Blair
Eric Blair

1. The two sections from 'I can't possibly agree' to 'to recast the whole thing' and from 'I suppose it will be disappointing' to 'make my point of view clear to them' are marked and the letter has been annotated in Moore's office: 'Quoted Harcourt Brace 21/3/48.' The precise sections suggested for omission are not now known but they evidently included Goldstein's *The Theory and Practice of Oligarchical Collectivism*—the 'book within the book.'

3576. To Sir Richard Rees

18 March 1949   Typewritten

Cranham

Dear Richard,

I'm sorry I didn't answer directly your previous letter. It was very kind of you to offer to lend me money, but really I don't need it. I am quite comfortable for some time to come. The only thing that worries me about my financial position is the possibility that I might become like some of the people here, ie. able to stay alive but unable to work. However it's not very likely. Re. your other query, I didn't think a great deal of Slater's book.[1] It seemed to me perfunctory, and I thought, as you did yourself, that the sex stuff was out of place and in poor taste. I really think that this modern habit of describing lovemaking in detail is something that future generations will look back on as we do on things like the death of Little Nell.

I haven't any reason to think my letters are tampered with. On one occasion ten years ago a letter of mine actually was opened by the police, but that was because it was addressed to a Paris publisher whose books were banned en bloc.[2] Other people have sometimes told me they thought theirs were opened, and at one time I tried to devise an envelope which couldn't be opened without the fact becoming apparent. But I don't think there's any reason to think the CP have any hand in that kind of thing or any power of getting at people's letters.

Thanks for sending the "Highway."[3] I thought the article quite good, but I didn't think a great deal of de Weidle's° book when I tried to read it some time back—actually it seemed to me that he had got himself into rather a muddle.

Robert Wheeler[4] looked in this afternoon. He has just been to Switzerland.

Yours
Eric

P.S. Did you read my article on Gandhi in the PR?[5] If so, did you agree with what I said?

1. *The Conspirator* (1948), by Humphrey Slater; Orwell does not list it amongst his reading for 1949.
2. Orwell records that on 12 August 1939 all his books from the Obelisk Press were seized by the police, his mail having been opened; see Orwell's Diary of Events Leading Up to the War, *565, 12.8.39* and *12.8.39, n. 2.*
3. *Highway*, organ of the Workers' Educational Association. In its February number, 1949, there was a review by J. M. Cameron of *The Dilemma of the Arts* by Vladimir Weidlé.
4. Robert Wheeler, a Gloucestershire farmer living near Cranham, had been asked by his friend Richard Rees to visit Orwell.
5. 'Reflections on Gandhi,' see *3516.*

3577. To David Astor

19 March 1949   Typewritten

Cranham

Dear David,

Thanks very much for your letter.[1] It's very kind of you to offer to get one of those wire recorders for me. If later on I did decide I could use one, I would be very glad of your help in getting one, provided of course you let me pay for it in sterling this end. At present I couldn't use anything of the kind, but when I first read about them I thought I could possibly make use of one—not, probably, for actual composition but for making final drafts and also for notes which I am normally too lazy to write down. The old dictaphones with cylinders were no good, but this thing I suppose will take large quantities at a time and can be switched on and off as you want it. Incidentally there is a story about one in James Thurber's new book.[1a]

I heard from Barnhill just recently. It seems Richard has now found out about money, ie. that you can buy sweets with it, and always goes about with some in his pocket, although of course he can't spend it locally. He will have to go to school soon, and my sister thinks that for this winter he might go to the village school in Ardlussa, but next year I shall have to take him to the mainland some where° where he can go to a better day school. I can't make any plans however until I am surer about my own movements.

Karl[2] tells me you are thinking of getting Kravchenko[3] as your Russian correspondent—if he wins his case, I assume!

Yours
George

1. Astor had written to Orwell on 15 March 1949 to say *The Observer* was getting into touch with Franz Borkenau regarding an article on the Spanish civil war (see *3562*) and offering to obtain for Orwell's use a wire-recorder machine (an antecedent of the tape recorder, clumsier but with similar characteristics, including the capacity to delete and re-record). 'I was thinking,' he wrote, 'that this machine might enable you to start writing without the use of any physical effort as soon as you felt inclined to do so . . . if you feel any inclination to try it, please let me get one of these things.' See also *3621, n. 6.*

1a. Perhaps *The Beast in Me*, which Orwell records reading in March 1949 (see p. 220).

2. Karl Schnetzler; see *2893*.

3. Viktor Andreevich Kravchenko (1905–1966), former Soviet official who wrote the best-seller *I Chose Freedom: The Personal and Political Life of a Soviet Official* (New York, 1946: London, 1947; written in Russian in 1945), in which he attacked the process of government in Soviet Russia. In 1947–48, *Les Lettres Françaises*, edited by Claude Morgan, published a series of attacks on Kravchenko's integrity which included much personal abuse. Kravchenko sued Morgan in his own name and his pseudonym, Sim Thomas, and André Wurmser for writing these articles. The trial opened on 24 January 1949 in Paris; judgement was given for Kravchenko, with heavy damages, on 4 April 1949. An account of the trial was published in 1950 as *Kravchenko versus Moscow*, with an introduction by the famous judge, Sir Travers Humphries. Among aspects of interest from this trial are the appearance in support of the defence of Konni Zilliacus, the left-wing Labour M.P. (see *2990, n. 2*) and Albert E. Kahn, co-author with Michael Sayers of *The Great Conspiracy* (and other books), about which Orwell asked Ruth Fischer on 21 April 1949 (see *3603* and *3603, n. 3*). Margarete Buber-Neumann, whose book *Under Two Dictators* Orwell told Tosco Fyvel he had 'read with interest' (see *3598*), gave evidence for Kravchenko and described her ordeal as a German Communist whose husband, presumed killed by Stalin, had been Ernst Thaelmann's right-hand man. She endured five years in a Siberian prison camp and was then handed over by the NKVD to the SS and sent to Ravensbrück (202–07). Another witness for those found guilty of libel was the Very Reverend Dr. Hewlett Johnson, the 'Red' Dean of Canterbury, who spoke in defence of Stalin and assured the court that under Stalin there was complete religious freedom. He said that if Kravchenko's book was right, his (Hewlett's) were wrong (208). Kravchenko appeared before the United States House of Representatives Un-American Activities Committee in 1947. Kravchenko wrote about his trial in *I Chose Justice* (1951). See also *3215, n. 8.*

3578. To *The New Leader* (New York)

21 March 1949

CAN YOU SEND ME CHURCHILL BOOK[1]   ORWELL

1. *Their Finest Hour*, see *3559, n. 2*, and, for Orwell's review, *3624*.

3579. Cranham Sanatorium Routine

Orwell's last Literary Notebook (see *3725*) contains a few handwritten entries relating to his time at Cranham Sanatorium and University College Hospital. The routine is given for each hospital, as it was for Hairmyres (see *3352*), and there are brief, dated, descriptive details. The entries for Cranham are dated 21 and 24 March and 17 April 1949. The first entry is given here and the last at its chronological point (*3602*). That for 24 March 1949 refers to Orwell's treatment with streptomycin at Hairmyres and is placed at 8/9 April 1949 (see *3378*), where it is more relevant to the medication Orwell was then receiving.

<u>21.3.49.</u>   *The routine here (Cranham Sanatorium) is quite different from that of Hairmyres Hospital. Although everyone at Hairmyres was most kind & considerate to me—quite astonishingly so, indeed—one cannot help feeling at every moment the difference in the* texture *of life when one is paying one's own keep.*

The most noticeable difference here is that it is much quieter than the hospital, & that everything is done in a more leisurely way. I live in a so-called chalet, one of a row of continuous wooden huts, with glass doors, each chalet measuring about 15' by 12'. There are hot water pipes, a washing basin, a chest of drawers & wardrobe, besides the usual bed-tables etc. Outside is a glass-roofed verandah. Everything is brought by hand—none of those abominable rattling trolleys which one is never out of the sound of in a hospital. Not much noise of radios either—all the patients have headphones. (Here these are permanently tuned in to the Home Service. At Hairmyres, usually to the Light.) The most persistent sound is the song of birds.
The day's routine:—

7 am.   Pulse & temperature taken. For this I don't wake up further than is necessary to put the thermometer in my mouth, & am usually too sleepy to take the reading then.

7.30.   Sputum cups changed.

8.00.   Breakfast. After breakfast I get up & wash. I am only allowed a bath twice a week, as it is supposed to be "weakening."

9.30. (about).   Beds made.

11.00.   Cup of coffee.

12.00. (about).   Room swept & dusted.

12.00.–12.40.   Rest hour. One is supposed to lie down during this period. Doctor generally arrives about this time.

12.40.   Lunch.

2.00–2.40.   Rest hour. Actually I usually sleep from about 2.30 to 3.30.

3.30.   Tea.

6.00.   Temperature & pulse taken.

6.00.–6.40.   Rest hour.

6.40.   Dinner.

9.30. (about).   Cup of tea.

10.30.   Lights out.

One is only weighed, screened etc. about once a month. The charge here is £12–12–0 a week, but this does not cover much more than one's board & lodging, special medicines, operations etc. being extra.

3580. To Leonard Moore

22 March 1949   Typewritten

Cranham

Dear Moore,
Thank you for your letter, and thanks so much for supporting me over the proposed alterations.[1]

Yours sincerely
Eric Blair

1. These were proposals to cut *Nineteen Eighty-Four* to suit the wishes of the Book-of-the-Month Club in the United States; see *3575*.

3581. To [Christy & Moore][1]

24 March 1949   Handwritten

Cranham

[No addressee]
Many thanks. I should be glad for "Animal Farm" to be broadcast by Radio Italiana.

Geo. Orwell

1. The provenance of this note indicates that it was sent to Orwell's agents. That it was not intended for Leonard Moore personally is suggested by the signature. Orwell always signed himself 'Eric Blair' when writing to Moore.

3582. To Tosco Fyvel

25 March 1949   Typewritten

Cranham

Dear Tosco,
In *one* issue of "What's Happening:"[1]
"Reticent to impose the ban"
"Without printing hardly any."
"Guaranteeing a cure against cancer or tuberculosis or painless childbirth."
"HeiNwehr."[2]
I think I am going to be in this place till about July. I make progress slowly, but they can't do much for me as they can't operate and daren't use streptomycin a second time. I am not really doing any work at present but hope to start in a month or so. Please give everyone my love.

Yours
George

1. Orwell wrote to Fyvel in the latter's role as literary editor of *Tribune*, which ran a feature called 'What's Happening.'
2. Mistake for Heimwehr, Home Guard (German).

3583. To Fredric Warburg

30 March 1949   Handwritten

Cranham

Dear Fred,

Thanks for your letter.[1] I read "We" about a couple of years ago & don't think I particularly want the galleys. I didn't wish to force it on you, & I merely thought it might be worth your while & at any rate ought to be re-issued by somebody. Certainly it has faults, but it seems to me to form an interesting link in the chain of Utopia books. On the one hand it debunks the super-rational, hedonistic type of Utopia (I think Aldous Huxley's "Brave New World" must be plagiarised from it to some extent), but on the other hand it takes account of the diabolism & the tendency to return to an earlier form of civilization which seem to be part of totalitarianism. It seems to me a good book in the same way as "The Iron Heel", but better written. But of course there's no knowing whether it would sell & I have no wish to land you with a white elephant. I just think *somebody* ought to print it & that it is disgraceful that a book of this kind, with its curious history as well as its intrinsic interest, should stay out of print when so much rubbish is published every day.

I have been rather poorly & have been having "haemoptyses".[2] That is why I have written this by hand. They have forbidden me to use my typewriter for a week, as it is supposed to tire me. Please give everyone my love.

Yours
George

1. Gleb Struve had written to Orwell on 1 January 1949 from Berkeley, California (where he was teaching), explaining that John Westhouse Ltd, the publishing house which was to bring out Zamyatin's *We*, was in the hands of liquidators. Various amounts were unpaid, though Madame Zamyatin (in Paris) had received an advance of £25. Struve asked Orwell whether he had heard anything from Warburg. On 26 January 1949, Warburg wrote to Struve. Some two months earlier, Orwell had spoken to Warburg about the problems associated with the publishing of *We*, and Warburg had obtained from the liquidators an assurance that he could see the proofs with a view to taking over from Westhouse. In the third week of January, Orwell had shown him Struve's letter of 1 January, and Warburg then assured Struve that he was keenly interested in publishing *We*. Struve, who was then at Harvard as a visiting lecturer, wrote to Warburg on 22 February. He explained that the translation into English had been unsatisfactory but on his recommendation it had been revised and he thought it would now be accurate. He remarked that 'Mr. Prost's translation [as revised by Mr. Sieff] is better than the awful American translation which appeared in 1925 and the knowledge of which the American publisher (Dutton) now seems to deny.' Warburg replied on 8 March, telling Struve that the liquidators 'hope in the near future to put the whole question of Zamyatin's book before us.' See also *3524, n. 1*.
2. Spitting blood from the lungs.

3584. To Sir Richard Rees

3 1 March 1949   Handwritten

Cranham

Dear Richard,

Thanks so much for your letter. I send herewith a copy of PR with the article I spoke of.[1] I'd have sent it before, as I thought it would interest you, but I was under the impression that you took in PR. Celia Kirwan was here the other day & she will send me a copy of that number of "Polemic" which I lost & which has the essay on Tolstoy in it. It really connects up with the Gandhi article.

Yes, I must get this will business sewn up. I had my will properly drawn up by a solicitor, then, as I wanted to make some alterations, re-wrote it myself, & I dare say this second draft, though duly witnessed etc., is not legal. Have you got a solicitor in Edinburgh? I am out of touch with my London ones. It is important to get the literary executorship sewn up properly, & also to be quite sure about Richard's position, because there is some legal difference, I forget what, in the case of an adopted child. In addition I must bring up to date the notes I left for you about my books, which editions to follow, etc. When Avril came back from town she brought some box files marked "Personal" which I *think* have all the relevant stuff in them. Do you think when you are at Barnhill you could go through these files & send the relevant papers to me. I want my will, ie. the second will, dated about the beginning of 1947 I think, the notes I left for you, & a notebook marked "Reprintable Essays"[2] which wants bringing up to date. It's important that your powers should be made clear, ie. that you should have the final say when any definitely literary question is involved. For example. The American Book of the Month people, though they didn't actually promise, half promised to select my present book if I would cut out about a quarter of it. Of course I'm not going to do this, but if I had died the week before, Moore & the American publishers would have jumped at the offer, ruining the book & not even benefiting my estate much, because whenever you make a large sum you are in the surtax class & it is all taken away again.

I have been very poorly, spitting up quantities of blood. This doesn't necessarily do any harm, indeed Morlock,[3] the specialist I went to before the war, said it might even do good, but it always depresses & disgusts me, & I have been feeling rather down. There is evidently nothing very definite they can do for me. They talked of doing the "thora" operation, but the surgeon wouldn't undertake it because you have to have one sound lung which I haven't. Evidently the only thing to do is to keep quiet. It worries me not to see little R., but perhaps later I can arrange somehow for him to visit me. If I do get up this year I want to take him for a trip to London.

Yours
Eric

Excuse this writing. They've forbidden me to use a typewriter at present because it is tiring![4]

1. 'Reflections on Gandhi'; see *3516*; and see postscript to letter to Rees of 18 March 1949, *3576*.
2. See *3728*, which includes a section on 'Reprintable Essays.'
3. Dr. H. V. Morlock.
4. The postscript (which is not so designated) was written at the head of the first page of the letter.

3585. 'Evelyn Waugh'

Unfinished essay; April (?) 1949   Typescript with handwritten notes

It has not proved possible to date precisely when Orwell prepared the first part of the typescript of his essay on Evelyn Waugh, nor to date exactly the notes he wrote in his last Literary Notebook, though all are from 1949. On the cover of a red folder Orwell has written 'Waugh / by end of April / 3000–4000 / 15,000 max).' If these notes refer to the essay on Waugh, which seems likely, a date of April 1949 for the typed opening would be reasonable. The 5½-page typescript looks to be Orwell's own work. He was typing up to 25 March 1949, was then very ill, typed again from 14 April but did little typing after the beginning of May 1949 and for much of the time was forbidden to write. His letters in May show he found it impossible to put pen to paper except for personal and minor business matters. He had been reading Waugh in February and March (*Robbery Under Law, When the Going Was Good, Rossetti: His Life and Works,* and *Work Suspended*), but only one of these is touched upon in what survives of this essay. The essay was certainly typed at Cranham, for it is headed with Orwell's name and the address of the sanatorium, typed above the upper typed line of the two that enclose the title, 'Evelyn Waugh.'

In his final Literary Notebook, Orwell drafted some notes 'For article on E. Waugh.' Earlier in that notebook he also wrote out three passages from Waugh. These passages and the notes, follow this item, as *3586*.

Evelyn Waugh visited Orwell at Cranham. Crick records: 'Many people came to visit [Orwell], some fearing that he was dying, others simply to entertain him in his isolation. [Anthony] Powell and [Malcolm] Muggeridge, who did their share of visiting persuaded Evelyn Waugh, who neither knew Orwell nor particularly cared for his writing, to visit him; simply because he lived nearby [about eighteen miles away]. As one worthy in the world of English letters to another, he did this kindness several times. "I should have loved to see them together," wrote Muggeridge, "his country gentleman's outfit and Orwell's proletarian one both straight out of back numbers of Punch" (Crick, 556). In the entry to his diary for 31 August 1945, Waugh says that his 'Communist cousin Claud [Cockburn]' warned him against Trotskyist literature, 'so that I read and greatly enjoyed Orwell's *Animal Farm*' (*Diaries 1911–1965*, edited by Michael Davie). Unfortunately, Orwell seems not to have kept a diary in 1949.

Within the last few decades, in countries like Britain or the United States, the literary intelligentsia has grown large enough to constitute a world in itself. One important result of this is that the opinions which a writer feels frightened of expressing are not those which are disapproved of by society as a whole. To a great extent, what is still loosely thought of as heterodoxy has become orthodoxy. It is nonsense to pretend, for instance, that at this date there is something daring and original in proclaiming yourself an anarchist, an atheist, a pacifist, etc. The daring thing, or at any rate the unfashionable thing, is to believe in God or to approve of the capitalist system. In 1895, when Oscar Wilde was jailed, it must have needed very considerable moral courage to defend homosexuality. Today it would need no courage at all: today the equivalent action would be, perhaps, to defend antisemitism. But this example that I have chosen immediately reminds one of something else—namely, that one cannot judge the value of an opinion simply by the amount of courage that is required in holding it. There is still such a thing as truth and falsehood, it is possible to hold true beliefs for the wrong reasons, and—though there may be no advance in human intelligence—the prevailing ideas of one age are sometimes demonstrably less silly than those of another.

In our own day, the English novelist who has most conspicuously defied his contemporaries is Evelyn Waugh. Waugh's outlook on life is, I should say, false and to some extent perverse, but at least it must be said for him that he adopted it at a time when it did not pay to do so, and his literary reputation has suffered accordingly. It is true, of course, that he has had immense *popular* success (a thing that does not seem to have any connection, positive or negative, with critical acclaim), and also that he has been underrated partly because he is a "light" writer whose special gift is for something not far removed from low farce. But his main offence in the eyes of his fellow-writers has always been the reactionary political tendency which was already clearly apparent even in such light-hearted books as *Decline and Fall* and *Vile Bodies*. Chronologically Waugh belongs to the generation of Auden and Spender, though he would be about five years older than most of the leading members of the group. This generation, almost en bloc, was politically "left," in a Popular-Front style, with Communist leanings. There were, of course, a few writers of about the same age who did not fit into the pattern—for instance, there were William Empson, William Plomer, V. S. Pritchett and Graham Greene. But of these, the first three were merely lacking in political zeal and not in any way hostile to the Popular-Front orthodoxy, while Graham Greene—the fact has passed almost unnoticed, no doubt because of the unjustified assumption that a Catholic is the same thing as a Conservative—was himself politically "left," in an ill-defined, unobtrusive way. In the whole of this age-group, the only loudly discordant voice was Waugh's. Even his first book, the life of Rossetti, published in 1927, displays a sort of defiant Conservatism, which expresses itself, as was natural at that date, in aesthetic rather than political terms.

Waugh is the latest, perhaps the last, of a long line of English writers whose real driving force is a romantic belief in aristocracy. At a casual glance, *Decline and Fall*, *Vile Bodies*, and considerable passages, at least, in nearly all the subsequent books, appear to consist of nothing but a sort of high-spirited foolery, owing something to Norman Douglas and perhaps a little to "Saki," and tinged by the kind of innocent snobbishness that causes people to wait twenty-four hours on the pavement to get a good view of a royal wedding. If one looks only a little way below the surface, however, one sees that though the approach is at the level of farce, the essential theme is serious. What Waugh is trying to do is to use the feverish, cultureless modern world as a set-off for his own conception of a good and stable way of life. The seeming immoralism of these books (the jokes turn not merely upon adultery but upon prostitution, homosexuality, suicide, lunacy and cannibalism) is merely a reversion to the older tradition of English humour, according to which any event can be funny provided that it either didn't happen or happened a long time ago. In *Decline and Fall*, for instance, the funniest episode is the sawing-off of a clergyman's head. If one were asked to believe this it would be merely disgusting, but being impossible it is acceptable, like the events in, for instance, the *Miller's Tale*, which would seem by no means funny if they happened in real life. Waugh's books certainly owe some of their popularity to their air of naughtiness, but none of them (except, perhaps, to some small extent, *Decline and Fall*) is intended to be morally subversive. They are really sermons in farcical shape, and kept in farcical shape by avoidance of comment. In *Decline and Fall*, *Vile Bodies*, *Scoop* and, to a less extent, *A Handful of Dust* the central character is a passive figure who simply lets things happen to him and hardly appears to notice the difference between good and evil, or even between pain and pleasure: in *Black Mischief* and *The Loved One* he is not passive, but his motives are unexplained. The general outline of these books resembles that of *Candide*, and in very broad terms the "moral" is also the same: "Look, this is what the world is like. Is it really necessary to behave quite so foolishly?" But, of course, Waugh's notion of reasonable conduct is very different from Voltaire's.

In all Waugh's books up to *Brideshead Revisited*, which perhaps indicates a new departure, the idea of sanity and moral integrity is mixed up with the idea of country life—upper-class country life—as it was lived a couple of generations ago. Already in *Vile Bodies* there is an irrelevant outburst in favour of the older kind of minor aristocracy, the people who still have, or used to have, a sense of obligation and a fixed code of behaviour, as against the mob of newspaper peers, financiers, politicians and playboys with whom the book deals:

> . . . a great concourse of pious and honourable people (many of whom made the Anchorage House reception the one outing of the year), their women-folk well gowned in rich and durable stuffs, their men-folk ablaze with orders; people who had represented their country in foreign places and sent their sons to die for her in battle, people of decent and temperate life, uncultured, unaffected, unembarrassed, unassuming, unambitious people, of independent judgement and marked eccentricities, kind people who cared for animals and the deserving poor, brave and rather unreasonable people, that fine phalanx of the passing order, approaching, as one day at the Last Trump they hoped to meet their Maker, with decorous and frank cordiality to shake Lady Anchorage by the hand at the top of her staircase. . . .

Here "animals and the deserving poor" may perhaps be meant ironically, but the note of affection and esteem, out of tune with most of the rest of the book, is unmistakeable. In *A Handful of Dust* the theme is made more explicit. On the one side the foolish, glittering life of fashionable London: on the other the country house, the succession that must be maintained, the fields and woods that must not be allowed to decay. As an earlier writer in the *Partisan Review* has pointed out, whenever the action of Waugh's books takes place in England, a house, an old house, always plays an important part in it. In *Decline and Fall* the house, in process of being ravaged, is already there. In *A Handful of Dust*—this time a somewhat ridiculous house but beautiful in its owner's eyes—it is the pivot of the story. In *Brideshead Revisited* it appears in more magnificent form. But it is probably as it appears in *Scoop* and *Vile Bodies* that it corresponds most closely with Waugh's private ideal. Everyone knows, at least traditionally, the kind of house that is there described—the middle-sized country house which required, in the days of its glory, about ten servants, and which has now, if it is not merely derelict, been turned into a hotel, a boarding school or a lunatic asylum. All the familiar scenery is there, whether or not Waugh mentions it in detail: the "wet, bird-haunted lawns" and the walled garden with its crucified pear-trees; the large untidy porch with its litter of raincoats, waders, landing-nets and croquet mallets; the plastery smell of the flagged passage leading to the gunroom; the estate map on the library wall; the case of stuffed birds over the staircase. To Waugh, this is magic, or used to be magic, and it would be [a] waste of time to try to exorcise it from his mind merely by pointing out that

The typescript breaks off at this point.

3586. Notes for 'Evelyn Waugh'
Handwritten

These notes were written by Orwell in his last Literary Notebook. The extract from *Brideshead Revisited* is on folio 1ᵛ and those from *Robbery Under Law* are on folio 2ʳ. The notes for the essay are on folios 9 and 10. (This numbering has been added by the Orwell Archive.) The ellipses are Orwell's.

He said: "I hope it's dipsomania. That is simply a great misfortune that we must all help him bear. What I used to fear was that he just got drunk deliberately when he liked & because he liked."
"That's exactly what he did—what we both did. It's what he does with me now. I can keep him to that, if only your mother would trust me. If you worry him with keepers & cures he'll be a physical wreck in a few years."
"There's nothing *wrong* in being a physical wreck, you know. There's no moral obligation to be Postmaster-General or Master of Foxhounds or live to walk ten miles at eighty."
"*Wrong*," I said. "*Moral obligation*—now . . . . etc.
("Brideshead Revisited.")

Let me, then, warn the reader that I was a Conservative when I went to Mexico & that everything I saw there strengthened my opinions. I believe that man is, by nature, an exile & will never be self-sufficient or complete on this earth; that his chances of happiness & virtue, here, remain more or less constant through the centuries &, generally speaking, are not much affected by the political & economic conditions in which he lives, that the balance of good & ill tends to revert to a norm, that sudden changes of physical condition are usually ill, & are advocated by the wrong people for the wrong reasons; that the intellectual communists of today have personal, irrelevant grounds for their antagonism to society. I believe in government; that men cannot live together without rules but that these should be kept at the bare minimum of safety; that there is no form of government ordained from God as being better than any other; that the anarchic elements in society are so strong that it is a whole-time task to keep the peace. I believe that inequalities of wealth & position are inevitable & that it is therefore meaningless to discuss the advantages of their elimination; that men naturally arrange themselves in a system of classes . . . . . I do not think that British prosperity must necessarily be inimical to anyone else, but if, on occasions, it is, I want Britain to prosper & not her rivals . . . .

(Evelyn Waugh, "Robbery Under Law.")

There is no more agreeable position than that of dissident from a stable society. Theirs are all the solid advantages of other people's creation & preservation, & all the fun of detecting hypocrisies & inconsistencies.

(ibid.)

For article on E. Waugh.

The advantages of not being part of the movement, irrespective of whether the movement is in the right direction or not.

But disadvantage in holding false (indefensible) opinions.
The movement (Auden etc.)[1]
W.'s driving forces. Snobby.[2] Catholicism.

Note even the early books not anti-religious or demonstrably anti-moral. But note the persistent snobbishness, rising in the social scale but always centreing° round the idea of continuity/aristocracy/a country house. Note that everyone is snobbish, but that Waugh's loyalty is to a form of society no longer viable, of which he must be aware.
Untenable opinions Cf. Poe[3]
Catholicism. Note that a Catholic writer does not have to be Conservative in a political sense. Differentiate G. Greene.
Advantage to a novelist of being a Catholic—theme of collision between two kinds of good.
Analyse "Brideshead Revisited." (Note faults due to being written in first person.)[4] Studiously detached attitude. Not puritanical. Priests not super-human. Real theme—Sebastian's drunkenness, & family's unwilling° to cure

this at the expense of committing a sin. Note that this is a real departure from the humanist attitude, with which no compromise possible.

But. Last scene, where the unconscious man makes the sign of the Cross. Note that after all the veneer is bound to crack sooner or later. One cannot really be Catholic & grown up.

Conclude. Waugh is about as good a novelist as one can be (ie. as novelists go today) while holding untenable opinions.

1. Sidenote, arrowed to be placed in this position.
2. Possibly 'Snobbery.'
3. Sidenote, arrowed to be placed in this position.
4. See Orwell's notes 'For & against novels in the first person,' written in his last Literary Notebook, *3725*. The notes on Waugh followed immediately after those on novels in the first person.

3587. Una Marson to Orwell

2 April 1949

Una Marson had been a producer in the West Indies Section of the BBC Overseas Service when Orwell was working in the Eastern Service. She had read her poem 'The Banjo Boy' in Orwell's programme 'Voice, 4,' 3 November 1942; see *1630*. After a hectic tour of the West Indies and a further visit to London, she had returned to her home island, Jamaica. She wrote in this letter of her progress from ill health to recovery and of her response to visiting the mission house where her father had worked for twenty-seven years. 'I have talked a lot about myself,' she wrote, 'because I know you have some little interest in me and must be wondering a bit.' She also described the political and social developments and the problems faced by the West Indies. She concluded, 'Get Creech Jones to send you out to write a book on the West Indies. You would love Jamaica, politics apart.' Arthur Creech Jones was Secretary of State for the Colonies.

3588. To David Astor

4 April 1949   Handwritten

Cranham

Dear David,
Thanks so much for your letter.[1] I'd love to come & stay with you for a bit when I get out of here, if I ever do, & bring Richard. As to my sister I'm not sure. She seems to be so stuck into the farm work at Barnhill that I don't know whether she'd ever be able to get away. But I can easily make some arrangement to have a temporary nurse for R. or for that matter look after him myself. I have been wanting to take him for a trip south this year, as I think it is time he started to see the world a bit. But if we come & stay with you, *please* don't alter anything round. We'll fit in quite easily.

I look forward to being profiled[2] with a certain alarm—however! If you want photographs I have some.

I am a bit better now but I was very poorly for about a week, with haemoptyses (polite name for spitting blood). I can't get any picture of when I shall be well enough to get up & about, so it's impossible to make any plans. They talked of operating on me but they can't do it because you have to have one reliable lung, which I haven't. So I suppose there is nothing for it except to keep quiet. Everything seems well in Jura & they are very busy.

Yours
George

1. Astor wrote on 2 April telling Orwell that Harold Nicolson, not Bertrand Russell, would review *Nineteen Eighty-Four*. Though Russell was believed to be willing, Nicolson had 'complained that there were so few books worth reviewing' it was 'felt unfair to deprive him of one which he had expressed an active interest in reviewing.' The reporter for the Profile was to be Karl [Schnetzler]. Astor said that opinion at *The Observer* was that Borkenau's article on the civil war, 'Spain: Whose Victory?,' 27 March 1949, was a great success. There is nothing in the letter about Orwell, Avril, and Richard visiting Astor.
2. No Profile was published. However, an unsigned article, 'George Orwell: A Life of Independence,' with a photograph by Vernon Richards, appeared on 22 January 1950, the day after Orwell died, and, one week later, 'A Rebel's Progress' by Arthur Koestler. See final paragraph of *3621*.

3589. To Ruth Fischer

4 April 1949

A letter from Orwell of this date is reported to exist but it has not been traced. There may be no such letter.

3590. To Fredric Warburg

5 April 1949   Handwritten

Dear Fred,

Thanks for your letter.[1] I would be pleased to see Mr Curran & give him any information I can. All that matters is that he should let me know what day & time he is coming, so that I can arrange for a car.

Yours
George

1. Warburg wrote on 4 April. He said that the *Evening Standard* had chosen *Nineteen Eighty-Four* as its Book of the Month for June but had turned down the book for serialization. They wanted their feature editor, [Charles] Curran, to spend an hour with Orwell to get personal background for a big feature. Warburg wanted to know whether Orwell felt fit enough to see Curran. If he wasn't, he would put him off.

3590A. Orwell and the Information Research Department:

see Appendix 14

3590B. Orwell to Celia Kirwan, 6 April 1949: see Appendix 14

3591. To Sir Richard Rees

6 April 1949   Handwritten

Cranham

Dear Richard,
Thanks so much for your two letters. I hope you got to Barnhill O.K.—Avril
said you would probably have to walk from the New Stable.
    When you're sending those documents, do you think you could also send
me a quarto notebook with a pale-bluish cardboard cover, which I *think* was
in my bedroom, but might have been in the sitting-room. In either case it
would probably be in one of the wire boxes among a mass of other papers. It
contains a list of crypto-Communists & fellow-travellers which I want to
bring up to date.[1]
    No more blood-spitting, but I am feeling ghastly most of the time. They
are going to take my photo[2] again today & we will see what they say on the
basis of that.[3]

Love to all
Eric

1. See *3590A* and *3590B* (in Appendix 14) and *3732*.
2. X-ray.
3. On the verso of Orwell's letter is a draft (in Richard Rees's hand) of a letter to an unnamed
   addressee proposing the sale of the lorry used at Barnhill. It was 'supposed to be new (600
   miles)' and had cost £895, which included tax, insurance, and delivery charges.

3592. To Vernon Richards

7 April 1949   Handwritten

Cranham

Dear Vernon,
Thanks so much for your letter. Please excuse handwriting—I've been very
poorly lately & they have told me not to use a typewriter.
    I had heard about your misfortune from the people at Whiteway here.[1] It
was a miserable thing to happen. I don't in any way want to press the
suggestion upon you, but if you badly want a baby you might do worse than
do what I did, ie. adopt one. It seems an unnatural thing to do, but it does
seem to work, ie. one becomes as fond of the child as one could be of a
"natural" child, & that almost from the start.
    What I partly wrote about was to ask whether, among the prints of photos
that you have of me, there are any that are sufficiently full-face to do for

passport photographs. My passport has expired, & I have been meaning for a long time to get it renewed, but have never been anywhere near a photographer. It says in the instructions that the photographs have to be full face. I suppose I *could* get someone to come & take one here in bed, but it would be an awful nuisance. Please remember me to Marie Louise.

Yours
Geo. Orwell

1. At the end of 1948, Marie-Louise Berneri (wife of Vernon Richards) gave birth to a still-born child. She died unexpectedly, aged thirty-one, of a virus infection less than a week after Orwell wrote to Richards (*Freedom*, Centenary Number, 1986, 25). Whiteway lies some five miles northeast of Stroud and about two miles from Cranham. It gave its name to an anarchist and craft colony where Lilian Wolfe (see *3600, n. 3*) lived from the early 1920s until 1943, but also visiting thereafter. Her companion, Thomas Keell (1866–1938), brought the Freedom Press to Whiteway when the continuance of *Freedom* was put in doubt by the London County Council's demolition of the area where the journal's London offices were located. Whiteway served as the Freedom Press address from September 1928 to December 1932; June 1937 to January 1938; and November 1939. Keell was secretary of the colony from 1928. Orwell arranged for Richard to stay at Whiteway for a time so he could see him (information about Whiteway from *Freedom*, Centenary Number, 1986, 22, 24, 30).

3593. Medical Superintendent, The Cotswold Sanatorium, to the Editor, *Partisan Review*
7 April 1949   Typewritten

MR. GEORGE ORWELL is seriously ill and will be unable to write the article which he had promised you, at any rate for the time being. He hopes you will forgive him for not fulfilling his engagement.

[Signed] Geoffrey A. Hoffman

3594. To Sir Richard Rees
8 April 1949   Handwritten

Cranham

Dear Richard,
I thought you'd all like to know that I have just had a cable saying that the Book of the Month Club have selected my novel after all, in spite of my refusing to make the changes they demanded. So that shows that virtue is its own reward, or honesty is the best policy, I forget which. I don't know whether I shall ultimately end up with a net profit, but at any rate this should pay off my arrears of income tax.

I've had the sanatorium cable the magazines to which I had promised articles saying I am unfit to do any work, which is the truth. Don't depress the others too much with this, but the fact is I am in a bad way at present. They are going to try streptomycin again, which I had previously urged them

82

to do & which Mr Dick thought might be a good idea. They had been afraid of it because of the secondary effects, but they now say they can offset these to some extent with nicotine, or something, & in any case they can always stop if the results are too bad. *If* things go badly—of course we'll hope they won't, but one must be prepared for the worst—I'll ask you to bring little Richard to see me before I get too frightening in appearance. I think it would upset you less than it would Avril, & there may be business deals to talk over as well. If the stuff works, as it seemed to do last time, I shall take care this time to keep the improvement by leading an invalid life for the rest of the year.

I forgot to say, I wish some time you'd have a look at my books & see they're not getting too mildewy (I asked Avril to light a fire from time to time for that reason) & that the magazines in the bottom shelf are in some sort of order. I want to keep all the magazines that are there, as some of them have articles of mine that I might want to reprint. The books are piling up here & I'm going to start sending them home some time, but I can't do up parcels at present.

Love to all
Eric

3595. To [*The New Leader*, New York]

9 April 1949   Typewritten

Cranham

[No addressee]
I hope this[1] does not come too late. I have been very ill and almost unable to do any work of any kind.

G.O.

1. This was the covering note for Orwell's review of Winston Churchill's *Their Finest Hour*. It was published by *The New Leader*, New York, 14 May 1949 (see *3624*). The executive editor, S. M. Levitas, wrote a grateful note of thanks on 21 April 1949 and offered 'some kind of compensation' for the review and for future articles, either by cheque or by CARE parcel (Cooperative for American Relief to Everywhere, an organisation for providing aid to those in need). Levitas explained how he saw the journal's relationship with Orwell:

    We of the NEW LEADER, and I am sure that I speak in the name of the bulk of our readers, consider you our own in every respect. I know of no other publication in our country where you can feel as much "at home" as you can with the NEW LEADER group. We are in the battle together for a decent and humane world and not only are we in the same trenches combatting totalitarianism but we think in unison of the remedies that are so vital in building a new and better world.

    I know that at the moment you are ill and can't do as much as you would like to, nevertheless I sincerely hope that when your fingers itch to write on any subject, you will think of us and give us the preference over other publications.

    Orwell replied to Levitas's letter on 2 May 1949; see *3616*.

3596. To Vernon Richards

13 April 1949   Handwritten

Cranham

Dear Vernon,

Thanks so much for the photos. But please send me a bill for them! It isn't business to give things away.

I hadn't noticed the misprints in the uniform edit. of "Burmese Days".[1] It's no doubt because I was ill when I corrected the proofs. It's annoying, I do hate misprints.

I hope Marie-Louise is going on all right. I have really been very ill indeed. They started to give me a second course of streptomycin, but just one dose had the most dire effects. Evidently I've become resistant or allergic or something.

Yours
George

1. The Uniform Edition published by Secker & Warburg in January 1949 introduced many errors, though it is, on occasion, correct against its source, the Penguin edition of 1944. See *CW*, II, Textual Note, especially 310–12 and the list of variants.

3597. To Robert Giroux

14 April 1949   Typewritten

The Cotswold Sanatorium
Cranham
Glos.

Dear Mr Giroux,

Many thanks for your letter of the 11th. Naturally I am delighted that the Book of the Month Club selected "1984" after all. A little before publication date I am going to ask you to be kind enough to send complimentary copies to about a dozen people in the USA. I will send you the names through Leonard Moore. Actually I dare say some of them are on your list already.

The essay on "Lear" that you asked after (actually it's on Tolstoy's essay on Shakespeare) appeared about two years ago in a shortlived magazine called "Polemic."[1] Unfortunately I haven't a copy myself, and have been trying to get hold of one, as I might want to reprint it some time. I would be interested to know where Empson's essay appeared, as I'd like to know what he has to say about "Lear."[2] He has disappeared into China[3] the way people do, and I did not even know he was writing anything at present.

I have been very ill the last few weeks, but am now somewhat better. I trust that I am now on the way to recovery and shall be out of here before the summer is over, but it is certain to be a slow job at best. I have my next novel mapped out,[4] but I am not going to touch it until I feel stronger. It is not only that it tires me to work, but also that I am afraid of making a false start and getting discouraged.

Yours sincerely
[Signed] Geo. Orwell
George Orwell

1. 'Lear, Tolstoy and the Fool,' *Polemic*, 7, March 1947; see *3181*.
2. 'The Fool in Lear,' *Sewanee Review*, 57 (April 1949); reprinted in *The Structure of Complex Words* (1951), in the chapter with the title of the essay.
3. William Empson (see *845, n. 3*), with whom Orwell had worked at the BBC, had held a professorship in English Literature at Peking University, then part of the South-Western Combined Universities, in Hunan and Yunan, 1937–39; he returned there in 1947, after being Chinese editor for the BBC, 1941–46. See Orwell's letter to Giroux, 19 May 1949, *3627*.
4. This is presumably 'a novel dealing with 1945' that Orwell told Tosco Fyvel he had 'in his head but which he wouldn't touch until 1950'; see *3598*. He told Sonia Orwell that he had two novels in mind. Only fragments of one, 'A Smoking-room Story' (see *3723*), survive. This Orwell sets in 1927 (xx, 189), but see *3723, ns 7 and 8*. In his obituary of Orwell, *The Bookseller*, 11 February 1950, Warburg says: 'Two new novels were already simmering in his mind, and a long essay on Joseph Conrad. . . .'

3598. To Tosco Fyvel

15 April 1949

Fyvel lost the original of this letter after most of it had been printed in *Encounter*, January 1962. It is reproduced here as printed in *Encounter* ('Some Letters of George Orwell,' 64–65), except that in *Encounter*, 'millionaires' is followed by an apostrophe instead of a comma.

Cranham

Dear Tosco,

Thanks so much for sending Ruth Fischer's book.[1] I had intended buying it, but perhaps after reading a borrowed copy I shan't need to. I'll see you get it back. I read Margarete Neumann's book[2] with some interest. It wasn't a particularly good book but she struck me as a sincere person. Gollancz also has a quite remarkable novel about the forced-labour camps coming along, by someone calling himself pseudonymously "Richard Cargoe"[3]—a Pole I should say—how authentic I couldn't be sure, but quite a striking book, in the Slav manner.

There were several points in your articles that I had been meaning to take up with you. One is about Graham Greene. You keep referring to him as an extreme Conservative, the usual Catholic reactionary type. This isn't so at all, either in his books or privately. Of course he is a Catholic and in some issues has to take sides politically with the church, but in outlook he is just a mild Left with faint CP leanings. I have even thought that he might become our first Catholic fellow-traveller, a thing that doesn't exist in England but does in France, etc. If you look at books like *A Gun for Sale, England Made Me, The Confidential Agent* and others, you will see that there is the usual left-wing scenery. The bad men are millionaires, armaments manufacturers etc., and the good man is sometimes a Communist. In his last book there is also the usual inverted colour-feeling. According to Rayner Heppenstall, Greene somewhat reluctantly supported Franco during the Spanish civil war, but *The Confidential Agent* is written from the other point of view.

The other thing is that you are always attacking novelists for not writing about the contemporary scene. But can you think of a novel that ever was written about the strictly contemporary scene? It is very unlikely that any novel, *i.e.* worth reading, would ever be set back less than three years at least. If you tried, *in* 1949, to write a novel about 1949 it would simply be "reportage" and probably would seem out of date and silly before you could get it into print. I have a novel dealing with 1945 in my head now, but even if I survive to write it I shouldn't touch it before 1950.[4] The reason is not only that one can't see the events of the moment in perspective, but also that a novel has to be lived with for years before it can be written down, otherwise the working-out of detail, which takes an immense time and can only be done at odd moments, can't happen. This is my experience and I think it is also other people's. I have sometimes written a so-called novel within about two years of the original conception, but then they were always weak, silly books which I afterwards suppressed. You may remember that nearly all the worth-while books about the 1914 war appeared 5, 10 or even more years after it was over, which was when one might have expected them. I think books about the late war are about due to appear now, and books about the immediate post-war at some time in the fifties.

I've been horribly ill the last few weeks. I had a bit of a relapse, then they decided to have another go with streptomycin, which previously did me a lot of good, at least temporarily. This time only one dose of it had ghastly results, as I suppose I had built up an allergy or something. I'm a bit better now, however, but I can't work and don't know when I shall be able to. I've no hope of getting out of here before the late summer. If the weather is good I might then get up to Scotland for a few weeks, but not more, and then I shall have to spend the autumn and winter somewhere near a doctor, perhaps even in some kind of residential sanatorium. I can't make plans till my health takes a more definite turn one way or the other. Richard is blooming, or was when I last saw him. He will be five in May. I think he will go to the village school this winter, but next year I shall have to remove him to the mainland so that he can go to a proper day school. He is still backward about talking but bright in other ways. I don't think he will ever be one for books. His bent seems to be mechanical, and he is very good at farm work. If he grew to be a farmer[5] I should be pleased, though I shan't try to influence him. . . .[6]

Yours,
George

1. *Stalin and German Communism*, by Ruth Fischer; see *3603* and *3603, n. 1*. Orwell includes it in his list of reading for April.
2. *Under Two Dictators*, by Margarete Buber-Neumann; see *3577, n. 3*. Orwell includes it in his list of reading for April.
3. *The Tormentors*; listed by Orwell under February in his reading list for 1949. It is marked as a proof copy, and Orwell wrote a question mark against it (as he did against several titles in the

list), but the significance of the query is not known. See also *3544, n. 1.* Cargoe's real name was Robert Payne (1911–1983). Orwell apparently did not know him by his pseudonym, but he may have known him as Payne without realising that he was the author of this book. Payne had been a war correspondent in Spain in 1938 (the year after Orwell fought there) and in 1941–42 he worked for the British Ministry of Information in Chungking, China, when Orwell was at the BBC.

4. This was the second of the two books Orwell had in mind at his death. See *3597, n. 4.*
5. Richard Blair did initially take up farming as a career. In 1964 he married Eleanor Moir, a schoolteacher; they have two sons. See *3736.*
6. The letter was cut here by *Encounter.*

3599. To Brenda Salkeld

16 April 1949   Handwritten

The Cotswold Sanatorium
Cranham
Glos.

Dear Brenda,
It is so nice of you to come & see me. I have booked you a room for the nights of 26 & 27 April at the Royal George, Birdlip, which is not far from here. This place isn't on the map, but the nearest villages are PAINSWICK and BIRDLIP (near Cheltenham.) I don't know how you're coming—if by car, it's simple enough, but if by train you will want a car from Gloucester or Stroud or wherever it is you come to. In that case can you let me know time of arrival so that I can order a car. You can see me here any time after about 12.30. You can have lunch & tea here. I'm in bed of course, but may be allowed to sit out in a deck chair shortly. I have been horribly ill but am a little better I think.

With love
Eric

3600. To Sir Richard Rees

17 April 1949   Typewritten

Cranham

Dear Richard,
Thanks so much for sending on the things. It doesn't matter much about the book marked Essays. I can remember most of the items I wanted to note down, and I dare say the book itself will turn up among the papers which were sent to Pickfords. You might ask Avril whether, when she cleaned out my papers at Canonbury, she threw any notebooks away. There was another one, a dirty old red book,[1] which had notes that I might need some time.

I am somewhat better I think. The streptomycin after only one dose had the most disastrous results, so they dropped it promptly. Evidently I had built up an allergy or something. However I've now got over that, and today for the first time I was allowed to sit out in a deck chair for an hour or two. When I'll get to the point of putting some clothes on, lord knows. However, I've ordered myself a few new clothes, just to keep my morale up. I have discovered that there is a stream just near here with trout in it, so when I am somewhere near the point of getting up I'll ask Avril to send me my fishing things. I do hope I'll be able to get up to Jura for a few weeks some time in the summer, perhaps in August or so, and that the motor boat will be running then. I can't make plans till I know more about my health, but I suppose I'll have to spend this winter in some kind of institution, or at any rate near a doctor, and conceivably abroad. Probably somewhere like Brighton would be better, but in case of going abroad I'm taking steps to get my passport renewed. And after that I'm going to look about for a flat somewhere. It's evident that from now on I must spend the winters in civilized places, and in any case Richard will soon have to spend most of his time on the mainland, because of schooling. But I needn't remove anything from Barnhill, except perhaps my books, or some of them, because I think I could afford to furnish a second establishment now.

Inez is coming to see me next week and Brenda[2] the week after. I asked Inez to get me a birthday present for R., or at least to go to Gamage's and see what they've got. I can't think what to get him. I suppose he's almost ripe for a pocket knife, but somehow I don't fancy the idea.

I get visits occasionally from the people at Whiteway, [which] seems to be some sort of Anarchist colony run, or financed, by the old lady whose name I forget[3] who keeps the Freedom Bookshop. One of them is old Mat Kavanagh, whom you perhaps know, an old Irish I.R.A. Anarchist hairdresser, a figure at meetings for many years, who used to cut my hair in Fleet Street. He now tells me, what I hadn't known, that when a person with my sort of hair comes into the shop there is a sort of competition not to deal with him. He said he always used to cut my hair because the others pushed me off onto him, feeling that I wasn't the sort of person they could do themselves credit with.

Re. the cryptos and fellow travellers. I don't think Laski[4] is a fellow traveller, much as he has aided them by his boosting of Russia. *In this country* he loathes the CP, because they menace his job. I suppose he imagines they are different elsewhere. I also think he is too integrally a part of the LP, and too fond of being in an official position, to go over to the enemy if, for instance, we were at war with the USSR. The thing one can't imagine Laski doing is breaking the law. Cole[5] I think should probably not be on the list, but I would be less certain of him than of Laski in case of a war. Martin[6] of course is far too dishonest to be outright a crypto or fellow-traveller, but his main influence is pro-Russian and is certainly intended to be so, and I feel reasonably sure he would quislingise in the case of a Russian occupation, if he had not managed to get away on the last plane. I think there *must* be two Niebuhrs.[7] I saw an unmistakeable fellow-traveller statement over that name, quoted in the New Leader about two years ago. The whole business is very tricky, and one can never do more than use one's judgement and treat each case individually. I feel reasonably sure that Zilliacus,[8] for instance, is a crypto, but I would concede perhaps a twenty-five percent chance that he is not, whereas about Pritt[9] I feel completely certain. I feel less sure about ——[10] than about Z., but I feel pretty sure of Lester Hutchinson[11] after meeting him once. Mikardo[12] is I should say simply a fool, but he is also one of those who think they see a chance of self-advancement in making mischief and are quite ready to flirt with the cryptos.

I'm just reading Ruth Fischer's enormous book, "Stalin and German Communism." It's extremely good—not at all the sort of doctrinaire Trotskyism I would have expected. Have you seen the new Catholic magazine, the Month? It's lousy. I also read Margarete Neumann's book (the woman who gave evidence for Kravchenko), but it's about the Russian and German concentration camps, not about the party squabbles in Germany. I must send some books home soon. They're piling up fast here. Ask Avril to wipe the books now and then, will you, and to light a fire in those rooms. Otherwise the covers end by bending.[13]

Love to all
Eric

1. See 3729.
2. Inez Holden (see 1325, n. 1) and Brenda Salkeld (see 107, n. 2).
3. Lilian Wolfe (1875–1974), born in London, worked for twenty years as a Post Office telegraphist. She became a socialist and women's suffragist in 1907, and in 1913 an anarcho-syndicalist. She was active in the anti-war movement, 1914–16, and was imprisoned, as was her companion, Thomas Keell (1866–1938). She paid a fine in order to be released from prison, having become concerned for the well-being of the child she carried (her son, Tom). After the war she ran health-food shops in London and Stroud, living in the main at the anarchist colony at Whiteway (see 3592, n. 1). She earned enough to keep her husband and son and support the anarchist journal, Freedom. She gave up the shop in Stroud in 1943 and from then on administered the Freedom Press in London until, in 1969, personal differences led to her withdrawal. In 1966 the anarchist movement gave her a holiday in the United States as a ninetieth birthday present. She lived a spartan life but saved from her meagre pension money to help anarchist causes and political prisoners. After a lifetime devoted to anarchism, always behind the scenes, she died at her son's home in Cheltenham at ninety-eight (from Nicolas Walter's account of her life, Freedom, Centenary Number, 1986, 23–24).
4. Harold Laski; see 3526, n. 8. For Orwell's list of crypto-Communists and fellow-travellers, see 3732.
5. G. D. H. Cole (1889–1959), economist and prolific author; his books include The Intelligent Man's Guide to the Post-War World (1947) and The Meaning of Marxism (1948), based on his What Marx Really Meant (1934). See also 497, n. 2.
6. Kingsley Martin (1887–1969) then editor of The New Statesman; see 496, n. 4 and 2266.
7. One was presumably Reinhold Niebuhr (1892–1971), American theologian and professor at Union Theological Seminary, 1930–60, for a time a socialist and pacifist; later a supporter of the war against Hitler. His important books include The Nature and Destiny of Man (2 vols., 1941–43), Faith and History (1949), The Irony of American History (1952), The Self and the Dramas of History (1955), and The Structure of Nations and Empires (1959). His essays have been collected in several volumes. Although he favoured recognition of Communist China and was an early opponent of the war in Vietnam, he supported anti-Communist policies in The Irony of American History, which, though published two years after Orwell's death, might have reflected his attitudes about this time. In his list, Orwell noted against 'the famous R.N.' that he did not think he was a fellow-traveller: 'He has a great deal of sense.' Regarding a second Niebuhr, it is possible that there is confusion between Reinhold and his brother, Helmut Richard (1894–1962), who was ordained as a minister of the Evangelical & Reformed Church in 1916 and from 1931 pursued a distinguished career at Yale, culminating

in his appointment as Sterling Professor of Theology and Christian Ethics in 1954. He wrote a number of books, translated Paul Tillich's *The Religious Situation* into English, and in 1957 was involved in the union of the Congregational and the Evangelical & Reformed churches.

8. Konni Zilliacus; see *2990, n. 2.*
9. Dennis Noel Pritt (1887–1972), Labour and then Independent Labour M.P. and chairman of the Society for Cultural Relations with the USSR; see *560, 27.7.39, n. 2.*
10. Name withheld because the person is alive.
11. Hugh Lester Hutchinson (1904–1950), journalist and author, studied in Switzerland and at Edinburgh University, and served in the Navy, 1942–44. He was elected Labour M.P. in 1945, but was expelled in 1949 for his criticism of the Labour government's foreign policy. In 1950 he stood against the leader of the Labour Party (and Prime Minister), Clement Attlee; he polled only 704 votes out of nearly 35,000 cast.
12. Ian Mikardo (1908–1993), management consultant, author of *Centralised Control of Industry* (1942), and politician. He was a left-wing Labour M.P., 1945–59 and 1964–87, and was a prominent follower of Aneurin Bevan and a rumbustious debater with a strong sense of comedy. He was often considered to be unduly sympathetic to Communism, but his passionate Zionism ensured that he never forgot or forgave Stalin for his treatment of Jews. Among his books were *The Labour Case* (1950) and an autobiography, *Back-Bencher* (1988). He was much appreciated by fellow M.P.s of all parties in his role as 'unofficial bookmaker' to Parliament, offering odds on contentious issues and the fortunes of political figures.
13. In a letter to Ian Angus of 10 June 1967, Richard Rees described this exchange of names with Orwell as 'a sort of game we played – discussing who was a paid agent of what and estimating to what lengths of treachery our favourite bêtes noires would be prepared to go.'

3601. To Dr. Gwen O'Shaughnessy

17 April 1949   Typewritten

The Cotswold Sanatorium
Cranham
Glos.

Dear Gwen,

I have been meaning for ages to write to you. Among other things I owe you money for some things you got for Richard. I can't remember what they were but I have an idea they included an overcoat. Please let me know and I'll pay you.

I have been here since January and am getting a little better I think. I was really very ill in December, and again recently. I had a relapse and they decided to try another go of streptomycin, with dreadful results after only one dose. I suppose I had built up a resistance to it or something. However the last few days I have felt better and have even been sitting out in a deck chair a little. They can't really do much for me except keep me quiet. They can't do the "thora" operation (somewhat to my relief I must say) because you need one reliable lung which I haven't got. It looks as though I shall be here till well into the summer, and if I do get up to Jura this year it will only be for a week or two in August or September. I shall have to spend the winter somewhere warm and near a doctor, perhaps in some kind of sanatorium, and I imagine shall always have [to] regard myself as an invalid in the winters from now on. I can't make plans till I am surer about my health, but evidently I shall have to get a flat somewhere and only go to Scotland in the summer. Richard in any case will have to go to school next year, which means removing him to the mainland. This winter I think he will go to the village school in Ardlussa, but that is only possible as a temporary arrangement. At worst we can keep on Barnhill as a summer cottage, but Bill Dunn wants to go on farming it, and I daresay Avril will want to stay on and help, which means we shall have to split up for part of the year. However, as I say, I shall have to see how my health develops.

I have remade my will,[1] or rather I have sent the will I made some years ago to a solicitor to be redrafted, as it occurred to me it might not be in proper legal order. I have made you my executor, which I don't think will involve much nuisance, as Richard Rees is my literary executor and he will see to all the business of dealing with publishers etc. I have also requested—this is one of the things that I want the solicitor to put in good order—that you and Avril shall decide between you about Richard's upbringing, but that if there is any dispute the decision shall lie with you. I don't suppose any disagreement is likely to arise between you. Avril is very fond of him and I know will want to bring him up, but if anything should happen to her, or if she should wish to live in any place where he can't go to school, I wish you would take charge of him. I don't think you would be financially out of pocket. I have put aside enough to see him through his childhood in a modest way. If I should die in the near future, there are considerable income tax claims to be met, but there is also a good deal of money coming in and I think the "estate" would be easily cleared without encroaching on my savings. There should also be at any rate a small income from royalties for some years to come. I trust that all this won't become urgent yet awhile, but after these two illnesses I don't imagine I can last very many years, and I do want to feel that Richard's future is assured. When I am able to get up to London I shall go and see Morlock[2] or somebody and get an expert opinion on how long I am likely to live. It is a thing doctors usually will not tell you, but it affects my plans, for future books as well as for Richard.

Richard was extremely well when I came away, and is evidently enjoying himself with the spring ploughing etc. He really seems quite fond of farm work. I have been trying to think what to give him for his birthday next month. I suppose he is almost old enough to have a pocket knife, but somehow I don't fancy the idea. Avril says he has found out about money, ie. knows you can get sweets[3] for it, so I have started him on regular pocket money, which I hope may teach him the days of the week. I am going to get her to bring him down here to see me, but it is no use till I am out of bed.

I am not doing any work at present. I have cancelled everything, but I hope to start again next month. My new book is coming out in June, here and in the USA. I had a line from Doreen and George[4] announcing their new baby, but otherwise haven't heard from them. Please remember me to the kids.

Yours
George

1. Orwell made a new will on 18 January 1950, before the flight he hoped to make to Switzerland; see *3730*.

2. Dr. H. V. Morlock, the specialist whom Orwell had consulted before the war.
3. Sweets and chocolate were still rationed when Orwell wrote, but just one week later restrictions were lifted. Unfortunately, this freedom did not last long. Confectionary was rationed again (4 ounces per week) on 14 July, the sugar ration was cut to 8 ounces, and tobacco imports were reduced.
4. Doreen and George Kopp; see *359, n. 2.*

3602. Diary Entry, Last Literary Notebook

Cranham, 17 April 1949

<u>17.4.49.</u>   *Curious effect, here in the sanatorium, on Easter Sunday, when the people in this (the most expensive[1]) block of "chalets" mostly have visitors, of hearing large numbers of upper-class English voices. I have been almost out of the sound of them for two years, hearing them at most one or two at a time, my ears growing more & more used to working-class or lower-middle class Scottish voices. In the hospital at Hairmyres, for instance, I literally never heard a "cultivated" accent except when I had a visitor. It is as though I were hearing these voices for the first time. And what voices! A sort of over-fedness, a fatuous self-confidence, a constant bah-bahing of laughter about nothing, above all a sort of heaviness & richness combined with a fundamental ill-will—people who, one instinctively feels, without even being able to see them, are the enemies of anything intelligent or sensitive or beautiful. No wonder everyone hates us so.*

1. The National Health Service began its 'cradle to grave' care on 5 July 1948 but there was still also private care for those who wished to pay for it.

3602A. To Lydia Jackson

18 April 1949   Handwritten

> The Cotswold Sanatorium
> Cranham
> Glos.

Dear Lydia,
I wonder how you have been getting on all this time. I haven't written earlier because I really haven't written many letters at all. I was very ill for some time, but I think I am somewhat better. I have begun to sit up a little in a deck chair, & soon I hope they may let me out a little. Perhaps when they do you would like to come & see me. There is a hotel near here where I can get rooms for you. It has been wonderful weather so far all this spring. I hear fairly frequently from Barnhill, where evidently everything is going fairly well. From what they say I don't suppose I shall get out of here till well into the summer, so if I do go up to Barnhill this year it will only be for a few weeks in August or thereabouts. This winter I shall have to spend somewhere near a

doctor—possibly in London, or Brighton, or possibly abroad—but I can't make any arrangements till I am surer about my health. I think Richard will go to the village school in Ardlussa this winter, but next year he'll have to go to a proper day school in London or Edinburgh or somewhere. When I came away he was still backward about talking, but Avril says he is improving as he has become fond of listening to the radio. She says he has also found out about money, ie. that you can get sweets for it. I hope to get him down here to see me sometime, but it's no use till I'm up & about. He doesn't understand why I have always to be lying down. He used to come to see me & say, "where you hurt yourself?"—as hurting himself is about the only kind of illness he has experience of. One time when he fell off a cart & bruised his forehead badly, he came up to my room & solemnly put the thermometer in his mouth. I said "Why do you do that?" & he said, "Make my head better," because he knows that when people are ill they have their temperature taken.

My book is coming out in June. It has again been chosen in the USA by the Book of the Month Club, so that at any rate I shall be able to pay off my arrears of income tax. I haven't been able to do any work yet this year, but I hope to start again next month or so. Please remember me to Pat & let me know how you are getting on.

With love
Eric.

3603. To Ruth Fischer

21 April 1949   Typewritten

The Cotswold Sanatorium
Cranham
Glos. England

Dear Miss Fischer,[1]
No doubt you have been overwhelmed with congratulations, but I would like to tell you how much I enjoyed reading your book "Stalin and German Communism." I am sorry that a year or two ago when you were in London I got a message asking me to come and see you, and didn't answer it; but so far as I remember I didn't receive the message until it would have been too late to answer. Most of the time during the past two years or more I have been either in a rather remote part of Scotland, or else in hospital (tuberculosis.) I wonder what became of the paper you started about that time? I think I asked my New York agents to take out a subscription for me, but they may not have done so, as they always seem to think I ought to get every American periodical free.

One or two footnotes to your book:—
You mention that Berthold Brecht[2] tries to stay abroad as much as possible. Isn't he back in Germany now? I saw a report a year or two ago that he had gone back to the Russian Zone and was part of the literary front there.

"The Great Conspiracy." I would like to know more about this book, which has never appeared in this country, I imagine because of something libellous in it. I think the Michael Sayers[3] who is part-author of it must be the same Michael Sayers whom I knew in London in 1934–5 as a very out-at-elbow young Irish poet. About 1938 he suddenly disappeared to America, and in 1945 was over here again, talent-scouting for some periodical or publishing house. He wanted me to write something, although well aware of my views. In ten years he had changed in the most astonishing way, turning into a fat prosperous business-man, completely Americanised and somewhat ashamed of having once tried to be a poet, and did not even get his Irish accent back until softened by drink. He was very pro-USSR, but in what struck me as a curious way, ie. from the angle of a business-man who saw Russia as a powerful and potentially rich country with which America could do a profitable deal. One could not possibly have credited him with any proletarian sympathies. I would like to know what line his book takes.

There is a novel of mine coming out shortly that might possibly interest you, and I will see that they send you a copy.

Yours sincerely
[Signed] Geo. Orwell
George Orwell

1. Ruth Fischer (1895–1961), former General Secretary of the German Communist Party, 1923–26, when she was expelled as a Trotskyist. She fled Nazi Germany and lived in France and the United States, writing on political subjects. Her book *Stalin and German Communism* was published by Harvard University Press in 1948.
2. Bertolt Brecht (1898–1956) returned to Europe in 1947 and from 1949 directed the Berliner Ensemble in East Berlin. In her reply of 9 May, Ruth Fischer said that when she wrote her book, Brecht was still in Hollywood but 'since then, without formal proceedings, he was deported because of his connection with the Eisler case.' Although Brecht was subpoenaed to appear before the House of Representatives Committee on Un-American Activities on 30 October 1947, he ran rings round his questioners and was congratulated for being so co-operative; the next day he left for Europe of his own volition. He went to Moscow in May 1955 to receive the Stalin Peace Prize.
3. Michael Sayers (1912–) shared a flat with Orwell and Rayner Heppenstall at 50 Lawford Road, Kentish Town, London, NW5 (illustrated in John Thompson, *Orwell's London*, 47), from August 1935 to January 1936. He reviewed *Burmese Days* and *A Clergyman's Daughter* in *The Adelphi*, August 1935. Dr. Fischer, in her 9 May letter, described *The Great Conspiracy* as 'an interpretation of world history as a general conspiracy to overthrow the Stalinist regime.' She sent Orwell a copy on 23 May 1949; see *3632*. Sayers's co-author was Albert E. Kahn, who gave evidence on behalf of those who were found guilty of libelling Viktor Kravchenko; see *3577, n. 3*. He and Sayers also wrote *Sabotage!: The Secret War against America* (1942) and *The Plot against the Peace: A Warning to the Nation!* (1945).

3604. To Fredric Warburg

22 April 1949   Typewritten

The Cotswold Sanatorium
Cranham
Glos.

Dear Fred,

Thanks so much for sending the copy of "1984." It seems very early for advance copies. I think the jacket and general-make-up are very nice. You say you had sent proof copies to the people I had named, who were, I think:

Bertrand Russell
Lancelot Hogben
C. D. Darlington
Anthony Powell (for the Times Lit. Supp.)

and also some American ones, but these don't matter as I can get copies of the American edition sent to them. I wonder then if you could send copies to:

Arthur Koestler
David Astor
Professor R. H. Tawney
Herbert Read
André Malraux
T. S. Eliot.

I suppose I can get some more copies at the time of actual publication.

I am somewhat better, and have been sitting out a little in a deck chair when the weather is fine. I have still no definite plans nor any idea of when I shall get out of here, but it doesn't look as though I shall get out till late into the summer, and if I do go up to Scotland this year it will only be for a few weeks in August or September. Could you tell Michael[1] that if he would like to go and stay at Barnhill this year they will be delighted to have him, only to give notice in advance. There is now a motor boat which would enable him to get at the lochs he didn't fish last year. It is generally out of order, but with his mechanical genius he could no doubt get it running.

A friend in New York has procured me a copy of Gissing's "New Grub Street." I forget whether you yourself had read it or not, though I know Roger[2] has. It seems easier to get hold of out-of-print books over there, and I am going to have a try at getting other books of Gissing's. Perhaps some time we could talk over again the idea of reprinting "New Grub Street." I suggested to Gollancz that he might like to reprint "We" and referred him to you to find out how to get hold of the MS.

Please remember me to everyone.

Yours
George

1. Michael Kennard; see *3371, n. 3*. He had stayed at Barnhill whilst Orwell was in Hairmyres Hospital in 1948.
2. Roger Senhouse, a director of Secker & Warburg; see *375, n. 2*.

3605. To Leonard Moore

22 April 1949   Typewritten

The Cotswold Sanatorium
Cranham
Glos.

Dear Moore,
I have just had an advance copy of "1984" from Warburg, and have given him the list of people I want advance copies sent to. I suppose I can get some more copies at the time of publication.

As for the American edition, I don't know how soon they will be sending out advance copies, but when they do, I wonder whether you could ask Harcourt Brace[1] to make sure that copies get to the following:

Edmund Wilson (care of the New Yorker.)
Dwight Macdonald ("Politics," 45 Astor Place, New York 3.)
Ruth Fischer (Harvard University Press).
Henry Miller ("New Directions" would know his address.)
Aldous Huxley (I think he is [in] the USA now?)
Gleb Struve (2851 Buena Vista Way, Berkely° 8, California.)

I see that the Italian translation of "Homage to Catalonia" appeared recently, also I think two other books previously.[2] Have we had any copies of these Italian translations? I would like to see what they are like.

Yours sincerely
[Signed] Eric Blair
Eric Blair

1. Annotated in Moore's office: 'Wrote 27.4.49.'
2. *Omaggio alla Catalonia* was published by Mondadori in December 1948, translated and with an introduction by Giorgio Monicelli. *Animal Farm* appeared in Italian as *La Fattoria degli Animali*, published by Mondadori, October 1947, translated by Bruno Tasso and with an introduction by Giorgio Monicelli. *Burmese Days* was published by Longanesi as *Giorni in Birmania*, November 1948, translated by Giovanna Caracciolo. (Willison.)

3606. To Harcourt, Brace

25 April 1949

REFERENCE NINETEEN EIGHTYFOUR° ONE MISPRINT SHOULD BE CORRECTED IF NOT TOO LATE STOP PAGE TWO SIX THREE LINE THIRTEEN AFTER HE EXISTS SHOULD BE STOP NOT QUERY[1]

ORWELL

1. The cable has been annotated in Harcourt, Brace's office: 'Too late.' The edition appeared with the question-mark. The English edition has the full-point (261, line 5), as has *CW*, IX, 272, line 18). The U.S. edition was published on 13 June 1949. Later printings corrected this error.

3607. To Sir Richard Rees

25 April 1949   Handwritten

Cranham

Dear Richard,

Thanks for your letter. I have been sort of up & down in health but on the whole am a little better, I think. I still can't make any plans, but if I am up & about for the winter, I thought it might not be a bad idea to go abroad somewhere, & Orlando[1] (I don't know if you know him, he writes for the Observer sometimes) suggested Capri as a good place to stay. It sounds as if it would have good food & wine, & Silone,[2] who is a friend of mine & lives there, would no doubt be able to arrange somewhere for me to stay. Any way° it's worth thinking over. The Tawneys came in the other day. I think they're going back to London almost immediately, so I'm afraid I may not see them again. For little Richard's birthday, Inez is going to try & get me one of those children's typewriters you see advertised now, if not too impossibly expensive. I thought if he could be kept from smashing it, it would come in useful when he begins to learn his letters in earnest, & it would also keep him off my typewriter. The Tawneys took that book of yours[3] I had & are going to send it to you. When Brenda comes I am going to get her to make up some parcels for me & send home some of the books, which are piling up fearfully. I still can't do any work. Some days I take pen & paper & try to write a few lines, but it's impossible. When you are in this state you have the impression that your brain is working normally until you try to put words together, & then you find that you have acquired a sort of awful heaviness & clumsiness, as well as inability to concentrate for more than a few seconds. I am reading Mr Sponge's Sporting Tour, which I had never read before. I don't think it's as good as Handley Cross. I also recently re-read Little Dorrit[4] for the first time in a good many years. It's a dull book in a way, but it contains a really subtle character, William Dorrit, quite unlike most of Dickens's people. Someone in the USA has managed to get me a copy of Gissing's New Grub Street at last. Don't lose The Odd Women,[5] will you.

Yours
Eric

1. Ruggiero Orlando (1907–1994), journalist, broadcaster, poet, and critic. His passionate, slightly anarchic political views led to his fleeing Italy in 1939 for Britain. He was engaged by the BBC to broadcast in its external service and did so with great success, achieving a legendary status with colleagues and listeners. After the war he worked for RAI, the Italian state broadcasting service, and was its correspondent in the United States for eighteen years. He returned to Italy in 1972 and was elected to the Chamber of Deputies. He was, when in England, a frequent contributor to *Poetry Today*, and he translated Dylan Thomas into Italian.

2. Ignazio Silone (1900–1978), Italian novelist; see *2870, n. 3*. In his essay on Arthur Koestler, Orwell claimed that there had been nothing in English writing to resemble Silone's *Fontamara* (1933; English translation, 1934) or Koestler's *Darkness at Noon* (1940): 'there is almost no English writer to whom it has happened to see totalitarianism from the inside.' See *2548*.
3. Probably David Jones's *In Parenthesis*; see Orwell's letter to Richard Rees, 18 January 1949, *3529, n. 3*. It is not included in Orwell's list of his reading for 1949.
4. Orwell's list of his reading for April 1949 includes Dickens's *Little Dorrit* and Surtees's *Mr Sponge's Sporting Tour*; see *3727*.
5. *The Odd Women* by George Gissing (1893).

3608. To Leonard Moore

27 April 1949   Typewritten

Cranham

Dear Moore,

I have just had a letter from Mr Roger Sauvé, a young Frenchman who translated "Coming Up for Air"[1] for Editions Fontaine and subsequently had some mix-up about it. He says:

I have just received a letter from Odile Pathé, who asks me to get in touch with you as soon as possible, about that new book of yours which is due to appear next June. I had understood that that new book was "1984", but Odile Pathe° assures me that "1984" was published at the beginning of this year, and that she has had it for over two months. . . . She seems to want to publish a translation of "1984", and must have applied for an option from Christy & Moore.[2]

Evidently there is some mix-up here. But what I would like to know is whether Mlle. Pathé has an option on "1984" or whether any other arrangement has been made about translating the book into French. If Odile Pathé do take it, I should like Mr Sauvé to be the translator if it can be arranged, as it is evident from the dealings I have had with him that he is a painstaking translator and knows English well. But in any case, if the book is translated, I want to be kept in touch with the translator. The neologisms in the book would, I should think, present difficulties in a foreign language, and one would have to think out a way of tackling them. If this book is translated, we must not let them make a mess of it as happened with "Burmese Days."

Yours sincerely
[Signed] Eric Blair
Eric Blair

1. This translation and the transactions relating to it have not been traced. Sauvé made none of the published translations of Orwell's books. That of *Coming Up for Air* was made by Claude de Leschaux (as *Journal d'un Anglais Moyen*) and published by Amiot Dumont, April 1952. It was serialised in *Le Monde*, August–September 1952 (Willison).
2. *Nineteen Eighty-Four* was translated into French (as *1984*) by Amélie Audiberti and published by Gallimard, 30 June 1950. Gallimard bought the rights from Odile Pathé, publishers of the French translation of *Animal Farm* (Willison).

3609. To Leonard Moore

28 April 1949   Handwritten

Cranham

Dear Moore,

Many thanks for your letter. I have a copy of the French translation of "Animal Farm," but I would like copies of the other translations you mention. I like to have one among my books,[1] also to see what sort of job they have made.

Yours sincerely
Eric Blair

1. There were many translations of his books among Orwell's effects at his death. Sonia Orwell selected some, and the rest, under the terms of Orwell's will, passed to Sir Richard Rees. At Rees's death, those not already held by the Orwell Archive went to its collection.

3610. To Dwight Macdonald

29 April 1949   Handwritten

The Cotswold Sanatorium
Cranham
Glos.

Dear Dwight,

Thanks so much for sending the book.[1] I asked Miss Otis to pay you what I owe you, plus a small contribution for "Politics" & I hope she has done so. Thanks also for sending the interesting paper on the Waldorf Conference,[2] which had been very poorly reported in the press here.

I'm glad you liked "New Grub Street". I have been fighting hard for some years to get Gissing into print again, but without much success. I don't in the least want you to make an expedition on my behalf, but if when poking about in bookshops you ever do come across a copy of Gissing's "Born in Exile," I will pay anything in reason for it.[3]

Yours sincerely
George Orwell

1. Not identified.
2. The Cultural and Scientific Conference for World Peace sponsored by Communist-inspired organisations at the Waldorf Astoria Hotel, New York, 25–27 May 1949. Much of the time was spent denouncing the Atlantic Pact and U.S. 'warmongering.' There were strong protests in the U.S.A. against the Conference. Among those refused entry to attend by the United States were J. D. Bernal (see *1005, n. 1*), J. G. Crowther (*1117, n. 1*), and the novelist Louis Golding (1895–1958); Professor Olaf Stapledon (*2824, n. 1*) was admitted. All four are included in Orwell's list of crypto-Communists and fellow-travellers. Orwell's list queries whether the critic and anthologist Louis Untermeyer (1885–1977), whom he describes as 'very silly,' chaired the Conference; more probably he took the chair at a sectional meeting. This was one of a series of such meetings about this time, which many of the same people attended. Bernal and Crowther, with Zilliacus, Pritt, and Platts-Mills, attended the World

Partisans for Peace Congress, Paris, 20–25 April 1949—at which Zilliacus attacked the Labour Party and Winston Churchill, and Platts-Mills attacked 'American imperialism.' See *Keesing's Contemporary Archives* (1949), 10,007; and for the Wroclaw Conference of Intellectuals, *3617*, n. 9.
3. No copy was found among Orwell's books at his death.

3611. To Leonard Moore

29 April 1949   Handwritten

Cranham

Dear Moore,
I am sorry to say I seem to have lost the letter with Roger Sauvé's present address, & I only have an earlier one from which a letter probably would not be forwarded. However, Odile Pathé has his address, & I think he will probably write to you himself as I suggested that he should do so.[1]

Yours sincerely
Eric Blair

1. Annotated in Moore's office: 'wrote 3/5/49.'

3612. 'A Prize for Ezra Pound'

Partisan Review, May 1949

On 14 February 1949, Ezra Pound was awarded the Bollingen Prize for Poetry. Pound (1885–1972) had supported Mussolini in the 1930s. During World War II he had lived in Italy and from 1941 had broadcast in support of the Fascist powers. He was arrested by U.S. forces in 1945, but was declared insane at his trial for treason and was confined to St. Elizabeths Hospital in Washington, D.C., until 1958. In its issue for April 1949, *Partisan Review* published a Comment by William Barrett. This began:

The awarding of a prize is a public act usually surrounded with many difficulties. When the prize is literary, there are not only all the difficulties that attend literary judgment, but the further complications from the fact that the judges, because of the public nature of the award, act both as citizens and literary critics.

The Bollingen Foundation has recently announced that the Bollingen Prize for Poetry, the first of an annual series, has been awarded to Ezra Pound for *The Pisan Cantos* as the best book of poetry published during 1948. The judges were the Fellows in American Letters of the Library of Congress, among whom are T. S. Eliot, W. H. Auden, Allen Tate, Robert Penn Warren, Katherine Anne Porter, and Robert Lowell. In the public statement accompanying the award the judges tell us that they were aware that the choice of Pound was likely to provoke objections, and their brief

statement implies that they have given these objections careful consideration, ending with something like an affirmation of a general principle:

"To permit other considerations than that of poetic achievement to
sway the decision would destroy the significance of the award and would
in principle deny the validity of that objective perception of value on which
any civilized society must rest."

The sentiments behind this declaration seem to us admirable. Our only
interest here is to insist on the application of this principle. . . .

Several writers, one of them George Orwell, were asked to discuss the issues
connected with this award. These were published in the May issue of *Partisan
Review*. This was Orwell's response:

I think the Bollingen Foundation were quite right to award Pound the prize,
if they believed his poems to be the best of the year, but I think also that one
ought to keep Pound's career in memory and not feel that his ideas are made
respectable by the mere fact of winning a literary prize.

Because of the general revulsion against Allied war propaganda, there has
been—indeed, there was, even before the war was over—a tendency to claim
that Pound was "not really" a fascist and an antisemite, that he opposed the
war on pacifist grounds and that in any case his political activities only
belonged to the war years. Some time ago I saw it stated in an American
periodical that Pound only broadcast on the Rome radio when "the balance of
his mind was upset," and later (I think in the same periodical) that the Italian
government had blackmailed him into broadcasting by threats to relatives.
All this is plain falsehood. Pound was an ardent follower of Mussolini as far
back as the nineteen-twenties, and never concealed it. He was a contributor to
Mosley's review, the *British Union Quarterly*, and accepted a professorship
from the Rome government before the war started. I should say that his
enthusiasm was essentially for the Italian form of fascism. He did not seem to
be very strongly pro-Nazi or anti-Russian, his real underlying motive being
hatred of Britain, America and "the Jews." His broadcasts were disgusting. I
remember at least one in which he approved the massacre of the East
European Jews and "warned" the American Jews that their turn was coming
presently. These broadcasts—I did not hear them, but only read them in the
BBC monitoring report—did not give me the impression of being the work
of a lunatic. Incidentally I am told that in delivering them Pound used to put
on a pronounced American accent which he did not normally have, no doubt
with the idea of appealing to the isolationists and playing on anti-British
sentiment.

None of this is a reason against giving Pound the Bollingen Prize. There
are times when such a thing might be undesirable—it would have been
undesirable when the Jews were actually being killed in the gas vans, for
instance—but I do not think this is one of them. But since the judges have
taken what amounts to the "art for art's sake" position, that is, the position
that aesthetic integrity and common decency are two separate things, then at
least let us keep them separate and not excuse Pound's political career on the

ground that he is a good writer. He *may* be a good writer (I must admit that I personally have always regarded him as an entirely spurious writer), but the opinions that he has tried to disseminate by means of his works are evil ones, and I think that the judges should have said so more firmly when awarding him the prize.

3613. A Look into the Future: 1984 and Newspeak

World Review, May 1949

This abridgement of the Appendix to *Nineteen Eighty-Four*, 'The Principles of Newspeak,' was published before the novel was issued in June and was made insensitively. Thus, Orwell had written, 'The grammar of Newspeak had two outstanding peculiarities' (*CW*, IX, 314). The abridgement included this and Orwell's account of the first peculiarity but cut completely all details of the second peculiarity. Orwell described this as 'a most stupid extract, abridged in such a way as to make nonsense of it'; see his letter to Fredric Warburg, 16 May 1949, *3626*.

3614. To Melvin Lasky

2 May 1949   From typed copy of handwritten letter.[1]

The Cotswold Sanatorium
Cranham
Glos., England

Dear Mr. Lasky,
I am sorry I have delayed so long in answering your letter of about a month ago, but I really have been and still am most desperately ill, and I can't do any work at all. I don't even know, as yet, when I shall be able to do any, but when I start again I think I shall have to concentrate on my next novel, which should have been begun early this year. It occurs to me that "Der Monat" might possibly care to translate a passage or two from my novel "1984" which is due to be out in June.[2] If you are at all interested, my agent could tell you all about it and no doubt could procure a proof copy for you. I'm sorry being so unhelpful.

Yours sincerely
Geo. Orwell

This address will continue to find me.[3]

1. The copy may not be wholly reliable because 'The Cotswold Sanatorium' is given as 'The Colywold Sanatorium.'
2. *Der Monat* serialised *Nineteen Eighty-Four*, November 1949–March 1950.
3. Written at the head of the letter.

3615. To Celia Kirwan

2 May 1949   Typewritten

The Cotswold Sanatorium
Cranham
Glos.

Dear Celia,

Thanks so much for your letter. I'd be delighted to see you next Sunday (the 8th isn't it?) If you're coming by car I don't know what time you'll arrive, but unless I hear to the contrary I'll assume that you and Dr Hahndel[1] are arriving in time for lunch and will order lunch for you.

I enclose a list with about 35 names.[2] It isn't very sensational and I don't suppose it will tell your friends anything they don't know. At the same time it isn't a bad idea to have the people who are probably unreliable listed. If it had been done earlier it would have stopped people like Peter Smollett[3] worming their way into important propaganda jobs where they were probably able to do us a lot of harm. Even as it stands I imagine that this list is very libellous, or slanderous, or whatever the term is, so will you please see that it is returned to me without fail.

I was beastly ill not long after you last came to see me, as a result of another attempt with streptomycin, which I have now, it appears, built up a "resistance" to. I am getting better very slowly, I think, but lord knows when I shall get out of bed.

With love
George

1. Dr. Hans Hahndel, a German physician, whom Celia Kirwan and her twin sister, Mamaine Koestler, got to know when living in Florence in 1934. He later lived in Calcutta, but was visiting London at this time and had volunteered to drive Celia Kirwan to Cranham. She was then at the Foreign Office, doing research into Communism world-wide, and had the day off to consult Orwell—hence his reference to his list of names.
2. Of crypto-Communists and fellow-travellers; see 3732 and especially 3590A and 3590B (last appendix of this volume) for letters and notes on Orwell's relationship with the Information Research Department, for which Celia Kirwan was working.
3. Peter Smollett (Harry Peter Smollett-Smolka, 1912–1980; OBE), author and journalist born in Vienna, attended the University of Vienna and the London School of Economics. He worked for the *Exchange Telegraph*, 1934–39, the Ministry of Information, (head of the Russian Department), 1939–45, and then was the *Times* correspondent in Vienna. Orwell held him in deepest suspicion; see 3732. His suspicions were correct; after his death he was denounced as a Soviet agent, and this accusation has never been denied (Richard Cockett, *David Astor and 'The Observer,'* 102). Smollett may have been the 'important official in the Ministry of Information' who persuaded Jonathan Cape not to publish *Animal Farm* for fear of offending the Russians (see 2494, n. 1).

3616. To S. M. Levitas

2 May 1949   Handwritten

The Cotswold Sanatorium
Cranham
Glos., England

Dear Mr Levitas,
Many thanks for your letter of the 21st April. I will do something for you later on when I can, but I really am most deadly ill & quite unable to work, & I don't know how soon this state of affairs will change. I don't want any payment & certainly not Care packages—the truth is I have no appetite & can't eat the food I am given already. But next time I do something for you I'll ask you to pay me by sending me one of the books I see advertised in American papers & which one can't get over here.[1]

 The above address will continue to find me, I'm afraid.

Yours sincerely
Geo. Orwell

1. Levitas replied on 3 June, offering to get 'any and every book which you would like to have and I shall without hesitation, indeed with great pleasure, forward them to you immediately.' He had received a review copy of *Nineteen Eighty-Four* on 2 June and congratulated Orwell on its being a Book-of-the-Month Club selection. He hoped Orwell's health had improved sufficiently for him 'to write an original piece for us.' *The New Leader* was establishing a 'Guest Columnist Editorial,' and Levitas asked Orwell if he could send one thousand words 'on any subject you desire.'

3617. To Sir Richard Rees

2 May 1949   Handwritten

Cranham

Dear Richard,
I have to hand-write because there is a patient further down the row who is in articulo mortis, or thinks she is, & the typewriter worries her.
 About this business of Barnhill etc. I cannot make any real plans until I know if & when I shall get out of bed, but the governing facts are:
  1. I can't in future spend the winters in Jura.
  2. Richard must go to school next year, which means somebody being with him, as I don't want him to go to a boarding school till he is at any rate 10.
  3. I don't want to disrupt the Barnhill ménage.
  4. Avril will probably want to stay on at Barnhill, & Bill in any case couldn't get on without her, or without some female helper.
 All this being so, it seems to me that if I am in circulation again later this year, I had best go abroad or somewhere like Brighton for the winter, & then next spring set up a second establishment in London or Edinburgh where I

can have Richard with me & where he can go to day-school. He can spend his holidays in Jura, & I hope I shall be able to spend my summers there as well. This will mean having another nurse-maid or housekeeper or something. However, *provided* I can work I can easily earn enough money for this; in any case it was agreed between Avril & me that if she stopped looking after R. I should reduce the amount I paid her. If I remain bedridden, or at any rate have to remain under medical care, which I suppose is a possibility, I shall move to a sanatorium somewhere near London, where it is easier for friends & business associates to come & see me, & set up an establishment for Richard near there, with a housekeeper or something. That is as much as I can plan at present.

Thanks so much for drying off all the books.[1] I don't agree with you about "The Great Gatsby"—I was rather disappointed by it. It seemed to me to lack point,[2] & "Tender is the Night", which I read recently, even more so.[3] I've just read Geoffrey Gorer's book on the Americans—very amusing & shallow, as usual. I've at last got hold of May Sinclair's "The Combined Maze"—a forgotten good bad novel which I've been trying to get a copy of for years. I must get some more books rebound before long. Re my unsuccessful efforts to get Gissing reprinted, it's struck me that the Everyman Library might do one of them. They have no Gissing on their list. I wonder how one approaches them, & whether there is a string one can pull.

In spite of his chumminess with "Zilli"[4] (who he of course thinks can help him in his political career), I don't believe Mikardo is a crypto. Apart from other things, if he were a crypto, Michael Foot[5] would probably know it & wouldn't have him on Tribune. They got rid of Edelmann[6] for that reason. It's of course true that "objectively" people like Laski are a lot more useful to the Russians than the overt Communists, just as it is true that "objectively" a pacifist is pro-war & pro-militarist. But it seems to me very important to attempt to gauge people's *subjective* feelings, because otherwise one can't predict their behaviour in situations where the results of certain actions are clear even to a self-deceiver. Suppose for example that Laski had possession of an important military secret. Would he betray it to the Russian military intelligence? I don't imagine so, because he has not actually made up his mind to be a traitor, & the nature of what he was doing would in that case be quite clear. But a real Communist would, of course, hand the secret over without any sense of guilt, & so would a real crypto, such as Pritt. The whole difficulty is to decide where each person stands, & one has to treat each case individually.

The weather has rather gone off here. I sat outside in a deck chair one or two days, but latterly it's been too cold. A man came from the E. Standard to "interview" me,[7] rather an intimidating experience, also Paul Potts,[8] who has just got back from Palestine, together with the wife of A. J. P. Taylor,[9] the chap who turned traitor at the Wroclaw conference. I gather from her that Taylor has since turned a good deal more anti-CP.

Yours
Eric

1. Some of Orwell's books had become damp at Barnhill; see *3594*.
2. Orwell's letter has been annotated here, 'NO!'
3. Orwell's letter had been annotated here, 'Yes.'
4. Konni Zilliacus; see *3600*, and also *2990, n. 2.*
5. Michael Foot (1913–), then Labour M.P. and editor of *Tribune*; see *1241, n. 2* and *2955, n. 2.*
6. Maurice Edelman (1911–1975), educated at Trinity College, Cambridge, entered the plywood business which led to visits to the USSR, about which he then wrote. He was a war correspondent in North Africa and in Normandy and a Labour M.P. in 1945, re-elected in 1950. His surname has only one 'n', not two as Orwell spelt it.
7. Charles Curran, who 'tired me so . . . arguing about politics'; see Orwell's letter to Fredric Warburg, 16 May 1949, *3626.*
8. Paul Potts (1911–1990), Canadian poet and author. In his *Dante Called You Beatrice* (1960) is a chapter on Orwell, 'Don Quixote on a Bicycle.' He visited Orwell at Barnhill; see *3027, n. 1*, and also Orwell's letter on his behalf, *3619.*
9. A. J. P. Taylor (1906–1990), historian and journalist. At this time he was Tutor in Modern History, Magdalen College, Oxford (to 1963); Fellow, 1938–76. He wrote prolifically and authoritatively (if not always uncontroversially), especially on Germany and World Wars I and II; also *English History, 1914–45* (1965), *Politicians, Socialism and Historians* (1980), and *A Personal History* (1983). The Wroclaw Conference (cf. the Waldorf Conference, *3610, n. 2*) was a Communist-front Conference of Intellectuals, August 1948, attended by scientists, writers, and cultural leaders from forty countries. It passed a resolution condemning the revival of Fascism. The conference backfired on the organisers. Some participants saw through the proceedings, Taylor among them, and walked out, hence Orwell's description of his turning traitor is ironic.

3618. To Charles Curran

3 May 1949   Handwritten

Cranham

Dear Mr Curran,
Many thanks for your letter of the 2nd. Thanks for the name of the book—I will note it down & get a copy from the USA. Either May 28th or 29th would suit me—but would you let me know which day you intend coming, &, if it is the Sunday, what time you expect to arrive, so that I can arrange for the car.
Yours sincerely
Geo. Orwell

3619. To David Astor

7 May 1949   Handwritten

Cranham

Dear David,
Paul Potts,[1] whom I dare say you know of, recently came back from Palestine & is very anxious for journalistic work of some kind. He has done a certain amount of journalism, mostly in rather obscure highbrow papers, & has written a book on Israel which I think is coming out in the USA. He asked me

whether I would give him an introduction to you, which I said I would, though of course explaining that I couldn't give any sort of assurance that you would be able to make use of him. I really don't know whether you could, but I suppose you often dispose of various kinds of hack-work which he could do as well as another. At any rate, if he writes to you, you or somebody at the Obs. would perhaps grant him an interview. He is an old friend of mine, a person who has been unfortunate but has gifts which he has not yet been able to use very successfully. I hope this kind of thing doesn't put you out.

Yours
George

1. See *3617, n. 8.* Potts fought on the Jewish side in the Israeli War of Independence.

3620. Anthony Powell on George Orwell

Britanskii Soyuznik, 8 May 1949

Britanskii Soyuznik, subtitled Izdanie Ministerstva Informatzii Veliko Britanii [*British Ally*: A Publication of the Ministry of Information of Great Britain], was a weekly newspaper published in Russian in Moscow. Its 'responsible editor' was given as 'the Press Attaché of the British Embassy in the USSR,' and it was printed by the Soviet government printer. This issue included an article, 'The Younger Generation of British Novelists—The Opinions of Four Eminent Critics' (in Russian): Arthur Calder-Marshall, Raymond Mortimer, Daniel George, and Anthony Powell. There is so much overlap that the choice of authors discussed must have been left to each critic without any guidance from the MOI.[1] Powell had nine paragraphs; the first was a tactful explanation that, though his three choices, Evelyn Waugh, Graham Greene, and George Orwell, were the three most prominent 'novelists of middle age,' there were others who were in some respects no less interesting. However, his chosen three combined 'a high degree of talent with considerable literary success.' He devoted three paragraphs solely to Orwell; the last ended his account.

George Orwell to some extent presents a contrast to writers like Waugh and Greene, who are first and foremost novelists but who have written travel books and Waugh has experimented with historical subjects.

Orwell has created for himself a reputation with books of another kind, for the greater part autobiographical and describing the life of those who for one reason or another live in particularly unfavourable circumstances. His first book, "Down and Out in Paris and London", is an account of his experiences when he tried to make a living after he had resigned from military service as an officer in the Burma Police.

In another of his books he writes about the Spanish civil war in which he took part on the Republican side.

In short, Evelyn Waugh, Graham Greene and George Orwell have all already made their individual mark on the history of the English novel.

They are still comparatively young and it will be interesting to watch the further development of their talents.

1. Evelyn Waugh was discussed by Calder-Marshall and Mortimer, who both also chose Elizabeth Bowen and Graham Greene. Daniel George selected P. H. Newby, Alex Comfort, and Howard Clewes. Some direction from the MOI might have enabled some of, say, H. E. Bates, Joyce Cary, Henry Green, James Hanley, L. P. Hartley, Rosamund Lehmann, L. A. G. Strong, or V. S. Pritchett to be introduced. And, of course, Anthony Powell should himself have been included.

3621. To David Astor

9 May 1949   Handwritten

Cranham

Dear David,

I've been rather bad & I can't write much of a letter.

I think Philip Toynbee[1] is a good idea. I don't know him well, but he seems to me quite gifted & politically OK. I don't suppose he has much *editorial* experience, though he did have something to do with the editorship of a monthly, Contact or something. I believe he drinks a bit, ie. not soaks steadily but is easily knocked out by a few drinks—however, I don't suppose that would affect.° One advantage of having Toynbee would be that he would bring you in contact with the *younger* writers, which I do feel is important.

Failing Toynbee, what about Pritchett?[2] Or couldn't he leave whatever he is doing? Or just possibly William Plomer.[3] Did you ever consider having a woman for the job? I should think C. V. Wedgwood[4] could do it quite competently. Or conceivably old Rebecca West.[5]

I've been making my will, & the lawyers tell me it is better to name two executors in case the first dies. Would you object to being my second string? It's not likely to involve you in anything. The first executor is not likely to die before I do, & even if she does there is not much of an "estate" to administer. Somebody else is doing the literary executorship, which is the tiresome job. If you *don't* object, I'll put a codicil naming you as my alternative executor.

I've really been very bad. If you haven't already done so, I don't know whether it is worth ordering that "sound mirror",[6] at least on my account. God knows when I should start using it, or anything else. It really wouldn't surprise me if you had to change that Profile into an obituary (ie. if the Obs. considered me worthy of one.) Even if it isn't as bad as that, it looks rather as though I may have to stay in bed for months or years. If so, I shall move to a sanatorium nearer London where people can come & see me more easily. However I can't make any plans yet.[7]

Yours
George

1. Philip Toynbee (1916–1981), novelist, critic, and poet, was literary editor of Contact Publications, 1945–46, and became a leading reviewer for *The Observer* in 1950. Best known for *Tea with Mrs Goodman* (1947), *Friends Apart: A Memoir of Esmond Romilly and Jasper Ridley in the Thirties* (1954), and *Pantaloon* (1961), which was the first of four experimental novels in verse. In 1984 Jessica Mitford published an affectionate memoir of him, *Faces of Philip*.
2. Victor Sawdon Pritchett (1900–) author and critic; see *1835, n. 1*.
3. William Plomer (1903–1973), South African novelist who came to live in England in 1929.
4. Cicely Veronica Wedgwood (1910–1989; DBE, 1968), historian and author.
5. Rebecca West (1892–1983; DBE, 1959), novelist, critic, and political writer; see *2907, n. 1*.
6. A recording machine; see Astor's offer of a wire-recorder, 19 March 1949, *3577, n. 1*.
7. He had, however, just applied for a passport to enable him to go abroad for the winter; see *3622* and *3622, n. 8*.

3622. To Anthony Powell

11 May 1949   Handwritten

Cranham

Dear Tony,

Thanks so much for your letter. I at last (only yesterday as a matter of fact) got hold of a copy of John Aubrey[1] & am reading it with interest. I had not realised he was such an all-round chap—had simply thought of him in connection with scandalous anecdotes. I look forward to seeing your selections.[2] Yes, I read Margarete Neumann's book.[3] I thought it was quite good, obviously written by a sincere person. Tell Malcolm[4] if he hasn't seen it that he ought to read Ruth Fischer's book ("Stalin & German Communism")—at any rate it is a useful book to have by one as a reference. I am so sorry about poor old Hugh Kingsmill.[5] I don't know if you see him, but if you do, tell him I just re-read his book on Dickens, which I got hold of with some difficulty, & that I think the same as before—it's a brilliant book, but it's the case for the prosecution.[6] I wonder why somebody doesn't reprint "After Puritanism".[7] I put in a mention of it when I reviewed that other book of his that they reprinted, but it got cut out the way things do in reviews. I have by the way at last got hold of a copy of "New Grub Street" & am having another try at getting someone to reprint it. One would think the Everyman Library would have at least one book of Gissing's, but I don't know how one approaches them—at least I have no wire I can pull there.

I have been beastly ill, on & off. I can't make any firm plans. If I'm reasonably well this winter I shall go abroad for some months.[8] If I'm able to walk but can't face a journey I shall stay in somewhere like Brighton. If I have to continue in bed I shall try to move to some sanatorium near London where people can come & see me more easily. It looks as if I may have to spend the rest of my life, if not actually in bed, at any rate at the bath-chair level. I could stand that for say 5 years if only I could work. At present I can do nothing, not even a book review.

Please give everyone my love.

Yours
George

1. Powell's *John Aubrey and His Friends* (1948).
2. *Brief Lives and Other Selected Writings by John Aubrey*, edited by Anthony Powell (1949). Powell sent him a copy, which Orwell acknowledged on 6 June 1949; see *3641*. It is not listed in his reading for 1949.
3. Margarete Buber-Neumann, *Under Two Dictators*.
4. Malcolm Muggeridge.
5. Hugh Kingsmill (pseudonym of Hugh Kingsmill Lunn, 1889–1944), critic, editor, and anthologist. Orwell had copies of his book *The Dawn's Delay* (1924), three short novels, reviewed by Orwell in *The Observer*, 18 July 1948 (see *3425*), and *After Puritanism* (1929). Kingsmill had entered hospital on 14 April 1949 and died on 15 May. In his *Progress of a Biographer* (1949) Kingsmill wrote that *Animal Farm* 'revealed the poetry, humour and tenderness' of Orwell, and he discussed Orwell's categorising him as a Neo-Tory in 'Notes on Nationalism' (*2668*); reprinted in *The Best of Hugh Kingsmill*, edited by Michael Holroyd (1970), 287–91.
6. Orwell does not list Kingsmill's *The Sentimental Journey: A Life of Charles Dickens* (1934; New York, 1935) among books read in 1949.
7. *After Puritanism 1850–1900* (1929) is on Dean Farrar (author of *Eric, or Little by Little*). Samuel Butler, Frank Harris, and W. T. Stead, the crusading journalist.
8. Orwell was issued Passport No 1243051 on 10 May 1949. This, unlike one and probably two earlier passports, gave his year of birth correctly as 1903; see *3103*.

3623. To Celia Kirwan

13 May 1949   Handwritten

Cranham

Dear Celia,

Thank you ever so much for that lovely bottle of brandy, which arrived here two days ago. I would have written earlier, but I've been most horribly ill. Sonia[1] was coming tomorrow but I've put her off because I'm just a misery when I'm like this. I'll write again when I'm a bit better. Any way° thanks so much.

Much love
George

1. Sonia Brownell, whom Orwell would marry later in the year; see *3212, n. 1*.

3624. Review of *Their Finest Hour* by Winston Churchill

The New Leader (New York), 14 May 1949

It is difficult for a statesman who still has a political future to reveal everything that he knows: and in a profession in which one is a baby at fifty and middle-aged at seventy-five, it is natural that anyone who has not actually been disgraced should feel that he still has a future. A book like Ciano's diaries, for instance, would not have been published if its author had remained in good standing. But it is fair to Winston Churchill to say that the political reminiscences which he has published from time to time have always been a great deal above the average, in frankness as well as in literary quality. Churchill is among other things a journalist, with a real if not very discriminating feeling for literature, and he also has a restless, enquiring mind, interested both in concrete facts and in the analysis of motives, sometimes including his own motives.

In general, Churchill's writings are more like those of a human being than of a public figure. His present book does, of course, contain passages which give the appearance of having escaped from an election address, but it also shows a considerable willingness to admit mistakes.

This volume, the second in the series, covers the period between the opening of the German attack on France and the end of 1940. Its main events, therefore, are the collapse of France, the German air attacks on Britain, the increasing involvement of the United States in the war, the stepping-up of the U-boat warfare, and the beginning of the long struggle in North Africa. The book is heavily documented, with excerpts from speeches or despatches at each step, and though it leads to a great deal of reduplication, it makes it possible to compare what was said and thought at the time with what actually happened.

As he himself admits, Churchill had underestimated the effect of recent changes in the technique of war, but he reacted quickly when the storm broke in 1940. His great achievement was to grasp even at the time of Dunkirk that France was beaten and that Britain, in spite of appearances, was not beaten; and this last judgment was not based simply on pugnacity but on a reasonable survey of the situation.

The only way in which the Germans could win the war quickly was to conquer the British Isles, and to conquer the British Isles they had to get there, which meant having command of the sea over the Channel. Churchill, therefore, steadily refused to throw the whole of the British metropolitan air force into the Battle of France. It was a harsh decision, which naturally caused bitterness at the time and probably weakened Reynaud's position against the defeatists in the French government, but it was strategically correct. The twenty-five fighter squadrons held to be indispensable were kept in Britain, and the threatened invasion was beaten off. Long before the year was over the danger had receded sufficiently for guns, tanks and men to be transferred from Britain to the Egyptian front. The Germans could still defeat Britain by the U-boat, or conceivably by bombing, but it would take several years, and in the meantime the war could be relied upon to spread.

Churchill knew, of course, that the United States would enter the war sooner or later: but at this stage he does not seem to have expected that an American army of millions of men would ultimately arrive in Europe. He foresaw even in 1940 that the Germans would probably attack Russia, and he rightly calculated that Franco, whatever promises he might make, would not come into the war on the Axis side. He also saw the importance of arming the Palestine Jews and of fomenting rebellion in Abyssinia. Where his judgment went astray, it was chiefly because of his undiscriminating hatred of "Bolshevism" and consequent tendency to ignore political distinctions.

He says revealingly that when he sent Sir Stafford Cripps as Ambassador to

Moscow, he did not realize that Communists hate Socialists more than they hate Conservatives. No British Tory, indeed, seems to have grasped this simple fact until the advent of the Labor government in 1945: failure to do so was partly responsible for the mistaken British policy during the Spanish civil war.

Churchill's attitude towards Mussolini, although it probably did not affect the course of events in 1940, was also based on a miscalculation. In the past he had admired Mussolini as a "bulwark against Bolshevism," and had belonged to the school that believed it possible to draw Italy out of the Axis by means of bribes. He would never, he says frankly, have quarrelled with Mussolini over such an issue as Abyssinia. When Italy entered the war, Churchill did not, of course, pull his punches, but the over-all situation would have been better if the British Tories could have grasped ten years earlier that Italian Fascism was not just another version of Conservatism but must of its nature be hostile to Britain.

One of the most interesting chapters in *Their Finest Hour* deals with the exchange of American destroyers for bases in the British West Indies. The letters that passed between Churchill and Roosevelt form a sort of commentary on democratic politics. Roosevelt knew that it was in the American interest that Britain should have the destroyers, and Churchill knew that it was not to the disadvantage of Britain—rather the contrary— that the United States should have the bases. Nevertheless, apart from the legal and constitutional difficulties, it was impossible for the ships to be simply handed over without haggling.

With the election ahead of him, and with one eye on the Isolationists, Roosevelt had to give the appearance of driving a hard bargain. He also had to demand an assurance that even if Britain lost the war, the British fleet would in no circumstances be handed over to the Germans. This, of course, was a senseless condition to impose. It could be taken as certain that Churchill would not hand over the fleet: but, on the other hand, if the Germans succeeded in overrunning Britain, they would set up some kind of puppet government, for whose actions Churchill could not answer. He was unable, therefore, to give as firm an assurance as was demanded, and the bargaining was prolonged accordingly. The one quick solution would have been to secure a pledge from the whole British people, including the crews of the ships. But Churchill, curiously enough, seems to have shrunk from publicizing the facts. It would have been dangerous, he says, to let it be known how near Britain was to defeat—perhaps the only occasion through-out this period when he underrated public morale.

The book ends in the dark winter of 1940, when unexpected victories in the desert, with vast hauls of Italian prisoners, were offset by the bombing of London and the increased sinkings at sea. Unavoidably, as one reads, the thought moves to and fro in one's mind: "How freely is Churchill capable of speaking?" For the main interest of these memoirs is bound to come later, when Churchill tells us (if he does decide to tell us) what really happened at Teheran and Yalta, and whether the policies there adopted were ones that he himself approved of, or whether they were forced upon him by Roosevelt.

But at any rate, the tone of this and the preceding volume suggests that when the time comes, he will tell us more of the truth than has been revealed hitherto.

Whether or not 1940 was anyone else's finest hour, it was certainly Churchill's. However much one may disagree with him, however thankful one may be that he and his party did not win the 1945 election, one has to admire in him not only his courage but also a certain largeness and geniality which comes out even in formal memoirs of this type, much less personal than a book like *My Early Life*.[1] The British people have generally rejected his policies, but they have always had a liking for him, as one can see from the tone of the stories about him that have been told throughout most of his life. Often, no doubt, these stories were apocryphal, and sometimes they were also unprintable, but the fact of their circulating is significant. At the time of the Dunkirk evacuation, for instance, when Churchill made his often-quoted fighting speech, it was rumored that what he actually said, when recording the speech for broadcasting, was: "We will fight on the beaches, we will fight in the streets. . . . We'll throw bottles at the b——s, it's about all we've got left"—but, of course the BBC's switch-censor[2] pressed his thumb on the key at the right moment. One may assume that this story is untrue, but at the time it was felt that it ought to be true. It was a fitting tribute from ordinary people to the tough and humorous old man whom they would not accept as a peacetime leader[3] but whom in the moment of disaster they felt to be representative of themselves.

1. Churchill's *My Early Life: A Roving Commission* (1930; New York, 1930) and, as *A Roving Commission: My Early Life*, preface enlarged for U.S. readers (New York, 1939).
2. Whilst Orwell worked for the BBC Eastern Service, he became accustomed to the presence of a censor during broadcasts who could cut off the transmission when a speaker departed from a script that had been passed by the censors. That a switch censor was present when Churchill made this broadcast seems unlikely.
3. Churchill was to serve as a peacetime Prime Minister after Orwell's death—from 1951 to 1955.

3625. Review of *Dickens: His Character, Comedy and Career* by Hesketh Pearson

The New York Times Book Review, 15 May 1949

Literary men are apt to make poor subjects for biography, especially when, as in the case of Dickens, their careers are successful from the start. The most truly adventurous and dramatic part of Dickens' life was behind him by the time he was 25; from then onward his energy, which was enormous—all but frightening, indeed—was expended almost entirely in writing and lecturing and in such semi-literary pursuits as editing magazines and quarreling with publishers. Moreover, his middle years are an almost unbroken chronicle of triumphs, and success is on the whole less interesting than failure. But Hesketh Pearson, as in his biographies of Wilde and Shaw, manages to make the story readable, and supplies incidentally a good deal of information, not easily accessible elsewhere, about John Forster, Thackeray, Wilkie Collins and others of Dickens' contemporaries.

Books about Dickens tend to be vehemently "for" or "against", and Mr. Pearson belongs to the "for" school. Where possible, he sides with Dickens, not only against his publishers ("scaly-headed vultures" was the kind of phrase that Dickens liked to apply to them), but also against his family and against the various colleagues and rivals with whom Dickens quarreled from time to time. However, even Mr. Pearson's very sympathic handling does not disguise the fact that Dickens was a tiresome person to have any dealings with, and that the gap between his private character and his literary personality was even wider than it is in the case of most writers.

He was vain, restless, egotistical, generous in money matters but completely selfish in an emotional sense, an inconsiderate and ultimately an unfaithful husband, and—though Mr. Pearson does not say so—probably an oppressive and not very understanding father. In his defense it should be said that if he had not acted like a tyrant toward his family he could never have got through so immense a quantity of work. And though in some ways he failed to grow up, his literary personality did develop, more markedly than one might gather from the short accounts that Mr. Pearson gives of certain of the novels.

Dickens was born into a lower-middle-class family which, like countless similar families at that time, was socially and economically on the up-grade. His father, who was the son of a butler, had a fairly well-paid clerkship in the Navy Pay Office, and seems to have continued drawing his salary even when he was in prison. He was a pretentious, kindly, improvident man, who appears in his son's novels as Mr. Micawber and (a far more damaging portrait) John Dorrit.[1] In 1824 his creditors managed to get him thrown into the Marshalsea, and little Charles, aged about 12, went to work in a blacking warehouse, in circumstances very similar to those he describes in "David Copperfield."

But this episode, which wounded Dickens so deeply that until he was almost middle-aged he kept it secret even from his wife, only lasted six months, and it seems to have been only for about two years that he experienced real poverty. He left school at 15 and entered a lawyer's office, but gravitated into journalism and quickly made his name as a brilliant reporter. From the moment when he tried his hand at creative writing, everything he touched turned to gold. At 30 he was already a rich and famous novelist, touring in triumph through an America which had just cried its eyes out over Little Nell and was ready to do anything for Dickens except pay royalties on his books.

Out of this first American tour arose the American chapters in "Martin Chuzzlewit," the only grossly unfair piece of satire in Dickens' works, and the only occasion when he attacked a race or community as a whole. No doubt the unpaid royalties were at the bottom of the trouble, but there were other grounds for antipathy, not all of them on one side; for we learn that Dickens' flamboyant manners and loud clothes (a scarlet waistcoat with apple-green trousers, for example) made a bad impression in Boston. The

American public was understandably not pleased by "Martin Chuzzlewit" but Dickens was soon forgiven, and on his second tour, a quarter of a century later, he was received even more rapturously than before.

Dickens spent a great deal of his life in travelling, but chiefly in search of quiet places to work in. The main non-literary event of his middle years was the break-up of his marriage. He had married very young and very hastily, and out of a large family of sisters had managed to choose exactly the one who was least suited to him. The situation, or something resembling it, is reproduced in "David Copperfield" where the pretty and silly Dora corresponds to Catherine,[2] Dickens' wife, and the saintly Agnes to Georgina, his sister-in-law. There was never any suggestion of a direct sexual relationship between Dickens and Georgina, but she succeeded by degrees in completely ousting her sister from Dickens' affections.

For many years she lived in the Dickens home, managing all the household affairs and acting as Dickens' intellectual companion, while the less-talented Catherine wore herself out in bearing ten children. It ended by Dickens turning his wife out-of-doors—with an allowance of £600 a year, certainly—and publishing in the press a sort of manifesto in which he justified this entirely indefensible action. Although, of course, he denied it, it was probably before this date that the actress Ellen Ternan had become his mistress. She bore him one child, which died. Estella Provis, in "Great Expectations"; Bella Wilfer, in "Our Mutual Friend," and Helena Landless, in "Edwin Drood" are all thought to be portraits of her. Georgina remained with Dickens as his housekeeper until his death.

In his last ten years of life Dickens produced only two completed novels, partly because by this time he had developed his public readings to the point at which they almost amounted to a second profession. He had always been fascinated by the stage, and had great powers of mimicry, and the readings—it was really acting rather than reading—seem to have been almost as remarkable a performance in their way as the books themselves. Unfortunately, they imposed a tremendous strain on his vitality while at the same time whetting his appetite for more public appearances and yet more. Throughout his second American tour, in which he never shirked an engagement, he was too weak to take solid food and lived mainly on stimulants.

Mr. Pearson thinks that Dickens in effect committed suicide by deciding to add the murder of Nancy (in "Oliver Twist") to his repertory. This scene—so terrifying that it was always liable to cause anything up to twenty faints among the audience—exhausted Dickens disastrously, but he insisted on including it in almost every performance. In the middle of 1870, aged only 58, he collapsed, so suddenly that he was dead within twenty-four hours of doing a normal morning's work. His body, against his clearly expressed wish, was buried in Westminster Abbey. In spite of the scaly-headed vultures, he left over £90,000, having lived for many years in a lavish style and supported a large family, as well as various poor relations.

There has never been a completely satisfactory life of Dickens. Forster's "official" biography is unreadable and leaves out important facts; Dame Una

Pope-Hennessy's is very full and fair-minded, but is spoiled by an unsuccessful effort to summarize all the novels in turn. Hugh Kingsmill's book is perhaps the most brilliant ever written on Dickens, but it is so unremittingly "against" that it might give a misleading impression to anyone not acquainted with Dickens' work.

Mr. Pearson's book, more "popular" than any of these, keeps the story in perspective and is fairly successful in relating the changes in Dickens' work to the changing circumstances of his life. As a critic Mr. Pearson is perhaps less reliable than as a biographer. He prefers Dickens in his picaresque mood, and seems seriously to underrate some of his later novels, even going so far as to describe "Great Expectations" as a partial failure.

One should also, perhaps, be on one's guard against his tendency to present Dickens in too rosy a light. Dickens did, for instance, caricature his friends in a merciless way, and Mr. Pearson seems to excuse him too easily by saying that good taste is not to be expected from men of genius. And one would have liked to hear a little more of Dickens' treatment of his children and of that unobtrusive, almost invisible figure, his wife. But in general this is a well-balanced, as well as a very readable, book, which will be of interest to anyone with even a partial knowledge of the novels.

1. An error for William Dorritt, 'Father of the Marshalsea'; see *3607*, p. 97.
2. Spelt 'Catherine' in the original.

3626. To Fredric Warburg

16 May 1949   Handwritten

Cranham

Dear Fred,

Thanks so much for your letter. As she may have told you, I had to put Sonia Brownell off. I am in most ghastly health, & have been for some weeks. I am due for another X-ray picture, but for some days I have been too feverish to go over to the X-ray room & stand up against the screen. When the picture is taken, I am afraid there is not much doubt it will show that both lungs have deteriorated badly. I asked the doctor recently whether she[1] thought I would survive, & she wouldn't go further than saying she didn't know. If the "prognosis" after this photo is bad, I shall get a second opinion. Can you give me the name of that specialist you mentioned? Then I will suggest either him or Dr. Morlock, another specialist whom I consulted before the war. They can't *do* anything, as I am not a case for operation, but I would like an expert opinion on how long I am likely to stay alive. I do hope people won't now start chasing me to go to Switzerland, which is supposed to have magical qualities. I don't believe it makes any difference where you are, & a journey would be the death of me. The one chance of surviving, I imagine, is to keep quiet. Don't think I am making up my mind to peg out. On the contrary, I have the strongest reasons for wanting to stay alive. But I want to get a clear idea of *how long* I am likely to last, & not just be jollied along the way doctors usually do.

Yes, do come & see me. I hope & trust by the beginning of June I may be a bit better, at any rate less feverish. I am glad "1984" has done so well before publication. The "World Review" published a most stupid extract, abridged in such a way as to make nonsense of it.[2] I wouldn't have let Moore arrange this if I'd known they meant to hack it about. However I suppose it's advertisement. That Evening Standard man, Mr. Curran, came to interview me, & had arranged to come again, but I'm thinking of putting him off, because he tired me so last time, arguing about politics. Please give everyone my love.

Yours
George

1. Dr. Margaret Kirkman, one of the two resident physicians at Cranham; see *3520, n. 1*
2. See *3613.*

3627. To Robert Giroux

19 May 1949   Handwritten

The Cotswold Sanatorium
Cranham
Glos., England

Dear Mr Giroux,
Thank you so much for sending the Sewanee Review, also Empson's Poems. I note with interest from the Sewanee Review that Empson has decided to stay on in Pekin.°[1] I wonder if you are in touch with him? I should certainly be glad of any news of him. I had had vague ideas of writing, but I thought it might be embarrassing for foreigners in China to get letters from outside at this moment. Hetta, Empson's wife, is or used to be a Communist, & he himself was not particularly hostile to Communism, but I doubt whether that would do them much good under a Chinese Communist régime.

I have been horribly ill for the last month or so—a little better now, I think, but I am still feverish for part of every day, & very weak. No prospect of getting up yet awhile, I am afraid, nor even of doing any work in the immediate future.

Yours sincerely
Geo. Orwell

1. See *3597, n. 3.*

3628. To David Astor

20 May 1949   Handwritten, headed paper[1]

> Cranham Lodge,
> Cranham,
> Gloucester.

Dear David,

Thanks so much for your letter. Do come on Sunday the 29th. I'll look forward to seeing you both. If you can, let me know beforehand time of arrival, so that I can arrange for the car. Better have lunch here, if you arrive in time (it's quite eatable.)

I have been absolutely ghastly. I am getting a second opinion, a London specialist, supposed to be very good. Of course they can't actually do anything but I don't want to feel I'm letting my case go by default, also a specialist called in for one consultation might be willing to give an expert opinion on whether I'm likely to stay alive, the thing most doctors will only hum & haw about.

I'm arranging for Richard to come & stay near here, near Stroud. I suppose it will take weeks to fix up, but it's quite a good arrangement, the people he is going to stay with have 2 children, & he can go to kindergarten with them & come over & see me in the afternoons sometimes.

> Yours
> George

1. The paper Orwell used here had Cranham Lodge and the address as its printed heading, and, in addition, 'Telegrams: "Hoffman, Birdlip"' and 'Telephone: Witcombe 2195.' Letters on this paper can be distinguished by the use of this punctuation.

3629. To Charles Curran

20 May 1949   Handwritten

> Cranham Lodge,
> Cranham,
> Gloucester.

Dear Mr Curran,

I wonder if you would mind putting off the visit you kindly proposed making me on the 28th or 29th. My health has deteriorated seriously since I last saw you, & at present it tires me to sit up or talk for more than a few minutes. I hope you will forgive me.[1]

> Yours sincerely
> Geo. Orwell

1. No more letters to Curran have been traced. Five years later, in the *Daily Mirror* for 14 December 1954, Curran wrote a short piece headed 'Orwell: The man behind 1984—and all that.' The last two paragraphs state: 'I spent a day with Orwell just before he died. I sat on his

sanatorium bed, tried to smoke the frightful cigarettes he insisted on making for himself. I heard him say: "The problem of the world is this: Can we get men to behave decently to each other if they no longer believe in God?" Orwell was evidently still smoking his 'frightful cigarettes' despite the state of his lungs.

3630. To Fredric Warburg
20 May 1949   Handwritten

> Cranham Lodge,
> Cranham,
> Gloucester.

Dear Fred,

I've spoken to the doctor here. She has no objection to a second opinion (she says she knows Dr. Morland.) Do you think you could be kind enough to get in touch with him on my behalf & get him to fix up a suitable date with Dr. Kirkman here for him to come & see me. If you know him well, could you impress on him that I *don't* want to be cheered up but to be given an expert opinion on whether I am likely to stay alive, & if so, how long. I know doctors hate committing themselves on that, but I won't hold it against him if he's wrong.

> Love to all
> George

3631. To Jacintha Buddicom
22 May 1949   Handwritten

> Cranham Lodge,
> Cranham,
> Gloucester.

Dear Jacintha,

Thanks so much for your letter. I'd have written before, but I've been most horribly ill & am not very grand now. I can't write much of a letter because it tires me to sit up. Thanks awfully for the offer, but I am generally pretty well supplied with books & things. It looks as if I am going to be in bed for months yet. I have sent for my little boy to come & stay with friends near by. I think he'll like it, & as he is now 5 he can perhaps start going to day school. I hope to see you when I am in Town if I ever am.

> Yours
> Eric

This is the last of Orwell's letters to Jacintha Buddicom to survive. She replied on 2 June, and he wrote again on the 8th. Both letters have been lost, but she describes Orwell's letter in *Eric & Us*: 'My diary records: "Letter from Eric about

Nothing Ever Dies." As I remember . . . it defined his faith in some sort of after-life. Not necessarily, or even probably, a conventional Heaven-or-Hell, but the firm belief that "nothing ever dies", and that we must go on *somewhere*. And it ended with our old ending, *Farewell and Hail*. He probably wrote it because I had told him that my mother was ill: though I had not stressed this unduly, since he was in such poor health himself' (157). See also final paragraph of *3643*.

3632. Ruth Fischer to Orwell

23 May 1949

Ruth Fischer (see *3603, n. 1*) wrote to Orwell on 23 May 1949 acknowledging the receipt of a copy of *Nineteen Eighty-Four* (ahead of publication). She proposed reading it on the boat to England from the United States. She sent him with her letter a copy of *The Great Conspiracy* (see *3603, n. 3*). Orwell does not list this book among his reading for 1949.

3633. To Sonia Brownell

24 May 1949   Handwritten

Cranham Lodge,
Cranham,
Gloucester.

Dear Sonia,
I was so very sorry to put you off, but at the time I was in a ghastly state. Now I seem to be somewhat better. I do hope you'll come & see me soon. Any day would suit me except the day you think Cyril[1] might be coming, on the 29th, when I think someone else is coming. But any way when & if you can come let me know in advance because of ordering a car.

I've just had what is called a "second opinion", incidentally the doctor who attended D. H. Lawrence in his last illness.[2] He says I'm not so bad & have a good chance of surviving, but it means keeping quiet & doing no work for a long time, possibly a year or more. I don't mind very much if I could then get well enough to do say another 5 years° work. Richard is coming down soon to stay near here. He will start going to kindergarten school in the mornings, & can sometimes come over & see me in the afternoons.

Please give everyone my love. By the way I cut the enclosed out of the N.Y. Times. If you see Stephen,[3] tell him to get another photo taken, for the honour of English letters. Looking forward to seeing you.

With love
George

1. Cyril Connolly, for whom Sonia Brownell was working on *Horizon*.
2. Dr. Andrew Morland.
3. Stephen Spender.

3634. To Tosco Fyvel

26 May 1949   Handwritten

> Cranham Lodge,
> Cranham,
> Gloucester.

Dear Tosco,

Thanks so much for your letter. I'll expect you on Friday June 3rd, about 11.30. Unless I hear to the contrary I'll assume you are both staying to lunch. So looking forward to seeing you.[1]

> Yours
> George

1. In his *George Orwell: A Personal Memoir*, Fyvel describes a visit to see Orwell at Cranham. It is not quite clear if it is this occasion—it was a wintry day in spring—because in his account he goes on to discuss Orwell's views on writing contemporary novels, as expressed in his letter to Fyvel of 15 April (see *3598*) and then he later refers directly to that, as if it were after his visit to Cranham, saying, 'In a letter on° 15 April I got bad news from Cranham' (163). With these reservations, Fyvel's description does seem to relate to 3 June 1949 (a day when it rained heavily): 'On a wintry day the sanatorium looked a bleak place and the visit was a major shock to us: Orwell was so much worse, so much thinner and frailer in his critical illness than we had expected. True, mentally he seemed in perfect control, but in body, there he lay flat on his back in bed, looking terribly emaciated, his face drawn and waxen pale—without doubt he was dangerously ill. Constrained by the shock, I tried to tell him how much I had liked his book. He commented a little sadly that because of his illness, the book might have turned out duller and more pessimistic than intended.' Fyvel was accompanied by his wife, Mary, and by Olga Miller (also known as Olga Katzin; see *2744, n. 1*), who wrote 'entertaining satirical verses unfailingly each week in the *New Statesman* under the pen-name "Sagittarius."' On their way back to London, Olga Miller said that 'even in bed, Orwell seemed in his person and interests characteristically unchanged. However, that was his spirit. As for his physical state, we felt dismayed by the severe advance of his illness' (162–63).

3635. To Fredric Warburg

Friday, [27 May 1949]   Handwritten

> Cranham Lodge
> Cranham
> Gloucester.

Dear Fred,

Your friend Dr. Morland came here on Tuesday & examined me. He was very nice & quite encouraging. He says—& the latest X-ray apparently confirms this—that I have quite a good chance of staying alive for some years, but that it is necessary to stay still and do no work for what may be a long time, possibly as much as a year or two years. I don't think I could stick it, ie. not working, for two years, but could manage one year if absolutely necessary. At any rate the thing is to get right over the present disturbance before attempting to work. If this means, as it well may, that I shan't set pen

to paper again this year, I shall have nothing ready for next year. But perhaps
the time would be ripe in 1950 to publish a second volume of reprinted essays.
We can discuss that when I see you next. I hope you will come down again as
you suggested.

I am having Richard to stay nearby, near Stroud. I don't know how long
for, but we will see how it works out. I think he would like it, he can perhaps
start going to kindergarten, and he can come & see me sometimes in the
afternoons when it is fine.

Love to all
George

Dr. Andrew Morland sent this report to Warburg on 25 May 1949:

Mr. Eric Blair (George Orwell).

I have just returned from seeing this man at the Cotswold Sanatorium. I
found that he has rather severe disease of the left lung and a relatively slight
amount on the right. He has made some progress in the right direction
since January but his improvement has been slow and undulating.

I discussed his outlook with him as fully and frankly as possible but in a
case like this prognosis is hazardous.

Provided he rests properly he should continue to improve but it may
well be that after a number of months he will stagnate or even relapse. One
point I am quite clear about is that if he ceases to try to get well and settles
down to write another book he is almost certain to relapse quickly.

With further rest I do not anticipate a cure but he might well reach a stage
at which he could do several hours writing a day combined with physical
rest. He would then reach the stage which we call the "good chronic" i.e.
able to potter about and do a few hours sedentary work.

His resistance must be fairly good as he stabilised well last year and
should not have broken down had he not foolishly over-exercised.

Warburg thanked Morland on 30 May for his report and told him the gist of
what Orwell had said in his letter of the 27th. He quoted Orwell's statement that
'the thing to do is to get right over the present disturbance before attempting to
work' and continued: 'The danger probably is that he will be good and quiet for
two to three months and then, feeling much better, set to work and collapse
again. Can this danger be guarded against? Has he made arrangements to see you
at three-monthly intervals? Would it be possible or desirable once he [is]
somewhat recovered from the present collapse to come to a sanatorium nearer
London? Is it good for him to see friends? His friends love seeing him, but it is a
long way for them to go right down to Gloucestershire.[1] If he were 30–40 miles
out of London, this would be much simplified.' He concluded by suggesting
they 'might have a chat over the 'phone about the best way to handle this difficult
patient,' especially because Warburg intended seeing Orwell in mid-June shortly
after the publication of *Nineteen Eighty-Four*.

1. Journeys by motorway nowadays tend to make us forget how long-drawn-out was the trail
from London to Cranham and for those living away from London to the north and south even

more tiresome. And, of course, the ownership of cars was far less common in 1949 than it is now. Many who went to see Orwell made a considerable effort to do so.

3636. Orwell on Marie-Louise Berneri

Freedom, 28 May 1949

Volume 10, Number 11 of *Freedom*, 28 May 1949, was devoted in large part to the memory of Marie-Louise Berneri, wife of Vernon Richards. She had been ill since the birth of their child and died of pneumonia on 13 April 1949. Orwell had written to Richards on 7 April, suggesting that, in the light of their loss, they might consider doing what he had done: adopting a child; see *3592*. He wrote again on the 13th asking about Marie-Louise's health, unaware that she had died; see *3596*.

Marie-Louise Berneri (see *3042, n. 4*) was greatly loved and admired, and *Freedom* published seventeen letters of condolence as well as articles about her and her work. *Freedom* printed this excerpt from Orwell's letter, sent from Cranham, evidently to Richards:

I can't say much either, but you will know I feel for you. She was always so much alive that it is difficult to believe it can have happened. . . .

3637. To Leonard Moore

31 May 1949   Handwritten

Cranham Lodge,
Cranham,
Gloucester.

Dear Moore,

Many thanks for your letter of the 30th.

Could you please make my apologies to the Saturday Review of Literature & tell them I am quite unable to do anything. I am told here that I may have to keep quiet & do no work for as much as a year (I hope it won't be so long, of course). It's worth while if it means getting well. Of course I can attend to small matters of business & like to be kept in touch with what is going on, but I can't write anything. So could you please refuse on my behalf any offers you get—making it clear, of course, that this won't be for ever.

I am so glad to hear about the Reader's Digest.[1]

Yes, I had one advance copy of "1984" from Harcourt Brace & they are sending some more. I thought they had got it up very well. As to copies of the English edition I think Warburg has sent out the advance complimentary copies I asked for (to Professor Tawny° & others). When there are some author's copies available, I wonder whether you could save me some trouble by sending some out for me, as follows:

Miss Brenda Salkeld, 71 Goldington Avenue, Bedford.

Mrs E. K. Adam, 56A Craven Avenue, Ealing.[2]
Mrs Celia Kirwan, care of the Foreign Office.[3]
Mrs Lydia Jackson, 370 Russell Court, Woburn Place, W.C.1.
And say 4 copies for myself.

Yours sincerely
Eric Blair

1. In October 1949, *The Reader's Digest* published a lengthy extract from Part I of *Nineteen Eighty-Four* (129–55).
2. Orwell's aunt, Nellie Limouzin Adam.
3. An annotation made in Moore's office gives the address as '10 Downing St. S.W.1.'—the address of the Prime Minister. Each of the addressees is ticked, indicating copies despatched.

3638. To Sir Richard Rees

1 June 1949   Handwritten

Cranham Lodge,
Cranham,
Gloucester.

Dear Richard,

Thanks so much for your letter. Avril & R. arrived on Saturday & I think he's settling in all right. I hope to see him once or twice this week. He seemed to me to have grown (his weight is now 3st 5lb.) & to be extremely fit.[1] I think Avril returns to Jura on today's boat, but I am not certain.

I have been a good bit better this last week, & after seeing my last plate they decided I am not so bad as they thought. Dr. Morland said the same, but he said I shall have to keep still for a long time, possibly as long as a year (I trust it won't be so long as that) & not attempt to work till I am definitely better. Another doctor[2] whom David Astor brought along, although a psychologist, said much the same as the others.

I enclose a copy of that article I wanted you to read.[3] The magazine itself seemed quite unprocurable, but someone managed to get it typed out. Actually some of what I said in it I also said appropos of Gandhi. I've just read the 4th vol. of Osbert Sitwell's memoirs—not so good as some of the others, I think. I know nothing about Goethe, nor indeed about any German writer. I'm trying to read Henry James's "The Spoils of Poynton," but it bores me unbearably. Also read a short book by Rex Warner "Why was I killed?"— very silly, I thought.

So looking forward to seeing you.

Yours
G

1. Richard stayed at Whiteway, the colony run by Lilian Wolfe; see *3600, n. 3*. In *Remembering Orwell*, Richard Blair recalls: 'When I saw my father at Cranham I used to say, "Where does it hurt, Daddy?" because I couldn't understand why he said it didn't hurt, but he was in bed. I couldn't relate to that at all' (203).

2. Unidentified.
3. 'Lear, Tolstoy and the Fool,' see *3181*. See also Orwell's letter to Rees, 31 March 1949, *3584*.

3639. To Fredric Warburg

2 June 1949   Handwritten

Cranham Lodge
Cranham
Gloucester.

Dear Fred,

Thanks so much for your letter. I'll look forward to seeing you on the 12th. Could you confirm nearer the time just when you are arriving, so that I can arrange about the car. I think on Sundays the train gets to Stroud at 12.30. I've been feeling a good deal better the last few days. Richard is staying near Stroud, & I think will remain there for about 3 months. He comes over and sees me once or twice a week. If possible he is going to start kindergarten school while here. Tosco Fyvel is coming to see me tomorrow. Love to all.

George

3640. To Robert Giroux

3 June 1949   Handwritten

Cranham Lodge,
Cranham,
Gloucester.

Dear Mr Giroux,

It is extraordinarily kind of you all to take so much interest in my case, & it is more than generous of Dr de Kruif & Dr O'Brien to offer their services. But actually I am a good deal better & I doubt whether much more could be done for me than is being done at present. As to streptomycin, I was treated with it last year with some success, but I have now developed a resistance against it. However, after being really very ill for a couple of months, I have taken a turn for the better during the last 2 weeks. I had one of the leading English chest specialists, Dr Morland, to examine me, & both he & the doctors here say the same thing, ie. that I should make a good recovery but that I must keep quiet & not attempt to work for a long time, possibly for as long as a year. It is a great nuisance, but worth while if it means I can go on working afterwards. I wonder if you would be kind enough to convey my thanks to Dr de Kruif & Dr O'Brien for their offer & the interest they have shown in me.

I wonder if there is any news of the Empsons? There was a rumour in London that William had reached the USA, but I can't get it confirmed.

"1984" has come out here & seems to be getting quite good notices.

Yours sincerely,
George Orwell

3641. To Anthony Powell

6 June 1949   Handwritten

Cranham Lodge,
Cranham,
Gloucester.

Dear Tony,

Thanks ever so for sending me the 'Aubrey' book. I'm so glad you *did* put in my favourite Mrs Overall after all, also the story about Sir W. Raleigh & his son.[1] I was so sorry about Hugh Kingsmill.[2] If they are trying to get a pension for his widow, if my signature would be useful in any way, of course include me. I'm a good deal better, & trust this will continue. I had a specialist from London, who said much the same as the people here, ie. that if I get round *this* corner I could be good for quite a few years, but that I have got to keep quiet & not try to work for a long time, possibly as long as a year or two years—I trust it won't be as long as that. It's a great bore, but worth while if it means I can work again later. Richard is staying nearby for the summer, & comes over & sees me once or twice a week. Please remember me to everybody. I hope you & Malcolm[3] will come & see me some time—but of course don't put yourselves out. I know what a tiresome journey it must be.

Yours
George

P.S. I'm reading Dante! (with a crib of course.)[4]

1. *Brief Lives and Other Selected Writings of John Aubrey*, edited by Anthony Powell (1949); see 2985, *n. 1*, where it is suggested that Powell may have sent Orwell a typescript of John Overall's life when considering whether or not to include it. The reference here to Sir Walter Raleigh and his son may support that, although Orwell could have been recalling Andrew Clark's nineteenth-century edition. Aubrey's life of Raleigh does not refer to his son. If Orwell was recalling that life from memory he may have confused two anecdotes retailed by Aubrey. He says that when Raleigh was at Oxford University and seriously short of money he borrowed a gown from Mr. Thomas Child 'which he never restored, nor money for it.' As the life begins with that anecdote it might easily be recalled. But Aubrey also tells how, when Raleigh was Captain of Her Majesty's Yeoman of the Guard, a father approached him begging that his son be admitted though only about eighteen or nineteen. Sir Walter answered that though he would accept the father—a goodly man himself—he took no boys. But the father called in his son, who was 'such a goodly proper young fellow' and taller than any in the Guard that he 'swears him immediately.' Further, he had him carry in the Queen's first dish at dinner 'where the Queen beheld him with admiration, as if a beautiful young giant had stalked in with the service.'
2. See *3622, n. 5*.
3. Malcolm Muggeridge.
4. Among Orwell's books at his death were Volumes 2 and 3 of the Bodley Head bilingual edition of Dante's *Divina Commedia*, the 'Purgatorio' and the 'Paradiso'; the English translation is by John Sinclair. He also had a bilingual edition of the 'Paradiso,' with an English translation by Laurence Binyon (1943), and Volumes 2 and 3 in an Italian edition published in Florence in 1827. The other volumes may have been lost in the course of Orwell's several moves in 1949; he could have had the 'Inferno' with him at Cranham.

3642. To Fredric Warburg

6 June 1949   Handwritten

Cranham Lodge,
Cranham,
Gloucester.

Dear Fred,

Thanks so much for your letter. I'll expect you on Wednesday the 15th,[1] and will send the car to meet the 12.5 at Stroud. Do bring Michael[2] if he'd like to come.

Yours
George

1. Warburg had written a long letter to Orwell on 30 May 1949. He said that Dr. Morland's report was 'far more encouraging than I had dared to hope' but 'this disease is one which apparently you cannot cheat'; however much better Orwell felt, 'for God's sake don't start working until you are given the all-clear.' He proposed coming on the 12th (later changed to the 15th), by when reviews of *Nineteen Eighty-Four* would be available. He was convinced it would earn far more than *Animal Farm* in England and America, which should provide Orwell with enough money, even after tax and 'the heavy expenses of treatment in a sanatorium,' to last, say, three years or more. He would be interested in publishing a second volume of essays, in the autumn of 1950, say, and by then Orwell might have recovered and had time to write his next novel. (This letter is almost fully reproduced in *All Authors Are Equal*, 113–14.) He saw Orwell on the 15th and noted that his being so ill 'some weeks ago . . . appear[s] due to pleurisy rather than the tubercular infection. George's present condition is shocking, but he is hopeful.' See Warburg's Report, *3645*.
2. Michael Kennard; see *3371, n. 3*.

3643. Publication of *Nineteen Eighty-Four*

Nineteen Eighty-Four was published by Secker & Warburg on 8 June 1949. It was published five days later by Harcourt, Brace and Company in New York. Secker & Warburg printed 26,575 copies for the first edition; a second impression, of 5,570 copies, was issued in March 1950, and a third impression, of 5,150 copies, in August 1950. A second edition, entirely reset, was ordered in December 1950. Harcourt, Brace ordered 20,000 copies for its initial print run, and two further impressions, of 10,000 copies each, were issued on 1 July and 7 September 1949; fourth and fifth impressions, of 4,100 and 5,000 copies, were issued on 3 February and in June 1950. A Book-of-the-Month Club edition was issued in the United States in July 1949, and by March 1952 had sold 190,000 copies (Willison). Warburg gives figures for later printings and initial reactions to the book in *All Authors Are Equal*, 114–18.

The novel was very widely reviewed. Crick summarises initial reactions (563–68) and devotes a long section of his annotated *Nineteen Eighty-Four* (1984) to 'The Contemporary Reaction' (92–105) (See also his Appendix F), 150–51, for a useful account of the texts of the English and American dust-jackets. On 31 July 1949, *The New York Times Book Review* stated that some sixty reviews, coast-to-coast, were 'Overwhelmingly (90 per cent) admiring, with cries of terror rising above the applause. . . . Few paid more than passing attention to the novel as fiction. . . . The emphasis was on the political 'prophecy' involved. . . . Even the ordinarily breezy *New Yorker* was so shaken that it found itself endorsing something awesome called Orwell's "moral centrality."' L[ouis] A[deane] in *Freedom* (11 June 1949) began by suggesting: 'If it is true that satire admits an element of hope, then this novel is not satirical: it is a grim and convincing attack on the centralised State and on modern warfare, and its power is due to the complete pessimism with which every page is stamped'; he concluded: 'Only an honest man could have written this book, and it is desolating that in our world such honesty should lead to such despair. Out of his despair, Orwell has made a protest more complete and more sustained than any other writer of his generation, and for this he deserves our praise and gratitude.' Praise, with a summary of the book, marked most reviews. G. M. Thompson, in the *Evening Standard* (7 June), which made it its Book of the Month, also remarked on the savagery of the satire. Some reviews applauded Orwell's vision but pointed to what they regarded as weaknesses in the novel. Bruce Bain, in *Tribune* (17 June 1949), did not think that *Nineteen Eighty-Four* was a great novel, because Orwell was 'not in full command of his material, and the importance of what he has to say splits the novel at the seams.' *The Observer*'s review (12 June)—by Harold Nicolson, who had asked to review it—whilst finding the book impressive, thought it was not convincing, lacking 'either the high imaginative force of Aldous Huxley's "Brave New World," or the self-contained logic of Mr. Orwell's own "Animal Farm."' In particular he thought that those who were twenty-five in 1960, when Ingsoc was established, could not have lost all remembrance of the past by the time they were forty-nine in 1984. Also, the task set 'the staff of Thinkpol'° was beyond fulfilment. 'Such inconsistencies of detail prevent our surrendering ourselves wholly to Mr. Orwell's thesis: but it is an excellent thesis none the less.'

A fierce attack on Orwell, which arose from the publication of *Nineteen Eighty-Four*, was launched by Arthur Calder-Marshall (see *856, n. 3*) in *Reynold's News* (12 June 1949), a Sunday paper which supported the Labour Party. This was a biographical denigration of Orwell, accusing him, for example, of indulging in the thirties in 'a peculiar, personal politics, playing the conflict between Comrade Orwell and Mr. Blair out on the political scene.' He claimed that *Animal Farm* adopted 'the cheap Tory thesis that Fascism and Communism are the same thing; a thesis which the lunatic fringe of the Labour Party has also adopted.' *Nineteen Eighty-Four* made the same equation and would serve as election propaganda for the Tories. Calder-Marshall concluded: 'The sooner Comrade Orwell assumes the pen-name of Eric Blair, the better. Except, of course, that Mr. Blair, ex-Etonian, ex-civil servant, has no literary reputation at all.' The following week, H. Greville strongly defended Orwell against this 'despicable attack,' made because Calder-Marshall could not 'stomach attacks on the realm of the great Stalin.' Two more letters followed on 26 June, one from a person who signed a defence of Orwell as 'Jewish Socialist,' and one defending Calder-Marshall's stance from the Labour M.P. Woodrow Wyatt; he claimed that Orwell's 'blank hopelessness' made it impossible for him to count himself 'among those who identify themselves with the aims and beliefs of the Labour Party.' (Woodrow Wyatt, 1918–, was knighted in 1983 and created a life peer as Baron Wyatt of Weeford in 1987; in 1976 he was appointed Chairman of the Horserace Totalisator Board; he has not for some time been a supporter of the Labour Party.) For Orwell's reaction to Calder-Marshall's attack, see his letter to Mr. Shaw, 20 June 1949, *3650*.

Calder-Marshall's spite apart, he was correct in seeing that *Nineteen Eighty-Four* would be taken by some to be an attack on socialism and the Labour Party; this was especially so in the United States. *Life* published a descriptive summary of the novel, largely made up of illustrations drawn by Abner Dean (4 July 1949, 78–85). This had a prominent sub-heading: 'An Englishman writes a frightening satire about the cruel fate of man in a regimented left-wing police state which controls his mind and soul.' Orwell was much concerned at this misunderstanding and particularly by an article in the New York *Daily News* which, he had been told, stated that *Nineteen Eighty-Four* was an attack on the Labour government (see letter to Leonard Moore, 13 July 1949, *3657*). He therefore prepared a statement that this was not his intent (see *3646*) and a summary was sent to *Life* by Warburg and evidently to others (see *3646*). On 25 July, *Life* published two letters about *Nineteen Eighty-Four*. One, from A. D. Crane, of Kingsport, Tennessee, said nobody should be scared by 'Orwell's prediction,' because such forecasts never came true, and every decade since 1880 had shown 'an improvement and advancement in real freedom and in every other respect'; the world had never gone backward. A more thoughtful letter came from Arthur Schlesinger, Jr. (1917–), whose *The Age of Jackson* had won a Pulitzer Prize in 1945:

> Your description of George Orwell ("who fought in the Spanish civil war, saw firsthand what the Communists were up to and has since devoted all his talents to warning the world of the fate which awaits it if it confuses liberalism with regimentation") is liable to misunderstanding. Orwell fought on the Republican side in Spain. He was outraged by the behavior of Communists whose attacks on the non-Communist majority of Republicans played such a large part in delivering Spain to fascist tyranny. But Orwell hated Franco fully as much as he did the Communists.
>
> The essence of Orwell's position is a warning against totalitarianism—not, as your editorial writer puts it, just against "left-wing" totalitarianism. Your description would have been much more accurate if you had written of Orwell: "who fought in the Spanish civil war, saw firsthand what the fascists and the Communists were up to and has since devoted all his talents to warning the world of the fate which awaits it if it confuses conservatism or liberalism with regimentation."

In that same issue, immediately below Schlesinger's letter, *Life* published a summary of Orwell's statement. This was not based on Warburg's telephoned summary, but on a statement prepared for the United Automobile Workers (see endnote to *3646*).

Two early responses to *Nineteen Eighty-Four* were among Orwell's papers at his death. Lawrence Durrell wrote from the British Legation, Belgrade, complimenting Orwell. It was, he wrote, 'intellectually the bravest and cruellest book you've done. Reading it in a Communist country is really an experience because one can see it all around one—the ever-present fact which no left-wingers of my acquaintance will dare to look in the eye.' On 12 June 1949, Bernard Sankey wrote from Belleville, New Jersey, enclosing the *New York*

Times review; he had not yet been able to get hold of the book. He had gone to the United States because he thought it would be easier to earn a living there, he says, and he describes paradoxical characteristics of American life as they struck him, especially admiring 'the wonderful library system.' He evidently knew Orwell, for he twice refers to his state of health, showing some indication that he knew how very ill Orwell was. Unfortunately he has not been traced.

A third, more personal, response to *Nineteen Eighty-Four* is recorded by Jacintha Buddicom in her *Eric & Us.* On 11 June 1949, she went to Shiplake (where Orwell had lived before World War I) to see her mother, then very frail, who showed her daughter a copy of *Nineteen Eighty-Four*, which she had had Bumpus (a London bookseller) send her as soon as it was published. Mrs. Buddicom reminisced about Eric 'with affection,' but his book she found morbid: 'She had been very fond of Eric, and the defeatist destruction of all individuality portrayed by him in the nightmare world of *Nineteen Eighty-Four* upset her very much. So when I left on the Sunday evening, I left with her his letter declaring that *nothing ever dies* [see *3631 endnote*]—to comfort her that perhaps he would have better luck next time.' Jacintha Buddicom never saw the letter again, nor her mother, for she died three days later. Thus, *Nineteen Eighty-Four* was inextricably tied up in her mind with her mother's death. Writing it had 'to all intents and purposes killed him' and 'it certainly did not make any happier her [mother's] last few days of life. . . . So I never answered his final lost letter' (*Eric & Us*, 157–58).

Finally, writing to Orwell on 26 August 1949, Arthur Koestler described the novel as 'a glorious book' (*3681A*, Appendix 14).

3644. To William Phillips

8 June 1949   Handwritten

Cranham Lodge,
Cranham,
Gloucester.

Dear Mr Phillips,[1]

I received your letter of the 2nd today. I need hardly tell you that I am delighted as well as very much astonished at your picking me out for the Partisan Review Award. It is the kind of honour I am quite unused to. Perhaps you will convey my thanks to the rest of the Advisory Board. I will not tell anyone about it until you make the announcement.

I will send you something when I can, but I have done no work since December & may not be able to work for a long time to come. The doctors tell me the best chance of recovery is to lie in bed & do nothing, possibly for as long as another year—I hope it won't be as long as that, of course.

With very many thanks again, & best wishes to everybody.

Yours sincerely
Geo. Orwell

1. Co-editor with Philip Rahv of *Partisan Review*.

3644A. To Lydia Jackson

10 June 1949   Handwritten

Cranham Lodge,
Cranham,
Gloucester.

Dear Lydia,

Thanks so much for your letter.[1] You must have wondered why I have not written for so long, but (as I dare say you didn't know) I was most horribly ill for a long time, about 2 months. In fact for a while I almost thought I was a goner. However I'm glad to say I'm much better, & the various doctors I have seen do not think too badly of my case. But they all say I must remain an invalid & not try to work for a long time, possibly as long as a year—I hope it won't be so long, of course. It's a great bore, but worth while if it means getting better.

Yes, do come & see me. I'd love just to see you & talk to you. Either of the week ends you suggested would suit me. But let me know well in advance wht date, because I have to arrange about cars etc.

Richard is staying for the summer near here & comes over & sees me once a week. He is extremely well. He is starting kindergarten school, mornings only, & in the winter he will go to the village school in Jura. But I can't make plans much ahead until I know more about my own movements.

Looking forward to seeing you.

With love
Eric.

1. This may have been prompted by the receipt of a complimentary copy of *Nineteen Eighty-Four*, which Orwell asked to have sent her on 31 May; see *3637*.

3645. Fredric Warburg's Report on His Visit to Orwell

15 June 1949

CONFIDENTIAL

Visit to George Orwell June 15th, 1949

Health.

He is undoubtedly better than at his low point of some weeks ago when he saw Dr. Andrew Morland. The high temperature of that date, the general feeling of exhaustion and disintegration, appear to have been due to pleurisy rather than a worsening of the tubercular infection. George's present condition is of course shocking, but he is hopeful, and prepared at the moment to do whatever the doctor tells him for a period of up to twelve months. If he does not or cannot improve within this period there cannot in my opinion be much hope. He is thinking of moving to a sanatorium nearer London when he is feeling better, in two or three months time, provided he feels that his stay in a sanatorium must be continued over a longish period.

Sales & Prospects.

I told him of the position and suggested to him that from British and American sources digest rights, etc., he would make very large sums of money, probably between £10,000 and £15,000. He spoke reassuringly of the auditors who handle his financial affairs, and told me they were turning him into a Limited Company. Until this is done he is not anxious to receive further royalties, and I shall therefore instruct Miss Murtough[1] to withhold the payment of £800 odd due to Christy & Moore on publication. Obviously this payment is merely withheld for a month or two.

Statement.

I took down from him a note on the American cables and have already given over the 'phone to "Life" a summary. The statement is typed on the attached sheet, and a copy is being sent to George for his approval.[2] Subject to this it can be used I imagine in any way that appears useful.

Literary Work.

He has quite come round to the idea of a new volume of essays, but these will be more miscellaneous than the earlier volume, CRITICAL ESSAYS. He could give us material for a volume right away, approximately 40,000 words, but is anxious to include one or two new essays not hitherto printed. One of these would be a piece he did for "Politics & Letters" on Gissing, which has been lost during the liquidation of this little Company. I suggest J. G. P.[3] gets from George the name of the solicitors who are liquidating it and does a little detective work if he can to find the typescript. Another unprinted contribution would be an essay on Conrad which he has been working on for some months and which he could write quite quickly when he is allowed to do so. The book would probably be called ESSAYS AND SKETCHES and would presumably include the piece about his private school which we have seen here.[4] R. S.[5] *must* find this during the next few days and hand it to Sonia Brownell or send it to George. This is important.

This material we might wait for until the end of the year, as it is possible that he may do the Conrad essay in the next 8 or 9 months. The idea would then be to publish in the autumn of 1950.

I asked him about a new novel, and this is formulated in his mind—a nouvelle of 30,000 to 40,000 words—a novel of character rather than of ideas, with Burma as background. George was naturally as reticent as usual, but he did disclose this much.[6]

Ability to Write.

The effort of turning ideas in his head into a rough draft on paper is, according to George and Dr. Morland, work which he cannot afford to attempt for a number of months. At best I doubt whether anything can or should be done by George until the autumn of this year.

This about covers the main points that arose, and I am greatly encouraged by my visit. At worst he has a 50/50 chance of recovering and living for a number of years. Probably everything depends on himself and he does at last realize what is involved and what he has got to do.

Warburg's manuscript notes for his report on his visit to Orwell and for the Statement on *Nineteen Eighty-Four* (see *3646*) have survived. The second set of notes is written on Cranham Lodge stationery; the first on an unheaded sheet. There is little doubt that Warburg made both either at Cranham or on the return journey home. The Statement is a carefully filled-out version of the notes; the only exception in the omission of a name. Whereas in the last sentence it is said that it would be 'invidious to mention names,' the notes have one name: 'Cf Henry Wallace as possible friend.' For a note on Wallace, see *3215, n. 1*.

The notes on the visit are headed <u>GO</u> and are numbered 1 to 12. Two are expanded below note 12 in Warburg's hand, but in smaller, neater writing; they were possibly added later, when Warburg returned to his office. There are also two side- notes; these are discussed below. Two headings, 'Sales & prospects' and 'Health' are repeated in the report (in reverse order). Some other headings, and the two paragraphs written below note 12, which relate to 'Essays and Sketches' and the 'nouvelle' (as 'novella' in these notes) are worked into the typed report, reproduced here. There are, however, other notes which are not reflected in the report. Note 5 is 'Richard's future.' This is crossed through (presumably because Warburg did not think it appropriate for the report). One of the side-notes has 'Roy Harrod / at [?] Westminster / 5 years old.' Orwell is not known to have had any links with Harrod (1900–1978; Kt., 1959), though Warburg certainly did. Warburg was two years older than Harrod, and both were at Westminster School before they went up to Oxford. In *An Occupation for Gentlemen*, Warburg speaks of Harrod as being one of his closest friends (66). Harrod became a distinguished economist and worked in Churchill's office, 1940–42, and then as statistical adviser to the Admiralty, 1943–45. Richard was just five years old at this time. Orwell did not want him to go to a boarding school until he was ten (see *3481*). Shortly after Warburg's visit he decided to enrol Richard to enter Westminster School in 1957 (see *3647* and *3678*). Warburg's association with this decision is a little strange, because he wrote that, owing to his being a Jew, his five years at Westminster ('or [at] least the first two of them') were among the most hateful of his life (*An Occupation for Gentlemen*, 30). The other side-note is an instruction to Warburg himself: 'Send GO "The Wrong Set."' This was a book of stories by Angus Wilson published by Secker & Warburg in 1949. It may have been suggested to Orwell by Sonia Brownell; she had published Wilson in *Horizon* and they had become friends. It was among Orwell's books at his death. The other headings are 'Georgina Coleridge'; 'Geo. Gissing' (which may refer to Orwell's wish to have Gissing's novels reprinted, rather than his essay on Gissing, which is separately noted); 'Trip to Copenhagen'; 'Curran of E. Standard' (perhaps associated with Orwell's wish to put off a second visit from Curran, who tired him so; see *3617* and *3629*); and 'Are you seeing Morland regularly,' presumably a reminder to Warburg himself to check that Orwell was seeing Morland. The two puzzling headings are 'Georgina Coleridge' and 'Trip to Denmark.' The latter could hardly be an alternative for Orwell to the proposed stay in Switzerland; Orwell's link with Georgina Coleridge is not known. For Warburg's account of this visit and for Dr. Andrew Morland's reports, see *All Authors are Equal*, 111–14, 118–19.

1. Miss P. Murtough was a secretary at Secker & Warburg. It was she who offered to borrow a copy of *Coming Up for Air* from Kensington Public Library so that a reprint could be made; see *3155, n. 2*).
2. See *3646*.
3. John G. Pattisson; he joined Secker & Warburg as an office boy and remained with the firm when Warburg took over. After serving in the tank corps in North Africa and Italy, he returned to Secker & Warburg in 1945. He later became a director of the publishers Barrie & Rockliffe.
4. The mislaid essay was 'Such, Such Were the Joys.'
5. Roger Senhouse, of Secker & Warburg.
6. The initial draft is titled 'A Smoking-room Story'; see *3722, 3723*, and *3724*.

3646. Orwell's Statement on *Nineteen Eighty-Four*

It has been suggested by some of the reviewers of NINETEEN EIGHTY-FOUR that it is the author's view that this, or something like this, is what will happen inside the next forty years in the Western world. This is not correct. I think that, allowing for the book being after all a parody, something like NINETEEN EIGHTY-FOUR *could* happen. This is the direction in which the world is going at the present time, and the trend lies deep in the political, social and economic foundations of the contemporary world situation.

Specifically the danger lies in the structure imposed on Socialist and on Liberal capitalist communities by the necessity to prepare for total war with the U.S.S.R. and the new weapons, of which of course the atomic bomb is the most powerful and the most publicized. But danger lies also in the acceptance of a totalitarian outlook by intellectuals of all colours.

The moral to be drawn from this dangerous nightmare situation is a simple one: *Don't let it happen. It depends on you.*

George Orwell assumes that if such societies as he describes in NINETEEN EIGHTY-FOUR come into being there will be several super states. This is fully dealt with in the relevant chapters of NINETEEN EIGHTY-FOUR. It is also discussed from a different angle by James Burnham in THE MANAGERIAL REVOLUTION. These super states will naturally be in opposition to each other or (a novel point) will pretend to be much more in opposition than in fact they are. Two of the principal super states will obviously be the Anglo-American world and Eurasia. If these two great blocks line up as mortal enemies it is obvious that the Anglo-Americans will not take the name of their opponents and will not dramatize themselves on the scene of history as Communists. Thus they will have to find a new name for themselves. The name suggested in NINETEEN EIGHTY-FOUR is of course Ingsoc, but in practice a wide range of choices is open. In the U.S.A. the phrase "Americanism" or "hundred per cent Americanism" is suitable and the qualifying adjective is as totalitarian as anyone could wish.

If there is a failure of nerve and the Labour party breaks down in its attempt to deal with the hard problems with which it will be faced, tougher types than the present Labour leaders will inevitably take over, drawn probably from the ranks of the Left, but not sharing the Liberal aspirations of those now in power. Members of the present British government, from Mr. Attlee and Sir Stafford Cripps down to Aneurin Bevan will *never* willingly sell the pass to the enemy, and in general the older men, nurtured in a Liberal tradition, are safe, but the younger generation is suspect and the seeds of totalitarian thought are probably widespread among them. It is invidious to mention names, but everyone could without difficulty think for himself of prominent English and American personalities whom the cap would fit.

[Initialled] F. J. W.

Orwell's statement was prepared following misunderstandings about his intentions in *Nineteen Eighty-Four*. These arose especially from an article in the New York *Daily News* which, he had been told, interpreted his novel as an attack on the Labour government. He had also been asked for a statement by the United Automobile Workers, an American trade union (see letter to Moore, 13 July 1949, *3657*). *Life* did not publish the statement that Warburg had telephoned to it (see *3643*; Orwell writes of a démenti being cabled; see *3657*), but used part of the version sent to Francis A. Henson of the UAW, having telephoned Orwell at Cranham again to seek his permission (see *3657*). *Life* published that statement on 25 July 1949; the lead-in made it seem as if Orwell had written a letter to the editor of *Life*.

In a recent letter Orwell wrote: My novel *Nineteen Eighty-four*[o] is *not* intended as an attack on socialism, or on the British Labor party, but as a show-up of the perversions to which a centralized economy is liable, and which have already been partly realized in Communism and fascism. I do not believe that the kind of society I describe necessarily *will* arrive, but I believe (allowing of course for the fact that the book is a satire) that something resembling it *could* arrive. I believe also that totalitarian ideas have taken root in the minds of intellectuals everywhere, and I have tried to draw these ideas out to their logical consequences. The scene of the book is laid in Britain in order to emphasize that the English-speaking races are not innately better than anyone else and that totalitarianism, if not fought against, could triumph anywhere.

A slightly different account was given by *The New York Times Book Review* on 31 July 1949 in the same column in which it summarised reactions to *Nineteen Eighty-Four* (see *3643*). This included Orwell's statement that he was a supporter of the Labour Party and italicised 'if not fought against.' The *Book Review* opening read: 'Certain reviewers, incidentally, thought that "Nineteen Eighty-Four" might be an attack on the British Labor party. Mr. Orwell himself has settled that question in a letter to Francis A. Henson of the United Automobile Workers:'

My recent novel is *not* intended as an attack on socialism or on the British Labor party (of which I am a supporter) but as a show-up of the perversions to which a centralized economy is liable and which have already been partly realized in communism and fascism. . . .

The scene of the book is laid in Britain in order to emphasize that the English-speaking races are not innately better than anyone else and that totalitarianism, *if not fought against*, could triumph anywhere.

The ellipses between the two paragraphs are the *Book Review*'s.

The Socialist Call, New York, 22 July 1949, most fully refuted the charge that *Nineteen Eighty-Four* was an attack on the Labour government. The New York *Daily News*, it reported, 'no citadel of intellectualism, printed a lead editorial praising this "intellectual" novel as further proof of its oft-reiterated thesis that "Socialism and Communism are brothers under the skin." *Life* magazine echoed this capitalist "party" line.' *The Socialist Call* said that it had asked George Orwell for a statement. Presumably what was sent them, through Leonard Moore, was a copy of the statement Orwell had prepared for the UAW: see postcript to *3657*. It published this in full on its front page, making the change of verb Orwell had mentioned in his letter to Moore, under the heading: 'Orwell Tells CALL "1984" Does NOT Attack Socialism.'

My recent novel "1984" is NOT intended as an attack on socialism, or on the British Labor Party (of which I am a supporter) but as a show-up of the perversions to which a centralized economy is liable and which have already been partly realized in Communism and Fascism.

I do not believe that the kind of society which I described necessarily will arrive, but I believe (allowing of course for the fact that the book is a satire) that something resembling it could arrive. I believe also that totalitarian ideas have taken root in the minds of intellectuals everywhere, and I have tried to draw these ideas out to their logical consequences.

The scene of the book is laid in Britain in order to emphasize that the English speaking races are not innately better than anyone else and that totalitarianism, **if not fought against**, could triumph anywhere.

On 8 July 1950, Tosco Fyvel wrote to Margaret M. Goalby of Presteigne, Radnorshire (see *355A*), answering some questions about Orwell's responses to the events in the last months of his life and the meaning of Ingsco. 'Certainly,' he wrote; 'Orwell believed in the old Liberal principles and the value of truth and ordinary decency. He was also firmly of the view that these principles demanded a democratic socialist structure of society. It is true that he was pessimistic about the extent to which these principles could prevail in most parts of the world. But I know that he was pleasantly surprised at the firmness with which the Labour Government here at home continued in office after mitigating the worst harshnesses of British society by means of the Health Service, the National Social Insurance Act, the nationalisation of the mines, the development of the depressed areas, and so on. All these measures were steps in the direction Orwell desired . . . . Even during his last weeks in hospital, Orwell was keenly interested in the coming election and the chances of his various friends among Labour M.P.s. He also said that one point in *1984* had been misunderstood by the critics. "Ingsoc", the totalitarian society, was not represented as arising out of democratic socialism. On the contrary: his imaginary totalitarians who arose in England after an atomic war merely adopted the name of "English Socialism" because they thought it had popular appeal—in the same way as the Nazis, while allying themselves in 1933 with the Ruhr industrialists and smashing the German trade unions and Socialist Party, called themselves "National-Socialists" to dupe the German working class.'

3647. To Julian Symons
16 June 1949   Handwritten

Cranham Lodge,
Cranham,
Gloucester.

Dear Julian,

I think it was you who reviewed "1984" in the T.L.S.[1] I must thank you for such a brilliant as well as generous review. I don't think you could have brought out the sense of the book better in so short a space. You are of course right about the vulgarity of the "Room 101" business. I was aware of this while writing it, but I didn't know another way of getting somewhere near the effect I wanted.

I have been horribly ill since last seeing you, but a lot better in the last few weeks, & I hope perhaps now I have turned the corner. The various doctors I have seen are all quite encouraging but say I must remain quiet & not work for a long time, possibly as much as a year—I hope it won't be so long, of course. It's a bore, but worth while if it means recovering. Richard is staying nearby for the summer & comes & sees me every week. He has started kindergarten school & this winter is going to the village school in Jura, I don't know for how long. I have been thinking about Westminster for him when he is older. They have abandoned their top hats, I learn. It is a day school, which I prefer, & I think has other good points. Any way I'm going to make enquiries & put his name down if it seems suitable. Of course god knows what will have happened by then, say 1956, but one has to plan as though nothing would change drastically.

Have you any news of the Empsons, who were in Pekin°? I don't know whether you knew them. There have been various rumours, & I am trying to get some news from Empson's American publishers.

Did you read Ruth Fischer's book "Stalin & German Communism"? She's coming to see me tomorrow, I think.

Hope all is well & baby flourishing. Please remember me to your wife.

Yours
George

1. The review had appeared (unsigned, as was then the practice) in *The Times Literary Supplement* on 10 June 1949.

3648. To Leonard Moore

18 June 1949   Handwritten

Cranham Lodge,
Cranham,
Gloucester.

Dear Moore,
Many thanks for your letter. I have got a diary I kept during the war years, but it is among my papers which are in store with Pickfords. I don't know how to dig it out & I don't think it's worth while at this moment. At some future time it might be worth publishing. Could you please explain this to Schimanski?[1]

Yours sincerely
Eric Blair

1. Orwell and Inez Holden had intended to make a joint publication out of their war diaries. Gollancz refused to publish them, and they passed to another publisher, Lindsay Drummond, for whom Stefan Schimanski worked. Drummond published a section of Inez Holden's diary in *Leaves in the Storm*, edited by Stefan Schimanski and Henry Treece, in 1947. Schimanski later wrote the editorial in *World Review*, June 1950, which published 'From the Notebooks of George Orwell,' and he there explained that he had first read Orwell's diary in 1944 but that it was not then felt to be a propitious time for its publication. See *2634, n. 3*. In 1941 Schimanski had edited *Kingdom Come* with Treece, and he edited the annual, *Transformation*, 1943–47. He was killed in Korea when working as a war correspondent.

3649. To Tosco Fyvel

20 June 1949   Handwritten

Cranham Lodge,
Cranham,
Gloucester.

Dear Tosco,
Thanks ever so for that wonderful talk on the 3rd programme. I am sure it would sell at least 1000 copies. Would you please thank the others at *Tribune* for putting in such a kind par about me?[1]
I've just read Deutscher's book on Stalin.[2] It's very good & less pro-Stalin than I would have expected. Ruth Fischer came & saw me the other day. She's become something of an old gossip (a typical old German Jewess—not so very old actually) but it was fun meeting somebody who had known Radek[3] & Bukharin[4] & others intimately.

Yours
George

1. *Tribune* for 17 June published not only a review of *Nineteen Eighty-Four*, by Bruce Bain (pseudonym of Richard Findlater; see *3643*), but also two 'news' paragraphs on pages 3 and 5. The first contrasted the manner in which the human brain was rigidly controlled in the

totalitarian state depicted by Orwell with the creation at Manchester University of a mechanical 'brain'—the word is printed within quotation marks. This brain was currently working on mathematical problems, but might even be developed to write sonnets. At least, *Tribune* comforted itself, Orwell's 'brain is still human.' The second paragraph noted that the author of *Nineteen Eighty-Four* (which had proved such an outstanding success) had long been 'intimately connected with *Tribune*' and it expressed good wishes for his speedy recovery from illness.

2. Isaac Deutscher, *Stalin: A Political Biography* (1949). Orwell lists it in his reading for June 1949.
3. Karl Radek (1885–1939?) accompanied Lenin in the sealed train for the return to Russia that led to the October revolution. However, he left the train in Sweden, where he organised propaganda in French and German for the revolution and was active in the leadership of the Comintern and in fomenting revolution in Germany in the 1920s (unsuccessfully). He was expelled from the party as a Trotskyist in 1927 and sentenced to internal banishment. Readmitted, he was appointed to the editorial board of *Izvestia*, but was again arrested, confessed guilt at the second show trial in the Stalin purge of 1937, and was sentenced to ten years' imprisonment. He was the author of *The Architect of Socialist Society* (1933), which purports to be written in 1967. Its aim is the glorification of Stalin. Radek was small and was described by Trotsky as 'monkey-like' (R. Payne, *The Rise and Fall of Stalin*, 1966, 493). His talent for propaganda, and especially for inverting facts, suggests he might lie behind the 'little Rumpelstiltskin figure, contorted with hatred' who switched from one party line to another 'actually in mid-sentence' in *Nineteen Eighty-Four* (*CW*, IX, 188–89).
4. Nikolai Ivanovich Bukharin (1888–1938), a Bolshevik from 1908 who worked with Lenin on *Pravda* before the October revolution, edited *Novy Mir* (New World) in New York in 1916, but after the October revolution he became editor of *Pravda*. He was the author of several theoretical publications in the early 1920s. For a time an ally of Stalin's, he later opposed him when Stalin changed his policies, and was expelled from the Politburo in November 1929. He regained some measure of acceptance when he was appointed editor of *Izvestia* in 1934, but in 1937 he was expelled from the party as a Trotskyist and in the following year was a defendant in one of Stalin's purge trials, found guilty, and executed. Bukharin's fate was effectively sealed when, in 1936, he charged Stalin with wanting to establish absolute power over party and state and claimed that the NKVD, not the Communist Party, ruled the country (see R. Payne, *The Rise and Fall of Stalin*, 481).

3650. To Mr. Shaw

20 June 1949   Handwritten

Cranham Lodge,
Cranham,
Gloucester.

Dear Mr Shaw,[1]
Thank you so much for your letter. I am sorry to say I am very ill (T.B.) so I can't write much of a letter in return. The review in Reynolds's[2] was stupid. My feeling when reading it was that if I was going to smear somebody I would do it better than that. Any way° thank you for troubling to write, and please forgive this short scrawl.

Yours sincerely
Geo. Orwell

1. Not identified, but see *3061*.
2. *Reynold's News*; the review was by Arthur Calder-Marshall; see *3643*.

3651. To Leonard Moore

22 June 1949   Handwritten

Cranham Lodge,
Cranham,
Gloucester.

Dear Moore,

Many thanks for the press cuttings. The book seems to have had a good reception, ie, even when unfriendly I should say they are mostly "selling" reviews.

Could you please send to

Mr. Jordi ARQUER[1]
Boite° Postale 6
Paris VIII[eme]

a copy of the Italian edition of "Homage to Catalonia" (I suppose the Italian publisher could send it direct if you haven't got one) & a copy of the Observer for Sunday February 27th.[2] I presume one can get hold of back numbers as recent as that.

Yours sincerely
Eric Blair

1. Jordi Arquer had been sentenced to eleven years' imprisonment in 1938, ostensibly for having helped organise the 'May Events' in Barcelona, though in reality it was simply because he was a member of the POUM. See *497* and *3238, n. 1*.
2. It is difficult to know which item particularly caused Orwell to ask for a copy of this issue: the award of the Bollingen Prize to Ezra Pound (see *3612*); anarchy in Burma; an article by Edward Crankshaw (see *3467, n. 5*) on forced confessions in totalitarian countries; an 'extraordinary speech' by Maurice Thorez (see *2579, n. 3*) in which 'he openly envisaged a military invasion of France by the Red Army'; an attack by the Kremlin on the Indian government of Pandit Nehru which it accused of attempting to create a 'Far Eastern variant of an aggressive Western Union'; Rajani Palme Dutt, Vice-Chairman of the Communist Party (see *913, n. 1* and *2096, n. 3*), as the 'final interpreter' in Britain of the Kremlin's wishes. But that is only a selection of what might have interested Orwell.

3652. To Vernon Richards

22 June 1949   Handwritten

Cranham Lodge,
Cranham,
Gloucester.

Dear Vernon,

Thanks so much for your letter, & the press-cuttings. Yes, I got the copy of the memorial number[1] all right.

Sell as many photos as you can. It doesn't cost *me* anything, & is all advertisement. I had a lot of fuss with Life, who wanted to send interviewers here etc., but I put them off because that kind of thing tires me too much. I am afraid some of the U.S. republican papers have tried to use "1984" as propaganda against the Labour Party, but I have issued a sort of démenti which I hope will be printed.

Yes, send me the list of questions & I'll do my best. You will understand that I cannot answer at great length. The more this issue is cleared up, the better.

I'd love to see you some time. But let me know when you're coming (I think there are people coming the next 3 week-ends) so as not to clash with anyone else, & so that I can arrange about a car.

Yours
George

1. Richards's wife, Marie-Louise Berneri, died on 13 April 1949. *Freedom* for 28 May paid tribute to her: see *3636*.
2. A denial; Orwell, in his Second Literary Notebook, 1948 (see *3515*), includes '*Issue a* dementi' in the section 'Foreign words and phrases used unnecessarily in English.' Orwell forgot to add an acute accent to démenti.

3652A. To Lydia Jackson

27 June 1949   Handwritten

Cranham Lodge,
Cranham,
Gloucester.

Dear Lydia,

I assume you are coming here on Saturday the 2nd, & I am going to book a room for you at the George, the local hotel which is somewhere near this sanatorium (but I am not sure how near). I assume also that as you are bringing your bike you will ride from Stroud (it's about 5 miles I believe.) If any of this is wrong, please let me know, would you. I don't know what time you'll reach Stroud, but if you are likely to get here, ie. to the sanatorium, in time for lunch on Saturday, could you let me know, because I am supposed to order lunch beforehand.

I am getting better, but it is a slow business & I am afraid it will be a long time before I am able to work again. Look forward to seeing you, with love

Eric.

3653. To Mamaine Koestler

27 June 1949   Handwritten

Cranham Lodge,
Cranham
Gloucester.

Dear Mamaine,

Thank you ever so for that lovely bottle of brandy, which arrived here on Saturday, appropriately for my birthday (46!) I hope you are a bit better.[1] Sonia gave me a very poor account of you when she came on Saturday. I didn't also realise that Celia had already had her operation. I'm writing to her, but am a bit doubtful about the address. I am a good deal better, but it appears I may be laid by the heels & unable to work for a long time, possibly as much as a year. Richard is staying near by for the summer & comes & sees me once a week. He goes to kindergarten school in the mornings, & seems to be enjoying it. He is so big & strong now I think you would hardly know him. Please give Arthur my love.

Yours
George

1. Mamaine Koestler and Celia Kirwan, twin sisters, both suffered from asthma. Mamaine underwent a bronchoscopy in November 1949.

3654. To Celia Kirwan

27 June 1949   Handwritten

Cranham Lodge,
Cranham,
Gloucester.

Dearest Celia,

I'm a bit vague where to send this to, because Sonia thought letters wouldn't be forwarded from Stewart's Grove & I gather from your letter that you have left the nursing home. However, I'll try Stewart's Grove.

I hadn't realised you were going to have your operation[1] so soon—any way, I'm so glad to hear it's gone off all right. Sonia was here on Saturday, which was my 46th birthday by the way.[2] Richard is now staying with friends near Stroud & is going to be there till about the end of August when he will go back to Jura & go to the village school in the winter term. At present he goes to kindergarten school in the mornings, & comes & sees me once a week. All he seems to learn at school is "counting," but he does know a good many more of his letters than he used to. He is getting very big, & is tremendously healthy. I have him X-rayed from time to time, but no signs of T.B., thank goodness.

I hope you are taking care of yourself & getting strong. I am better, but it is a slow business.

With love
George

1. Like her twin sister, Mamaine, Celia suffered badly from asthma; she had just undergone a bronchoscopy operation.
2. It was typical of Sonia Brownell to surprise Orwell on his birthday.

3655. To Leonard Moore

27 June 1949   Handwritten

Cranham Lodge,
Cranham,
Gloucester.

Dear Moore,

Thank you for your letter of the 24th. Yes, let the BBC go ahead with the German version of "1984."

Did anything transpire about the "Life & Letters" people & that mislaid manuscript?[1]

Yours sincerely
Eric Blair

1. Orwell presumably means *Politics and Letters*, which was to have published his article on George Gissing. However, the journal ceased publication before it appeared, and the typescript was not found until 1959. The essay was published in the *London Magazine*, June 1960. See *3406*.

3655A. To C.V. Wedgwood

5 July 1949   Handwritten

Cranham Lodge,
Cranham,
Gloucester.

Dear Miss Wedgwood,

Thanks so much for your letter. I am afraid I can't write anything or even promise anything. I am fearfully ill (T.B.) & have been for some time.

The doctors tell me not to do any work at all, & I have no doubt they are right. Of course I trust this won't continue for ever, but at present I prefer not to make any commitments.

Yes, I read your review in Time & Tide (of "1984") & almost wrote and thanked you for it, but I know that is considered "bad form." I thought it was one of the best reviews, ie. the most understanding, that the book had.[1]

Yours sincerely
Geo. Orwell.

1. Cicely Veronica Wedgwood (1910–1989; DBE 1968), historian specialising in seventeenth-century history. Among her books published by this time ere *Strafford* (1935; revised as *Thomas Wentworth*, 1961); *The Thirty Years War* (1938); *Oliver Cromwell* (1939); and *William the Silent* (1944) for which she was awarded the James Tait Black Prize. Her review of *Nineteen Eighty-Four* was published in *Time and Tide* on 11 June 1949. It is not known what she wished Orwell to do.

3656. To S. M. Levitas

11 July 1949   Handwritten

Cranham Lodge,
Cranham,
Gloucester.

Dear Mr Levitas,
Very many thanks for your letter of the 5th July,[1] & the cuttings. I honestly *cannot write anything*. All the doctors tell me that my chance of staying alive depends on resting & doing nothing for a long time, possibly as long as a year. The "Progressive" did put my name in a list of prospective contributors, but I told them that I could not do anything.

Yours sincerely
Geo. Orwell

1. Levitas had written expressing pleasure at the 'chorus of praise' that had greeted *Nineteen Eighty-Four*, the only exception being the *Daily Worker*. He remarked that Orwell had not replied to his letter of 3 June: he would be willing to send any books Orwell cared to review. The announcement that Orwell was to contribute to *Progressive* made him envious and, though he realised Orwell was plagued by poor health, he asked him to find time to send copy for *The New Leader*. He enclosed a *New Leader* article by Norbert Muhlen and asked Orwell if he would 'care to comment on it in a few hundred words.'

3657. To Leonard Moore

13 July 1949   Typewritten; handwritten postscript

Cranham Lodge,
Cranham
Gloucester.

Dear Moore,
Many thanks for your three letters, and the various enclosures. I am so glad you fixed up the Spanish and Swedish translations,[1] and the serialisations. I enclose the contract and exemption certificates duly signed.
    With reference to the Socialist Call. I believe all this trouble started with the New York Daily News, which I am told wrote up "1984" as an attack on the Labour government. I issued a sort of démenti through Warburg and

something of the same kind in a cable to "Life." Meanwhile the United Automobile Workers had written saying they were encouraging their members to read the book and asking for a statement. I gave them a few lines of which they then issued a cyclo-styled copy. But I see that it contains a stupid slip, either of theirs or mine (possibly caused by my handwriting.) I had written "I do not believe that the kind of society which I described necessarily will arrive, but I believe . . . that something resembling it could arrive." The latter phrase appears in their version as "that something resembling it will arrive." Yesterday "Life" rang up again and asked whether my statement to the U.A.W. could be quoted. I told them it could, and pointed out the error which I trust they will rectify.[2]

Could you tell the Socialist Call people as politely as possible that I would gladly write them an article if I were well, but that I am really too ill to write anything and that my statement to the UAW covers my position, provided that it is understood that I wrote "could arrive" and not "will arrive."

Yours sincerely
Eric Blair

P.S. I enclose a copy of the UAW Statement.[3]

1. No Spanish translation was published in Orwell's lifetime. Kraft, of Buenos Aires, intended to publish a translation but asked for certain cuts; see 3710. A Swedish translation by Nils Holmberg, *Nittonhundraättiofyra*, was published in May 1950 by Albert Bonniers Förlag, Stockholm (Willison).
2. *Life* did change the verb as Orwell requested; see 3646, and also 3643.
3. The copy of the UAW Statement has not survived; it was, presumably, sent by Moore to the *Socialist Call*; see the text printed in *Socialist Call*, 3646.

3658. To David Astor

14 July 1949   Handwritten

Cranham Lodge,
Cranham,
Gloucester.

Dear David,

I've just seen Leo Robertson, my old friend from Burma of whom I spoke to you, & I told him to write to you & ask if you could give him an interview. He is a man of about 55, was born & partly brought up in India, but educated in England, & was in business in Burma & in the army in India. Practiced as a lawyer & then a judge in Burma up to 1942, then for a short while after the liberation. Besides having a good knowledge of Burma & some of India, he knows Chinese & has been in China, but I think only in Yunnan. He translates from the Chinese, but his real subject is Hindu philosophy. He has done a good deal of writing, but mostly not of [a] very journalistic kind. I am pretty sure you could use him & his background knowledge in *some* capacity. Any way I think he will write to you.

I'm getting on fairly well. It's a slow business, but I think I am better.

Richard is extremely well. He is staying near here & comes & sees me once a week.[1]

Yours
George

1. Annotated: 'Mr Astor sent personal reply to this.' This has not been traced.

3659. To Ruth Fischer

15 July 1949   Handwritten

Cranham Lodge,
Cranham,
Gloucester.

Dear Miss Fischer,
It was extremely kind of you to send me those chocolates, which arrived several days ago.[1] I hope you have been having an interesting & not too depressing time in Germany. I am about the same—a little better, I think. I don't know whether you will still be at Frankfurt or whether this will have to be forwarded after you, but if you are still there I should be interested to hear whether you have seen a Russian D.P. paper named POSSEV[2] which is published in Frankfurt. They sent me a file of the paper containing a Russian translation of "Animal Farm" made by Gleb Struve, whom I know quite well. They say they would like to issue the translation in book form, which of course would be a good idea, but it would have to be financed somehow. I suppose the editors of this paper are bona fide people, & also not whites?[3]

Yours sincerely
Geo. Orwell,

1. According to Orwell's letter to Julian Symons, 16 June 1949 (see *3647*), Ruth Fischer was to visit Orwell on 17 June. On 4 July, she wrote to thank him for sending her a copy of *Burmese Days*, which had arrived 'several days ago.' She appreciated his having given her several hours of his time but feared it was 'somewhat too tiring' for him.
2. See Orwell's letter to Moore, 20 July 1949, *3662*, and its *n. 1* for *Possev*'s letter of 16 July 1949. For *Possev*, see *3496, n. 1*.
3. Whites were anti-revolutionary; thus the White Army, which opposed the Red Army in the Russian civil war, 1917–21. 'White' also alludes to the royalist forces of the Vendée, which opposed the French Revolution and whose badge was a white lily.

3660. To David Astor

15 July 1949   Handwritten

Cranham Lodge,
Cranham,
Gloucester.

Dear David,
It was very thoughtful & kind of you to send me that Oxford marmalade, which I am so fond of. I never seem able to get it myself. I trust all goes well with you. There's no news here except that we've had some rain at last.

Yours
George

3661. To David Astor

18 July 1949   Handwritten

Cranham Lodge,
Cranham,
Gloucester.

Dear David,
I wonder how you are getting on. I was slightly dismayed to hear from Charoux[1] that you were getting along "as well as can be expected." I had thought the operation you were having was something very minor.[2] Let me know how you are when you get a chance to write.

Richard went back to Jura yesterday, as he is going to the village school at Ardlussa for the Xmas term & it starts at the end of this month. He enjoyed himself at the kindergarten & had a good report, I am glad to say, though I didn't notice that he learned very much.

I have been so-so, up & down. I get what they call flare-ups, ie. periods with high temperatures & so on, but on the whole I am better I think. I have got Morland, the specialist, coming to see me again next week. When I am well & about again, some time next year perhaps, I intend getting married again. I suppose everyone will be horrified, but it seems to me a good idea. Apart from other considerations, I think I should stay alive longer if I were married & had someone to look after me. It is to Sonia Brownell, the sub-editor of "Horizon," I can't remember whether you know her, but you probably do.

It is evident that I shall be under medical care for a long time yet, & I shan't even be able to get out of bed until I stop being feverish. Later on I might move to a sanatorium nearer London, & Morland may have some ideas about that, but at present I don't think I could face a journey.

147

Have you read "The Naked & the Dead"?[3] It's awfully good, the best war book of the last war yet.

Write when you can.

Yours
George

1. Charoux was a picture-framer and restorer recommended to Orwell by Astor to repair one of Orwell's pictures damaged in the move to Jura; see *3490*.
2. Astor's operation was relatively minor but very painful.
3. *The Naked and the Dead* by Norman Mailer (1948). Orwell lists it as having been read in August 1949.

3662. To Leonard Moore

    20 July 1949   Typewritten

Cranham Lodge,
Cranham,
Gloucester.

Dear Moore,

Recently some Russian DPs who run a Russian-language paper called POSSEV in Frankfurt sent me a file of the papers containing a Russian translation of "Animal Farm."[1] They want to issue it as a booklet and say, what is no doubt true, that it would be quite easy for them to get a few thousand copies of it through the Iron Curtain, I suppose via Berlin and Vienna. Of course I am willing enough for them to do this, but it will cost money, ie. for the printing and binding. They want 2000 deutsch marks, which represents about £155. This is more than I can pay out of my own pocket, but I wouldn't mind contributing something. As a start it occurs to me that the American army magazine "Der Monat" must owe me something.[2] There was their serialisation of "A.F.," but in addition there was a mix-up about a previous article (reprinted from "Commentary") which I believe has never been paid for. They sent some kind of official form which I thought was the cheque, and I believe I incorrectly told Melvyn Lasky, the editor, that I had received the cheque.[3] Their bank account would show whether the money has actually been paid over. But any way, if "Der Monat" do owe me something which they have not yet paid to you, it would be a convenient way of financing the Russian translation of "A.F." if they paid the money over in marks which wouldn't have to leave Germany. I can't remember whether there is anything else of mine appearing in Germany, but at any rate, could you let me know how many marks you think I could realise there? In the case of our carrying through any transaction of this kind, naturally you will draw your commission as usual.[4]

I am also trying to pull a wire at the Foreign Office to see if they will subscribe a bit. I'm afraid it's not likely. They will throw millions down the drain on useless radio propaganda,[5] but not finance books.

If all this comes to anything we shall have to make sure that these "Possev" people are O.K. and not just working a swindle. Their notepaper etc. looks all right, and I know the translation must be a good one as it was made by Gleb Struve whom I know well. They gave me as the address of their English agent Mr Lew Rahr, 18 Downs Road, Beckenham, Kent, and suggested he should come and see me. I don't think I want to see him at this stage, but do you think you could write to him, say tentatively that we are trying to get this scheme financed and see from his answer whether he seems O.K. I have also asked a friend who is I think in Frankfurt[6] to contact the "Possev" people.

Yours sincerely
Eric Blair

1. Vladimir Gorachek, who described himself as the 'Authorized DP-Publisher' of *Possev* (the sub-title of which was 'Social and Political Review in Russian Language. Germany'), wrote to Orwell on 16 July 1949 with proposals for publishing *Animal Farm* in Russian for distribution gratis among Russian readers behind the Iron Curtain. It was planned to distribute the books through Berlin and Vienna 'and other channels further E[a]st.' The cost of distribution was to be met from selling 1,000 to 1,200 copies in West Germany. There was still a need for 2,000 DM (or £155), and Orwell was asked if he could collect such a sum. It was also suggested that Orwell's earnings in Deutschmarks might be conveniently applied to this purpose. Calculations showing how the costs were arrived at were enclosed but have not been traced. Gorachek apologised for the fact that an earlier letter (that sending the file of papers) had been written in Russian: 'We thought that such a perfect understanding of all events occurred° in our country after the revolution and of the very substance of the regime now established there could not be acquired without the knowledge of Russian language.' See also *3496, n. 1*, especially for *Possev*.
2. Annotated in Moore's office: 'Paid £50 for A.F.'
3. See letter to Moore, 12 March 1949, *3571*.
4. Annotated in Moore's office: '£250 owing from U.S. Army 1984.' This was money due for the serialisation of *Nineteen Eighty-Four* in *Der Monat*, November 1949 to March 1950; see *3663* and *3695*.
5. The reference to 'useless radio propaganda' may have been prompted by Orwell's experience of broadcasting to India and the Far East during the war for the BBC. The Foreign Office (the Information Research Department) made no contribution; see *3590A* and *3590B* (in Appendix 14) and *3695*.
6. Ruth Fischer; see *3659* and *3603, n. 1*.

3663. To Leonard Moore
21 July 1949[1]   Handwritten

Cranham Lodge,
Cranham,
Gloucester.

Dear Moore,

Thank you for two letters date the 19th, with various enclosures.

I enclose the photostats of the McGill article. I don't object to its being published in this form *provided it is stated that this is an abridgement* (they needn't of course say why it has been abridged.)[2] Could you please make this clear to Harcourt Brace?

I am of course very pleased about the NBC broadcast of "1984", & the serialisation in "Der Monat." This last would at need solve the difficulty I wrote to you about yesterday, of getting some marks to pay for the Russian translation of "Animal Farm." Of course I'm not going to pay this myself if I can help it, but I haven't very great hopes of the government coming to my aid. Meanwhile, could you ask the editor of "Der Monat" to hold over the necessary sum (2000 deutsch° marks) in case we want to disburse it in Germany. The editor, Melvyn Lasky, would be sympathetic to this idea & can no doubt make the necessary arrangements. As I said before, your commission will not be affected by this.

Yours sincerely
Eric Blair

P.S. On the photostats I made two more slight alterations on pp. 130, 134.[3]

1. This letter was dated 20.9.49 but is date-stamped as having been received in Moore's office on 22 July 1949. The month is clearly incorrect, and Orwell seems also to have misdated the day of the month, since he refers to 'the difficulty I wrote to you about yesterday.'
2. 'The Art of Donald McGill,' *Horizon*, September 1941 (see *850*), was published in an abridged form in *A Writer's Reader*, edited by P. W. Souers and others (New York, 1950).
3. On page 130, the editors had omitted Orwell's description of a card captioned 'They didn't believe her' (some seven lines). The original text says that it is doubtful whether any paper would print 'a joke' of this kind. This makes no sense with the description of the joke cut out, so Orwell altered the text to read 'would print jokes of this kind.' Page 134 is a list of questions on the essay and an assignment; it is not now possible to know what alteration Orwell made.

3664. Ruth Graves to Orwell

23 July 1949

Among the letters in Orwell's possession at his death was one from Ruth Graves, whom he had known twenty years earlier, in Paris. She had, she said, read all his essays but had been prompted to write on hearing *Animal Farm* described on the radio by Christopher Morley as the 'outstanding political satire of all time.' She remembered the evenings in Paris when they took turns preparing Saturday dinner 'and the hours of good talk later in my little cluttered place in Rue de la Grande Chaumière.' She was looking forward to reading *Nineteen Eighty-Four*. Having heard that Orwell was seriously ill, she offered to get him anything that medical science could offer and, if there were difficulties in importing things into England, she would herself act as courier. She recalled Orwell's aunt, Mrs. Adam, and another friend in common, Edith Morgan. Although she had returned to America in October 1939, she still did not feel at home. In conclusion, she said she treasured her memories of her time in Paris, 'including the very good talk of a tall young man in a wide-brimmed pair of Breton hats,° who was as kind as he was keen of mind.'

3665. To Leonard Moore
24 July 1949   Typewritten

> Cranham Lodge,
> Cranham,
> Gloucester.

Dear Moore,
Thank you for your letter of the 22nd.
   With regard [to] this business of a Russian translation of "Animal Farm." I should like to hear some more about the negotiations you have in hand, because there are two points that arise. In the first place, if you do fix up something with these people, it might save some time for them to use the translation already published in "Possev." I know it must be a good translation, as it is by Gleb Struve, whom I know well. Secondly, the important thing is that if any Russian translation is published in book form, copies should get into the Soviet Zone. It is not much use publishing it for refugees only, especially as I don't imagine there are many Russian-speakers among the Soviet D.Ps. The Possev people say they would know how to get quite a few copies across, and no doubt they do know, as they are actually in Germany. It is this that I am prepared to subsidise, up to a reasonable amount, for of course copies distributed in that manner wouldn't be paid for. Could you find out whether the people you are dealing with have any ideas about distributing the book in the Soviet Zone? Possibly they and the Possev people might co-operate in this. Of course some discretion is needed. I don't want the story of the Ukrainian translation repeated.[1]

> Yours sincerely
> Eric Blair

1. The American Military Government had seized copies and given them to the Soviet authorities. According to Secker & Warburg 5,000 copies were handed over (Willison). Orwell had heard that the number was 1,500, according to his letter to Arthur Koestler, 20 September 1947; see *3275.*

3666. To Jack Common
27 July 1949   Handwritten

> Cranham Lodge,
> Cranham,
> Gloucester.

Dear Jack,[1]
Herewith cheque for £50—reply if when° you can, no hurry.
   This place is a sanatorium. I've been under treatment for TB for the better part of 2 years, all of this year here, & half of last year in a hospital near Glasgow. Of course I've had it coming to me all my life. The only real

treatment, it seems, is rest, so I've got to do damn-all, including not trying to work for a long time, possibly as long as a year or two, though I trust it won't be quite as bad as that. It's an awful bore, but I am obeying orders, as I do want to stay alive at least 10 years, I've got such a lot of work to do besides Richard to look after.

Richard is now 5 & very big & strong. He's been spending the summer here, so that I can see him every week, & going to kindergarten school, but shortly he's going back home so that he can start attending the village school in the winter term. We've lived since 1946 in Jura, but I'm afraid I personally shall only be able to spend the summers there from now on, because it's too remote & inconvenient in the winter for a semi-invalid. I suppose Richard, too, will have to start going to school on the mainland before long, as you can imagine what a village school in the Hebrides is like. So I shall probably have to have some sort of establishment in London or Edinburgh or somewhere—however, I can't make plans till I know when I shall be on my feet again.

I'm glad to hear you've been so philoprogenitive, or at any rate, progenitive. I haven't ever remarried, though I sometimes think I would if I could get some of my health back.[2] Richard Rees spends part of each year with us in Jura as he is sort of partner with the chap who farms the croft our house is on. Otherwise he is more & more wrapped up in painting.[3]

All the best
Eric

1. Jack Common (1903–1968), author of novels based on his working-class upbringing, met Orwell frequently in the 1930s when he was working on *The Adelphi* (hence the reference to Richard Rees). He had taken over the cottage in Wallington when Orwell and his wife were in North Africa, 1938–39. See *95* and *295, n. 1*. Common's recollections of Orwell, found among his papers, are printed in *Orwell Remembered*, 139–43. The amount lent Common remained unpaid at Orwell's death; see *3726*.
2. Orwell suggests, contrary to what happened, that he might remarry if his health improved; see *3693*.
3. One of Rees's paintings of Barnhill is held in the Orwell Archive.

3667. To Gleb Struve

27 July 1949[1]   Typewritten

Cranham Lodge,
Cranham,
Gloucester.

Dear Struve,
Thanks so much for your letter. The Possev people sent me a complete file of the paper containing your translation of Animal Farm. They now want to bring out an edition in book form to distribute in the Soviet Zone. This of course would cost money as the copies so distributed wouldn't be paid for. Meanwhile my agent tells me that he was already in negotiation with some other Russian publisher to bring out a translation. It's all in the air as yet, but

I've suggested that if he does close with this other publisher your translation should be used, as it would save time and I know the translation would be a good one. In that case I suppose you would be paid something—but, as I say, nothing is settled yet. But at any rate I shall see to it that the book appears in book form, even if I have to finance it myself.

Warburg decided against publishing "We." I then wrote and told Gollancz about it and suggested that he should get hold of the MS, which he said he would—with what result, I don't know.

I am so glad you are going to enlarge your book on Soviet literature.[2] I shall take care to get hold of the new edition when it comes out. I am somewhat better, but I am afraid I am likely to be in bed and unable to work for a long time to come. Rest seems to be the only cure.[3]

Yours sincerely
Geo. Orwell

1. Dated originally 27.8.49 but the '8' was overwritten (by Orwell?) with a seven.
2. Struve wrote several books on Russian literature. Orwell learned of the origins of We from Struve's Twenty-five Years of Soviet Russian Literature; see 2841. The revision to which Orwell refers is Soviet Literature 1917–1950. The Russian translation of Nineteen Eighty-Four was made by Struve and M. Kriger.
3. Of Orwell's letters that have survived, this is probably the last one he typed himself; see 3683, n. 1.

3668. To Leonard Moore

28 July 1949   Handwritten

Cranham Lodge,
Cranham,
Gloucester.

Dear Moore,
Herewith the Japanese contracts,[1] duly signed.

I have heard from the F.O.,[2] who of course won't help to finance the Russian translation of A.F. However, they confirm that the "Possev" people are well known to them & are reliable. So we can use them for helping to distribute a Russian edition of A.F., or at need for printing it. Would you arrange with Laskey° of "Der Monat" to hold over some marks in case they are needed for this purpose. And could you keep in touch with "Possev's" English representative (Mr. Lahr,[3] is it not?) & keep him posted as to what is happening. It is important to get this book distributed in one way or another, even if it does cost a bit.

Yours sincerely
Eric Blair

1. The Japanese translation of Animal Farm had been published on 15 May 1949, so this almost certainly refers to the translation of Nineteen Eighty-Four. It was published as 1984 on 20 April 1950 by Bungei Shunjū Shinsha, Tokyo, and translated, with a preface, by Yoshida, Kenichi, and Tatsukuchi Naotarō (Willison).

153

2. The Foreign Office.
3. The representative was Lew Rahr; see *3662*.

3669. To Sir Richard Rees

28 July 1949   Handwritten

> Cranham Lodge,
> Cranham,
> Gloucester.

Dear Richard,

Thanks so much for your letter, with cutting. Do you think you could get your Mr Roberts to make me a bookcase, same dimensions as yours but 5' feet° wide, if he can manage it. If, as I assume, it will be of white wood, I suppose it should be stained or painted, I don't much mind which, except that if painted I think off-white is the best colour. I'd be much obliged if you could get him to do this & send it up to Barnhill.

I think you'll find at Barnhill one novel by Charles Williams, called "The Place of the Lion"[1] or something like that (published by Gollancz.) He's quite unreadable, one of those writers who just go on & on & have no idea of selecting. I think Eliot's approval of him must be purely sectarian (Anglo-Catholic). It wouldn't surprise me to learn that Eliot approves of C. S. Lewis as well. The more I see the more I doubt whether people ever really make aesthetic judgements at all. Everything is judged on political grounds which are then given an aesthetic disguise. When, for instance, Eliot can't see anything good in Shelley or anything bad in Kipling, the real underlying reason must be that the one is a radical & the other a conservative, of sorts. Yet evidently one does have aesthetic reactions, especially as a lot of art & even literature is politically neutral, & also certain unmistakeable standards do exist, e.g. Homer is better than Edgar Wallace. Perhaps the way we should put it is: the more one is aware of political bias the more one can be independent of it, & the more one claims to be impartial the more one is biassed.

"1984" has had good reviews in the USA, such as I have seen of them, but of course also some very shame-making publicity. You'll be glad to hear "Animal Farm" has been translated into Russian at last, in a D.P. paper in Frankfurt. I'm trying to arrange for it to be done in book form.

> Yours
> Eric[2]

1. Charles Williams (1886–1945), poet, novelist, dramatist, and writer on theological subjects. He worked for the Oxford University Press for much of his life. Orwell remembered the title correctly; the novel was published in London in 1931 and in New York in 1951.
2. 'Eric,' not 'G' as in the transcription published in *Encounter*, January 1962, 65.

3670. To Leonard Moore

30 July 1949   Handwritten

> Cranham Lodge,
> Cranham,
> Gloucester.

Dear Moore,

Many thanks for your letters & the book.

Naturally I have no objection to a stage version of "1984" being made, though I should not have thought it lent itself to stage treatment. On the other hand I should think it ought to be filmable.[1] Of course I must see the script when & if it is made, but could you make it clear that I can't collaborate or help in any way, in case that should arise.

With ref. to the translation of A.F. All my books are at Barnhill. I think at present I have copies of translations in about 10 languages, but in some case° I may have only one copy. My friend Richard Rees is going up to Barnhill in about a week, & I'll get him to look & see what translations I have. Where I have only one copy I can't let it go. But in some cases you may have a spare copy.

> Yours sincerely
> Eric Blair

1. Orwell's instinct was correct. The proposed adaptation came to nothing, but *Nineteen Eighty-Four* was filmed in 1956 and in 1984. For the adapter of the first film, see *3671*. The BBC made a television adaptation in 1954.

3671. To Leonard Moore

4 August 1949   Handwritten

> Cranham Lodge,
> Cranham,
> Gloucester.

Dear Moore,

Thanks for your letter. I am writing to Mr Sheldon.[1] I shouldn't have thought it was worth his coming to see me, as I can't really help with the adaptation, but of course he can if he wants to. I don't know how these things are done, but I suppose you can fix it so that the adaptation, if finally accepted for the stage, is one that I approve. Or does one have to sell the thing outright?

Could you please deal with Knopf & tell them I can't write anything about that book.[2] I refuse to write blurbs in any case, but at present the state of my health is a quite sufficient excuse.

> Yours sincerely
> Eric Blair

1. Sidney Sheldon (1917–), screenwriter and best-selling novelist, won an Academy Award in 1947 for best original screenplay. His address is given in Orwell's address book as 1225 Westholme Avenue, Los Angeles 24, California, USA.
2. Unidentified.

3672. To Fredric Warburg

4 August 1949   Handwritten

Cranham Lodge,
Cranham,
Gloucester.

Dear Fred,
Thanks so much for your letter. I'm glad you had a good holiday. I am so-so—I have been rather poorly with a touch of pleurisy the last few days, but better on the whole. Richard is going back to Jura on the 15th, as the village school to which he is going next term will be re-opening about the end of the month. I have put him down for Westminster, but as he wouldn't in any case go there till 1957 it is a very tentative arrangement. I hope Michael[1] caught some fish even if there weren't any trout.

Love to all
George

1. Michael Kennard; see *3371*, *n. 3*. He had, presumably, been to stay at Barnhill again.

3673. McIntosh and Otis, Inc. to Dwight Macdonald

10 August 1949

Orwell's U.S. agents for publishing his work in journals wrote to Dwight Macdonald, editor of *Politics*, on 10 August to say that they had been instructed by Orwell to send him $3.00 for a subscription to *Politics* and $1.35 for a book. At Orwell's request, they asked for an invoice for outstanding money due for expenses incurred on his behalf.

3674. To Tosco Fyvel

11 August 1949   Handwritten

Cranham Lodge,
Cranham,
Gloucester.

Dear Tosco,
It was so awfully kind of you & Mary to send me those wonderful crystallised fruits, which must be very difficult to get hold of nowadays, in fact I hardly

156

knew such things still existed. I was very sorry indeed to put you all off last Sat. & I hope I did not throw your arrangements out too much by doing so. I had what they call a "flare-up," meaning a sudden burst of high temperatures etc. It doesn't usually last very long but it is very unpleasant & of course I am barely human while it is happening.

Richard is going back to Jura at the end of this week, as he is going to start attending the village school & the term starts at the end of this month. I think he has profited by going to the kindergarten though I can't discover very much in the way of booklearning that he has acquired. Tentatively I have put him down for Westminster, but he wouldn't be going there till 1957 & god knows what may have happened by that time.

I can't write any more, it's absurd but it tires me even to write a letter. Please give everyone my love & thanks so much again.

Yours
George

3675. To Leonard Moore

12 August 1949   Handwritten

Cranham Lodge,
Cranham,
Gloucester.

Dear Moore,

The Japanese contracts are herewith. I am sorry that on one of them, not noticing it was made out "Eric Blair" I started to initial it "G.O.", but I presume the crossing-out doesn't matter.

As to the translations of "A. F." I have more than one copy of the following:

German	Ukrainian
Portuguese	Polish
Danish	Persian.[1]
Dutch	

I also have copies of Italian, French, Swedish & Norwegian, but only 1 each. I think translations are also being made in Spanish, Japanese, Korean, modern Hebrew & several Indian languages, but I haven't seen copies & doubtless shan't in some cases. I think the Spanish one must have appeared as I saw a review[2] of it.

Possibly in some of the cases where I have only 1 copy you have a duplicate, or could get one?

I have written to the "Possev" people telling them to go ahead & that you are getting in touch with Mr Lew Rahr. I made further enquiries about them & evidently they are all right.

Yours sincerely
Eric Blair

157

1. Annotated in Moore's office: 'Already sent—Persian: Italian: French: Dutch: Swedish.' The languages German, Portuguese, Danish, Ukrainian, and Polish have been marked with a cross and in the margin is the annotation: 'send these when they arrive' and, on the opposite side of the letter, 'Sent 26.8.49.' At the head of the letter is an annotation: 'Told Stechert-Hafner on phone.' Stechert-Hafner was a New York publisher with a London office; it also ran a very big periodicals-ordering agency patronised by British universities in the 1940s and '50s.
2. Orwell originally wrote 'copy.'

3676. To Leonard Moore

16 August 1949   Handwritten

Cranham Lodge,
Cranham,
Gloucester.

Dear Moore,
Thank you for your letter. I enclose the Swiss contract duly signed.[1] I will see that copies of the other translations of "A.F." are sent on to you from Jura. I don't know what arrangements if any you have made about a French translation of "1984" but possibly the people whose letter I enclose[2] may be of use. At any rate perhaps you could give them an answer.

Yours sincerely
Eric Blair

1. Presumably for the German-language translation published by Diana Verlag, Zürich, not later than 17 May 1950 (the date of Christy & Moore's file copy). The German national bibliographies give this edition priority over that published in March 1950 by Ullstein Verlag, Vienna. The translation was that serialised in *Der Monat*, Berlin, November 1949 to March 1950, made by Kurt Wagenseil (Willison, who gives first serialisation date as February 1949).
2. Calmann-Levy, Paris, responsible for the French translation of Arthur Koestler's *Darkness at Noon*. See Koestler's letter to Orwell, *3681A* in Appendix 14.

3677. To Leonard Moore

22 August 1949   Handwritten

Cranham Lodge,
Cranham,
Gloucester.

Dear Moore,
I wonder if you could deal with the enclosed.[1] (Sheldon, you will notice, refers to "Mr John Smith,"[2] but I suppose this is your representative in the USA.) What Sheldon says in the passage I have marked is reasonable. It would put him in an intolerable position if I had to approve all last-minute changes suggested for producers etc. I would be satisfied if I could see & approve the first draft, provided that it is agreed that the general tendency of

the adaptation is not radically altered thereafter. I suppose this can be written into the contract somehow, & perhaps you could make clear to him that I am not just trying to make trouble. What I was afraid of was that the meaning of the book might be seriously deformed, more than is unavoidable in any stage adaptation of a novel, but from the letter he wrote me recently[3] I don't think he intends doing this.

Yours sincerely
Eric Blair

P.S. I haven't signed these contracts, but will do so if you think that they cover my position sufficiently as they stand.

1. 'the enclosed' has not been traced.
2. John Smith was a member of the staff of Orwell's agents, Christy & Moore.
3. This letter has not been traced.

3678. To Fredric Warburg

22 August 1949   Handwritten

Cranham Lodge,
Cranham,
Gloucester.

Dear Fred,
Could you please send one copy each of "Burmese Days" & "Coming Up for Air" to Sonia Brownell, care of "Horizon".

I have Morland coming to see me again this evening. On & off I have been feeling absolutely ghastly. It comes & goes, but I have periodical bouts of high temperatures etc. I will tell you what Morland says. Richard has just gone back to Jura & is going to the village school for the winter term. Beyond that I can't make plans for the moment. I have put him down for Westminster, but he wouldn't be going there till 1957, heavens° knows what may have happened by then. As I warned you I might do, I intend getting married again (to Sonia) when I am once again in the land of the living, if I ever am. I suppose everyone will be horrified, but apart from other considerations I really think I should stay alive longer if I were married.

I have sketched out the book of essays I would like to publish next year, but I want it to include two long new essays, on Joseph Conrad and George Gissing, & of course I can't touch those till I am definitively better.

Love to all
George

An extract of Warburg's reply on 23 August, made in his office, states: 'As regards the rest of your letter, I am sending a copy of BURMESE DAYS and COMING UP FOR AIR to Sonia, as requested. As for the book of essays, if it is necessary to wait for new essays by yourself on Conrad and Gissing it hardly seems likely that the book can be published in 1950. Whether the book could be published without these essays, you know better than I, but it would be a good idea, when things are a little easier with you, if you would let me have a list of essays already complete and ready for inclusion in the volume—perhaps with the number of words in each contribution.'

3679. To Fredric Warburg

24 August 1949   Handwritten

Cranham Lodge,
Cranham,
Gloucester.

Dear Fred,

Thanks so much for your letter & good wishes. I arranged with Moreland° to come to his London hospital for a month or two, but haven't fixed a date yet—I suppose in 2–3 weeks. I don't know if there is really any other treatment they can try on me, but both he & the people here seem to think that a change would do me good.

As to the proposed book of essays. Apart from those on Conrad and Gissing, which I intend to be long essays, perhaps 15,000 words the two combined, I propose reprinting the following:

"Lear, Tolstoy & the Fool" (Polemic 1947) about 6,000
"Politics vs. Literature" (on Swift) (Polemic 1947[1]) about 6,000
"Reflections on Gandhi" (Partisan Review 1949) about 3000
"Politics & the English Language" (Horizon 1946) about 6000
"Shooting an Elephant" (New Writing 1936) about 3000
"How the Poor Die" (Now 1945[2]) about 3000

It needs the two new essays, which in any case I want to write, when I can.

Love to all
George

Warburg replied on 26 August, thanking Orwell for the good news that he hoped soon to come to London; he hoped that Orwell would not be left 'to drag along down in Cranham any longer than need be.' He was sure the change would do Orwell good and things would improve when he was 'firmly established in University College Hospital.' Orwell's proposals for the book of essays would be borne in mind, 'but obviously there is nothing to be done until you have got well enough to tackle the last two contributions.'

1. Actually published in 1946.
2. Actually 1946.

3680. To David Astor

25 August 1949   Handwritten

Cranham Lodge,
Cranham,
Gloucester.

Dear David,
I feel so ghastly I can't write more than a scrawl to thank you for sending those two nice vases & the flowers. Some beautiful gladioli & scabius° arrived from Stroud, I suppose ordered by you. You shouldn't really, but it's nice having them.

I have these ghastly temps. every day, sometimes up to 103. Moreland° nevertheless thinks I am not doing badly & says he doesn't notice any deterioration in me between his two visits. He wants me to move to his own hospital, University College Hospital. It's doubtful whether there's any other treatment they can try on me, but he thinks, & the people here seem to agree, that a change might do me good. So I shall probably be moving there soon—don't know when, in two weeks perhaps.

I can't write more, I'm really quite shaky, as you can see from my handwriting perhaps.[1]

Yours
George

1. Orwell always seemed conscious that his handwriting might deteriorate when he was ill, but it is as firm and clear as ever in the original of this letter.

3681. Catherine Karot to Orwell

25 August 1949

Among Orwell's papers is a letter from Catherine Karot in Paris; she had heard that Orwell was soon leaving Cranham and, assuming his health was improving, suggested he recuperate in a small village in Haute-Savoie, France, near Chamonix, Assy sur Pasq. This, she said, had an excellent climate, a sanatorium, and small chalets which could be rented inexpensively and one was independent of the sanatorium. She offered to send Orwell a prospectus. In a postscript she asked him what he thought of 'l'affaire Toulaëff,' which she had evidently had sent to him to read. He was asked not to return it to Francesca Wilson[1] (who had left London) but to her, in Paris. Did not Orwell, she asked, think it ought to be translated into English.

1. Francesca Mary Wilson (1888–1981), best known for *In the Margins of Chaos: Recollections of Relief Work in and between Three Wars*, with a foreword by J. L. Hammond (1944). She wrote, for Penguin Books, *Aftermath: France, Germany, Austria, Yugoslavia* (1945) and *1946* (1947), and compiled *Strange Island: Britain through Foreign Eyes 1350–1940* (1955).

3681A. Arthur Koestler to Orwell, 26 August 1949: see Appendix 14

3682. Allan Dowling to Orwell

27 August 1949

Allan Dowling had helped finance *Partisan Review* and was on its editorial board. He wrote from Monaco to advise Orwell that he was sending him a cheque; it was the first *Partisan Review* Annual Award. He had hoped to come to England before returning to New York in order to hand it to him personally, but would not now be able to do that. If Orwell wished the award to be given in any other manner, 'for tax reasons or any other.' that could be arranged. This award to Orwell 'lifts the magazine above the level of a coterie,' he said, which, in his view, had always been 'the most serious charge leveled against it.'

3683. To Leonard Moore

30 August 1949   Typewritten[1]

Cranham Lodge,
Cranham,
Gloucester.

Dear Moore,
I am leaving here for a London hospital on 3rd September, and my address as from then will be, The Private Wing, University College Hospital Gower Street, W.C.1.[2]

I enclose three copies of the Telegu translation of ANIMAL FARM. You could, perhaps, send one copy to those people in America. There is, of course, no question of our receiving any money for a translation of this type.

William Empson[3] in China has asked for a copy of 1984. I think it might be wise to get two copies sent, one from London and one from New York. He already seems uncertain as to whether his letters are being opened, so could you ask both publishers *not* to enclose the usual card saying "Compliments of the Author", as this might just conceivably be embarassing° to him.

When I am in London we can perhaps get this business of company formation sewn up, but I don't think I shall be equal to long interviews or to anything more than signing the necessary documents. Meanwhile I seem to be running short of money. If there are any sums you are holding over until the company is formed you could, perhaps, pay something into my account. I think, incidentally, the *New Yorker* and Miss Otis both have some money of mine. I dare say those sums would do. At any rate I could do with a couple of hundred to go on with.

Did that lost essay on George Gissing ever turn up?[4]

I don't know whether you have fixed anything about a French translation of 1984, but if nobody else bites,[5] Arthur Koestler tells me that Calmann-Levy, whose previous letter I sent to you,[6] are very enterprising and sold 400,000 copies of DARKNESS AT NOON.

Yours sincerely,
[Signed] Geo. Orwell
George Orwell

P.S. Empson's address is: 11, Tung Kao Fang, Near Peking National University, Peiping 9, China.

1. Two letters from Orwell were typewritten on 30 August, but it is unlikely that he typed them. The layout and style are different from his. They give the date in the form '30th August, 1949,' whereas he customarily used only figures and without a final full-point. Orwell always indented the salutation up to about half the width of the page. These letters have the salutation flush with the left-hand margin. See also *3667, n. 3* and *3695*.
2. An annotation in the margin indicates that this was noted by Moore's office.
3. Although in different sections of the BBC's Eastern Service, Orwell and Empson had worked together from time to time, for example in the production of 'Voice, 2,' 8 September 1942; see *1464*. For Empson, see *2568, n. 9*.
4. Annotated in Moore's office: 'Have reminded Critic Press twice, but no reply.' The typescript was not recovered until 1959; see *3406*.
5. 'writes' was first typed for 'bites' at the end of one line and crossed through in ink; 'bites' was then typed at the beginning of the next line.
6. Sent on 16 August 1949; see *3676* and *3681A*. Annotated at the foot of the letter, in Moore's office: 'Gallimard,' the publisher who would bring out the French translation, 30 June 1950.

3684. To Sir Richard Rees

30 August 1949   Typewritten

Cranham Lodge,
Cranham,
Gloucester.

Dear Richard,
I am removing to a London hospital on September 3rd, and my address will be: Private Wing, University College Hospital, Gower Street, London, W.C.1. This is Morland's own hospital and the idea is that I shall go there probably for about two months. I don't think you need fear my having too many visitors—in fact it may be easier to keep them off in London where people don't have to come for the whole day.
Of course its° perfectly O.K. about the old Austin. Anything you can get for her should go towards the jeep. As to the motor boat it seems to me that it would be a good idea to leave her in the boat-yard at Ardrishaig for the winter unless they need her at Barnhill. I suppose you can do that with boats like leaving a car in a garage, and then next year it would be in good order when we picked it up.
I am going to send on the remaining books I have here. Could you be kind enough to see that the magazines etc., go in the right place. There are various bundles of papers which I have asked Avril to put in my desk upstairs.
I hope the harvest is going O.K. Avril told me she had started, or was starting another pig. If nothing has been decided yet you might suggest to Avril to think seriously about a sow which I am very in favour of, and would willingly pay the initial costs of. The only difficulty is about getting her to a hog once a year. I suppose one would buy a gravid sow in the Autumn to litter about March, but one would have to make very sure that she really was in pig the first time.

Do make Bill go to the dentist. It is nonsense to put it off when they can come across in the boat and go to Lochgilphead. He was already having trouble with that tooth when I came away in January, and at the last moment refused to go to Glasgow.

Love to all,[1]
Eric

1. Although this and the letter to Moore of the same date are the last extant letters typed over Orwell's signature, they were almost certainly not typed by him. See *3683, n. 1*.

3684A. To Arthur Koestler, 1 September 1949: see Appendix 14

3685. For Freedom in Spain

Tribune, 2 September 1949

A committee for the help and protection of Spanish democrats has been founded on the initiative of the "Fédération Espagnole des Déportés et Internés Politiques". The sole object of this committee is to help the victims of an historical injustice, which is perpetuated through the complicity or silence of those who have the possibility to end it.

The men who compose this committee feel that they have the duty to limit, as far as is possible, the effects of this injustice. Being unable as yet, to re-establish freedom in Spain, they want, at least, to preserve Spanish lives in order to assure the future of this freedom. This is not a political question, but one of the solidarity of free men. The committee calls on these free men, whatever their viewpoint may be, to join in, so that an international force may be created which will help to preserve as much as possible of that Spain in exile or in the prisons, which is, for us, the real Spain.[1]

Albert CAMUS, J. P. SARTRE, André GIDE, François MAURIAC,
Rémy ROURE, René CHAR, Ignacio SILONE, Carlo LEVI,
Georges ALTMAN, Claude BOUET,[2] André BRETON, George ORWELL,
Pablo CASALS, Fernand DEHOUSSE, Jef LAST,
Henriette ROLAND-HOLST,[3] C. SCHILT,[4] and L. de BROUCKERE.

51, Rue de Boulainvilliers, Paris, XVI.[5]

1. This statement also appeared in French on 27 October 1949, in the newspaper *Le Populaire de Paris*, with nine additional signatories, including Stephen Spender. Brouckère should have a grave accent.
2. Claude Bourdet in *Le Populaire de Paris*.
3. Roland-Holts in *Le Populaire de Paris* (incorrect).
4. M. Schilt in *Le Populaire de Paris*.
5. This was the address of the offices of FEDIP, the Fédération espagnole des déportés et internés politiques. The French text invited support and gifts.

3686. To David Astor

5 September 1949   Handwritten

U.C.H.[1]

Dear David,

Thanks ever so for sending those beautiful crysanths° & the box of peaches that actually met me on my arrival here. I feel ghastly & can't write much, but we had a wonderful journey down yesterday in the most ritzy ambulance you can imagine. This beastly fever never seems to go away but is better some days than others, & I really quite enjoyed the drive down.[2]

What a bastard that doctor[3] must have been. It seems that there's a regular tradition of with holding° anaesthetics & analgesics & that it is particularly bad in England. I know Americans are often astonished by the tortures people are made to go through here.

I hope you're feeling better & that soon you will be able to meet Sonia. Morland says I mustn't see people much, but here in London it's easier for people to just look in for half an hour, which they hardly can at Cranham. Sonia lives only a few minutes away from here. She thinks we might as well get married while I am still an invalid, because it would give her a better status to look after me especially if, eg., I went somewhere abroad after leaving here. It's an idea, but I think I should have to feel a little less ghastly than at present before I could even face a registrar for 10 minutes. I am much encouraged by none of my friends or relatives seeming to disapprove of my remarrying, in spite of this disease. I had had an uneasy feeling that "they" would converge from all directions & stop me, but it hasn't happened.[4] Morland, the doctor, is very much in favour of it.

I remember visiting you when you had the sinus but I didn't know it was this hospital. It seems very comfortable & easy-going here. Can't write more.

Yours
George

1. University College Hospital, one of London's major teaching hospitals.
2. Orwell was transferred from the sanatorium at Cranham to U.C.H. on 3 September 1949 (Crick, 571).
3. The doctor attending Astor; see *3661, n. 2.*
4. See Koestler's letter of congratulation, *3695A* in Appendix 14.

3687. University College Hospital Routine

The following is the entry Orwell made in his last Literary Notebook about the daily routine at the hospital. It also gives a description of his room.[1]

Daily Routine at University College Hospital (Private Wing)

7–7.30 am. Temperature taken. Routine question: "How did you sleep?"
7.30–8. Blanket bath. Bed made. Shaving water. "Back" rubbed.

8.45. (about)   Breakfast. Newspaper arrives.
9.30. (about)   Wing sister arrives with mail.
10.   Temperature taken.
10.30.   (at present) my bed is "tipped". Ward maid comes to sweep room.
11. (about)   Orderly arrives to dust.
12.30.   Bed taken down.
12.45. pm.   Lunch.
2.   Temperature taken
2.30.   Bed "tipped."
3.30.   Bed taken down.
3.45.   Tea.
5.   Temperature taken.
5.30. (about)   am washed as far as waist. "Back" rubbed.
6.45.   Dinner.
10.   Temperature taken; a drink of some sort.
10.30. (about)   Bed "tipped" & light put out shortly after.

No fixed hour for visits of doctor. No routine daily visit.

Room has: washbasin, cupboard, bedside locker, bed table, chest of drawers, wardrobe, 2 mirrors, wireless (knobs beside bed), electric fire, radiator, armchair & 1 other chair, bedside lamp & 2 other lamps, telephone. Fees 15 guineas a week, plus extra fee for doctor, but apparently including special medicines. Does not include telephone or wireless. (Charge for wireless 3/6 a week.)

1. Orwell's room, Number 65 in the Private Wing, is illustrated in Thompson's *Orwell's London*, 102; the Private Wing is shown on 101.

3688. C. E. M. Joad to Orwell

8 September 1949

C. E. M. Joad (1891–1953), head of the Department of Psychology and Philosophy, Birkbeck College, University of London, and a prominent figure in the popular BBC radio programme 'The Brains Trust,' wrote to Orwell from Paris to congratulate him on *Nineteen Eighty-Four*. It was, he said, 'terrifying and very subtle.' It had, he continued, upset him more than anything he had read since *Brave New World* in the early 1930s. He had tried in an amateurish way to write that sort of thing himself in his book *Decadence* (London, 1948; New York, 1949; see *3372, n. 2*), 'but it was only for one chapter.' Joad said he could not understand why, after Winston's confession, didn't they 'let the rats eat his face?' It was surely not a mark of O'Brien's affection that he had been spared.

No reply has been traced, but on 16 September Joad wrote a brief note to Orwell to say how very sorry he was to learn that he was ill, and sent best wishes for his rapid recovery.

Joad broadcast for Orwell in the BBC's Eastern Service; see *1469*. For Orwell on 'The Brains Trust,' see *2490*.

3689. To Leonard Moore

[7] September 1949[1]   Handwritten postcard

U. C. Hospital

Dear Moore,

I think I forgot to say in my last letter that I have no objection to the 25¢ edition[2] of "1984" provided that Harcourt Brace think it a good idea.

Yours sincerely
Eric Blair

1. Postmarked 8 September, a Thursday; Orwell simply dated the letter 'Wed.'
2. Paperback edition published by the New American Library for twenty-five cents. Warburg states it sold 1,210,000 copies between 1950 and 1957; 2,052,000 between 1958 and 1965; and 5,571,000 from 1965 to 1969 (*All Authors Are Equal*, 115). The first printing was issued in July 1950. The cover was garish and the title given as *1984*. A third printing of November 1950 was marked as Canadian.

3690. Franz Borkenau to Orwell

14 September 1949

Borkenau had been reminded of Orwell by a visit from Ruth Fischer (see *3603*, *n. 1*). She told him he was ill. At about the same time he had managed to obtain a copy of *Nineteen Eighty-Four* for a few days. Whereas he thought Orwell in *Animal Farm* had handled the Aesopian fable brilliantly, he queried the sociological interpretation, particularly what he took to be the 'return to capitalism.' *Nineteen Eighty-Four* was immeasurably more powerful: 'I felt that behind every detail there was a bulk of correct analysis and at the same time such an evocation of horror that it makes one doubt the value of living at this period. The problem for all of us is of course that the horrors of the totalitarian regime are such that they defy both scholarly analysis and artistic creation. . . . Yours is the only book which seems to me to convey fully what a totalitarian regime means in terms of the individuals living under it.'

The bearer of the letter was 'an unusually alert and serious young German university student,' Miss Edith Schmidt, a Sudeten refugee. Borkenau felt that if Orwell was well enough, he would enjoy meeting her, especially for what she could tell of the totalitarian regime in Czechoslovakia.

3691. To Philip Rahv

17 September 1949   Handwritten

> Room 65
> Private Wing
> University College Hospital
> Gower Street
> London WC.1

Dear Philip Rahv,
About two weeks ago Alan° Dowling wrote to me from France,[1] informing me that I had been selected for P.R's literary award & forwarding a cheque for 1000 dollars, signed by you. I wrote to him then, & would have written to you earlier if it were not that I have been so beastly ill that writing letters is still something of an effort. I really do feel very deeply honoured, & only wish I could repay you a little by sometimes writing for P.R. again. As it is I am quite incapable of doing any work, even if the doctors would allow me to, & in fact I have hardly set pen to paper since last December. This beastly disease (T.B.) works very slowly, & though I am supposed to be getting on fairly well it is possible that I shall be incapacitated for the better part of another year.

I must also thank you for your very long & kind review of "1984" in P.R. I expect you will forgive me for not writing a better letter. At any rate, very many thanks again.[2]

> Yours sincerely
> George Orwell

1. 27 August 1949; see *3682* for a summary of Allan Dowling's letter.
2. William Phillips, Rahv's co-editor, wrote on 28 September saying he hoped the cheque for the award had arrived and that Orwell was feeling better. He wondered if Orwell could review Arthur Schlesinger, Jr.'s *The Vital Center*, which had just been published. For Schlesinger's letter on *Nineteen Eighty-Four*, see *3643*.

3692. To Sir Richard Rees

17 September 1949   Handwritten

> Room 65
> Private Wing
> U.C. Hospital
> Gower St.   WC.1

Dear Richard,
Thanks so much for seeing about the boat & for re-arranging my books. I suppose by the way they'll send on the bill for the bookcases to you—if so, forward it to me, won't you.°

It's all right about the literary executorship. You & Sonia wouldn't quarrel

168

about anything. Some time I'll have to make another will, & then I'll regularise it.

I am getting on quite well & have felt distinctly better since being here. The only new treatment they have done to me is to make me lie all night & part of the day with my feet higher than my head. Sonia comes & sees me for an hour every day & otherwise I am allowed one visitor for 20 minutes. Sonia thinks that when I am a little better it would be a good idea for us to get married while I am still in hospital, which would make it easier for her to accompany me wherever I have to go afterwards. Someone, I think Fred Warburg, told the press about this & there was some rather nasty publicity.[1]

I'm afraid I haven't a copy of Trilling's review of "1984."[2] The only copy I had was among some press cuttings I sent up to Barnhill. I've just had back that picture that went to be restored.[3] He's made a beautiful job of it, & it is almost like a new picture. Apparently they can lift a picture right off & stick it onto a new piece of canvas. I have another old picture which I thought was past praying for, as the canvas is sort of moth eaten, but perhaps this chap could do something with it. He also put the picture in a quite nice new frame, & only charged 12 guineas for the whole job.

Things seem to be going O.K. at Barnhill. R. evidently hasn't started going to school yet, as Mrs Angus[4] was ill. He sent me a "letter" which showed that he knows at any rate 12 letters of the alphabet. Unless I am out of England by then, I will have him down for the Xmas holidays, & then he can start getting to know Sonia a bit better. I do not think there need be any complications about his upbringing. We have agreed that if I should die in the near future, even if I were already married, Avril shall be his guardian. Beyond that I can't make plans at present.

Yours
Eric

1. For publicity in *The Star* and *Daily Mail*, see *3693*.
2. The review by Lionel Trilling (1905–1975) appeared in *The New Yorker*, 18 June 1949. He praised the 'intensity and passion' of this 'momentous book' (Crick, 564).
3. David Astor had recommended a Mr. Charoux, a picture-restorer; see *3490*. Rees, as a painter, might be expected to be particularly interested in what Charoux had been able to do.
4. Presumably the teacher on Jura.

3693. Announcement of Orwell's Engagement to Sonia Brownell

The Star and *Daily Mail*, 17 September 1949

'Star Man's Diary' for 17 September reported:

A specialist's verdict will decide whether fair-haired Miss Sonia Brownell,[1] engaged to novelist George Orwell, will have a bedside wedding in hospital.

Mr Orwell who has been ill for two years is now in University College Hospital.

He is expected to be there for at least another three months but Miss Brownell told me today: "If the doctors say he is well enough we shall be married within the next few weeks."

Blue-eyed 30-year-old Miss Brownell, assistant editor of the literary magazine "Horizon," became engaged to Mr Orwell some two months ago but their engagement was not disclosed until today.

They have known each other for five years.

In her Bedford-square office today Miss Brownell, in a white lace-work blouse and grey flannel skirt, was wearing her Italian engagement ring of ornamental design with rubies, diamonds and an emerald.

She chose it herself because she thought it pretty.

Her hope is that her husband-to-be—his real name is Eric Blair—will be well enough to leave hospital so that they can go abroad early in the new year.

The *Daily Mail* story referred to Orwell as the 'brilliant satirical novelist whose last book, "Nineteen Eighty-Four," was highly praised by British critics and banned in Eire.'

A brief review of Orwell's life was given, and the statement by an American critic that *Nineteen Eighty-Four* was as 'timely as the label on a bottle of poison.' It was said, the story added, that the book had sold 750,000 copies.

The *Mail* reported that Orwell's bride-to-be, who 'met the 45-year-old novelist about five years ago,' had said they would marry when he was well enough to leave hospital; friends, however, believed 'there may be a hospital wedding soon, as he is not expected to recover for some time.' In addition to describing Sonia Brownell as assistant editor of *Horizon*, the story added: 'In 1936 she was the only survivor of a canoeing tragedy at Neuchatel, Switzerland. A girl and two youths were drowned. Miss Brownell swam ashore.'

The death of Eileen, Orwell's wife, in 1945 was mentioned and that their adopted son, Richard, lived with Orwell and his sister 'in their remote home on Jura Island.'

1. Sonia Mary Brownell was born on 25 August 1918 at Ranchi, Bihar, India, the daughter of Beatrice and Charles Neville Brownell, a freight broker in Calcutta. Ranchi is some 230 miles from Motihari, Orwell's birthplace, and—a closer link—Orwell's father served as an officer in World War I in the 51st India Labour Company, the 'Ranchi Company.'

Ian Angus writes: 'Sonia's father died of a heart attack a few months after she was born. In 1920, her mother married Edgar Geoffrey Dixon, a successful chartered accountant, who became an alcoholic. The family returned to England in 1927, but from 1931 Sonia's mother was forced to bring up her children unaided. In 1933 she bought and ran a private guest-house at 29/31 Tregunter Road, South Kensington, London. Sonia had an older sister, Bay, and a younger half-brother, Michael. Michael Dixon served in the army during the war, then studied medicine and became a consultant psychiatrist. Sonia greatly admired him and was strongly attached to him. She was born a Roman Catholic and was educated at the Convent of the Sacred Heart, Roehampton, and then went to Neuchâtel, Switzerland, where she perfected her French. After the fatal boating accident referred to by the *Daily Mail*, Sonia was distraught and was brought home by her mother. She took a secretarial course, becoming a fast and accurate typist, and in 1938 worked for Professor Eugene Vinaver on his edition of Malory's *Morte d'Arthur*. About this time she acquired the soubriquet, "The Euston Road Venus", as a result of her sitting for portraits for the Euston Road school of painters, then recently opened by William Coldstream, Victor Pasmore, and Claude Rogers. In the late summer of 1939, Coldstream painted her portrait and he and Sonia were lovers for the next two years. Through Coldstream she became friends with Cyril Connolly and Stephen Spender, co-editors of *Horizon*, and its financial backer, Peter Watson. She contributed a short article on "The Euston Road Group" to *Horizon*, May 1941. That year she worked for a few months as John Lehmann's secretary on *New Writing*, before starting war work in the shipping section of the Ministry of War Transport. She joined *Horizon* in 1945 as editorial secretary. Until it ceased publication, a decision taken in October 1949, she was in effect Connolly's working partner when Connolly (then sole editor) and Watson were absent. For a good account of her association with *Horizon*, see Michael Shelden, *Friends of Promise: Cyril Connolly and the World of "Horizon"* (1989).'

It is not certain precisely when Orwell and Sonia met (see Crick, *449*). In her accounts to Ian Angus the date varied, but the setting was always the same: a dinner given by Cyril Connolly at which Diana Witherby was one of those present and it was held shortly after Sonia had read *Burmese Days* in a copy Diana Witherby had borrowed from a public library. On one occasion Sonia told Ian Angus that she had known Orwell for eight years and had met Eileen and liked her, this accords with William Coldstream's statement to him in 1982 that Coldstream was sure that Sonia had met Orwell by 1941. Thus she met Orwell through the *Horizon* group in the early 1940s, but came to know him well only after Eileen's death in 1945. She had a very brief affair with Orwell in late 1945 and later a prolonged and unhappy affair with the French philosopher Maurice Merleau-Ponty.

For an accurate account of Sonia Orwell's life, see Hilary Spurling, *The Girl from the Fiction Department*, 2002

3694. To Julian Symons

[c. 19 September 1949][1]   Handwritten

> Room 65
> Private Wing
> U.C. Hospital
> Gower St.   WC.1

Dear Julian,

Thanks so much for your letter. I've been here a fortnight & was meaning to write or ring up, but till a day or two ago I was not supposed to have visitors. I was really ghastly ill for some months. Now I'm slightly better, but it's a very slow business & lord knows when I shall be able to get up or work again. As you saw from those nasty pars in the newspapers, Sonia & I contemplated getting married while I am still an invalid, among other things because it would make it easier for her to come & look after me wherever I go after leaving here.

Do come & see me some time. I'm supposed to have only 1 visitor a day for 20 minutes (of course it stretches itself out a bit) so[2] it's not worth making a special expedition. Perhaps you could ring up & arrange a day that suited you. If you ring up the hospital they'll put you through to my room. In the evening, any time after 5, is the best time to come. I'd like very much to see the biography of your brother if you'll bring it along.[3]

I can sympathise with you trying to write in a flat with a small child.[4] If you don't find a suitable place in Essex you might try Hertfordshire. It's a very attractive county in places, very agricultural. I should say Gollancz is talking rot about having to produce your novel under another name. I suppose it might be true if you were Peter Cheyney or James Hadley Chase.[5]

Richard was staying near me for the summer (at the anarchist colony at Whiteway) & has now gone back to Jura. He is attending the village school, which I think he will enjoy. He is getting enormous & is extremely active, though still a bit backward in talking. He loves farming & boats, & even last year he helped with the farm work to the extent of being quite useful. I shan't influence him if I can help it, but if he does grow up to be a farmer, a sailor, a civil engineer or something useful of that description I should be very pleased.[6]

What do you think of devaluation?[7] I imagine they had to do it sooner or later, but I wasn't expecting it till after the election.

Please remember me to your wife.

Yours
George

1. The date is based on the facts that Orwell had been in the hospital for a fortnight (second sentence) and devaluation took place on 18 September 1949; see *n. 7*.
2. Orwell first wrote 'but,' crossed it through and continued on the line with 'so.'
3. *A. J. A. Symons: His Life and Speculations* (1950). Symons brought a proof copy, and Orwell listed that in his reading for September 1949.
4. See Orwell's letter to Michael Meyer, 12 March 1949, *3570*, in which he refers to Thomas Hood's poem on the distractions caused to a writer by a small child.
5. Writing to Rees on 4 February 1949, Orwell said he had read one of Cheyney's novels; see *3540, n. 8*. James Hadley Chase wrote *No Orchids for Miss Blandish*, discussed by Orwell in 'Raffles and Miss Blandish'; see *2538* and *2538, n. 3*.
6. Richard Blair did take up farming.
7. On 18 September 1949, Sir Stafford Cripps, the Chancellor of the Exchequer, announced a devaluation of the pound sterling against the dollar of 30.5%. The shock was the greater, not because of the degree of the devaluation (£1 = $2.80), but because Cripps had denied on nine occasions in 1949 that the pound would be devalued. A general election was held on 23 February 1950. At the dissolution of Parliament, discounting seven vacant seats and the Speaker, Labour had an overall majority of 136; after the 1950 election, discounting the Speaker, its majority was six. Devaluation was only one element leading to this decline in the Labour Party's fortunes.

3695. To Melvin Lasky

21 September 1949   Copy (from typed original?)[1]

The Private Wing,
University College Hospital,
Gower Street,
London, W.C.1

Dear Mr. Lasky,

Many thanks for your letter of the 13th.[2] I think Leonard Moore hasn't made my meaning quite clear about the marks. The position is this. A Russian D.P. paper in Limburg called POSSEV has recently serialised ANIMAL FARM in a Russian translation, and are now printing an edition in book form. I have to finance this myself, and in order to avoid the fuss about changing pounds into marks I told Moore to ask you to pay the required amount directly to the POSSEV people in marks and the balance to me in pounds. So far as I remember you agreed to pay me £250.0.0. for the serialisation of "1984", and I believe the printing of ANIMAL FARM is to cost the equivalent of £155.0.0[3] This will therefore leave a considerable balance which I do not want changed into marks. I imagine that you already know the POSSEV people. I know that they are politically OK and the translation is probably a good one. So this venture obviously deserves encouragement.[4]

Thank you very much for sending me DER MONAT each month. The above address will find me for a month or two.

Yours sincerely,
[Signed] Geo. Orwell
George Orwell

1. The letter was probably typewritten by someone (Sonia Brownell?) for Orwell. If the copy is accurate, the address is not in his style—it is fully punctuated; and his name is typed under his signature. It also has Lasky's address in full at the foot of the letter; that was not Orwell's practice. The address is 'Office of Military Government for Germany (U.S.) / Information Control Division, APO 742, Berlin. Germany.' See 3683, n. 1.
2. Lasky's letter (on Der Monat headed paper) explains that Deutschmarks will be paid into a non-convertible, blocked account. He says that he has seen Ruth Fischer, who gave him news of Orwell, and that Animal Farm was still being talked about. He proposed using the translator responsible for Animal Farm for the serialisation in Der Monat of Nineteen Eighty-Four. (Der Monat had re-worked the translation by N. O. Scarpi, the pen-name of Fritz Bondy, who had made the German translation for the Swiss edition, Farm der Tiere (1946); the name of the translator for the version published by Der Monat is not known.) Lasky said that the version in Der Monat had been widely praised by German literary critics, 'which was gratifying because the Swiss edition is quite poor.' He had bought half a dozen copies of Nineteen Eighty-Four and 'set up a small circulating-library.' One copy had just gone to Ortega y Gasset (1883–1955), the Spanish philosopher and writer, who was in Berlin giving several lectures. He said everyone was amused that 'Ingsoc' was preferred to something like 'Am-Way,' American Way of Life, 'which might have been more descriptive.'
3. See letter to Leonard Moore, 20 July 1949, 3662.
4. The edition was published by Possev at an unknown date in 1950. There were two simultaneous issues, one on ordinary paper of 1,000 copies for Western Europe, and one, probably also of 1,000 copies, on thin paper for distribution behind the Iron Curtain (Willison).

3695A. Arthur Koestler to Orwell, 24 September 1949: see Appendix 14

3696. Condensed Book Version of *Nineteen Eighty-Four*

October 1949

The Reader's Digest condensed book for October 1949 was *Nineteen Eighty-Four*. It was preceded by this statement:

'Most reviewers of this powerful book have given particular attention to Part One, the story of everyday life in the "Oceania" of *1984*. Due to space limitations, only this first section (of the three which comprise the novel) is here condensed. Readers generally have found the remainder of the book of equal interest.'

Part One, pages 3 to 107 of *CW*, IX, comprises about 33,000 words; the *Reader's Digest* condensation runs to approximately 12,500 words.

3696A. To Mọna Harrofs McElfresh, 2 October 1949: see Appendix 14

3697. To Leonard Moore
2 October 1949   Handwritten

Room 65
Private Wing
U.C. Hospital

Dear Moore,
Please settle this,[1] would you?

Yours sincerely
Eric Blair

1. Unidentified.

3698. John Dos Passos to Orwell
8 October 1949

John Dos Passos (1896–1970), American author, best known for his innovative trilogy *U.S.A.* (1937) and social historian, wrote to Orwell to tell him '1984 is a wonderful job. I read it with such cold shivers as I haven't had since as a child I read Swift about the Yahoos. Had nightmares all the next week about two way television. I certainly have to hand it to you. . . . Please accept my most sincere plaudits and bouquets.' He hoped Orwell's health was improving and asked him to let him know if he came to the United States.

3699. Dwight Macdonald to Orwell
10 October 1949

At the head of a circular announcing that the publication of *Politics* was to be suspended for reasons 'partly financial, partly personal,' Macdonald wrote, 'Dear George — Congratulations on your marriage — *and* on "1984"! Dwight.'

3700. To Leonard Moore
11 October 1949   Handwritten

Room 65
Private Wing
U. C. Hospital

Dear Moore,
I wonder if you could deal with the enclosed letters.[1]

I am still very weak & ill, but I think better on the whole. I am getting married very unobtrusively this week. It will probably be a long time before I can get out of bed, but if I am equal to travelling by the end of the year the doctor suggests that I should spend the worst of the winter abroad, probably in France. They will no doubt allow me some currency,[2] but probably not enough & I want to wangle some more francs if possible. If I have any francs due to me (eg. from the French translation of "1984"), do you think you could arrange for them to remain in France, after deducting your commission.

Yours sincerely
Eric Blair

1. Unidentified.
2. Owing to the financial crisis in Britain, the amount of foreign currency that could be bought was extremely limited.

3701. To Roger Senhouse

12 October 1949   Handwritten

U. C. Hospital

Dear Roger,
Here is that elucidation of a passage in "1984" that the Danish translator wanted.

Yours
George

The passage on p. 170 (English edition)[1] beginning "Items one comma five comma" could be rendered in standard English as follows:—

Items one, five & seven are fully approved. The suggestion contained in item six is ridiculous in the extreme & almost amounts to political deviation. Cancel it. Do not proceed with construction (ie. building) before getting fuller estimates of the cost of machinery & other overhead expenses. This is the end of the message.

1. The passage will be found on 176, lines 6–10, of *CW*, IX. Senhouse transcribed this, not quite accurately, into his own copy of *Nineteen Eighty-Four* (now in the Orwell Archive). This passage was originally written in Standard English in the draft of *Nineteen Eighty-Four* (see Facsimile, folio 168, 141) and in Newspeak (verso of folio 168, 143). It is not referred to in Paul Monrad's Danish translation (Steen Hasselbalchs Forlag, published 21 January 1950). See also *CW*, IX, 341.

3702. Marriage to Sonia Brownell

13 October 1949

George Orwell and Sonia Brownell were married in University College Hospital on 13 October 1949. David Astor had obtained a special licence for the marriage from the Archbishop of Canterbury (necessary if the place where the marriage was to be performed was not licensed for that purpose by the Church of England). The hospital chaplain, the Reverend W. H. Braine, officiated. As 'The Londoner's Diary' reported (*Evening Standard*, 14 October 1949), 'Only intimate friends were present. Mr. David Astor, editor of the Observer, gave away the bride.' The witnesses were David Astor and Janetta Kee (née Woolley see *3212, n. 2*), a friend of Sonia's and wife of Robert Kee (1919–), author and broadcaster. Orwell was forty-six and Sonia thirty-one. After the ceremony, David Astor was host to Sonia and a few friends at a wedding luncheon at the Ritz.

3703. John Braithwaite to Orwell
20 October 1949

Among Orwell's papers at his death was a letter signed 'Jock.' This referred to times the writer and Orwell—as Eric Blair—shared in the Spanish civil war; it has been identified by Stafford Cottman (who was in the same section of the POUM) as being from John, or Jock, Braithwaite (or Branthwaite; see *378* and *399*). Braithwaite was one of the signatories to Orwell's letter of 24 September 1937 to *The New Leader* refuting F. A. Frankfort's allegations in the *Daily Worker* (see *399*). He also attended the Independent Labour Party's summer school at Letchworth in 1937, at which Orwell, Cottman, and Douglas Moyle (see *3564*) were present (see Crick, 347–48).

Evelyn Anderson, who worked on *Tribune*, had evidently told Orwell that the writer had called at the hospital, but because of the restrictions on visiting, he had been unable to see Orwell. Orwell wrote to him and this letter is a reply. Braithwaite tells of what he had done since leaving Spain. For a time he had stayed with Robert Smillie, the Scottish miners' leader and grandfather of an ILP colleague, Bob Smillie, who had died in 1937 of appendicitis in a Spanish gaol to which he had been sent without cause (see *Homage to Catalonia*, CW, VI, 171, where Orwell describes how he was allowed to die 'like a neglected animal'). Braithwaite had joined the army when war broke out, was at Dunkirk, and then became a member of the Parachute Regiment. He was temporarily in hospital as 'mentally unsound,' but recovered and was discharged with a pension. He improved so much that he told the authorities; they ignored this and actually increased his pension: 'telling the truth proved insanity.' He was now married and worked as a setter in a factory, which he disliked. He thought Russia was choosing Hitler's methods: 'bloodless victories, to start, and then he [they] will, like Hitler overstep the mark, and off we go again.' He often thought of 'that horrible little Russian in Spain. I think we saw enough of their methods.' He asked if there was anything he could do for Orwell, anything that might help. He would be glad of a chance to visit him but didn't want to stand in the way of 'more important visitors.'

For another of Orwell's visitors from his past, see *3590B, n. 15* in Appendix 14.

3704. Aldous Huxley to Orwell
21 October 1949

Orwell had arranged for a copy of *Nineteen Eighty-Four* to be sent to Aldous
Huxley, whose failing eyesight meant it took him a long time to read it. He now
wrote a long letter, in which he said 'how fine and how profoundly important
the book is', and discussed his philosophy of the ultimate revolution, in a
manner not dissimilar to his introduction to *Brave New World Revisited* (1954).
The world's rulers would discover that 'infant conditioning and narco-hypnosis
are more efficient, as instruments of government, than clubs and prisons, and
that the lust for power can be just as completely satisfied by suggesting people
into loving their servitude as by flogging and kicking them into obedience . . .
the nightmare of Nineteen Eighty-Four is destined to modulate into the
nightmare of a world having more resemblances to that which I imagined in
Brave New World. The change will be brought about as a result of a felt need for
increased efficiency.'

3705. To Tosco Fyvel
25 October 1949   Handwritten

Room 65
Private Wing
U. C. Hospital

Dear Tosco,
I have to write to you instead of Mary, because I can't remember or find your
Amersham address, so have to send this to Tribune. It was so awfully kind of
you both to send me that beautiful box of crystallised fruits, & then on top of
that for Mary to send me those packets of tea. Sonia asks me to thank you
from her too.
   I am getting on pretty well, but they evidently won't let me out of bed for a
long time to come. However, I enjoy my food very much more than I did,
which makes a great difference. I hope you will come & see me again some
time, & please convey my thanks to Mary. I tried to ring up Evelyn[1] the other
day to ask her to come & see me, but she was out.

Yours
George

1. Evelyn Anderson had been deputy editor of *Tribune*, and a close friend of Orwell's, at the time
he wanted to give up the literary editorship of *Tribune* in 1945. Between them they arranged
for Tosco Fyvel to take over (*George Orwell: A Personal Memoir*, by Tosco Fyvel, 139). For
Evelyn Anderson, see *2638, n. 8*, for a biographical note.

3706. William Barrett to Orwell

4 November 1949

William Barrett, an associate editor of *Partisan Review*, wrote to ask Orwell if he could participate in a symposium, the deadline for which was 3 January 1950. Since contributors were limited to 1,500 words, it was hoped this would be within his strength.

3707. To Leonard Moore

4 November 1949   Typewritten for Orwell

Private Patients Wing,
University College Hospital,
Gower Street,   W.C.1.

Dear Moore,
Many thanks for your letter of the 2nd. I am glad that the Danish paper would like to serialise "The English People".[1] As for the photographs in "The Road to Wigan Pier", I have no objection to their being reproduced, but I am not certain about the copyright. Gollanz° put them into the book without consulting me when I was in Spain.[2] I have an idea that they have been reproduced at some time before. At any rate Gollanz° would know about the copyright.

I don't know who is doing the translation of "1984" for Gallimard, but could you please ask them to make sure that the translator consults me if he is in difficulty, and particularly that he lets me know what he is going to do about the appendix. Obviously this couldn't be translated into French so it would be necessary to put some kind of explanatory footnote early in the book.[3]

Yours sincerely,
[Signed] Eric Blair
Eric Blair

1. *The English People* had been translated into Danish by Paul Monrad and published on 11 February 1948 by Steen Hasselbalchs Forlag.
2. For an account of how these photographs came to be included, see the General Introduction to this edition, *CW*, I, xxxii–v.
3. The letter was annotated in Moore's office: 'Wrote Gallimard 8.11.49'; the last sentence of the letter has been marked off by quotation marks.

3708. To Robert Giroux

17 November 1949   Typewritten for Orwell

> Private Patients Wing,
> University College Hospital,
> Gower Street,
> London, W.C.1.

Dear Mr. Giroux,

Thank you very much for your letter and the poster for ANIMAL FARM. It was nice to know the sales of 1984 have been so good.

> Best wishes,
> Yours sincerely,
> [Signed] Geo. Orwell
> George Orwell

3709. G. van der B. Lambley to Orwell

21 November 1949

Mr. Lambley wrote from Epping Garden Village, Vasco, Cape Province, South Africa. It was in reply to a letter Orwell had written him from the hospital, but it is not clear whether this was Cranham or University College Hospital; the latter is the more likely. From his letter, it would seem that Lambley had first written to Orwell to offer 'a word of praise' for *Nineteen Eighty-Four*. He had also planned to say what an impact Orwell's other books had had on him and his wife, in particular *The Road to Wigan Pier*, *Coming Up for Air*, and *Homage to Catalonia*. He had not been in England since 1932, and had not fought in Spain, though he now wishes he had gone. In those days, he said, it was possible to do useful political activity in South Africa. It is almost certain this correspondence was initiated simply by someone wishing to praise and thank Orwell for his writings.

3710. Proposed Cuts to *Nineteen Eighty-Four*

On 22 November 1949, Leonard Moore sent Orwell a request from his representative in Buenos Aires for certain cuts to be made in *Nineteen Eighty-Four*. Editorial Kraft had completed the translation but feared that, published as it stood, it would be banned. It wished to omit about 140 lines. The representative explained that, although there was no censorship in Argentina, books were seized by the police on moral grounds. There was no appeal, and the publisher and author suffered the resulting loss. The passages Kraft wished to cut were 'too realistic.' There was no intention of 'interfering with the ideas of the book,' it was simply that 'the Spanish language is cruder than the English.' *Nineteen Eighty-Four* had a 'basic philosophy . . . aimed directly against some of the most powerful movements of our time,' and it would be regrettable if those who found such ideas 'distasteful' could procure the book's withdrawal 'on some quite irrelevant point of morality.' The representative pointed out that ninety per cent of foreign publishers would have made such cuts without informing the author. This request arose, therefore, because Editorial Kraft was so conscientious.

The passages objected to are listed by page and line numbers from the first English edition. There has evidently been a one-line miscalculation for all but the first cut to be made on page 127. The passages to be cut are set out below. Where it seems intended, the ensuing part-line is included even though its line number is not mentioned.

[68/34–9 and 69/1–19:]   As soon as he touched her she seemed to wince and stiffen. To embrace her was like embracing a jointed wooden image. And what was strange was that even when she was clasping him against her he had the feeling that she was simultaneously pushing him away with all her strength. The rigidity of her muscles managed to convey that impression. She would lie there with shut eyes, neither resisting nor co-operating, but *submitting*. It was extraordinarily embarrassing, and, after a while, horrible. But even then he could have borne living with her if it had been agreed that they should remain celibate. But curiously enough it was Katharine who refused this. They must, she said, produce a child if they could. So the performance continued to happen, once a week quite regularly, whenever it was not impossible. She used even to remind him of it in the morning, as something which had to be done that evening and which must not be forgotten. She had two names for it. One was "making a baby", and the other was "our duty to the Party": (yes, she had actually used that phrase). Quite soon he grew to have a feeling of positive dread when the appointed day came round. But luckily no child appeared, and in the end she agreed to give up trying, and soon afterwards they parted.

[126/22–39:]   Quickly, with an occasional crackle of twigs, they threaded their way back to the clearing. When they were once inside the ring of saplings she turned and faced him. They were both breathing fast, but the smile had re-appeared round the corners of her mouth. She stood looking at him for an instant, then felt at the zipper of her overalls. And, yes! it was almost as in his dream. Almost as swiftly as he had imagined it, she had torn her clothes off, and when she flung them aside it was with that same magnificent gesture by which a whole civilization seemed to be annihilated. Her body gleamed white in the sun. But for a moment he did not look at her body; his eyes were anchored by the freckled face with its faint, bold smile. He knelt down before her and took her hands in his.

"Have you done this before?"

"Of course. Hundreds of times—well, scores of times, anyway."

"With Party members?"

[127/1–6:]   "Yes, always with Party members."

"With members of the Inner Party?"

"Not with those swine, no. But there's plenty that *would* if they got half a chance. They're not so holy as they make out."

His heart leapt. Scores of times she had done it: he

[127/14:] weaken, to undermine! He pulled her down so that they were kneeling face to face.

[127/18:] "Yes, perfectly."
"I hate purity, I hate goodness! I don't want any

[127/23–5:] the bones."
"You like doing this? I don't mean simply me: I mean the thing in itself?"
"I adore it."

[127/29–38:] the simple undifferentiated desire: that was the force that would tear the Party to pieces. He pressed her down upon the grass, among the fallen bluebells. This time there was no difficulty. Presently the rising and falling of their breasts slowed to normal speed, and in a sort of pleasant helplessness they fell apart. The sun seemed to have grown hotter. They were both sleepy. He reached out for the discarded overalls and pulled them partly over her. Almost immediately they fell asleep and slept for about half an hour.
Winston woke first. He sat up and watched the

[128/1–17:] freckled face, still peacefully asleep, pillowed on the on the[1] palm of her hand. Except for her mouth, you could not call her beautiful. There was a line or two round the eyes, if you looked closely. The short dark hair was extraordinarily thick and soft. It occurred to him that he still did not know her surname or where she lived.
The young, strong body, now helpless in sleep, awoke in him a pitying, protecting feeling. But the mindless tenderness that he had felt under the hazel tree, while the thrush was singing, had not quite come back. He pulled the overalls aside and[2] studied her smooth white flank. In the old days, he thought, a man looked at a girl's body and saw that it was desirable, and that was the end of the story. But you could not have pure love or pure lust nowadays. No emotion was pure, because everything was mixed up with fear and hatred. Their embrace had been a battle, the

[128/24–6:] She became alert and business-like, put her clothes on, knotted the scarlet sash about her waist and began arranging the details of the journey home. It seemed

[129/18–20:] bloody? Give me a brush-down, would you. Have I got any twigs in my hair? Are you sure? Then good-bye, my love, good-bye!"

[134/6–18:] "I could have stood it if it hadn't been for one thing," he said. He told her about the frigid little ceremony that Katharine had forced him to go through on the same night every week. "She hated it, but nothing would make her stop doing it. She used to call it—but you'll never guess."
"Our duty to the Party," said Julia promptly.
"How did you know that?"
"I've been at school too, dear. Sex talks once a month for the over-sixteens. And in the Youth Movement. They rub it into you for years. I dare say it

works in a lot of cases. But of course you can never tell; people are such hypocrites."

[137/3–37:] "Then why are you sorry you didn't do it?"

"Only because I prefer a positive to a negative. In this game that we're playing, we can't win. Some kinds of failure are better than other kinds, that's all."

He felt her shoulders give a wriggle of dissent. She always contradicted him when he said anything of this kind. She would not accept it as a law of nature that the individual is always defeated. In a way she realized that she herself was doomed, that sooner or later the Thought Police would catch her and kill her, but with another part of her mind she believed that it was somehow possible to construct a secret world in which you could live as you chose. All you needed was luck and cunning and boldness. She did not understand that there was no such thing as happiness, that the only victory lay in the far future, long after you were dead, that from the moment of declaring war on the Party it was better to think of yourself as a corpse.

"We are the dead," he said.

"We're not dead yet," said Julia prosaically.

"Not physically. Six months, a year—five years, conceivably. I am afraid of death. You are young, so presumably you're more afraid of it than I am. Obviously we shall put it off as long as we can. But it makes very little difference. So long as human beings stay human, death and life are the same thing."

"Oh, rubbish! Which would you sooner sleep with, me or a skeleton? Don't you enjoy being alive? Don't you like feeling: This is me, this is my hand, this is my leg, I'm real, I'm solid, I'm alive! Don't you like *this*?"

She twisted herself round and pressed her bosom against him. He could feel her breasts, ripe yet firm, through her overalls. Her body seemed to be pouring some of its youth and vigour into his.

[140/25–7:] "To-morrow afternoon. I can't come."

"Why not?"

"Oh, the usual reason. It's started early this time."

1. The first edition duplicates 'on the'.
2. The first edition duplicates 'and'.

3711. Emilio Cecchi to Orwell

26 November 1949

The Italian journalist, Emilio Cecchi (see *3178, n. 1*), had visited Orwell several times in London and had reviewed several of his books in Italian journals. He now sent Orwell two articles, one about the Italian translation of *Burmese Days* (*Giorni in Birmania*, November 1948) and the other on the English original of *Nineteen Eighty-Four*. The former had appeared in 'a big weekly issuing in Milan' called *Europeo*, 30 January 1949; the latter in its issue for 27 November 1949. He concluded: 'Always I remember the talks I had with you in London two years ago.'

3712. Otto G. von Simson to Orwell

27 November 1949

Otto G. von Simson, managing editor of *Measure: A Critical Journal*, wrote on 27 November 1949 to say that he was greatly distressed to hear of Orwell's illness and that they would be as patient as Orwell might have to be. He was, presumably, expecting an article from Orwell. He said he intended to send Orwell the first number of *Measure* shortly.

3713. Nancy Parratt to Orwell

8 December 1949

Nancy Heather Parratt (1918–) joined the BBC on 13 June 1941 and worked initially in the North American Service. She became Orwell's secretary shortly after he was appointed and worked for him until mid-December 1942 (see *847*, *n. 3* and *1707, n. 1*). She then transferred to the Secretarial Training Reserve and on 15 March 1943 joined the Women's Royal Naval Service (WRNS); she was released in May 1946. She had served in the United States and later married the American Bill, of her letter. She wrote from Geneva. As she says in her letter, she had telephoned Orwell early in November, and he apparently asked her for a photograph, which she was now enclosing. This shows her rowing and is dated August 1949. Her description of life in the United States has been omitted here. Despite many inquiries, and the help of the Ministry of Defence and *Navy News*, it has not proved possible to trace her.

Dear George,
Just a line to send you the enclosed [photograph]. I wonder which will amuse you most. It must be a pretty strange sensation to be quoted so approvingly by men who, a couple of years ago, would have been on very different ground from you. I must say I at least find it strange to see you turning up so often in such respectable places! You presumably know that the Philadelphia Inquirer is serializing 1984 in its Sunday supplement starting 4 December. I wonder if it is the only one or if a whole gang of them are doing it.

Bill told me after I talked to you at the beginning of Nov. that he had sat next to a very pretty girl at a Hallow'en° party who told him she was reading a v. g. book—1984, but it was too strong meat for her. She couldn't remember the name of the author but Bill happened to know it, and she said—Yes, he just got married recently. So Bill knew you were married before I did! *And* he forgot to tell me. . . .

You see I have one of these new fangled ball point pens—I only just succumbed to the fashion last week—it seems quite good, only cost $1[1] but sometimes I get carried away by it and it writes funny things!

I hope you are getting on well and not finding the time goes too slowly. If you are allowed visitors being in London must have its compensations I should think. Next time we come we hope to stay at least twice as long. By that time I am sure you will be moved on to the country or to some mountains or other.

All the best
Nancy

I don't really talk American but it was such a lousy line I had to talk loudly & then I do sound a bit peculiar! If I can mutter I can usually get away with it!

1. Orwell had started to use a Biro early in 1946; see *2904*. Even by the end of 1947 he was paying £3 for a new one.

3714. To Harry Roskolenko

13 December 1949

SORRY AM SERIOUSLY ILL QUITE UNABLE TO INTERVIEW ANYBODY PLEASE FORGIVE ME

ORWELL

This telegram was addressed to Harry Roskolenko (1907–1980), c/o American Express, 11 rue Scribe, Paris. On 15 December, Sonia Orwell wrote to him from her flat at 18 Percy Street, W.1 (illustrated in Thompson, *Orwell's London*, 112). 'I am writing on behalf of my husband—Mr. George Orwell—to say that he is extremely ill at the moment and is unable to have visitors. He is very sorry not to be able to see you, and asked me to thank you for your letter. Yours sincerely, Sonia Orwell.'

3715. Desmond MacCarthy to Orwell

29 December 1949

The last letter among Orwell's papers from a well-wisher was from the critic and literary journalist Desmond MacCarthy (1877–1952; Kt., 1951; see *2973, n. 3*). He said that he had written two letters which he had torn up because they did not express what he really wished to say. Now that he was meeting Sonia for lunch, he was sending a greeting by her. He wanted Orwell to know that he thought he had made 'an indelible mark in English literature' and that in his judgement 'you are among the few memorable writers of your generation.' He concluded, 'We hardly know each other but I want you to know how much I respect you as a writer.'

3715A. 'The Best Novels of 1949', *The Observer*, 1 January 1950: see Vol. XX, Appendix 15

3716. Sonia Orwell to Yvonne Davet

6 January 1950   Handwritten

Yvonne Davet had known Orwell before the war and had corresponded with him about the translation of his books into French, of *Homage to Catalonia* in particular; see *389, n. 1*. In this letter, where accents were omitted, they have been added and one or two slight corrections have been made. The letter was written on *Horizon*-headed notepaper.

18, Percy Street.   London.   W.1.

Chère Madame Davet,

Je vous écris de la part de mon mari George Orwell qui est assez malade en ce moment et n'a donc pas la force d'écrire lui-même. Il me prie de lui excuser le long delai en répondant à votre lettre mais elle ne lui ai pas parvenue qu'il y a deux jours. Je crois que nos amis Alexei et John Russell[1] vous ont donné des nouvelles de mon mari—qu'il est toujours malade etc. Nous espérons bientôt pouvoir aller en Suisse, parcequ'il n'est vraiment pas possible de se guérir de cette maladie en Angleterre.

Mon mari m'a prié de vous remercier très vivement de toute la peine que vous avez pris pour son compte. Il espère pour vous autant que pour lui-même que le traduction de Homage à Catalonia paraîtra enfin.[2] Quant à votre article, il dit qu'il n'y a absolument rien d'intéressant à dire en sa vie, mais en tout cas cette lettre arrivera probablement beaucoup trop tard pour vous aider pour cela.

Il me prie de vous envoyer ses meilleurs vœux pour la nouvelle année, et espère vivement pouvoir venir vous voir quant il sera à Paris de nouveau.

Je vous prie de croire, chère Madame, a l'expression de mes sentiments les meilleurs.

Sonia Orwell

Translation

Dear Madame Davet,

I'm writing to you on behalf of my husband, George Orwell, who is rather ill at the moment and so isn't strong enough to write himself. He has asked me to apologise for his long delay in replying to your letter, but it only reached him two days ago.

I think you will have heard about my husband from our friends Alexei and John Russell[1]—he is still ill etc. We hope to go to Switzerland soon, as it really isn't possible to get over this disease in England.

My husband asks me to thank you most sincerely for all the trouble you have taken on his behalf. He hopes as much for your sake as for his own that the translation of *Homage to Catalonia* will finally appear. As for your article, he has absolutely nothing interesting to say about his life, but in any case this letter will probably arrive too late to be of much help.

He asks me to send you his best wishes for the New Year, and hopes very much to be able to come and see you when he is in Paris again.

Yours sincerely,
Sonia Orwell

1. John Russell (1919–; CBE, 1975), art critic, then married to Alexandrine Apponyi (dissolved 1950), worked at the Ministry of Information, 1941–43, and for Naval Intelligence, 1943–46. He was art critic of the *Sunday Times*, 1949–74, and later for the *New York Times*. In 1958, he was a witness at Sonia's marriage to Michael Pitt-Rivers.
2. Madame Davet's translation of *Homage to Catalonia* was published in 1955. It took in many of the changes Orwell had requested. See Textual Note to *CW*, VI, 251–53.

3717. Donald Brace to Fredric Warburg

13 January 1950

Fredric Warburg had cabled Harcourt, Brace and Company in order to seek their assistance in obtaining urgently a supply of Aureomycin with which to treat Orwell. Donald Brace made the arrangements. This is an extract from his letter to Warburg of 13 January.

Bob Giroux has shown me your letter to him of December 28th. I am very happy to hear that the aureomycin arrived so promptly. Out of my own experiences I have become something of a specialist in these drugs, and from the medical director of the pharmaceutical house which manufactures the aureomycin I was able to get the supply to send to you during the morning your cable arrived. I hope it has been benefiting Orwell. In cases where it is effective the results from it are almost miraculous.

3718. Orwell's Last Will

18 January 1950

Orwell signed his last will on 18 January 1950. It was witnessed by Sister J. Wood, SRN, of the University College Hospital nursing staff, and a solicitor, Norman H. Beach. For the will, see *3730*.

3719. U.S. Edition of *Coming Up for Air*

The first U.S. edition of *Coming Up for Air* was published by Harcourt, Brace and Company on 19 January 1950; 8,000 copies were printed and were sold at $3.00. At the same time, Harcourt, Brace reprinted 3,000 copies of *Down and Out in Paris and London*, at $2.75, and 3,000 copies of *Burmese Days*, at $3.00. These reprints were produced by photo-offset-litho from the English Uniform Edition (Willison).

3720. Orwell's Death

21 January 1950

George Orwell died of a massive haemorrhage of the lung in the early hours of Saturday, 21 January 1950. Death came very quickly. Although Sonia had been with him much of the preceding day, he died alone.

Orwell had asked in his will of 18 January 1950, made just before he had expected to fly to Switzerland for treatment, that he be 'buried (not cremated) according to the rites of the Church of England in the nearest convenient cemetery, and that there shall be placed over my grave a plain brown stone bearing the inscription, "Here lies Eric Arthur Blair born June 25th, 1903, died . . . ."'

A funeral service, arranged by Malcolm Muggeridge, took place on 26 January at Christ Church, Albany Street, London, NW1, conducted by the Reverend W. V. C. Rose. Later that day Orwell was buried in the churchyard of All Saints, Sutton Courtney, Berkshire, the arrangements having been made by David Astor.[1]

Fredric Warburg wrote to Robert Giroux on the 26th: 'This morning I attended the funeral service for George Orwell, one of the most melancholy occasions in my life, and feel not only that a good author and a good friend has passed from this list but that English literature has suffered an irreparable loss. I am sure that you and your colleagues feel in the same way.'

1. See Crick, 570–81; *Remembering Orwell*, 216–20; Thompson's *Orwell's London*, 104, for an illustration of Christ Church; Lewis, 113, for an illustration of Orwell's gravestone, inscribed as he had requested. On 22 January, *The Observer* published a tribute, 'George Orwell: A Life of Independence.' On the 27th, *Tribune* reprinted 'As I Please,' 68, 3 January 1947 (see *3146*), as 'The best tribute we think we can pay to his memory.'

3720A. Avril Dunn to David Astor

18 June 1950   Handwritten

Dear David,

Thank you very much for the copy of World Review, which naturally I read with great interest. However Fyvel's article[1] made me rather cross! It seems to me that this insistance° on Eric's unhappiness at school, & the unsuitability of his education, is a reflection on our parents, who, in actual fact, made every kind of sacrifice to give him what they thought & hoped would be a good education. If they had given him the sort of education they could afford, that is, elementary school followed by grammar school or third-rate Public school, I don't suppose the biographers would have liked that any better!

Sorry to visit you with this diatribe, I dare say I am being too touchy.

Yours
Avril.

1. T. R. Fyvel, 'A Writer's Life', *World Review*, June 1950. This issue is devoted to Orwell. As well as Fyvel's article, there is a short article on Orwell by Bertrand Russell; Orwell's then unpublished notebooks are printed; and there are re-evaluations of *Burmese Days* (Malcolm Muggeridge), *The Road to Wigan Pier* (John Beavan), *Homage to Catalonia* (Stephen Spender), *Animal Farm* (Tom Hopkinson), and *Nineteen Eighty-Four* (Herbert Read, with 'a footnote' by Aldous Huxley). One of Vernon Richards's portraits of Orwell is reproduced, full page. *World Review* had published an abridgement of 'The Principles of Newspeak' (as 'Language of Tomorrow') in May 1949. Orwell described it as 'a most stupid extract, abridged in such a way as to make nonsense of it' (see above, p. 102).

APPENDIX 1

3721. Unfinished Projects

In the last nine months of his life Orwell had in mind four major pieces of writing: long essays on Waugh and Conrad, and two novels, one short, set in Burma earlier in the century, and one long, set in 1945.

The fragment of the essay on Waugh that was typed and the notes for the whole essay are reproduced at *3585* and *3586*.

The essay on Conrad did not get beyond Orwell's list of reading in 1949 (see *3727*) and a few notes (see *3725*). Orwell's last formal opinion on Conrad is to be found in the answers he gave to a questionnaire about Conrad sent by the Polish journal *Wiadomości* (London) to several English writers, to which Orwell responded on 25 February 1949 (see *3553*).

After his visit to Orwell at Cranham Sanatorium on 15 June 1949, Fredric Warburg wrote a confidential report on Orwell's state of health and on other matters affecting him (see *3645*). In this he stated: 'I asked him about a new novel, and this is formulated in his mind—a nouvelle of 30,000 to 40,000 words—a novel of character rather than of ideas, with Burma as background. George was naturally as reticent as usual, but he did disclose that much.'

The words 'formulated in his mind' may, perhaps, indicate more than that, given Orwell's reticence. The outline and detailed layouts accord with 'formulated' but show that Orwell had got a little further than 'in his mind.' Warburg went on: 'The effort of turning ideas in his head into a rough draft on paper is, according to George and Dr. Morland, work which he cannot afford to attempt for a number of months. At best I doubt whether anything can or should be done by George until the autumn of this year.'

By the autumn, Orwell was worse and he was certainly in no state in May to be drafting his new novel. It seems probable, therefore, that the draft reproduced here (see *3723*) and the notes and the layouts (see *3722*) date from March–April 1949.

In his obituary of Orwell, published in *The Bookseller*, 11 February 1950, Warburg said that at his death Orwell had two novels 'simmering in his mind' as well as the long essay on Conrad. One of these novels is 'A Smoking-room Story'; the other, Orwell referred to in letters to Robert Giroux and Tosco Fyvel on 14 and 15 April 1949 respectively. He told Giroux that he had his next novel 'mapped out' but he would not touch it until he felt stronger; see *3597*. To Fyvel he said he had 'a novel dealing with 1945' in his head but 'I shouldn't touch it before 1950'; see *3598*. Nothing has survived in writing of this novel.

3722. Notes and Details of Layout for 'A Smoking Room Story'

Last Literary Notebook, 16–21; see 3725

The title is given as above. Words crossed through are placed within square brackets.

To be brought in:—

1   The bungalow at Nyaungbinzeik (miserable bachelor atmosphere.) The drip–drip on the roof. The grazing grounds beside the river. The game of football. Hamid's grocery store. The lined bed. Girls.

2   The plantation. The little club beside the lake. The flying beetles. [Ma Yi. The sandals.] The planters. Their girls. The one married member.

3   The Mission. The bare patch in the jungle (beaten earth all round). The raw looking red-brick tin roofed buildings. The smell of earth oil. The ducks' eggs fried in sessamum oil. The vegetable gardens (NB. what time of year?). The rasping taste of red wine.

4   B. J. His [sleeve] arm filling his sleeve. One short visit to France. The other brothers, the little scrubby-faced one & the enigmatic yellow one. No payment, only food, wine & cigars.

5   Getting there. The soft dust of the jungle path, the old pony neighing & breaking into a sort of slow gallop. The arrival. The boys marching out behind the brass band (some of the smaller ones almost invisible behind their instruments) & at once bursting deafeningly into "Rule Britannia." Followed up by "La Marseillaise" without even waiting to shake the spittle out of the trombones.

6   The ship. The lascar throwing the bulb into the sea. Return towards the bows. Screaming passengers. The contrast between the Burma, Ceylon & Soudan passengers. The charming little widow smacking Mr ——'s behind. C's feeling of dismay. The overheard remark: "That's the boy that's being sent home."

7   The smoking saloon. Its geography (pews.) The four Englishmen & the four American oil drillers. Thick fingers of the Americans stuffing sandwiches & pouring whisky between thick lips. Their implied belief that Man is naturally in a state of playing poker & drinking whisky. The four Englishmen. Mr McGillivray. The supercilious offensive I.C.S. man. The dreary elderly judge. The soldier with sticking out teeth. Competition in offensiveness between the two branches of the Anglo-Saxon race — the English worse.

8   Mr McGillivray's laugh. Snortings, then gorilla-like roarings. Echoes in it from Singapore & Shanghai, from 1886[1] & 1857.[2]

9   The young people, esp. from Colombo. Cockney imitations. "Laugh? I thought I should have died." (Some secretly uneasy about their own accents.)

10   Short skirts. Songs of the period (1927). "Bye bye, blackbird." "When it's night-time in Italy." "Avalon"?

11   C's home. The era of the 2nd class carriage.[3] High-crowned bowler hat?[4] To them, C's job a step up ("with a lot of natives under him, of course.")

12   School (Merchant Taylors?) Ought to have got into the XV. Dimly aware that his being left out was due to favouritism, but not the less ashamed of this. Lack of "grit", lack of "drive" (& so throughout life.)

13   Some snobbish remark by one of the other passengers about what they will do in London while on leave. C. unaware of their prompt scattering to poky suburban homes etc. Vision of his father meeting him at Victoria (?) in the high-crowned hat.

14   The deck passengers. The priest. Fleeting memory of another priest in similar garment.

15   Mr McG's anticlericalism. The type of the colonial (better word) millionaire. Though rich, not respectable.

16   First meeting with Brother J. Vast figure, cassock, fanshaped brown beard, small white topi stuck incongruously on back of head. Like many missionaries of long standing, features slightly Mongolian.

17   The brothers had built the Mission themselves, with the first contingent of boys. "We were living in tents for nearly two years."

18   Brother J's gift to C. "The Forsyte Saga?" (Better make it something older.) "Best novel ever written. All my knowledge of English society I owe to that book."

19   C's highbrow period. The Rangoon Library. "A box of books." "Simon Called Peter." "Daddy Longlegs." "Freckles." "A Girl of the Limberlost." (Get others.) Tried & failed with "The Constant Nymph" (Qy. what else?) ("Sinister Street?")[5]

20   Coming away from the Mission. Sudden turning aside at the road leading to the plantation. The planters offended if one was still sober at 11. Breakfast next morning. Ma Yi. The sandals. Vague feeling of something distasteful.

21   His feeling towards the Mission. Chief feeling, boredom. Shrinking from the austerity. But constant feeling that it had something his life lacked. Change of habits. Visits of girls ceased. Reading instead of gramophone. Vague classification of phenomena into two schools. On the one hand B. J., the Rangoon Library (also, curiously, Ma Yi.) On the other, the dust & squalor of his house, the worn gramophone records, the piled-up whisky bottles, the whores.

22   The planters talking about B. J. "What about women?" Suggested he had boys instead – prompt indignation of P. Like all men addicted to whoring, he professed to be revolted by homosexuality. (NB. Important question whether to make C. remember the incident of the picture only in [connection with this]? this context?)

23   The other ship of the same line passing. The exchange of greetings, & the shout "You're going the wrong way!" C's sudden dread of getting home. Sudden looming-up of the word "unemployment." (This would do to introduce a chapter.)

24   The incident with the picture. C's complete theological vagueness.

The flash of blue (deeper blue than in the picture) catching the corner of his eye. Make clear that owing to similarity of garments it is sometimes possible to mistake one sex for the other in the case of *young* Burmese. As he falls asleep, thought detaching itself: blue is an unusual colour, a man would not wear blue, it must have been a girl. From this no further inference drawn. It is just one of the innumerable unanswered & uninteresting questions in his mind, along with the question of why the picture was put on top of the almirah.[6]

25   C's general inefficiency. Emphasise that *sometimes* he can get along very well, lounge against a bar & shake the poker dice in just the right manner, dance elegantly, chip in when everybody bursts out singing, etc. At other times overwhelmed with gaucherie & shyness. Emphasise also that in his mind his inability to shine socially among people of his own age is indistinguishable from his lack of "grit" & consequent failure to get on. It is not what you do but what you *are*.

26   In his dim vague mind C. could not be sure whether he liked B. J. or not. But what he was aware of was there was something that B. J. had *not said*, something he would have had a right to say & which he did not say & could not be imagined as saying. It was this that was at the bottom of C.'s short-lived attempt to live more decently. (The mother & daughter episode.)

27   The passengers singing "Avalon." The moon on the sea. Glitter of a lascar's eyes. Mrs —— quite softened by the song & the soft night air. "Isn't it *beautiful!*" she said (referring to the song.)

28   The time when the servant brought two women who turned out to be a mother & a daughter, & C. & friend threw poker dice for first pick. The point was that the mother was the one they both wanted (the daughter aged only 12.) (Could use this to illustrate C's revulsion of feeling & vague perception that B.J. stands for something better.)

29   The occasion of C. telling the story. It must be round about cocktail time, at a moment when the two strata, the older men surrounding Mr McGillivray, & the younger set, are more or less in one group, one lot shading off into the other (the girls sitting on the companionway outside.) Conversation just general enough for C. to chip in without being snubbed by the older men.

30   Throwing the book out of the porthole. NB. to make C. *completely unconscious* of any symbolical significance in this.

General lines of lay-out.
The ship. Establish C.'s situation & general hopelessness.
The mission.
The ship. C's yearning to adjust himself.
Second thoughts on the Mission.
Uncertainty of C.'s position.
The opportunity. Finale.

More detailed lay-out.

The ship. The other passengers. C's inadequacy — 1 chap.
More about the ship, connecting up Mr McG., C's ambition to "get on," &
the younger passengers — 1 chap.
His memories — the bungalow at N'zeik.[7] — 1 (2?) chap.
First meeting with B. J. The Mission — 1 chap.
Return — the planters — his reactions to the Mission. — 1 chap.
Incidents on the ship. The other ship passing. C's line — 1 chap.
The incident with the picture — 1 chap.
C's highbrow period — 1 chap.
The ship — 1 chap.
The opportunity — 1 chap.
Finale — 1 chap.   11 chaps?

Chaps of v. variable length — perhaps 30–40000 altogether.

1. The ship. Deck passengers. Lascar at the stern, etc. (6) (14). The saloon
   and the 4 men in the corner (7 & 8, part of.) C's vague feeling of
   helplessness. The younger passengers coming in. (9). Bugle for dinner.
   (C's final thoughts as he sits on his bunk—fan, smell of paint—then bugle
   blaring.)
2. The dancing on deck. Songs. C. I was *not* sent here! Memories of N'zeik.
   The bungalow (1, part of). The lecture on grit & initiative. Schooldays.
   More songs. (10). Hopeless aspiration towards the young widow. (25)
3. Mr M's anticlericalism. C's awe of him. His laugh. (8) (15) Geography of
   the smoking room. The oildrillers (7. But they must be mentioned in 1).
   C's thoughts wandering away to the bungalow & his first meeting with
   B. J. (16)
4. The Mission. (5) (3) (4) (17) (18)
5. Coming back. The plantation. (20).
6. Overheard remarks of other passengers. The other ship passing. (13)
   (23). Meeting with father at rly. station, & home. (11) (12).
7. The incident with the picture, C.'s feeling towards B. J., & his highbrow
   period. Possibly better to split up into several chaps., but keep
   continuous so as not to make the incident over-conspicuous. But end
   chapter with some back-reference to it? (21) (22) (24) (26) (28) (19).
8. The ship.
9. Telling the story (29)
10. Finale (30).

1. 1886 = 1866? By an Act of Parliament passed in 1866, effective 1867, the then Straits
   Settlements, of which Singapore was a part, were separated from the jurisdiction of the
   Governor-General of India and established as an independent community under their own
   Governor-General. Neither Sir Richard Winstedt, in *A History of Malaya* (rev. 1962), nor N. J.
   Ryan, in *A History of Malaysia and Singapore* (1976), gives 1886 special significance for Malaya
   and Singapore.
2. Shanghai stands at the mouth of the Yangtze River. In 1857 the British obtained rights of
   navigation on the Yangtze to facilitate and protect the development of their commercial
   interests in that area. Both 1886 and 1857 suggest the expansion of imperial interest. 1857 was
   also the year in which the 'Indian Mutiny' broke out.

3. Until 3 June 1956, British railways operated three classes of transportation for passengers. Third class was abolished on that date, the old third becoming standard class, and ending permanently the railways' three-class system. That had symbolised the class structure in Britain, and also 'knowing one's place'—and accepting it. T. W. Robertson, in his social comedy *Caste* (1867), puts into the mouth of a hard-working plumber a speech making precisely these points. As time passed, second-class compartments became less and less common—almost an anachronism. They were used by, and typified, those with claims to 'a certain position' but who could not afford first-class tickets. The death knell of second class was sounded by World War II. In the 1840s there had even been a fourth, 'parliamentary,' class.

4. In the final sentence of 'Grandeur et décadence du roman policier anglais', 17 November 1943 (see 2357), Orwell refers to such hats as 'des chapeaux melons à la calotte surélevée.'

5. *The Forsyte Saga* was published as a trilogy in 1922; it comprised *The Man of Property* (1906), *In Chancery* (1920), and *To Let* (1921). Perhaps *Box o'Books: A Book of Verse*, edited by C. Platt (1930); or, less likely, *Black's Box of Books* (traditional tales) (1930); Robert Keable, *Simon Called Peter* (1921); Jean Webster (pseudonym of Alice Jane Chandler Webster), *Daddy Long Legs* (1913); Gene Stratton-Porter, *Freckles* (1904) and *A Girl of the Limberlost* (1909); Margaret Kennedy, *The Constant Nymph* (1924); and Compton Mackenzie, *Sinister Street* (1913). In *Enemies of Promise* (1938), Cyril Connolly records that when he and Orwell were at St Cyprian's they alternately won Mrs Wilkes's prize for having the best list of books borrowed from the school library. However, 'we were both caught at last with two volumes of *Sinister Street* and our favour sank to zero' (chap. 19). Orwell, writing to Julian Symons, 10 May 1948 (see 3397), recalls that they 'got into severe trouble (and I think a caning—I forget).'

6. An almirah is a cupboard or chest of drawers (Anglo-Indian from Urdu).

7. N'zeik is Nyaungbinzeik; see Orwell's first note.

3723. 'A Smoking-room Story'

Spring(?) 1949   Unfinished draft

The draft, with the title as given above, is written in a red hard-backed notebook, approximately 12 × 7 inches, with five gatherings of 32 pages each, the first and last pages pasted to the boards; there are 42 ruled lines to a page. Orwell wrote the draft on three rectos, starting with the second, and on the facing versos wrote the inserts. The rest of the pages are blank. The notes and details of the lay-out were written in his last Literary Notebook, pages 16–21; see 3722. In transcribing the draft here, passages that were crossed through are placed within square brackets; words substituted for crossed-through sections follow the closing square bracket; simple false starts have been ignored; passages to be inserted from facing versos are preceded by 'Insert' in italic within square brackets. 'NP' is Orwell's indication for a new paragraph; these are not reproduced but note is taken of this instruction in the transcript. All the inserts start a new paragraph, and a new paragraph begins after each insert. A dot within two concentric circles is used as it was in the draft of *Nineteen Eighty-Four*, to indicate a place requiring revision. It is represented here by ○. False starts and pen rests have not been indicated, and interlineation is not noted. Orwell uses a number of abbreviated forms—&, abt, vy—and these are transcribed here as they are in the manuscript. It is not always clear whether could/would/should are abbreviated and, if they are, precisely how. Where an abbreviation is indicated it is represented by the form 'wld' or 'cld' though the letter forms may indicate 'wuld' and 'culd'; in doubtful cases the full spelling is given. The text was written in blue ink but most of the revisions are in blue Biro. For a conjectural fair copy of the draft, prepared for ease of reading, see 3724.

i.

The serang,[1] in his white uniform & scarlet sash, swarmed up the lamp-standard like a monkey, plucked the electric bulb out of its socket, rattled it against his ear to make sure that it was defective, & tossed it into the foaming wake of the ship. It disappeared & then broke water again a hundred yards away, glittering like a diamond.

Curly Johnson (his Christian name was Geoffrey, but somehow the nickname had followed him abt since childhood) turned away from the stern. Scattered abt the deck, forlorn-looking° Indians squatted on bamboo mats with little tightly-tied bundles of possessions surrounding them. Some of the women were rolling out curry paste for the evening meal. They were deck-passengers — a party of Indian Christians who for some reason were travelling [to East Africa.] from Colombo to Port Said. A priest, an enigmatic, darkish figure in a cassock, slipped with an air of furtiveness through a doorway into the seamens'° quarters. Curly watched him with a faint, fleeting curiosity.

O [He had already heard some of the other passengers talking abt the priest in a disapproving way. The boats of the Bathurst Line, although they usually carried a few deck passengers between Colombo and Port Said, were advertised as "all one class," & there was evidently something irregular abt the priest's position on board. He did not sleep on deck with his Indian charges, but on the other hand he did not come to the saloon for meals & did not appear to have a cabin. It was rumoured that he berthed with the stewards, or with the European quartermasters.]

[Insert] There was something irregular abt the priest's position on board [, & questions had already been asked abt it.]. He was travelling with the Indians as their guide & spiritual director, [though he did not actually sleep on deck with his charges] & it appeared that he was not exactly either a deck-passenger or a cabin passenger. He never appeared in the saloon for meals, & it was rumoured that he shared a cabin either with the assistant-purser or with one of the junior engineers.

The ship was a day out from Colombo, [westward] homeward bound. From the bow there floated shrill screams of feminine laughter. [End insert]

[O]² [From the bow end of the ship screams of feminine laughter.]

[The ship was a day out from Colombo, homeward bound.] Curly made his way towards the [bow, drawn by the sound of [yell] screaming feminine laughter. He was] sound — a tallish, [well-built] shapely youth, moving with a grace of which he was not conscious. His soft, curly black hair, clinging close to his head, was almost like [the fur of a water-spaniel], a water-spaniel's coat, & there was something doglike also abt his vague, freckled face, which even at the age of four-&-twenty did not need shaving more than three times a week. As he passed along the upper deck two [scrawny] dried-up middle-aged women, lying in deck chairs under the shade of the smokestack, eyed him [unfavourably] disapprovingly.

"Is that the boy who's being sent home?" said one.

"Yes. He was in Peterson's. Quite a good job, I believe. . . . . Oh, the usual thing, I suppose. Drunkenness, & so on."

Their [whispers] whispering voices easily bridged the gap between Curly & themselves. Perhaps they were meant to do so. Curly [flushed], blushed, a habit of which he could not cure himself. He wanted to turn round, [stride masterfully] march across to the two women[, & say] & shout at them in a [manner] voice that wld [silence them for good & all]: shrivel them up: "I am not being sent home! Peterson's were reducing staff, [that is all] that's all. [They have given me the best possible references. I am going home of my own accord:] It was a thing that might [happen] have happened to anybody. I am not being sent home: will you be [kind] good enough to [remember] understand that?" — but [of course] he did nothing of the kind. Instead[,] he paused at the [rail & beside the] top of the companionway that led down to the fore-deck, & gazed with a sort of envious friendliness at the [mob of] mob of passengers disporting themselves below.

The ship[, like all those of the Bathurst Line] had a long clear foredeck° on which, as there were no hatches to get in the way, games of skittles were played when the sea was calm enough. [At [the] this moment] Evidently a game had just ended[.], [A] for a lascar was carrying the skittles away under his arm. [A mob of abt twenty passengers, most of them very young — the youths in khaki shorts, the girls in light summery frocks — with vy short skirts —[3] was milling round Charlie Bowles, the delightfully witty young tea-broker who had already constituted himself the life & soul of the ship. Mr Greenfield, of the I.C.S.,[4] the only middle-aged person in sight, [—] a bulky, placid man in a tussore suit [—] leaned against the rail, gazing thoughtfully at the jade-green water, like some large, harmless animal chewing the cud. A girl caught sight of Curly at the top of the companionway & gave him a wave of her hand.][5]

["Hullo, Curly!" she squealed in an affected little voice.]

[Curly smiled shyly back, but he did not go down. The group of people on the foredeck were the Younger Set, the acknowledged arbiters of fashion & elegance. They intimidated him a little, partly because most of them were people he did not know. Since yesterday the [Colombo] Ceylon passengers had dominated the ship. They seemed somehow younger & fresher & richer than the Burma people. They were a week's sail nearer Home, & they got Home [earlier]: [oftener]: their faces were less yellow, their clothes a year newer.]

[Insert] It was cocktail-time, or nearly. In the still brilliant sunshine a group of ten or twenty passengers, nearly all of them vy young, the youths in khaki shorts, the girls in light summery frocks, was screaming with laughter at some witticism that had just been uttered by Charlie Bowles, the young Colombo tea-broker, who was already recognized as the life & soul of the ship. Mr Greenfield, of the I.C.S.,

the only middle-aged person in sight, a bulky, placid man in a baggy
tussore suit, leaned against the rail, gazing dreamily at the jade-green
water. A girl caught sight of Curly at the top of the companionway &
gave him an affected little wave of her hand.

"'lo, Curly!" she squealed in a high, silly voice.

Curly smiled shyly back, but he did not go down. The people down
there all looked so handsome & elegant, so conscious of belonging to a
privileged minority. They were "the gang," the acknowledged leaders
of fashion, the people who set the tone for the rest of the younger
passengers. They intimidated him somewhat, partly because most of
them were people he did not know. Since yesterday it was the
Colombo passengers who had dominated the ship. They were
markedly younger & fresher than the Burma people. They lived a
week's sail nearer [home] Home, & most of them got [there] Home[6]
once in four years instead of once in five. Their faces were less yellow,
their dinner-jackets a year younger. [*End insert*]

Up to Port Soudan the contrast would persist, & then [suddenly] the
ship would be flooded [with] by Soudanese officials, [— people who
went Home every year & who wore what looked like brand-new
clothes & had the real European red in their cheeks —] people in
brand-new clothes with the real European red in their faces — people
who went Home for three months in every year — & then even the
[girls from] élite of Colombo wld suddenly look yellow & [dowdy]
shrunken.

There were fresh screams of laughter. Curly caught the words,
"Laugh? I thought I shuld have died." It was Charlie Bowles[.], [He
was really too funny with his cockney° imitations.] giving some of his
Cockney° imitations again. He was a scream, was Charlie Bowles. He
culd take off a bus conductor, a coster, a charwoman — anybody. You
just culdn't help laughing at him. Almost at the same moment, as
spontaneously as a flock of birds, the whole group of people burst out
singing. [It was a habit that they had. Someone wuld strike up, &
promptly everyone else wuld join in. It seemed to emphasise the fact
that they were "the gang," that they were perfectly in tune with one
another & outsiders were not wanted. The song was "Bye-bye,
Blackbird." It was the song of the year:[7] for months past it had been
impossible to get away from it.]

[*Insert*] It was a thing that they were constantly doing, & in some way
it emphasised the fact that they were "the gang",° the élite, the arbiters
of fashion & elegance. They were in tune with one another: [foreigners]
outsiders culd not join in. The chorus of youthful voices ebbed away
with a sort of pleasant sadness — "Bye-bye — Blackbird!" It was the
tune of the year:[8] for months past it had been impossible to get out of
the sound of it. [*End insert*]

Curly gazed with yearning, hopeless admiration at the beautiful Mrs
Kendrick (even in his secret thoughts he did not dare to call her by her
Christian name), the twenty-three year old widow who at this moment

was singing tunefully at the far end of the group, arm in arm with [her][9] her almost equally pretty friend, Miss Cherry. Mrs Kendrick, whose husband had died three months ago, & who was [now] presumably on her way home[,], [presumably] in search of another, was a vivid-looking girl, with [short dark hair,] dark hair as short as a boy's, a bold, aquiline little face, a perfect figure & swift, [graceful movements. The words of the song "Bye-bye — Black — bird!" ebbed out[10] slowly, tunefully, but sorrowfully. And just as the last note died away, Mrs Kendrick] darting movements like those of a dragon fly. As the last note of the song died away she suddenly disengaged her arm from her friend's, came dancing lightly down the deck [in her fairy-like way], twitched up the tail of Mr Greenfield's tussore jacket & caught him a playful smack across the bottom. [There was another yell of laughter. Mr Greenfield] turned round,[11] [wearing the] [a smile forming slowly on his face — the sort of benign, tolerant smile that one might expect to see on the face of some large ruminant animal — & lumbered away in the direction of the smoking saloon.]

[*Insert*] There was another burst of laughter, this time of half-scandalised laughter. Even Mr Greenfield seemed amused by the delightful impertinence that had been played upon him. He turned round, a smile forming slowly upon his face — the sort of smile that you culd imagine on the face of some large harmless antediluvian reptile — & lumbered aimiably° away in the direction of the smoking saloon. [*End insert*]

"Isn't she *too* sweet?" murmured the [dried-up] lady in the deck-chair.

[Manuscript ends.]

1. A serang is a lascar bosun.
2. Roundel crossed through.
3. 'with vy short skirts' is heavily crossed through with zig-zag line.
4. Indian Civil Service.
5. The insert is marked (as are all inserts) as a new paragraph, starting after 'a lascar was carrying the skittles away under his arm.' The text as first written did not then begin a new paragraph with 'A mob of abt twenty passengers' but ran straight on. When first written out, the paragraph break began at "Hullo, Curly!"
6. Orwell's deliberate capitalising of 'Home' (crossing out 'home') and his repetition of 'Home' in place of 'there' are characteristic of the weight he gives the capitalised form of this word (and of 'Canal,' for Suez Canal, and 'War,' for the Great War of 1914–1918) in *Burmese Days*; see *CW*, II, Textual Note, 315, note 26/35.
7. In his Notes of items to be brought in, Orwell gives the year as 1927. Orwell returned from Burma by ship in August 1927. 'Of the voyage home nothing is known, except that he got off the P&O liner at Marseilles and returned to London via Paris'; he 'was in Marseilles a few days before 23 August 1927' (Crick, 174–75).
8. 'Bye Bye Blackbird' was one of the hit songs of 1926. It is included in Orwell's list of popular songs in his Second Literary Notebook, 1948 (*3515*).
9. '[her]' is reasonably certain, but heavily crossed through.
10. 'out' is uncertain.
11. 'turned round' should have been crossed through.

3724. 'A Smoking-room Story'
Conjectural fair copy

This editorial fair copy has been provided for ease of reading. Orwell did not see his draft in this 'clear' form and he marked the draft for further revision. His contractions have been expanded, slight errors have been corrected, and there is some reparagraphing.

The serang, in his white uniform and scarlet sash, swarmed up the lamp-standard like a monkey, plucked the electric bulb out of its socket, rattled it against his ear to make sure that it was defective, and tossed it into the foaming wake of the ship. It disappeared and then broke water again a hundred yards away, glittering like a diamond.

Curly Johnson (his Christian name was Geoffrey, but somehow the nickname had followed him about since childhood) turned away from the stern. Scattered about the deck, forlorn-looking Indians squatted on bamboo mats with little tightly-tied bundles of possessions surrounding them. Some of the women were rolling out curry paste for the evening meal. They were deck-passengers—a party of Indian Christians who for some reason were travelling from Colombo to Port Said. A priest, an enigmatic, darkish figure in a cassock, slipped with an air of furtiveness through a doorway into the seamen's quarters. Curly watched him with a faint, fleeting curiosity. There was something irregular about the priest's position on board. He was travelling with the Indians as their guide and spiritual director, and it appeared that he was not exactly either a deck-passenger or a cabin passenger. He never appeared in the saloon for meals, and it was rumoured that he shared a cabin either with the assistant-purser or with one of the junior engineers.

The ship was a day out from Colombo, homeward bound. From the bow there floated shrill screams of feminine laughter. Curly made his way towards the sound—a tallish, shapely youth, moving with a grace of which he was not conscious. His soft, curly black hair, clinging close to his head, was almost like a water-spaniel's coat, and there was something doglike also about his vague, freckled face, which even at the age of four-and-twenty did not need shaving more than three times a week. As he passed along the upper deck two dried-up middle-aged women, lying in deck chairs under the shade of the smokestack, eyed him disapprovingly.

"Is that the boy who's being sent home?" said one.

"Yes. He was in Peterson's. Quite a good job, I believe. . . . Oh, the usual thing, I suppose. Drunkenness, and so on."

Their whispering voices easily bridged the gap between Curly and themselves. Perhaps they were meant to do so. Curly blushed, a habit of which he could not cure himself. He wanted to turn round, march across to the two women, and shout at them in a voice that would shrivel them up: "I am not being sent home! Peterson's were reducing staff, that's all. It was a thing that might have happened to anybody. I am not being sent home: will you be good enough to understand that?"—but he did nothing of the kind.

Instead he paused at the top of the companionway that led down to the foredeck, and gazed with a sort of envious friendliness at the mob of passengers disporting themselves below.

The ship had a long clear foredeck on which, as there were no hatches to get in the way, games of skittles were played when the sea was calm enough. Evidently a game had just ended, for a lascar was carrying the skittles away under his arm.

It was cocktail-time or nearly. In the still brilliant sunshine a group of ten or twenty passengers, nearly all of them very young, the youths in khaki shorts, the girls in light summery frocks, was screaming with laughter at some witticism that had just been uttered by Charlie Bowles, the young Colombo tea-broker who was already recognized as the life and soul of the ship. Mr Greenfield, of the I.C.S., the only middle-aged person in sight, a bulky, placid man in a baggy tussore suit, leaned against the rail, gazing dreamily at the jade-green water. A girl caught sight of Curly at the top of the companionway and gave him an affected little wave of the hand.

"'lo, Curly!" she squealed in a high, silly voice.

Curly smiled shyly back, but he did not go down. The people down there all looked so handsome and elegant, so conscious of belonging to a privileged minority. They were "the gang," the acknowledged leaders of fashion, the people who set the tone for the rest of the younger passengers. They intimidated him somewhat, partly because most of them were people he did not know. Since yesterday it was the Colombo passengers who had dominated the ship. They were markedly younger and fresher than the Burma people. They lived a week's sail nearer Home, and most of them got Home once in four years instead of once in five. Their faces were less yellow, their dinner-jackets a year younger.

Up to Port Soudan the contrast would persist, and then the ship would be flooded by Soudanese officials, people in brand-new clothes with the real European red in their faces—people who went Home for three months in every year—and then even the élite of Colombo would suddenly look yellow and shrunken.

There were fresh screams of laughter. Curly caught the words, "Laugh? I thought I should have died." It was Charlie Bowles, giving some of his Cockney imitations again. He was a scream, was Charlie Bowles. He could take off a bus conductor, a coster, a charwoman—anybody. You just couldn't help laughing at him. Almost at the same moment, as spontaneously as a flock of birds, the whole group of people burst out singing. It was a thing that they were constantly doing, and in some way it emphasised the fact that they were "the gang", the élite, the arbiters of fashion and elegance. They were in tune with one another: outsiders could not join in. The chorus of youthful voices ebbed away with a sort of pleasant sadness—"Bye-bye—Blackbird!" It was the tune of the year: for months past it had been impossible to get out of the sound of it.

Curly gazed with yearning, hopeless admiration at the beautiful Mrs Kendrick (even in his secret thoughts he did not dare to call her by her Christian name), the twenty-three-year-old widow who at this moment was singing tunefully at the far end of the group, arm in arm with her almost equally pretty friend, Miss Cherry. Mrs Kendrick, whose husband had died three months ago, and who was presumably on her way home, in search of another, was a vivid-looking girl, with dark hair as short as a boy's, a bold, aquiline little face, a perfect figure and swift, darting movements like those of a dragon fly. As the last note of the song died away she suddenly disengaged her arm from her friend's, came dancing lightly down the deck, twitched up the tail of Mr Greenfield's tussore jacket and caught him a playful smack across the bottom. There was another burst of laughter, this time of half-scandalised laughter. Even Mr Greenfield seemed amused by the delightful impertinence that had been played upon him. He turned round, a smile forming slowly upon his face—the sort of smile that you could imagine on the face of some large harmless antediluvian reptile—and lumbered amiably away in the direction of the smoking saloon.

"Isn't she *too* sweet?" murmured the lady in the deck-chair.

[Manuscript ends.]

APPENDIX 2

3725. Notes from Orwell's Last Literary Notebook

The last of Orwell's literary notebooks is a cash book measuring approximately 12½ × 8¼ inches; it has two vertical ruled columns on the left (for the date) and four on the right, the first for references and separated by a double rule from the remaining three columns (for pounds, shillings, and pence). There are thirty-four horizontal ruled lines. Orwell wrote on thirty rectos and thirteen versos. One leaf was abstracted but was later recovered (see 'Separated leaf' below). The draft of 'A Smoking-room Story' (3723) is in a different notebook. Some of the items have been transferred to the main run of this edition where their significance is more immediately apparent. These are:

Quotations from *Brideshead Revisited* and *Robbery Under Law*; see *3586*
Notes for essay on Evelyn Waugh; see *3586*
Diary entry, 21.3.49: Cranham Sanatorium Routine; see *3579*
Diary entry, 24.3.49 on experience with streptomycin; see *3378*
Experience at the BBC in 1943; see *892*
Notes and Details of Layout for 'A Smoking-room Story'; *3722*
University College Hospital Routine; see *3687*
Diary entry, 17.4.49: Hospital Journal; see *3602*.

The transfer of these items is noted at the point where they appear in the last Literary Notebook.

In transcribing the manuscript the more important revisions are shown and words crossed out, where they can be deciphered, are within square brackets. False starts are not noted. Lines indicating suppressed names or words are as in Orwell's manuscript. Interlineations are not marked. Orwell wrote these notes in ink and Biro. He numbered each leaf at the top right-hand corner of rectos. In this transcription they are within brackets at the first line of the appropriate page. Versos (which Orwell did not number) are numbered as the appropriate rectos (e.g., 1ᵛ) in the same position. Notes related to the text are given at the foot of the relevant pages; editorial notes are at the end.

[1]   His perennial subjects of conversation:
What happens to the compass at the North Pole?
What would happen (effects on gravitation) if you could cut a hole right through the centre of the earth?
Why does a ball thrown upwards on the deck of a moving ship not come down behind you?
How can sound, if a movement of the atmosphere, come through an airtight wall?
Achilles & the turtle. (He came upon this problem late in life, & felt sure there must be a fallacy somewhere, but could not see where.) (Earlier in life he would have rejected it because of the suggestion of classical learning implied by acquaintance with Achilles.)
If you could travel round the world in 24 hours would you not arrive at the same time as you started? (Towards the end of his life it occurred to him that if you could do it in less than 24 hours, you should arrive *before* you started.)
Flying fishes. Whether they flap their wings. (Grasshoppers, Bats, snipe, cuckoos, homing pigeons).
His reading   Winwood Reade: "Martyrdom of Man." The "Origin of Species?". Renan? H. G. Wells: "Outline of History." (Qy. What else?) He had not actually read these books, but he venerated them & his ideas were drawn from them, or so at least he believed. (He possessed a complete set of the Thinker's Library.)
    The Pyramids. How they were got into place.

North of the Equator, the water in a whirlpool moves clockwise, & South of it, anticlockwise (or the other way about?) (Magnetism of ships).

[1ᵛ–2]   [Quotations from *Brideshead Revisited* and *Robbery Under Law*; see 3586.]

[3]   Vanguard.   Quietus
       Lay the foundations.
       Pave the way for.
       Spearhead.
       Play into the hands of.
       Sole criterion.
       Sorry commentary.
       Crusade.
       Hamstring.
       Dynamic (n).
x*   Torpedo (v.)

* The small 'x' against certain words appears in Orwell's notes.

buckle to
[Lay the foundations]
Beck & call
Dance to the tune (of)
Hold a pistol at the head (of)
x   Bottleneck
x   Ceiling
x   Target
x   Catalyst
x   Unscramble
Passionate conviction.
Scourge.
Sinews of war
Cinderella.
Shibboleth
Ranks
Vacuum
Jumping-off place
Rally (the progressive forces)
Powder — magazine
x   Iron out

[4] With suicide, as with murder: the great difficulty, disposal of the body.

Probably there was some truth in Pétain's remark, at the time when he became ruler of France,[1] that the French defeat was due partly to the low birth-rate. Where families are small, the civilian population cannot regard the killing of their sons with indifference, & the soldier's own attitude is probably affected by his having learned to think of himself as more of an individual, & more important, than if he had had to scramble for survival in a hungry peasant family of five or ten children.

One great difference between the Victorians & ourselves was that they looked on the adult as more important than the child.* In a family of ten or twelve it was almost inevitable that one or two should die in infancy, & though these deaths were sad, of course, they were soon forgotten, as there were always more children coming along. In St. John's Church, near Lord's, there are many memorial tablets of East India nabobs, etc., with the usual column of lies in praise of the dead man, then a line or two about "Sarah, relict of the above," and then perhaps another line saying that one male & two female children, or words to that effect, are buried in the same vault. No names given, & in one case the inscription reads *two or three children*. By the time the stone was put up, it had been forgotten how many had died.

Nowadays the death of a child is the worst thing that most people are able to imagine. If one has only *one* child, to recover from losing it would be

* But NB. what abt Little Nell etc.? (Compensation for guilty conscience.) [Orwell's note, marked by asterisk, and written on 3ᵛ.]

almost impossible. It would darken the universe, permanently. Even two generations ago I doubt whether people had this feeling. Cf. in "Jude the Obscure," in the preposterous incident where the eldest child hangs the two younger ones & then hangs itself. Jude & Sue are, of course, distressed, but they do not seem to feel that after such an event their own lives must cease. Sue (I think Hardy realises that she is an intolerable character, but I don't think he is being ironical in [5] this place) says after a while that she sees why the children had to die: it was to make her a better woman & [able] help her to begin her life anew. It does not occur to her that the children were more important creatures than herself & that in comparison with their death, nothing that can now happen to her is of much significance.

I read recently in the newspaper that in Shanghai (now full of refugees), abandoned children are becoming so common on the pavement that one no longer notices them. In the end, I suppose, the body of a dying child becomes simply a piece of refuse to be stepped over. Yet all these children started out with the expectation of being loved & protected, & with the conviction which one can see even in a very young child that the world is a splendid place & there are plenty of good times ahead.

Qy. are you the same again if you have walked home stepping over the bodies of abandoned children, & not [even] succouring even one of them? (Even to take care not to tread on them is a sort of hypocrisy.) M. M.[2] says that anyone who has lived in Asia has in effect done this kind of thing already. Perhaps not quite true, insomuch that when he & I lived in Asia we were young men who wd hardly notice babies.*

Aldous Huxley. The more other-worldly & "non-attached" he becomes, the more his books stink with sex. Above all he cannot keep off the subject of flagellating women. It would be interesting to know whether there is a connection between this & his pacifism. [Perhaps that is the solution to the problem of war—ie., if we culd develop an interest in individual sadism we might work off our surplus energy in that way instead of by waving flags & dropping bombs.] Cf. also Alex Comfort, another pacifist, always brooding on the idea of stamping on people's faces.

Death dreams. Very frequent throughout the past two years. Sometimes of the sea or the sea shore—more often of enormous, splendid buildings or streets or ships, in which I often lose my way, but always with a peculiar feeling of happiness & of walking in sunlight. Unquestionably all these buildings etc. mean death — I am almost aware of this even in the dream, & these dreams always become [worse ever]† more frequent when my health gets worse & I begin to despair of ever recovering. What I can never understand is *why*, since I am not afraid of death (afraid of pain, & of the moment of dying, but not extinction), this thought has [6] to appear [under] in my dreams under these various disguises. Cf. also my ever-recurrent fishing dream. Obviously this has a sexual meaning. The water, I suppose,

---

* From 'Qy. are you the same again . . .' to '. . . hardly notice babies.' is on 4ᵛ.

† worse ever] unclear; possibly a comma is required between 'worse' and 'ever,' or this is the start of 'worse every time'; or perhaps 'ever' is 'even.'

means woman, & the fish are phallic symbols. But why do sex impulses which I am not frightened of thinking about when I am awake have to be dressed up as something different when I am asleep? And then again, what is the point of the disguise if, in practice, it is always penetrable?

It is now (1949) 16 years since my first book was published, & abt 21 years since I started publishing articles in the magazines. Throughout that time there has literally been not one day in which I did not feel that I was idling, that I was behind with the current job, & that my total output was miserably small. Even at the periods when I was working 10 hours a day on a book, or turning out 4 or 5 articles a week, I have never been able to get away from this neurotic feeling that I was wasting time. I can never get any sense of achievement out of the work that is actually in progress, because it always goes slower than I intend, & in any case I feel that a book or even an article does not exist until it is finished. But as soon as a book is finished, I begin, actually from the next day, worrying because the next one is not begun, & am haunted with the fear that there never will be [another one] a next one—that my impulse is exhausted for good & all. If I look back & count up the actual amount that I have written, then I see that my output has been respectable: but this does not reassure me, because it simply gives me the feeling that I once had an industriousness & a fertility which I have now lost.

One of the things which, at the crucial moment, prevented him from committing suicide, was the fact of suddenly realising that after twelve years of marriage he did not know what colour his wife's eyes were. It seemed almost impossible not to go home & find out.

[7] Recently I was reading somewhere or other abt an Italian curio–dealer who attempted to sell a 17th century crucifix to J. P. Morgan. It was not at first sight a particularly interesting work of art. But it turned out that the real point was that the crucifix took to pieces & inside it was concealed a stiletto. What a perfect symbol of the Christian religion.

There were two great facts about women which it seemed to him that you could only learn by getting married, & which flatly contradicted the picture of themselves that women had managed to impose upon the world. One was their incorrigible dirtiness & untidiness. The other was their terrible, devouring sexuality. This was disguised by the fact that women usually remained chaste till marriage, & were more or less monogamous by instinct. But within any marriage or regular love affair, he suspected that it was always the woman who was the sexually insistent partner. In his experience women were quite insatiable, & never seemed to be fatigued by no matter how much love-making. In the long run even the motive behind their sexuality became uncertain. Perhaps it was sheer sensuality, but perhaps again they simply felt that sexual intercourse was a way of keeping the man under control.* At any rate, in any marriage of more than a year or two's standing, intercourse was thought of as a duty, a service owed by the man to the woman. And he

* 'Sign that he "really loves me"' written in left-hand margin.

suspected that in evy marriage the struggle was always the same—the man trying to escape from sexual intercourse, to do it only when he felt like it (or with other women), the woman demanding it more & more, & more & more consciously despising her husband for his lack of virility. (Diferent° in the working class?)

[8] For & against novels in the first person.[3]

Actually, to write a novel in the first person is like dosing yourself with some stimulating but very deleterious & very habit-forming drug. The temptation to do it is very great, but at [any] every stage of the proceedings you know perfectly well that you are doing something wrong & foolish. However, there are two great advantages:—

i. In the first person, one can always get the book actually written, & fairly quickly, as the use of the "I" seems to do away with the shyness & feeling of helplessness which often prevent one from getting well started. In the first person, one can always get somewhere near the conception with which one starts out.

ii. In the first person *anything* can be made to sound credible. This is so in the first place because whatever he writes seems credible to the author, for you can daydream abt *yourself* doing no matter what, whereas third-person adventures have to be comparatively probable. The reader, again, finds anything told in the first person credible, because he either identifies himself with the "I" of the story, or, because an "I" is talking to him, accepts it as a real person.

Disadvantages:—

i. The narrator is never really separable from the author. It is impossible to avoid crediting him with one's own thoughts occasionally, &, since even in a novel the author must occasionally comment, one's own comments unavoidably become those of the narrator (which would not be so in a third-person novel.) At the least, the narrator must have the author's prose style (example, *Great Expectations*, which is otherwise not a very autobiographical book.)

[9] ii. If the arrangement is strictly kept to, the events of the story are seen only through the consciousness of one person. Merely in order to find out what is happening, this involves the narrator in eavesdropping & amateur detective work, or makes it necessary for people to do things in company which in real life they would only do alone. If the thoughts of the other characters are to be revealed, then they have to be made to talk more freely than any real person would do, or else the narrator has to say something which amounts to, "I could see what he was thinking, namely," etc., etc. (Cf. fearful scene in E. Waugh's "Brideshead Revisited.") But in general an "I" novel is simply the story of one person—a three-dimensional figure among caricatures—& therefore cannot be a true novel.

iii. Range of feeling much narrowed, as there are many kinds of appeal that you can make on behalf of others but not for yourself.

[Notes for essay on Evelyn Waugh, pages 9–10, transferred to *3586*]

[10]   The conversations he overheard as a small boy, between his mother, his aunt, his elder sister (?) & their feminist friends. The way in which, without ever hearing any direct statement to that effect, & without having more than a very dim idea of the relationship between the sexes, he derived a firm impression that women *did not like* men, that they looked upon them as a sort of large, ugly, smelly & ridiculous animal, who maltreated women in every way, above all by forcing their attentions upon them. It was pressed deep into his consciousness, to remain there till he was abt 20, that sexual intercourse gives pleasure only to the man, not to the woman. He knew that sexual intercourse had something to do with the man getting on top of the woman, & the picture of it in his mind was of a man pursuing a woman, forcing her down & jumping on top of her, as he had often seen a cock do to a hen. All this was derived, not from any remark having a direct sexual reference—or what he recognized as a [11] sexual reference—but from such overheard remarks as "It just shows what beasts men are," "My dear, I think she's behaving like a perfect fool, the way she gives into° him," "Of course she's far too good for him," & the like. Somehow, by the mere tone of these conversations, the hatefulness—above all the physical unattractiveness—of men in women's eyes seemed to be established. It was not till he was abt 30 that it struck him that he had in fact been his mother's favourite child. It had seemed natural to him that, as he was a boy, the two girls should be preferred to him.

"I hold no brief for —." This remark invariably used to mean the opposite of what it appears to mean. When somebody says that he holds no brief for something or other, one can safely infer that he does hold a brief for just that thing.

[11–13]   Diary entry, 21.3.49: Cranham Sanatorium Routine, transferred to *3579*. Diary entry, 24.3.49 on experience with streptomycin, transferred to *3378*.
[14–15]   [Experience at the BBC in 1943, transferred to 892.]

[15]   Swing, child Elizabeth; under the apple tree,
Few shall escape from the jaws of the crocodile, (? blast of the hurricane)
As you are, so were we, as we are, you must be —
Swing, swing, swing!

The time when they stopped sacrificing to (? his name should mean "he-who-receives-without-giving"), the lord of the islands. And a black cloud coming hovering down over the island, & a voice coming out of it saying:
"Sacrifice unto —, lord of the islands!"
Then the people answered: "We have sacrificed to you for three hundred years. What have you done for us in return?"
And the voice from the cloud said: "Nothing."

Then the people said: "And what will you do for us if we continue sacrificing?"
"Nothing," said the voice.
"Then why shld we sacrifice?" said the people.
"Because of what will happen to you if you do not," said the voice, & after that there were no more answers.

LIFE IS BAD BUT DEATH IS WORSE. This constituted the whole of their religious literature.

[16–22, (excl 21ᵛ)]   [Notes and Details of Layout for 'A Smoking Room Story,' transferred to *3722*.]

[21ᵛ]   And what was his astonishment to find that Proudhon & Carlyle were not the flawless champions of human liberty that the progressive Left had assumed them to be. True, they hated the plutocrats who ruled the roost. But they hated much more the proletarians whom the roost was choking to death. They had no use for those doctrines of equality, popular sovereignty, & Trade Unionism which were then helping the underdog to pull himself out of the morass.

(Felix Grendi, U.S. "New Leader" 27.8.49)

It was apparent from the Bridlington Congress, therefore, that a head-on attack on the present wages structure will not be made by the General Council or by individual unions. . . . The adventitious aids of forms of compulsion like compulsory arbitration & linkages between unions operating in the nationalised industries will also have to be relied on to bear their fruit.

(George Green, "Socialist Commentary" October 1949)

I think I may add here, that he who would overcome (the false materialist philosophy which has so often been denounced as the real reason for the present situation in our relations with Leon Chestov's native land, the philosophy of the Communist intellectuals leading the great Party which claims to represent the toiling Russian masses, the philosophy which drove Chestov into exile after 1920), will be unable to get very far until he sees that Materialist Idealism, which does not yet realise that it might truly to be thus so-called, confuses reflection & reflector.

(David Gascoyne, article on Leon Chestov, Horizon, October 1949.)
Between [Orwell's] brackets
53 words = "Marxism."

[22]   D. C. Thomson (Dundee)

Evg. Telegraph & Post	[Cutting from *Daily Telegraph*]
Sporting Post	'abt 24.ii.49'
Weekly News	[A letter from Sir Crawford Douglas-Jones
W. Welcome & W. Way	describing how when big-game shooting in
Red Letter	Portuguese East Africa about 1906 he had shot
Red Star Weekly	at a wildebeest about fifty yards away. To his
Family Star	surprise his bullet killed two bucks, for a
Sunday Post	second was covered by the one he had aimed at.
The Rover	Both heads were displayed in the Royal West
Adventure	Kent drill hall, Maidstone, and he had the tails
The Wizard	mounted as fly-whisks.]
The Hotspur	
Dandy Comic	
Beano ..	

With all its ugliness & tragedy, the war has brought to Americans—if they have the wisdom to sieze° it—the prospect of a step forward which may give them that moral leadership out of which the world could wrest the chance of making secure the foundations of civilization.
          Laski (New York Nation. "America, Good & Bad" 25.6.49)

[22ᵛ]   (In Czarist Russia in mid-nineteenth century) there was only one executioner, a certain Frolov of Moscow, & it is significant that when he was not available there was great difficulty in finding a substitute. We know of a case when Frolov [who] went sick shortly before an execution at Kharkov. The authorities looked for a volunteer throughout the Army & Police but failed to find one. Then they tried the various prisons. Only one prisoner, a murderer, was willing to undertake the task. His terms were 250 roubles in cash, the countermanding of a flogging on the soles of the feet to which he had been condemned, & immediate transfer to Siberia. His offer was considered, but the authorities received a better one at the last minute from a NOVOBELGOROD peasant who was willing to act for [*] sixty roubles, free transport in a three-horse carriage from N'gorod to Kharhov & back, one rouble sixty kopecks a day subsistence while absent from home, & twenty-two glasses of vodka immediately before the execution.
(D. Footman, "Red Prelude.")
     (N.B. Bears more than one meaning. Cf. in Burma jails, difficulty of getting hangmen—job always done by another convict, usually (or always?) an Indian.)

[23]   Gross unfairness & misleadingness of much criticism of both USA & USSR, because of failure to allow for the *size* of those countries. Obvious absurdity of comparing a small homogeneous population, eg. of Britain,

---

* Figure scored through; possibly '100.'

packed together in a small area, with a multi-racial state sprawling across a continent. Clearly one cannot reasonably compare conditions in Britain with those in, say, Siberia. One might compare Siberia with Canada, or Turkestan with Northern India, or Leningrad with Edinburgh. Ditto with USA. People in Britain vy high-minded abt American treatment of Negroes, but cf. conditions in South Africa. Certainly we, in Britain, have no control over S. Africa, but neither have the people in the Northern States much control over what happens in Alabama. Meanwhile we profit indirectly from what happens in S. Africa, in Jamaica, in Malaya etc. But these places are separated from us *by water*. On this last fact the essential hypocrisy of the British labour movement is based.

George Garrett[4] ("Adelphi" June 1936) re. J. Conrad's "Nigger of the Narcissus."

"The true artist is supposed to portray life whole, but it is next to impossible for an artist or anyone else to see life whole. Seeing is determined by an awareness of intense experience, but does not always exclude personal prejudices. And personal prejudice must not pass as whole truth.

"Conrad had his. He could write romantically & vividly of a ship in a heavy sea, but when it came to the men aboard he wrote as a conservative-minded ship's officer, as shown in *The Nigger of the Narcissus*."

"Conrad could not hide his personal dislike of (Donkin)."

"Yes, Donkin was Conrad's scapegoat; the villain of the piece. Perhaps at some time in his sea career a Donkin had told Conrad 'where to get off.' And Conrad probably wrote *The Nigger of the Narcissus* to let a reading public know exactly what he thought about the Donkins." (Cf. *The Secret Sharer*.)

[23ᵛ–24]   [University College Hospital Routine, transferred to *3687*.]
[24]   [Diary entry for 17.4.49: Hospital Journal, transferred to *3602*.]

[24]   The big cannibal critics that lurk in the deeper waters of American quarterly reviews.

Critical jargon: Values. Alienated. Disoriented. Reductions. Frame of reference. Avant–garde. Kitsch. Motivation. Evaluate. Discrete. Dichotomy. Aesthetic (noun.) Creativity. Criteria. Epigone. Psyche. Schizoid. Revaluation. Modes. Significant. Artform. Perspectives.

American subjunctive. It is essential that our programme can, with courage & mutual encouragement & mutual aid, be put into effect by our own effort, to a degree at once & progressively more & more, without recourse to distant party or union decisions.

(Paul Goodman, "Now" No 6[5] 1945)

[24ᵛ]   I was once walking home with Smeed, his (C. F. Gill's) clerk, from a police court in which Gill had been appearing on such [a] charge,* as we

* At the top of the page, with a line drawn to this punctuation mark, Orwell has written 'NB. this is a comma'

crossed the Park we came to a very brilliant electric light standard of obvious recent origin, & one which would render all adjacent love-making impossible.

(Autobiography of Sir Patrick Hastings)

(NB. Gill was "appearing" in the case as an advocate.)

[25] He remembers suddenly the squalid little rooms of the working-class hotel in the Latin Quarter—rooms which had probably been made by partitioning off larger rooms & which were divided only by the thinnest kind of matchboarding, through which one could see cracks of light & hear every sound. And the 18-year old girl in the room next to him who was living with a lusty redfaced errand boy of abt the same age. Each evening at 6 the boy's vigorous step & loud whistle coming up the stairs. Then the door opening, the loud smack of a kiss, the picking-up of the tin slop-pail & a pissing of a strength & loudness one would not have thought it possible for a human being to achieve. It was like a horse urinating into a bucket or a hose playing against a tin shed. Then, immediately following on this, a storm of kisses & then the creaking of a bed followed by groans.

(Emphasise that this youth & girl are living in a room measuring about 12' by 8'. Also the sameness of the routine every evening & the promptitude with which one event followed on another. Perhaps better miss out the first kiss.)

Coming back from church after the wedding, he did manage to make her come by the lane so as to see the chaffinch's nest on the trunk of the elm-tree. She wanted to go in the car with the others, but he was so anxious for her to see the nest that she rather impatiently did come with him. And it was a beautiful early June morning, & the mother chaffinch was doing her stuff, sitting there on the nest & not budging even when they were standing only a couple of yards away from her. The only bit of real married life that they ever had.

[25^v] Your mother was a spinster, say the bells of the Westminster,
Don't keep talking balls, say the bells of St Paul's.

[26]   [Draft of a Poem]

[NB: the words have been reproduced in the approximate position of the manuscript. There is a heavily scored-through word, or part-word, before 'stumps' and before 'dirty,']

Joseph Higgs, late of this parish,
Who pushed the plough till he became the ploughshare,
Exists no longer as the memory of a memory.
His wooden graveboard vanished in a cold winter,
A mishap with the inkpot blotted him from the register,
And
                         where the lost graves are visible,
Still

His raised right shoulder at the Day of Judgement
Might absolve him for the milkmaid's strangled daughter,
But

     the middle years (30–40? years)
When (boots were teeth were stumps of misery)
    March mornings
Seven separate pains played in his body like an orchestra
Till
A dirty old man in a stinking cottage
Where the panes grew darker & the mice grew bolder.

Three days running no smoke from the chimneys
       (burst the door in)
And broke his back to fit him in the coffin.

Ne me perdas illa die[6]

(Either here or there—I would prefer it here, but let it be there)
Without
I see no justification
For Joseph Higgs, late of this parish.

[26ᵛ] In modern English & American literature, poetry does not rhyme, but prose does. (Put better: rhyme has been transferred from poetry to prose.)

Round & round like a mouse in a chamberpot.

[Anything you can do I can do twice as well,
I can do anything better than you (Current song?)][7]

 He once noted on the proof of an article on his voyages which I had written:
 "Do try to keep the damned sea out if you can. My interests are terrestrial, after all."
 And again in a letter dated July, 1925, he wrote to me:
 "You knew very well that in the body of my work barely one-tenth is what may be called sea stuff, & even of that, the bulk, that is *Nigger & Mirror*, has a very special purpose, which I emphasise myself in my Prefaces. Of course, there are seamen in a good many of my books. That doesn't make them sea stories any more than the existence of de Barral in *Chance* (and he occupies there as much space as Captain Anthony) makes that novel a story about the financial world. I do wish that all those ships of mine were given a rest."
 To be called a novelist of the sea always annoyed him beyond endurance . . . .
    (R. Curle "The Last Twelve Years of J. Conrad" 1928)

[27]   J. D. Bernal—Letter answering A. J. Cummings (Russian education, etc.) News-Chronicle° 15.9.49.

For Conrad essay:[8]

Under Western Eyes.
(uniform edit.) p. 23
"They shot him in '28."
verify date—misprint?

*The Secret Agent**
Under Western Eyes   [The Good Soldier.]
Chance   [(F. M. F.)][9]
The Nigger of the Narcissus.
Richard Curle: Last 12 years of J. C. (?)
Jessie C.: Memories of J. C. (?)
F. M. Ford: Essay (?) on J. C.
Sales (reception) of: The Secret Agent (1907), Under Western Eyes (1911)
            Victory (1914)†
Victory. Dramatic version. What year made, by whom, whether successful,
        whether orientated anti-German, what effect on J. C's popularity.
        H. L. Mencken—essay—7–6.
J. C.   T. U. affiliations (in early '80's?)
Assassination of Alexander II.[10] Whether rumoured done by Ochrana (cf.
                        French film). Name of head of reactionary
        MOROZOV   faction (POBYEDONOSTSEV)
(N.A.) Morozov. (Formation of Social-Revolutionary Party, about 1879).

Possible candidates for co-option (to Executive Committee of S.R.P) were to be vy strictly scrutinised. Approved candidates were to have the programme read to them paragraph by paragraph. If they did not wholeheartedly approve of any point the reading was stopped & their admission refused. At least that was the rule. In practice, however, Morozov says: "When admitting a new member we never asked his views on socialism or anarchism. We asked, 'Are you ready at once to offer your life, your personal freedom & all you have?' If he said yes, & if we believed him, we took him on."

(D. Footman, "Red Prelude.")

The greatest of all the disadvantages under which the left wing movement suffers: that being a newcomer to the political scene, & having to build itself up out of nothing, it had to create a following by telling lies. For a leftwing party in power, its most serious antagonist is always its own past propaganda.

(Inherent in all democratic politics to some extent.)

---

* Orwell ticked this title and the next five.
† There was a query against each of these dates initially, but the question-marks were crossed through when the dates 1907 and 1914 were confirmed and 1911 filled in.

One law for the young & another for the old. (in sexual matters esp.)

It is one of Herzen's[11] weaknesses that he was seldom blinded by enthusiasm. (E. H. Carr in "The Romantic Exiles.")

Greater & ever-increasing softness & luxuriousness of modern life.

Rise in the standard of physical courage, improvement in health & physique, continuous supersession of athletic records.
    Qy. how to reconcile?

At 50, everyone has the face he deserves.

[*Separated leaf*[12]]   The unduly high standard of living of western working class. Wants constantly being translated into needs. Eg. films, unheard-of 50 years ago, radio, unheard-of 30 years ago, etc., now priorities which have to be provided even if necessities run short. Television now similarly being translated into an everyday household necessity. But the trouble is that if you ask the high-standard races to abandon their luxuries, you are asking them not only to become less luxurious but also *less civilized*. Eg. bathrooms, WCs, abundance of clean linen, separate bedrooms, medical attention, etc., etc. The European working class could not come anywhere near equalising their status with that of Asiatics without in the process making themselves dirtier, more diseased; more ignorant & generally more barbarous. To considerable extent, civilization is glass, linen, paper, water-piping, drugs, roads & transport. It is right, therefore, for the western working class to resist actual equality, which would only mean common misery. (Contained in this is the assumption that the average European is objectively superior to the average Asiatic, which one is not now permitted to say.)

Underlying facts which have never been admitted in Socialist literature (or more particularly are not mentioned before the acquisition of power), but which nevertheless govern the world situation:—

[*Separated leaf*ᵛ]   No guilty person is ever punished. So far as subjective feelings go, a person who is in a position to be punished has become the victim, & has therefore become innocent. This is perfectly well understood, internally, by everyone concerned. When a murderer is hanged, there is only one person present at the ceremony who is not guilty of murder. The hangman, the warders, the governor, the doctor, the chaplain*—they are all guilty: but the man standing on the drop is innocent. Everyone who has ever seen an execution knows this, & indeed even the public which gloats over the reports in the News of the World knows it after a fashion; the vast bulk of what is said & written in favour of capital punishment is simply a hypercritical cover for continuing to enjoy the pleasures of *being* guilty & indulging in murder, while remaining respectable.

* In the margin, alongside this sentence, Orwell has written 'other prisoners?'

'Twas never good days but when great tables were kept in large halls, the buttery hatch always open; black jacks, & a good smell of meat & March beer; with dogs' turds & marrow bones as ornaments in the hall. These were signs of good housekeeping. I hate to see Italian fine buildings with no meat or drink in 'em.

> Shadwell, "The Lancashire Witches", 1681 (quoted in "A Calendar of British Taste" by E. F. Carritt.)

[Cutting from *News Chronicle*]
16.12.49

"WHEAT CAN BECOME RYE"

—Lysenko
Moscow, Thursday.

Lysenko,[13] the Russian scientist, says in "Izvestia" today it has been proved that "in mountainous areas possessing unfavourable wintry conditions winter wheat can turn into rye."

This, he says, confirms Stalin's teaching based on "dialectic laws" and appears to corroborate his own theory of the influence of environment in heredity.—B.U.P.

And two physicians, like a pair of oars,
Conduct him faster to the Stygian Shores.
(Quoted in "Hard Cash". Author?)[14]

[28] The room stank as only a bachelor's room can stink. It was immediately clear that no female odour, not even a female bad odour, had ever [been admitted into] invaded it. —— inferred in his wordless way that even the cousin-housekeeper was not admitted into this room. There was in any case hardly space to move about in it, the walls being piled to the ceiling with books & magazines, broken only by a glass case containing a stuffed polecat, another containing some predatory bird (perhaps an osprey) devouring a salmon, & a plaster cast of the archeopteryx ——.[15] Evidently a fresh stuffing operation was in progress on the table under the window, the skin of some small animal being pegged out on a board & adding its bacon-like reek to the general stench. For the rest—though a smell cannot really be analysed—the room smelt of naphthaline; raw alcohol, dust, mice, the fusel oil that collects on homemade wines, & the peculiarly disgusting, sour, cold smell of pipes which are smoked with strong tobacco & never cleaned.*

Who has not felt when talking to a Czech, a Pole—to any Central European, but above all to a German or a German Jew—"How superior their minds are to ours, after all?" And who has not followed this up a few minutes later with the complementary thought: "But unfortunately they are all mad?"

---

* Against the last sentence of this paragraph, Orwell has written, in the left-hand margin, 'dirty socks   old breadcrusts.'

Importance of realising that —— (Taylor)* feels the bouncing of the cheque to be immensely less important than his father's inability to pay the bill. In fact the dud cheque, with its tinge of criminality & hence of picturesqueness, is the sole redeeming feature in the whole affair.

[28ᵛ]   As soon as the house had quietened down, X., who had been sitting waiting in his dressing-gown, slipped across the passage & into Portia's room. This happened, with reasonable regularity, about six times a year. It had happened ever since Portia, now thirty-eight, was twenty-five, & it had happened all through the seven years of his marriage without any inter-mission (he had first been unfaithful a fortnight after the wedding, he remembered), &, so far as he knew, without —— ever entertaining any suspicion. The reason for it was simple & unmentionable. It was that —— not frequently, but, say, once in two months it was necessary for him (but, he felt, truly necessary) to have dealings with a woman who was large, brawny, peasant-like & frankly animal. It was no defect in his eyes that Portia was now thirty-eight, nor that even in her young days she had never been pretty so far as her face went. Actually he rather enjoyed the plainness of her face, & he definitely valued the fact that she now bulged more than ever at the appropriate places. (At the times when he desired her)† the last thing he wanted was a pretty doll of a woman. What he wanted—& happily Portia was always there to fill the bill—was a large, mature, peasant-like woman, with monstrous thighs, with breasts that menaced you through her dress like the fore-guns of a battleship, & with arms that almost cracked your ribs when she embraced you.

Only twenty minutes after entering Portia's room he slipped out of it again. He did not even give her a farewell kiss—indeed, she was already asleep. Throughout all the years of their association there had never been any word of endearment between them—no suggestion & indeed no thought of marriage even after —— had died. Tomorrow they would not [29] mention this encounter, & would perhaps have almost forgotten it. They were not lovers,‡ they were merely old friends who occasionally enfolded one another in a ferocious embrace. In between times X. was fond of Portia in a mild way. At times her impenetrable stupidity was very trying, & indeed it was difficult to explain anything complex to her without losing one's temper, but she was genuinely kind-hearted, affectionate, obliging, reliable. That was why he had planted the Lerinski family upon her, well knowing that she wld never dream of refusing to shelter them. If she had now betrayed Dr Lerinski's identity & whereabouts to Z. it was out of stupidity pure & simple. (In the at first uncomfortable coldness of his own bed, he starts thinking uneasily about

* The name has been written, in parentheses, above the long dash.
† These brackets are squarish and appear to have no syntactical significance.
‡ Against the line including 'They were not lovers' Orwell has written, in the left-hand margin, 'other lovers.'

Z. then, as the bed warms & he begins to fall asleep,* eases the situation by regarding Z. as a psychological problem.)

Taylor
Miss Driver

[29^v]   a dead cock (cockerel?)
[29^v]   Far away an owl hooted, like the ghost of a cockerel crowing from beyond the Styx.
          across?

What Portia needed, he thought, was to be given a beating with a dogwhip—but a really terrible beating, which she would remember till her dying day—& then to be set to work with a pail & scrubbing brush for the rest of her life. (A moment later, in a terrible flash of self-knowledge (Q. what caused this? The jolting of the cab or something) he realises that it is not Portia's fault at all. It is his own fault for entrusting Dr. Lerinski to Portia, & this only happened because of his intimacy with Portia, which should never have existed. It was really his own unfortunate weakness for women with fat legs that had led to Dr Lerinski's destruction.)

[Orwell's 'Statement of Assets' is written on the back page of his last Literary Notebook; see 3726.]

1. Marshal Henri Pétain (1856–1951) concluded an armistice with the Germans in June 1940, and in the following month took office at Vichy as head of state. See 644, n. 1.
2. Malcolm Muggeridge; he was assistant editor of the Calcutta Statesman, 1934–35; see 3537, n. 1.
3. See Orwell's notes for his essay on Evelyn Waugh (3586), particularly his proposal to discuss the faults of Brideshead Revisited 'due to being written in the first person.'
4. George Garrett, a seaman who wrote for The Adelphi under the pseudonym 'Matt Low'. Orwell had 'some long talks' with him when he visited Liverpool, 29 February 1936; see 287, n. 2. The round brackets around 'Donkin' are square in the original.
5. Now, n.s., no. 6, was not published until 1946; it was the issue in which Orwell's essay 'How the Poor Die' appeared.
6. 'Do not destroy me on that day': a plea to Christ for salvation on Judgement Day. From 'Dies irae, dies illa,' attributed to Thomas of Celano (1200?–1255?), biographer of St. Francis of Assisi; 'originally conceived as a pious meditation, [it] has become the sequence for the Mass of the Dead' (The Oxford Book of Medieval Latin Verse, edited by F. J. E. Raby, 1961, 393; 498 for the note).
7. 'Anything you can do I can do better' is from Annie Get Your Gun, book by Herbert and Dorothy Fields; lyrics by Irving Berlin (New York, 1946; London, 1947).
8. In his report of 15 June 1949, Fredric Warburg stated that Orwell had been working on an essay on Conrad 'for some months' and that 'it is possible that he may do the Conrad essay in the next 8 or 9 months'; see 3645. From the date of the issue of the New Chronicle to which Orwell refers at the head of this page it would seem he was actively considering writing this essay in the second half of September 1949, after his transfer to University College Hospital.
9. Ford Madox Ford, author of The Good Soldier: A Tale of Passion (1915).

* Against the line including 'the bed warms & he begins to fall asleep' Orwell has written, in the left-hand margin, 'Goebbels   Hitler.'

10. Alexander II (1818–1881), reformist czar; assassinated by the Narodnaya Volya, or People's Will (a revolutionary group) on the day he signed the proclamation establishing a measure of constitutional reform.
11. Aleksandr Ivanovich Herzen (1812–1870), Russian revolutionary who lived abroad after 1847. In his writings he attacked the tsarist system of government.
12. This leaf was taken out of the last Literary Notebook by Sonia Orwell in order to raise money for the campaign to promote the abolition of capital punishment and prison reform. The sale, at the O'Hana Gallery, London W.1, was held on 30 May 1956. The leaf was described as 'Entry from Diary on the subject of Capital Punishment, written just before he [George Orwell] died.' It was re-united with the body of the Notebook on 16 July 1984.
13. Trofim Denisovich Lysenko (1898–1976), Soviet advocate of Lamarckism (roughly, the ability in nature to develop acquired characteristics). His views, supported by Stalin, dominated Soviet biology from the 1930s, leading to the elimination of rival (and far sounder) biologists, and became official in 1948 when the Central Committee of the Soviet Union decreed that 'Lysenkoism' was correct. Lysenko and his theories were totally discredited following the fall of Khrushchev. The penultimate book read by Orwell in 1949 was Julian Huxley's *Soviet Genetics and World Science: Lysenko and the Meaning of Heredity* (1949); see *3590A*. In this, as Gary Werskey puts it, 'Huxley attempted to relate the overnight ascendancy of this doctrine to the vicissitudes of the Cold War' (*The Visible College*, 296).
14. The author of *Hard Cash*, a novel exposing the iniquitous way lunatic asylums were being run, was Charles Reade (1863).
15. The archeopteryx was the oldest-known fossil bird; it had a long vertebrate tail. The two long dashes are in Orwell's manuscript; see headnote.

APPENDIX 3

3726. Statement of Orwell's Assets

These details are written on the back page of the last Literary Notebook, recto and verso. Square brackets are placed round items crossed through.

For Harrison, Son, Hill & Co.[1] Statement of Assets on the assumption of my dying during 1949.

Present. [Current account. £500? (In April abt £800).]	[£500]
["B" account. £1000 (more, I think).]	[£1000]
R's insurance policy. Abt £150	£150
[In New York. Abt £150.]	[£150]
Savings Certificates. £500	£500
Defence Bonds. £2000	£2000
	[£4300]

Future. Book of Month Club edition of "1984." Uncertain, but if equal to "Animal Farm." abt £10,000, spread over abt a year.?	£7500 [£10,000]
English edit. of "1984." If this sells according to W's expectations, ie. 25,000 or more, not less than £500.	£500

3

VOL XX Our Job is to Make Life Worth Living

Other royalties, translation fees etc. now accumulating,
perhaps £200?   £200
American reprints (Harcourt Brace) of "Burmese Days" &
"Coming Up   £400
for Air," some time within the next few years, not less than
£400
Royalties on English reprints after my death, & on another
selection   £200
of essays: very uncertain, say £200, spread over several
years.
Owed to me by various persons (not necessarily all   £520
recoverable)   [£370]
£370 + £100 (£470) + £100 (£570)[2] + £75 (£545)
Personal effects (furniture, books etc.) say £300   £300
[Income from Defence Bonds, if left intact, £50 per annum.]

[Total over say next 5 years]   [£11,970]
                                                                                   [£50 per annum.]

[Less perhaps £2,500[3] Income Tax.?]
Motor boat. Say £100. less abt £50 for repairs   £50

1. Orwell's accountants.
2. Orwell put an asterisk between '(£570)' and '+ £75' and on the verso of the page
   on which he had written these accounts he noted:
   Loans. George Kopp   —   £250
           [Sonia Brownell   —   £100—to be paid off by banker's order]
           Paul Potts   —   £120
           Inez Holden   —   £ 75
           Humphrey Slater   —   £ 25
                                    _____
                                    £470[a]
           [Aunt N.[b]   [£ 50]   £25]
           Jack Common[c]   £ 50
                                    _____
                                    [£545][d]
                                    £520
   a.   Written over £570 (allowing for deduction of £100 from Sonia Brownell).
   b.   Orwell's Aunt Nellie Limouzin; evidently paid off in two instalments of £25.
   c.   Orwell sent Jack Common a cheque for £50 on 27 July 1949; see 3666.
   d.   Written over £670 (though '7' is very faint) allowing for deduction of £100 paid back by
        Sonia Brownell and first £25 from Aunt Nellie.
3. The figures are very faint; they are deduced from Orwell's deduction of £2,500 from £10,000
   expected from sales of Nineteen Eighty-Four.

APPENDIX 4

3727. Orwell's Reading List for 1949

Orwell listed what he had read during the year, but the list is not complete. For example, on 4 February 1949 he told Richard Rees that he had 'read a Deeping' (see *3540*) but no book by Warwick Deeping is listed. Writing to Celia Kirwan a little later (see *3555*) he says he has just received a copy of Arthur Koestler's 'book from America,' *Insight and Outlook*, but this is not listed; he may not, of course, have read it, but that is unlikely. The asterisks and question marks appear in Orwell's original manuscript. In reproducing Orwell's list, authors' names have been corrected and filled out and capitalisation of titles regularised. See also *3728*.

JANUARY

Author	Title	Remarks
F. Scott Fitzgerald	Tender Is the Night	
* D. H. Lawrence	Sons & Lovers	
E. Arnot Robinson	Four Frightened People	
J. L. & B. Hammond	The Town Labourer	Skimmed only
T. S. Eliot	From Poe to Valéry	
Barry Pain	The Eliza Books	
* Arnold Bennett	Riceyman Steps	
* V. Sackville West	The Edwardians	
* E. A. Poe	Tales	Most of them
E. C. Webster	Ceremony of Innocence	
Bertrand Russell	Human Knowledge, Its Scope & Limits	Tried & failed
Peter Cheyney	Dark Hero	
Harold Nicholson	Public Faces	
James Cain	The Postman Always Rings Twice	

FEBRUARY

Author	Title	Remarks
Thomas Hardy	Jude the Obscure	
Julian Symons	Bland Beginning	
* D. H. Lawrence	The Prussian Officer	
Markoosha Fischer	The Nazarovs	Skimmed only
Aldous Huxley	Ape & Essence	
* W. Barbellion	The Journal of a Disappointed Man	
?R. Cargoe	The Tormentors	Proof copy
P. Gosse	A Naturalist Goes to War	
* J. D. Beresford	A Candidate for Truth	
M. Aldanov	The Ninth Thermidor	
* Thomas Hardy	Tess o'the D'Ubervilles	
Evelyn Waugh	Robbery under Law	

Evelyn Waugh	When the Going Was Good	
Tanya Matthews	Russian Child & Russian Wife	Skimmed only
Evelyn Waugh	Rossetti: His Life & Works	

MARCH

?M. McCarthy	The Oasis (in "Horizon")	
Hesketh Pearson	Dickens, His Character, Comedy	
★	& Career (in proof)	
Philip Gibbs	Both Your Houses	
Delisle Burns	The First Europe	Skimmed
"Saki"	The Chronicles of Clovis	
★ I. Zangwill	Children of the Ghetto	
James Thurber	The Beast in Me	
Joseph Conrad	Notes on Life & Letters	
G. Fairley	Captain Bulldog Drummond	
★ J. Frazer	Folk Lore in the O.T.	Dipped into
Winston Churchill	Their Finest Hour	
Evelyn Waugh	Work Suspended	
G. Bernard Shaw	Sixteen Autobiographical Sketches	

APRIL

★ Charles Dickens	Little Dorrit
C. A. Alington	Archdeacons Afloat
M. Buber-Neumann	Under Two Dictators
M. Bloch	Strange Defeat
R. Fischer	Stalin & German Communism
?Hans Scherfig	The Idealists
Sidney Horler	High Hazard
Peter Cheyney	Try Anything Twice
R. Surtees	Mr Sponge's Sporting Tour

MAY

★ Hugh Kingsmill	The Sentimental Journey	
Geoffrey Gorer	The Americans	
★ George Gissing	New Grub Street	
F. Tennyson Jesse	A Pin to See the Peepshow	
W. White	A Man Called White	Skimmed
R. T. Gould	The Story of the Typewriter (pamphlet)	
S. Labin	Stalin's Russia	Skimmed only
★ M. Sinclair	The Combined Maze	
★ Arnold Bennett	Clayhanger	
Edmund Wilson	The Triple Thinkers	
D. Shub	Lenin	Skimmed
Anthony Powell	John Aubrey & His Friends	
Lancelot Hogben	The New Authoritarianism (pamphlet)	
C. D. Darlington	The Conflict of Science & Society (pamphlet)	
Henry Green	Loving	

Patrick Hastings	Autobiography	
C. Brooks	Modern Poetry & the Tradition	Skimmed
Henry Green	Concluding	
J. M. Keynes	Two Memoirs	
Osbert Sitwell	Laughter in the Next Room	
Rex Warner	Why Was I Killed?	

JUNE

J. Guest	Broken Images	
B. Cobb	Early Morning Poison	
Geoffrey Trease	Tales Out of School	
G. Santayana	The Genteel Tradition at Bay (pamphlet)	
William Empson	Seven Types of Ambiguity	
J. J. Farjeon	Seven Dead	
★ Cyril Connolly	Enemies of Promise	
N. West	Miss Lonelyhearts	
?A. Wilson	The Wrong Set	
J. Gloag	Documents Marked Secret	
G. M. Trevelyan	An Autobiography & Other Essays	Skimmed
I. Deutscher	Stalin: A Political Biography	
★ E. Raymond	We, the Accused	
★ Arnold Bennett	Whom God Hath Joined	
?William Sansom	The Body	

JULY

W. Somerset Maugham	The Razor's Edge	
★ Rudyard Kipling	The Day's Work	
H. G. Wells	The Autocracy of Mr Parham	
Philip Guedella	The Duke	
W. Somerset Maugham	Then & Now	
J. M. Keynes	The Economic Consequences of the Peace	Skimmed
?★ T. Dreiser	Chains	Skimmed
Nevil Shute	No Highway	
George Woodcock	The Paradox of Oscar Wilde	
★ T. Dreiser	Sister Carrie	
E. Sackville West	A Flame in Sunlight	Skimmed
★ T. Dreiser	An American Tragedy	
J. Curtis	The Gilt Kid	

AUGUST

J. Cousins	Secret Valleys	
M. Joseph	The Adventure of Publishing	
Dorothy Sayers	Mystery Omnibus	Most of
H. M. Hyde	Trials of Oscar Wilde	Most of
Nigel Balchin	The Small Back Room	

* Norman Mailer	The Naked & the Dead	[Large asterisk]
M. Davidson	Astronomy for Beginners	Skimmed
Philip Guedella	The Hundred Days	
Raymond Chandler	The Little Lady[1]	
A. Berkeley	Murder in the House	
F. M. Montgomery[2]	Normandy to the Baltic	Dipped into
J. Langdon-Davies	Russia Puts the Clock Back	
* Compton Mackenzie	Sinister Street	
Agatha Christie	Sparkling Cyanide	

SEPTEMBER

Arthur Koestler	Promise & Fulfilment	
J. M. Burns	The Gallery	Most of
Philip Toynbee	The Savage Days	
W. H. Sheldon	The Varieties of Temperament	Skimmed
C. Sykes	Character & Situation	
R. West	The Meaning of Treason	
Truman Capote	Other Voices, Other Rooms	
F. Utley	Lost Illusion	
R. Stout	How Like a God	
Nancy Mitford	Love in a Cold Climate	
Julian Symons	A. J. Symons (in proof)	

OCTOBER

F. Urquhart	The Year of the Short Corn	
?Alberto Moravia	The Woman of Rome	
C. Sykes	Four Studies in Loyalty	
D. Footman	Red Prelude	
Leonard Woolley	Digging Up the Past	
L. A. S. Salazar	Murder in Mexico (proof)	Skimmed
Rayner Heppenstall	The Double Image	

NOVEMBER

Oscar Wilde	De Profundis (new edition)	
* R. Kee	The Impossible Shore	[Large asterisk]
T. Hopkinson	Down the Long Slide	
R. Kee	A Crowd Is not Compulsory	
A. Menen	The Stumbling-Stone	

DECEMBER

E. H. Carr	The Romantic Exiles	
* Joseph Conrad	Chance	
* Joseph Conrad	The Secret Agent	
* Joseph Conrad	Under Western Eyes	
* Joseph Conrad	The Nigger of the Narcissus	
Julian Huxley	Soviet Genetics[3]	

Malcolm   Affairs of the Heart
Muggeridge

144 books, of which 27 read before, & 3 or 4 merely pamphlets

1. The correct title is *The Little Sister* (see p. 289, line 6). Orwell may have conflated two Chandler books, *The Lady in the Lake* and *The Little Sister* (so L. J. Hurst).
2. 'F. M.' stands here for Field-Marshal; Montgomery's initials were B. L.
3. See *3725, n. 13*.

APPENDIX 5

3728. Orwell's Notes on His Books and Essays

Orwell prepared these notes on his books and essays, and summarised changes he wished to have made to *Homage to Catalonia*, at some time in the second half of 1949. On 31 March 1949 and 6 April 1949, he wrote to Richard Rees about materials at Barnhill (see *3584* and *3591*). Among other matters, he had in mind collecting items for a new book of essays, and he asked for a notebook marked 'Reprintable Essays.' In these notes he refers to the cheap edition of *Animal Farm* (dated May 1949) and to the Uniform Edition of *Down and Out in Paris and London*, published 15 September 1949. He may have made these notes before the latter date, since he would probably have known the edition was about to come out, but it is at least as likely that the notes were typed up after the middle of September

The typing cannot be Orwell's, for the sidenote typed under 'Leonard Merrick' in 'Reprintable Essays Etc.,' which lines up precisely with the rest of the text, has the date 16 January 1951. Orwell typed little after the first few days of May 1949; the last surviving letter he typed is that to Gleb Struve, 27 July 1949 (see *3667* and *3667, n. 3*). To type this lengthy document would have proved a great strain for Orwell then. The text may have been written out by him or he may have dictated some or all of it. The frequent use of 'I think' indicates a draft form. Quite possibly these notes were put down by Orwell and Sonia when she made her daily visits to him at University College Hospital and they were typed up later—in this version after 16 January 1951. One or two of the errors (for example, 'Telegu' for 'Telugu' twice) might reflect a dictated version as much as Orwell's uncertainty. This is strongly supported by the error of 'MB' for 'MG' for 'Military Government.' Orwell's written 'B' is distinct from his 'G,' but when spoken they can easily be mistaken. It would be very surprising if Orwell forgot the initials for the American (or Allied) Military Government of Germany.

Orwell marked up a copy of *Homage to Catalonia* with changes he wished made. It was probably from that that he summarised the changes reproduced here. He sent the book to Roger Senhouse, a director of Secker & Warburg, with the two pages of errata. He hoped that these changes would be made in the Uniform Edition reprint of 1951. Unfortunately, Senhouse ignored this request, and Orwell was not alive to see that these changes were made; thus the 1938 edition was reprinted unchanged except for the introduction of new errors. After Senhouse died, Orwell's marked-up copy of *Homage to Catalonia* and his notes were sold to a bookseller. They then came into the possession of Rita

Blocke; the editor is grateful to her and to her husband, George Blocke, for an opportunity to examine Orwell's annotations when preparing the edition of *Homage to Catalonia* for the Complete Works Edition.

This was not the only list of notes on his work that Orwell prepared. Reference should also be made to his notes for his literary executor prepared in or about 1945 (see *2648* and *2649*) and to those probably prepared in 1947 (see *3323*).

· · Textual Notes to the volumes of the Complete Works Edition should be consulted for an account of procedures followed in the light of Orwell's instructions regarding his novels.

BOOKS — editions

DOWN & OUT. English 1933. American 1934 or 1935. Penguin 1944 [should be 1940]. Uniform edition 1949. Banned in Australia (I think).

BURMESE DAYS. American (Harpers) 1934. This is the true first edition. English (Gollancz) 1935. This is a garbled version and should NOT be followed. Penguin 1944. This follows American edition. Uniform edition 1949. Follows American, but said to contain misprints. The following slip (interpolation of American compositor) has persisted through all editions: P. 271 (Uniform edit.) line 1, "sat down" should be "knelt down."

THE ROAD TO WIGAN PIER. English (Left Book Club) 1937. Ordinary edition has misprints, corrected in later LBC editions. The first half of the book many times reprinted as LBC supplement. NB that though the book as a whole would hardly be worth reprinting, the first half is detachable, and in particular the first chapter might be put into a collection of sketches.

HOMAGE TO CATALONIA. English 1938. Never reprinted (see notes on reprints.) If reprinted, it would be better to put Chaps V and XI at the end as an appendix. The political parts of the book were deliberately concentrated into these two chapters so as to make them excisable at need, but Chap. XI in particular contains historically valuable material. The book if ever reprinted could do with a preface, preferably by a Spaniard. Vide list of misprints etc.

COMING UP FOR AIR. English 1939. Uniform edition 1948.

INSIDE THE WHALE. English 1940. Name Essay was I believe reprinted by New Directions (New York) in 1941. Also I think translated into Italian. Publication of CRITICAL ESSAYS cuts out re-publication of this book, but the name essay might be reprinted some time. NB it is very difficult to get hold of, as stocks of the book were destroyed in the blitz. One or two slips want correcting. Slip in name essay, attribution of Day Lewis poem to Auden.[1]

ANIMAL FARM. English 1945. American 1946. No difference of text except that in later editions of English edition, statement that some pigeons "dropped their dung" has been altered (without my consent) to "muted", a piece of pedantry which I should like cut out if the book is ever reprinted. Cheap edition 1949.

CRITICAL ESSAYS. English 1946, American (Dickens, Dali and Others) 1946. No difference of text, but American edit. has bad misprints. Marked copy somewhere among my books,[2] also correcting some misquotations. These corrections should be made if the book is reprinted. See remarks about reprinting the essays: it might also be worth considering including Frank Richards's reply (in Horizon) to Boys' Weeklies.

N.B. Misquotation of Kipling. ("White hands cling" etc.)[3]

NINETEEN EIGHTY-FOUR. English 1949, American 1949. Same text except that phrase "negroid lips" excised from American edition. Banned in Eire.

TALKING TO INDIA. Allen & Unwin, 1944. I edited and largely wrote this. (Tripe.)

BRITISH PAMPHLETEERS Vol. I. With Reg. Reynolds. Wingate 1948. I am advertised as part-editor of this, though actually I only wrote the introduction.

N.B. COMING UP FOR AIR contracted for by "Albatross Books" (Europe) but publication coincided with fall of Paris in 1940.[4] Edition may exist (was slightly bawdlerised°).

Also a few *poems*: One beginning "A dressed man and a naked man" (Adelphi 1931). Another beginning "Not the pursuit of knowledge" (Tribune 1943 or 1944). Another beginning "A happy vicar I might have been" (Adelphi 1936).[5]

NOTES ON REPRINTS

Secker & Warburg have contracted to reprint the following books in the Uniform Edition:—

COMING UP FOR AIR
BURMESE DAYS
DOWN & OUT
HOMAGE TO CATALONIA
ANIMAL FARM
CRITICAL ESSAYS

of which to date (1949) the first two have appeared. To these presumably will be added NINETEEN EIGHTY-FOUR, possibly a second collection of essays, and perhaps later books, if any.

I do NOT want Warburg kept to his agreement with reference to HOMAGE TO CATALONIA, which is commercially no good. At the same time I do not want the book simply to disappear, as it has minor historical value. I suggest that if copies still exist, it would be worth making sure that the national libraries (museums, universities) have copies, as they will preserve them.

Harcourt Brace have contracted to reprint COMING UP FOR AIR, BURMESE DAYS and I think one other (Moore has contracts.) They will probably lose money by this, but I suggest they should be kept to the contract, as they must have made a good deal of money out of me.

If a second volume of essays, or essays and sketches, is issued at some time before CRITICAL ESSAYS has been reissued in the Uniform Edition, it might be better to make a new selection and divide the essays between the two books so as to get a more balanced selection, instead of keeping CRITICAL ESSAYS just as it is.

The following books are NOT to be reprinted:[6]

A CLERGYMAN'S DAUGHTER
KEEP THE ASPIDISTRA FLYING
THE LION AND THE UNICORN
THE ENGLISH PEOPLE

NOTES ON TRANSLATIONS

DOWN AND OUT.   French (NRF 1934 or 1945. Good translation.)
Czech (1935.)

BURMESE DAYS.   French (Nagel 1946. VERY BAD translation.)
Italian (Mondadori 1948)
Burmese? (May exist.)

HOMAGE TO CATALONIA.   Italian (Mondadori 1949.)
French? (translated by Yvonne Davet but not sure whether ever published.)[7]

COMING UP FOR AIR.   French? (translated by Roger Sauvé on commission for Editions Fontaine, but apparently refused by them. Not sure whether accepted elsewhere.) [See 2357 and 3036]

CRITICAL ESSAYS.   Spanish (Sur, Buenos Ayres, 1949. Appears good translation.)
French? (Contracted for I think.) Italian?

ANIMAL FARM.   French (Odile Pathé.) (Also serialised & in Belgium.)
German (Amstedt, Switzerland.) Also serialised (different translation) in Der Monat 1949.)
Italian (Mondadori 1948. Also serialised I think.)
Spanish (Kraft, Buenos Ayres).
Portugese° (Livraria de Francisco Franco.)
Swedish (Albert Bonniers. Also I think in interleaved Swedish-English edition.)
Dutch
Norwegian (Branns Forlag.)
Danish. (Vilhelm Priors Forlag.)
Polish (World League of Poles Abroad, London.)
Ukrainian (by Ukrainian DPs.[8] Printed in Belgium and distributed through DP bookshop in Munich.

MB authorities[9] seized about half of the edition of 5000 and handed them over to the Soviet repatriation commission (1947) but the others said to have been distributed successfully.)

Estonian? (serialised in DP paper in Stockholm I think.)

Persian. (By British Council, Teheran.)

Korean. (U.S. Army.)

Japanese. (U.K. Liaison Mission, Tokyo.)

Gujerati? Bengali? Telegu?* Modern Hebrew? (requests received for leave to translate into these languages.)

Curacao (serialised in Catholic Workers' bi-lingual paper. Language appears to be dialect of Portugese.°)

Czech translation of ANIMAL FARM made but refused publication by Czech M.O.I.[10] (before the Communist coup d'état).

Icelandic (Prentsmidjor, Austurlands H.F.)

Russian ("Possev", Limberg, Germany)

NINETEEN EIGHTY-FOUR.   Italian (Mondadori)

Spanish (Kraft, Buenos Ayres — slightly bawdlerised°)[11]

Greek (newspaper serialisation)

Swedish (Bonnier, Stockholm)

Danish (Steen Hasselbalchs Forlag)

German (serialisation in Der Monat)

Dutch (N. V. Drukerij)

German (Diana Verlag, Zurich)

? Telegu° (Ranakrishna, A.I.R., Madras)

French (Gallimard)

Norwegian (Gyldendal Norsk Forlag, Oslo)

THE LION AND THE UNICORN and THE ENGLISH PEOPLE — various foreign translations.

Braille versions of one or two books exist I think.*

NOTE. Some of the above translations, chiefly of ANIMAL FARM, were not paid for. I most particularly do not wish payment to be demanded for translation of any book, article, etc., by groups of refugees, students, working-class organisations, etc., nor in any case where the translation will only be made if the rights are given free.

Ditto with reprints in English (I don't think Braille versions are ever paid for, but in any case I don't want payment for any that may be made).

REPRINTABLE ESSAYS ETC.

Shooting an Elephant.   (Sketch) New Writing 1936. Reprinted several times but not recently. Should be reprinted. (N.B. whether copyright disposed of).

---

* [in margin] 'Telegu [Telugu] of Ranakrishna, A.I.R., Madras.'

A Hanging (Sketch).   Adelphi about 1931 and Savoy 1947. Danish trans.
    ditto Swedish.
How the Poor Die (Sketch).   Now, 1947 (I think.)[12] N.B. I have no copy of
    this number of Now.
Politics v. Literature.   Polemic 1946. Should be reprinted. In S. America?
The Prevention of Literature.   Polemic 1945. Has been reprinted or translated,
    I think. (Atlantic Monthly.)
Lear, Tolstoy and the Fool.   Polemic 1947. Should be reprinted.
Notes on Nationalism.   Polemic 1945. Reprinted in Australian magazine in
    which all the footnotes are treated as passages in brackets.
    Reprintable, but was written in bad circumstances and
    could do with revision. Finnish translation. Ditto French?
    (Yes.)
Politics & the English Language.   Horizon 1946. Reprinted a number of times
    in USA. Moore would know whether copyright disposed
    of. Horizon version probably only complete one. (Version
    in New Republic much abridged.)
Second Thoughts on James Burnham.   ? Polemic 1946. Also as pamphlet.
George Gissing.   Written in 1948 for Politics and Letters, which then expired.
    LOST[13]   Have never been able to secure return of MS, but should be
    printed if recoverable.
Leonard Merrick.   ? ? Introduction written for Merrick's "The Position of
    Peggy Harper", in series of reprints issued by Eyre &
Paid—not yet   Spottiswoode. Written in 1946, but up to date (1949) the
published.   book has not appeared. My introduction was paid for (I
(D. Jerrold   think) but should be recoverable if the book has been
16.1.51)[14]   scrapped, and might be worth reprinting.
Jack London.   ? ? Introduction to collection of stories issued by Paul Elek.
    Just possibly worth reprinting.
Reflections on Gandhi.   ? Partisan Review 1949. Translated into Spanish (Sur,
    Buenos Ayres).[15]
Why I Write.   ? Gangrel, 1947. (Reprinted somewhere I think). (Also in
    Italian translation I think.)
Marrakesh.°   ? New Writing 1939. (Sketch).
Antisemitism in Gt. Britain.   ? ? Commentary (then called Contemporary
    Jewish Record) 1945.
Writers & Leviathan.   ? ? Politics & Letters 1948. (Reprinted in U.S. New
    Leader.)
Such, such were the Joys.   (Long sketch). Written as pendant to Cyril
    Connolly's book ENEMIES OF PROMISE but never printed or
    shown to C. C. Unprintable (libellous) until certain people
    are dead, but should be printed some time. Warburg has
    copy: another among my papers.
London Letters.   Partisan Review 1940–46. Fragments of these would be
    reprintable. Ditto occasional fragments from As I Please
    (Tribune 1943–47) See list of possibly usable fragments.[16]
Looking Back on the Spanish War.   New Road 1943.

Britain's Struggle for Survival (not my title)   ? ? Commentary 1948.
Gandhi in Mayfair.   Horizon 1943. Reprinted once (in P.R.)
Poetry & the Microphone.   ? ? (New Saxon Pamphlets?)
Propaganda & Demotic Speech   ? ? Scope 1944[17]
Herbert Read. (Long review) ? Poetry Quarterly.
The Detective Story   ? ? Fontaine (In French translation only)

ARTICLES ETC. NOT TO BE REPRINTED

Long review of T. S. Eliot's Four Quartettes° (or rather of first 3 of them). Poetry
    London 1942, and Little Reviews Anthology.
My Country Right or Left.   New Writing 1940.
Introduction to British Pamphleteers.
Culture and Democracy.   In Victory or Vested Interest (1941?)   This was
    substantially altered and deformed all the way through
    without my knowledge or consent *after* I had corrected the
    proofs.
Any article of less than 1000 words, except as fragment.
Essays in "The Betrayal of the Left."

PAMPHLETS

At present (1949) the bulk of these are in store with Pickfords, in about 20
boxes. There are also about a dozen others in the bookcase in my bedroom at
Barnhill, and a few more among my papers. Total number would be between
1200 and 2000 I should say.

These pamphlets were collected between 1935 and 1945 but do contain
some of earlier date. A few of them must be great rarities. They have been
sorted into boxes under about a dozen headings and the contents of each box
is listed. In any box, if any pamphlets are found on top of the sheet with the
list of titles, these are ones that have not yet been entered up.

These pamphlets are of no value now, but are bound to be of historical
interest in 50 years time. I suggest presenting them to the British Museum
library.[18] If the BM is not interested in having them, they might be put into
some kind of watertight case, e.g. a uniform trunk, and put in some place
where they will not be destroyed.

DIARIES

War Diary kept between 1940 and 1942 might be publishable at some date.
Other fragmentary diaries, eg one I kept in Morocco in 1938–9, might be
worth preserving if any papers are kept.

N.B. There are a lot of signed letters from celebrities which some signature
fan would like.

Errata in HOMAGE TO CATALONIA[19]

Pp. 3–4. "Tipping . . . lift-boy". Should be excised or in some way altered so as not to suggest that prohibition of tipping dated from the civil war (actually from Primo de Rivera's time).

P. 7. Near bottom of page (and perhaps elsewhere). "Puron". Should be "poron".

P. 29. Lines 5–7. "but occasionally . . . (red-yellow-purple)". Am not now completely certain that I ever saw Fascists flying the republican flag, though I *think* they sometimes flew it with a small imposed swastika. Could be verified. There is also a back-reference to this passage on pp. 193–4.

P. 29. Line 15. "Position". Should be "possession".

P. 62. Footnote. Should be verified. Am not completely certain whether the names of the 3 premiers are correct.

P. 85. Heroices — Heroics.

P. 153. Footnote. Remark should be modified. I have no good evidence that prostitution decreased 75% in the early days of the war, and I believe the Anarchists went on the principle of "collectivising" the brothels, not suppressing them. But there was a drive against prostitution (posters etc.) and it is a fact that the smart brothel and naked cabaret shows were shut in the early months of the war and open again when the war was about a year old.

P. 156. Top line. "26 mm". Should be ".26 inch".

P. 158–9. "At Puigcerda . . . was killed". I am told my reference to this incident is incorrect and misleading. Might be verified.

P. 159. Line 13 and bottom line. "Roldan". Should be "Roldan Cortada".

Pp. 161–242. All through these chapters are constant references to "Civil Guards". Should be "Assault Guards" all the way through. I was misled because the Assault Guards in Catalonia wore a different uniform from those afterwards sent from Valencia, and by the Spaniards referring indifferently to all these formations as "la guardia". The remarks on p. 213 lines 14–17 and footnote should be regularised. The undoubted fact that Civil Guards often joined Franco when able to do so makes no reflection on the Assault Guards who were a formation raised since the 2nd Republic. But the general reference to popular hostility to "la guardia" and this having played its part in the Barcelona business should stand.

P. 272. Wallowed — walloped.

P. 298. Line 11. "El colonel". Should be "el coronel".

In addition, if this book is ever reprinted the spelling of Spanish names should be regularised throughout.

Last page. Contains the phrase "under your brun". Unnecessary obscenity which might be altered to "underneath you".

1. See *600, n. 33*; also *596*.
2. Not traced.
3. See headnote to *948*.
4. For Albatross, see *561, n. 1*.
5. The leaf giving details of poems that might be reprinted was folded with the two leaves of errata for *Homage to Catalonia* inside a copy of that book which had been marked up by Orwell with the changes he wanted made. Possibly the leaf about the poems had been

inserted by mistake; it is the only copy to have survived. Roger Senhouse, to whom the book and leaves were sent, summarised the errata on the fly-leaf of the book and changed the misspelling 'brun' to 'bum' in the list of errata (in green ink). A second edition of *Homage to Catalonia* was published by Secker & Warburg in 1951, the year of the note about the 'Leonard Merrick' introduction (see headnote). It must have been for that reset edition that these instructions were sent to Senhouse by Sonia Orwell. Unfortunately, Senhouse ignored Orwell's wishes and compounded his disinterest by removing many of Orwell's books and documents from the offices of S&W. These were sold by various auctioneers at his death, including this marked-up copy of *Homage to Catalonia*.

6. In his 'Notes for My Literary Executor,' 1945 (see *2648*), Orwell said, with particular reference to these four books, 'Of course, after I am dead I do not object to cheap editions of any book which may bring in a few pounds for my heirs.' Orwell may have taken against the two novels because of the way they had been 'garbled' by his publishers; see Textual Notes to *CW*, III and IV, and Orwell's Will, *3730*, section 6.

7. The French edition was published in 1955.

8. Displaced Persons.

9. This must be 'MG'—Military Government.

10. Orwell has used the initials for the British Ministry of Information.

11. See *3710* for the cuts demanded.

12. It was published in 1946.

13. Found in 1959; see *3406*.

14. See headnote. Jerrold did not publish *The Position of Peggy Harper* in 1950–51.

15. Orwell does not mention the abridgement published in *Mirror*; see *3516*, n. 2.

16. See *2649*. The bulk of these notes was prepared before Orwell went to France, 15 February 1945. He seems to have annotated the list in 1949.

17. It appeared in *Persuasion*, not *Scope*.

18. The pamphlets were passed to the British Library; they are held in forty-six boxes (one seems to be missing): 1899 ss 1–21, 23–47; an index made about 1950 is at 1899 ss 48. See *3733*.

19. For problems arising from these instructions, see Textual Note to *CW*, V.

* Willison records Braille editions of *Homage to Catalonia* (1940), *Critical Essays* (1949), *Nineteen Eighty-Four* (1949–50), and *Shooting an Elephant* (1953).

APPENDIX 6

3729. Orwell's Notes on Inside Covers of Red Book-Cover

All that is left of this notebook is the outer casing (or book binding). The cover is red; the inside linings are brown paper. Orwell has written notes in ink on the linings. These are in part water-damaged. The front and back covers, each approximately 28 × 21.5 cm, are joined by a back strip 6.3 cm in width. The notes all seem to have been written in 1949. They are of four kinds: books Orwell wished to read; those to whom he wished to give proof or complimentary copies of *Nineteen Eighty-Four*; notes on three contributions to be written; and three sets of initials and dates (see *n. 12*).

Many of the books are ticked and the tick is crossed through. Collation with Orwell's list of reading in 1949 indicates that nearly all the books so marked were read by him in that year. For convenience, the month when he read such books is given in abbreviated form within square brackets at the end of the listing; if the book does not appear in the reading list a short dash is given within square brackets. From this it would seem, as had been noted earlier (for example, *3529*, *n. 3*), that his list of reading reproduced in *3727* is not complete. Many of the books listed are included in the list of books in his possession at his death; see *3734*. Books only ticked may have been ordered but not delivered or read yet.

For letters referring to proof and complimentary copies of *Nineteen Eighty-Four*, see *3604*, *3605*, and *3637*.

The article on Waugh due 'by the end of April' 1949 was not completed; see *3585*. The reference to Dickens is to Orwell's review of Hesketh Pearson's biography, published in *The New York Times Book Review*, 15 May 1949; see *3625*. It is not known what article Orwell was proposing for *Commentary* 'by the end of May' 1949. His last article for that journal appeared in October 1948 ('Britain's Struggle for Survival'; see *3462*) and copy was due by 20 July 1948. Of surviving materials the only possible article would be that on Conrad which Orwell was working on in 1949: see last Literary Notebook, *3725*, *n. 8*. However, that subject would not be in accord with the other articles Orwell wrote for *Commentary*, though that magazine did publish literary articles in the 1950s. In March 1949 Orwell read one Conrad book and began to read (or reread) Conrad seriously in December 1949. That might suggest that May 1950 is intended. This entry, like those for Dickens and Waugh, is crossed through, so Orwell may have decided he was too ill to write this essay and abandoned the attempt. *Commentary* no longer has its correspondence for 1949, so cannot tell whether Orwell was working on anything for it.

In his letter to Richard Rees, 17 April 1949 (see *3600*), Orwell refers to 'a dirty old red book, which had notes that I might need some time.' Because so many of these titles refer to months earlier than April, this cover cannot have been removed from that book.

Inside front cover:

Eight Famous Plays √ A. Strindberg (Duckworth 15/-). [–]
The Strange Life of A. Strindberg. Eliz. Sprigge (H. Hamilton 15/-).[1] [–]
Mayhew London Life? Pilot Press [–]
$$\sqrt{}{}^{2}$$
R. Surtees. Mr Sponge (2nd hand). √ [Apr]
J. Conrad. The Arrow of Gold. √ [–]   ⎫
     The Rescue[3] √ [–]   ⎬ Dent 7/6
     Notes on Life & Letters [√][4] [Mar] ⎭
C. Dickens. Little Dorrit (2nd hand) √ [Apr]
H. Kingsmill. Dickens (title? second hand.)[5] √ [May]

America. David Shub. √ Biography of Lenin (Doubleday) [May]
     A. Koestler. √ Outlook & Insight (Macmillan?)[6] [–]
     E. Wilson. The Triple Thinkers (? Recent) [May]
          Churchill   B. Gitlow
          ?[7]   "The whole of their Lives"[8] [–]

"Commentary"
4000–5000
by end of May.[9]

Dickens	*Waugh*
April 25 in	by end of April
1000–2000[10]	3000–4000
	(5000 max)[11]

Inside back cover:

I. Zangwill. ꝟ "Children of the Ghetto" (2nd hand). [Mar] J. S. 23.2.49[12]
    "Grandchildren ditto [··] √ ··   [–]   T. P. 19.2.49
       ꝟ [crossed out]   L. S. ? 25–26?
W. N. P. Barbellion. The Diary (Journal?) of a Disappointed Man. [Feb]
   ꝟ[13]
B. Russell. Human Knowledge — its Scope & Limits. (Allen & Unwin 18/–).
[Jan]
Delisle Burns. ꝟ The First Europe. (new?) [Mar]
M. Aldanov. ꝟ The Ninth Thermidor (2nd hand). [Feb]
Tennyson Jesse. ꝟ A Pin to see the Peepshow. (second hand) [May]

F. Engels. √ Condition of the Working Class in England. (L & W?)[14] [–]
A. Bennett. ꝟ Clayhanger (2nd hand.) [May]
M. Sinclair. ꝟ The Combined Maze. (second hand). [May]
Sir J. Frazer. ꝟ Folk Lore of the O. Test. [Mar]
G. Flaubert. Madame Bovary, La Tentation, d'Education [–][15]

The remaining notes are in three columns: the first two list those to whom
Orwell wished to give proof or complimentary copies of *Nineteen Eighty-Four*;
the third is a final list of books. For convenience, the third list is given below and
is followed by the two columns of names against some of which Orwell has
marked an 'x' some of which are ringed.

T. Matthews. ꝟ Russian Child & Russian Wife. (Gollancz 15/–) [Feb]
Tchernani. √ "I speak for the Silent." (2nd hand). [–][16]
M. Beerbohm. A Christmas garland [–]
I. Rosenberg. √ Poems ("Complete Works.") (Ch. & W. 1937) [–]
A. Powell. √ John Aubrey. (new) [May]
Saki. ꝟ Chronicles of Clovis (2nd) [Mar]
M. Bashkirtseff. ꝟ Journal (Eng. trans.) [–]

Complimentary copies[17]

x Russell [crossed through] √	x A. Powell √	R. Rees
x Hogben √	Darlington √	M. Muggeridge
⊗Huxley √	R. Fischer √	R. H. Tawney
⊗Koestler √	[added later]	J. Symons [crossed through]
⊗Edm. Wilson √		A. Malraux? √
		J. Burnham
⊗D. Macdonald √		H. Read √
		R. Postgate [crossed through]
S. Hook?		A. Gide
⊗O. Sitwell		Mrs Adam
Forster		R. Fletcher
E. Waugh		
C. Kirwan		

1. Crossed through except for "(H. Hamilton 15/–)."
2. Tick could refer to either Mayhew or Surtees.
3. On the same line as, and immediately before 'The Rescue,' *Chance* has been crossed through. Orwell read *Chance* in December 1949.
4. The crossed tick is slightly conjectural because the surface has been badly affected by water.
5. The title of Kingsmill's book was *The Sentimental Journey*.
6. The title should be *Insight and Outlook: An Inquiry into the Common Foundations of Science, Art and Social Ethics* (1949). See letter to Michael Meyer, 12 March 1949, *3570*.
7. Probably *Their Finest Hour*, reviewed in *The New Leader*, 14 May 1949 (see *3624*); Orwell read it in March.
8. B. Gitlow, *The Whole of Their Lives: Communism in America: A Personal History and Intimate Portrayal of its Leaders* (1948).
9. Not published; see headnote. This entry is crossed through.
10. See *3625*. This entry is crossed through.
11. See *3585*. This entry is crossed through.
12. Arrangements for visits. Julian Symons was to visit Orwell on 23 February; see *3546*. Anthony (Tony) Powell was to visit on 19 February; see *3545*. L. S. is probably Louis Simmonds, the bookseller who was, with colleagues, raising money to enable Orwell to recuperate in Switzerland; see *3530*. No letters from Simmonds to Orwell have survived.
13. The crossed tick could refer to Barbellion or Russell.
14. L & W: the publishers Lawrence & Wishart.
15. *La Tentation de Saint Antoine*; *L'Éducation sentimentale*.
16. Not traced. The author may be Odette Tchernine, then a features agent in London. Her books include *Thou Shalt Not Find* and *Wild Morning*.
17. Most of the names listed have obvious associations with Orwell and are referred to in letters and annotations. Mrs. Adam was Orwell's Aunt Nellie Limouzin, who had lived in Paris when Orwell was there in 1928–29 but was living in London in 1949. Robin Fletcher was Orwell's landlord on the Isle of Jura. The one unusual name is that of Sidney Hook, and it is a later insertion. Sidney Hook (1902–1989), a distinguished philosopher and associate editor of *The New Leader* (to which Orwell contributed), was a contributor to *Partisan Review* and *Commentary*, among other journals. His books include *Towards the Understanding of Karl Marx* (1933), and *Education for the Modern Man* (1946). He vigorously opposed both Stalinism and McCarthyism. In 1949 he was Chairman of the Philosophy Department at New York University.

APPENDIX 7

3730. Orwell's Will of 18 January 1950, and Estate

I, ERIC ARTHUR BLAIR, of Barnhill, Isle of Jura, Argyllshire, Author and Journalist, hereby revoke all former wills and codicils made by me and declare that this is my last will made the 18th day of January 1950.

1.   I appoint GWEN O'SHAUGHNESSY of Cranglegate, Swaffham, in the County of Norfolk, General Practitioner, to be executrix[1] and trustee of my will (and jointly with my wife Sonia Mary Blair and my sister Avril Nora Blair guardians of my infant adopted son RICHARD HORATIO BLAIR)

2.   I declare that in the interpretation of this my will the expression "my trustees" shall (where the context permits) mean and include the trustee or trustees for the time being hereof whether original or substituted and if there shall be no trustees or trustee shall (where the context permits) include the persons or person empowered by statute to exercise or perform any power or trust hereby or by statute conferred upon the trustees hereof and willing or bound to exercise or perform the same.

3.   I give to my wife SONIA MARY BLAIR such of my books, periodicals, press cuttings, manuscripts and documents as she may within six months after my decease select and the residue thereof not selected by her I give and bequeath to my friend SIR RICHARD LODOWICK MONTAGUE REES[2] c/o Messrs. Coutts & Co. of 440 Strand, London, W.C.2 with the exception of the small collection of leather-covered books which are kept in a wooden travelling case and were originally the property of my great-uncle HORATIO BLAIR which excepted books shall form part of my residuary estate.

4.   I give and bequeath unto my trustees the policy of insurance relating to the education of my adopted son RICHARD HORATIO BLAIR upon trust to sell call in and convert the same into money (with power in their discretion to postpone such sale calling-in and conversion) and to invest the proceeds in any of the investments authorised by law and to stand possessed of such investments upon trust to provide out of the interest and of capital from time to time funds to be applied in and towards the education of my adopted son and upon my adopted son attaining his majority to pay the sum remaining (if any) of such proceeds to my said son. In the event of my son dying before attaining his majority the residue of such proceeds of sale as shall not have been applied towards the education of my said son shall be paid to my wife, SONIA MARY BLAIR.

5.   In the event that my son dies before attaining his majority and my wife predeceases him, the residue of the proceeds of sale of the Insurance policy as shall not have been applied towards the education of my son shall be paid and divided in equal shares between my nephew Henry Dakin and my nieces Jane Dakin and Lucy Dakin, all of Ten Westgate, Southwell, Nottinghamshire.

6. It is my desire that my Trustees shall entrust to the said SIR RICHARD LODOWICK MONTAGUE REES and the said SONIA MARY BLAIR (hereinafter referred to as "my literary Executors") the fullest powers of administration and control over the property assets and effects of my literary business or profession of writer and journalist including (without prejudice to the foregoing generality) all unprinted manuscripts, printed material, pamphlets, leaflets, manifestos, copies of rare periodicals, press cuttings, diaries, unpublished statements on contemporary events and all other books, documents and papers of every description whether published or unpublished having any connection with my literary business or profession of Writer and Journalist, together with the benefit of all contracts subsisting in relation to my said business at the time of my death and all book debts which shall then be owing to me in connection therewith and all copyrights, film rights and rights of publication belonging to me at the time of my death, and all ledgers, accounts, vouchers and correspondence relating thereto, or, in so far as these relate to other matters full right of access thereto (all which property assets and effects are hereinafter referred to as "my literary estate"), and for this purpose I direct that immediately after my death my Trustees shall give to my Literary Executors full right of access to my literary estate and, in the case of any delay occurring between my death and, the arrival of my Literary Executors to take charge of my literary estate, I particularly request that my literary estate be left intact and that no books, press cuttings, back numbers of periodicals or other documents shall be destroyed or thrown away; and further my Trustees shall as soon as possible after my death deliver and make over to my Literary Executors my literary estate and that in trust for the following purposes and with the following powers to my Literary Executors to be exercised by them as they in their uncontrolled discretion shall think fit; (One) full power to carry out all negotiations with Publishers, Editors and others and with my literary Agents concerning publication of unpublished material, re-prints, film rights and all other literary business whatsoever and to make such contracts and enter into such engagements as they in their absolute and uncontrolled discretion shall think fit; and so decide which of my unprinted manuscripts shall or shall not be published and which of my published works shall or shall not be re-printed and what alterations or re-arrangements if any shall be made[;] (Two) to decide which documents are to be preserved and which are to be destroyed, but I specially direct that if it is in any way avoidable my collection of pamphlets shall not be destroyed; (Three) to sell or dispose of my literary estate or any part thereof in any way that may seem proper, and to collect all royalties, fees or other monies arising from my literary estate; (Four) my Literary Executors, after deducting all expenses properly incurred by them shall, when called upon by my Trustees and in any event annually, give a full accounting for and shall pay over all sums in their hands arising from the administration or disposal of my literary estate to my Trustees who shall apply such sums as part of my said means and estate.

7.   I devise and bequeath all the residue of my property including my literary estate unto my wife SONIA MARY BLAIR absolutely.

8.   I express the hope that my wife will execute a testamentary disposition of my residuary estate in favour of my adopted son but expressly negative any presumption that this clause gives rise to a trust or settlement.

9.   I direct that my body shall be buried (not cremated) according to the rites of the Church of England in the nearest convenient cemetery, and that there shall be placed over my grave a plain brown stone bearing the inscription "Here lies Eric Arthur Blair born June 26th 1903, died — "; in case any suggestion should arise I request that no memorial service be held for me after my death and that no biography of me shall be written .

SIGNED by the above-named ERIC   )
ARTHUR BLAIR as his Last Will in   )
the joint presence of himself   )
and us, who at his request and in   )
such joint presence have hereunto   )
subscribed our names as witnesses:[3]—   )
)

Orwell's Estate

Except that it was after April 1949, it is not known when Orwell made out the Statement of Assets reproduced in 3726, nor are the figures by any means clear. Ignoring what he may have had in the bank—possibly much reduced by the time of his death—and the figures he crossed out, he seems to have had

Savings	£2,500	
Anticipated Royalties	8,800	(spread over about a year)
Owed	520	
Effects etc	300	
Richard's Insurance	150	
TOTAL	£12,270	

It must be stressed that there is no way of knowing how accurate this is, and it does not represent a sum actually at hand but includes an estimate of what might be forthcoming.

However, in the light of that figure, the value of Orwell's estate when probate was granted in May 1950—£9,908. 14s 11d—suggests that Orwell had estimated his financial position in the later part of 1949 fairly well. Of course, no allowance was made for expenditure, for example on hospital bills. Unfortunately, it was only after his death that the value of his estate grew markedly, from the proceeds of *Animal Farm* and *Nineteen Eighty-Four*.

1. Gwen O'Shaughnessy and Sonia Mary Blair (Sonia Orwell) each signed as an executrix; their signatures were witnessed by two commissioners for oaths.
2. For the division which was made, see 3734.
3. Orwell signed as Eric Blair. The two witnesses were a State Registered Nurse from University College Hospital, Miss (?) J. Wood, and a solicitor, Norman A. Beach.

APPENDIX 8

3731. Names in Orwell's Address Book

In addition to names, addresses are also given if these might help in identification or in some way be of interest. When Orwell gives an indication of why a name is entered (as for A. G. Allan), this is noted. The order is as in the address book. For clarity, some conventional punctuation marks have been added. Editorial notes are in square brackets. Many of the addresses are in Sonia's hand, so she evidently helped compile the list; a few addresses are in the hands of the addressees.[1]

David Astor
Mrs E. K. Adam
Allen & Unwin
A. G. Allan (lamps), 102 Islington High St., N.1.
Austin & McAslan, 91–95 Mitchell St., Glasgow C. 1.
Sonia Brownell, 18 Percy Street, W.1. [Written in her hand]
Boss, M. A. (*Picture Post*)
Laurence Brander, O.U. Press, Amen Corner, Warwick Sq., E.C.4.
Alec Brown, c/o A. M. Heath.
Mark Benney
Blair & Binnie Ltd., 95 Hope St., Glasgow, C.2.
[Cyril] Connolly
Cooke, Diana
Christy & Moore
Commentary, 425 Fourth Avenue, New York 16, N.Y.
Mrs W. Cox, 7 Avenue Marc Marnier, Geneva, Switzerland (temp?)
Charoux, 65 Holland Park Rd., W.14. [picture restorer]
C. D. Darlington, John Innes Horticultural Institute, Mostyn Road, Merton Park, S.W.19.
Dobbie's, The Scottish Seed Establishment, Edinburgh 7.
Douglas & Foulis, Printers & Bookbinders, Castle St., Edinburgh 2.
William Empson, 11 Tung Kao Fang, Near Peking National University, Peiping 9, China.
Editions Nagel-Paris (F. Erval), 47 Rue Blanche, Paris.
Eyre & Spottiswoode
Ruth Fischer
T. R. Fyvel [probably in his hand]
Daniel George
Geoffrey Gorer
Victor Gollancz
Harrison, Son, Hill & Co [Accountants]
Hancock & Scott, The Outer Temple, 222 Strand, W.C.2
Inez Holden
Horizon

Harper's
Harcourt Brace°
Rayner Heppenstall
Celia Kirwan, 3 Stuart's Grove, Fulham Road, S.W. [and Foreign Office telephone number]
[Arthur] Koestler, Verte Rive, Fontaine-le-Port, France.
Betty King, 16 Clabon Mews, Cadogan Sq., S.W.1 (Care of *Tribune*)
Jennie Lee [telephone number only]
Geo. Lowther (Care of *World Review*, Garrick Club)
L. P. Moore, The Ride Annexe, Duke's Wood Avenue, Gerrard's Cross, Bucks.
Michael Meyer, Oure Slottsgatan 14c, Upsala,° Sweden
Malcolm Muggeridge (Care of *Daily Telegraph*)
McIntosh & Otis (Miss Elizabeth Otis) [New York agent]
Nation
New Republic
New Yorker
New Leader [New York]
New York Times (London) (Miss Tania Lang Daniell)
Gwen O'Shaughnessy, Cranglegate, Swaffham, Norfolk
Partisan Review
Anthony Powell
Ruth Pitter
Possev (V. Goracheck & E. Romanov) Limburg, Lahn, Germany
Kathleen Raine
Richard Rees, 14 Douglas Crescent, Edinburgh 12
J. Ramakrishna, M.A., All India Radio, Egmore, Madras 8, India
Herbert Read
Secker & Warburg
Karl Schnetzler, 5 Breakspear Rd, Ruislip, Middx.
Gleb Struve
Julian Symons
Sidney Sheldon, 1225 Westholme Avenue, Los Angeles 24, California, USA [who proposed to adapt *Nineteen Eighty-Four* for the stage; see *3671*]
Roger Sauvé, ? 3 Rue Leon Lhermitte, Paris 15
Brenda Salkeld, 71 Goldington Avenue, Bedford (Bedford 3661)
L. Simmonds, Bookseller, 16 Fleet St., EC.4
Soho Wine Supply Ltd
Pastor Sevilla, 16 Winchester Rd., NW.3
Thomson, Skinner & Hamilton, 137 Sauchiehall St., Glasgow C.2 [supplier of methylated spirit]
Tribune
Professor R. H. Tawney [London address and Gloucestershire telephone number]
Susan Watson
Henry W. Whitney, 535 5th Avenue, New York 17, N.Y.
Robert Wheeler [telephone number] Burford 273

C. A. Wells [telephone numbers] HAM 0893 [and] GUL 5555; 4 Telegraph Hill, Platts Lane, NW. 3
Cyril Wilson Ltd (trees?), Market Harborough, Leicestershire

1. Names that might have been expected to be included are those of Jack Common (*3666, n. 1*), Stafford Cottman (*2984, n. 1*), Lydia Jackson (*534A*), Michael Koestler (Kennard) (*3371, n. 3*) and Helmut Klöse (*3083, n. 1*).

APPENDIX 9

3732. Orwell's List of Crypto-Communists and Fellow-Travellers

On 6 April 1949, Orwell wrote to Richard Rees from Cranham Sanatorium asking him if he would send him 'a quarto notebook with a pale-bluish cardboard cover' which he thought was in his bedroom: 'It contains a list of crypto-Communists & fellow-travellers which I want to bring up to date'; see *3591*. On 17 April he wrote again, commenting on some of those included; see *3600*. Shelden describes this as a random list: 'much of it is based on pure speculation'; he was, says Shelden, 'doubtful that some of the names on his list really belonged there, but he included them anyway because he was engaged in a continuous exercise of determining who was sincere and who was not' (468, 469; U.S.: 428, 429). Orwell's attitude is well summed up in his two letters in *Tribune* of 17 and 31 January 1947 replying to Konni Zilliacus's protestations of innocence following Orwell's accusation that he was a Communist in London Letter, *Partisan Review*, Summer 1946; see *2990*. In the second of these letters he says, 'I believe that he is reliably sympathetic to the Communist Party and can be counted on to support its policies in all major issues: I believe that his main allegiance is to the U.S.S.R., and that when Soviet and British interests appear to clash, he will support the Soviet interest.' In his London Letter he had referred to 'crypto-Communists' and 'fellow travellers'[1] and he went on: 'it is clear that a combination of open Communists like Arthur Horner at the head of big trade unions, "underground" Communists like Zilliacus in Parliament, and "sympathisers" like Priestley in the popular press, could be very dangerous.' If such people 'could get inside the Labour Party as an organised body, they might be able to do enormous mischief. Even the worst kind of split could hardly result in a Communist-controlled government, but it might bring back the Conservatives.' However, Orwell was wholly opposed to the suppression of the Communist Party 'at any time when it did not unmistakably endanger national survival': such suppression 'would be calamitous' ('Burnham's View of the Contemporary World Struggle,' *The New Leader*, 29 March 1947; see *3204*).

In a later letter to Rees, 2 May 1949 (see *3617*), Orwell discussed the political stance of several of those on his list and concluded: 'The whole difficulty is to decide where each person stands, & one has to treat each case individually.' On the same day he sent Celia Kirwan (then working at the Foreign Office on world-wide Communism) a list of thirty-five names, commenting, 'it isn't a bad idea to have the people who are probably unreliable listed'; see *3615*. See note on

Orwell's use of asterisks, below. In a letter to Ian Angus, 10 June 1967, Rees described his and Orwell's exchange of names as 'a sort of game we played – discovering who was a paid agent of what and estimating to what lengths of treachery our favourite bêtes noires would be prepared to go.'

On 13 September 1994, the Library and Records Department of the Foreign & Commonwealth Office advised the editor that Orwell had been consulted from time to time by its Information Research Department (IRD). This had been 'set up in January 1948 primarily to give a "lead and support to genuinely progressive and reformist elements withstanding the inroads of Communism" by means of a new anti-Communist publicity policy based on information concerning Communist policy, tactics, and propaganda.' Orwell was too ill to contribute directly but was in touch with the department. (Note Celia Kirwan's telephone number at the Foreign Office in his address book; see 3731.) For a letter and a report that became available after page proofs had been made up, see 3590A and 3590B in Appendix 14.

Studied nearly half a century after Orwell compiled his list, when the fear of Soviet power and nuclear war has diminished greatly, such listing may make uncomfortable reading. Orwell, however, had had experience of infiltration and unreliable allies in Spain; see 374A; he knew only too well, what politicians and publishers were desperate to ignore, of the treachery perpetrated by the Soviets at Katyn; he saw through the charade of the New York, Paris, and Wroclaw conferences (see 3610, n. 2 and 3617, n. 9), and witnessed how easily people were duped and traitors were created; and, by no means least, the Czech coup (see Upton Sinclair in the list below) showed plainly how a democratic society could be subverted. Earlier still, he had had an eye on those who might 'go over' to the Nazis if the Germans conquered England; see 913, where he says he could 'make out at least a preliminary list' of such people.

The notebook has stiff board covers and measures approximately 19.8 × 16.5 cm. It is made up of six thirty-two-page gatherings, each page having twenty-two ruled lines; the first and last pages are pasted to the inside of the covers. The alphabetical lists take the first sixty-five pages (excluding the page pasted to the inside front cover) but many versos are blank. A written list is on the final page of the notebook and a printed list is pasted to the inside back cover. All the intervening pages are blank. The alphabetical list is in the order given in the notebook. It has 135 names and is as complete as the laws of libel allow; thirty-six names have been withheld.[2] Omissions are not indicated because the alphabetical order might arouse real or unfounded suspicions that could be damaging. Orwell begins each letter of the alphabet on a fresh recto page headed by the appropriate letter in a large capital. This division has not been followed here.

Three kinds of brackets are used. Round brackets are Orwell's; square brackets are editorial; and half-brackets enclose passages Orwell crossed through. Editorial notes have been given with each name listed, rather than at the end of the list, for the convenience of readers. The asterisks are Orwell's. The entries are very much in note form, and in order to preserve something of the character of the original no editorial smoothing has been made. The narrowness of the columns of the original makes it unclear whether new lines are intended; a new line begins in the transcript only if it is quite plain in the original. The punctuation is often irregular, but it has been reproduced as in the original.

The entries were made at many different times, but no attempt has been made to suggest by describing the different colours of inks when these were and how entries made at different places might be related in time. Such a study can only be made from the original manuscript. There are two exceptions: Orwell's asterisks are in either red or blue inks; those in red are so indicated. A few entries are in pencil; this is noted, since it *may* indicate when Orwell was too ill to use ink or had no Biro. The reason for the red and blue asterisks is not known. The fact that there are thirty-five may tally with the thirty-five names Orwell sent Celia Kirwan on 2 May 1949. According to *The Mitrokhin Archive*, Smollett's codename was 'Abo' and Driberg's was 'Lepage' (see 158 and 522–6).

See also Shelden, 467–69; U.S.: 428–29), and Alok Rai, *Orwell and the Politics of Despair* (1988), 155–57. Also *3590A* and *3590B* in Appendix 14.

1. 'Fellow-travellers' is the English equivalent of the Russian *poputchik*, a word Trotsky used to describe writers sympathetic to the Revolution who were not members of the Communist Party. The OED notes the first usage in English in this sense as occurring in *The Nation*, New York, 24 October 1936. In *Comintern Army*, R. Dan Richardson states that Willi Münzenberg, a German political exile living in Paris after 1933, 'invented and made use of the "fellow traveller," a new species which was to have a significant future, especially during the popular front period.' Münzenberg was chief of agitprop for Western Europe for the Comintern. Arthur Koestler worked with him in those days and called him the 'Red Eminence of the international anti-fascist movement.' He 'produced International Committees, Congresses and movements as a conjurer produces rabbits out of his hat,' according to Koestler in *The God That Failed*, edited by Richard Crossman (1950), 56, whom Richardson quotes (9–10). Thomas also states that Münzenberg 'really invented the fellow traveller' (341, n. 3); he quarrelled with his masters and left the Party in 1937, to be mysteriously murdered in southern France in 1940 (Thomas, 452, n. 2).

2. Sir Richard Rees, who was involved in the compilation of Orwell's list, maintained that, although Orwell took the infiltration of crypto-Communists and fellow-travellers very seriously, there was an element of a game about the project. One name which has been withheld, because the person cannot be traced, suggests that this is so. Orwell lists the name, without initials; in the second column he gives 'Income Tax Dept.'; and in the third, a question-mark. One cannot help but wonder whether or not Orwell's wry sense of humour motivated the inclusion of a man who may, perhaps, have been his income tax inspector.

NAME	JOBS	REMARKS
Anderson, John [1911–81]	Manchester Guardian (correspondent.) [for 20 years, becoming industrial ed. and leader writer]	Prob. sympathiser only. Good reporter. Stupid.
Adamic, Louis [1899–1951] (U.S.) (Jugo-Slav origin)	U.S.A. (Croat). Author. Pns "Trends & Tides." "Dinner at the White House." Still very anti-British. [Awarded Yugoslav Order of Unity by Tito; editor-in-chief, *Common Ground*, New York, 1940–42; editor as well as publisher of *Trends & Tides*.	Some kind of agent (prob.) ⌈Qy. attitude re Tito?⌉ Pro-Tito (same line as Zilliacus.) (more so.)

Contributed to many
U.S. newspapers &
magazines, inc. *Times,
Herald Tribune,
Saturday Evening Post,
Nation, Harper's,
Women's Home
Companion, New
Masses, Yale Review.*
Born in Slovenia, not
Croatia.]

Beavan, John [1910–94; Baron Ardwick; see *1781*, n. *1* and *2844*, n. *1*.	Manchester Evening News (editor). Previously Observer (news editor).	Sympathiser only. Anti British C.P. Might change???
[red]★ Bernal, Professor J. D. (Irish extraction) [1901–1971; see *1005*, n. *1*]	Scientist (physicist) Birkbeck College, London University. President, Association of Scientific Workers. Scientific staff of Combined Operations during war. ["Science & Society."] "The Social Function of Science".	Qy. open C.P.? Very gifted. Said to have been educated for R.C. priesthood. [in pencil:] I am pretty sure he *is* an open member.
Braddock, Mrs. E. M. [1899–1970; see *2946*]	M.P. (Lab)	??
★Blackett, Professor (initials?) [in pencil:] P.M.S. [1897–1974]	Physicist. Atomic expert.	Open C.P. member?
Braddock Tom [1887–1976]	M.P. Mitcham (Lab)	? [Listed in Second Literary Notebook, 1948; see *3515*, n. *49*]
Bailey, Gerald [1903–72]	Acting Chairman, International Liaison Committee of Organisations for Peace. (18 years Director of British National Peace Council [1930–49].)	? [A Quaker and a member of the Liberal Party]

Burhop (initial) [E.H.S.] (Australian) [1911–80] [red]*	Scientist (physicist)	?
Carr, Professor E.H. [1892–1982; see *2454*, *n. 3*]	Times. Aberystwith° University. Various books.	Appeaser only.
⌈Cummings, A. J.⌉ [1882–1957]	⌈News-Chronicle (commentator.⌉	⌈Uncertain whether definitely F.T. Strong sympathiser, but appears somewhat anti British C.P. *Changed line.*⌉
Chaplin, Charles [1889–1977] (Anglo- American). (Jewish?)	Films.	[?? — crossed out in error when note above crossed through; then reinstated:] ??
Cunard, Nancy [1896–1965; see *386A*]	Anti-fascist & anti- imperialist organisations. Pamphlets.	Probably only sentimental sympathiser. Silly. Has money.
Crossman, Richard [1907–74]	M.P. (Labour) Coventry. Save Europe Now. Books New Statesman ⌈helps to direct⌉. Sunday Pictorial.	?? Political climber. Zionist (appears sincere about this.) Too dishonest to be outright F.T.
⌈Cocks, Seymour⌉ [1882–1953]	⌈M.P. (Labour)⌉	⌈?? Pacifist leanings⌉
Calder-Marshall, Arthur [1908–92; see *856, n. 3*]	Novelist. Contrib. Time & Tide, Tribune etc. Knowledge of Mexico, Jugoslavia. Reynolds's [Sunday newspaper] (book reviews [see *3650*])	? Previously close F.T. May have changed. Insincere person.
Crowther, D. J. [1899–; Orwell gives initials correctly as J.G. at *1117*; see *n. 1*]	Scientist (Biologist?)	?? Brother of Geoffrey Crowther (of the Economist.) Yes.

Childe, Prof. Gordon (Edinburgh University?) [1892–1957; see *1057, n. 1*]	Scientist (anthropology & history of science). Popular booklets on prehistoric man etc.	? [Professor of Prehistoric Archaeology, Edinburgh, 1927–46; London, 1946–56]
*Cole, G. D. H. [1889–1959; see *3600, n. 5*]	Economist, author of many books.	Sympathiser only. Shallow person. Diabetic. ??
*Coates, W. P. & Zelda K. [Mrs Zelda Coates b. 1886]	"A History of Anglo-Soviet Relations", & other books. [Many on Soviet affairs; *The Second Five-Year Plan of Development in the U.S.S.R.* (1938) had a preface by a leading Labour Party politician, Herbert Morrison. W. P. Coates's compilation on the trial of Vitviskii (1933) had a foreword by D. N. Pritt; see below.]	Q. Open CP?
Deutscher ⌈(initial?)⌉ I. (Polish Jew) [1907–67]	Economist. Observer (previously foreign correspondent). Life of Stalin. (Life of Stalin moderately objective.)	Only sympathiser, & recent development only (previously Trotskyist leanings.) Could change?? ⌈Polis⌉
[red]* Duranty, Walter (Anglo–American). [1884–1957; see headnote to *2378*]	American papers. Correspondent in USSR many years. Various books.	Discreet F.T. Probably no organisational connection, but reliable.

Driberg, Tom (English Jew) [1905–76; see *1025, n. 12*; *1931, n. 1*] [red★ against Driberg crossed out in blue ink]	M.P. (Ind) Malden Reynolds's News (Commentator).	Commonly thought to be underground member. Shows signs of independence occasionally. Homosexual. *Makes occasional anti-C.P. comments in his column.*
[red]★ Dover, Cedric (Eurasian) [1905–51; see *926, n. 1*]	Writer. ("Half Caste," etc.) Some training as biologist.	Main emphasis anti-white but reliably pro-Russian on all major issues. Dishonest, and a good deal of a careerist. In USA? (1949)
Dean, Vera M. (U.S. Russian origin). [1903–72]	Research Director, Foreign Policy Association. Books on USSR.	⌈?⌉
⌈Dark, Sidney,⌉ [later note:] Died Nov. 1947 [1874–1947; see *2347, n. 2*]	⌈Journalist. Books⌉ ⌈Previously editor of "Church Times".⌉ ⌈Anglo-Catholic (layman).⌉	⌈??⌉ ⌈Warm-hearted & stupid.⌉
Davies, Joseph E. (U.S.). [1876–1958]	Previously ambassador to USSR. "Mission to Moscow" (& film of ditto.)	Very stupid.
[later entry:] Davenport, John [1906–66; see *3481, n. 2*]	"Arena". British Council (?) in Eire during war.	Well-disposed person, rather silly. Old Etonian.
Edelman, Maurice [1911–75; see *3617, n. 6*]	M.P. (Lab). Reynolds' News.	Was for a very brief period "Jack Wilkes" in Tribune. ? Changed views (?1949)
Fraenkel, Heinrich [1897–?]	Articles in N.S. & N.	?
[entry in pencil:] Fletcher	Labour Party agent for Stroud	Knew him in Spain.

[? George Fletcher, newspaper canvasser, who briefly commanded the British Battalion of the International Brigade, October 1937; during World War II commanded the Home Guard at Rolls-Royce (Alexander, *British Volunteers for Liberty*, 1982, 79, 154, 247.) This Fletcher is deceased; verbal communication from Bill Alexander, 10.12.92.]

Flanner, Janet (U.S.) [1892–1978]	New Yorker ("Genêt.")	Previously violent red-baiter, changed vews about war years. Dishonest careerist. Appears to have swung back somewhat recently (1949.)
Goldring, Douglas. [1897–1960; see *2412*, *n. 4*]	Writer (mainly novels).	Disappointed careerist. Genuine hatred of British upper class. Probably venal. Shallow person.
Grozer, Fr. (initials?) [Rev. Fr. St John Groser, 1891–1966; see *2144*, *n. 3*]	Anglo-Catholic (priest).	? People's Convention. Said to have done good work during air-raids.

[The People's Convention, founded January 1941, was a Communist-front organisation ostensibly to fight for public rights, higher wages, friendship with USSR, then recently allied to Nazi Germany—but was strongly suspected of aiming to undermine the British war effort. In July 1941, when Russia was attacked by Germany, it ceaselessly demanded the opening of a Second Front.]

Golding, Louis [1895–1958; see *3610*, *n. 2*]	Novelist (Magnolia Street)	? Attitude at Wroclaw Conference? [see *3617*, *n. 9*] [in pencil:] only a vague sympathiser, I should say.
[red]* Hewlett-Johnson (initials?) [1874–1966; 'Hewlett' was forename, not hyphenated surname]	Dean of Canterbury [nicknamed 'The Red Dean']. Training as engineer. Various books, pamphlets.	Almost certainly underground member.

*Hopkinson, Tom. [1905–90; see *2836*, *n. 2*]	Picture Post (editor)	Appeaser only. Subjectively hostile to USSR? Anti-American.
[red]* Hutchinson, Lester [1904–50; see *3600*, *n. 11*]	M.P. (Labour) [later note:] (Rusholme) Cancelled visit to J'slavia after Tito split.	Imprisoned in Meerut trial. Generally considered to be underground C.P. member. Refused re-nomination 1949. [interlinear note:] Expelled 1949. [The government of British India prosecuted 30 alleged Communists for conspiracy at Meerut in 1929.]
Hindus, Maurice (U.S. Russian extraction). [1891–1969]	Writer & journalist ("Red Bread," etc.)	? Often attacked in C.P. press. General effect of writings is strong pro-Soviet propaganda.
Hughes, Emrys [1894–1969]	M.P. (Ayrshire). Editor of "Forward". Votes with crypto group.	? Probably not. Well-meaning, wrong-headed. [Listed in Second Literary Notebook, 1948; see *3515, n. 50*]
Ingersoll, Ralph (U.S.) [1900–85]	P.M. (editor) "Top Secret" (anti-British). [See also *Report on England*, 1940; founded *PM* & editor, 1940–46; Vice-President & Gen Mgr of *Time*, 1935–38]	Probably no organisational tie. Dishonest demagogic type.
Kirchwey, Freda (U.S.) [1893–1976]	"Nation" etc. (Editor of "Nation".)	

[red]★
Litauer, Stefan (Polish) [1892–1959; served in Polish diplomatic service, in USSR and Polish Foreign Ministry, 1922–27; President of Foreign Press Association, London, 1936–41; Polish Chargé d'Affaires, Washington, 1945]

News-Chronicle Polish correspondent circa 1944–46.

Some kind of agent. Was previously Pilsudski supporter. Probably careerist. [Jozef Pilsudski (1867–1935), Polish patriot, Marshal, statesman; declared Poland's independence, 1918; President until 1922; established dictatorship, 1926.]

Lewis, C. Day [1904–72]

Poet etc. Selector of Book Club (with Priestley & Daniel George). Orion (helps to edit). M.O.I. during war.

Previously C.P. Probably not now completely reliable. Said to have changed since Czech coup d'état.

⌈La Guardia, F.⌉ (U.S. Italian) [1882–1947]

Mayor of New York. UNRRA.

?? Died September 1947.

Leslie, Kenneth (U.S.) [1892–1974]

The Protestant (editor). [Listed as Communist-front organisation by *New Leader*]

Longden, Fred [1886–1952]

M.P. (Lab)

?

[entry in pencil:]
LASKI! [1893–1950]

[See *3600*; and biographical note, *3526, n. 8*]

Liebling, A. J. (U.S.) [1904–63]

New Yorker ("Our Wayward Press")

?

[red★] Morley, Iris. [1910–53]	Observer (previously corresp. in Moscow). [Moscow correspondent for *Observer* and *Yorkshire Post*, 1943–45; later ballet critic for *Daily Worker*; novels include *Nothing but Propaganda*, 1946]	Qy. open C.P. member?
[red]★ ★Macmurray, Professor John [1891–1976; see *3392, n. 5*]	Author (vide esp. The Clue to History.) Connections with S.C.M. Also Nat. Peace Council. Personalist move-ment. [See *3392, n. 4*]	Probably sympathiser only. Decayed liberal.
[red]★ ★Martin, Kingsley [1897–1969; see *3600*; *2105*]	New Statesman (editor). Pamphlets & books.	Probably no definite organisational connection . . . Decayed liberal. Very dishonest.
McLeod, Joseph [1903–84]	BBC announcer. Book on Soviet theatre.	??
[red]★ ★Moore, Nicholas. [1918–86; see *854*, headnote & *1195, n. 9*]	Poet.	?? (People's Convention.) Anarchist leanings.
McCabe, Joseph. [1867–1955]	Books & pamphlets.	Main emphasis anti-Catholic. V. stupid on all other subjects.
McDiarmid, Hugh (Christopher Murray Grieve) (Scottish). [1892–1978]	Poet & critic. "Scottish Writing" (?)	Dissident Communist but probably reliably pro-Russian. Main emphasis Scottish nationalism. Very anti-English.

⌐Mackay, Ian⌐ | ⌐News-Chronicle (columnist & industrial correspondent.)⌐ | ⌐?? Prof journalist.⌐
[1898–1952] | | ⌐No.⌐

Manning, Mrs Leah | M.P. (Lab) Epping. Went with Zilliacus on Tito split. | ? Very active in Spanish civil war. [in pencil:] Probably only a vague F.T.
[1886–1977]

★ [blue asterisk appears between Manning and May]

May, Dr Alan Nunn | Physicist. (In prison) | Vide Blue Book on Canadian spy trials. Has brother also politically active?
[see 3042, n. 3]

Mathieson, F. O. | Journalist (U.S.) Books on Modern verse etc, [The Achievement of T. S. Eliot, 1935]
[F.O. Matthiessen, 1902–50]

[Entry in pencil] Mikardo, Ian (Jewish?) [1908–93; see 3600, n. 12; 3617] | Labour M.P. (Reading). Column in "Tribune." [later addition:] (Resigned from editorial board of Tribune May 1949. On political grounds.) | ? I dont know much about him, but have sometimes wondered Prob. not. Silly.

Mounier, E. (France) | "Esprit." Personalist Movement. [See 3392, n. 4] | Slimy person.
[1905–50; see 3392, n. 6]

Neumann, Robert (German) [1897–1975] | Novelist. Manager of "International Authors" (Russian propaganda) for Hutchinson's for some years. [Complained about Gollancz's treatment of his Children of Vienna in 1947; see Ruth Dudley Edwards, Victor Gollancz, 524.] | Q. whether merely careerist. (Qy. still in Britain?)

Niebuhr, (initials?) [in pencil:] Reinhold [1892–1971; see *3600, n. 7*]	Theologian (Protestant)	? NB. Two people of this name? [There may be confusion with his brother, Helmut Richard; see *3600, n. 7*.] [in pencil:] I don't believe the famous R.N. is a F.T. He has a great deal of sense
Nearing, Scott (U.S.) [1883–1983]	Old figure in the leftwing movement. Journalist & writer.	Qy. whether open C.P. member? [in pencil]: I should have thought he had dropped out long ago, like Horrabin (whom I thought he rather resembled when I met him. A nice type) [For J. F. Horrabin (1884–1962), see *2908, n. 3*]
O'Donnell, Peader (Eire) [1893–1986]	Critic. The Bell (helps to edit?) (now extinct?) [Publication suspended between May 1948 and October 1950]	Qy. open C.P.?
[red]* O'Casey, Sean (Eire, lives in England). [1880–1964]	Playwright.	Q. open C.P.? Very stupid. [See O'Casey's letter, *2774*]
[red]* O'Flaherty, Liam (Eire, usually in USA). [1896–1984]	Novelist.	Qy. whether open C.P.?

[entry in pencil]
[red]★
Parker, Ralph(?)
[1908–64]

News-Chronicle (Moscow Correspondent 1947). Also Times. "Moscow Correspondent" (1949). "Plot Against Peace" (pub. Moscow 1949.) [Also wrote for *New York Times*, 1942.]

Underground member or close F.T.? Stayed on in Moscow [where he died] (became Soviet citizen.) [Listed in Second Literary Notebook, 1948; see *3515, n. 51.*]

[red]★
Pritt, D. N. [1887–1972] [See *2393* & *3600, n. 9*]

M.P. (independent— expelled L.P.) for West Hammersmith. Barrister. Author of many books, pamphlets etc. "Choose Your Future" issued 1940, withdrawn 1941.

Almost certainly underground member. Said to handle more money than is accounted for by his job. Good M.P. (ie. locally). Very able & courageous.

Priestley, J. B. [1894–1984; see *1391, n. 1*] [red★ against Priestley crossed out in blue ink with large ? added]

Novelist, broadcaster. Book Club selector. [later note:] Appears to have changed latterly (1949).

Strong sympathiser, possibly has some kind of organisational tie-up. Very anti-USA. Development of last 10 years or less. Might change. Makes huge sums of money in USSR.
?? [large question-marks; may refer specifically to making money in USSR.]

[red]★
Padmore, George (Negro. Qy. African origin?) [Pseudonym of Malcolm Nurse, b. Trinidad, 1903–59; died London but buried in Ghana; see *2518, n. 2.*]

Organiser League against Imperialism & kindred activities. Books, pamphlets.

Expelled C.P. about 1936. Nevertheless reliably pro-Russian. Main emphasis anti-white. Friend (lover?) of Nancy Cunard. [Left C.P. 1934; founded Pan-African Federation 1944]

[red]* Platts-Mills, J.	M.P. (Labour)	Expelled from L.P. New Zealander.
Pepper, Claude (U.S.) [1900–89]	Senator.	Said to have modified views recently.
Pares, Sir Bernard [1867–1949]	Expert on Russian affairs. Various books.	? Very pro-Russian culturally. Many years in Russia. Changed views over sabotage trials [trial of British engineers working in Russia, 1933]. Recently denounced by Russian press.
[later addition] PARKER [actually B. T. Parkin, 1906–69]	Labour M.P. for Stroud	? Dont know much about him, but have sometimes wondered.
Redgrave, Michael [1908–85]	Actor	?? (People's Convention) [set up by Communist front]
Robeson, Paul (U.S. Negro) [1898–1976]	Actor, Singer.	[??] (People's Convention.) Very anti-white. Wallace supporter. [Henry Wallace, 1888–1965, U.S. Vice-President, 1941–45; later advocated co-operation with USSR; see 3215, n. 1 & Wallace below.]
Reavey, George [b. Russia, 1907–76; educated Belfast and Cambridge Univ.]	Critic (expert Russian literature) "Soviet Literature Today." [Founded European Literary Bureau, Paris, 1932]	?? Probably not.

[red]★
Smollet, Peter
(Smolka?) (Austrian)
[Harry Peter Smollett°
= Smolka; 1912–80;
see *3615, n. 3*]

Beaverbrook Press
(correspondent).
Russian section
M.O.I. during war
[awarded Order of the
British Empire for his
services].

Almost certainly
agent of some kind.
Said to be careerist.
Very dishonest.
[Exposed as Soviet
agent by Chapman
Pincher; see Richard
Cockett, *David Astor
and The Observer*,
102.]

Spender, Stephen
[1909–95; see *411, n. 2*]

Poet, critic etc.
Literary organisations
of various kinds.
(UNESCO).

Sentimental
sympathiser, & very
unreliable. Easily
influenced. Tendency
towards
homosexuality.

[red]★
Shaw, G. B. [1856–
1950]

Playwright.

No sort of tie-up, but
reliably pro-Russian
on all major issues.

Swingler, S. T. [1915–
69]

M.P. (Labour)
Stafford

Brother in C.P. ??

Snow, Edgar. (U.S.)
[1905–72]

Reporter &
Correspondent.
Books ("Red Star over
China.")

No organisational
connection?

Strong, Anna Louise
(U.S.) [1885–1970]

Novelist(?) &
publicist.
Many years in USSR.

F.T. Expelled from
USSR (charge of
espionage) 1949.
Views unchanged?

⌈Sinclair, Upton⌉
(U.S.) [1878–1968]

⌈Novelist.⌉

⌈Perhaps was strong
sympathiser only.
Unreliable. Very
silly.⌉
No. Denounced
Czech coup &
Wroclaw Conference.

[Czech coup: seizure of power by Communists,
February 1948, and the elimination of democratic
Czech government, culminating in murder or
protest-suicide of Jan Masaryk, son of founder of
Czechoslovakia. For Wroclaw Conference, see
3617, n. 9.]

255

Schuman, Maurice L. (U.S.)   Journalist (P.M., New Republic).

[Perhaps confused with Frederick Lewis Schuman, 1904–81; b. Chicago. Maurice Schumann, 1911–; b. Paris. Both were concerned with foreign affairs. F. L. Schuman wrote *Soviet Politics: At Home and Abroad*; *Design for Power*; *Night over Europe*; and *American Policy Toward Russia since 1917*. Maurice Schumann wrote *Honneur et Patrie*; *Mussolini*; *Le Germanisme en marche*; and *La France vent la liberté*. Both contributed to many journals. It is likely that Orwell had F. L. Schuman in mind.]

Stapledon, Olaf [1886–1950; see *2824*, *n. 1*]	"First & Last Men", etc. [*Last and First Men*]	?? Took equivocal line at Wroclaw and New York Conferences 1948–9. [See *3610*, *n. 2* and *3617*, *n. 9*]
Steinbeck, John (U.S.) [1902–68]	Novelist ("The Grapes of Wrath," etc.)	?? Spurious writer, pseudo-naif.
[probably later addition] Solley (inits.) [L. J. Solley, 1905–68]	M.P. (Lab.) Thurrock.	Expelled from party 1949. Subsequently applied for re-admission.
⌈Taylor, A. J. P.⌉ (1906–90]	⌈Foreign policy expert (east Europe).⌉ ⌈Manchester Guardian. (Contrib.)⌉ ⌈B'casts.⌉	⌈?? Anti-American.⌉ ⌈*Took anti-CP. line at Wroclaw Conference.*⌉ ⌈See *3617*, *n. 9*.⌉
Thomson, George [1903–87; honoured by Eastern bloc countries]	Anthropologist & archaeologist (sub. Ancient Greece). [Professor of Greek, University of Birmingham]	Q. C.P. member.
Untermeyer, Louis (U.S.) [1885–1977]	Poet, critic, anthologist.	? Took the chair at Waldorf Conference 1949. [See *3610*, *n. 2*.] Very ⌈stupid⌉ silly.
"Vicky" (name?) [Victor Weisz, 1913–66]	Cartoonist, News-Chronicle.	⌈??⌉ ⌈(Don't thinks so.)⌉ Yes.

[red]*
Warbey, William
[1903–80]

M.P. (Lab.)
Books on Norway
campaign, etc.

Q. whether more than
sympathiser.
Appears shallow
person.

Wallace, Henry.
[1888–1965; see 3215,
n. 1]

U.S.A. Previously
vice-president.
Editor in Chief New
Republic.
Many books (on
farming etc.)
Unofficial connection
with P[rogressive]
C[itizens of]
A[merica].

Probably no definite
organisational
connection.
Very dishonest (ie.
intellectually). [His
Progressive Party was
endorsed by the U.S.
Communist Party.]

Werth, Alexander
(Russian origin)
[1901–69]

Manchester Guardian
(& many other
papers.) Recent (1949)
book on Russian
music said to be
markedly critical.)

Said to be privately
disappointed by turn
of events in USSR.
?

Welles, Orson (U.S.)
[1915–85]

Film producer
("Citizen Kane" etc.)

??

[red]*
Zilliacus, K. (Finnish?
'Jewish'?) [1894–1967;
see 3600 & 2990, n. 2]

M.P. Gateshead
(Labour).
"Vigilantes."
Author of many
books.
Previously League of
Nations official.
Expelled from L.P.
1949
Made equivocal
remark (re Tito) Sept.
1949. Attacked in
Moscow press.
Continued F.T.
activities.

Possibly no
organisational
connection. Close
fellow-traveller only
since about 1943.
Anti-Russian during
Finnish war [1939–
40].
Good M.P. (locally.)
Refused re-
nomination by L.P.
1949. Nominated
candidate for E.C.
[Labour Party
Executive
Committee?] by
D.L.P. [Democratic
Labour Party?]

| Zuckermann, S. (English Jew). [Solly Zuckerman,° 1904–93; Kt. 1956; life peer 1971] | Biologist (Bristol University?) [Professor of Anatomy, Un. of Birmingham, 1943–68] Books on apes. On scientific staff of RAF [and for Combined Operations HQ and SHAEF] during the war. | Strong sympathiser only. Could change Politically ignorant. [Chief Scientific Adviser to the British Government, 1964–71] |

At the end of the volume are two lists. The first is on the final page of the notebook and is in Orwell's handwriting; it gives the names of seven front organisations. The second is pasted on the inside back cover and is a cutting from *The New Leader*, New York, 14 June 1947; Orwell has marked it 'N.B. not exhaustive.'

U.S.A.

American Jewish Labor Council
The Council on African Affairs
The Congress of American Women
P.C.A. (Progressive Citizens of America.)
National Council of the Arts, Sciences & Professions
[no heading]
International Peace Congress (British Peace Committee).
International Liaison Committee of Organisations for Peace?

The cutting from *The New Leader* lists the following organisations:

*List of Communist-front organizations:
The National Committee to Win the Peace; The American Youth for Democracy; The National Federation of Constitutional Liberties; The Civil Rights Congress; The National Negro Congress; The Joint Anti-Fascist Refugee Committee; The Samuel Adams School for Social Studies; The Thomas Jefferson School of Social Science; The American Committee for the Protection of Foreign Born; The National Council of Soviet-American Friendship; The American Slav Congress; "The Protestant"; The American Youth Congress; The National Free Browder Congress; The Japanese-American Committee for Democracy; The Committee for a Democratic Far Eastern Policy; American Committee for Spanish Freedom; United American Spanish Aid Committee; North American Spanish Aid Committee; Spanish Refugee Committee; Puerto Rico's Right to Freedom; American Soviet Membership; Emergency Peace Mobilization;

American Peace Mobilization; American People's Mobilization; Congress of Youth; "The Yanks Are Not Coming," and others.

APPENDIX 10

3733. Classified List of Orwell's Pamphlets

[1946–47?]

On 9 January 1943, Orwell reviewed fifteen pamphlets for *The New Statesman and Nation*; see *1807*. In this article he refers to his own collection, made 'during the past six years, [which] would run into several hundreds, but probably does not represent anywhere near 10 per cent. of the total output.' On 3 December 1943, in his first 'As I Please,' *2385*, he wrote of collecting since 1935 'when pamphleteering revived.' Writing to Geoffrey Gorer on 22 January 1946, *2870*, Orwell said that he had taken on a secretary (Siriol Hugh-Jones, see *2689*): 'I am using her to arrange and catalogue my collection of pamphlets. I find that up to date I have about 1200.' Then, in his 'Notes for My Literary Executor,' signed 31 March 1945 (see *2648*), Orwell says, 'I have been collecting pamphlets since 1935 and must have at least 1000. They are only very roughly classified and some are unclassified.' Orwell thought that some of the pamphlets 'must be great rarities' and refers to 'a little Trotskyist pamphlet published in Paris in 1937 or 1938 about the fate of Kurt Landau' (see below, Spanish Civil War, 2, for Katia Landau's *Le Stalinisme en Espagne*, 1937). In a note about the pamphlets written in 1949 for his literary executors (see *3728*), Orwell said he thought there were between 1,200 and 2,000 pamphlets. About twenty boxes of pamphlets were stored at Pickfords and there were 'about a dozen others' (presumably boxes) in his bedroom at Barnhill and 'a few more' (pamphlets?) 'among my papers.' He said that he had collected pamphlets between 1935 and 1945. The pamphlets had, he said, been sorted into boxes 'under about a dozen headings and the contents of each box listed.' If pamphlets were found 'on top of the sheet with the list of titles,' they were ones 'that have not yet been entered up.' Thus, there were once, evidently, separate lists of contents for each box, but these have disappeared. Orwell hoped that his collection could be deposited in the British Museum (the name by which the British Library was then known), and it is now held by the British Library, call number 1899 ss 1–21, 23–48. Item 48 is a typed catalogue (discussed below), dated by the Library as 'c. 1950'; this records items in boxes 1–21, 23–26, and 28–30.

Precisely when Orwell began to collect pamphlets is uncertain. From the above, there seem to be two starting dates, 1935 (given twice) and 1937. Looking back, it is easy to confuse dates. The year 1937 might be supported by the possibility that his experience in Spain prompted his interest in pamphlets, and several of those in his collection are related to the Spanish civil war in that year. Items 10 and 19 under the heading 'Spanish Civil War' below might well have been picked up in Spain, but caution is necessary in making such an assertion. The inscription on *Tempête sur l'Espagne* (item 15) shows that it was bought in Paris in 1936 by Henry Swanzy, whom Orwell came to know at the BBC in 1941. The earliest letter found in the pamphlet boxes is one from Michael Fraenkel of 14.2.36; the latest is from Ihor Szewzenko of 25.3.47.

If Orwell had started collecting in 1935, that might explain a seeming conflict about what knowledge of Marxism he acquired before he went to Spain. Richard Rees says that when Orwell attended the Adelphi Summer School at Langham, Essex, in August 1936, he 'astonished everybody, including the Marxist theoreticians, by his interventions in discussions. Without any parade of learning he produced breathtaking Marxist paradoxes and epigrams, in such a way as to make the sacred mysteries seem almost too obvious and simple. At one of the sessions I noticed a leading Marxist eyeing him with a mixture of admiration and uneasiness' (*George Orwell, Fugitive from the Camp of Victory*, 147).

Professor Crick finds this unlikely: '"Leading Marxist" and "theoretician" must have been relative terms among Middleton Murry's followers. . . . To judge by the second half of *The Road to Wigan Pier*, Orwell had not studied the classic texts of Marxism closely; and there is no evidence elsewhere in his writings, letters or among the books he possessed that his knowledge of Marxism was anything but secondary' (305).

These two statements may not be irreconcilable. As Crick states, Orwell may not by then have read 'the classic texts of Marxism' nor possessed its books; but the 'breathtaking Marxist paradoxes and epigrams' may have been suggested by pamphlets, pro- and anti-Communist. Did Orwell have by then, for example, any of his Socialist Party of Great Britain pamphlets published between 1933 and 1936? Or Litvinoff's *The Bolshevik* (1918), G. A. Aldred's *For Communism* (1935), *The Witchcraft Trial in Mosco°* (1936), the Communist Party's *Where is Trotsky Going?* (1928), or Harry Pollitt's *Save Spain from Fascism* (1936), and the like?

Whether Orwell began collecting pamphlets in 1935 or 1937, what is certain is that this is no mere chance collection. The pamphlets provide clues as to what he read at a crucial period in his life, from the composition of *Homage to Catalonia* to *Nineteen Eighty-Four*, and they also, perhaps, suggest insights into his thinking about personal matters. Do the brochures about cremation and the Golders Green Garden of Remembrance imply that he considered (and rejected) cremation, leading to his requiring in his will that he be buried (not cremated) according to the rites of the Church of England? The pamphlets might repay more attention than they have so far received.

Sonia Orwell asked her friend Angus Wilson, Deputy to the Superintendent of the Reading Room, 1949–55, whether the British Museum would, as Orwell wished, accept the collection. Wilson (1913–1991, Kt., 1980), who later achieved great distinction as a novelist and academic, arranged for the collection to be received, and a memorandum of 5 April 1955 from the Department of Printed Books to the Trustees of the British Museum reports that forty boxes of pamphlets had been offered to the Museum and, because 'at least half of these pamphlets are not at present in the library,' recommended acceptance of the offer. A written receipt dated 16 April 1955 indicates that these forty boxes had been received. The boxes are numbered 1 to 47; there is neither a 22 nor a 27 (and these are not included in the typed catalogue). An undated Museum memorandum suggests that 22 and 27 'are probably two of the boxes 31–34 and possibly 35.' Boxes numbered 24 and 25, 28 and 29, and 42 and 43 are housed in pairs, and 45–47 are together in a single box; this accounts for the total of forty boxes offered and received. Boxes up to and including 30 were numbered by Orwell; those from 31 to 47 were numbered by Ian Angus, according to the memorandum.

When Ian Angus examined the boxes in December 1963, he discovered that they contained letters and documents as well as pamphlets. Sonia Orwell then wrote to Sir Frank Francis (Director and Principal Librarian of the British Museum, 1959–68) on 21 January 1964, requesting that these be transferred to the Orwell Archive, which she had set up at University College London; they could there be more conveniently used by scholars. Francis replied on 5 January 1965 to explain that the Act of Parliament under which the Museum operated forbade the release of this material, but he ensured that the Archive was supplied with photocopies. A memorandum shows that this material included 76 letters and postcards to Orwell and two to Eileen; Orwell's BBC and *Polemic* contracts; the typescripts of his adaptation of *Little Red Riding Hood* for the BBC; six lectures for the Home Guard; two articles on the Home Guard; proofs of an unpublished book review for *The Observer* (see *1447*) and of a letter to *Tribune* (see *2685*), the latter not having been published 'because *Tribune* changed its political line,' according to the memorandum; a carbon copy of a letter that *The Times* refused to publish (see *1564*); carbon copies of three more letters; press cuttings; a list of Gissing's work; five insurance cards, and a copy of Orwell's father's will. The same memorandum also notes that '29 letters to Orwell and 1 letter by him and possibly another by him' had been removed from the pamphlet collection and deposited in the Department of Manuscripts (Add. 49384).

The British Museum memorandum lists the boxes and their titles. The titles of boxes 1–17, 19–21, 23–26, 28, 30, 35, 38–42, and 45 are stated as being Orwell's own. Boxes 31–34, 36, 43, 44, 46, and 47 are not Orwell's originals, but Museum pamphlet slip-cases. Their titles are also probably Orwell's, however, 'because it seems likely that Orwell's own titles have been copied on to the B.M. slip-cases,' though the title of 47, 'Orwelliana—Postcards,' hardly sounds like Orwell's. The titles of boxes 18 and 37 were supplied by Ian Angus. As the rest of this introduction shows, the pamphlet collection is, as the Museum memorandum suggests, contained in boxes 1–34 and probably 35. The list that follows gives the details of the collection as they are listed in the Museum's memorandum. Square brackets enclose additions to titles or numbering of boxes by the Museum and Ian Angus.

1. Pacifist: 75 items, all listed.
2. Pacifist: 49 items, all listed.
3. Trotskyist, Anarchist: 70 items, all listed.
4. Trotskyist, Anarchist, ILP: 51 items listed, 2 not listed.
   There is a note that item 7, Czapski's *Souvenirs de Starobielsk*, was to be found as item 1 in box 37; Orwell had more than one copy of this pamphlet, and item 7 here was probably not to be identified, as the Museum thought, with 37/2; it was probably the copy sent to Arthur Koestler at the end of February or early in March, 1946; see *2919*.
5. Labour Party and Socialist: 27 items, all listed.
6. Labour Party and Socialist: 57 items, all listed (except the second item numbered 37).
7. Labour Party and Socialist: 40 items, all listed.
8. Labour Party and Socialist: 57 items, all listed.
9. Fascist, Vansittart, Ext[remist]: 26 items, all listed.
10. Currency Reform: 21 items listed; 8 not listed.
11. Conservative [+ War, Poland, Greece, Norway, Atrocities]: 61 items, all listed.
12. Conservative: 62 items, all listed.
13. Religious and Anti-Clerical: 64 items listed; 65th item listed by Ian Angus.

14. Communist: 68 items, all listed.
15. Communist: 128 items listed; 42 newspapers and periodicals not listed.
16. Liberal and Radical: 35 items, all listed.
17. Liberal and Radical: 68 items, all listed.
18. [Education and post-war reconstruction]: 79 items, all listed; 29 and 30 missing.
19. Miscellaneous—Political: 61 items, all listed.
20. Zionism and Anti-Semitism: 48 items, all listed.
21. Lunatic [mainly Jehovah's Witness and British Israelite]: 40 items, all listed.
[22. Neither box nor list.]
23. Trotskyist, Anarchist, ILP: 34 items, all listed.
24. Labour Party and Socialist: 20 items, all listed.
25. Fascist, Vansitattite° and Extreme Tory: 8 items, all listed.
26. Leaflets: India, Burma, Foreign, Colonial, etc.: 27 items listed; 3 not listed.
[27. Neither box nor list.]
28. Communist: 11 items + 7 items from Box 29 listed; 5 not listed.
29. [Merged—by Orwell?—with Box 28.]
30. Miscellaneous—Political: 40 items listed; 5 not listed.
[31.] Political [Trotskyist, Communist, Common Wealth Party, ILP]: 25 pamphlets and octavo-size newspapers; 31 newspapers and periodicals.
[32.] Political [Communist; Refugees]: 15 periodicals and newspapers, 9 pamphlets and 8 reports.
[33.] Political [Burma, India; Pacifism, Post-War Reconstruction]: 23 periodicals and newspapers; 16 pamphlets and leaflets.
[34.] Miscellaneous—Non Political: 10 newspapers; 28 pamphlets and leaflets.
[35.] War [Europe, especially France]: 12 Resistance French newspapers; 12 leaflets.
[36.] Miscellaneous—Non Political [personal, e.g. proof-reader's chart, hints on law of libel].
[37.] [Home Guard; War Office booklets, battalion instructions, Orwell's lecture notes.]
[38.] War, etc. [Wartime official leaflets].
[39.] Miscellaneous Papers Relating to USSR [Press-cutting of the Munich Crisis and the War; election blurbs].
[40.] Maps 1: 18 maps and booklets.
[41.] Maps 2: 25 maps.
[42.] Gardening, Household, etc.
[43.] Miscellaneous Typescripts, etc.: Typescript of *Sluggards' Comfort*, by Morwenna Pendour and literary odds and ends.
[44.] Theatre Programmes, Song Sheets.
[45.] Press Cuttings Miscellaneous—Personal.
[46.] Correspondence Literary: Exercises in map drawing, i.e. trash.
[47.] Orwelliana—Postcards: unsigned picture postcards.

Orwell's 'Rough Classification'

It is not certain what Orwell meant by 'only very roughly classified' in his 'Notes for My Literary Executor,' 31 March 1945. He probably meant the initial sorting of pamphlets into the boxes in which they are, in the main, still stored in the British Library (some have been reboxed). The grouping is quite rough and, as Orwell seems to imply, some of the boxes contain unclassified batches of pamphlets. Although Orwell said in 1949 that he collected pamphlets from 1935 to 1945, some pamphlets in the typed catalogue in the Library are dated 1946 and a few are dated 1947. One press cutting is dated 1.1.47 in Orwell's hand. A date of publication is only the earliest date when Orwell could have obtained a pamphlet; pamphlets dated 1945–47 may have been acquired in 1948 or 1949. However, the absence of any pamphlets for those last two years suggests that Orwell was not then collecting pamphlets. Many of the items are pre-war. It is difficult to give an unqualified total of pamphlets because many items might or might not be considered pamphlets—for example, a batch of small, single-sheet, 1945 election leaflets—but a figure of about 1,340 might be fair.

The Typed Catalgue

The typed catalogue, 1899 ss. 48, has been dated c. 1950 by the British Library, but it was probably earlier. There are five ruled columns, headed No., Title, Author, Source (publisher and price), and Remarks (date). Some of it may have been typed by Orwell, but since he had engaged Siriol Hugh-Jones 'to arrange and catalogue' his collection it is reasonable to assume that the bulk of the typing is hers. She worked for Orwell until he left for Jura in May 1946; that would mean that the catalogue should be dated 1945–46. There are quite a number of manuscript notes and additions. Orwell seems to have confined his annotating to adding dates or 'wartime,' instead of a precise date, but the list for Box 15 has two additions in Orwell's hand. All the other additions are in an unidentified hand. The catalogue is composed of 82 unnumbered sheets of quarto typing paper which have been mounted and bound by the Library. Some of the sheets have the watermark 'PLANTAGENET BRITISH MADE' within a double circle in the centre of which is a crest. The watermark was in use throughout the 1930s and 1940s. Watermarked sheets appear throughout the catalogue. Evidence that might indicate Orwell's typing is to be found in the use of the abbreviations 'Gov.t' and 'Dep.t,' but a typist may have copied his style, perhaps from a manuscript. Orwell tended to use a capital X for crossing out words, and this appears for item 17 of Box 7, and there is the typical amateur's fault of page slip when typing has proceded too far down a page. None of this is conclusive. Since it cannot with any certainty be attributed to Orwell, the typed catalogue has not been included in this appendix.

Orwell's Handwritten Classified List

The list printed here is Orwell's handwritten classified list. The cataloguing is almost certainly his work. It is written in a cash-book measuring 32 cm tall × 12.8 cm wide and contains 364 items. There are 25 duplicates and both *The Kronstadt Revolt* and *The British General Strike* appear three times. Thus there are 335 different pamphlets grouped according to subject. Many pamphlets listed were published in 1945; none is dated later than that. Because several section-headings given on the first page have no pamphlets listed against them and the final entry is incomplete, this list must have been a first stage in the process of categorising the collection. Giving the location of leaflets, that is, in which box the numbered pamphlets are to be found, is dependent upon the existence of the typed catalogue; this can be confirmed by the location errors, all of which can be explained by reference to the typed catalogue. So, although no pamphlet listed here is later than 1945, the list must have been made, at the earliest, at the end of 1946 and probably in 1947. (The single 1947 item in the typed catalogue in Box 24 could have been added after the classified handwritten list was made.) It is possible that Orwell took the typed catalogue with him to Jura in May 1946 and started his handwritten classification whilst at Barnhill; or he may have undertaken this task in the summer of 1947.

Orwell wrote a list of categories in alphabetical order on the first verso of the cash book followed by a list of abbreviations. The entries are numbered starting at one in each category, but something has gone wrong in Pacifism: History and Theory, where the numbering runs from 1 to 39 and then continues from 18 to 30 without a break. Some categories have no pamphlets listed. Orwell identified the sources of pamphlets, but four of the seven abbreviations listed are not used—those for Conservative, Communist, Fellow Traveller, and Fascist—all indicative of the incomplete state of this list. The list goes no further than the first eight boxes. The location of each pamphlet is indicated by its box number and by a number showing its position in the box. Of the eight boxes, Box 1 held 74 pamphlets, located from 1 to 75; no item 62 is listed (and there is no 62 in the typed catalogue). Box 2 held 30 pamphlets, originally numbered 1–31 in the typed catalogue, item 14 being omitted (*Why Blunder On?* by the Duke of Bedford); two pamphlets are located at 28 but the typed catalogue shows that one should be 29; the typed catalogue has an item 32 added in an unidentified hand and then a fresh page is started with typed contents originally numbered 1–15 but renumbered, in a hand other than Orwell's, 33–49, none of which are in Orwell's classified handwritten catalogue; ten of these are by the Duke of Bedford. Box 3 held 70 pamphlets, 1–70; there are two 23s, one of which should be 22, and two 62s, one of which should be 63. As originally typed, Box 4 held items 1–48 (one, 32, evidently missed in typing, was written in); of these, 7 and 41 were omitted, 41 because it was a duplicate of *The Russian Myth*, the first item under Trotskyism: History & Theory; and item 7, Joseph Czapski's *Souvenirs of Starobielsk* (of which Orwell had more than one copy); for the absence of this important pamphlet, see the British Museum list of the pamphlet collection, box 4, above. Box 5 held pamphlets 1–27, but 2 and 25 were omitted from the classified list: *The Education of the Backward Child*, a Fabian Research pamphlet of 1941, and *Allies and Equals*, published by the China Campaign Committee, 1943; the latter should have appeared under China in Orwell's handwritten list, so its absence is probably an oversight. Box 6 held pamphlets 1–57 but 17, 20, and 49 were omitted from the handwritten list; the first two refer to Austria, *Austrian Labour and the Moscow Conference* and O. Pollak's, *It Started in Vienna*, both 1944; 49 is a duplicate of 23, which is included elsewhere. Box 7 held 36 pamphlets, 1–36, one of the two 36s in the handwritten list should be 34; and of 57 pamphlets in Box 8, only five were catalogued. These net totals come to 340 but include pamphlets entered at more than one location, reducing the 340 to 335.

The Catalogued Boxes

The contents of the 28 boxes that are listed in the typed catalogue (1–30 minus 22 and 27) are similar in general pattern to those which Orwell started to categorise. There are some groupings of particular interest, however. Boxes 8, 11, 14, and 26 have concentrations of pamphlets about foreign countries. Box 10 has a number of pamphlets on economics, poverty, and the control of industry; 20, pamphlets on the Jews and Palestine; 21, the 'lunatic' collection, includes Nostradamus, astrological prophecies, *Why Eve was Left in the Garden: A Textbook on Genesis for the Classroom*, by 'Janet' and so forth; 23, Scottish National Party pamphlets and others. Individual boxes invariably have items out of line with the general run.

A few individual pamphlets are particularly relevant to Orwell. Box 9, item 14, has Maj-Gen J. F. C. Fuller's *March to Sanity*, published by the British Union of Fascists (see *1316, n. 1*); Box 14/65, *Gagged by Grigg*, by William Rust, published by the *Daily Worker* (for Sir James Grigg, see *1043, n. 1*); 15/22, *Patriots of France: An Account of the Martyrdom of Twenty-seven French Working Men at Chateaubriant, October 22 1941,* by An Unnamed Frenchman, and *The Execution and Victory of Pierre Semard, Secretary of the French Railwaymen's Union* by André Marty, 1942? (a single pamphlet; for Marty, the 'Butcher of Albacete,' see *374A*); 16/33, *Gems of German Propaganda,* cyclostyled in two colours, with illustrations, 1939; two pamphlets indicative of Orwell's interest in artificial languages (*cf.* Newspeak); 18/28, *Basic English* (in Basic), a prewar pamphlet and 18/29, *Budao (Esperanto),* by P. L. Narasu, probably printed in Japan, 1933; and 28/11, George Thomson, *Marxism and Poetry,* 1945.

The Uncatalogued Boxes
   The first six uncatalogued boxes have much the same kind of contents as those catalogued. Most are wartime pamphlets, but some go back to 1931 and there are a number from 1946–47. Siriol Hugh-Jones had probably stopped working for Orwell before she could deal with boxes 31–36. Box 33 includes pamphlets on cremation; 35 contains copies of the French underground newspaper *Combat,* 1943; 36 has a lengthy, untitled typescript report on 'the situation of the American Negro.'
   Boxes 37–45 are a very mixed bag, and although pamphlets are included, their contents are often quite different. The contents noted below indicate only items of particular interest.
   37: Home Guard booklets and army instruction manuals.
   38: Food recipes; duplicated letter from Rt Hon Alfred Duff Cooper (Minister of Information) to Civil Service staff (including Eileen?) about the dangers of careless talk.
   39: A red folder containing newspaper cuttings with written on it, in Orwell's hand, 'Cuttings etc. re the war-crises,' mainly from the *News Chronicle;* election leaflets; wartime press cuttings; a cutting from the *Daily Herald,* dated 1.1.47 (in Orwell's hand), about two Indians, Brijlal Mukerjee and Sirdar Anjit Singh, who had attended a reception in London on their way back from Berlin en route for India—Mukerjee is described as Subhas Bose's 'chief emissary to Hitler' (see *1080, n. 1*)—and a small newspaper cutting showing a group of men in civilian clothes practising throwing hand grenades; one is clearly Orwell and the setting might be Regent's Park, London. On the verso are references to the past 1939–40 football season and fixtures for the opening of the Scottish season for 1940; the cutting must date from the last week of August 1940. This illustration has never been reproduced.
   40: European and English county maps; also a copy of J. F. Horrabin's, *An Outline of Political Geography,* 1942, inscribed by the author for Orwell.
   41: English County Maps; maps of North Africa (Marrakech), and Spain: Michelin 42, Burgos—S. Sebastián (includes Huesca), and 45, Madrid—Zaragoza; also the Ward Lock Guide to Southwold and District, 4th edn., n.d.
   42: Cuttings from *The Smallholder,* 1938–39.
   43: *Household Repairs,* 1932; Martin Walter's *Scientific System of Fiction-Writing; Specimen Plot; Plot Formula,* 1944; for Orwell's comments on Walter's method, see 'As I Please,' 48, 17 November 1944, *2579.* Also a cutting of an advertisement by the Panacea Society, 'The Sealing on the Forehead of 144,000' (re *Revelations* vii,3), which Orwell annotates, 'Rather quaint—Sounds a bit like an air-raid. According to Rev. There were sealed the 144,000 but Panacea says the sealing is now in progress.'
   44: Theatre programmes and film preview story-sheets of plays and films Orwell had reviewed in 1940–41. On the verso of the film preview sheet for *Little Men,* reviewed by Orwell, 10 May 1941 (see *798*), he has written four

telephone numbers: 'Chatty [?] PRI 2783; Battalion HQ 16 Mansfield St. W.1 LAN 4197; Police Newcourt St. N.W.8 PRI 1113; Adjutant 56 Grove End Gdns MAI 7570.' The telephone numbers and addresses all border Regent's Park. Battalion HQ and Adjutant would be in connexion with the formation of the Local Defence Volunteers (later the Home Guard) which Sir Anthony Eden called for in a broadcast at 9:15 P.M. on 14 May. Orwell's response was clearly immediate.

45: Press Cutting for *Critical Essays*, 1946.

46: School exercises showing drawing of a freehand map of Europe by schoolchildren aged 13–17; ten pages of shorthand notes on tuberculosis and thoracic illness (coronary thrombosis, coronary sclerosis, cardiac ischaema, angina pectoris), with references to 'O'Shaughnessy 1937'—presumably Eileen's brother's revision of F. Sauerbruch's *Thoracic Surgery*.

47: 13 picture postcards in an envelope.

Orwell's handwritten classified list is reproduced *as written* (including his use of lower-case letters in titles). Additional information derived from the typed catalogue and from the pamphlets themselves is given within square brackets; longer notes, in smaller type, are added after the item; reference numbers to biographical information in *CW* on those associated with Orwell are given in italic after the first appearance of that person's name. Most pamphlets entered in more than one category are marked with an asterisk at one of the listings. Four duplicates are not asterisked: *Family Allowances* (which is only entered once but is given two locations), *Bolshevik Bogey in Britain, Towards a New Poland* and *Cauchemar en URSS* (also written as U.S.S.R.). Orwell began each category on a fresh page but allowed several pages for later additions. He underlined section headings. Lower-case roman numerals were double underlined, as was Orwell's regular practice; here they are underlined once. A few minor variations in accidentals—for example, the addition or omission of final full points—have been ignored, as have one or two instances where Orwell began by entering a location in the wrong column. However, those alterations, even though trivial, which may indicate the order of composition of the list have been described. The spelling of proper names is occasionally uncertain: Orwell's usage varies.

After the list of (italicized in original), Orwell gave the abbreviations he intended to use although not all were found necessary for the pamphlets he had time to classify. These abbreviations are sometimes, but not regularly, punctuated. Such full-points as are used in the original have been omitted here.

[Categories]

Anarchism: History & Theory.
Britain: i. Internal Affairs. ii. Foreign Affairs.
British Empire & Commonwealth.
Catholic Church.
China
Communism: History & Theory.
Fascism: History & Theory.
France: i. Internal Affairs. ii. Foreign & Colonial Affairs.
Germany: i. Internal Affairs. ii. Foreign Affairs. iii. Post-war treatment of.
India & Burma.
Italy.

Japan: <u>i.</u> History & Policy. <u>ii.</u> Post-war treatment of.
Minor Asiatic States.
Minor European States.
Nationalism: History & Theory.
Pacifism: History & Theory.
Poland.
Religion & Politics.
Science & Politics.
Socialism: History & Theory.
Spanish Civil War.
Trade Unionism: History & Theory.
Trotskyism: History & Theory.
U.S.A. <u>i.</u> Internal Affairs. <u>ii.</u> Foreign Policy & Affairs.
U.S.S.R. <u>i.</u> Internal Affairs. <u>ii.</u> Foreign Affairs.
War of 1914–18.
War of 1939–45.
Russian Revolution: History of
Zionism & Antisemitism: History & Theory.

Orwell's Abbreviations

Con. Conservative. L.P. Labour Party. L.S. Left Socialist. C. Communist. F.T. Fellow Traveller. Tr. Trotskyist. An. Anarchist. P. Pacifist. F. Fascist

Editorial Abbreviations

ACLU   American Civil Liberties Union
AF   Anarchist Federation
APF   Anglican Pacifist Fellowship
Au   Published by the author
BRC   Bombing Restriction Committee
CBCO   Central Board for Conscientious Objectors
COPC   Co-Operative Copartnership Propaganda Committee
CSC   Community Service Committee
CSYH   Clarion Socialist Youth Hostel
FP   Freedom Press
FPC   Friends' Peace Committee
FPDC   Freedom Press Defence Committee
FR   Fellowship of Reconciliation
FRS   Fabian Research Series
FS   Fabian Society

IAA   Italian Anti-Fascist Action Committee
IFC   India Freedom Campaign
ILP   Independent Labour Party
LBAS   London Bureau of the Austrian Socialists
LL   Leninist League
LP   Liberty Publications
LRD   Labour Research Department
NCC   No Conscription Council
NMWM   No More War Movement
NPC   National Peace Council
NFPB (or C)   Northern Friends' Peace Board (or Council)
PCG   Peace Community Group
PN   Peace News
PNP   Peace News Pamphlet
PPU   Peace Pledge Union.
PPUn   Pacifist Publicity Unit
PSG   Pacifist Socialist Group
PWDP   Post-War Discussion Pamphlets

SC Socialist Correspondence	WAP Workers' Age Publications
SLP Socialist Labour Press	WIL Workers' International League
SP The Strickland Press	WIP Workers' International Press
SPGB Socialist Party of Great Britain	WRI War Resistance International
UDC Union of Democratic Control	

Anarchism: Theory & History

* 1. The British General Strike (Tom Brown) 3 [FP,   Box 3 (10)
1943]

The figure 3 indicates the number of copies Orwell had. See also
item 12 below.

2. The Anarchist Revolution (G. Barrett) [FP, 1920]   (An) Box 3 (12)
3. Anarchy (Malatesta) [FP, 1942]   (An) Box 3 (13)

Errico Malatesta (1850–1932), Italian Anarchist. FP also
published his *Anarchy*.

4. Objections to Anarchism (G. Barrett) [FP, 1921]   (An) Box 3 (20)
5. Revolutionary Government (Kropotkin) [*2346*,   (An) Box 3 (56)
n. 1] [FP, 1941]
6. What is Anarchism° (Woodcock) [*1270, n. 2*] [FP,   (An) Box 4 (1)
1945]

Orwell initially wrote Box 3.

7. The Struggle in the Factory [AF, 1945]   (An) Box 4 (8)
8. Vote For What? (Malatesta) [FP, 1945]   (An) Box 4 (28)
9. Freedom—Is it a Crime? (H. Read) [*953, n. 1*]   (An) Box 4 (29)
[FPDC, 1945]
10. Selections from Godwin's 'Political Justice' [FP,   (An) Box 4 (39)
1945]
11. Peter Kropotkin—His Federalist Ideas (Berneri)   (An) Box 4 (42)
[FP, 1942]

First published in Italian, 1922. Camillo Berneri (1897–1937),
Italian anarchist, father of Marie-Louise Berneri, *3042, n. 4*; took
refuge in France, 1926, following Mussolini's rise to power.
Murdered in Barcelona.

12. The British General Strike [Tom Brown, FP, 1943;   (An) Box 4 (45)
as item 1]
13. Socialism versus Anarchism (Daniel de Leon) [SLP,   (An) Box 4 (19)
Prewar]

Daniel de Leon, intellectual Marxist initially involved in
formation in the U.S. of I.W.W. (International Workers of the
World); broke away in 1908 because committed to political
action through the Socialist Labour Party. (James Joll, *The
Anarchists*, 201–02.) Typescript spells name 'D. de Lion.'

Britain: Internal Affairs

1. Memorandum of the Avoidance of Violence in the   (P) Box 1 (4)
Control of Insanity [PPU Prewar]
2. Conscription of Children (Education) (J. H.   (P) Box 1 (58)
Jackson) [PPU, Wartime]

3. Labour's Black Manifesto (Preston Benson) [PPU,   (P) Box 1 (72)
   Prewar]

★ 4. Why We Oppose Conscription ([James] Maxton   (P) Box 1 (73)
   [*424, n. 2*] [George] Lansbury, *[2633, n. 2]* etc.
   [James McGovern, Aneurin Bevan]) [ILP, Prewar]

★ 5. The C.O. and the Future [CBCO, 1944]   (P) Box 2 (2)

6. A Mechanistic or a Human Society? (W[ilfred]   (P) Box 2 (4)
   Wellock) [PPU, Wartime]

★ 7. The C.O's Hansard [CBCO, 1942]   (P) Box 2 (31)

8. The Real Battle for Britain [W. Padley, ILP,   (Tr) Box 3 (31)
   Wartime]

9. What's This National Service? [ILP, 1939]   (Tr) Box 3 (36)

10. Pensions Can be Raised to 20/– (C. Stephen) [ILP,   (Tr) Box 3 (41)
    Prewar]

11. Scotland—Nation or Desert? (O. Brown) [Scottish   (Tr) Box 3 (48)
    Socialist Party, 1942]

12. Hitlerism in the Highlands (O. Brown) [Au,   (Tr) Box 3 (49)
    Wartime]

13. Better Pensions Now ([D.] Caradice & [C.]   (Tr) Box 3 (54)
    Stanfield) [ILP, Wartime]

14. Homes or Hovels (Woodcock) [FP, 1944]   (An) Box 4 (6)
    Orwell originally wrote 'Tr' for 'An.'

15. Family Allowances: A Socialist Analysis. 2 [SPGB,   (Tr) Box 4 (10
    Wartime]   & 43)

★16. The French Cooks' Syndicate (W. McCartney)   (An) Box 4 (31)
    [FP, 1945]
    Reviewed by Orwell, 8 September 1945, *2746*.

17. Under the Banner of Connolly (P. Dooley) ['Irish   (An) Box 4 (32)
    Freedom,' Wartime]
    This is a manuscript addition to the typed catalogue. The hand is
    unidentified (Siriol Hugh-Jones's?).

18. The Assistance Board (J. S. Clarke) [FRS, 1941]   (LS) Box 5 (4)

19. Back to Work? (H. Levy) [FRS, 1941]   (LS) Box 5 (5)

20. Labour Fights for Workmen's Compensation ([J.]   (LP) Box 5 (16)
    Lawson) [Labour Publications Department, 1938]

21. Letter to an Industrial Manager ([G. D. H.] Cole)   (LS) Box 5 (19)
    [*3600, n. 5; 3732*] [FS, Wartime]

★22. Behind the Scenes of the Great Strike ([H.] Fyfe)   (LP) Box 5 (21)
    [Labour Publications Co., 1926]
    Orwell first wrote 'LS' for 'LP.'

23. The Railways—Retrospect & Prospect ([G.]   (LP) Box 5 (26)
    Ridley) [Labour Publications Department, 1942]

24. British Railways & Unemployment ([E.R.B.]   (LS) Box 6 (18)
    Roberts) [Industrial Transport Publications, Pre-
    war]

25. How will planning affect land ownership? ([E.S.]   (LS) Box 6 (22)
    Watkins) [Planning Bogies° Series, 1945]

7. You Remember Abyssinia? [Reg Reynolds; *1060,*   (P) Box 2 (25)
   n. 1. NMWM, 1936]
8. Towards a New League ([H.N.] Brailsford) [*424,*   (LS) Box 5 (12)
   n. 3] [New Statesman, 1936]
9. Planning World Trade ([G.D.H.] Cole) [PWDP,   (LP) Box 6 (46)
   1944?]
10. Bolshevik Bogey in Britain (E[mrys] Hughes)   (LP) Box 7 (19)
    [*3732*) [Civic Press, 1943]
11. The Dying Peace (Vigilantes) [New Statesman,   (LS) Box 7 (32)
    1933]

British Empire & Commonwealth

1. Come & See the Empire by the All Red Route [ILP,   (Tr) Box 3 (37)
   Prewar]
   <small>The layout of the cover suggests that 'By the All Red Route' ('B' is capitalised) is both title and 'author.'</small>
2. Stepmother Britain (O. Brown) [Scottish Socialist   (Tr) Box 3 (47)
   Party, Wartime]
3. The Forgotten Island—Newfoundland ([Lord]   (LS) Box 6 (38)
   Ammon) [FRS, 1944]
4. The Colonies & Us ([R.] Hinden) [FS, Wartime]   (LS) Box 7 (17)

Catholic Church

1. The Roman Catholic Church & the Modern Age   (Tr) Box 3 (66)
   (F. A. Ridley) [FP, nd]

China

1. Allies & Equals—Extraterritoriality in China   (LS) Box 5 (25)
   [China Campaign Committee, 1943]

Communism: History & Theory

1. People's Front Illusion (J. Lovestone) [WAP, USA,   (Tr) Box 3 (15)
   1937]
2. For Communism (G. A. Aldred) [Au (Glasgow),   (Tr) Box 4 (22)
   1935]
   <small>This is one of the pamphlets missing from its Box in 1994.</small>
3. Songs of the People [verse; Various, University   (LS) Box 5 (9)
   Labour Federation, n.d.]
4. Communist Circus (T. Wakley) [CSYH, Wartime]   (Tr) Box 3 (5)
5. Defend Socialism from the Communists ([T.]   (Tr) Box 3 (42)
   Taylor) [ILP, 1942]

Fascism: History & Theory

1. Why Hitler? (H. R[unham] Brown) [WRI,   (P) Box 1 (18)
   Wartime]
2. Facism° Comes like This (J. H[ampden] Jackson)   (P) Box 1 (22)
   [PPU, Prewar]

France: Internal Affairs
1. Une Circulaire du Syndicalisme Français [Groupe   (Tr) Box 3 (55)
Syndicale Française, 1941]
2. France—the Political Problem ('Gabriel') 2 [ILP,   (Tr) Box 4   (3)
1944]

[Although Orwell's list of contents has a section for France, Foreign &
Colonial Affairs, no pamphlets are listed under this heading.]

Germany: Internal Affairs
1. Germany's Record 2 [Parliamentary Peace Aims   (LS) Box 6 (11)
Group, Wartime]
2. La Otra Alemania [Alemanes antinazis de   (LS) Box 6 (10)
Sudamerica, 1942]
3. What Buchenwald *really* means ([V.] Gollancz)   (LP) Box 6 (56)
[Gollancz, 1945]
4. The Other Germany [cyclostyled; Trade Union   (LS) Box 7 (36)
Centre for German Workers in Great Britain, 1943]
5. Forces of Resistance Inside Germany [as 4. above]   (LS) Box 7 (35)
6. Germany & the Hitlerite State ([Bishop of]   (LS) Box 8   (2)
Chichester) [Gollancz, 1944]

[Although Orwell's list of contents has a section for Germany, Foreign
Affairs, no pamphlets are listed under this heading.]

Germany: post-war treatment of
1. —And So the Peace Was Lost (F. E. Pollard) [FPC,   (P) Box 1 (44)
1942]
2. The War Has Come—Must Peace be Left Behind?   (P) Box 1 (56)
[FPC, 1941]
3. What about Germany? [NPC, 1944]   (P) Box 2   (3)
4. What Shall [Should] We Do About Germany? (Carl   (P) Box 2   (9)
Heath) [FPC, 1943]
5. Germany? We Must Make Up Our Minds   (P) Box 2 (23)
(G[erald] Bailey) [NPC, 1945]
6. For a German October!   (Tr) Box 3 (27)
7. Commonsense versus Vansittartism (D. Brown) 2   (Tr) Box 3 (46)
[ILP, Wartime]
For this and 19 below, see opening section of 'London Letter,'
1.1.42, *913*.
8. Germany—the Key to the International Situation   (Tr) Box 4 (16)
([L.] Trotsky) [Fourth International, 1944]
9. Is the German Working-Class Guilty? [SLP?,   (Tr) Box 4 (20)
Wartime, duplicated]
The typescript has 'S.A.P.'
10. Help Germany to Revolt! ([H.] Monte [and H. von   (LP) Box 5   (6)
Rauschenplat]) [FRS, 1942]
The party affiliation was first written as 'C'; then what looks like
'LS' (cf. 18 below).

11. Restive Austria ([J.] Kostmann) 2 [Austrian Centre   (LS) Box 5 (14)
and Young Austria, 1942]
12. The Case of Austria [Free Austria Movement,   (LS) Box 5 (18)
1942]
13. Making Germany Pay? ([H. N.] Brailsford) [NPC,   (LS) Box 6 (7)
1944]
14. Mr. Deakin & German Responsibility ([J.] Walker)   (LS) Box 6 (26)
['Fight for Freedom,' 1943]
15. Sudeten Deutsche Wohin ([G.] Beuer) [Lofax   (LS) Box 6 (27)
(London) Ltd, 1943]
16. Austria—Conditions of Prosperity ([K.] Ausch)   (LS) Box 7 (7)
[LBAS, Wartime]
17. The Future of Austria ([J.] Braunthal) [Gollancz,   (LS) Box 7 (8)
1943]
18. Help Germany to Revolt! ([H.] Monte [and H. von   (LS) Box 7 (20)
Rauschenplat]) 2 [FS, Wartime]
19. Vansittart's Gift for Goebbels (H. Fraenkel) [FS,   (LS) Box 7 (22)
1941]
See *758, n. 1* and *913*, section 1.

India & Burma
1. The Indian Problem (A. K. Jameson) [PNP, 1945]   (P) Box 2 (26)
2. The New Indian Rope Trick (R[eg] Reynolds)   (Tr) Box 3 (8)
[IFC, 1943]
3. The Road to India's Freedom [E. Grant and A.   (Tr) Box 3 (26)
Scott; WIL, 1941]
4. Indians in Britain—Should They be Compelled to   (Tr) Box 4 (11)
Fight? [Fenner Brockway; *363, n. 4*; IFC, 1944]
5. India & British Commonwealth [C. Akbar Kahn   (Tr) Box 4 (13)
(Khan?); Hindustani Press. 1944]
6. India & the Atlantic Charter ([R.] Sorensen) [India   (LS) Box 5 (20)
League, 1942]
7. The Way Out (Rajagopalachari) [Oxford   (LS) Box 6 (2)
University Press, 1944]
Chakravarti Rajagopalachari (1879–1974), Indian nationalist
who nevertheless supported the Allied cause, 1939–45; last
Governor-General of India, 1948–50.
8. Indian Famine [LRD, 1944]   (LP) Box 6 (3)
9. Dundee & Calcutta (T. Cook) [Dundee Trades &   (LP) Box 6 (54)
Labour Council, 1945?]
Orwell first entered 'Italy's Struggle for Liberation' here; see
next section, 5.
10. Violence in India. Is Congress to Blame? [IFC,   (LS) Box 7 (5)
1943]
11. Famine? ([N.] Gangulee) [*1861, n. 1*] [Swaraj   (LS) Box 7 (3)
House, London, 1943]

Italy

1. The Italian Revolution ([G.] Russell & [Hugh]   (Tr) Box 3 (11)
   Brannan) [Militant Scottish Miner, 1944]
2. We Must Reconquer Italy ([A.] Caltabiano) [IAA,   (Tr) Box 3 (62)
   1942; duplicated]
3. Italy After Mussolini ([John] Hewetson) [FP, 1945]   (An) Box 4 (35)
4. A Free Italy in a Free Europe (I. Thomas) 3 [Friends (LS) Box 6 (43)
   of Free Italy, 1944]
5. Italy's Struggle for Liberation [Various;   (LS) Box 6 (30)
   International Publishing Co., 1944]
6. Italy Works her Passage ([G. V.] Selsey) [British-   (LS) Box 6 (57)
   Italian Society, 1945]
7. Italy's War Crimes in Ethiopia 2 [New Times &   (LS) Box 8 (1)
   Ethiopian News, Prewar?]
8. Rise and Fall of Italy's Fascist Empire ([J.T.]   (LS) Box 8 (5)
   Murphy) [J. Crowther, 1943]

Japan: History & Policy

1. Japan—the Problem of Asia (D. Woodman) [Pilot   (LS) Box 6 (41)
   Press, 1944]

[Although Orwell's list of contents has a section for Japan, Post-war treatment of, and a section for Minor Asiatic States, no pamphlets are listed under these headings.]

Minor European States

1. Belgium (Roy Walker) [PPU, Wartime]   (P) Box 1 (14)
2. Luxemburg [American, 1943]   (LS) Box 6 (19)
3. Greece Fights for Freedom! [Greek-American   (LS) Box 6 (15)
   Labour Committee, 1944]
4. The Truth about Greece [Greek Unity Committee,   (LS) Box 6 (16)
   1944]
5. Report[s] on the [Underground] Resistance   (LS) Box 7 (34)
   Movement in Austria [LBAS, 1943; cyclostyled]
   Orwell gave the position as 36 but the typed catalogue makes
   plain that this should be 34.

[Although Orwell's list of contents has a section for Nationalism: History & Theory, no pamphlets are listed under this heading.]

Pacifism: History & Theory

1. The Wisdom of Ghandi° (Roy Walker) [Dakers;   (P) Box 1 (1)
   signed copy]
2. An Open Letter (Rose Macaulay) (600, n. 29]   (P) Box 1 (3)
   [PPU, 1937]
3. Income & the Community [PSG, 1940]   (P) Box 1 (12)
4. Pacifism, Revolution & Community (A[lexander]   (P) Box 1 (13)
   Miller) [PSG; Proof copy of banned pamphlet]
5. Pacifists over the World (H[arold] Bing) [WRI,   (P) Box 1 (15)
   1943]

6. The Unknown Soldier (H. E[merson] Fosdick)   (P) Box 1 (16)
   [PPU 1943; written 1933]
7. What are You Going to Do About It? (1) (A[ldous]   (P) Box 1 (19)
   Huxley) [*600, n. 43*] [PPU, 1936]
   <small>Orwell initially entered *Why Hitler?* here; see Fascism: History & Theory. 1.</small>
8. Peace Service Handbook [PPU, Prewar]   (P) Box 1 (20)
9. Encyclopaedia of Pacifism (A[ldous] Huxley)   (P) Box 1 (23)
   [Chatto & Windus, 1937]
10. Conscience & the War (U.S.A.) [ACLU, 1943]   (P) Box 1 (26)
11. The Economics of Peace (J. M. Murry) [*95*] [PPU]   (P) Box 1 (27)
12. Sanctions Junction, Change Here for Peace (R. Fry)   (P) Box 1 (28)
    [Au, 1936; rptd 1939]
    <small>Ruth Fry responded to Orwell's review of pamphlet literature (see *1807*) with a charming letter in which she said she was 'a pretty ardent pamphleteer' whom Orwell would probably describe as 'a crank who passionately wants to say something.' She sent Orwell some of her pamphlets for his collection and to give him 'the pleasure of laughing at them.'</small>
13. State Housekeeping (R. Fry) [Au, 1937]   (P) Box 1 (29)
14. Force & Failure (R. Fry) [Au, 1938]   (P) Box 1 (30)
15. The Great If (R. Fry) [Au, 1940]   (P) Box 1 (31)
16. The Spectacles of Faith (R. Fry) [Au, 1938]   (P) Box 1 (32)
17. The Atlantic Charter (R. Fry) [SP, 1941]   (P) Box 1 (33)
18. Vision or Prison? (R. Fry) [Au, 1941]   (P) Box 1 (34)
19. The Storm (R. Fry) [Au, 1940]   (P) Box 1 (35)
20. Women's Responsibilities with Regard to   (P) Box 1 (36)
    International Problems (R. Fry) [Au, 1940]
21. Fish or Bear's Paws? (R. Fry) [Au, 1940]   (P) Box 1 (38)
22. But . . . (R. Fry) [Au, 1939]   (P) Box 1 (39)
23. Jupiter's Moons (R. Fry) [Au, 1939]   (P) Box 1 (40)
24. Boomerangs (R. Fry) [Au, n.d.; priced at three   (P) Box 1 (41)
    farthings]
25. Quite Impossible (R. Fry) [Au, 1938]   (P) Box 1 (42)
26. The Moral Challenge of M. K. Ghandhi° [D.   (P) Box 1 (54)
    Hogg; FPC, 1942]
27. What Are You Going to Do About It? (2) (A.   (P) Box 1 (61)
    Huxley) [PPU, Prewar]
    <small>The typed catalogue gives the author as 'Aldous Huxley' but this is x-ed through (with small x's).</small>
28. The Meaning of Rearmament (M[ax] Plowman)   (P) Box 1 (64)
    [*95*] [PPU, Prewar]
29. Some Things We Must Realise if War is to Cease   (P) Box 1 (67)
    [PPU, Oct. 1939]
    <small>Orwell first entered 'Religion & Politics' here but crossed it out. There is no such pamphlet title; this is a section heading.</small>
30. Pacifism & Civil War [PPU, Prewar]   (P) Box 1 (69)
31. The Pacifist Believes: — [PPU, Prewar]   (P) Box 1 (70)

Poland

1. Problems of the Exiled Governments ([E.] Puacz)   (LS) Box 6 (21)
["Free Poland" Library, 1943]
2. The Labour Movement & the Polish Cause (P. J.   (LP) Box 6 (25)
Dollan) [LP, 1944]
3. Polish Labour Underground Press 2 [LP, 1944]   (LP) Box 6 (28)
4. Towards a New Poland [LP, 1943?]   (LS) Box 6 (31)
5. Warsaw Fights Alone ([Z.] Nagórski [jnr., Polish   (LS) Box 6 (32)
Pubs. Ltd., 1944]

Orwell's typed catalogue has 'H,' for 'Z' Nagórski, who, between September 1946 and February 1947, sent Orwell a letter from a Scot about the presence of Polish exiles in Scotland. Nagórski was then working for the Polish Press Agency, Edinburgh. See *3171*.

6. Warsaw—a Warning ([Z.] Litynski) 2 [Max Love   (LS) Box 6 (33)
Co., 1944; signed copy]
7. Democratic Poland Answers [Various; LP, 1944]   (LS) Box 6 (34)
8. Socialists & Poland (P. J. Dollan) [LP, 1944]   (LS) Box 7 (9)
9. Towards a New Poland [LP, Wartime]   (LS) Box 7 (13)

Also entered as item 4 above in typed catalogue without specific date.

10. Underground Poland Speaks [LP, 1941]   (LS) Box 7 (25)
11. Slavery under Hitler's 'New Order' [LP, 1941?]   (LS) Box 7 (31)

Religion and Politics

1. Retribution & the Christian (S. Hobhouse) [FR,   (P) Box 1 (5)
1942]
* 2. The Archbishop of Canterbury & Pacifism (P.   (P) Box 1 (6)
Hartill)

See Pacifism, 30. In the typed catalogue a note states, 'York altered to Canterbury in ink.'

3. Religion & the Quest for Peace (G[eorge] M. Lloyd   (P) Box 1 (7)
Davies) [PPU, 1942]
4. Christianity & the State (G[lyn] Lloyd Phelps) [FR,   (P) Box 1 (8)
1942]
5. Economics & the Christian (L[eslie] Artingstall)   (P) Box 1 (9)
[FR]
6. Christ & Our Enemies (S. Hobhouse) [FR, 1941)   (P) Box 1 (10)
7. Anglicans & War (A[rchdeacon] Hartill [APF,   (P) Box 1 (11)
1941]
8. Social Control & Personal Freedom (L[eyton]   (P) Box 1 (17)
Richard] [FR]
9. God or the Nation? (J. M. Murry) [PPU, Prewar]   (P) Box 1 (21)
10. Religion & Science & Co. Unlimited (R. Fry) [Au]   (P) Box 1 (37)
11. The Quakers: Who Are They? (R. Fry) [Au, 1942]   (P) Box 1 (43)
12. Retribution or . . .? (W. E. Wilson) [FPC,   (P) Box 1 (46)
Wartime]

13. The Church & the War (E[velyn] Underhill) [APF.   (P) Box 1 (47)
    Wartime]
14. The Logic of Faith (Fr. Andrew) [APF]   (P) Box 1 (48)
15. How Shall the Christian Church Prepare for the   (P) Box 1 (49)
    New World Order? (V[era] Brittain) [*2473, n. 1*]
    [APF, Wartime]
16. Justice & Love (T. C. Hume) [FPC, 1936]   (P) Box 1 (50)
17. Christian Responsibility in the Present War   (P) Box 1 (51)
    Situation [K. C. Capper-Johnson; FPC, Wartime;
    price a halfpenny]
18. Our Peace Testimony in Total War (S. C. Farrar)   (P) Box 1 (52)
    [FPC, 1942]
19. Peace Aims & War Methods (C. Catchpool) [FPC,   (P) Box 1 (53)
    1940]
20. Community as the Social Application of Pacifism   (P) Box 1 (57)
    (C. S. Stimson) [CSC, 1942]
21. Christian Pacifism & Rearmament (Alex Wood)   (P) Box 1 (60)
    [PPU, 1943]
22. Conscripting Christianity ([Canon] S. Morris)   (P) Box 1 (65)
    [PPU, 1937; Broadcast]
23. For Christ's Sake (Laurence Murfitt) [Au, Prewar]   (P) Box 1 (74)
24. Remain in the Church of England (S[ybil]   (P) Box 2 (5)
    Thorndike) [APF, Wartime]
25. Big Powers and Little Powers (L[aurence]   (P) Box 2 (15)
    Housman) [PN, 1944]
26. Whited Sepulchres[: a Political Record of the   (Tr) Box 3 (50)
    Church of Scotland] (O. Brown) [Scottish
    Secretariat, Wartime]
*27. The Roman Catholic Church & the Modern Age   (Tr) Box 3 (66)
    ([F. A.] Ridley) [FP]
28. The Foundation of Economic Reconstruction [J.   (LS) Box 6 (14)
    Macmurray; NPC, 1942]

    John Macmurray, Grote Professor of the Philosophy of Mind and
    Logic, University of London, 1922–44 (see *2071, n. 1*), was
    described by Orwell in a letter to Dwight Macdonald, 2.5.48, as a
    fellow traveller 'of a peculiarly slimy religious brand' (see *3392*).

29. Letter to a Country Clergyman (S[idney] Dark)   (LS) Box 7 (11)
    [*2347, n. 2*] [FS, Wartime]

    In his review of pamphlet literature (see *1807*), Orwell
    mentioned this pamphlet and referred to Dark as a 'left-wing
    Anglican.'

Science and Politics

1. War on the People (B. Edwards), (*363, n. 2*) [ILP,   (Tr) Box 3 (32)
   1943]

   Orwell started to enter 'Friends' Ambulance' here; see War of
   1939–45, 9. The pamphlet is subtitled 'An Exposure of the
   Chemical Kings and their Nazi Associates.' Edwards was
   General Secretary of the Chemical Workers' Union, 1947–71.

2. Atoms & Socialism ([Richard] Rodnight) [The   (Tr) Box 4 (34)
   Engels Society, 1945]
3. New Weapons Against Tuberculosis [LRD, 1943]   (LP) Box 6 (48)
   This does not refer to modern drugs (which might have been
   particularly relevant to Orwell's needs), but to mass
   radiography and new financial allowances for those with TB.

Socialism: History & Theory

1. The Death Agony of Capitalism ([L.] Trotsky)   (Tr) Box 3 (1)
   [WIL, 1938]
2. Towards the British Revolution (F. A. Ridley) 2   (Tr) Box 3 (3)
   [ILP, Wartime]
3. Should Socialists Support Federal Union? 2   (Tr) Box 3 (4)
   [Barbara Wootton and E. Hardy; SPGB, 1940]
* 4. Communist Circus (T. Wakley) [CSYH, Wartime]   (Tr) Box 3 (5)
5. The World Revolution [WIL, 1943]   (Tr) Box 3 (9)
6. What I Stand for ([I.] Silone) [856, n. 1] [IAA, 1943]   (Tr) Box 3 (14)
   Orwell initially entered here 'The British General Strike (Tom
   Brown) 3 (An) Box 3 (10).'
7. War or Socialism? [ILP, Prewar]   (Tr) Box 3 (16)
8. The I.L.P. in War & Peace [ILP, 1940; fourpence]   (Tr) Box 3 (18)
9. The I.L.P. in War & Peace [ILP, 1942; sixpence]   (Tr) Box 3 (19)
*10. Does Russia's Entry Alter Britain's War? (A. Scott)   (Tr) Box 3 (21)
   [WIL, 1941]
11. We Carry On (D. McArthur) [ILP, 1937]   (Tr) Box 3 (23)
*12. Wall Street versus Wilhelmstrasse (F. A. Ridley) 2   (Tr) Box 3 (24)
   [ILP, 1941]
13. War & the Working Class [SPGB, 1936]   (Tr) Box 3 (29)
14. Make Britain Socialist Now! (J. McNair) 363, n. 5)   (Tr) Box 3 (39)
   [ILP, 1942]
*15. Defend Socialism from the Communists ([T.]   (Tr) Box 3 (42)
   Taylor) [ILP, 1942]
*16. Socialism Can Defeat Nazism ([F.] Brockway &   (Tr) Box 3 (58)
   [J.] McNair) [ILP, 1940]
   Orwell initially repeated item number 1 in this category as 16.
17. The Socialist Challenge to Churchill [ILP, 1941]   (Tr) Box 3 (61)
18. Beveridge Reorganises Poverty [SPGB, 1943]   (Tr) Box 3 (63)
   The location, '63', was written as '62' by Orwell, perhaps
   running on from '61' above.
19. Questions of the Day [SPGB, 1942]   (Tr) Box 3 (64)
20. The Way Out ([F.] Brockway) 2 [ILP, 1942]   (Tr) Box 3 (65)
21. Peoples & Charlatans (A. Caltabiano) 2 [IAA, 1944]   (Tr) Box 4 (2)
22. Socialism Isn't Enough [University Labour   (Tr) Box 4 (14)
   Federation, Wartime]
23. Reform or Revolution (Daniel de Leon) [SLP,   (Tr) Box 4 (18)
   Prewar]

*24. Socialism versus Anarchism (Daniel de Leon) (An) Box 4 (19)
[SLP, Prewar]

Orwell first described this as a Trotskyist pamphlet: the
overwriting makes the categorisation unclear but it has been
given here as at Anarchism item 13.

25. Spartacus—A Study in Revolutionary History (F. (Tr) Box 4 (21)
A. Ridley) [National Labour Press, 1944]

26. Trial of a Working-class Representative ([A. E.] (Tr) Box 4 (24)
Dent) [Rydal Press]

27. The Truth About Socialism ([N.] Thomas. U.S.) (Tr) Box 4 (26)
[American Socialist Party, 1943]

28. Socialism [SPGB, 1933] (Tr) Box 4 (33)

29. The Socialist Party Exposes Mr. Chamberlain & his (Tr) Box 4 (44)
Labour Critics [SPGB, 1938]

30. The Socialist Party—Its Principles & Policy [SPGB, (Tr) Box 4 (47)
1934]

31. Labour on the March (G. Ridley) [Labour (LS) Box 5 (8)
Publications Dept., Wartime]

32. Let's Talk It Over ([R.] Postgate) [497, n. 2] (LS) Box 5 (22)
[Socialist Propaganda Committee, Wartime]

33. Two Approaches to Co-operation (J. Thomas) (LS) Box 5 (24)
[COPC, 1942]

34. The Rise of Capitalism ([Lester] Hutchinson,) (LS) Box 6 (8)
[NCLC Publications Committee, 1941]

'Lester' also as 'Leicester'; see 2946. Orwell started to enter item
5 of Trade Unionism: History & Theory here. The abbreviation
NCLC is Orwell's

35. The Future of International Socialism 2 [Socialist (LS) Box 6 (29)
Vanguard Group, 1943]

36. The New World Order ([F.] Leeman) [Nottingham (LS) Box 6 (35)
Co-op Political Committee, Wartime]

37. Imperialism? ([G.] Cornes) [Prestwick Labour (LS) Box 6 (36)
Party, Wartime]

The manuscript has '?' before 'Imperialism.'

38. What the Workers Expect of the International (LP) Box 6 (37)
Labor Organization ([B.] Ibañez) [American Labor
Conference on International Affairs, 1944]

Bernardo Ibañez, Secretary General, Chilean Confederation of
Workers; Vice-President, Latin-American Workers' Federation.

39. Dumbarton Oaks [FS, 1944] (LS) Box 6 (39)
40. England has Risen (W. Morris) [Red Flag (LS) Box 6 (40)
Fellowship, Wartime]
41. Social Security ([J.] Smyth) [PWDP, 1943?] (LS) Box 6 (51)
42. Your Future [LP, 1944] (LP) Box 6 (52)
43. Thomas Blandford[, the Man and his Message] ([J. (LS) Box 6 (47)
J.] Worley) [COPC, 1943]

44. The Labour Party—the Party with a Future   (LP) Box 7 (1)
[Morgan Phillips; LP, 1945]
45. Letter to a Woman Munition Worker ([A. S.]   (LS) Box 7 (18)
Lawrence) [FS, Wartime]
46. James Keir Hardie (G. D. H. Cole) [FS, 1941]   (LS) Box 7 (23)
47. The Old World & the New Society [LP, 1941]   (LP) Box 7 (28)
50. Can We Afford 'Beveridge' ([H. W.] Singer) [FS,   (LS) Box 7 (33)
1943]

[Orwell omitted 48 and 49.]

Spanish Civil War

1. Civil War in Spain (B[ertram] D. Wolfe) [*2932, n.*   (Tr) Box 3 (2)
5] [WAP, USA, 1937]

Crick quotes from Wolfe's eulogy of Andrés Nin; this, he says, 'has several obvious parallels to *Nineteen Eighty-Four*' (634).

2. Le Stalinisme en Espagne (K[atia] Landau) [Edition   (Tr) Box 3 (7)
Spartacus, 2 francs, 1937]

The typed catalogue notes, 'very rare'; see headnote; for Kurt Landau, see *2648, n. 4*.

3. Spotlight on Spain (J. Hatz) [ILP, 1938]   (Tr) Box 3 (17)
4. Democracy or Revolution in Spain? (J. Matteo) 2   (Tr) Box 3 (33)
[ILP, 1937]
5. The Lesson of Spain ([L.] Trotsky) [WIP, 1937]   (Tr) Box 3 (34)
6. The Truth About Barcelona (F. Brockway) [ILP,   (Tr) Box 3 (35)
1937]
7. Terror in Spain (J. McGovern) [*424, n. 2*] [ILP,   (Tr) Box 3 (44)
1937]
8. Why Bishops Back Franco (J. McGovern) [ILP,   (Tr) Box 3 (45)
1936]
9. The Trotskyist Position on Spain [LL, 1943]   (Tr) Box 3 (67)
10. Buenaventura Durruti [CNT-FAI, Barcelona,   (Tr) Box 3 (70)
1937]

CNT: 'Syndicalist unions controlled by the Anarchists'; FAI: 'an actual Anarchist organisation'; Orwell, *Homage to Catalonia*, *CW*, VI, 195, 203.

11. Spain—Anarchism [Anarcho-Syndicalist Union   (An) Box 4 (37)
(CNT), 1937]
12. Social Reconstruction in Spain [Gaston] (Leval) [;   (Tr) Box 4 (38)
Spain and the World, 1938]

French anarchist who went to Moscow in 1921 with a Spanish delegation led by Andrés Nin, and wrote on the Spanish civil war. See Thomas, 67, 117, 1025. Orwell wrote 'Level' in the manuscript but typescript has Gaston Leval.'

13. Catholics & the Civil War in Spain [National   (LP) Box 5 (10)
Council of Labour, 1936]
14. A Catholic Looks at Spain [S. Gurrea; Labour   (LP) Box 5 (11)
Publications Dept., 1937]

15. Tempête sur l'Espagne [L'Homme Réel, 1936, 3   (LS) Box 6 (6)
   francs]

    This is inscribed 'Henry Swanzy, Paris 1936.' Swanzy was one
    of Orwell's colleagues at the BBC; see *845*, *n. 2*.

16. Impressions of Franco's Spain (J. R. Vega) 2   (LP) Box 6 (9)
    [United Editorial Ltd., 1943]

17. Franco's "Neutrality" & British Policy [UDC,   (LS) Box 6 (13)
    1944]

18. Spain: the moral touchstone of Europe (C. Duff) 2   (LS) Box 6 (23)
    [Gollancz, 1944]

19. Romancero de la Guerra Civil (Series 1) [verse;   (LS) Box 7 (6)
    Madrid Gov.t, 1936]

Trade Unionism: History & Theory

1. Workers! Freedom or Servitude? (B. Edwards)   (Tr) Box 3 (60)
   [ILP, 1941]

2. The Next Step for Trade Unionists [SPGB,   (Tr) Box 4 (4)
   Prewar]

3. Trade Unionism & the South Wales Miner [pbd by (Tr) Box 4 (5)
   Ted Merriman, 1944]

4. Trade Unions in the Epoch of Imperialist Decay   (Tr) Box 4 (17)
   ([L.] Trotsky) [Fourth International, Wartime]

5. The Essential Work Order [LRD, 1941]   (LP) Box 6 (4)

6. Postal Trade Unionism against Pioneering [Union (LS) Box 7 (10)
   of Post Office Workers, 1943]

7. The Essential Work Order ([H.] Samuels) [London (LS) Box 7 (14)
   Trades Council, 1943]

8. The Battle for Britain's County Workers [B.   (LP) Box 7 (15)
   Roberts; National Union of Public Employees,
   1941?]

* 9. Post-War Education ([J. P. M.] Millar) [N.C.L.C. (LP) Box 7 (16)
   (Orwell's abbreviation), 1943]

10. Union of Post-Office Workers & Workers' Control (LP) Box 7 (24)
    [UPW, 1942]

11. The British General Strike (Tom Brown) [FP,   (An) Box 3 (10)
    1943]

12. Behind the Scenes of the Great Strike ([H.] Fyfe) (LP) Box 5 (21)
    [Labour Publications Co., 1926]

13. The French Cooks' Syndicate (W. McCartney)   (An) Box 4 (31)
    [FP, 1945]

    Reviewed by Orwell in *Freedom—through Anarchism*, 8
    September 1945; see *2746*.

Trotskyism: History & Theory

* 1. The Russian Myth [FP, 1941]   (An) Box 3 (25)

    'An' is overwritten what looks like 'Tr'; an 'x' has been written
    above.

★ 2. The Kronstadt Revolt (A. Ciliga) [FP, 1942]   (Tr) Box 3 (28)

In his review of pamphlet literature, 9 January 1943, (see *1807*), Orwell describes this as 'Anarchist pamphlet, largely an attack on Trotsky.' Anton Ciliga is referred to by Orwell in his Editorial, *Polemic*, 3, May 1946; see *2988*. For a later reference to the Kronstadt Revolt, see Orwell's letter to Dwight Macdonald regarding the meaning of *Animal Farm*, 5 December 1946, *3128*. See also letter to Macdonald, 15 April 1947 (*3215*).

★ 3. The End of Socialism in Russia ([M[ax] Eastman)   (Tr) Box 3 (30)
[Secker & Warburg, 1937]

Crick suggests that Orwell might have read this (especially since it was published by Secker & Warburg) before writing *Homage to Catalonia* 'and it would have refortified all he meant to say' (634).

4. Trotskyism, Left Flank of the Reformist [LL, 1943]   (Tr) Box 3 (43)
★ 5. I Stake My Life! ([L.] Trotsky) [Fourth   (Tr) Box 3 (53)
International, 1937]
★ 6. Cauchemar en U.R.S.S. ([B.] Souvarine) [Plon,   (Tr) Box 3 (69)
1937, 2 francs]

Boris Souvarine, Russian-born naturalised Frenchman (pseudonym of Boris Lifchitz, 1895–1984), had been a founder of the Parti Communiste Français, a member of the Executive Committee of the Comintern, and editor of the Communist newspaper *L'Humanité*. After about 1935 he became highly critical of Stalin's Soviet Union. This is expressed in this item, first published in *Revue de Paris*, 1 July 1937—just as Orwell returned from Spain. As William Steinhoff shows, it was influential on *Nineteen Eighty-Four*; see *George Orwell and the Origins of 1984*, USA, 1975, 32–34. In the manuscript, the French form 'U.R.S.S.' is written 'U.S.S.R.': the typed catalogue has a (typed) note: 'prob, rare.'

7. The Case for Socialist Revolution [WIL, Wartime]   (Tr) Box 4 (12)

U.S.A.: Internal Affairs

1. Defence Policy in the Minneapolis Trial [G. Munis   (Tr) Box 3 (57)
and J. P. Canon, Pioneer Publishers, USA, 1942]
Orwell's manuscript has 'Trials.'

2. Victory's Victims? The Negro's Future ([A. P.]   (Tr) Box 4 (25)
Randolph [and N. Thomas]) [(American) Socialist
Party, 1943]

[Although Orwell's list of contents has a section for U.S.A., Foreign Policy & Affairs, no pamphlets are listed under this heading.]

U.S.S.R.: Foreign Affairs
[Orwell's list of contents places the Internal Affairs of the U.S.S.R. before Foreign Affairs.]

1. Bolshevik Bogey in Britain (E[mrys] Hughes)   (LP) Box 7 (19)
[Civic Press, 1943]

U.S.S.R.: Internal Affairs

* 1. The Kronstadt Revolt ([A.] Ciliga) [FP, 1942]   (Tr) Box 4 (30)
2. Why Did They "Confess"? (U.S.) [Pioneer   (Tr) Box 4 (36)
Publishers, 1937]

Orwell annotated the typed catalogue that this has an Introduction by James Burnham. For Orwell's first reference to Burnham and Burnham's response, see 'As I Please,' 7, 14 January 1944, *2404*; for Burnham, see *2404, n. 1*. The subject of the pamphlet is the trial in January 1937 of Karl Radek and sixteen alleged co-conspirators, of whom thirteen, but not Radek, were executed. A chapter is devoted to the trial in Robert Payne, *The Rise and Fall of Stalin*, 1966. See also *3649, n. 3*.

3. Summary of the Final Report on the Moscow Trials   (Tr) Box 4 (46)
[WIP, 1938?]

The typed catalogue gives the title as 'Summary of the final report of the Commission of Enquiry into the charges made against Trotsky in the Moscow Trials.' The date has been added in Orwell's hand.

4. How the Russians Live [W. Miller; Socialist   (LP) Box 5 (1)
Propaganda Committee, 1942]
5. Stalin–Wells Talk (Shaw, Wells etc) 2 [New   (LP) Box 5 (7)
Statesman, 1934]

'LP' appears to be written over 'Tr.'

6. Towards an Understanding ([B.] Czernetz)   (LS) Box 5 (13)
[LBAS, 1942]
7. The Russian Myth [FP, 1941]   (An) Box 3 (25)
8. The End of Socialism in Russia (M. Eastman)   (Tr) Box 3 (30)
[Secker & Warburg, 1937]
9. I Stake my Life! (L. Trotsky) [Fourth International,   (Tr) Box 3 (53)
1937]
10. Cauchemar en URSS (B. Souvarine) [Plon, 1937]   (Tr) Box 3 (69)

War of 1914–18

1. What Happened in the Great War (W. T. Colyer)   (P?) Box 1 (66)
[No Conscription League, Prewar]
2. The Wilhelmshaven Revolt (Icarus) [FP, 1944]   (Tr) Box 4 (15)

War of 1939–45

1. Stop Bombing Civilians [BRC, 1943]   (P) Box 1 (2)
2. Seed of Chaos (V. Brittain) [BRC, 1944]   (P) Box 1 (24)
3. Why Blunder On? (Duke of Bedford) 2 [SP, 1942]   (P) Box 1 (45)
4. Freedom is in Peril (R. S. W. Pollard) [FPC,   (P) Box 1 (55)
Wartime]
5. Victory for Humanity (U.S.A.) (A. W. Palmer)   (P) Box 1 (59)
[PPU, Wartime]
6. Poison Gas (U.D.C.) [Prewar]   (P) Box 1 (63)
7. Why Have This War? (Marquis of Tavistock) [Au.   (P) Box 1 (68)
Wartime]
8. What a Game! (Duke of Bedford) [SP, 1941]   (P) Box 2 (13)

9. Friends' Ambulance Unit [Annual Report, FAU,   (P) Box 2 (21)
   1945]
10. The Red Army (F. Maitland) [Tait Memorial   (Tr) Box 3   (6)
    Pubs., 1943]
11. The Way to Win [ILP, 1941]   (Tr) Box 3 (38)
12. War for Freedom or Finance? (O. Brown) [ILP,   (Tr) Box 3 (51)
    1941]
13. Arms—& the Men (O. Brown) 2 [Au, Wartime]   (Tr) Box 3 (52)
14. Secrets of the Second Front ([F.] Maitland) [Tait   (Tr) Box 3 (59)
    Memorial Committee, 1942]
15. The Secret International (Armament) [UDC, 1932]   (Tr) Box 3 (68)
    'Armament' appears only in this list; it is omitted from the typed
    catalogue. The full title is 'The Secret International Armament
    Firms at Work.'
16. The Meaning of Total War ([F.] Lohr) [Au,   (Tr) Box 4 (9)
    Wartime]
17. Marcus Graham's Tissues in the Present War [R.   (Tr) Box 4 (23)
    Rocker; Workers' Friend Printing and Publishing
    Association, 1944]
18. The Peace We Lost (U.S.) [Keep America Out of   (Tr) Box 4 (27)
    the War Campaign, post-1941]
19. Wall Street versus Wilhelmstrasse ([F. A.] Ridley)   (Tr) Box 4 (40)
    [ILP, 1941]
20. War & the Working Class [SPGB, 1936]   (Tr) Box 4 (48)
?21. The Distribution of Fish ([J.] Atkins) [FRS, 1941]   (LS) Box 5   (3)
    This item is not queried in the typed catalogue. Because Box 5 is
    currently missing from the British Library, it is not possible to
    check the pamphlet, nor to ascertain whether this was written by
    J. A. Atkins, Orwell's predecessor as literary editor of *Tribune*;
    see 1340, n. 1).
22. Shaping the Future [Education Dep.t, Birmingham   (LS) Box 5 (15)
    Co-Op, Wartime]
23. European Revolution—How to Win the Peace (M.   (LS) Box 5 (17)
    Saran) [International Publishing Co., pre-June
    1941]
24. Victory Through Socialism [Socialist Discussion   (LP) Box 5 (23)
    Group, Wartime]
25. Labour & Defence [National Executive, LP, May   (LP) Box 5 (27)
    1939]
26. Terror in Europe—the Fate of the Jews (Tobtir)   (LS) Box 6   (1)
    [National Committee for Rescue from Nazi
    Terror, 1942?]
    The typed catalogue gives the authors as A. Tolstoy, a Polish
    Underground worker, and T. Mann.
27. Fire-Watching for Men & Women [LRD, 1942]   (LP) Box 6   (5)

28. Justice Outlawed (H. Slesser) [Liberty   (LS) Box 6 (12)
Publications, Wartime]

The Rt. Hon. Henry Slesser wrote only a foreword; no other authors are named.

*29. Greece Fights for Freedom! [Greek-American   (LS) Box 6 (15)
Labour Committee, 1944]

*30. The Truth About Greece [Greek Unity   (LS) Box 6 (16)
Committee, 1944]

31. Letter to a Soldier [A Comrade in Arms; FS,   (LS) Box 7 (12)
Wartime]

32. Herbert Morrison's Work in the War Govt. 1940–   (LP) Box 7 (29)
45 [LP, 1945]

For Herbert Morrison, see 763, n. 28.

*33. Reports on the [Underground] Resistance   (LS) Box 7 (34)
Movement in Austria [LBAS, 1943]

Noted in typed catalogue as cyclostyled. Orwell mistakenly gave the pamphlet's position as 36 in the handwritten list.

34. Does Russia's entry alter Britain's War? (A. Scott)   (Tr) Box 3 (21)
[WIL, 1941]

35. Wall Street versus Wilhelmstrasse (F. A. Ridley)   (Tr) Box 3 (24)
[ILP, 1941]

36. Socialism can defeat Naziism ([F.] Brockway & [J.]   (Tr) Box 3 (58)
McNair) [ILP, 1940]

Russian Revolution: History of

1. The Kronstadt Revolt (A. Ciliga) [FP, 1942]   (Tr) Box 3 (28)

Orwell entered under this heading the first two titles of U.S.S.R.: Internal Affairs, this title, and 'Why Did They "Confess"?'; crossed them out, then re-entered *The Kronstadt Revolt*—which also appears under Trotskyism, its third appearance.

Zionism & Antisemitism: History & Theory

1. "Nowhere to Lay Their Heads" ([V.] Gollancz)   (LP) Box 6 (55)
[Gollancz, 1945]

2. What Bu

The manuscript list breaks off after the start of the entry 'What Buchenwald *really* means'; see Germany: Internal Affairs, item 3.

APPENDIX 11

3734. Books Owned by Orwell in 1950

This list records books known or believed to have been owned by Orwell at the time of his death. Some degree of uncertainty is inevitable in compiling such a list. It cannot be complete and books may be included that were not Orwell's. For example, though some of the books he read during 1949 (see *3727*) were borrowed, an item such as C. D. Darlington's *The Conflict of Science and Society* (a pamphlet) would hardly be likely to be found in a hospital library, and if, as is possible, it came from its author—Orwell sent him a copy of *Nineteen Eighty-Four* (see *3542*)—it would almost certainly have been given, not merely lent. It does not appear in this list, and it is probable that many of Orwell's books that he had in hospital never got back into his 'library.'

In 'Books *v.* Cigarettes,' *Tribune*, 8 February 1946 (see *2892*), Orwell said he had nearly 900 books, of which fifteen were borrowed and not returned or temporarily on loan. The list that follows, excluding *Horizon* and the *Quarterly Review*, comprises 523 titles (counting multi-volume sets as one title). Of these, 134 are questionable, leaving 389 as certainly Orwell's. Orwell's will (see *3730*) gave his wife, Sonia, six months to choose which books she would like, and then Richard Rees was to be the beneficiary. The distribution of books is indicated here by 'S' for Sonia, 'R' for Rees, and 'A' for Avril (Mrs. William Dunn, Orwell's sister). A few books were originally Eileen Blair's (Eileen O'Shaughnessy's) or her brother Laurence's; this is indicated where it is known. A few titles have been added of purchases made much later by the Orwell Archive, but only where they can reasonably be identified as Orwell's; some of these are queried. Some books have two publication dates; the second, in round brackets, gives the date of re-issue of an edition first published in the year of the first date. Undated books are indicated by 'n.d.' Editorial annotations are placed within square brackets. A question-mark indicates that there is doubt whether a book was Orwell's. Place of publication is London (including Harmondsworth) unless stated otherwise.

It must be reiterated that this list, though it may include books that are not Orwell's, certainly omits many he owned. In addition, he had a very large collection of pamphlets, which was passed, at his request, to the British Library (see *3733*), and his will refers to 'the small collection of leather-covered books which are kept in a wooden travelling case and were originally the property of my great-uncle Horatio Blair,' which were excepted from the division of books between Sonia Orwell and Richard Rees; see *3730*.

A R. Aldington. *Death of a hero.* 1937.
? S R. Aldington. *Four English portraits, 1801–1851.* 1948. [Selected by Orwell for review in *The Observer*, about 20.11.1948.]
S R. Andom. *The marvellous adventures of me.* n.d.
R W. H. Auden. *For the time being.* 1945.
S N. Ault. *Elizabethan lyrics.* 1925. [Eileen O'Shaughnessy.]
? R J. Austen. *Lady Susan and The Watsons.* n.d.
? R J. Austen. *Love and friendship and other early works.* 1922.
? R J. Austen. *Mansfield Park.* n.d.

? S F. Bacon. *Advancement of learning and The new Atlantis.* 1929.
? S J. O. F. Ball. *Poems.* n.d.
? S A. Barea. *The Clash.* [*Horizon* review copy.]
S M. Bashkirtseff. *Journal* 1891.
S H. W. Bates. *The naturalist on the River Amazon.* 1914.
R C. Baudelaire. *Les fleurs du mal*; édition prefacée et annotée par M. E. Raynaud. Paris, n.d. [Blue binding;[1] 8 or 9 poems are ticked in the index. 2 are used in KTAF.]
R Beaumont and Fletcher. *Plays.* n.d. [Inscribed "Eileen O'Shaughnessy."]

? R I. de Beausobre. *The woman who could not die.* 1948.
S W. Beckford. *Vathek.* 1905. [Inscribed E. A. Blair, 1922.]
A A. Bennett. *Clayhanger.* [Not earlier than August 1910.]
R ··   ··   *Hilda Lessways.* 1911.
? S ··   ··   *The old wives' tale.* 1936.
A ··   ··   *The old wives' tale.* 1939.
A ··   ··   *Riceyman Steps.* 1946.
? S N. Berdyaev. *The Russian Revolution.* 1931.
A J. D. Beresford. *A candidate for truth.* n.d.
? R G. Bernanos. *A diary of my times.* Trans. P. Morris. 1938.
? R W. H. Beveridge. *The Beveridge Report in brief.* 1942.
S R. D. Blackmore. *Lorna Doone.* 1914. [Avril Blair Winton House.]
R R. P. Blackmur. *Dirty hands; or The true-born censor.* Cambridge, 1930.
R W. Blake. *The poetical works.* 1925.
? R L. Bloy. *Pilgrim of the absolute.* Intro. Jacques Maritain. 1947.
A B.M.A. *Secret remedies, what they cost & what they contain. Based on analyses made for the B.M.A.* 1909.
S R. Boldrewood. *The squatter's dream.* 1892.
R F. Borkenau. *The Spanish cockpit.* 1937.
? R Bossuet. *Oraisons funèbres.* Paris, 1874.
R J. Boswell. *The Life of Samuel Johnson.* Ed. G. B. Hill, revised L. F. Powell. 4 vol. Oxford, 1934.
S Major Boulton. *Reminiscences of the North-West rebellions.* 1886.
S G. Bourne. *Memoirs of a Surrey labourer.* 1907.
R V. W. Brooks. *The ordeal of Mark Twain.* New York, 1920.
S V. W. Brooks. *The world of Washington Irving.* 1944.
R B. Brown. *The Readies.* 1930.
S F. Browne. *Granny's wonderful chair.* 1940.
S Sir T. Browne. *Religio Medici.* [Eileen O'Shaughnessy.]
R E. B. Browning. *Poems.* 1890.
S O. Browning. *Charles XII of Sweden.* 1899.
R R. Browning. *Works.* 8 vols. 1914. [Inscribed "E. A. Blair, from his Tutor [A. S. F. Gow], Eton, Dec., 1921."]
S H. T. Buckle. *History of civilisation in English.* Vol. 1. 1930.
S J. Bunyan. *Grace abounding.* Ed. S. C. Freer. 1903. [Eileen O'Shaughnessy.]
S J. Bunyan. *Pilgrim's progress.* 1924. [Eileen O'Shaughnessy.]
S J. Burnham. *The machiavellians.* 1943.
S J. Burnham. *The managerial revolution.* 1945.
R C. D. Burns. *The first Europe; a study of the establishment of medieval Christendom.* 1947.
S S. Butler. *Erewhon.* 1935.
S ··   ··   *Erewhon revisited.* 1926. [Eileen O'Shaughnessy.]
A ··   ··   *The notebooks of Samuel Butler.* 6th imp. 1921. [Orwell blue-rebinding?][1]
A ··   ··   *The way of all flesh.* 1924. [Signed: Eileen O'Shaughnessy.]
? S H. Butterfield. *Napoleon.* 1947.
? S Lord Byron. *Conversations of Lord Byron with the Countess of Blessington.* 1834.
R Lord Byron. *The poetical works.* n.d. [Blue binding.]

R R. Campbell. *The Georgiad.* 1931.

? S R. Campbell. *The Georgiad.* 1931.
? S N. Carrington. *Popular art in Britain.* 1945.
  S C. Carswell. *The savage pilgrimage.* 1932.
? R J. Cary. *The horse's mouth.* 1948.
? R C. Caudwell. *Illusion and reality.* 1946 (1947).
  A R. Chandler. *The little sister.* 1949.
  R G. Chaucer. *The works.* Ed. Skeat. 1920. [Inscribed "Eileen . . . ."]
  A G. K. Chesterton. *The Father Brown stories.* 1947.
  S R. Church and M. M. Bozman. *Poems of our time, 1900–1942.* 1945.
  S J. Collier (ed). *The scandal and credulities of John Aubrey.* 1931.
  A V. H. Collins. *Ghosts and marvels.* 1927.
  A *Concise Guide to Decorating.* 1946
  R C. Connolly. *The condemned playground.* 1945.
? R Jessie Conrad. *Joseph Conrad as I knew him.* 1926.
  S Joseph Conrad. *Almayer's folly and Tales of unrest.* 1947.
  R   ··   ·· *The arrow of gold.* 1947.
  R   ··   ·· *Chance* n.d.
  R   ··   ·· *Lord Jim.* 1946.
  S   ··   ·· *The mirror of the sea.* 1946.
  S   ··   ·· *The nigger of the "Narcissus."* 1948.
  R   ··   ·· *The nigger of the Narcissus, Typhoon and The shadow line.* 1945.
  R   ··   ·· *Nostromo.* 1947.
  R   ··   ·· *Notes on life and letters.* 1949.
  S   ··   ·· *The rescue.* 1920.
  R   ··   ·· *The rescue.* 1949.
  S   ··   ·· *The rover.* 1923.
  A   ··   ·· *The secret agent.* 1943.
  R   ··   ·· *The secret agent.* 1947.
  R   ··   ·· *A set of six.* 1908.
  R   ··   ·· *Tales of unrest.* 1921.
  R   ··   ·· *Twixt land and sea.* 1947.
  R   ··   ·· *Under western eyes.* 1947.
? R   ··   ·· *Youth and other stories.* n.d. [Wartime.]
  R   ··   ·· *Youth, Heart of darkness and The end of the tether.* 1946.
  R J. Conrad and F. M. Hueffer. *Romance.* n.d.
  S G. G. Coulton. *Social life in Britain.* 1918.
  R G. Crabbe. *Selected poems.* 1946. [Inscribed "George Orwell, from M . . . Henderson, 1947."]
  R Sir E. Creasy. *The fifteen decisive battles of the world.* 1894.
  R A. Cruden. *A concordance to the Old and New Testament.* 1903.
  S W. Cunningham. *The industrial revolution.* 1917. [Marjorie Dakin.]
  R R. Curle. *Joseph Conrad; a study.* 1914.

? S D. Daiches. *Virginia Woolf.* 1945.
  A R. H. Dana. *Two years before the mast.* 1948.
  R Dante. *La divina commedia.* 3 vols. Firenze, 1827. [Vol. 2 missing.]
  R Dante. *Paradiso.* [English and Italian.] Trans. L. Binyon. 1943. [Inscribed "C. Lawrence, 1944."]
  S Dante. *The divine comedy.* Vols. II & III. 1948.
  R C. Darwin. *Charles Darwin and the Voyage of the Beagle.* Ed. and intro. N. Barlow. 1945. [Damaged by damp on Jura.]

A C. Darwin. *The origin of species*. Popular imp. of the corrected copyright edn. 1901.

A C. Darwin. *Voyage of the Beagle*.

A D. Defoe. *Adelaide Murray*. 1823.

R ·· ·· *A journal of the plague year*. 1909.

R ·· ·· *Moll Flanders*. n.d.

R ·· ·· *Robinson Crusoe*. n.d.

R T. Dekker. *Plays*. n.d. [Inscribed "Eileen O'Shaughnessy."]

? R W. De La Mare. *Memoirs of a midget*. 1932.

R T. De Quincey. *Confessions of an English opium eater*. 1902. (1934).

R I. Deutscher. *Stalin; a political biography*. 1949.

R C. Dickens. *The Works*. [5 vols. only.] 1890.

R C. Dickens. [Another 10 vols., to make a complete set; various publishers.]

S J. Dos Passos. *The ground we stand on*. 1942.

R F. Dostoevsky. *The Brothers Karamazov*. Trans. C. Garnett. 1912 (1945).

R ·· ·· *Crime and punishment*. Trans. C. Garnett, 1914 (1945).

? R ·· ·· *The Idiot*. Trans. E. M. Martin. 1914 (1929).

? R ·· ·· *Poor folk, and The gambler*. Trans. C. J. Hogarth. 1915 (1944).

R ·· ·· *The possessed*. Trans. C. Garnett. 2 vols. [Vol. 2 only.] 1931.

A A. C. Doyle. *The return of Sherlock Holmes*. 1925.

R T. Dreiser. *An American tragedy*. 1926 (1928). [Damaged by damp on Jura.]

S ·· ·· *Best short stories*. Ed. Howard Fast. 1947.

S ·· ·· *Chains*. 1928.

R ·· ·· *The color of a great city*. 1930.

S ·· ·· *Tragic America*. 1932.

? R C. Du Bos. *Journal 1924–1925*. Paris, 1948.

R L. Du Fresnoy. *Chronological tablets*. 1801.

R G. Du Maurier. *Trilby*. 1895.

A F. M. Duncan. *British shells*. 1943.

R *Early English lyrics*. Ed. E. K. Chambers and F. Sidgwick. 1921. [Inscribed "Eileen . . . 1926."]

? R G. Eliot. *Middlemarch*. 2 vols. 1930.

? R G. Eliot. *The mill on the floss*. n.d.

R G. Eliot. *Scenes of clerical life*. n.d.

? R T. S. Eliot. *After strange gods*. 1934.

? R ·· ·· *Ash-Wednesday*. 1930.

? R ·· ·· *Burnt Norton*. 1941.

? R ·· ·· *Collected poems, 1909–1935*. 1936.

? R ·· ·· *Dante*. 1939.

? R ·· ·· *The Dry Salvages*. 1941.

? R ·· ·· *East Coker*. 1940.

? R ·· ·· *The family reunion*. 1939.

? R ·· ·· *The four quartets*. 1944.

? R ·· ·· *The idea of a Christian Society*. 1939.

? R ·· ·· *Murder in the cathedral*. 1935.

? R ·· ·· *Notes towards the definition of culture*. 1948.

? R ·· ·· *Poems 1909–1925*. 1925.

? R ·· ·· *The rock*. 1934.

? R ·· ·· *The sacred wood*. 1920 (1934).

? R ·· ·· *Selected essays*. 1932.

? R T. S. Eliot. *Sweeney Agonistes.* 1932.
? R [Elizabeth von Arnim]. *Elizabeth and her German garden.* 1901.
? S *English comic album, The.* [Selected by Orwell for review in *The Observer* about 20.11.48.]

S J. T. Farrell. *The league of frightened Philistines.* 1948.
S J. T. Farrell. *Studs Lonigan.* 1943.
? S W. Faulkner. *Intruder in the dust.* [*Horizon* review copy.]
? R R. Fénelon. *Les aventures de Télémaque.* Paris, 1787.
S L. Fielden. *Beggar my neighbour.* 1943.
R H. Fielding. *The works.* 1853.
? R F. Scott Fitzgerald. *The great Gatsby.* 1948.
Fletcher. See Beaumont.
R J. Ford. *Plays.* n.d. [Inscribed "Eileen O'Shaughnessy."]
R E. M. Forster. *The longest journey.* 1947.
R J. Forster. *The life of Charles Dickens.* 2 vols. 1927.
S M. Fraenkel. *Death in a room. Poems 1927–30.* New York, 1936. [Inscribed 'To Eric Blair from Michael Fraenkel. September 1936.']
? R A. France. *Les contes de Jacques Tournebroche.* Paris, 1921.
A A. France. *The amethyst ring.* 1924.
R J. G. Frazer. *Folk-lore in the Old Testament.* Abridged. 1923.

R M. K. Gandhi. *The story of my experiments with truth.* Trans. M. Desai. 1948.
S M. Geismar. *Last of the provincials.* 1947.
R E. Gibbon. *The decline and fall of the Roman Empire.* 12 vols. 1791.
S A. Gide. *Journal des faux-monnayeurs.* Paris, 1927.
? R ·· ·· *Les caves du Vatican.* Paris, 1922.
? R ·· ·· *L'École des femmes.* Paris, 1929.
R ·· ·· *Les faux-monnayeurs.* Paris, 1925. [Blue binding.]
? R ·· ·· *Retour de l'U.R.S.S.* Paris, 1936.
R G. Gissing. *Charles Dickens.* 1926 (1929).
A ·· ·· *In the year of jubilee.* Intro. William Plomer. 1947.
R ·· ·· *A life's morning.* 1947.
A ·· ·· *New Grub Street.* Intro. Morley Roberts. New York edn., n.d.
A ·· ·· *The odd women.* n.d.
A ·· ·· *Private papers of Henry Ryecroft.* 1906.
? R Goebbels. *The Goebbels diaries.* Trans. L. P. Lochner. 1948.
S Goldoni. *Commedie scelte.* 1,5,6. Prato, 1826. [Blue binding & greened.]
R O. Goldsmith. *Works.* 18??.
? R I. A. Goncharov. *Oblomov.* Trans. N. Duddington. 1932.
S G. Grassi. *James-Grassi dictionary of the Italian and English languages.* 19th ed. 1945.
? S R. Graves. *Good-bye to all that.* 1931.
S T. Gray. *Poems.* 1920. [Inscribed 'Hunc librum Erico A. Blair ab Etona discedenti dono dedit Cyrillus Alington Magister Informator. Etonae A.D. MCMXXI']²
A G. Greene. *England made me.* [1935.]
A G. Greene. *The heart of the matter.* 1948.
? R G. Greene. *Nineteen stories.* 1947.
S J. and W. Grimm. *Household tales.* 1930.

S J. Habberton. *Helen's babies.* n.d.

S J. B. S. Haldane. *Science and everyday life.* 1941.
R T. Hardy. *The dynasts.* 1923. [Blue binding.]
A T. Hardy. *Jude the obscure.* 1923.
A T. Hardy. *Tess of the D'Urbevilles.* 1896.
A B. Harte. *Stories, sketches, & bohemian papers.* n.d. [Cross against 'Luck of Roaring Camp,' 'Outcast of Poker Flat,' 'Miggles,' 'M'liss,' 'Idyll of Red Gulch.']
A B. Harte. *Tales, poems, & sketches.* n.d. [Tick against 'How Santa Claus came to Simpson's Bar.']
R B. Harte. *Tales, poems and sketches.* n.d.
R G. Herbert. *The poetical works.* Edinburgh, 1853.
S H. Hesse. *In sight of chaos.* 1923.
R T. Heywood. *Plays.* n.d. [Inscribed "Eileen O'Shaughnessy."]
? R J. A. Hobson. *The evolution of modern capitalism; a study of machine production.* [1916.]
A Homer. *Odyssey.* Trans. E. V. Rieu. 1945.
? S E. Honig. *Garcia Lorca.* [Selected by Orwell for review in *The Observer* about 6.9.45.]
? S H. L. Hopkins. *The White House papers.* 1948.
R *Horizon.* [Various copies, to 1950.]
R H. House. *The Dickens world.* 1941.
R A. E. Housman. *Last poems.* ?
S A. E. Housman. *The name and nature of poetry.* 1933.
A W. H. Hudson. *Green mansions.* 1941.
    F. M. Hueffer. See J. Conrad.
A R. Hughes. *High wind in Jamaica.* 1929.
R [T. Hughes]. *Tom Brown's schooldays.* 1892. [Inscribed "Robert Blair . . . Christmas 1892."][3]
A P. Hunot. *Man about the house.* n.d.
? S E. Aldington Hunt. *The aristocratic cur.* [1917].
? R A. Huxley. *Mortal coils.* 1922 (1931).
S J. Huxley and others. *Science and religion.* 1931.
? R J.-K. Huysmans. *Là-bas.* Paris, 1891.

? R H. Ibsen. *A Doll's house and two other plays.* 1910 (1912).
R N. M. Iovetz-Tereshenko. *Friendship-love in adolescence.* 1936. [Inscribed "Eileen, 10.3.36."]
R C. Isherwood. *Prater Violet.* 1946.

R H. James. *Daisy Miller; A Study, Four meetings, Longstaff's marriage, and Benvolio.* 1883. [Inscribed "Freeman."]
R ·· ·· *Fourteen stories.* 1947.
R ·· ·· *In the cage* 1898.
R ·· ·· *The jolly corner.* 1918. [Inscribed ". . . ?, 1936."]
R ·· ·· *The lesson of the master and other stories.* 1948.
R ·· ·· *The middle years.* n.d. [Inscribed "E. M. Cutting."]
R ·· ·· *The outcry.* 1911. [Inscribed "Bourne 12/12/11."]
R ·· ·· *The spoils of Poynton.* 1897.
R ·· ·· *Stories revived.* 3 vols. [Vol. 2 only.] 1885.
R ·· ·· *Ten short stories.* Ed. M. Swan. 1948.
R ·· ·· *The turn of the screw and The Aspern papers.* 1935.
R ·· ·· *What Maisie knew.* 1947.

A M. R. James. *More ghost stories of an antiquary*. 1930.
S W. James. *Selected papers on philosophy*. n.d. [Ex libris L. O'Shaughnessy.]
? R R. Jeffries. *The story of my heart*. 1938.
R E. Jenkins. *Jane Austen*. 1948.
A J. K. Jerome. *Observations of Henry*. 1901.
R J. Joyce. *Haveth childers everywhere*. 1931.
R ·· ·· *A portrait of the artist as a young man*. 1916 (1946).
R ·· ·· *Two tales from Shem and Shaun*. 1932.
R ·· ·· *Ulysses*. Paris, 1925. [Blue binding.]

? R Harry Kemp, Laura Riding, et al. *The Left heresy in literature and life*. 1939.
? S S. Keyes. *The collected poems*. 1945.
? S A. W. Kinglake. *Eothen*. 1920.
S H. Kingsmill. *After puritanism*. 1931.
S H. Kingsmill. *The dawn's delay*. 1948.
A R. Kipling. *Captains courageous*. 1905.
R ·· ·· *A choice of Kipling's verse*. Ed. and intro. T. S. Eliot. 1941.
A ·· ·· *The day's work*. 1898.
R ·· ·· *Many inventions*. 1947.
S ·· ·· *The seven seas*. 1896.
R ·· ·· *Soldiers three and other stories*. 1895.
A ·· ·· *Something of myself*. 1937.
R ·· ·· *Stalky and Co*. 1947.
R ·· ·· *Traffics and discoveries*. 1904.
R A. Koestler. *Arrival and departure*. 1943.
R ·· ·· *Darkness at noon*. 1940 (1947).
R ·· ·· *Insight and outlook*. 1949.
R ·· ·· *Thieves in the night*. 1946.
R V. Kravchenko. *I chose freedom*. 1947. [Damaged by damp on Jura.]

? S E. Lampert. *Nicolas Berdyaev and the new middle ages*. n.d.
R W. S. Landor. *Imaginary conversations*. n.d.
A J. Langdon-Davies. *Russia puts the clock back*. 1949.
? S H. J. Laski. *Communist manifesto: Socialist landmark*. 1948.
? R D. H. Lawrence. *Assorted articles*. 1930.
? R D. H. Lawrence. *Etruscan places*. 1932.
A D. H. Lawrence. *The white peacock*. 1932.
S S. Leacock. *Nonsense novels*. 1920. [Avril Blair.]
R F. R. Leavis. *For continuity*. Cambridge, 1933.
R F. R. Leavis. *The great tradition*. 1948.
A J. S. Le Fanu. *In a glass darkly*. 1923.
R J. Lemprière. *A classical dictionary*. n.d.
R D. Leon. *Tolstoy; his life and work*. 1944.
S Sinclair Lewis. *Ann Vickers*. 1933.
S ·· ·· *Dodsworth*. 1929.
S ·· ·· *Elmer Gantry*. 1927.
S ·· ·· *Main Street*. 1946.
S ·· ·· *The prodigal parents*. 1938.
A J. London. *Love of life and other stories*. Intro. G. Orwell. 1946.
R F. L. Lucas. *Time and memory*. 1929.
R Earl of Lytton. *Antony*. 1935 (1947).

R T. B. Macaulay. *Macaulay's historical essays*. n.d.

? S N. Macchiavelli. *The prince.* 1903.
A E. Macglagen. *The Bayeux tapestry.* 1943.
A C. Mackenzie. *Sinister Street.* Vol. 1. 1914.
A M. Maclennan. *A pronouncing and etymological dictionary of the Gaelic language.* 1925.
A N. Mailer. *The naked and the dead.* 1949.
S Sir T. Malory. *Le Morte d'Arthur.* Vol. 2. 1923 ["Eileen O.S."]
R A. Malraux. *Man's estate.* Trans. A. Macdonald. 1948. [Appeared 1934, as *Storm in Shanghai.*]
R K. Mansfield. *The garden party and other stories.* 1928. [Inscribed "Eileen . . ."]
S Marcus Aurelius Antoninus. *The thoughts.* Trans G. Long. 1912. [Inscribed 'E. A. Blair. Eton 1917–1921. With good wishes.']
? R K. Marx. *Capital.* Trans. E. and C. Paul. 2 vols. 1930 (1934).
S R. Matthews. *English messiahs.* 1936.
A W. S. Maughan. *Creatures of circumstance.* 1947.
R W. S. Maugham. *Cakes and ale.* 1948.
A Maupassant. *Short stories.* 1934.
? R F. Mauriac. *Thérèse.* Trans. G. Hopkins. 1947.
S G. Mazzini. *Selected writings.* Ed. N. Gangulee.[4] 1945.
? R T. McGreevy. *Thomas Stearns Eliot: A study.* 1931.
A H. Melville. *Moby Dick.* 1930.
? R H. Melville. *Moby Dick.* 1907 (1933).
R L. Melville. *The life of William Makepeace Thackeray.* n.d.
? R J. de Menasce. *Quand Israël aime Dieu.* Paris, 1931.
S G. Meredith. *Poems and lyrics of the joy of earth.* 1895.
S G. Meredith. *The poetical works.* 1919. ["Eileen O'S. I.A.S. 1926."]
R J. S. Mills. *Autobiography.* 1924 (1935).
S H. Miller. *The colossus of Maroussi.* San Francisco, 1941.
H. Miller. *The cosmological eye.* 1945.
S *The Minor Elizabethan Drama.* 2. *Pre-Shakespearean Comedies.* 1923. [Eileen O'Shaughnessy.]
R D. S. Mirsky. *Contemporary Russian literature.* 1926.
? R J. B. P. Molière. *Le bourgeois gentilhomme.* Paris, 1688.
S G. Moore. *Aphrodite in Aulis.* 1931.
R ·· ·· *Celibate lives.* 1927.
? R ·· ·· *Confessions of a young man.* 1939.
A ·· ·· *Esther Waters.* 1947.
R ·· ·· *Héloise and Abélard.* 1928.
A ·· ·· *A mummer's wife.* n.d.
S ·· ·· *Ave.* 1947.
·· ·· *Salve.* 1947.
S ·· ·· *Vale.* 1947.
S T. Moore. *Lalla Rookh.* 1854. [Emily Blair,[5] Jan 28, 1857.]
? R W. Morris. *Hopes and fears for art.* 1919.
A A. Morrison. *A child of the Jago.* 1911.
A A. Morrison. *Tales of mean streets.* 1906.
R M. Muggeridge. *The earnest atheist: a study of Samuel Butler.* 1936.
S M. Muggeridge. *The thirties in Great Britain.* 1940.
? R Muir. *The story and the fable.* 1940.

R J. M. Murry. *The free society.* 1948. [Inscribed "To G.O. from J.M.M.[6] . . . Feb., 1948."]

A *The Newgate Calendar.* Intro. Henry Savage. 1928.
R J. H. Newman. *Apologia pro vita sua.* 1912 (1946).
A J. R. Norman. *Fishes of Britain's rivers and lakes.* 1943.
S L. Norris. *Tongue of beauty.* n.d.
A *Novels of High Society from the Victorian Age.* Intro. Anthony Powell. 1947. [*Henrietta Temple*, by B. Disraeli; *Guy Livingstone*, by G. A. Lawrence; *Moths*, by Ouida.]

R C. K. Ogden and I. A. Richards. *The meaning of meaning.* (5th edn.) 1938.
A G. Orwell. *Burmese days.* 1934.
A   ··   ··   *Burmese days.* 1949.
A   ··   ··   *A clergyman's daughter.* 1935.
A   ··   ··   *Down and out in Paris and London.* 1933. [Ida Mabel Blair's copy.[7]]
A   ··   ··   *The English people* 1947.
A   ··   ··   *Homage to Catalonia.* 1938. [Ida Mabel Blair's copy.]
A   ··   ··   *Nineteen eighty-four.* 1949.
A   ··   ··   *The road to Wigan pier.* 1937. [With dust jacket.]
R *Oxford book of English verse.* Ed. A Quiller-Couch. 1923. [Inscribed "Eileen . . . 1923."]

A B. Pain. *The Eliza books.* 1931.
A B. Pain. *The octave of Claudius.* 1897.
? S T. Paine. *The selected works.* Ed. Howard Fast. 1948. (*Horizon* review copy].
R "Palinurus" [Connolly]. *The unquiet grave.* 1944.
S E. Partridge. *A dictionary of Forces' slang, 1939–1945.* 1948. [Review copy.]
R *The Paston Letters, 1422–1509*, 3 vols. Ed. J. Gairdner. 1872–1875.
? S H. Pearson. *Dickens.* 1949.
R H. Pearson. *The life of Oscar Wilde.* 1946.
? R C. Peguy. *Men and saints.* Trans. A. and J. Green. 1947.
? R S. Pepys. *The diary of Samuel Pepys.* 2 vols. 1906 (1943).
S T. Percy. *Reliques of ancient English poetry.* Vols. I and II. 1926.
R F. Petrarca. *Rerum vulgarium fragmenta.* 1907.
A Petronius. *The satyricon.* n.d.
A *Philip's Record Atlas.* 13th edn. Ed. G. Goodall. 1947.
R R. Pitter. *A mad lady's garland.* 1934. [Inscribed "To Eric from Ruth."]
? W. Plomer. *Notes for poems.* 1937. [With annotations claimed to be Orwell's but possibly those of the original owner, H. E. du Plessis.]
R Plutarch. *Lives.* 3 vols. Revised A. H. Clough. n.d.
R E. A. Poe. *The complete tales and poems.* New York, 1938.
R T. Polner. *Tolstoy and his wife.* Trans. N. Wreden. New York, 1945.
S K. R. Popper. *The open society and its enemies.* Vols. I & II. 1945.
R P. Potts. *A ballad for Britain on May Day.* 1945. [Inscribed "To George Orwell, 25.5.45."]
? S P. Potts. *A poet's testament.* 1940.
S A. Powell. *John Aubrey and his friends.* 1948.
S W. H. Prescott. *History of the reign of Philip II.* Vol. 1, 2 & 3. 1878.

R M. Proust. *Remembrance of things past*, 12 vols. [Missing vols. 1, 5, 9 & 10.] Trans. C. K. S. Moncrief. 1943–4.

R *Quarterly Review*. Vols. V, VI, XI, XV, XVIII, XIX, XXVII, XXVIII, XXXVI, XLVI. (1811–1832).

? S Rabelais. *Oeuvres*. 2 vols. Paris, n.d.
A E. & M. A. Radford. *Encyclopaedia of superstitions*. 1947.
S B. Rajan. *Monsoon*. 1943. [103rd copy of limited edition.]
S Sir Walter Raleigh. *Remains*. 1681. [Ex Libris L'O'Shaughnessy.]
A J. Ramsbottom. *Poisonous fungi*. 1945.
S H. Read. *A coat of many colours: occasional essays*. 1945.
A C. Reade. *It is never too late to mend*. n.d.
A C. Reade. *Put yourself in his place*. n.d.
R *Restoration plays from Dryden to Farquhar*. 1932.
   I. A. Richards. See C. K. Ogden.
S H. H. Richardson. *Maurice Guest*. 1931. [Blue binding greened.]
? R L. Riding. *Experts are puzzled*. 1930.
   L. Riding. See Harry Kemp.
? R A. Rimbaud. *Oeuvres*. Paris, 1929.
? R M. Roberts. *The recovery of the West*. 1941.
? R M. Roberts. *T. E. Hulme*. 1938.
S I. Rosenberg. *Collected works*. 1937.
   G. Rosenthal. See J.-P. Sartre.
   D. Rousset. See J.-P. Sartre.
? R B. Russell. *The history of Western philosophy*. 1946.
? R ·· ·· *Mysticism and logic, and other essays*. 1919.
A ·· ·· *Mysticism and logic, and other essays*. 1949.
? R ·· ·· *Philosophy and politics*. 1947.
? R ·· ·· *The theory and practice of Bolshevism*. 1920.
? ·· ·· *Roads to freedom*. 1918. [Notes, said to be Orwell's but they may be those of the original owner, Emrys Jones.]
R M. Rutherford. *The autobiography of Mark Rutherford*. n.d.
S M. Rutherford. *Last pages from a journal*. 1915.
S M. Rutherford. *Mark Rutherford's deliverance*. 1885.

R M. Sadleir. *Trollope; a commentary*. 1945.
? R G. Saintsbury. *Prefaces and essays*. 1933.
A "Saki." *Chronicles of Clovis*. 1937.
? R "Saki." *The unbearable Bassington*. 1947.
R J.-P. Sartre. *Portrait of the anti-Semite*. Trans. E. de Mauny. 1948.
? J.-P. Sartre. *Huis Clos*. 1945.
R R. D. Sartre, D. Rousset, and G. Rosenthal. *Entretiens sur la politique*. Paris, 1949.
A *Saturday Book*. 4th year. [Contains 'Benefit of Clergy.'] 1944.
A *Saturday Book*. 5th year. 1945.
R Shakespeare. *The comedies*. 1922. [Inscribed "Eileen . . . 1922."]
R Shakespeare. *Histories and poems*. 1906 (1937).
R Shakespeare. *Shakespeare's tragedies*. 1911. [Inscribed "Eileen, 1920."]
R *The Shakespeare Apocrypha*. Ed. C. F. Tucker Brooke. Oxford, 1908.
R G. B. Shaw. *John Bull's other island, Major Barbara*. 1907. [Blue binding.]
R G. B. Shaw. *Plays pleasant and unpleasant*. 1906. [Blue binding.]
R P. B. Shelley. *Poetical works*. 2 vols. 1907 (1917).

? S Mrs. Sherwood. *The history of the Fairchild family.* 1854.

R J. Shirley. *Plays.* n.d. [Inscribed "Eileen . . ."]

S *Shorter novels.* Vol. 1. *Elizabethan & Jacobean.* 1929.

S *Shorter novels [of the] eighteenth century. Rasselas; The Castle of Otranto; Vathek.* 1930.

S *Shorter Oxford English Dictionary.* 1933.

S D. Shub. *Lenin.* 1948.

S E. Sitwell. *Alexander Pope.* 1930. [Blue binding.]

S Osbert Sitwell. *Before the bombardment.* 1949.

A ·· ·· *Dumb animals.* 1932.

R ·· ·· *Left hand, right hand.* 4 vols. 1945–1949. [Inscribed in each vol., 'To George Orwell from Osbert Sitwell, 1949.']

S ·· ·· *A letter to my son.* 1944. [Inscribed 'For George Orwell, with best wishes, even though he might not agree with all the sentiments, from Osbert Sitwell, August 1944.']⁸

? S ·· ·· *Triple fugue.* 1940.

S ·· ·· *The true story of Dick Whittington.* 1945. [Inscribed 'For George Orwell with best wishes from Osbert Sitwell. 26.11.46.']

? R S. Sitwell. *All summer in a day.* 1949.

R J. Skelton. *Poems.* 1924.

R H. Slater. *The heretics.* New York, 1947.

A W. Smith. *A classical dictionary of biography, mythology & geography.* 1859.

R T. Smollett. *Ferdinard Count Fathom.* 1905.

R T. Smollett. *Humphrey Clinker.* n.d.

S G. Sorel. *Reflections on violence.* 1925.

R S. Spender. *Poems.* 1938.

R S. Spender. *Spiritual exercises.* Privately printed, 1943. [Inscribed "To George Orwell, with best wishes for 1944, Stephen Spender."]

R S. Spender. *Trial of a judge.* 1938. [Inscribed "To Eric Blair with admiration from Stephen Spender, 5.4.38."]

S Arthur Stanley, ed. *The bedside book.* 1932. [Eileen O'Shaughnessy.]

? R E. Starkie. *Arthur Rimbaud.* 1947.

? S L. S. Stebbing. *Ideals and illusions.* 1948. [*Horizon* review copy.]

R G. Stein. *Three lives.* Norfolk, Conn., 1933.

? R L. Sterne. *Tristram Shandy.* 1912 (1938).

R C. G. Stillman. *Samuel Butler; a mid-Victorian modern.* 1932.

? R L. Strachey. *Books and characters.* 1922. [Inscribed "Madame Revel, 1948."]

? R L. Strachey. *Eminent Victorians.* 1948.

? R A. Strindberg. *Eight famous plays.* 1949.

? S Sir John Suckling. *A ballad upon a wedding.* 1932.

R R. S. Surtees. *Handley Cross.* 1903 (1914). [Blue binding.]

A R. S. Surtees. *Mr. Sponge's sporting tour.* 1949.

S [R. S. Surtees.]. *Plain or ringlets? Ask mamma.* Two facsimiles. [1892]. [Both inscribed 'To George & Sonia, on the occasion of their wedding, with love, Malcolm Muggeridge Oct. 1949.']

S J. Swift. *Miscellanies.* 1,2,3,4,5,6,7,8,9,10,13. 1738–1744.

R J. Swift. *Gulliver's travels and Selected writings.* 1944. [Inscribed "From Paul Potts to George Orwell, 2.8.46."]

R Swinburne. *Poems and ballads.* 1917 (1924).
S J. M. Synge. *Plays, poems, and prose.* 1941.

A G. Tabori. *Original sin.* 1947.
S J. Taylor. *The rule and exercise of holy living.* 12th ed. 1680.
R Tennyson. *Complete works.* 1894. [Inscribed "R. C. Blair."]
R W. M. Thackeray. *Works.* 10 vols. n.d.
? S H. D. Thoreau. *Walden.* 1886. [Southwold carving class.]
? S M. A. Titmarsh. *The Paris sketch-book.* 1886.
? S Countess Tolstoy. *The final struggle.* 1936.
R Leo Tolstoy. *A landed proprietor, The Cossacks, and Sevastopol.* Trans. L. Wiener. 1904.
? S Leo Tolstoy. *The slavery of our times.* Trans. A. Maude. 1948.
A Leo Tolstoy. *War and peace.* 3 vols. n.d.
? S G. M. Trevelyan. *An autobiography.* 1949.
? S G. M. Trevelyan. *England under Queen Anne.* Vol. 3: *Peace under the Protestant Succession.* 1934.
? S G. M. Trevelyan. *English social history.* 1946.
A Anthony Trollope. *An autobiography.* 1924.
A   ··   ·· *Cousin Henry.* 1929.
A   ··   ·· *Framley parsonage.* 1939.
A   ··   ·· *Last chronicles of Barset.* Vols. 1 & 2. 1932.
A   ··   ·· *Miss Mackenzie.* 1924.
A   ··   ·· *Rachel Ray.* 1924.
A   ··   ·· *Tales of all countries.* 1931.
A   ··   ·· *Vicar of Bullhampton.* 1924.
? R   ··   ·· *The Vicar of Bullhampton.* 1924 (1942).
? S J. Tschichold. *An illustrated history of writing and lettering.* 1946.
? R I. Turgenev. *Fathers and sons.* Trans. C. J. Hogarth. 1921 (1929).
? S Mark Twain. *The adventures of Huckleberry Finn.* 1916.
R   ··   ·· *Huckleberry Finn* 1924 (1945).
R   ··   ·· *The innocents abroad.* [1871.]
R   ··   ·· *Life on the Mississippi.* 1914.
R   ··   ·· *Roughing it and The innocents at home.* 1898.

R N. Udall. *Ralph Roister Doister.* 1907.

? S E. Vacandard. *L'inquisition.* 1912.
? S B. de Verville. *Le moyen de parvenir.* Paris, n.d.

S I. Walton. *Lives of Donne, Wotton, Hooker and Herbert.* n.d. [L. O'Shaughnessy.]
A Evelyn Waugh. *Black mischief.* 1948.
R   ··   ·· *Brideshead revisited.* 1945 (1947).
R   ··   ·· *Decline and fall.* 1947.
R   ··   ·· *Put out more flags.* 1942. [Inscribed "J. Kimche."][9]
R   ··   ·· *Scott-King's modern Europe.* 1947.
R   ··   ·· *Vile bodies.* 1947.
A   ··   ·· *Work suspended & other stories.* 1948.
R C. S. Waverley. *Works.* 1901.
R Webster and Tourneur. *Plays.* n.d. [Inscribed "Eileen O'Shaughnessy."]
S H. G. Wells. *First and last things.* 1932.
A   ··   ·· *Island of Dr. Moreau.* 1927.

	S	H. G. Wells.	*Mind at the end of its tether.* 1945.
?	R	·· ··	*The new America: The new world.* 1935.
	R	·· ··	*Tono-Bungay.* 1909. [Inscribed "A.? B. from R. ? ? February, 1909."]
	A	G. E. Whitehead.	*Plain vegetable growing.* 1941. [Contains slip "With the author's compliments."]
	R	W. Whitman.	*Leaves of grass.* 1912. [Inscribed "E. B. from R.? B., 1919."]
?	S	Oscar Wilde.	*The soul of man under socialism.* 1948.
	R	Oscar Wilde.	*Stories.* n.d.
?	R	A. Wilson.	*The wrong set and other stories.* 1949.
?	R	E. Wilson.	*Axel's Castle.* New York, 1947.
	R	E. Wilson.	*To the Finland Station.* n.d. [Contained a letter from L. P. Moore to Blair, 15.7.48.]
?	R	E. Wilson.	*The triple thinkers.* New York, 1948.
	A	P. G. Wodehouse.	*Psmith in the City.* 1923.
	A	P. G. Wodehouse.	*Ukridge.* 5th printing. n.d.
	R	George Woodcock.	*The paradox of Oscar Wilde.* 1949.
	S	George Woodcock.	*William Godwin.* 1946. [Inscribed 'To George Orwell from George Woodcock. 16.12.46.']
	S	George Woodcock.	*Imagine the south* [verse]. Pasadena, 1947. [Inscribed 'For George Orwell. George Woodcock. 2nd March 1948.']
	R	Wordsworth.	*Poems.* 1892. [Inscribed "R. C. Blair."]
	R	Wordsworth.	*Poetical works.* n.d.
?	S	W. Wycherley.	*Plays.* 1888.
	A	J. D. Wyss.	*Swiss family Robinson.* [After December 1944.]
?	S	M. Yearsley.	*The story of the Bible.* 1933.
?	S	*The Year's Poetry 1935.* 1935.	
	R	W. B. Yeats.	*The collected poems.* 1939.
	A	I. Zangwill.	*Children of the Ghetto.* 1926.

1. A number of the books listed have rebindings in dark blue. Orwell told Leonard Moore, on 19 March 1948, with reference to the Uniform Edition of his books, that he favoured dark blue; see *3362.* Writing to Julian Symons on 21 March 1948, he said, 'I think a uniform edition should always be very chaste looking & preferably dark blue'; see *3363.* Orwell's preference has been followed in the binding of this edition.
2. C. A. Alington (1872–1955) was appointed Head Master of Eton in 1916. He took over from John Crace in giving Orwell religious instruction. The *DNB* states, 'Undoubtedly his greatness lay in his genius for teaching, especially for teaching religion as distinct from theology.' He retired from Eton in 1933 and until 1951 was Dean of Durham. This copy was offered for sale by George S. MacManus, Philadelphia, for $1,750.00 in 1983. In his reading list for 1949 (see *3727*), Orwell noted that he had read Alington's *Archdeacons Afloat* in April.
3. No relationship of Robert Blair with Orwell has been established.
4. Professor N. Gangulee worked with Orwell at the BBC; see *1861, n. 1.*
5. Emily Blair (b. 1838) was the daughter of Frederick and Mary Blair; Frederick Blair was a younger brother of Orwell's grandfather. She married the Reverend Austen Gourlay.
6. John Middleton Murry; see *95, headnote.*
7. Orwell's mother.
8. Orwell's initial reaction was given in 'As I Please', 41, 8 September 1944; see *2547.* He also discussed Sitwell's little book—'For a book of 32 pages,' Orwell commented, it 'contains a quite astonishing quantity of invective'—in 'As I Please', 44, 13 October 1944; see *2562.* See also Orwell's 'Authors Deserve a New Deal,' 5 July 1945, *2697.*
9. Jon Kimche worked with Orwell at Booklovers' Corner and on *Tribune;* see *212, n. 8.*

APPENDIX 12

3735. Mrs. Miranda Wood's Memoir

In the summers of 1946 and 1947, whilst he was at Barnhill, Orwell let his London flat to Mrs. Miranda Wood (then Mrs. Christen). This memoir, written in 1984, throws light on the production of *Nineteen Eighty-Four*, 'Such, Such Were the Joys,' and on Orwell. It also says something about the bleakness of London in 1947–48, reflected in *Nineteen Eighty-Four*. It is printed, for the first time, by kind permission of Mrs. Wood; see also *3308, n. 3*.

1947 was the year of my second summer at the flat in Canonbury Square. At intervals of a fortnight or so batches of manuscript posted in the island of Jura dropped through the letterbox for me to type. I had to do the work in the evenings and at weekends because I had a regular nine to five job in the City. I do not think I kept the author waiting long for the return package enclosing clean new typescript and one carbon copy. I was paying a nominal rent for the flat and from this I made what I considered to be an appropriate deduction for the typing. Both parties were satisfied with the arrangement. Or so I assumed. It all seemed fair and square.

Years passed. I was on the other side of the world for some of them. Near and far I heard people saying "Big Brother is watching you," as if it were some radio comic's catchphrase. I began to feel like the girl who danced with the man who danced with the girl who danced with the Prince of Wales. In fact I made sparing capital of the gambit and only in company where the impact was assured.

Twenty years on I was being interviewed by Woodrow Wyatt, who needed a new secretary. I told him I was experienced in deciphering writers' rough manuscripts. He wanted to know what writers. I played my ace and this time I got back more than I bargained for. Over the next five years a variety of visitors, including MPs of all persuasions, trade union leaders, Mr Bernard Levin, a prime minister even were invited to a brief bask in my reflected glory. While in one way gratifying this always left me feeling curiously uneasy—as if George Orwell himself were glowering down from above, amazed at the presumption.

Back in the 'thirties I had worked for two publishers — Gerald Duckworth in London and the O.U.P in India. I had seen authors' MSS in all conditions and had typed or re-typed not a few. Orwell's was the easiest that ever came my way. The version he sent to me, presumably the initial draft, was partly self-typed, partly handwritten, not difficult to follow at all. The writing was neat and legible with alterations and inserts carefully indicated and unfamiliar names and words spelled out meticulously. I was also provided with a separate glossary of Newspeak.

On 22 October 1948, Orwell wrote to his publisher about the again-worked-over typescript, "I can't send it away because it is an unbelievably bad MS and no one could make head or tail of it without explanation. On the other hand a skilled typist under my eye could do it easily enough"; [see 3477]. My impression makes this statement hard to credit. Perhaps he was failing to do justice to both the clarity of his work and the savvy of an ordinarily intelligent typist. So far as I was concerned it was simply a matter of copying out what was plainly set forth.

Unlike 1946, the second peacetime summer was a scorcher. The days were unbrokenly sunny and seemed endless, it being still double summer-time. It was stifling in the flat, a conversion ranging across the attics of two nineteenth-century houses. The roof soaked up the heat of the day, conducting it into the rooms below. In the living room the pedestal table wobbled and rocked as I pounded the keys of the portable typewriter I had taken from the box sized office cum workshop across the passage. Orwell, of course, had a machine with him in Jura so perhaps the one I used had been the property of his dead wife.

All through the hot months on I typed. I was rivetted from the start. There were analogies with my recent past. Invaders who could promote slogans like "Great East Asia Co-Prosperity Sphere" to a cowed and penurious native population would have taken to the Ministry of Truth like ducks to water. I was too awestruck to volunteer any admiring opinion with the typescripts however. Nor was any reaction, good or bad, expressed regarding the quality of the work I turned in. Satisfactory or not, the brown envelopes kept on coming.

One day there was a separate sheaf of papers in the package. It was a bleary typescript of the essay "Such, such were the joys" to be re-done. It looked as if it had been lying around for a considerable time. I know now that this memoir is believed by some to be the source of '1984' and it is important to establish exactly when it was written. I can only clear up the mystery of when it was re-typed and by whom.

When I read this piece echoes of a long ago rumpus at Duckworths stirred in my memory. Osbert Sitwell had once done a similar hatchet job on his prep school. Writs had flown, an edition was withdrawn. There were apologies, if not damages, and red faces all round. I was emboldened to transmit this cautionary tale with my next delivery. The short answer I received was that publication was not contemplated until the protagonists were safely dead.

In a letter to F. J. Warburg dated 31st May 1947 (and I cannot be sure if this date would have been before or after the copy was sent to me: on the whole I think it was probably before) Orwell writes, "I am sending you separately a long autobiographical sketch . . . I think it is really too libellous to print . . . But I think it should be printed sooner or later when the people concerned are dead . . . I must apologise for the typescript. It is not only the carbon copy but is very bad commercial typing which I have had to correct considerably."[1]

When I came upon this, ten years or so ago, I failed to pay due regard to the date of the letter and I felt decidedly aggrieved. I assumed he was referring to my typescript. Undeniably it was commercial. But very bad? I have typed for a living all my working days and reflections on my competence came very much amiss.

I was somewhat appeased to read more recently in Prof. Crick's *George Orwell: A Life* (Appendix B)

"*The Dating of SSWTJ* — The typescripts . . . that survive are remarkably clean with only occasional and small corrections of literals and those not in Orwell's hand . . ."

I would lay odds on whose hand it was. Prof. Crick also states there is no record of anyone at Secker & Warburg's having done the work. There wouldn't be. And "There is moreover no record or memory of him farming out any work while at Jura . . ."

But he did.

To explain how it was that, like Goldilocks, I came to be sitting in Orwell's chairs, sleeping in his bed, reading his books and using his typewriter means introducing a segment of personal history.

I had landed in England from the Far East in 1946, with three and a half years in Japanese occupied territory behind me. I had not been interned because technically (through marriage) I was of German nationality. I had come home intent on getting myself re-admitted to the British fold and also on obtaining a divorce. Achieving these objects was clearly going to be a protracted business in the conditions of the time and I was resigned to a longish sojourn in London before they were accomplished. I was looking for a place to stay at the same time Orwell was making plans to vacate his flat and spend the summer in his house on the Scottish island.

It is reasonable to suppose that Anthony Powell, the activator of the transaction, had provided a rundown of my antecedents when he put forward the suggestion. On the face of it my record hardly added up to the most solid and dependable of characters and many a householder would have thought twice before entrusting his goods and chattels to a tenant so doubtful. Not Orwell. He invited me to tea to discuss matters.

I had read *Down and Out in Paris and London* and *The Road to Wigan Pier* before the war. The prospect of solving my accommodation problems for the next few months aside I was not a little excited to be about to meet an author whose work I had found so interesting.

The front door opened into a long, narrow passage, with doors to two large rooms on one side and four small rooms the other. The complete household was present — Orwell, the cherubic two year old Richard and Susan Watson, the girl who housekept and attended the baby.

All I took in of Orwell himself was that he was very tall and had a moustache. There was something about him that brought to mind schoolmasters, librarians or similar, usually benign, figures of authority. One would not take liberties with him.

He greeted me quite warmly and then directed Susan to take both children — I had brought my seven year old daughter with me — to buy buns for tea.

Long accustomed to the mistrustful probings of professional landladies I did not at first catch on that he had in fact decided in advance to let me have the flat. He didn't only look like Don Quixote. He said I could pay £3 a week which would just about cover his outgoings for controlled rent and the utilities. I dared hardly believe my luck. I was paying double that for a single room in Kensington. He said I could re-address mail that came for him, perhaps send on papers he might want from the little office. There was no mention of typing at this stage.

This was the only interview of any length we had. I wish I could remember more. He asked if I had listened to Overseas Service broadcasts in Java. But apart from infrequent and jittery occasions when I had heard Big Ben and the News behind locked doors with friends I had done no radio listening during the Japanese occupation at all. In Surabaya and Bandung news circulated by word of mouth and more often than not it became distorted in the process. It was possible to draw one's own conclusions by day to day comparisons of the official bulletins, particularly those concerning the war in Europe. Although it was never admitted that the Axis had lost ground unexplained advances by the Allies were revealed a day or two later so it was not difficult to assess the way the war was going. Those bold enough to tinker with their officially-sealed radios did so in order to receive hard news and even resented the chimes as a dead giveaway if overheard. To be caught meant being hauled off by the Kempei Tai — with unspeakable consequences — worth the risk, perhaps, for information about the Second Front or battles in the Pacific, of more immediate consequence to us, but not for BBC talks, however enlightening. Orwell said he feared as much. I was speaking solely from my own experience: in the camps they were much more audacious, availing themselves of the full BBC overseas programmes on their forbidden, ingeniously concealed and constructed radio sets.

I was given a word or two of warning about the elderly widow who lived in the flat beneath. She was a habitual complainer and had recently been taking exception to the patter of Richard's tiny feet penetrating her ceiling. I was also advised about the local shops, the best places for rations, etc. He recommended the Canonbury Tavern as a decent pub and said there were no tolerable restaurants nearer than King's Cross.

After tea, which was substantial, came the ritual of Richard's bath. He was a lively roly-poly toddler with brown hair and bright pink cheeks. He wriggled and squealed as Orwell carried him into the living room to be dried off in front of the smouldering coal fire. A Victorian draught screen shielded Orwell's high backed chair. It was embellished with coloured cut-outs depicting angel children, carol singers, Newfoundland dogs, Persian kittens, all redolent of Christmases and childhoods past. The scene might have been lifted straight out of an old-fashioned ladies' journal. I boggled a bit that Orwell, least sentimental of writers, was clearly revelling in all this cosy domesticity.

I moved in the day they left for Scotland. When I collected the keys Susan and Richard were missing and Orwell and his sister, Miss Blair, were almost ready to depart. Neither had much to say.

The flat has been described as Spartan. I did not find it so except in the matter of heating and that was a common enough inadequacy in English homes until some years after WW2. By my standards it was provided with everything necessary and it was indeed luxurious compared with some habitations I had known. Later it did occur to me that the long climb to the top floor, burdened with provisions, buckets of coal or a heavy infant would not have been medically recommended for a case of impaired lungs.

At first I stayed alone in the flat, my daughter Julia having been packed off to school in Essex. The weather was still terrible. In the long, light evenings I took solitary walks through the dismal, blitzed streets of Islington and Pentonville, soon to be immortalised as Prole territory.

The Canonbury area itself must always have been several cuts above its surroundings. To step out of the ordered Northampton estate into bordering Upper Street or Essex Road was to enter the world of working class North East London. Gentrification had yet to come.

Always an avid reader, years of book deprivation now made me feel like Rip Van Winkle waking up in a gingerbread house. The bookshelves in the living room were weighed down with long lines of volumes, promising rich pickings. There were also piles of literary and political journals, English and American, mostly new to me. I sat up half the night gorging myself on issue after issue of *Horizon*.

An American friend from Java and her two children who were waiting for a passage across the Atlantic came to stay. The Dutch father of the children had been beheaded by Dyak tribesmen at his Borneo jungle post as he waited for the Japanese to take over the district administration. There was room for us all in the flat and it solved the problem of looking after Julia in the school holidays. Needless to say, all three children clattered up and down the linoleum covered hallway, scold as we might. There were unfriendly looks when we encountered the widow on the stairs.

Old friends began turning up bearing bottles of booze. After initial reunion celebrations at the Four Sisters pub we returned to the flat to continue roistering. On one fairly tumultuous occasion the Burmese sword hanging on the wall was taken down and brandished. It had reminded the perpetrator, an ex-prisoner-of-war, all too forcibly, of the weapons borne by his captors. He was disarmed and calmed down. Next morning the hangovers were fierce.

I was bored stiff in the City and my affairs still hung fire. For the Home Office I had to write to people I had known in Java, now widely scattered, to obtain testimonials that I had been neither aid nor comfort to the enemy. It was a slow process. The German divorce was urged on and financed by parcels of cigarettes and ground coffee, about one in three of which got through.

Summer's lease and that of the flat was running out. Julia went back to school. Our friends returned to the transit camp, still waiting to complete their interrupted journey across the globe that had started nearly a year before. I made another tour of the tobacconists' notice boards and eventually settled for an expensive and depressing 'flatlet' in Marylebone.

The children had broken one or two of the Jubilee and Coronation mugs that were in common kitchen use. I wrote a note apologising and saying I would try to replace them. My apprehensions grew. Would Orwell now regret his kindness? The night of the big booze-up lay heavy on my conscience.

Sadly, I packed up. I don't know what inspired me to leave a packet of (rationed) tea and a bottle of milk on the kitchen table.

The century's worst winter followed. In the poky room in Wyndham Street the only heat was dispersed from the dimmest glimmer of gas jets. In the City we worked in unheated offices by the light of candles stuck in bottles and ran in and out of the tiny snack bar at the side of the Royal Exchange, the only source of hot drinks, as often as possible. I yearned for the steamy tropics. If there had been a bus running from the Bank to Mandalay I would have been first aboard.

After months of coughs and colds and aching bones the snow eventually melted. Hesitantly, I approached Tony Powell again. Did he happen to know how I rated at Canonbury Square? The tea had gone over well, he said. So well, in fact, that I might be forgiven one or two little peccadillos. Information about the riotous nights and boisterous kids had indeed filtered through. But the old lady had been so glad to see us depart she had almost welcomed the Orwells back as the lesser evil. And they would be travelling North again shortly.

Encouraged but not really daring to hope, I sent off a letter timorously asking if I might borrow the flat again. Incredibly the answer came back Yes.

The 1947 handover took place on another raw Spring evening. As before, Orwell and his redoubtable sister were making final arrangements for their journey. Again he appeared morose and uncommunicative. All three, even little Richard, were wearing thumping great boots.

It was wonderful to be back. Soon the letter came asking if I knew of anybody who would be willing to type out the draft of some work in progress.

My situation was gradually straightening itself out. Naturalisation and divorce papers came through almost simultaneously. I applied for a new British passport and put my name down for a sea passage to Singapore. There were still long waiting lists for ships bound anywhere.

At some time I was requested to take a will out of a box file and send it to Jura. I remember noticing the bit at the end expressing the wish to be buried according to the rites of the Church of England, which surprised me a little. I cannot recall which summer this occurred.

I toiled on in the City, profoundly thankful that soon I would be seeing the last of it. Then home again to another session on the portable. This summer holiday there was no one to look after Julia in my absence. So mainly she looked after herself with flying ten minute visits from me at lunchtime to check up. After she returned to school I was alone a great deal. A man called Bobby Roberts, a veteran of Grub Street, sometimes kept me company. He eyed the flat covetously. When I was gone he wrote to Orwell asking if he might replace me there but was turned down flat.

Some water leaked through to the widow's bathroom. She waylaid me on the stairs, triumphant with righteous indignation. At last she had something tangible to complain about, though we had been as quiet as mice all summer. I paid for the redecoration but that didn't stop her carrying tales to the Northampton Estate. This accounts for the reference in a letter written to Anthony Powell six months later, ". . . they have been riding me like the nightmare for lending the flat to Mrs Christen."

That year the Northern Irish charlady Orwell had spoken of put in an appearance. She was robust and cheerful and more than a match for the enemy below. She doted on Orwell and astonished me by a reference to glamorous girl friends. Several, she said. I would never have suspected him of being a ladies' man.

The final batch of MS was typed up and sent off. I found it hard to get the rat torture scene out of my mind. The manuscript stopped a few hundred words short of the end. The Appendix was not included.

September, the month I had expected Orwell to return, came and went but nothing happened. I stayed put. A load of peat was delivered and I was urged to make use of it. Try as I might I could not coax the stuff to burn in the small grate. Unless Orwell had better luck the little boy was going to be in for some chilly bathtimes. (There was, fortunately, a gas fire in the main bedroom.)

November was foggy. These were the last years of the dense sulphurous pea-soupers. Swathed in smoky vapours and outwardly unchanged since Dickens's day, Canonbury Square presented a scene of quintessential London for a wanderer's mental baggage. My number came up on the shipping register and I was awarded two berths in a semi-troopship sailing for Singapore.

I sent Orwell the name and address of a reliable typist of my acquaintance. So far as I know he did not make use of it.

On 20th November, 1947, a letter from Jura records, "Apparently Mrs Christen has just sailed"; [see *3308*].

She had.

1. For a detailed reconstruction of the composition of 'Such, Such Were the Joys' in the light of later evidence, see *3408*.

APPENDIX 13

3736. After Orwell's Death

When Harper & Brothers was considering the publication of *Burmese Days*, Orwell was asked if he would make changes to the last two or three pages of the novel. He wrote to Leonard Moore, about 8 February 1934; see *192*: 'I will cut these out if it is absolutely insisted upon, but not otherwise. I hate a novel in which the principal characters are not disposed of at the end. I will, however, cut out the offending words "it now remains to tell" etc.' It is in this spirit that these notes are included.

Orwell provided in his will that his wife, Sonia, his sister, Avril, and his sister-in-law, Gwen O'Shaughnessy, should act as guardians of his son, Richard. Avril and Bill Dunn, whom she married in February 1951, brought up Richard (see Orwell's letter to Richard Rees, 17 September 1949, *3692*), and Sonia was meticulous in fulfilling her financial obligations to Richard both whilst she was alive and at her death. The Dunns moved from Barnhill to a farm at Gartcharron by Ardfern in Argyllshire on the Scottish mainland, and it was there that Richard grew up, very happily. Avril died in 1978, aged seventy; her husband died in 1992, aged seventy-one. Orwell's elder sister, Marjorie, had predeceased him in 1946, aged forty-eight, and her husband, Humphrey Dakin, died in 1970, aged seventy-four. They had three children, Jane, Henry, and Lucy. Gwen O'Shaughnessy, Eileen's sister-in-law, continued to work as a general practitioner and died in 1963.

Richard attended Loretto (near Edinburgh), where Bill Dunn had been educated, and then Sonia suggested he study at Lackham College of Agriculture in Wiltshire. After graduation he studied further at the North of Scotland Agricultural College, Aberdeen. He then took up farming, as Orwell had hoped, first in Herefordshire (where he was head ploughman and reserve milkman) and then in Warwickshire as assistant farm manager. Later he worked as an agricultural engineer. He has kept the name Blair. In 1964 he married Eleanor Moir, whom he met when she was working as a scientific assistant at an agricultural research station in Aberdeen. After their two sons, Gavin and Alastair, were born she trained as a schoolteacher and is now a magistrate. Gavin farms in Warwickshire; Alastair, after teaching outdoor pursuits, is studying boat-building.

Sonia Orwell
Ian Angus writes:
After Orwell's death Sonia Orwell divided her time between England and France, a country she loved and where she had many friends. Several years after her death she was recalled by one of them, the writer Michel Leiris: "Douée en vérité d'une sensibilité aiguë et d'un esprit prompt à l'enthousiasme, cette Anglaise née dans les lointaines Indes et qui ne portait nulle trace de l'éducation bigote que toute jeune elle avait reçue était—n'en déplaise à ses détracteurs—la générosité même et, cherchant sans doute à désarmer le tourment profond dont la présence se laissait deviner sans grand risque d'erreur derrière sa gaîté habituelle, semblait prendre le plus grand de ses plaisirs à réunir chez elle ceux et celles dont la compagnie lui agréait."[1]

In 1950 Sonia for a short time worked for the publishing firm, Skira, in Geneva; then from 1951 she worked as a consultant and reader for Weidenfeld & Nicolson and also worked for them as an editor from 1954 to 1956. She persuaded them to publish Nigel Dennis, Saul Bellow, Elisabeth Hardwick, Dan Jacobson, and Mary McCarthy. In 1958 she married Michael Pitt-Rivers but the marriage lasted barely four years and ended in divorce in 1965.

Her love of literature was intense but she set a low value on her own literary ability and as a consequence the output of her writing was meagre: a few reviews in *Horizon*, the *London Magazine* (1959–60), and in *Europa Magazine* (1971); some reports from abroad in the *Sunday Times* (in 1956 from Israel) and the *Twentieth Century* (from Paris in 1960); and her disagreement in *Nova* in 1969 with Mary McCarthy's assessment of Orwell. In 1964–65 she was a co-editor of the Paris-based international review *Art and Literature*. She translated many articles from French and in 1966 translated *Days in the Trees*, by her friend Marguerite Duras, for the Royal Shakespeare Company. To writers whom she befriended she was generous in encouragement and frequently helped them materially, realising that, in some cases, critical acclaim did not necessarily sell enough books to support them in their writing.

Shortly after Orwell died, Sonia arranged that the Library of the British Museum should receive his pamphlet collection, where, as he had wished, it is now preserved. Ten years later, in 1960, she made possible the creation of the George Orwell Archive by donating to it all Orwell's papers in her possession. She was a founder trustee of the Archive, with Sir Richard Rees (her co-literary executor), the Honourable David Astor, John Beavan (Lord Ardwick), and the Lord Northcliffe Professor of Modern English Literature, James R. Sutherland. The policy of the trustees has been to acquire material by and on Orwell and to develop the Archive as a centre for Orwell studies.

Early in the 1960s, William Jovanovich, the head of Harcourt Brace Jovanovich, Orwell's publishers at that time in New York, was eager to put more of Orwell's writings into print. This resulted, under his stimulus and encouragement, in the five-year collaboration of Sonia and myself (I was then in charge of the Orwell Archive) in editing the Collected Essays, Journalism and Letters of George Orwell, which was published in four volumes in 1968.

Passionate and impulsive as she was in her personal relations—indeed, in everything she did—she was nevertheless steadfast and scrupulous in carrying out her responsibilities as Orwell's literary executor. She sought to make her decisions on exclusively literary grounds and to be of the kind that she thought Orwell would have approved. She vigorously resisted any attempt to sentimentalise or distort his work or commercialise it.

In requesting in his will that he should not be the subject of a biography, Orwell unwittingly placed on Sonia a heavy burden which became a highly emotive matter for her and caused her constant anguish till the end of her life. For the first few years after his death she faithfully committed herself to observe his wish and thus unavoidably disappointed and upset aspiring biographers and publishers, the more so if they had been Orwell's friends or acquaintances. Then, when the growth of Orwell's fame made it seem certain that a life would in any case be published, she agonised over whom to authorise. She was unable to secure Richard Ellmann, and in 1955 Malcolm Muggeridge accepted her invitation to write a biography of Orwell, but he failed to produce one. Throughout 1980, when she was dying of cancer, Sonia was distressed and self-reproachful for having commissioned, eight years earlier, a biography by Bernard Crick; she found she disliked it but contractual arrangements ensured that she could not stop its publication. The book appeared in late November that year and was very well received by critics. She was also sorely tormented in her last year by an impending lawsuit over Orwell's literary estate which finally and reluctantly she was forced by her physical condition to settle out of court, also late in November. She died on 11 December 1980, aged sixty-two.

1. 'Chevauchées D'Antan,' L'Ire des Vents, nos. 15–16 (1987), 11–15: 'This Englishwoman, born in the far-distant Indies, and who bore no trace of the bigoted education she had received in earliest youth, was—whatever her detractors may say—generosity itself, truly gifted with acute sensitivity and a spirit quickly fired with enthusiasm. Yet, beneath her customary gaiety, there could be no mistaking the presence of deep torment; doubtlessly seeking to disarm it, she seemed to take her greatest pleasure in gathering at her house those friends—men and women—whose company she found congenial.' (Translated by Marina Warner.) Michel Leiris (1901–1990), ethnologist and writer of remarkable courage and honesty, was

described as 'The Modern Montaigne' when his *Journal 1922–89* was reviewed in the *Times Literary Supplement*, 5 March 1993. Sonia briefly reviewed his *Fourbis* in the *Sunday Times*, 11 March 1956.

APPENDIX 14

3737. Supplementary Items

During the course of making up this edition some items came to light after the volumes had been completed. Most of these have been included in chronological sequence, distinguished by an A or B after the item number. A few items (several of considerable importance) became available after the volumes had reached the stage of page proof and it was not practicable to include them in their chronological positions. Their item numbers are given at the places where they should be read and the items are printed here with the appropriate volume and page number.

Vol. XI, p. 102

413A. To H. N. Brailsford

10 December 1937   Typewritten

The Stores   Wallington   Nr. Baldock   <u>HERTS.</u>

Dear Mr Brailsford,[1]

I cannot exactly claim your acquaintance, though I believe I did meet you for a moment in Barcelona, and I know you met my wife there.

I have been trying to get the truth about certain aspects of the May fighting in Barcelona. I see that in the "New Statesman" of May 22nd you state that the P.O.U.M. partisans attacked the Government with tanks and guns "stolen from Government arsenals." I was, of course, in Barcelona throughout the fighting, and though I cannot answer for tanks I know as well as one can be certain about such a thing that no guns were firing anywhere. In various papers there occurs a version of what is evidently the same story, to the effect that the P.O.U.M. were using a battery of stolen 75 mm. guns on the Plaza de Espana. I know this story to be untrue for a number of reasons. To begin with, I have it from eye-witnesses who were on the spot that there were no guns there; secondly, I examined the buildings round the square afterwards and there were no signs of gunfire; thirdly, throughout the fighting I did not hear the sound of artillery, which is unmistakeable if one is used to it. It would seem therefore that there has been a mistake. I wonder if you could be kind enough to tell me what was the source of the story about the guns and tanks? I am sorry to trouble you, but I want to get this story cleared up if I can.

Perhaps I ought to tell you that I write under the name of George Orwell.

Yours truly
Eric Blair

1. For H. N. Brailsford, see *424, n. 3.*

Vol. XI, p. 104

414B. To H. N. Brailsford

18 December 1937 Typewritten

The Stores Wallington Nr. Baldock <u>HERTS.</u>

Dear Mr Brailsford,

Thank you very much for your letter.[1] I was very interested to know the source of the story about tanks and guns. I have no doubt the Russian ambassador told it you in good faith and from what little I know myself I should think it quite likely it was true in the form in which he gave it you. But because of the special circumstances, incidents of that kind are apt to be a little misleading. I hope it will not bore you if I add one or two more remarks about this question.

As I say, it is quite conceivable that at some time or other the guns *were* stolen, because to my own knowledge, though I never actually saw it done, there was a great deal of stealing of weapons from one militia to another. But people who were not actually in the militia do not seem to have understood the arms situation. As far as possible arms were prevented from getting to the P.O.U.M. and Anarchist militias, and they were left only with the bare minimum that would enable them to hold the line but not to make any offensive action. There were times when the men in the trenches actually had not enough rifles to go round, and at no time until the militias were broken up was artillery allowed to get to the Aragon front in any quantity. When the Anarchists made their attacks on the Jaca road in March–April they had to do so with very little artillery support and had frightful casualties. At this time (March–April) there were only about 12 of our aeroplanes operating over Huesca. When the Popular Army attacked in June a man who took part in the attack tells me that there were 160. In particular, the Russian arms were kept from the Aragon front at the time when they were being issued to the police forces in the rear. Until April I saw only one Russian weapon, a sub-machine gun, which quite possibly had been stolen. In April two batteries of Russian 75 mm. guns arrived – again possibly stolen and conceivably the guns referred to by the Russian ambassador. As to pistols and revolvers, which are very necessary in trench warfare, the Government would not issue permits to ordinary militiamen and militia officers to buy them, and one could only buy them illegally from the Anarchists. In these circumstances the outlook everyone had was that one had to get hold of weapons by hook or by crook, and all the militias were constantly pilfering them from one another. I remember an officer describing to me how he and some others had stolen a field gun from a gun-park belonging to the P.S.U.C.,[2] and I would have done the same myself without any hesitation in the circumstances. This kind of thing always goes on in war-time, but, coming together with the newspaper stories to the effect that the P.O.U.M. was a disguised Fascist organisation, it was easy to suggest that they stole weapons not to use against the Fascists but to use against the Government. Owing to the Communist control of the press the similar behaviour by other units was kept dark. For instance there is not much doubt that in March some partisans of the P.S.U.C. stole 12 tanks from a Government arsenal by means of a forged order. La Battalla, the P.O.U.M. paper, was fined 5000 pesetas and suppressed for 4 days for reporting this, but the Anarchist paper, Solidaridad Obrera, was able to report it with impunity. As to the guns, if stolen, being kept in Barcelona, it seems to me immensely unlikely. Some of the men at the front would certainly have heard of it and would have raised hell if they had known weapons were being kept back, and I should doubt if you could keep two batteries of guns concealed even in a town the size of Barcelona. In any case they would have come to light later, when the P.O.U.M. was suppressed. I do not, of course, know what was in all the P.O.U.M. strongholds, but I was in the three principle° ones during the Barcelona fighting, and I know that they had only enough weapons for the usual armed guards that were kept on buildings. They had no machine guns, for instance. And I think it is certain that there was no artillery-fire during the fighting. I see that you refer to the Friends of Durruti[3] being more or less under P.O.U.M. control, and John Langdon-Davies[4] says something to the same effect in his report in the News Chronicle. This story was only put about in order to brand the P.O.U.M. as "Trotskyist." Actually the Friends of Durruti, which was an extremist organisation, was bitterly hostile to the P.O.U.M. (from their point of view a more or less right-wing organisation) and so far as I know no one was a member of both. The only connection between the two is that at the time of the May fighting the P.O.U.M. are said to have published approval of an inflammatory poster which was put up by the Friends of Durruti. Again there is some doubt about this – it is certain that there was no *poster*, as described in the News Chronicle and elsewhere, but there may have been a handbill of some kind. It is impossible to discover, as all records have been destroyed and the Spanish authorities would not allow me to send out of Spain files even of the P.S.U.C. newspapers, let alone the others. The only sure thing is that the Communist reports on the May fighting, and still more on the alleged Fascist plot by the P.O.U.M., are completely untruthful. What worries me is not these lies being told, which is what one expects in war-time, but that the English left-wing press has refused to allow the other side a hearing. Eg. the papers made a tremendous splash about Nin[5] and the others being in Fascist pay, but have failed to mention that the Spanish Government, other than the Communist members, have denied that there was any truth in the story. I suppose the underlying idea is that they are somehow aiding the Spanish Government by allowing the Communists a free hand. I am sorry to burden you with all this stuff, but I have tried to do all I can, which is not much, to get the truth about what has happened in Spain more widely known. It does not matter to me personally when they say that I am in Fascist pay, but it is different for the thousands who are in prison in Spain and are liable to be murdered by the secret police as so many have been already. I doubt whether it would be possible to do much for the Spanish anti-Fascist prisoners, but some kind of organised protest would probably get many of the foreigners released.

My wife wishes to be remembered to you. Neither of us suffered any ill-effects from being in Spain, though, of course, the whole thing was terribly distressing and disillusioning. The effects of my wound passed off more quickly than was expected. If it would interest I will send you a copy of my book on Spain when it comes out.

Yours sincerely
Eric Blair

1. For Brailsford's letter, 17 December 1937, see *424*.
2. Partido Socialista Unificado de Cataluña (The United Catalan Socialist Party, a communist party).
3. For the Friends of Durruti, see *424*, *n. 6* and *519*, *n. 24* (which has a note on Buenaventura Durruti.
4. For John Langdon-Davies, see *519*, *n. 16*.
5. For Andrés Nin, see *382*, *n. 5*.

Vol. XV, p. 268

2305A. To Lydia Jackson

8 October 1943   Original   07/ES/EB

Dear Lydia,[1]
Eileen[2] said that you might be interested in featurising a Russian short story for us. I have a feeling that that story you told me about – about the sailor who was marooned on an island in the Aleutian archipelago – might do very well if you have already translated it. These are half hour programmes and the story is broken down into narration and dialogue in such a way as to use not more than six or eight actors. I could send you specimen copies of earlier stories we have done so as to give you an idea of what is wanted. The chief difficulty in these stories is to find a suitable one. For the air they must have a strong plot, and as they are for an Indian audience they must be readily intelligible and not depend on local colour; for that reason I am inclined to think that European stories are better than English ones, and I would like very much to have a Russian story if a suitable one can be found. Do you think you can send me one or two specimens of the ones you have already translated, and let me

know about this pretty soon because the next story is due to go on the air in just under a month, which means having the script in less than three weeks.

Yours,
[Signed] Eric
(Eric)

1. For Lydia Jackson, see *534A, headnote.*
2. Orwell's wife.

Vol. XV, p. 276

2317A. To Lydia Jackson
15 October 1943   Original

Dear Lydia,
I am sending back the typescript of the story called "The Island of Birds" (I have shortened the title to that). I have not had time to read it very attentively but I am pretty certain it will do if boiled down to suitable length. I am sending together with it two copies of previous scripts in the same series. These will give you an idea of how we go to work. It is important that the same length should be kept and above all that the script should not be too long. The date of this one will be November 3rd, and it is most necessary that I should have the script ten days beforehand, that is, not later than October 24th. When I do these scripts myself I generally find that the boiling down and putting into radio shape is about two days work. I hope you will enjoy doing it.

With love,
[Signed] Eric
Eric Blair

Vol. XV, p. 301

2341A. To Lydia Jackson
28 October 1943   Original   07/ES/EB

Dear Lydia,
Many thanks for the story. I am afraid I only had time to look at it rather hurriedly as it had to be sent off to the producer, but I am pretty sure it will be all right. We are going to broadcast it live on Wednesday next at 11.0 a.m. They will also be rehearsing it the day before, but I think that if you came here on Wednesday you would see the final rehearsal and then the actual broadcasting and this would give you some ideas for future occasions. Could you be here at a quarter to ten on the morning of Wednesday 3rd? I think you know my office i.e. 200 Oxford Street.

With love,
[Signed] Eric
(Eric Blair)

Vol. XV, p. 305

2349A. To Lydia Jackson
11 November 1943   Original   07/ES/EB

Dear Mrs. Jackson,
Can you do a script similar to your last one using as a basis Galsworthy's story The Apple Tree? I am enclosing a copy of the story. The date of the programme would be December the 1st, which means that I would like the script by the 24th November.[1]

Yours sincerely,
ERIC BLAIR
Dispatched in Mr Blair's
absence by: [Signed] J E Light

1. The 24 November was Orwell's last day of service with the BBC. The letter is annotated (by Lydia Jackson): 'Script sent back on 18/11.'

Vol. XVI, p. 190

2470A. To Arthur Koestler
18 May 1944   Typewritten

Tribune

Dear Arthur,
The author of this[1] asked me to send it on to you if we couldn't print it (as we can't of course).

Yours
[Signed] Geo. Orwell
George Orwell.

1. Unidentified.

Vol. XVI, p. 279

2502A. To Arthur Koestler
         10 July 1944   Typewritten

Tribune

Dear Arthur,
Would you like to do us a short note on this?

                                                        Yours,
                                                        George

In a Strange Land – Jonathan Cape[1]

1. Eric Gill, *In a Strange Land: Essays*; it was not reviewed by Koestler.

Vol. XVI, p. 431

2563A. To Arthur Koestler
         13 October 1944   Typewritten

Tribune

Dear Arthur,
We should like it very much if you would become one of our regular reviewers. It would in all probability mean doing an article once every two or three months, but not in regular rotation. I will explain what it is that we want to do.

We feel that the practice of giving shortish reviews to a large number of books each week is unsatisfactory, and we intend to have each week a leading review of anything up to 1500 words, dealing with some current book which for one reason or another deserves serious criticism. With this much space to dispose of one can not only give a full criticism of the book in hand but can make one's article a worth-while piece of writing in itself. The reason why we cannot keep to a regular rotation is that we must send each book to the reviewer who seems most suitable. We should be able to give about a fortnight's notice. The fee for these articles will be 3 guineas.

A stamped addressed label is enclosed. I should be obliged if you would let me know as early as possible whether you are interested in this.

                                                        Yours truly,
                                                        [Signed] Geo. Orwell
                                                        George Orwell

Vol. XVII, p. 313

2765A. To Arthur Koestler

      17 October 1945   Typewritten

27 B Canonbury Square
Islington
London N 1

Dear Arthur,

I've no idea who the writer of the enclosed is. I should say a man (the name Evelyn is bi-sexual I think) and, as he or she seems to be domiciled in India, very likely a Eurasian.[1]

Do look me up if you're in town. It's ages since I saw you. I am nearly always at the above, as I don't go to an office now. I can't really remember when it was I last saw you. You knew I lost my wife early this year, didn't you? My little boy is 17 months old and very well, and walking quite strongly. I have just started writing for Tribune again, but I am not doing any editing. You must write for Polemic, the first number of which you saw, I dare say. I am doing an article on "The Yogi and the Commissar," at least on one aspect of it, for Common Wealth,[2] also going to lecture on it to some youth league or something. There's also a longish essay on you in the book of reprints I am publishing about the beginning of next year.[3] This was written for "Focus" but hasn't appeared there yet. The essay was written before "The Yogi and the Commissar" appeared.

Don't fail to ring up if you are here. I'd love to come to Wales some time but I can very rarely get out of London.

Yours
George

1. Koestler wrote to Orwell on 11 October asking him if he knew the writer of a letter he enclosed; he has not been identified. Koestler also invited Orwell to come to them for a break if he could spare the time. Orwell and Richard spent Christmas 1945 with the Koestlers in North Wales.
2. 'Catastrophic Gradualism,' 2778.
3. 'Arthur Koestler,' 2548. *Critical Essays* was published on 14 February 1946; see 2898.

Vol. XVIII, p. 338

3025A. Arthur Koestler to Orwell
2 July 1946   Typewritten; carbon copy

[No address]

My dear George,
When I was last in London I asked Foyles about the value of the 13th edition of the Encyclopaedia and was told that if I bought the 14th edition they would rebuy it for £15, otherwise the value depends on the free market. I am sending you enclosed cheque for £10 which would roughly correspond to its free market value, as a temporary payment; it being understood that you can of course always have it back for the same amount and that should I exchange it for the 14th edition I would ask your authorisation first and refund you the difference.
I hope that all is well with you.

Yours ever,
[Unsigned]

Vol. XIX, p. 216

3288A. From Arthur Koestler to Orwell
21 October 1947   Typewritten; carbon copy

Dear George,
We are back in Wales; I had considerable trouble in Paris about the scandalous translations of some of my books and as it is not the first time this has happened I had a bright idea and made the following arrangement with Sartre, Camus and Simone de Beauvoir.
These three French writers, plus three Italian writers (Silone, Carlo Levi and Moravia) plus three English writers – you, Cyril and I if you agree – plus one German-Swiss writer (Hermann Hesse), altogether ten authors, pledge themselves mutually to supervise the translations of each-other's books in their respective languages. "Supervision" doesn't mean reading proofs or the like, but discussing with the publishers which translator would be the most suitable for that particular book, giving the author an idea of the translator's particular qualifications, controlling samples and generally impressing upon the bloody publishers that translation is a serious business not to be entrusted to hacks, and that these ten authors are carefully watching over each other's interests.
As you know such experiments never work if one tries them on the muddled PEN level, and the arrangement in a smaller circle of ten fairly

well known authors has various advantages, i.la.[1] of setting an example, which I don't need to explain to you.

If you agree, please let me know; Sartre took it upon himself to work out a sort of statute with his lawyer so that none of us would have any bother with technicalities.

Another matter. You mentioned in your last letter that you want to spend the winter in the Jura to work on your book.[2] We shall spend January and February either in Palestine or in France, and it occurred to me that you might like for that period to have our house, which is slightly less in the wilderness and more comfortable than the Jura during the winter. We now have a telephone, electricity, constant hot water and sufficient fuel. The part of the house which was still uncompleted when you were here is now completed so that there are four sitting rooms, four bedrooms and two bathrooms. You could pay whatever rent you like, as there seems little chance of letting the house for a high rent during the winter anyway.

Love from both of us,
[Unsigned]

1. Presumably intended for *inter alia* – among other things.
2. See Orwell's letter of 20 September 1947 (*3275*). By 'the Jura' Koestler does not of course mean 'the Jura' of France, but Jura in the Hebrides. The Koestlers lived in a farmhouse near Blaenau Ffestiniog, North Wales.

Vol. XX, p. 80

3590A. Orwell and the Information Research Department

Celia Kirwan was the twin sister of Mamaine, the wife of Arthur Koestler. She had first met Orwell when she travelled with him and Richard to North Wales to spend Christmas 1945 with the Koestlers. He proposed marriage to her and although (as she put it) she 'gently refused him' they 'were always very close friends' (*Daily Telegraph*, 13 July 1996). She had for a time worked as an editorial assistant on *Polemic*, but when that collapsed she moved to Paris to work on *Occident*, a tri-lingual magazine. On 14 October 1947 she had written to Orwell asking whether he could write something for *Occident* (see *3298*). She wrote to Orwell in February 1949 to tell him she had returned to England (see *3549* and *3555*). Though now employed by the Information Research Department, she was, so far as her relationship with Orwell was concerned, far more a close friend than a government official.

Much of the information in *3590A* and *3590B* is based on documents in Foreign Office files released by the Public Record Office on 10 July 1996 under the Government's 'open government policy'. The permission of the Controller of Her Majesty's Stationery Office to reproduce Crown copyright material is gratefully acknowledged.

The Information Research Department was set up by the Foreign Office in 1948. 'Its creation was prompted by the desire of Ministers of Mr Attlee's Labour Government to devise means to combat Communist propaganda, then engaged in a global and damaging campaign to undermine Western power and influence. British concern for an effective counter-offensive against Communism was sharpened by the need to rebut a relentless Soviet-inspired campaign to undermine British institutions, a campaign which included direct personal attacks on the Prime Minister and members of the Cabinet and divisive criticism of government policies.'[1] Its first head was F. R. H. Murray (later, Sir Ralph Murray). It ran for nearly thirty years being closed down in 1977. Among the activities in which it engaged, it commissioned special articles and circulated books and journals to appropriate posts abroad. Thus, *Tribune*, because of its anti-Stalin stance, was widely distributed. A confidential letter of 4 March 1949 was sent to seventy-six missions and consulates throughout the world with copies of *Tribune* on the grounds that it combined 'the resolute exposure of Communism and its methods with the consistent championship of those objectives which Left-wing sympathizers normally support'. It was suggested that many of the articles could effectively be turned to IRD's purposes.[2] Among those who were commissioned to write articles were Harold Laski (see *3526*, *n. 8*), who compared British and Soviet trade unionism, and R. H. S. Crossman,[3] who re-assessed the Russo–German Pact of August 1939. Ruth Fischer (see *2591*, *n. 4* and *3603*) was commissioned to write a pamphlet on how the Soviets controlled Communist parties outside its borders and another article on the present aim of Soviet Russia in Germany.[4] Nine books were distributed in 1949. These included Julian Huxley's *Soviet Genetics and World Science* (which exposed the fallacy of Lysenko's genetic theories; see Orwell's suggestion reported in his interview with Celia Kirwan below, and *3725, n. 13*). However, the IRD found it difficult to find books 'projecting social democracy as a successful alternative to Communism, to compete with the subsidised publications of the Soviet Foreign Languages Publishing House.' It is the more surprising, therefore, that Orwell's request for the 2,000DMs required by *Possev* (see *3496, n. 1*) to publish a Russian-language version of *Animal Farm* came to nothing, even though Orwell wrote out for the IRD an impressive list of translations published and projected.[5] In the end, Orwell himself paid for the translation (see *3695*). There was more enthusiasm for an Arabic-language edition to be distributed in Egypt. Ernest Main of the Information Department of the British Embassy in Cairo reported to the Features Management Unit of the Central Office of Information in London on 4 April 1949 that the Embassy's Egyptian staff was 'very enthusiastic over the idea.' He himself told Ralph Murray on the same day that the idea was 'particularly good for Arabic in view of the fact that both pigs and dogs are unclean animals to Moslems.'[6]

On 29 March 1949, Celia Kirwan went to see Orwell at Cranham at the request of the IRD and Orwell's letter is the outcome of that meeting. She wrote this report on the following day.[7]

Yesterday I went to visit George Orwell, who is in a sanatorium in Gloucestershire. I discussed some aspects of our work with him in great confidence, and he was delighted to learn of them, and expressed his wholehearted and enthusiastic approval of our aims. He said that he could not agree to write an article himself at present, or even to re-write one, because he is too ill to undertake any literary work at all; also because he does not like to write 'on commission', as he feels he does not do his best work that way. However I left some material with him, and shall send him photostats of some of his articles on the theme of Soviet repression of the arts, in the hope that he may become inspired when he is better to take them up again.

He suggested various names of writers who might be enlisted to write for us, and promised to think of more in due course and to communicate them to us. The ones he thought of while I was there were:–

D'Arcy Gillie, the Manchester Guardian Paris correspondent, who he says is a serious opponent of Communism, and an expert on Poland as well as on French politics;

C. D. Darlington, the scientist.[8] Mr Orwell considers that the Lysenko case should be fully documented, and suggested that Darlington might undertake this;[9]

Franz Borkenau, the German professor, who wrote a History of the Comintern, and has also written some articles recently in the *Observer*.

Mr Orwell said that undoubtedly Gollancz would be the man to publish such a series of books as we had in mind. He would have been very willing to act as a go-between if he had been well enough; as it was, he would try to think of someone else who would do so, and he suggested that a glance at a list of Gollancz writers would probably recall to our minds someone who would be able to help us. He says, however, that Gollancz has a one-track mind, and at present it is running along the track of Arab refugees, so it might be a good plan to allow him to get these out of his system before trying to interest him in our plan. He said that Gollancz books always sell well, and that they are well displayed and given the widest publicity.

As Mr Orwell was for two° years in the Indian Police stationed in Burma, and as he ran a B.B.C. service to the Indians during the war, I asked him what in his view would be the best way of furthering our aims in India and Burma. He said that whatever was the best way, the *worst* was undoubtedly broadcasting, since hardly any of the natives had radio sets, and those who did (who were mostly Eurasians) tended only to listen in to local stations. He thought that one plane-load of leaflets probably did more good than six months broadcasting.

Indeed he did not think that there was a great deal of scope for propaganda in India and Pakistan, where Communism meant something quite different from what it did in Europe – it meant, on [t]he whole, opposition to the ruling class, and he thought that more good would be done by maintaining the closest possible links with these countries, through trade and through the interchange of students. He thought this latter aspect of Anglo-Indian relations very important, and was of the opinion that we ought to offer far more scholarships to Indian and Pakistan° students.

In Burma, he thought that propaganda should avoid 'atrocity' stories, since the Burmese were "rather apt to admire that kind of thing", or, if they did not actually admire it, to think "If that's what the Communists are like, better not oppose them."

Incidentally, he said that the Commander Young,[10] whose wife committed suicide the other day, is a Communist, and is the Naval equivalent, on a more modest scale, of the Archbishop of Canterbury[11] – that is, he is called in to confirm the Soviet point of view about matters relating to the Navy.

Also, his wife was a Czech; and Mr Orwell wonders whether there is any connection between these two facts and Mrs Young's suicide.

1. From opening paragraph of *History Notes, 9: IRD: Origins and Establishment of the Foreign Office Information Research Department 1946–48* (August 1995), p. 1.
2. FO 1110/221: PR 442.
3. R. H. S. Crossman (1907–74), Labour MP from 1949; Minister of Housing and Local Government. 1964–66; Secretary of State for Social Services and Head of Department of Health, 1968–70. His political diaries in four volumes were published in 1975–81.
4. FO 1110/264: 1634 G, June 1949.
5. FO 1110/221: PR 3361/33/913. Orwell's request for financial support was sent by Celia Kirwan on 11 November 1949 to Charles Thayer, Director of 'Voice of America' Broadcasts at Department of State, Washington, DC., USA. She does not mention a specific sum.
6. Information from FO 110/221 and IRD 'Notes on Developments in 1949', especially pp. 9–11.
7. Celia Kirwan's report is dated 30 March 1949; the reference for this and associated documents is FO 1110/189: PR 1135/11/G. It was circulated to the head of the IRD, Ralph Murray, and to other members of staff, Adam Watson, Assistant in the IRD, and Lt Col Leslie Sheridan, who made a few annotations; see, for example, *9, 10* and *3590B, n. 11.*
8. For C. D. Darlington, a specialist in plant breeding and genetics, see *1170, n. 1*: he had broadcast to India under Orwell's aegis.
9. For Lysenko and his theories, see *3725, n. 13.* It looks as if the IRD took up Orwell's suggestion but chose instead to circulate copies of Julian Huxley's *Soviet Genetics and World Science; Lysenko and the Meaning of Heredity* (1949). For two of Orwell's books chosen for the 'Books for Germany' scheme in 1947, and sent to the Foreign Office, see *3282.*
10. Lt. Col. Leslie Sheridan annotated this reference to Mrs Young's alleged suicide, 'The inquest is adjourned.' Orwell included Cdr. Edgar P. Young in his list of crypto-communists but his entry was withheld from *3732.* Now that his name has been published by the PRO, Orwell's notes can be printed here. Under 'Jobs' he wrote, 'Naval expert. Pamphlets'; under 'Remarks', 'F. T.? Active in People's Convention. Quite possibly an underground member I should think. Wife (Czech) committed suicide (in slightly doubtful circumstances) 1949.' Mrs Ida Young was found hanged in their flat on 23 March 1949. For a report on the inquest, see *The Times* 29 March 1949, 2A and 6 April 1949, 2D. There had been a Communist coup in Czechoslovakia on 27 February 1948. Two weeks later the charismatic Foreign Secretary, who opposed Communism, fell to his death in suspicious circumstances; see *3359, n. 5.* Cdr. Young presided over the Anglo–Bulgarian Committee. On 24 March, Lord Vansittart (see *758, n. 1*) suggested in the House of Lords that this Committee be suppressed in the light of the Bulgarian Government's demand that a member of the British Legation in Sofia be withdrawn. He asked whether the British Government was aware that, when it was protesting at the sentence of death passed on Nikola Petkov, leader of the Bulgarian opposition Agrarian Party, Cdr. Young said Petkov ought to be hanged 'to teach Mr Bevin [the British Foreign Minister] a lesson.' (Petkov was executed on 23 September 1947.) Vansittart was told that the Government could not take 'suppressive measures' against individuals because they expressed opinions which democrats disliked and repudiated. (*The Times*, 24 March 1949, 6.)
11. Sheridan annotated this (correctly), 'Dean, surely?' The Dean is included in *3732.*

Vol. XX, p. 80

3590B. To Celia Kirwan

6 April 1949   Handwritten

Orwell's letter to Celia Kirwan, which follows, should be read in the context of what the IRD was seeking: those who might reliably represent British interests in writing on its behalf to counteract Soviet propaganda designed to undermine democratic institutions (see *3590A*). This is the full text of the letter; the letter was first published in *The Guardian*, 11 July 1996, with the errors and omissions indicated in the footnotes.

Cranham

Dear Celia,
I haven't written earlier because I have really been rather poorly, & I can't use the typewriter even now, so I hope you will be able to cope with my handwriting.

I couldn't think of any more names to add to your possible list of writers except FRANZ BORKENAU (the Observer would know his address) whose name I think I gave you, & GLEB STRUVE (he's at Pasadena in California at present), the Russian translator and critic.[1] Of course there are hordes of Americans, whose names can be found in the (New York) New Leader,[2] the Jewish monthly paper "Commentary," & the Partisan Review. I could also, if it is of any value, give you a list of journalists & writers who in my opinion are crypto-Communists, fellow-travellers or inclined that way & should not be trusted as propagandists. But for that I shall have to send for a notebook which I have at home, & if I do give you such a list it is strictly confidential, as I imagine it is libellous to describe somebody as a fellow-traveller.[3]

Just one idea occurred to me for propaganda not abroad but in this country. A friend of mine in Stockholm[4] tells me that as the Swedes don't make many[5] films of their own one sees a lot of German & Russian films, & some of the Russian films, which of course would not normally reach this country, are unbelievably scurrilous anti-British propaganda. He referred especi[ally] to a historical film about the Crimean war. As the Swedes can get hold of these films I suppose we can: might it not be a good idea to have showings of some of them in this country, particularly for the benefit of the intelligentsia?[6]

I read the enclosed article[7] with interest, but it seems to me anti-religious rather than anti-semitic. For what my opinion is worth, I don't think anti-anti-semitism is a strong card to play in anti-Russian propaganda. The USSR must in practice be somewhat anti-semitic, as it is opposed both to Zionism within its own borders & on the other hand to the liberalism and internationalism of the non-Zionist Jews, but a polyglot state of that kind can never be officially anti-semitic, in the Nazi manner, just as the British Empire cannot. If you try to tie up Communism and anti-semitism, it is always possible in reply to point to people like Kaganovich[8] or Anna° Pauker,[9] also to the large number of Jews in the Communist parties everywhere. I also think it is bad policy to try to curry favour with your enemies. The Zionist Jews everywhere hate us & regard Britain as the enemy, more even than Germany. Of course this is based on misunderstanding, but as long as it is so I do not think we do ourselves any good by denouncing anti-semitism in other nations.

I am sorry I can't write a better letter, but I really have felt so lousy the last few days. Perhaps a bit later I'll get some ideas.[10]

With love
George

[Postscript at head of first side of letter] I did suggest DARCY GILLY,° (Manchester Guardian) didn't I? There is also a man called CHOLLERTON (expert on the Moscow trials) who could be contacted through the Observer.[11]

In a memorandum dated 21 April responding to Celia Kirwan's report, Adam Watson, Assistant in the IRD, said 'The point about anti-semitism is partly correct, partly mixed up with Mr Orwell's anti Zionist° views. We should not exaggerate anti-semitism in Russia, but we can expose what there is. It is irrelevant that some Jews are anti-British – we are not anti-semitic and the Russians are inclined to be.' He assumed Mrs Kirwan had thanked Orwell. Two days later, Watson added: 'Mrs Kirwan should certainly ask Mr Orwell for the list of crypto-communists.' It would be treated in confidence and returned in a day or two. Watson hoped the list gave reasons 'in each case.' On 30 April, Mrs Kirwan wrote to Orwell; she said that the suggestion that Chollerton be contacted had been particularly welcomed and she asked for his list of 'fellow-travelling and crypto journalists' (although Orwell used the term 'crypto-communists').

On 2 May 1949 (in a letter held by the Orwell Archive, UCL; see *3615*), Orwell wrote to say that he would be pleased to see Celia again (on 8 May) and he enclosed a list of about thirty-five names. A card has been placed in the PRO file holding Orwell's correspondence with Celia Kirwan indicating that a document has been withheld by the Foreign Office;[12] this document is presumably this list of names (but see *3615* and *3732*). He wrote that 'it isn't a bad idea to have the people who are probably unreliable listed' and he drew particular attention to Peter Smollett who, though head of the Russian Department at the British Ministry of Information (and awarded the OBE for his services) proved to be a Soviet agent (see *3615, n. 3* and *3732*). Orwell probably had in mind the influence exerted in June 1944 by 'an important official in the Ministry of Information' to have Cape refuse to publish *Animal Farm* because it might offend the Soviets (see *2494, n. 1*). He might well have suspected that 'important official' was Smollett. Despite the seriousness of the project, it had, as Sir Richard Rees pointed out, an aspect of a game (see *3600, n. 13*).

When Orwell's letter was released by the Public Record Office it created a stir in some newspapers, especially *The Guardian*, *The Times*, and the *Evening Standard* (11 July 1996), and *The Independent on Sunday* (14 July 1996). *The Guardian* printed Orwell's letter on the 11 July with one or two errors and two cuts marked by ellipses (see notes *3, 5, 6* and *9*). Although an account of Orwell's notebook containing names of crypto-communists and fellow-travellers had been published several years earlier, with a dozen photographs of those mentioned (*Sunday Telegraph*, 20 October 1991), it seemed to come as a surprise to the newspapers that featured the story and to some of their readers. The *Telegraph* having, through its sister paper, already featured the story ignored this 'news' and instead published an excellent interview of Celia Kirwan (now Mrs Celia Goodman) by Caroline Davies (13 July 1996). This, and a percipient account by Bernard Crick, a supporter of the Labour Party as well as Orwell's biographer (*Independent on Sunday*, 14 July 1996), put the letter into an intelligent context. Some Labour Party politicians took this opportunity to express surprise at Orwell's dealing with the secret services (Michael Foot, *The Guardian*, 11.7.96), to regret that Orwell had 'given in' (Tony Benn, MP, *Independent on Sunday*, 14.7.96), and even to declare that 'sickeningly, it turns out that Orwell himself was hounding those whose thoughts did not chime in with his own' (Gerald Kaufman, MP, *Evening Standard*, 11.7.96). A historian, Christopher Hill (whose work Orwell had reviewed in 1940, see *679*, and, in a single sentence in September 1944, see *2542*) went further: 'I always knew he was two-faced. There was something fishy about Orwell . . . it confirms my worst suspicions about the man' (*Independent on Sunday*, 14.7.96). For a correspondent to the *Evening Standard* it was 'a revelation about an English hero [he] could hardly believe' and he thought there were 'some things about great people of the past that perhaps it's better not to know, even if they're true' (S. Jarrett, 15.7.96). Although it should not be necessary for politicians and historians, it might be desirable for those unfamiliar with the history of the period, and especially of Soviet attempts to influence other countries, to give a brief reminder of Orwell's anxieties and of the context in which he was writing to Celia Kirwan and supplying names.

It is not relevant that Orwell was very ill; his brain was fully active and he was thoroughly resolute: he knew what he was doing. He wrote at a time when the Communist threat to the West was plainly apparent. Berlin had been blockaded by the Soviets for over nine months and a massive air-lift had been undertaken by the West to maintain life in the West's sector of Berlin. The blockade was only lifted on 12 May 1949, ten days after Orwell sent Celia Kirwan his list of about thirty-five names (*3615*). From Orwell's time in Spain he had witnessed the betrayal of good men and women by Soviet-inspired Communists who were ostensibly their allies. Much nearer to the time he wrote was the disgraceful behaviour of the left-wing press in playing down the treatment of Poles (whom Orwell and Arthur Koestler endeavoured to help and protect through the Freedom Defence Committee) for fighting for their country against the Germans by the Soviet-backed Lublin government ('As I Please,' 56, 26.1.45, XVII, 30); the trial of sixteen Poles in Moscow (see unpublished letter to *Tribune*, c. 26 June 1945, *2685*); and the future of those Poles who did not wish to return to their homeland ('Uncertain Fate of Displaced Persons,' 19 June 1945, *2675*, specifically, XVII, 174–75). Orwell was also distressed at the behaviour of successive British governments in covering up Soviet guilt for the massacre of some 15,000 Poles at Katyn, Starobielsk, and other camps, and the drowning of 7,000 more in the Kola peninsula. Orwell and Koestler tried desperately hard to get the latter exposed through the publication of Joseph Czapski's *Souvenirs de Starobielsk* in 1946 but, although it was published in Polish, Italian, and French, all their efforts were baulked in England (see *2919*, *2920* and *2956*).[13] Orwell saw treachery in the press and in government as due in part at least to Soviet influence. Even *Horizon* censored Orwell's work for fear of offending the

Soviets (see *2538, headnote* and notes *51* and *54*, and *2550*). For his general discussion of such issues, see 'The Freedom of the Press,' intended initially as a Preface to *Animal Farm (2721)*.

Orwell deeply distrusted the intelligentsia (so *The Guardian*'s omission of the reference to the intelligentsia – see *n. 6* below – is delightfully ironic) and especially left-wing intellectuals who transferred their loyalty to a foreign power, such as the USSR, and indulged in hatred of their own country; he did not share 'the average English intellectual's hatred of his own country' and he was not dismayed, as they were, by a British victory (London Letter, October 1944, xvi, 415 and 414 respectively). Such people, he wrote, saw the USSR as their Fatherland and felt it their duty to justify Russian policy and advance Russian interests at all costs ('Notes on Nationalism', xvii, 144). On the other hand he did trust the ordinary people of England. The last line of *The English People* says that if England is to survive as a great nation, 'it is the common people who must make it so' (xvi, 228), a sentiment echoed in *Nineteen Eighty-Four*: 'If there was hope, it *must* lie in the proles' (ix, 72). To Orwell, 'the important thing is to discover *which* individuals are honest and which are not, and the usual blanket accusation merely makes this more difficult' ('As I Please', 51, 8 December 1944; xvi, 495). In the light of the Soviet threat to democracy, and especially its malign influence on the Labour Party and socialism in Britain, and the insidious influence of the Soviets in high places, Orwell saw his duty to his country simply and straightforwardly. He knew well, and had experience of, the 'game' Soviet Russia was playing. And, of course, we now know, what Orwell feared in general terms, that some 1,500 writers perished at the hands of the NKVD and that thousands of manuscripts were destroyed (see headnote to 'The Prevention of Literature', *2792*).

A parallel aspect to this matter should be borne in mind. Orwell was himself the subject of Soviet surveillance. Miklos Kun, grandson of Bela Kun (1886–c.1939; see *556, 10.7.39* and *562, 7.8.39*), Communist leader of Hungary and a victim of Stalin's purges, told the editor in March 1996 that the GPU initiated a campaign to discredit Orwell and that the NKVD had a dossier on Orwell. Unfortunately, before copies of its contents could be photographed, access to such files was stopped.[14] (If this dossier becomes available, Orwell's Spanish diary, removed by the Communists from his hotel in Barcelona, might be found therein.)

Finally, if Orwell needs defending, this was done most effectively by Denzil Jacobs, who responded to Gerald Kaufman's article in the *Evening Standard*, referred to above. Writing in that newspaper he said:

I met George Orwell in 1940 when I joined the Home Guard. He was the sergeant in charge of seven men, of which I was one.

We became friends and I saw him regularly. We met for the last time a week before he died in University College Hospital. I deplore Gerald Kaufman's article. He vilifies a man of high principle whose views were very clear-cut and who, in my opinion, was a great patriot. In 1940 he was well aware that Stalin and Stalinism were no longer tolerable to a man of his ideals.

He was of the Left, but detested dictatorship, whether fascist or communist. I had many conversations with him during the nights we were on duty and I can quite see that he regarded it as his patriotic duty to give names of those supporting the Soviet Union to the Secret Service.

Gerald Kaufman did not know him and I trust will have second thoughts in the future.[15]

Anglo-Soviet relations in 1944–49 were different from those now seemingly ruling. Soviet subversive influence was widespread, innocents as well as the corruptible could be duped, and Stalin's attempts to undermine democracy went far beyond what the IRD was set up to try to counteract. Two significant sentences from the IRD's 'Notes on Developments in 1949' pertinently point to how widespread was the threat: 'Soviet activities throughout South East Asia were of concern. Both [Pandit] Nehru [Prime Minister of India] and the Prime Minister of Pakistan, Liaquat Ali Khan, had privately suggested at a Prime Ministerial meeting in the Autumn of 1948 that the theme of Soviet imperialism in the region was one on which we [the IRD] should concentrate.'[16] Orwell was only too well aware of the threat that some people in the intelligentsia posed for the country and the common people he loved so deeply.

1. Orwell greatly admired the work of Franz Borkenau. When reviewing his *The Communist International* on 22 September 1938 he remarked that Borkenau's *The Spanish Cockpit* remained 'the best book on the subject' (*485*). Gleb Struve was Professor of Slavic Languages and Literature at University of California, Berkeley (see *2421, n. 1*). On 19 November 1944 he had sent Orwell details of Soviet duplicity in recording its history – the omission of the Russo-German Pact of August 1939 from the Soviet *Reference Calendar for 1944* (see *2583*). He was one of the translators of the Russian-language version of *Animal Farm* published by *Possev*, referred to in these IRD files.
2. At the end of his list of Crypto-Communists and Fellow-Travellers in the notebook, Orwell pasted a cutting from *The New Leader* of what it called 'Communist-front organisations'; see end of *3732*.
3. *The Guardian* omitted 'as I imagine it is libellous to describe somebody as a fellow-traveller.'
4. Michael Meyer, then working as a Lecturer in English Literature at Uppsala University (45 miles north of Stockholm); see *2008, n. 1*. In a letter to Ian Angus, 30 July 1996, Michael Meyer recalled the Russian film he told Orwell about. He saw it in Uppsala, but does not now remember its title. However, he described its style: 'It was particularly crude propaganda, presenting Lord Raglan as a brandy-swilling effete and British soldiers as treacherous fellows who hid behind trees and stabbed honest Russian infantrymen in the back as they walked past.' Orwell, he concludes 'was obviously right to identify fellow-travellers at that stage of the cold war.'
5. *The Guardian* omitted 'many' (probably accidentally).
6. *The Guardian* omitted 'particularly for the benefit of the intelligentsia?'
7. Not identified.
8. Lazar Moiseyevich Kaganovich (1893–?), a Jew and originally a shoemaker but who went on to hold many important offices of state. He was a firm supporter of Stalin. He supervised the construction of the Dniepr hydroelectric power station and in 1938 was appointed Deputy Premier of the Soviet Union. During the war he had the important task of managing the nation's transport system. He was disenchanted by the changes brought about after the death of Stalin and lost his important offices; it was reported that he had been expelled from the Communist Party. His date of death is not known. Kaganovich was by no means the only Jew or person with Jewish connections on the Presidium of the Soviet Union (a point made by Robert Payne, *The Rise and Fall of Stalin*, 717–18).
9. Ana Pauker was born Ana Rabinsohn, 1894, daughter of a Jewish butcher. She joined the Communist Party in 1921 and was imprisoned and exiled from Romania. She spent some years in the USA with her husband, an engineer and an employee of the Soviet Trading Agency. She served as a Colonel in the Red Army during the war and was a signatory to the dissolution of the Comintern in 1943. The Soviet Army occupied Romania in 1944 and she became a leader of the Romanian Communist Party. From 1947–52 she served as Foreign Minister and was one of those instrumental in the formation of the Cominform, 1947. She

and Gheorghe Gheorghiu-Dej (First Secretary of the Communist Party, 1945–54) were the effective rulers of Romania until she disappeared towards the end of Stalin's life when anti-Semitism grew in the Soviet Union and its satellites and as Gheorghiu-Dej became more powerful. *The Guardian* gives her surname as 'Pauleer', but the 'k' is in Orwell's usual style (as in 'Stockholm' in the preceding paragraph). Orwell spells 'Ana' as 'Anna'.

10. That is, ideas for counter-propaganda.
11. Darsie Gillie, Paris correspondent *Manchester Guardian* (see Celia Kirwan's report). Adam Watson, Assistant in the IRD, annotating Celia Kirwan's report, said that Chollerton was 'an expert on Russia, & would be useful in various ways I think. I will try to contact him.'
12. FO 1110/189: PR 1135/11/G.
13. Although as early as 1951–52 a United States Congressional investigation had exposed the Soviets as guilty of these massacres (see Louis L. Snyder, *Historical Guide to World War II* (1982), 'Katyn Forest Massacre', 366), British Governments not only continued to blame the Germans but, when a memorial to those who were massacred was erected in Gunnersbury Cemetery, London, in 1976, the Labour government threatened British officers with court martial if they attended in uniform. It was another twelve years before British servicemen were permitted to attend in uniform (*Independent*, 19 September 1988).
14. Telephone conversation with Miklos Kun, March 1996.
15. *Evening Standard*, 16 July, 1996. Denzil Jacobs (born November 1921), with his uncle and guardian, Victor Jacobs, joined the Home Guard (then the Local Defence Volunteers) at Lord's Cricket Ground on 12 June 1940 (Crick, 396). In a conversation with the editor, 22 August 1996, Mr Jacobs described what he recalled of Orwell, the section he commanded, and visiting him in University College Hospital. Jacobs was in Orwell's section of the Home Guard for about eighteen months before he joined the RAF in 1941, in which he served as a navigator. He qualified as a chartered accountant and after the war joined his uncle's piano manufacturing business. Some of the section were wealthy men, including Len Chandler and his brother-in-law, Frank Haddrell (wholesale grocers) and Dennis Wells and his son, who owned a large garage. Other names he remembered were Luffman, Jones (a van driver for the Oxford Street department store, Selfridge's), and Davidson. The wealthy members would play poker and Orwell joined in on one occasion but having lost ten shillings (50p in today's coinage but worth approximately £20) found the stakes too high. Orwell was, he said, a fine section leader and particularly good on street fighting (see *733*). Though 'short on small talk,' to Orwell 'commitment was everything.' His uncle visited Orwell in University College Hospital a number of times and suggested to Denzil Jacobs that he also go to see Orwell. It proved to be a few days before Orwell died. Orwell was by then sure he was dying; he was convinced there would soon be an atomic war; and that because he wanted his son to survive he had found what he hoped would be a remote, safe place on a Scottish island where it would be possible to grow enough food to survive. He did not mention Jura or Barnhill by name.
16. The Notes quote from FO 1110/232: PR 622/41/G. In her report of her conversation with Orwell, Celia Kirwan says he thought there was little scope for propaganda in India and Pakistan (see above). An annotation by one of the staff of the IRD, Lt Col Leslie Sheridan, remarks that the IRD should respond to any brand of Communism.

Vol. XX, p. 161

3681A. Arthur Koestler to Orwell

26 August 1949   Typewritten; carbon copy

[No address]

Dear George,

Calman-Levy, my French publishers, are very keen on having 1984 but don't seem to get anywhere with your agents. So they asked me whether I could help.

I have now some experience with French publishers and my feeling is that if you have'nt° yet definitely committed yourself, Calman-Levy are probably the best choice. They are a couple of green grocers° only interested in profit, but extremely efficient and not subject to moods nor to intimidation. They have sold over 400,000 copies of Darkness at Noon – at a time when few publishers would have dared to touch it, and they are very keen indeed on you. Let me know, or tell your agents to let me know how matters stand. Just at present it is politically very important that 1984 should get a mass circulation in France. It is a glorious book.

If you want to make sure that it is well translated, get in touch with me.[1]

All the best,

Yours ever,
[Unsigned]

P.S. I have been kept au courant about you through David Astor, Celia, etc.

1. For Koestler's scheme for improving translations from English into French, see *3288A* in this appendix.

Vol. XX, p. 164

3684A. To Arthur Koestler

1 September 1949   Handwritten postcard

[No address]

[No salutation][1]

Thanks so much for your letter. I'm now moving to London & my address will be: Private Wing, University College Hospital, Gower St. WC.1.

Kalman-Levy° had already written to me. Following your letter I've again written to my agent.[2] I think he has been dickering with the NRF or somebody.

I have been ghastly ill on & off, but I suppose it can't last forever. I am told Mamaine's asthma is better, & I trust this is true.

Did you know I was going to get married again – though just when, lord knows.

Yours
George.

1. Koestler's name is taken from the address on the postcard.
2. See *3683*.

Vol. XX, p. 173

3695A. Arthur Koestler to Orwell

24 September 1949   Typewritten; carbon copy

[No address]

My dear George,
I thought that Mamaine had written to you and Mamaine thought that I had written to you, hence the delay. I was extremely happy to hear that you are going to marry Sonia. I have been saying for years that she is the nicest, most intelligent and decent girl that I met during my whole stay in England. She is precisely for this reason also very lonely in that crowd in which she moves and she will become a changed person when you take her out of it. I think I had a closer view of the Connolly set-up than you did; it has a steady stultifying effect which left its mark even on a tough guy like me. If a fairy had granted me three wishes for Sonia, the first would have been that she should be married to you, the second some dough for her, and the third a child – adopted or not makes little difference.

If you don't resent the advice of a chronically meddlesome friend, get through with it, the sooner the better, without waiting until your health is entirely restored. Delay is always a bore and as an amateur psychologist I have a feeling that having this settled will to a surprising extent speed up your recovery.

I hardly dare to hope of having you both down here in the near future, but whenever it is feasible it will be a great treat for me to see you both again and pop champagne corks into the Seine.

[No valediction or signature]

3696A. To Mona Harrofs McElfresh
2 October 1949   Handwritten

Room 65
Private Wing
University College Hospital
Gower St. London WC. 1

Dear Mrs Harrops,[1]
Many thanks for your letter & the review of "1984." My signature is below. I am afraid you must excuse bad hand writing, as I am in very poor health.
Yours sincerely
Geo. Orwell

1. Orwell addressed Ms McElfresh by her second name and mistook the spelling.

INDEX

Volume XX

This is an index of names of people, places, and institutions, and of titles of books, periodicals, broadcasts, and articles; it is not (with a very few exceptions) a topical index. This index lists titles of books and articles in the text, headnotes and afternotes; incidental references to people and places are unindexed. In general, references to England and Britain are not indexed nor are the names of authors and books significant to an author being reviewed but not necessarily to Orwell. Inhabitants of countries are indexed under their countries (e.g., 'Germans' under 'Germany'). Numbered footnotes are indexed more selectively; for example, books listed by an author who is the subject of a footnote are not themselves indexed unless significant to Orwell. This volume concludes with fourteen appendixes and some of these are not indexed or only partially indexed. Orwell's list of what he read in 1949 (*3727*) is fully indexed by author and by book (and the page reference to his list is followed by *Orwell's 1949 reading*). Orwell's pamphlet collection (*3733*), the list of books in his possession at his death (*3734*), and the names in his address book (*3731*) are not indexed; names, but not institutions, in his list of crypto-communists and fellow-travellers are indexed; the significance of half-brackets in that list should be particularly noted: they indicate that a person or item had been deleted from the list.

Orwell's book titles are printed in CAPITALS; his poems, essays, articles, broadcasts, etc., are printed in upper and lower case roman within single quotation marks. Book titles by authors other than Orwell are in italic; if Orwell reviewed the book (in this volume), this is noted by 'Rev:' followed by the pagination and a semi-colon; other references follow. Both books and authors are individually listed unless a reference is insignificant. If Orwell does not give an author's name, when known this is added in parentheses after the title. Preparatory Notes for the article on Evelyn Waugh have been abstracted from Orwell's Last Literary Notebook (*3515*) and placed immediately after the article. Articles and broadcasts by authors other than Orwell are placed within double quotation marks. Page references are in roman except for those to numbered footnotes, which are in italic. The order of roman and italic is related to the order of references on the page. Editorial notes are printed in roman upper and lower without quotation marks. If an editorial note follows a title it is abbreviated to 'ed. note:' and the pagination follows. First and last page numbers are given of articles and these are placed before general references and followed by a semi-colon; specific pages are given for reviews of books reviewed as part of a group. The initial page number is given for letters. Punctuation is placed outside quotation marks to help separate information. Salutations in letters to relatives and friends are not usually indexed. Items in two languages are indexed from the English version.

Letters by Orwell, and any written on his behalf, are given under the addressee's name and the first letter is preceded by 'L:', which stands for letters, memoranda, letter-cards, and postcards; telegrams are distinguished by 'T:' to draw attention to their urgency. Appendix 14 reproduces letters that came to light after the page-proofs for Volumes X to XX had been completed and paginated (25 July 1996). These letters are indexed here but to show they are out of chronological order, the years in which they were written is given in brackets after the relevant page numbers. Letters from someone to Orwell follow the name of the sender and are indicated by 'L. to O:'.

Index

References to letters are given before other references, which are marked off by a semi-colon. Letters by those other than Orwell are often summarised and this is shown by 'sy' after the page reference. References to Orwell are listed under 'Orwell, references to:'.

Items are listed alphabetically by the word or words up to the first comma or bracket, except that Mc and M' are regarded as Mac and precede words starting with 'M'. St and Sainte are regarded as Saint.

Three cautions. First, some names are known only by a surname and it cannot be certain that surnames with the same initials, refer to the same person. If there is doubt, both names are indexed. Secondly, the use of quotation marks in the index differs from that in the text in order to make Orwell's work listed here readily apparent. Thirdly, a few titles and names have been corrected silently and dates of those who have died in 1997 (after the page-proofs of the text were completed) are noted in the index.   P.D.; S.D.

Adam, Mrs E. K. (Aunt Nellie Limouzin), 124, 150, 218, 234
Adamic, Louis, 242
Address Book, Orwell's, ed. note: 238; 238–40 (*names not indexed*)
Adeane, Louis, 128
Adelphi, The, 209
Adelphi Summer School (1936), 260
Adventure of Publishing, The, 221 (*Orwell's 1949 reading*)
Affairs of the Heart, 31, 35, 223 (*Orwell's 1949 reading*)
After Puritanism, 109, 110
Agee, James, and Walker Evans, *Let Us Now Praise Famous Men*, 28, 28
A. J. A. Symons: His Life and Speculations, 172, 222 (*Orwell's 1949 reading*)
Albatross Books, 225
Aldanov, M., *The Ninth Thermidor*, 219 (*Orwell's 1949 reading*), 233
Alexander II, assassination of Czar, 212, 217
Alington, Dr Cyril, *Archdeacons Afloat*, 220 (*Orwell's 1949 reading*)
Allan Wingate (publisher), 21, 26
"America, Good and Bad", 208
American Military Government, 151
Americans, The, 220 (*Orwell's 1949 reading*)
American Tragedy, An, 221 (*Orwell's 1949 reading*)
Anarchists (in Spanish Civil War), 310–11
Anderson, Evelyn, 176, 177, 177
Anderson, John, 242
Anglo–Bulgarian Committee, 321
Angus, Ian, L. from Richard Rees, 90; On Sonia Orwell, 170–1, 307–9; 241, 260, 261, 307–9, 326
Anikst, Aleksandr, 18
ANIMAL FARM: Orwell's collection of translations, 155, 157 (languages not indexed), 158, 158, 162;
Individual references (*for details, see Vol. XIX index*):
French: 99
German: serialisation in *Der Monat*, 54, 54, 63, 158
Italian broadcast: 71
Russian: 146, 148, 149, 150, 151, 152, 153, 154, 172, 173
Swiss German: 158, 158
Telugu (India): 162;
74, 103, 127, 128, 150, 167, 172, 173, 179, 217, 223, 224, 225, 226, 319, 323
Anisimov, Ivan, 18
Annie Get Your Gun, 216
'Antisemitism in Great Britain', 228; for antisemitism, see Jews
"Anything you can do, I can do better" (*Annie Get Your Gun*), 211, 216
Ape and Essence, 53, 63, 219 (*Orwell's 1949 reading*)
"Apple Tree, The", 314
Apponyi, Alexandrine, 185, 186
Arabs, 320
Aragon, 310
Archdeacons Afloat, 220 (*Orwell's 1949 reading*)
Ardlussa, 68, 91, 147
Ardrishaig, 163
Argentina, 54, 179
'Armut und Hoffnung Grossbritanniens' ('The Labour Government After Three Years'), 64
Arquer, Jordi, 140, 140
Arrow of Gold, The, 232
'Articles etc. NOT to be Reprinted', 229
'Art of Donald McGill, The', 149
'As I Please', 228
Assets, Orwell's, 217–8
Astor, David, T: 15; L: 15, 24, 54, 68, 79,

332

Index

Index

Index

Index

Index

Marx, the Orwell's poodle, 56
Masaryk, Jan, 255
Matthews, Tanya, *Russian Child and Russian Wife*, 220 (*Orwell's 1949 reading*), 233
Matthiesen, F. O., 251
Maugham, Somerset W., *The Razor's Edge*, 221 (*Orwell's 1949 reading*); *Then and Now*, 221 (*Orwell's 1949 reading*)
May, Dr Alan Nunn, 251
May, Phil, 12
Mayhew, Henry, *London Life*, 232
Meaning of Treason, The, 222 (*Orwell's 1949 reading*)
Meccano (construction kit), 25
Memoirs of the Foreign Legion, 21
Menen, A., *The Stumbling-Stone*, 222 (*Orwell's 1949 reading*)
M. E. News: see *Manchester Evening News*
Meyer, Michael, L: 61; *The End of the Corridor*, 62; *62, 326*
Mikardo, Ian, 89, *90*, 105, 251
Miller, Henry, 96
Miller, Olga (= Olga Katzin, "Sagittarius"), *121*
"Miller's Tale, The" (Geoffrey Chaucer), 77
Ministry of Information, 323
Ministry of War Transport, *171*
Mirror: Monthly International Review, 10–12
Miss Lonelyhearts, 221 (*Orwell's 1949 reading*)
Mitford, Nancy, *Love in a Cold Climate*, 222 (*Orwell's 1949 reading*)
Modern Poetry and the Tradition, 221 (*Orwell's 1949 reading*)
Mohrenwitz (literary agent, Argentina), 57
Moir, Eleanor (Mrs Richard Blair), 307
Monat, Der, 54, 63, *64*, 102, *102*, 148, *149*, 150, 153, 173, *173*
Mondadori (Milan, Publisher), 40, *40*, 64, 65, *96*
Montgomery, Field Marshal Bernard, *Normandy to the Baltic*, 222 (*Orwell's 1949 reading*)
Month, The, 89
Moore, George, 38
Moore, Leonard, L: 19, 26, 39, 40, 49, 54, 57, 63, 64, 66, 71, 96, 98, 99, 100, 123, 138, 140, 143, 144, 148, 149, 151, 153, 155, 157, 162, 167, 174, 178; L. to Orwell, 179(sy); L. from Robert Giroux, *36*(sy); 18, 73, 84, 117, 136, 172, 226, 306; see also Christy & Moore
Moore, Nicholas, 250
Moravia, Alberto, *The Woman of Rome*, 222 (*Orwell's 1949 reading*); 317
Morgan, Charles, *69*
Morgan, Edith, 150

Morland, Dr Andrew, Report on Orwell, 122, *127*; L. from Fredric Warburg, 122; 24, 119, *120*, 121, 124, 125, *127*, 131, 159, 160, 163, 165
Morley, Christopher, 150
Morley, Iris, 250
Morlock, Dr H. V., 73, *74*, 91, *92*, 116
Morozov, N. A., 212
Morris, Alice S., 46
Morrison, Herbert, 245
Moscow, 324
Mosley, Sir Oswald, 101
Mounier, E., 251
Moyle, Douglas, L. to Orwell, ed. note: 56(sy)
Mrs Miranda Wood's Memoir (of Orwell), 300–6 (*selectively indexed*)
Mr Sponge's Sporting Tour, 63, 97, 220 (*Orwell's 1949 reading*), 232
'Mr Waugh Pays a Visit to Perilous Neutralia', 46
Muggeridge, Malcolm, *Affairs of the Heart*, 31, *35*, 223 (*Orwell's 1949 reading*); 30, 31, *31*, 33, 35, 109, 126, 176, 187, 203 (as M. M.), *216*, 308
Muhlen, Norbert, 144
Mundesley, 13, *14*
Murder in Mexico, 222 (*Orwell's 1949 reading*)
Murder in the House, 222 (*Orwell's 1949 reading*)
Murray, Sir F. Ralph H., *319*, *321*
Murtough, Miss, 132, *136*
Mussolini, Benito, 100, 101, 113
'My Country Right or Left', 229
My Early Life (Winston Churchill), 113, *113*
Mystery Omnibus (Dorothy L. Sayers), 221 (*Orwell's 1949 reading*)

Nadel, Enrique Marco, 51, *51*
Naked and the Dead, The, 148, *148*, 222 (*Orwell's 1949 reading*)
National Health Service, 92
Naturalist Goes to War, A, 219 (*Orwell's 1949 reading*)
Nazarovs, The, 219 (*Orwell's 1949 reading*)
NBC: US broadcast of *Nineteen Eighty-Four*, 149
Nearing, Scott, 252
Négrin, Dr Juan, 54, *55*
Nehru, Pandit Jawaharlal, 140, 326
Nelson, Margaret, *30*; and see Fletcher, Margaret
Neuchâtel, 170, *170*
Neumann, Margarete: see Buber-Neumann, Margarete
Neumann, Robert, 251

342

Index

Index

Index

CUMULATIVE AND SUPPLEMENTARY INDEXES

This Cumulative Index is a collation of the indexes provided for each of volumes X to XX. It is followed by four supplementary indexes.

The headnotes to the individual volume indexes give full details of the conventions used in compiling this Cumulative Index. Entries are indexed alphabetically to the first comma; titles are ignored. Some simplifications and rationalisations have been introduced but it is not thought that they will present readers with problems. Usually entry names are given once but if it is thought duplication will be helpful that has been done. Works by authors other than Orwell are given twice: first in their own right; second under the author within the appropriate volume entry.

The volume indexes were compiled manually on cards and then typed up; the Cumulative Index is a product of computer conflation of the computer-set individual indexes. Although the latter's print-out was modified to bring the alphabeticisation into line with that of the individually compiled indexes, there are inevitable variations. It is hoped that these will not present problems for readers.

The volume indexes (as explained in the headnotes) are name, place, and title indexes, not topical indexes. However, a number of topics have been included for readers' convenience. The first three Supplementary Indexes list such topics. The fourth Supplementary Index lists serials in which Orwell's work was published in his lifetime. Each of these four indexes has its own explanatory headnote.   P.D.; S.D.

Cumulative Index

Cumulative Index

Archdeacons Afloat, XX, 220 (*Orwell's 1949 reading*)
Archibald, Dorothy, XII, 530(L)
Arch of Triumph, XVIII, Rev: 478–9
Arciszewsky, Tomasz (Polish Premier, London), XVII, 223
Ardaschir, K. K., XIII, L: 289;
"The Sick Man Revives" (B), 264, *265*, 279, 289, 295, 344, 352, 353
"Forty[-three] years in England" (B), 264, 279
"The Rebirth of a Nation" (B), 317
"The Marriage of the Seas" (the Suez Canal) (B), 352, 375; text: *Talking to India*, XV, 321
"Turkey Past and Present" (B), 364, 469
"Byron", 469;
264, 265, 363–4, 364, 443
XIV, L: 62, 198, 306, 307, 312;
"The Moslem Minorities of Europe" (B), 3
"Rebirth of the Egyptian Nation" (B), 41
"The Highway of the World" (B), 50
"Status of Women in Europe" (B), (also as "Women of the West"), 98, 99
"President Inönü" (B), 99, 152, 328, *337*
"Byron" (B), 152
"French North Africa" (B), 176
"Victoria Station, Bombay, to Victoria Station, London" (B), 306, 329, 342, *347*
"The Storm nears Turkey" (B), *342*
XV, L: 17, 57, 121; 9, *121*, 153, 321;
"The Turkish University inaugurated in 1933" (B), 62, 76
"The Panama Canal" (B), 81, 90, 121
Ardlussa, XVII, 98, *103*
XVIII, 308, 327, 329, 337, *337*, 338, 339, 342, 377, 379, 392, 396, 398, 400, 411, 444
XIX, 9, 142, 145, 146, 159, 167, 168, 169, 174, 410, 449, 455, 457, 466, 489, 491, 492, 493, 494
XX, 68, 91, 147
Ardrey, Robert, XII, *Thunder Rock*, Rev D: 200–1
XV, *Thunder Rock* (B), 305
Ardrishaig, XX, 163
'Are Books Too Dear?', XVI, ed. note: 241, 242–4; end note: 244
Areopagitica, XVI, 489
XVII, *260*, 308–9, 370, 437
"Are you not weary of ardent ways", XVI, 492
Arganda Bridge, XI, 299
Argentina, XIII, 139
XIV, 47
XIX, 73

XX, 54, 179
Argentina (Buenos Aires), XVIII, 481, *481*
Argument of Empire, XV, *157*
Argument to Prove that the Abolishing of Christianity. . . , An, XVIII, 419
Arise, My Love, XII, Rev F: 438
Aristide Pujol, XVIII, 217
Aristippus, XVII, 21, *22*
Aristophanes, XVI, 481
Aristotle, *Complete Works*, XVII, 214
Aristotle, X, 329
Arklow, Damaris, XII, *Just as I Feared*, Rev: 276
Arlen, Michael, XIX, 499, *516*
Arliss, George, XIII, *128*
Armies and the Art of Revolution, Rev: XVI, 51–2
Armies of Freemen, XII, Rev: 305–7
Arminius, XVII, 227
"*Arms and the Man*" (B), XIV, 215, 248, *249*, 299, 312, 317–8, 323–7
Armstrong, Herbert Rowse, XVIII, 108
Armstrong, John, XVI, 368, 374
Armstrong, Martin, XI, *Spanish Circus*, Rev: 87; *88*
XIV, L: 25, 112; T: 108;
"Story by Five Authors, 4" (B), 25, 27, 75, 112, 133–6, 140;
25
'Armut und Hoffnung Grossbritanniens': see 'Labour Government After Three Years, XIX, The', ed. note: 435; *453*
'Armut und Hoffnung Grossbritanniens' ('The Labour Government After Three Years'), XX, *64*
Army Bureau of Current Affairs (ABCA), XVI, 311; XVII, 80, *80*
Arnold, Matthew, XII, *Culture and Anarchy*, *262*; "The Scholar Gypsy", 106; *134, 135*, 261, 485
XVI, 469
XVII, 34
Arnold, Dr Thomas, XVII, 442; XIX, 442
Aron, Robert, XVII, *83*
"Around the Courts" (B), XIII, 55, *56*, 63, *66*, 102
Around the World in Eighty Days, XII, 368, 369
ARP (Air Raid Precautions), XII, 259, 267, 549
XIII, 26
"ARP" (B), 300, 339
see Air raid precautions
Arquer, Jordi, XI, 226
XIX, 153, *154*
XX, 140, *140*
Arrival and Departure, XVI, Rev: 19–20; 393, 397, 398–9, 400

358

Cumulative Index

Cumulative Index

Bogart, Humphrey, XII, *543*
Boileau, Nicolas, XVI, 297
Boisson, Gen., XIV, 233
Bokhari, Prof. A. S., XVII, 186
Bokhari, Zulfaqar Ali (Indian Programme
 Organiser), XII, L: 451, 455, 464, 483;
 452, *513*, 544
 XIII, L: 241, 419; L to Orwell, 10; Letters
 to: J. Bahadur Singh, 99, 386; E. W. D.
 Boughen, 233 (summary), 270; Venu
 Chitale, 343; Cedric Dover, 231; L. F.
 Easterbrook, 378, 385; T. S. Eliot, 172;
 Empire Programme Executive, 233
 (summary); Mrs Hunt, 199; Princess
 Indira, 386; Bhupen Mukerjee, *50*; Sir
 John Russell, 379, 385; Noel Sircar, 386;
 Shridhar Telkar, 184, 191, 365, 386;
 Reading News Review: not specifically
 indexed; see News Review headnotes;
 9, *14*, 17, 18, 19, *50*, *52*, 84, 86, 87, 163,
 165, 166, 190, 198, *242*, *291*, *354*, 420,
 425, *430*, *439*, 447, 458, 523
 XIV, L. to E. W. D. Boughen, 289–90; L.
 to P. Chatterjee 237, 260; L. to M. R.
 Kothari, 55; L. to Rushbrook Williams,
 11 (summary), 37, 38, 39; *41*
 XV, L: 132, 175, 175(L);
 "The Sa Re Ga of Western Music" (B),
 121;
 L. to Oliver Bell, 246;
 L. to Ronald Boswell, *175*;
 L. to P. Chatterjee, 183 (summary);
 L. to Roger Falk, 124
 L. to J. C. Flugel, *276*;
 L. to C. E. M. Joad, 226 (summary);
 L. to C. Lawson-Reece, *175*;
 L. to Kingsley Martin, 229;
 L. to Orwell: "The World We Hope
 For", 148–50; *names not indexed*;
 Brander's response: 150–1;
 121, 153, *180*, 248, 300, 322
 XVI, L: *291*; L. to Orwell: *291*
Bolitho, Hector, XII, *America Expects*, Rev:
 179
Bollingen Foundation, XX, 100, 101
Bollingen Prize for Poetry, XX, 100–1, *140*
Bolloten, Burnett, XI, 36
Bologoye Concentration Camp, XVIII, 215
Bolzano (expulsion of foreigners), XI, 370,
 370
Bombay Presidency, XI, 383, *383–4*
Bomber Command Continues, XIV, 301
Bombing Restriction Committee, XVI, 193
Bonaparte, Joseph, XVIII, 475
Bondfield, Margaret, XVI, 270, 272
Bone, XIV, 231
Bone, Edith, XVII, *180*

Bonham Carter, Lady Violet, XI, *370*, *371*,
 371
Bonifas, P., XII, 519
Bonnet, Georges, XIII, 102, *102*
Bonora, Mrs Hastings, X, *457–8*
Bonsaver, Guido, XIX, *15*
"Booking Arrangements for Speakers",
 XIII, 343–4
Booklovers' Corner, X, ed. note: 354–5; *400*
 XVI, *3*, *379*
Book of Common Prayer, X, 485
 XII, Psalm 103, *113*
"*Book of Job, The*" (B), XIV, 215, 221, 227,
 237, 253, 261, *299*
Book of Miracles, A, XII, Rev: 165
Book of Snobs, A, XVI, 498
Book-of-the-Month-Club (USA), XVII,
 252, 457
 XVIII, 13, *133*, 248, 250, *250*, 254, 255,
 331, *332*, 340, 399
 XX, 67, 71, 73, 82, 84, *104*, 127, 217
Books and Authors (BBC Pamphlet 2), ed. T.
 O. Beachcroft and Laurence Brander,
 XIV, *248*, *299*, 323; texts of
 "Masterpieces of English Literature"
 (see *299*)
 XV, *82*, 164
 XVIII, ed. note: 454; *contributors not
 indexed*
Books and the People: series title, XVI, 456,
 459
 XVII, A New Year Message', 7–11; corr:
 Mrs O. Grant [9], 11(sy); A. Reid 11,
 12 (references); Adelaide R. Poole
 11(sy); Stephen Spender 11; John Atkins
 11; M. E. Farmer 12
Books for Germany, XIX, 211; XX, *321*
'Bookshop Memories', X, 510–3
Book Society, X, *532*
Books Owned by Orwell in 1950, XX, ed.
 note: 286–7; 287–99 (*not indexed*)
"Books That Changed the World" (B),
 XIII:
 Harriet Beecher Stowe: *Uncle Tom's
 Cabin*, 449
 Jonathan Swift: *Gulliver's Travels*, 450
 Jean-Jacques Rousseau: *The Social
 Contract*, 451
 Karl Marx: *Das Kapital*, 451
 XIV, series:
 "*The Descent of Man*" (B), 11
 "*Uncle Tom's Cabin*" (B), 11
 "*Gulliver's Travels*" (B), 12
 "*The Social Contract*" (B), 12
 "*War and Peace*" (B), 28, 70, 85
 "*Das Kapital*" (B), 71
 "*Mein Kampf*" (B), 29, 76

"The Koran" (B), 358
XV:
  The Koran (B), 20, 31
  The Bible (B), 38
  The Upanishads (B), 38
  The Analects of Confucius (B), 38, 79, 81
  The Bhagavat-Gita (B), 38, 41
  The New Testament (B), 94, 101, *102*
'Books *v.* Cigarettes', XVIII, 94–7; (corr)
  Joyce A. Sharpey-Shafer, 97; *262*
"Boomps-a-daisy", XVI, 507, *508*
Boom Town (film), XII, 523
Booster, The, XI, Rev: 90–1; *91, 91,* 92
  XII, 92, *112, 114, 219*
  XIV, 218
Booth, Gen William, X, 245
Booth, William, XVII, *In Darkest England,*
  236
Boothby, Guy, X, *Dr Nikola,* 268, 308
  XVII, *Dr Nikola,* 348
  XVIII, 216, 493
Boothe, Clare, XII, *Margin for Error,* Rev D:
  230–1
Boothroyd, John Basil ("Yaffle"), XI, 152
  XIX, 220, *220*
Boots the Chemists, XVII, 10, *12*
Bor: see Komorowski, Gen. Tadeusz
Borah, Gen. William, XIII, 102, *102*
'Borderline expressions & words', XIX, 498,
  505
Boris, King of Bulgaria, XIII, 252
Borkenau, Franz, XI, *The Spanish Cockpit,*
  Rev: 51–2; *The Communist International,*
  Rev: 202–4; *50,* 62, 88, 114, 116, 135
  XII, *The Totalitarian Enemy,* Rev: 158–60;
    The Communist International, 101, 553;
    The Spanish Cockpit, 553; 169, *170,* 176,
    181, 222, 538, 553
  XVI, 180, 392, *400*
  XVIII, *The Communist International,* 62, *63*
  XIX, *The Communist International,* 128;
    459, *459*
  XX, L. to Orwell, 167(sy); *54, 55, 69,*
    320, 322, *326*
Born in Exile, XIX, 322, 350; XX, 99
Born of the Desert, XVIII, Rev: 27
Borodino, Battle of, XII, 119
Borsley, L. R. (corr), XVII, 322, 323
Borstal, XII, 194, 397
Bos, Charles du, X, *Byron and the Need of*
  Fatality, Rev: 263–5
Bose, A. N., XVI, *83*
Bose, Ras Bihari, XIII, 261, *263,* 375, 513
  XVI, 36
Bose, Subhas Chandra, XIII, 229, *260,* 261,
  285–6, *286,* 323, 513
  XV, 34, 222, 321, 323

XVI, 159
XIX, *21*
Boswell, James, X, 513
Boswell, Ronald (Talks Booking Manager),
  XIV, 355
  XV, L: 15, 179; *174;*
    L. to R. R. Desai, 174;
    L. from Bokhari, 175;
  XVII, L: 199; *45,* 110
Both Your Houses, XX, 220 (*Orwell's 1949*
  reading)
Bottome, Phyllis, XII, *Masks and Faces,* Rev:
  258
Bottomley, Horatio, X, *429*
  XII, *Letters to the Boys in the Trenches,* 110;
    115, 420, *434*
  XVI, 481
Boucher d' Albacete, Le: see Marty, André
Boughen, Elsie W. D., XIII, L: *63;* 173, 295,
  449; L. from Bokhari, 233 (summary),
  270; *430–1*
  XIV, L: 211, 228, 309, 327, 330; L. as
    from Bokhari, 289–90
  XV, L: 40, 72; *41*
Bouillon Kub, X, *300*
"Boule de Suif" (Guy de Maupassant), X,
  369
  XVI, 246
  XVIII, 386, *386,* 400, 401, 448, *448*
Boulogne, XIII, 282
Bourne, George, XVI, *Memoirs of a Surrey*
  Labourer, 473; *473*
Bouvard et Pécuchet (Gustave Flaubert), XII, 52
  XIII, 28
Bovex, X, 415
Bow by-election, XII, 183
Bowdler, Dr Thomas, X, 245
  XIV, 157, 158, 159
Bowen, Elizabeth, XI, 356
  XVIII, *384*
  XX, *The Heat of the Day,* 46
Bower, Fred, X, *Rolling Stonemason,* Rev:
  489–90
Bowra, Maurice, XV, 181; *The Heritage of*
  Symbolism, 181
  XVI, 113
Bowyer, E. C. XIII, (B), Discussion on
  Aviation with Peter Masefield, 417,
  417, 418, 434, 437; 443
  XIV, L: 28, 29, 228, 270; L. from
    Bowyer: *29* (summary), *228*
    (summary), 270 (summary);
    "Air Transport" (B), 28, 41, 52–3, 70
    "Modern Aircraft" (B), 228, 240, 276,
    298, 310, *311* (L), 328, 332, 340, *340,*
    341, 343, 353; for topics, see "Modern
    Aircraft"

Cumulative Index

XV, L: 165; *The Future of British Air Transport*, 165
Boxer Rebellion, XVIII, 225; XIX, 481, *481*
Box o' Books: A Book of Verse (C. Platt), XX, 190, *193*
Boyd, D. F., XIX, L: 214; *407*
Boyer, Charles, XII, 495
Boyle, Francis (Francey), XIX, 451
   XX, 65, *66*
Boyle, Kay, XII, *The Crazy Hunter*, Rev: 143, 144, *144*
   XIX, 316
Boys' Friend Library, XII, 58
Boys in Brown, XII, Rev D: 194–5
Boy's Own Paper, XII, 59, *76*
   XVI, 60
'Boys' Weeklies', XII, 57–79; 6, *6*, 16, 18, 19; see "Frank Richards Replies to George Orwell", 79–85
   XVIII, *243*
Boys will be Boys, XIX, 450, 451
Bozman, Mildred M. and Richard Church, XVII, *Poems of Our Time 1900–1942*, Rev: 197–8
Brace, Donald, XVIII, L. from Fredric Warburg, 455(sy); *255*
   XX, L. to Fredric Warburg, 186
Bracken, Brendan, XVI, 259, *260*, 463
   XVII, 191, 193
Braddock, Mrs E. M. (Bessie), XVIII, 169
   XX, 243
Braddock, Tom, XIX, 516, *518*; XX, 243
Bradford, Bishop of, XIII, 391
Bradlaugh, Charles, XV, 259, *265*
Brady, Prof. Robert A., XVII, *The Spirit and Structure of German Fascism* (1937), 325
"Brahma" (B) (extract), XIV, 211
Braille editions of Orwell's books, XX, 227, *231*
Brailsford, H. N., XI, L: 102, 104; L to O: 119; 56, *60*, 117, 118, *119*
   XII, 531, *531*
   XIII, (B), Discussion on The Press with G. M. Young, 408, *409*
   XV, *Subject India*, Rev: 332–4; 159, *159*
   XVI, 3
   XIX, 296
   XX, L: 309 (1937), 310 (1937)
Braine, Rev. W. H., XX, 176
"Brains Trust, The", XIII, 18
   XIV, (B), 224
   XV, 186
   XVI, 258, *260*, 263, 314
   XVIII, 89, *90*, 104, 419, *431*
Braithwaite, John (died June 1997), XX, L. to Orwell, 176 (sy with extracts)

Bramah, Ernest, X, *Max Carados, The Eyes of Max Carados, The Wallet of Kai Lung*, 492, *492*
   XII, *The Secret of the League*, Rev: 212–3
   XV, 316–9; *The Eyes of Max Carados*, 316; *Max Carados*, 316
   XVII, *Max Carados*, 348
Bramahcharya, XX, 7
Branch Street, XVI, Rev: 334–5; 318
Brander, Laurence and T. O. Beachcroft (eds.), XVIII, *Books and Authors* and *Landmarks in American Literature*, ed. note: 454
Brander, Laurence, XIII, Reports from India: ed. note: 301; 18, 65, 85, 149, 174, 175, 176, *184*, 198, 236
   XIV, L. to Rushbrook Williams, 89, 173; "Resilience in Programmes", 173–4; "Report on Indian Programmes", 309; 39, 62, 76, 76–7, 100, 215, *215*, 299
   XV, L. to Bokhari re "The World We Hope For", 150–1; "Preferences of the English-Speaking Indian Audience", 247–8; "Report on Indian Programmes", 343–56 (which entry see for topics discussed); 79, 84, 96, 148, 300
   XVIII, *401*
Brandt, R. A., XVII, 213
Branford, Margaret, XII, *Wages for Wives*, Rev D: 216
Branthwaite, Jock (died July 1997), XI, 47, *50*, 63, 64, 85
Brass Bottle, The, XII, 360
Braunthal, Julius, XVII, *In Search of the Millenium*, Rev: 272–3
Brave New World, XII, Rev: 210–12, 213–4; 126, 540
   XIII, 216
   XVI, 38, 40
   XVIII, 14, 15, 270
   XIX, 471
   XX, 72
Brave New World Revisited, XX, 177
Bray, Berkshire, XVIII, 258
Brazil, XIII, 140, *140*, 148, 490, 491, 516
   XIV, 47, 204
Brea, Juan and Mary Low, XI, *Red Spanish Notebook*, Rev: 86–7
"Bread and Butter for the Teacher", XVI, 179
Bread and Wine, XVIII, 63
Breaking of the Seals, The, XVIII, Rev: 470
Brecht, Bertolt, XX, 93, *94*
Brecon & Radnor By-election, XI, 376, 385
Brehm, Eugen, XVII, 290, *290*
Brenan, Gerald XVI, (corr) 284 (sy)

Cumulative Index

Catalonia Infelix, XI, Rev: 103
"Cat-and-Mouse" Case: Campaign for
    Philip Sansom, The (petition), XVIII,
    48–9 (*signatories not indexed*)
'Catastrophic Gradualism', XVII, 342–5; 464
Cateau, Le, XII, 65, 77
Catholic Herald, XIII, 503
    XVI, 369, 373
    XVII, 30, 256
Catroux, Gen. George, XIV, 233, 234, 351,
    360
Cattell, David T., XI, 32
Caucasus, XIV, 171, 172
"Caucasus" (rejected script), XIII, 352
Cauchemar en URSS, XII, 359; XVI, 396, 401
Caudwell, Christopher, XI, 305
    XII, 297, 484
Caulaincourt, Louis, Marquis de, XVIII, 223
Caution and Warning, XIX, 114
Cavafy, C. P., XVII, 220
Cavalcade (Noel Coward), XVII, 251, 252
Cavalcade (journal), XVII, 418, 434
Cavell, Nurse Edith, XVI, 138, 139
Cavendish, Lord Frederick, XVI, 189
Cecchi, Emilio, XIX, L: 52, 80, 279; 52
    XX, L. to Orwell, 182(sy)
Cecil, Lord David, XIII, 167
    XIV, 287, 288, 289
    XV, L: 78, 82, XX, App. 15; 63, 133, 167;
    "Background to Modern English Verse"
    (B), 82
    "T. S. Eliot" (B), 152
    XX, 38
Cecil, Sir Robert, X, 236, 237
Celebes, XIII, 125
Céline (Louis-Ferdinand Destouches), XII,
    Voyage au Bout de la Nuit, 10, 89, 90,
    112; 109
    XIII, *Voyage au Bout de la Nuit*, 77, 78; 79
    XV, *Mea Culpa*, 127
    XVI, 81
Cellar (play), XVII, Rev: 450–1
C.E.M.A. (Council for the Encouragement
    of Music and the Arts), XVI, 388, 389,
    390, 391, 428
Censorship Department, Whitehall, XII, 169
    XVII, 463, 479
'Censorship in England' X, (English
    version), 117–9; (French version), 148–
    50
'Censure en Angleterre, La' X, (French
    version), 148–50; (English version),
    117–9
Central Africa, XIII, 34
Central Hotel, Glasgow, XVIII, 369
Central Labour College, XVII, 311

Central Office of Information: see COI and
    MOI
"Ceremonial, A", XIX, 315
Ceremony of Innocence, XX, 219 (*Orwell's 1949
    reading*)
Cervantes, Miguel de, XII, 40
    XVI, *Don Quixote*, 488; 408
    XVII, *Don Quixote*, 289
Ceylon, XII, 493; XV, 208
Chains, XX, 221 (*Orwell's 1949 reading*)
Chair on the Boulevard, A, XVIII, 217
Challaye, Félicien, XI, 117, 119, 189
Chalmers, T. W., XIII, 9
Chamberlain, Lady Austen, XV, 294
Chamberlain, Houston Stewart, XVI, 273
    XVII, 6, 7, 146
    XIX, 499, 516
Chamberlain, Neville, XI, 151, 179, 183,
    184, 200, 206, 207, 210, 216, 218, 222,
    227, 238, 239, 240, 240, 242, 244, 340,
    369, 369, 370, 373, 376, 384, 384, 400,
    403
    XII, 150, 151, 187, 271, 289, 344, 354,
    400, 404, 414, 416, 432, 460, 480
    XIII, 278, 393
    XIV, 30, 293
    XV, 294, 295
    XVI, 87, 300, 463, 470
    XVII, 51, 60
    XIX, 36, 281
Chambers, Arthur, XI, 63
Chambers' Farm, X, 219
Chamber's Papers for the People, XVI, 383
Champion, XI, 411; XII, 58, 76
Chamson, André, XII, 161
Chance, XVII, 190, 196
Chance, XX, 222 (*Orwell's 1949 reading*)
Chand, Prem, (Dhanpat Rāy Srīvastav),
    XV, "The Resignation", 181; "The
    Shroud", 169, 181; 169, 169, 180, 181,
    185
    XVII, 242
Chandler, Len, XX, 327
Chandler, Raymond, XX, *The Little Lady*,
    222 (*Orwell's 1949 reading*)
Chang Hsien Ch'Ung, XVI, 143–4
"Changing Britain" (B), XIII:
    "Clothes", 200
Changkufeng, XI, 393, 393
Changsa, XIII, 121
Channel, A. R., XII, *Phantom Patrol*, Rev:
    303
Channing, Mark, X, *Indian Mosaic*, Rev: 488
Chappelle, Bonnier de la, XVI, 22
Chapel Ridding, XI, 182
Chapiev (film), XII, 75, 79; XVIII, 520–1

Cumulative Index

Darlan, Adml Jean-François, XII, 501, *501*, 508

XIII, 86, 341, *341*

XIV, 193, 204, 208, 233, 244, 255–6, 290, 293, 296

XV, 296

XVI, 21, *21*, 27, 178

Darling, Sir Malcolm, XIII, L. to Rushbrook Williams, 190, 241 (summary); 8, 10, 12, 15, 17, 20, 21, 175, 177, *177*, 190, 191, 207, 241, 270, 457

XIV, *42*, 62, 309

XV, L: 79; *79*, 80, *229*

Darlington, C. D., XIII, "The Future of Science" (B), 321, 345, 512; "India in the Steel Age" (B), 361, 382, 512; 296, *321*

XV, L: 101; *89*, 169; "Plant or Animal Breeding" (B), 101

XVI, 180, *181*

XX, *The Conflict of Science and Society* (pamphlet), 220 (*Orwell's 1949 reading*); 36, *36*, 95, 320, *321*

Darlington, W. A., XII, *Alf's New Button*, Rev: 360

Darroch, Donald (and 'the D's'), XVIII, 313, *315*, 323, *323*, 354, 356, 357, 363, 378, 379, 380, 381, 394, 395, 398, 399, 400, 401, 406, 412, 445, 446, 448, *475*

XIX, (*usually as D. D. in Domestic Diary*), 125, 135, 136, *138*, 140, 141, 152, 156, 157, 168, 170, *171*, 175, 178, 186, 194, 197, 205, 210, 215, 266, *266*, 267, 332

Darroch, Katie (*as K. D. in Domestic Diary*), XVIII, *315*, 356, 395, *396*, 400

XIX, 138, *138*, 266, *266*

Darroch, Neil, XIX, 267

Dartford By-election, XI, 238

Dartington Hall, XII, 494; XVII, 415

Dartmoor Prison, X, 371

XI, 260

XII, 171, 194, 397

Darton, X, 454

Daruvala, F. R., XIV, L: 271

XV, L: 197; "The Problems Concerning the New Viceroy", *197*

Darwin (Australia), XIII, 186, *187*, 226, *227*; XIV, 234

Darwin, Charles, X, *Voyage of the Beagle*, 308; 340, 346

XIV, *The Descent of Man* (B), 11

XVI, 6, 239

XVII, 170, 302, 355

XVIII, *The Voyage of the 'Beagle'* (broadcast), 179–201; *The Descent of Man*, 181; *A Naturalist's Voyage Round the World*, 160, 161, 182;

The Origin of Species, 160, 181, 199; 55, 339, 386

XX, *The Origin of Species*, 201

Das, Ramaswami, XVIII, 84; (corr) 85

Datchworth, XI, 93

Date with Destiny, A, XII, Rev F: 316

Daudet, Alphonse, XII, *Tartarin of Tarascon*, 369

Daughters of Albion, X, *467*, 534

"Daughters of the Late Colonel, The", XVIII, 35

"Daughters of the Vicar", XVII, 387

Davenport, J. H., XIII, 301, *302*

XIV, 62, 100, 173, *174*

XV, 347

Davenport, John, XIX, 461, *462*; XX, 246

Davet, Yvonne, XI, L: 70, 89, 95, 101, 148, 156, 188, 192, 195, 201, 356; 54, *70*, *72*, *74*, *101*, *102*, 135, 365, *365*

XVII, 74

XVIII, L: 130, 173, 226, 360, 390; L. to Orwell, ed. note: 128; 128, 171, 404 (lost, see ed. note); *129*, *131*, *157*, 168, 173, 229, *321*, 391–2, *392*, 398

XIX, L: 13, 119; 30, *31*, 70, *70*, 130, *392*

XX, L. from Sonia Orwell, 185; *186*

Davey, Charles (corr), XVI, 114 (sy)

David and Joanna, X, Rev: 481

David, King of Israel, XII, 132

David, Wilfrid, XV, "Karl Peters: A Forerunner of Hitler" (B), text: *Talking to India*, 321

David Copperfield, X, 205, 325

XII, 167, 205

XIV, (B, extract), 81–3

XVI, 408

XX, 115

Davidson, Mr, XX, *327*

Davidson, Rev Harold (Rector of Stiffkey), XVII, 256, *260*

Davidson, J. L., (corr), XVIII, *81*(sy)

Davidson, John, XVI, 492

Davidson, M., XX, *Astronomy for Beginners*, 222 (*Orwell's 1949 reading*)

Davidson, Wilfred, XVII, 298, 305

Davies, Betty Ann, XII, 542

Davies, Clement, XX, *51*

Davies, E. Rowan, XIII, 17, 174, 198, 327

XIV, 180, *180*

XV, 74

Davies, Hilda, XVIII, 344

Davies, John Langdon, XVII, 20

Davies, Joseph E., XVIII, *Mission to Moscow* (book and film), 266

XX, 246

Davies, Dr Martin, XVI, *94*

Davies, Rhys, XVI, 471

Cumulative Index

'De toekomst van het socialisme', XIX, 162
Deutsch, André, XVI, *156*; XX, 26
Deutsch, Oswald, XIV, 35–6, 49
Deutschen Büros für Friedensfragen, XIX, *264*
Deutscher, Isaac, XX, *Stalin: A Political Biography*, 138, *139*, 221 (*Orwell's 1949 reading*); 245
Deutschland und der nächste Krieg, XVI, *140*
Deux Magots, Café aux, XIX, *257*, *258*
Deva, Jaya, XIII, "Open Letter to a Conservative" (B), 446
De Valera, Eamon, XVI, 190; XIX, 499
Devaluation of £, XX, 172, *172*
Development of William Butler Yeats, The, XIV, Rev: 279–83; responses, 283–9; 182
XV, Rev: 69–71
Devil and Miss Jones, The, XII, Rev F: 532–3
Devil and the Jews, The, XVI, Rev: 84–5
Devil's Disciple, The, XII, Rev D: 223–4
XIV, 326
Devon, XI, 216
Devonshire Baths, Eastbourne, XIX, 369
Dewey, Dr John, XVIII, 112
Dewey, Thomas, E., XVI, 24, *24*; XIX, *282*
D. H. Lawrence and Maurice Magnus: A Plea for Better Manners, XX, 21
Dial Press, XVI, 127, *127*, 135, 141, 142, 174, 175, 182, 232, 291, 358, 419
XVII, 47, *47*, 195, *196*, 208, 286, 289
XVIII, 11, 85, 123
Diamonds to Sit On, XII, Rev: 227–8
Diaries, Orwell's, XX, 229
Diaries of Cynthia Gladwyn, XVIII, *298–9*
Diary Entries (Second Literary Notebook), XIX, 307, 319–20, 339–40, 497, 498, 502, 503
Diary Entry (from Last Literary Notebook), XIX, 310–11
XX, 92, 200, 209
Diary of a Country Priest, The, XVIII, 65
Diary of a Nobody, The, XII, Rev: 241
XVI, 483, 487–8
XVIII, 10
'Diary of Events Leading Up to the War', XI, 361–5, 366–74, 375–8, 380–4, 385–90, 393–403, 403–4, 409–10
Diary of My Times, A, XVIII, 65
Diaz Ramos, José, XI, 32, 299
Dick, Dr Bruce, XIX, L. from David Astor, *272*(sy);
247, *248*, 262, 263, 272, 332, *394*, 450, 469, 476, *476*, 485
XX, L. to David Astor, 13; *14*, 83
Dick, Kay, (also as Edward Lane), XVII, L: 45, 290; *290*
XVIII, L:23, 37; *23*

Dickens, Charles, X, *Bleak House*, 187, *190*, 389; *David Copperfield*, 205, 308, 325; *Dombey and Son*, 389; *Little Dorrit*, 226; *Our Mutual Friend*, 349; 117, 118, 187, 188, *190*, 195, 205, 226, 308, 324–6, 348, 512, 519
XI, 365; *Barnaby Rudge*, 262; *Martin Chuzzlewit*, 262; *Our Mutual Friend*, 263; *Great Expectations*, 379
XII, *David Copperfield*, 167, 205; 9, 20, 20–57, 60, 62, 69, *85*, 97, 137, 140, 141, 205, 225, 295, 485, 538
XIII, *The Pickwick Papers*, 315; *Our Mutual Friend*, 315; 211, 314–5
XIV, 80, 149; *David Copperfield* (B, extract), 81–3
XV, *A Christmas Carol*, 4; 45
XVI, 'Charles Dickens', 37, 59, 135, 156; *Martin Chuzzlewit*, Rev: 95–6; *American Notes*, 96; *A Christmas Carol*, 37, 39; *David Copperfield*, 408; *Great Expectations*, 348, 498; *Hard Times*, 104; *Pickwick Papers*, 39, 95, 118, 162, 408, 483; *A Tale of Two Cities*, 451; *Dickens and Daughter* (Gladys Storey), 117; 14, 18, 39, 42, 117, 118, 251, 482, 484
XVII, *Charles Dickens*, Rev: 276–7; *The Cricket on the Hearth*, 357, 388; *Oliver Twist*, 277; *Pickwick Papers*, 277; 40, 68, 181, 335, 349, 400, 401
XVIII, *Oliver Twist*, 466; *Pickwick Papers*, 498
XIX, *30*, 347
XX, *David Copperfield*, 115; *Great Expectations*, 115, 205; *Little Dorrit*, 97, 220 (*Orwell's 1949 reading*), 232; *Pickwick Papers*, 64; 37, 38, 52, 62, 64, 65, 109, 233
Dickens and Daughter (Gladys Storey), XVI, 117
DICKENS, DALI & OTHERS: STUDIES IN POPULAR CULTURE (US title of *Critical Essays*), XII, 19
XIII, *30–1*, 150
XVI, 345, 391; US title of *Critical Essays* (which see)
XVII, *26*; see *Critical Essays* and 411–2 for other proposed US titles
XVIII, 53, 54, 85, 105, 396, 409. US title of *Critical Essays*, which see. The paperback edition dropped 'Studies in Popular Culture' from the title.
XIX, 106; rev. by Edmund Wilson, 253 (sy); and see *Critical Essays*
Dickens Fellowship Conference: Lecture (summary), XII, 167

Cumulative Index

Cumulative Index

European Union: see 'Toward European
Unity', XIX, 161–7
européen, l',° X, 114, *142*
'Europe's Homeless Millions', XVII, *123*
Eustace Diamonds, The, XI, 319
Evans, B. Ifor, XVII, 309
Evans, F. W., XV, L. to *Tribune*, 53–4
Evans, Myfanwy, XIX, Introduction to *The
Whirlpool* (George Gissing), 347
Evans, Walker, and James Agee, XIX, *Let
Us Now Praise Famous Men*, 317; 316
XX, *Let Us Now Praise Famous Men*, 28,
28
"Eve of Waterloo, The", XII, *432*
'Evelyn Waugh', XX, ed. note: 74; 74–7;
Preparatory Notes, 77–9
Evening News, XIII, 436; XVII, 416
Evening Standard, X, 114, 301, *304*
XII, 238, 418, *434*, 469, 471, 514
XIII, *56, 66, 363*
XIV, *174*
XV, 321
XVI, *34*, 146, 276, 337, 364
XVII, 253, 464
XVIII, *38, 53, 54*, 100–1, 467; "Saturday
Essay", 17, *19*
XIX, 20, 336, *337, 444,* 480
XX, *57, 66, 80,* 105, 117, 128, 133, 176,
323, 324
Events of May, Barcelona, XI, 31, 36, 41,
49, 53, *55–9, 60,* 64, 81, 82, 84, 88, 93,
102, 117, 118, 133, 172, 173, 226, 294,
295, 296, 297, 298–301; and see
Barcelona.
Everlasting Mercy, XII, 94, *113*
Evers, Harvey, XII, *237*; XVII, 96, 97, *102,*
112
"Everyday Chinese Heroes" (B), XV, 24
Everyman's Library, XVI, 273
'Examples of Critical English', XIX, 498,
504
Excess Profits Tax, XII, 432, *434*
Exchange and Mart, XII, 58, 232, 298
Excise Duty Notice, X, ed. note: 78
Experiment in Autobiography (H. G. Wells),
XIX, 352
"Extracts from the Diaries of Famous
Persons", X, 44
Eye of Osiris, The, X, 308
XV, 316
XVII, 348
Eyes of Max Carados, The, X, 492; XV, 316
Eyes of the Navy, XII, Rev F: 390
Eyes West, XII, Rev: 281
'Eye-Witness in Barcelona', XI, 54–60; *90,
96*
XVIII, *168*

Eyre & Spottiswoode (publishers), XVI,
127, 130, 155
XVIII, 216
XIX, 336, *336*

Faber & Faber, X, 235, 237, 238, 241, 243,
397
XI, 114, 169
XVI, 131, *131, 156,* 269, 282, 292
XVII, 120
Fabian (corr), XVII, 31(sy)
Fabian Research Pamphlets, XVIII, 260
Fabian Society, XII, 434
XIII, 424, 432
XVII, 31
XVIII, 39
XIX, 112, 399
'Face Behind the Page, The', XVII, 412
Facing the Odds, XII, Rev: 206–7
Fact, XI, 225, *226*
Faeroe Islands, XIX, 277–8, *278*
FAI (Federación Anarquista Ibérica), XI, 57,
144, 145, 194, 294, 295, 296, 297, 300,
301, *305*
Failure of Programmes for India (Brander's
Report), XV, 345–7
Fairbanks, Douglas, XII, 134
Fairchild Family, The (Mary M. Sherwood),
X, 268
XII, 29
Fairley, Gerard, XIX, *Captain Bulldog
Drummond*, 220 (*Orwell's 1949 reading*)
Fairley, Victor, XVIII, 179
Faith of the Roman Church, The, X, 247, 251
Faith, Reason and Civilisation, XVI, Rev: 122–
3; 19, *175,* 298, 313
Falange/Falangists, XI, 150, 151, *152,* 193,
194, *395*
Falconer, Freda, XV, 276, 278
Falcón Hotel, Barcelona, XI, 31, 57, 58, 72, 339
Falk W/Cdr Roger, XV, "My Visit to the
Indian Contingent in Great Britain"
(B), 124, *124*
"Interview with Indian Air Cadet
Officers" (B), 157
"The Fourth Indian Division" (B), 252
Fallada, Hans, XII, *Iron Gustav*, Rev: 164
Fallas, Carl, XVI, 19
Falls, Capt. Cyril, XIII, L: 421, *450; 421,*
422
Falstaff, XII, 37
Famel Cough Syrup, XII, 469
Family, The, XII, Rev: 437
Family Afloat, XII, Rev: 303
Family Colouring, XII, Rev: 286–7
Family Herald, X, 201
Famous Funnies, XVII, 221

407

53 bus, XVI, 46 47
Figaro, X, 119
Fight for the Charter, The, XI, Rev: 99
Fight Stories, XII, 58, 70
Fighters Ever, XIV, 301
Fighting French, XIV, 351, 360; and see Free
    French
Fighting French National Committee, XIV,
    193
FILLE DE L'AIR, LA, XV, 309; XVIII, *362*
"Film Commentary" (B), XIII, 371, 408
    XIV, series, 100, 121, 224
"Films of the Month" (B), XIV, 341
    XV, series, 30, 74, 98, 118, 151, 207, 229,
    246, 252, 269, 299, 320
Film Stories (H. G. Wells), XII, Rev: 191
'Final Years of Lady Gregory, The', XIX,
    80; and see *Lady Gregory's Journals*
Financial contribution to *The New Leader*,
    XI, ed. note: 250
Financial Times, XII, 74
"Fine Old English Gentleman, A", XVII, 78
Finerty, John P., XVIII, 112
Fink, Howard, X, 308–9; XVII, *264*
Finland, XII, 135–6, 138, *138*, 199, 303, 306,
    514, *514*
    XIII, 38, 77, 116, 307, 334, 347
    XVI, 436
    XVII, 20, 30
Finland's War of Independence, XII, Rev: 135–6
Finnegans Wake, XII, 53, 127, 128
    XIII, 316
    XVI, 109, 110, 111, 119
    XVII, 220, 331
Fires of St Dominic, The (play), XVIII, 17
"Fireworks", XIX, 315
Firing Squad, The, XVII, Rev: 438–40
First Europe, The, XX, 34, 220 (*Orwell's 1949
    reading*), 233
First Hundred Thousand, The (Ian Hay), XII,
    110, *115*
"First Jasmines" XIV, (B), 78, 79
First Men in the Moon, The, XII, 368
Firth household, X:
    Ellis Firth, *460*, 462, 463, 465, 466, 538
    Mrs Firth, 462, 465
    House, 558, *561*
    Weekly Budget, 565–7
Firth, Prof. John Rupert, XIII, "I Speak
    English", Discussion with Princess
    Indira, (B), 258;
    11, *15*, 20, 259
    XIV, 37, 38, 100, *297*
Fischer, Louis, XIII, *Men and Politics*, Rev:
    101–2
    XV, 341, 342, *342*; *A Week with Gandhi*,
    341

XVI, *Empire*, Rev: 186–7
XVIII, *Men and Politics*, 63, *63*; 62
XIX, *Gandhi and Stalin*, Rev: 452–3
XX, *Gandhi and Stalin*, 9
Fischer, Markoosha, XX, *The Nazarovs*, 219
    (*Orwell's 1949 reading*)
Fischer, Ruth, XVI, 498, *498*
    XX, L: 80 (*untraced*), 93, 146;
    L. to Orwell, *94*(sy), 120(sy), *146*(sy);
    Stalin and German Communism, 86, 89, 93,
    109, 137, 220 (*Orwell's 1949 reading*);
    85, *94*, 96, 138, *149*, 167, 319
Fisher, Dr Geoffrey, X, *252*
Fisher, Dr James, XIII, *355*, 376, *376*
Fisher, James, XVI, 181, *181*
Fisher, Norman George, XIII, "Education",
    Discussion with T. C. Worsley, (B), *495*
Fisher of Men, The, XVIII, *17*; XIX, *13*
Fisher, Vardis, X, *We Are Betrayed*, Rev: 480
Fishes of Britain, XVIII, 10
Fishing (Callow End), XIII, 384–5
Fiske, Dorothy B., XVII, *195–6*; XIX, 210
Fitter, R. S. R., XII, 434
    XVI, L: 85, 99, 380; *85, 380*
Fitton, Mary, XIX, 408
Fitzgerald, F. Scott, XVII, *314*, *398*
    XX, *The Great Gatsby*, 105, *106*; *Tender is
    the Night*, 105, *106*, 219 (*Orwell's 1949
    reading*)
Fitzgibbon, Louis, XVIII, 215
Fitzroy, Capt. Robert, XVIII, 160, 180–201
    passim, 339
Five Great Composers, XVIII, Rev: 480
'Five Specimens of Propaganda', text:
    Talking to India, XV, 321
Five-Year Plan (USSR), XII, 102, 104, 365,
    546
    XVII, 232
Flame in Sunlight, A, XX, 221 (*Orwell's 1949
    reading*)
Flame of New Orleans, The, XII, Rev F: 533
Flammarion, Camille, XVI, 473, *473*
Flanagan, Bud, XII, 488
Flandin, Pierre-Etienne, XII, 195, *200*
Flanner, Janet, XX, 247
Flannery, Harry, XVII, *Assignment in Berlin*,
    53; 52, 53, *53*, 54, 59, *62*
Flaubert, Gustave, X, 325
    XI, *Salammbô*, 261
    XII, *Bouvard et Pécuchet*, 53; *Salammbô*, 52;
    55, 485
    XIII, *Bouvard et Pécuchet*, 28; 211
    XVI, *Salammbô*, 305, 394, 451; *394*
    XVII, *Salammbô*, 167; *349*
    XX, *L'Education sentimentale*, 233, *234*;
    Madame Bovary, 233; *La Tentation de
    Saint Antoine*, 233, *234*

Cumulative Index

Cumulative Index

Jardin des Plantes (Paris), XIX, 344
Jarrell, Randall, XVIII, L. to Orwell, 299(sy)
    XIX, 313
Jarrett, S., XX, 324
Jasmine Garland, The (Indian play) (B), XV, 87
Jatha (= K. G. Jathar?; see XIV, 55), XIII, 91
    XIV, 103
Jathar, K. G., XIV, 55
Java, XIII, 186, 204, *207*, 389; XX, 303
Java Sea, XIII, 237, *239*
Jean Bart (French battleship), XIV, 244
Jeannie, XII, Rev F: 545–6
Jeans, Sir James, XIII, 459, *468*
Jeans, Ursula, XII, 383
Jeayes, Allan, XV, 187
Jedabaya, XIV, 204
Jedabla, XIII, 122
Jedeida, XIV, 231, 243
Jefferies, Richard, X, *The Amateur Poacher*, 308
    XII, 94, *113*
    XVI, 129
Jefferson, Thomas, XVI, *375*
Jeffery, Sydney, XIV, 288
Jehangir, Cowasjee, XIV, 38
Jeleńska, Teresa, XVIII, 237, *237*, 366
    XIX, 391, *392*
Jeleński, Konstanty A., XVIII, 236, *237*
Jellet, H. and Ngaio Marsh, X, *The Nursing Home Murder*, Rev: 474
Jellicoe, Admiral Lord, XI, 128, *130*
Jellinek, Frank, XI, L: 254; *The Civil War in Spain*, Rev: 172–4; Rev: 179; *The Paris Commune of 1871*, 172, 174; 82, 88, *88*, 175, *176*, 257, 258
Jena (bombed), XV, 129
Jenkin, May, XVIII, 345
Jenkins, Elizabeth, X, *The Phoenix' Nest*, Rev: 481
Jenkins, Roy, XIX, *Mr. Attlee: An Interim Biography*, Rev: 398–9; *394*, 399
Jenkinson, A. J., XII, *What Do Boys and Girls Read?*, Rev: 204–5, Rev: 224–5
Jennings, Humphrey, XII, *18*, *390*
    XIII, *The Silent Village* (film), 356
    XVIII, *251*
Jennings, John (corr), XVIII, 144
"Jenny kissed me", XIII, 158, *162*
Jermyn, J. Elizabeth, XV, L: 75, 89, *89*(L) (summary); 75
Jerrold, Douglas, *Mrs Caudle's Curtain Lectures*, XII, 53, *57*
    XVI, 482
Jerusalem, XVIII, 503
"Jerusalem, my happy home", XII, 150, *152*
    XIV, 66

XIX, 342
Jesse, F. Tennyson, XVIII, *The Story of Burma*, Rev: 124–5; corr: Orwell 125; F. Tennyson Jesse, 126; Orwell, 128, *126*
    XX, *A Pin to See the Peepshow*, 220 (*Orwell's 1949 reading*), 233
Je Suis Partout (journal), XIV, 208, *209*
Jesus Christ, X, 340
    XI, 328
    XVI, 105, 111
    XVII, 135, 417
    XVIII, 152, 161, 386, *386*
"Jeu Lugubre, Le", XVI, 235
"Jewish Socialist" (corr), XX, 128
Jews (and antisemitism), XIII, 26, 109, 111, 113, 405–6, 456
    XIV, 32, 72, 114, 193, 208, 234, 244, *245*, 246, 271, *272*, 295, 361–2
    XV, 34, 109–11, 303, 304
    XVI, 81, 83–5, 91–2, 93–4, 116, *116*, 191, 193–4, *280*, 386, 494, 502
    XVII, 5, 6, 64–70, *70*, *84*, 106, 147, *147*, 151–2, 204, 248, 325, 336, 340, 341, 361, 362
    XVIII, 266, 442, 482, 505, 510
    XIX, 19, 24, 27, *28*, *185*, 304–5, 443, 453, 457, 458, 461, *462*, 464–5, 500
    XX, Antisemitism in Great Britain', 228; 9, 101, 133, 322, 323
    and see Zionism
"Jews in the Polish Army", XVI, 194
Jew Süss, XII, 154
Jibouti, XIV, 203
Jinnah, Mohammed Ali, 186, XIII, *459*
    XVI, 446
J. Lyons & Co. Ltd. (restaurants and teashops), XVIII, 31, *32*
Joad, C. E. M., X, *315*
    XI, 225, 226
    XII, *Journey Through the War Mind*, Rev: 178–9; *179*, 179(L)
    XIII, "The Federal Idea" (B), Discussion with Cedric Dover, 231 (as "Utopias and Federations"), 233, 243
    XIV, 27, *27*
    XV, L: 131, 132(L), 137, 206, 226, 226(L); L. from Bokhari, 226 (extracts); 248; "What the West has Learned from the East" (B), 131
    "Why the West has not taken kindly to Indian Philosophy" (B), 171; *The Adventures of the Young Soldier in Search of the Better World*, Rev: 291–2
    XVI, 148, 258, *260*, 263, 445
    XVII, 80
    XVIII, 89, *89*, 419, *432*

438

Cumulative Index

"Mademoiselle de Maupin", XVII, 214

Madge, Charles and Tom Harrisson (eds.), *War Begins at Home*, XII, Rev: 17–18; *18*

Madjeski, M., XIX, 432

Madras, XIII, 281

Madrid, XI, 16, 21, 23, *23*, 28, 52, 58, 88, 113, 134, 144, 296, *382*, 387
   XII, 7, 183, 198, 468
   XVI, 289, 370
   XVIII, 167–8, 222

Madrid, Voice of (radio), XVIII, 167

Maginot Line, XI, 347
   XII, 344, *350*
   XVI, 27
   XVII, *143*

Magna Carta, XVI, 203

"Magna et Veritas", XI, 235, *236*

Magnet, The, XI, 365, 411
   XII, 10, 58, *76*, 80, 137, *374*
   XIII, 425, *425*
   XVII, 414–5, *416*
   XVIII, 241

Magnus, Maurice, XX, *Memoirs of the Foreign Legion*, 21; *20, 21*

"Maharao of Cutch", XIII, obituary; read by Orwell; ed. note: 133

Mahommed, Mahdjoub (servant), XI, 233, 250, 346

Maida Vale, London, XII, 246, *246*

Maidstone, X, 219, 220

Maikop, XIII, 476, 488

Mailer, Norman, XX, *The Naked and the Dead*, 148, *148*, 222 (*Orwell's 1949 reading*)

Maillart, Ella K., XI, *Forbidden Journey*, Rev: 78–9; *85*

Maillaud, Pierre, XVII, *The English Way*, Rev: 215–7

Main, Ernest, XX, 319

Main Street, XVI, 256; XVIII, 246

Mainz (bombed), XIII, 478

Mair, John, XII, *Never Come Back*, Rev: 359–60

Mairet, Philip, X, *246*
   XI, 92, 135, 158
   XVII, 27

Maisky, Ivan, XV, "M. Maisky" (B), 19, *19*
   XVI, *Before the Storm: Recollections*, 228; *228–9*

Maison de Madame Tellier, La, X, 369
   XVI, 246, 384

Majestic Hotel, Marrakech, XI, 198

Major Barbara, XIV, 325

Majorca, XI, 151; XVI, 9

Majuba, Battle of, XV, 319, *320*
   XVIII, 177, *179*

"Make Westing", XVII, 356

Making of the Indian Princes, The, XV, 227

Malaga, XI, 112
   XII, 8
   XVI, 393

Malan, Daniel, XIX, *227*

Mālatī Mādhava (B), XIV, 216, *216*, 227, 237, 250

Malaya, XIV, 9–10
   XVI, 454–6
   XVIII, 53, 485

Malaya Broadcasting Corporation, XVI, 454, *456*

Malaya, News Commentaries in English: see 'News Commentaries in English for Malaya'

"Malay News Commentary" (in Malay) (B), XV, 98, 99

'Malay Newsletter' (B), XIII, 13, 16, 83, 85, 174, 198

Malcolm: see Muggeridge, Malcolm

Malden by-election, XIII, 377

Mallarmé, Stéphane, X, 342–3

Mallock, W. H., *New Republic*, XVI, *439*, 440; *438, 439*
   XVIII, *New Republic*, 104, *431*; 419, *431*

Malmédy, XI, 318, *318*

Malraux, André, X, *352*, 356, 388
   XIII, 45, *48*, 399
   XVI, 392
   XVII, 74, *74*, 90, 402
   XVIII, *Days of Hope*, 63; *Storm over Shanghai*, 63; *61*, 70, *399*
   XIX, 120, *121*, 131, 169, *195*, 207, *331*
   XX, 95

Malta, XIII, 115, 122, 252, *253*, 435, 478, 489, *491*
   XIV, 31, 32, 111, 243, 303

Malta, G. C. (film), XV, 230, *230*

Maltz, Albert, XVIII, *The Cross and the Arrow*, Rev: 135

Malvern, XIII, 383, *384*

Malvern Torch, XVI, 152

Malyshkin, A. G., XVI, 250, *250*

Mamun, Caliph al, XVI, 281

Ma Mya Sein, *Burma*, XVI, Rev: 417

Man About the House, XIX, informal rev: 39–40

Managerial Revolution, The, XVI, 60–1, 62–3, 63–4, *64*, 74, 450
   XVII, 39, 320, 322, 323
   XVIII, 10, 59, 268, 270, 282
   XIX, 98, 104, 105
   XX, 134

Man and Superman, XIII, 160
   XIV, 327
   XVI, 279

'Man and the Maid, The', X, 31–44; *25*

Cumulative Index

Cumulative Index

Cumulative Index

Petronius, X, *The Satyricon*, 308; 511
Petrov, Eugene and Ilya Ilf, XII, *Diamonds to Sit On*, Rev: 227–8
Petsamo, XII, 514
Phalange: see Falange
Phantom Fame, X, Rev: 270
Phantom Patrol, XII, Rev: 303
Phatak, M., XIII, 85; XV, 74, 206
Phelan, Jim, XII, L to O: 384 (summary); *Jail Journey*, Rev: 171–2; 283, 298, 397
"Philharmonic Ensemble, The" (B), XIII, 330
Philip, André, XIV, 58
Philippines, XIII, 98, 115, 186, 205, 251, 313
Phillips, Miss (Empire Programme Executive), XIII, L. from Bokhari, 233 (summary)
Phillips, Mrs (Callow End), XIII, 383, *384*
Phillips, Morgan, XVIII, 523, *524*
Phillips, Rodney, XVII, 208
  XVIII, 165
  XIX, 223, *223*
Phillips, William, XII, 352
  XVI, 127
  XVIII, L: 85
  XIX, L: 193, 427; *427*
  XX, L: 130; L. to Orwell, *41*(sy)
"Phoenix, The", XIV, 288
"Phoenix and the Tortoise, The", XIX, 314–5
Phoenix' Nest, The, X, Rev: 481
'Photographer, The', X, 69; *44*
"Piano, The" (poem), (B), XIV, 61, 79
  XVI, 176
Piccadilly, XVI, 348, *357*
Pick, J. B., XVIII, *320*
Pickford, Mary, XVIII, 494
Pickfords (furniture removers), XVIII, L: 166(sy); 230, 249
  XIX, 468
  XX, 87, 138
"Pick of the Week", XV, *155*
Pickthorn, Kenneth, XVI, *Principles or Prejudices*, 465–6
Pickwick Papers, The, XIII, 315
  XVI, 39, 95, 118, 162, 408, 483
  XVII, 277
  XVIII, 498
  XX, 64
Picture of Dorian Gray, The (not *Grey*), XV, 335
  XVIII, 157
Picture Post, XII, 19, 156, *357*, 408, 418, *433*, 448–51, 474
  XIII, L: 391
  XIV, ed. note: 362; L: 362
  XV, 201, 202

XVI, 55, 216
XVII, 36, *89*
XIX, *119*
"Piece of Steak, A", XV, *8*
  XVI, 274
  XVII, 241, 298, 354, 356
Pierre Blanche, La, XVI, 262
Pigeon, The, X, 141
Piggling Bland, X, 45, 59
Pilcher, John, XIII, 65
Pile, Gen. Sir Frederick, XIII, 437
Pilgrim of Eternity, The, XV, *121*
Pilgrim's Progress, The, XVI, 437, 439, 442
Pilgrim's Regress, The, XVI, 443
"Pillicock sat on Pillicock Hill", XVII, 452
Pil'nyak, Boris, XVIII, 23, *23*
Pilsudski, Jozef, XX, 249
Pincher, Chapman, XX, 255
Pinero, Sir Arthur Wing, XVIII, 218
Pink 'un, X, 328, *329*; XII, 240, *241*
Pin to See the Peepshow, A, XX, 220 (Orwell's *1949 reading*), 233
Pioneer (Lucknow), XI, 120, 121, 122
Pioneer Corps, XII, 387, *387*, 465, *465*
Pioneer News, XI, 65
Piratin, Phil, XVII, 192; XIX, *310*
Pirie, J. R. K. (corr), XVII, 225
Pisan Cantos, The, XX, 100
Pitcairn, Frank C. (= Claud Cockburn, *q. v.*), XI, 291, 292, 293, 298, 301, 303, *303*, 386
Pitcher (of the *Pink 'Un*), XVII, 348
Pitter, Ruth, X, *Persephone in Hades*, Rev: 262–3; 87, *139*, *263*, 314, 347
  XII, *The Spirit Watches*, Rev: 10–12
  XVI, *231*, *260*
Pittock-Buss, G. B., XVI, Interview with Orwell on Burma, 358–62
Pitt-Rivers, Michael, XIX, 346
Pivert, Marceau, XI, 64, 66
"Place of Spiritual and Economic Values in the Future of Mankind, The", XVII, 309
Place of the Lion, The, XX, 154
Plack (Goebbels's assistant), XVII, 53, 54
Plain Tales from the Hills, XVII, 243
Plamenatz, John Petrov, XIX, *What is Communism?*, informal rev: 268–70, 497, 500
"Planning and Freedom": Public Meeting, XVIII, ed. note: 220
"Planning Music of the West for Indian Listeners", XV, *121*
"Planter of Malata, The", XVII, 190
"Plan Unfolds in Africa, The" (B), XIV, 174
Plassey, Battle of, XV, 113, *113*

Cumulative Index

Pound, Reginald, XVIII, *Running Commentary*, Rev: 492
'Poverty in Practice', XI, contract, ed. note: 164; *321, 322, 375*
Powell, Anthony, X, L: 484, *484*
   XVII, L: 124; *124*
   XVIII, *261*, 458
   XIX, L: 200, 217, 227, 259, 282, 393, 433, 466;
      Brief Lives . . . John Aubrey, 228; *From a View to a Death*, 467; *John Aubrey and His Friends*, 228, 467, *467*; *Novels of High Society from the Victorian Age*, 201; *231*, 326, 354
   XX, L: 30, 33, 39, 109, 126;
      "On George Orwell", ed. note: 107; 107–8;
      Brief Lives . . . of John Aubrey, 126, 233?; *John Aubrey and His Friends*, 109, *110*, 220 (*Orwell's 1949 reading*), 233?; 35, 36, 95, 176, *234*, 302, 305, 306
Powell, E. Alexander, X, *Aerial Odyssey*, Rev: 498
Powell, Lester, XV, "The Indian Red Cross" (B), 9, 17
Powell, Lady Violet, XVII, *124*; XX, 31
Powell, William, XII, 308
Power, Eileen, XVII, 367
Power, Hartley, XII, 231, 541, 542
Power and the Glory, The, XIX, 404, 405–6
Power: A New Social Analysis, XI, Rev: 311–12
   XVIII, 58, *59*
Power House, The, XVI, 471
Powisle, XVI, 368, *375*
Powley, Brian, XV, 231
Powys, John Cowper, XVI, 115
Powys, T. F., XX, 38
Pozas Perea, Sebastián, XI, 144, *145*, 298, *305*
PPU (Peace Pledge Union), XI, ed. note: 104; 331, *332*, 371, *372*, 372, 387, 394, 397, 400
   XII, 345, 353, 354, 417, 479, *538*
   XIII, 39, 43, 71, 112, 397
   XV, 340
   XVI, *274*, 279, 287, *317*, *319*, 493
   XVII, 151, 416
   XVIII, L: 114; *114*
P.R. = *Partisan Review, which see*
Practical Criticism, XVI, 175–6
Practical Engineering, XIX, 83
Practice and Theory of Bolshevism, The (not 'Theory and Practice'), XIX, 128
Prado, Mari, XI, 187, 188
"Praise to the Holiest in the height", XIX, 342, *343*

Pravda, XI, 32; XII, 522
Prebble, John, XIX, *The Edge of Darkness*, 274, *321*; 321
Prediction, XII, 58
Preedy, George R., X, *The Rocklitz*, Rev: 492
Preface to Prayer, A, Rev (by Rayner Heppenstall?), XVII, *238*(sy)
'Preface to Ukrainian Edition of *Animal Farm*', XIX, 86–9 (*biographical details not indexed*)
"Preferences of the English-Speaking Indian Audience", XV, 247–8
Preger, Leslie, XI, 34
'Preliminary to Autobiography', X, 95–6; *94*
"Prelude", XVIII, 35
Prelude to the Russian Campaign, XVIII, Rev: 222–4
Prelude to Victory, XII, Rev: 12–14
Premature Burial, The, XII, 372
"Prescribed Poetry" (B), series, XV, *339*
"President Inönü (B), XIV, 99, 152, 328, 237
Press, The, XIX, 116–7
Press, the: Ratings, XVIII, 499–501; Royal Commission, 499, 501
Press Censor, XVI, L. to Orwell, 411 (sy), *416*
Presse Marocaine, La, XI, 194, 252, 326
Preston, X, 540
Preston, Frank (corr), XVI, 147; *166*
Preston, Robert, XII, 524
Preston Hall Sanatorium, Aylesford, XI, 127, 127–8, *146*, 154, 164, 165, 187, 190, 192, 201, 335
Pretoria, XVII, 34
'Prevention of Literature, The', XVII, ed. notes: 368–9, 369–70; 370–81
   XVIII, ed. note: 5; *156*, 237, 432, 438, 451;
   and see Swingler, Randall, "The Right to Free Expression", annotated by Orwell, 432–43
   XIX, 33, 243
   XX, 228
Prévost, Abbé, *Manon Lescaut*, X, 308
   XII, 52, 130
Price, Harry, XIX, 389
Price, J. J. (corr), XVI, 489
Price, R. Philips (corr), XVI, 387; 427–8
Price, Vincent, XII, 370
Price, Ward, XV, 293
Pride and Prejudice, X, 327
Priest Island, XII, Rev: 190–1
Priestley, J. B., X, *Angel Pavement*, Rev: 186–8; 390, 512
   XII, *Cornelius*, Rev D: 250–2; 277, *277*, 348, *350*, 443

Cumulative Index

Prunier, M., XIX, 146
Prussian Officer and Other Stories, The, XVII, Rev: 385–8
Prussian Officer, The, XIII, 213
  XX, 219 (*Orwell's 1949 reading*)
Pruth, XII, 525
Pryce-Jones, David, XVII, *83*
Psmith in the City, XVII, 55, 56, 100–1, *103*
Psmith, Journalist, XVII, 55, 56
PSOP (Parti Socialiste Ouvriers et Paysans), XI, 387, *388*, *390*, 394
PSUC (Partido Socialista Unificado de Cataluña – Catalan Communists), XI, 57, 139, 141, 142, 143, *144*, 300
  XX, 311, *312*
Psychic News, XII, 526
Psychologist's Wartime Diary, A, XII, 179
"Psychology" (B), series, XV, 225, 254, *254*:
  "Psychology 1: The Uses of Psychology" (B), Prof. Pear, *255*, 255
  "Psychology 2. [untitled]" (B), J. C. Flugel, 266, 267, 276, *276*
  "Psychology 3. [untitled]" (B), Prof. Valentine, 269, 275, 291
  "Psychology 4. Intelligence Tests" (B), D. W. Harding, 288, *288*, 299, *300*, 301
  "Psychology 5. [Child Psychology?]" (B), Dr Susan Isaacs, 267, 291
  "Psychology 6. [untitled]" (B), May Smith, *300*;
  and see Laws, Frederick
Ptolemy (Claudius Ptolomaeus), XVI, 281
Pub and the People, The, XIV, Rev: 320–2
Public Assistance Committee, X, 443, *445*, 542, 543, 549, 568
Public Faces, XVI, Rev: 450
  XX, 219 (*Orwell's 1949 reading*)
Public Record Office, XX, 318, 323
Public Schools, XIX, 86, *86*
Publishing in Peace & War, XVI, 244, 436
Pucelle, La, XVI, 38, 41, 485
Pucheu, Pierre, XVI, 137–8, *141*
Puckle, Sir Frederick, XV, 343, 348, 351, *356*
Pugh, Richard (corr), XVI, 133 (sy); 134
Puigcerdá (Puiccerda), XI, 293, *304*
Pulleyne, Collett Cresswell, X, 232, *232*, 249, 269, 271
Punch, X, 405, 533
  XII, 40, 66, 98, 162, 240, 359
  XV, 125
  XVI, 90, *91*, 102, 216, 498, 499
  XVIII, 510
"Punjabi Newsletter" (B), XIII, 12
Purber, Eileen E. (corr), XVI, 78
Purges, French (1944–45), XVII, 83, *83*

Purges, German (June 1934), XVII, 5
Purges, Russian, XVII, 258
"Purloined Letter, The", XV, 317
  XVI, 383
"Purple Head, The", X, 268
Purple Land, The (H. E. Bates), XIX, 342
Pushkin, Aleksandr, XVII, 179–80
  XVIII, *Eugene Onegin*, 266
"Pushtu Newsletter" (B), XIII, 12
Put Our More Flags, XVII, 69
Putting Things Right (Brander's Report), XV, 347–53
Pyatakov, Grigory, XVIII, 111
Pyatigorsk, XIII, 476
Pygmalion, X, 307; XVI, 275
Pythagoras, XII, *135*

Qattara Depression, XIV, 138, 170, *172*
Quaint Companions, The, XVIII, 217
Quarterly Review, XII, 34
  XVI, 60, 246, 453
  XVII, 12–13, *15*, 23
  XVIII, 97
Quartermaine, Leon, XII, 383
Quartus (and Norah), XVII, 108, *109*
Quatar: see Katha
Queen Christine, X, 314
Queen Elizabeth (the Queen Mother), XVIII, 11
Queen Mary, XIX, 25, 27
Queen of the Spies, The, X, Rev: 412
Queipo de Llano y Serra, Gonzalo, XI, 112, 301, *305*, 376, *376*, 378, 380, 383
Quennell, Peter, XI, *175*
Quest for Corvo, The, XIX, *336*
Questionnaire: The Three Best Books of 1947, Orwell's response, XIX, 232–3
Quezon, Manuel Luis, XIII, 253, *253*
'Quick and the Dead, The' (projected novel title), XII, 148
'Quick & the Dead, The', XV, Orwell's Notes; ed. note: 356–61; 361–7
Quick Service, XII, Rev: 274–5
Quiet Wedding, XII, Rev F: 385–6; *386*
Quiller-Couch, Sir Arthur, XVI, 444, *445*
  XIX, *The Oxford Book of English Verse*, 68; see *69*
Quinn, John, XVI, *119*
Quiroga, Casares, XI, 291, *303*
Quisling, Vidkun, XII, 399, *433*; and see *532*
  XVI, 80, 194
  XVII, 53, 60, 61, *62*
  XIX, 18, 19
Quislings, XIII, 440, *442*, 446; XIV, 72
Quiver's Choice, XVII, Rev: 282–4; *284*
Quixote, Don, XII, 37

Cumulative Index

Son, 385, 388, 427, 476, 479; 30, 46, 385, 386, 388, *391*, 476, 477, 481
XVII, *A Letter to My Son*, 210
XVIII, 11
XIX, *Great Morning*, Rev: 395–8: *327;*
Before the Bombardment, 397, *398;* 326
XX, *Laughter in the Next Room*, 124, 221
(*Orwell's 1949 reading*), 301
Sitwell, Sacheverell, XII, L: 208; *Poltergeists*,
Rev: 246–8
XIV, "Four Variations upon William
Browne of Tavistock", 288
XV, 309
Sixteen Autobiographical Sketches (Bernard
Shaw), XX, 220 (*Orwell's 1949 reading*)
Skelton, John, XIX, 45, *46*
Sketch Map of Eastern and Southern Europe,
XIX, ed. note: 497, 498
Sketch Map of Jura: XVIII, p. xvii
XIX, p. xvii
Skin Game, The, X, 453
Skipper, XI, 411; XII, 58, 76
Skira (publisher), XX, 307
'Slack Bob, The', X, 46–7; *44*, 68, *72*
Slade, Miss, XV, 340
Slater, Hugh (Humphrey), XI, 34
XII, *Home Guard for Victory!*, Rev: 387–9,
Rev: 439–41; *War into Europe*, *331;* *241*,
329, 330, *331*, *337*, 337, 348, 468, 551
XIII, 452
XV, 274, *275*
XVII, 97, *102*, *156*, 178, 209
XVIII, L: 408; *The Heretics*, 376, *376*, 455;
12, 165, 214, *214*, 376, *376*, 397, *448*
XIX, 124, 223, *223*, 318, *319*
XX, *The Conspirator*, 68; *41*, 54, *55*, 67, 218
Sleeper Awakes, The, XV, 360; XVIII, 270
"Slip Under the Microscope, A" (H. G.
Wells), XII, 372, *372*
XV, (adapted by Orwell) (B), ed. note: 256;
256–65; *231*
XVI, 383
XVII, 241
XVIII, 400
Sloan, Pat, XVIII, 437, 443
Slovakia, XI, 385, *386*, 403; and see
Czechoslovakia
XII, 15
Small Back Room, The, XX, 221 (*Orwell's 1949 reading*)
Smallholder, XI, 362; XIX, 83
Small House at Allington, The, XII, 38
XVI, 449, *451*
Smallman, X, 8
Smedley, F. E., XII, *Frank Fairleigh*, 53, 57
Smiles, Samuel, XII, 33, *56*
XVII, *Self-Help*, 24, 25

Smillie, Bob, XI, 18, 33, *50*, 60, 63, *63*, 68
XX, 176
Smillie, Robert, XX, 176
Smith (Foreign Legion), XI, 343
Smith, A. Clark (corr), XVI, 284(sy)
Smith, C. A., XI, "Power and State", 40,
40; 60, *63*, 394, *394*
XIII, 60
XVI, 3, *152*, *155*
Smith, David Nichol, XIV, 253, *253*, *299*
XV, 306, *307*
Smith, Dodie, XV, *Dear Octopus*, 246, *246*
Smith, D. Pearson, XIII, 5
Smith, Frank (corr), XVI, 387
Smith, James C., XVI, L. to *Manchester
Evening News*, 241
Smith, J. C. and Herbert J. C. Grierson,
XVI, *A Critical History of English Poetry*,
Rev: 474–5
Smith, John, XX, *158*, *159*
Smith, Joseph (Brides-in-the-Bath murderer),
XI, 160
XVII, 400
XVIII, 108, 109
Smith, Lloyd Logan Pearsall, XIX, 408
Smith, May, XV, "Psychology 6?" (B), *300*
Smith, Mikeal, XI, 97, *98*
Smith, Peter Duval, XIX, 15
Smith, Stevie (= Florence Margaret Smith),
XIV, L: 113, 201, 274; 77, 85, *113*; "It
was a cynical babe" (B), 80–1
XIV, "Poems from France", 115; *114*,
115, *115*
Smith Sydney, X, *426*
Smithfields, X, 257
"Smoke Bellew", XVII, 303
Smoke Mortar, XII, 339
'Smoking-Room Story, A', XIX, *486*, *487*
XX, Notes and layout, 189–93, 200, 207;
Unfinished draft, ed. note: 193; *194–7*;
Conjectural fair copy, 198–200; *85*
Smolensk, XIII, 147, 171
Smollett, Peter, XX, 103, *103*, 255, 323;
NKVD codename, 242
Smollett, Tobias, X, *Peregrine Pickle*, 309; *Sir
Launcelot Greaves*, 521; 117, 195, 307
XII, 40
XVI, 'Tobias Smollett: Scotland's Best
Novelist', 408–10;
The Expedition of Humphry Clinker, 408;
Peregrine Pickle, 275, 408, 409; *Roderick
Random*, 408, 409, 410; *Sir Launcelot
Greaves*, 408
Smuts, Field Marshall Jan Chrisiaan, XIII,
283, *284*
XIV, *48*, 128, *129*
XIX, 227
Smyth, V. C., Brig. J. G., XVII, 205

Cumulative Index

XX, 54, 69, 128, 325
Stalin: An Appraisal of the Man and His
Influence, XVIII, 254, 304–5, *306*
Stalin and Eternal Russia, XVI, *427*
Stalin and German Communism, XX, *86,* 89,
93, 109, 137, 220 (*Orwell's 1949 reading*)
Stalin: A Political Biography, XX, 138, *139,*
221 (*Orwell's 1949 reading*)
Stalin Canal, XI, 369, *369*
Stalingrad, XIII, 412, 413, 440, 453, 476,
488, 489, 515
    XIV, 8, 32, 46, 56–7, 61, 71, 93, 109–10,
    126, 138–9, 171, 194, 202–3, 242, 257,
    258, 304, 305, 350, 361
    XVI, 414
Stalinisme en Espagne, Le, XVII, *115*
Stalino, XIV, 361
Stalin Prize (for novel), XVII, 295
"Stalin's Promise" (Warsaw Uprising),
    XVI, 362–3
Stalin's Russia, XX, 220 (*Orwell's 1949 reading*)
Stalin-Wells Talk: The Verbatim Record, and a
    Discussion (by G. B. Shaw, H. G. Wells,
    J. M. Keynes and others), XI, *160*
Stalky & Co, XII, 61, 62, 77, 80, 149
"Stalky at Beton", X, 54
Standing, Michael, XIII, 9
Stanwyck, Barbara, XII, 507
Stapledon, Olaf, XVII, L. to Orwell 455;
    455
    XX, *99,* 256
Stapledon, Sir R. George, XVI, *Disraeli and*
    the New Age, Rev: 71–2
Star, The, XVI, 386, 387
    XVII, 147
    XX, 169–70
Starkie, Enid, X, *Baudelaire,* Rev: 320–1;
    XVI, 510
Starkie, Walter, X, *Don Gypsy,* Rev: 487
Starobielsk massacre, XX, 324
Starobielsk Prison Camp, XVII, *90*
    XVIII, 137, *138,* 215
Statement of Orwell's Assets, XX, 217–8
Statistician (corr), XVI, 153–4
"Status of Women in Europe" ("Women of
    the West") (B), XIV, 98, 99
Stead, James, X, *Treasure Trek,* Rev: 486–7
Steadman, Ralph, XVII, *314;* XVIII, *123*
Stechert-Haffner (publisher), XX, *158*
Steedman, George, XVII, 298
Steel, Flora Annie, XVII, *On the Face of the*
    Waters, 244; *243*
Steel Man in India, A, XVII, Rev: 217
Steer, G. L., XI, *The Tree of Gernika°,* Rev:
    112
Stein, Gertrude, X, 268
Steinbeck, John, XIV, 141, 142, 311

XIX, *The Grapes of Wrath,* 448
XX, 256
Stellenbosch, XIII, 154, *160*
Stendhal (= Henri Beyle), X, *La Chartreuse*
    de Parme, 309, 314, 521; 395, 519
    XII, *La Chartreuse de Parme,* 274; *Le Rouge*
    et le Noir, 274; 121, 203, 274
Stendhal, XI, Rev: 378–80
    Le Rouge et Noir, 379; *La Chartreuse de*
    Parme, 379, 380
Sten gun, XIII, 452, *453,* 457
    XIV, 52
    XV, 93
Stepanek, Karl, XII, 543
Stephen, Campbell, XI, 63, *63*
Stephen Ayres, XII, Rev: 143–4
Stephen Hero XVI, *291*
Stephens, A. (corr), XIX, *119*
Stephens, James, XIV, "W. B. Yeats: *The*
    Hour Glass" (B), 357; 354, 355, *355, 357*
    XV, L: 170, 174; 23, 24, *186;*
    "Yeats: *The Hour Glass*" (B), 32, 71, *71;*
    "Shaw: [no topic]" (B), 170, 186
Stephenson, George, XVII, 25
Stephenson, James (= James Stephens?), XV,
    23
Stepney, XII, 273
Stern, Kultur Journal, Die, XIX, *416*
Sterndale-Bennett, Joan, XII, 365, 366
    XIII, 431, *431*
Sterne, Laurence, *Tristram Shandy,* XI, *160;*
    XVI, *385*
Stevens, Geoffrey W., X, 278
Stevens, George and Stanley Unwin, *Best-*
    Sellers, XI, Rev: 407–9
Stevenson, Robert Louis, XII, 205
    XVI, 293
    XVII, *Novels and Stories,* Rev: 389–90
    (*titles not indexed*)
Stewart, Andrew, XIX, 214
Stewart, Desmond Stirling, XVI, *453, 454*
Stewart, Neil, XI, *The Fight for the Charter,*
    Rev: 99
Stewart, Oliver, XIII, "Aviation" (B),
    Discussion with Peter Masefield, 372,
    373, 443
Stewart, P., XVII, 206
Stewart's Cafe, X, 213, 216
Stidwell, Charles, XV, 256
Stiffkey, Rector of, XII, 151; XVII, 256,
    260
Stilwell, Gen. Joseph ("Vinegar Joe"), XIII,
    251   XVI, 254
Stirling, Edward, XII, 519
Stirling, Pamela, XII, 519
Stirling W. F., XVI, L? 188, 261
Stockton-on-Tees, XVII, 101, 105

Cumulative Index

Szewczenko (and Sevcenko and Cherniatync'kyi), Ihor, XVIII, L. to Orwell, 235; *237*
XIX, L: 73, 85; L. to Orwell, 72 (sy and extracts), 85 (sy and extracts); *73*, 206, 224

Tablet, XVI, 81
XVII, 417
XVIII, 106–7
XIX, 339, *339*
Tabori, Paul, XVIII, L: 517; *517*
Tabouis, Geneviève, XI, 184, 368, *368*
Taddert, XI, *322*, 324, 325, 326, 425
Taganrog, XIV, 350, *352*
Tagore, Rabindranath, XIV, "First Jasmines" (B), 78, 79; *334*, 335
XV, "*The King of the Dark Chamber*" (Indian play) (B), 120
Tahmankar, D. V. (J?), XIII, "The News" (B), 103
Take Back Your Freedom, XII, Rev D: 242–3; *244*
Taki, Zahra, XIII, "The Hand that Rocks the Cradle", 53; *54*
XIV, Interviewing Leonora Lockhart, "Basic English" (B), 71
Takungpao ("The Imperial"), XVIII, 29
Talbot, XIV, 207
Talbot Rice, Tamara, XIII, L: 363; 289, *290*, 344, 352, *353*, 400
XIV, L. to Bokhari, *342* (summary); 327
Tale of a Tub, A, XVI, 280; XVIII, 418, 419
'Tale of John Flory, The', X, 94
Tale of Two Cities, A, XVI, 451
Tales (Edgar Allan Poe), XX, 64, 219 (*Orwell's 1949 reading*)
Tales of a Grandfather, XVI, 498
Tales of Mean Streets, XVIII, 10, *11*
Tales of Mystery and Imagination, X, 308, 389
Tales of St Austin's, XVII, 55
Tales Out of School, XX, 221 (*Orwell's 1949 reading*)
Tales Told by Shem and Shaun, XII, 128
'Talk' to Oxford University English Club, XV, ed. note: 10
TALKING TO INDIA: *A Selection of English Language Broadcasts to India*, ed. by Orwell: XIII, 86, 92, *94*, 209, 427
XV, ed. note: 320–1; 'Introduction', 322–3; A Note on Contributors, 323–4; Review by Narayana Menon, *324* (summary);
39,*40*, 43, 151, 172, 338, 339
XVI, *23*, 232
XVII, royalties, ed. note: 295, 463, 464
XVIII, 322

XX, 225
Talks Booking Forms, XIII, ed note: 51; not indexed as such
Talks for India (Brander's Report), XV, 353
Tallents, Sir Stephen, XIII, 7
Talmey, Allene, XVIII, "*Vogue* Spotlight [on Orwell]", 396; *396*
Tambimuttu, Meary J., XIII, "The Man in the Street" (B), 56, 60
"The British Press" (B), 79, 96
"T. S. Eliot" (B), 291; text: *Talking to India*, XV, 321
"Augustus John" (B), T: 366; *366*, 368
"An Open Letter to a Marxist" (B), 369, 492;
36, *56*, 165
XIV, 'Voice 5' (B), 211, 212; 15
XV, 57, 166, 172, 321, 323
XVI, 471
"Tamil Newsletter" (B), XIII, 13, 16, 83, 85, 174, 198
'Tamil Newsletter' (B), XV, 25, ed. note: 74, 103, 160, 161, 176, 226, 355;
1: 74; 2: 84; 3: 90; 4: 96; 5: 101; 6: 113; 7: 120; 8: 132; 9: 137; 10: 152; 11: 159; 12: 164; 13: 170; 14: 172; 15: 177; 16: 183; 17: 197; 18: 204; 19: 206; 23: 248; 24: 253; 25: 267; 26: 273; 27: 291; 28: 301; 29: 302; 30: 305; 31: 331; 32: 340
"*Taming of the Shrew, The*" (B), XV, 301
Taming of the Shrew, The, XII, Rev D: 526–7
Tanaka Giichi, Baron, XIII, 98, *99*
Tandy, Jessica, XII, 180
Tangier, XI, 193, 194, *195*, 197, 198, 199, 201, 269, 326, 345
XII, 183, 198, 313, 452, 469, 501, *501*
Tangier Gazette & Morocco Mail, XI, 194
Tanks: Churchill, XIV, 360, *362*; Tiger, 360, *362*
Tapsell, Walter, XI, 34, 35
Tara Arts Group, XIV, *339*
Tarakan, XIII, 125
Tarbert (and East and West Tarbert), XVIII, 308, 323
XIX, 8, 123, 167, 168, 410, 413, 469
Tarioff (USSR), XI, 381
Tarkington, Booth, XVII, 348
XVIII, *Penrod*, 494
Tarr, XVII, 349
Tartarin of Tarascon (Alphonse Daudet), XII, 369
Tarzan of the Apes (Edgar Rice Burroughs), XI, 408
XII, 60, 69, 216, 229, 257, 286
Tata Steel Works, XVII, 217
Tate, Harry, Jnr., XII, 166
Tate, Harry, Snr., XII, *167*

514

Cumulative Index

Cumulative Index

INDEX

As I Please Topics

Orwell's 'As I Please' columns have no indications of the topics discussed. Although names and places are listed in the indexes, it was thought that it might be helpful to readers if a list were given here of topics discussed. It is stressed that the descriptions given here are editorial.

INDEX

London Letters: Topics

Topics are not always given sub-titles in Orwell's London Letters for *Partisan Review* (January 1941 to May 1946). It was thought that it might be helpful to readers if editorial descriptions of topics Orwell discussed were provided for the Letters. Topics are not as readily separated out as they are for 'As I Please' so that, in addition to bearing in mind the caution that these are not Orwell's subject headings, it is important to appreciate how selective and arbitrary are the descriptions given here. The first page of a reference follows the volume number. Footnote references are in italic

Supplementary Index

INDEX OF TOPICS

The indexes to volumes 10–20 and the cumulative index in the main list names of people, places, institutions, books, articles, publishers, political parties, and the like; the indexes are not indexes of topics. However, it was thought that it might be helpful to index certain topics, e.g., rationing, and some other items listed might be argued as really being topics. As an aid to finding such items this list has been prepared. It includes what are certainly topics but also items that might not be thought by readers to fall within the strict interpretation of names of people, institutions, etc., for example, Albertine rose. Reference to the items listed here can be found in the cumulative index.

Supplementary Index

INDEX
Serials

This index lists all those serials (not books) in which Orwell's poems, articles, essays, and letters (including those of which he was only one of the signatories) were published in his lifetime. After each serial is the volume number in which an item appears, followed by the first (or only) page of text. Some publications changed their names but items are listed under the names of the journals at the time they appeared; cross-references are given to alternative names of periodicals. Items not published in Orwell's lifetime or untraced are so indicated. Some articles were printed in more than one serial and these are listed under each periodical with, where necessary, a reference to the page and footnote giving details of reprinting.

A few items closely associated with Orwell have been listed; their page numbers are enclosed in square brackets. Page numbers of letters and manifestos signed by a number of people are enclosed in round brackets. For correspondence arising from Orwell's articles and reviews, see the volume and cumulative indexes.

Supplementary Index

'every book is a failure'

George Orwell, 'Why I Write', XVIII, 320

3738. APPENDIX 15
Articles and Letters Additional to the Second Edition

Vol. XV, p. 249

2278A. Lord David Cecil to W. J. Turner
Handwritten; undated

On 23 September 1943, Orwell signed a contract with W. J. Turner (see *1743*, *n. 1*; XIV/237) as editor of the series 'Britain in Pictures', to be published by Collins. Although Orwell seems to have completed his text by 22 May 1944, the book was much delayed and not published until August 1947. See *2278*, *2475* and *3253*. The first letter from Lord David Cecil (see *1791*, *n. 6*, XIV/289) throws an interesting light on Cecil's attitude to Orwell. The letters are undated but must have been written between the time Orwell submitted his text and Turner's death in 1946. Cecil had broadcast on T. S. Eliot in June/July 1943 under Orwell's aegis: see *2042* and *2149* (XV/82 and 152). He wrote the first book in the 'Britain in Pictures' series, *The English Poets* (1941), and was to have written *English Conversation* with Lettice Fowler, but that was not published. The second letter can only be assumed to be referring to the first, but the words 'that you had the interest of the country at heart' may refer to Cecil's stating that publication of Orwell's book would be 'an unpatriotic act on our part'. The two letters are handwritten from New College, Oxford; the handwriting is not always easy to decipher.

Dear Turner,

I am most flattered you should ask me to write the book. But I literally cannot promise it: I haven't the time with a book of my own and couldn't consider hers. I should just let you down again if I promised. I am so sorry.

In these circumstances perhaps I should not advise. But, as a member of the advisory committee [of Britain in Pictures], I feel in conscience, bound to urge you strongly *not* to accept Orwell's book. Britain in Pictures has built itself up, under your most imaginative & judicious guidance, a great reputation at home & abroad as an impartial account of things English.

Now Orwell's book is not only extremely partisan but also presents England to the foreigner in the most unfavourable light, guilty of all the sins of feudal archaic snobbery of which she is most frequently accused especially in America. I spend a great deal of my time at Brains Trusts[1] etc in refuting precisely the attack he, Orwell, makes. I think it would be a really mischievous thing if his book came out under this auspicious and very impartial & respected a series. In any case some of this book, especially the extremely undesirable reference to the monarchy, must be cut. But cutting is no use. It is simply a political pamphlet and in no way an adequate picture of it's[0] subject. I do not think a counter [?] book meets the case. Britain in Pictures should not be a platform for political debate. It is a series for presenting England's achievements. This factious & inaccurate pamphlet only blackens England's reputation. I do sincerely feel that to publish it would be an unpatriotic act on our part.

Yours sincerely,
David Cecil

1. *The Brains Trust* was a popular BBC radio programme: see *2490, n. 1* (XVI/260).

2278B. Lord David Cecil to W. J. Turner
Handwritten;   undated

Dear Turner,
I am so very sorry to have offended you. Believe [me] it was quite unintentional: & I do not know why I have. Of course I did not doubt for a moment that you had the interest of the country at heart. Did I say anything that implied it? If so please accept my apologies. Why I wrote was that I felt [as] a member of the advisory committee & with my name on the list, you would expect rightly that I should give you my views on the matter.

As a matter of fact I was longing to know what you thought of what I said. I should be most interested to discuss it further.

Yours,
David Cecil

Vol. XVI, p. 99

2420A. To Daniel George
17 February 1944   Typewritten

Tribune

Dear Daniel George,[1]
I'm sorry I didn't write to thank you for the loan of "The New America[n] Credo",[2] which I have studied with interest, I will see that you get it back. I think it was from this that Nathan & Mencken[3] evolved their idea of collecting "Americana"[4] which the New Statesman afterwards copied.

Yours,
[Signed] Geo. Orwell
George Orwell

1. Daniel George Bunting, literary critic who wrote under his first two names; this letter and *2451A* and *2593A* are addressed to D. G. Bunting although their greetings are to Daniel George. He was principal reader to Jonathan Cape and strongly urged publication of *Animal Farm*; see *2494, n. 1* (XVI/266).
2. *The New American Credo: a contribution to the interpretation of the national mind* by G. J. Nathan and H. L. Mencken, 1930.
3. George Jean Nathan (1882–1958), very influential dramatic critic and journalist. H. L. Mencken (1880–1956), an important editor (particularly of the *American Mercury* 1924–28, for

which Nathan also wrote), literary and music critic, and journalist. He was the author of *The American Language* (1919; 4th edn, 1936).
4. *Americana*, edited by H. L. Mencken, 1925 and 1926.

Vol. XVI, p. 150

2451A. To Daniel George
10 April 1944   Typewritten

Tribune

Dear Daniel George,
Is the book in French?[1] If so I don't think we ought to review it, but it is O.K. if it is a translation.

Yours,
[Signed] Geo. Orwell
George Orwell

1. Unidentified.

Vol. XVI, p. 431

2563B. [Ivor Brown] to Dr Thomas Jones, CH
14 October 1944   Typewritten (unsigned carbon copy)

Dear T. J.,[1]
I would be very grateful for your opinion on this review by George Orwell, which I held out of the paper this week.[2] It came in very late and there was not time to talk it over with him. It seems to me that the whole tone of it breathes a distaste for christianity, which would be offensive to a great many of our readers and, almost certainly, to Lord Astor. I dont,[0] myself, complain as a member of the Faith who is pained, but simply as the Editor of a paper having a tradition of Protestant christianity, which I believe the Chairman of Directors is eager to maintain. That does not mean that a reviewer like Orwell need be barred from such topics, but it does mean that he should endeavour to express himself in a different way.

The effect his review had on me was this: I felt that the reader who is a churchman, or chapelman, would say to himself "This man so dislikes us and our ideas that we will never get any justice out of him". I may be quite wrong in feeling this and that is why I am asking your opinion. Do you think the review as a whole is likely to create the impression that I have suggested, and that a few minor alterations would put it right, or do you think that a few changes, such as I have pencilled in, would put the matter right?

I am sorry to trouble you, but this is a case where the atmosphere built up by a review is of great importance, and I very much want your sense of the atmosphere.

Yours ever,

1. Dr Thomas Jones (1870–1955; CH), was described by Crick as 'Lloyd George's famous Cabinet Secretary' (425). In 1939 he had been a prime mover in the establishment of the Council for the Encouragement of Music and the Arts, the forerunner of the Arts Council. Orwell wrote to him about 20 March 1943 (*1043*).
2. This must refer to *Beyond Personality* by C. S. Lewis, which *The Observer* did not publish. It was set in type and the review is published in XVI/437–9 (*2567*) from galley-proofs. When the first edition of *The Complete Works* was published it was not known why the review did not appear (see *2567, n. 1*). Following the appearance in 'As I Please', 46, 27 October 1944 (*2568*) of Orwell's discussion of C. S. Lewis's apologetics, there was a quite lively correspondence; see XVI/422–4.

Vol. XVI, p. 502

2593A. To Daniel George
28 December 1944   Typewritten

Tribune

Dear Daniel George,
George Orwell asked me to return the enclosed book, "The New American Credo"[1] to you and to thank you very much indeed for the loan. He enjoyed it immensely, but is very sorry that he kept it so long.

Yours sincerely,
[Signed] Sally McEwan[2]

1. See *2420A* above.
2. Sally McEwan (d. 1987) was Orwell's secretary at *Tribune*. For a hint at their relationship, see *2634, n. 1* (XVII/89). For her stay at Barnhill, see especially *3027, n. 1* (XVIII/340).

Vol. XVII, p. 64

2625A. Paris Puts a Gay Face on her Miseries
The Observer, 25 February 1945

Paris, February 24
One Paris correspondent after another has dilated on the food shortage, but it can hardly be mentioned too often. It is the dominant factor in most people's lives, and by diverting attention from larger issues—perhaps even by rousing resentment against Britain and the United States—it is capable of directly affecting the political situation.

Every newspaper one looks at contains complaints about food distribution. One must realise that for two months the average Parisian has not seen butter, and for far longer than that he has never had enough of anything except vegetables and a blackish bread, which probably contains rye and barley.

The tiny meat ration is often unobtainable, sugar is very scarce, coffee (even in the form of roasted acorns) is almost non-existent, and cigarettes are costly rarities unless you happen to be friends with an American soldier.

A litre of the coarsest wine, if you can get hold of it, costs the equivalent of eight shillings. More serious is the lack of milk, even tinned milk, for the children. And there is no coal for domestic purposes. There is gas for cooking at certain hours, but the gas situation has presumably not been improved by the recent flooding of the Seine, which has made it impossible for the coal barges to pass under the bridges.

With all this, the first remark of every newcomer is that Paris manages to put a very good face upon its miseries. In the centre of the town, where American money oozes in all directions and a lively Black Market flourishes, it would almost be possible to imagine that nothing is wrong. There are no taxis and the streets are only half lit, but the girls are as carefully made up as ever, and the hat shops and jewellery stores have almost their ancient glitter. Out in the working-class suburbs things are naturally worse. Glassless windows are common, many of the cafés are shut, the food shops have a miserable appearance.

A grocer's window will sometimes contain nothing at all except a list of the goods which are out of stock. Yet even in the poorest quarters the surface aspect of things is less bad than I would have expected. Paris is not dingier or more neglected than present-day London, and considerably less battered. And in several days of wandering to and fro in all kinds of quarters I have not yet seen a barefooted person, and not many who were conspicuously ragged. Probably half the women have stockings, and though wooden shoes are common they do not predominate.

The signs of privation are obvious enough if one knows where to look for them. The children of five or six look fairly sturdy, but the very young babies are terribly pale. The pigeons, once so numerous in Paris streets, have almost completely disappeared. They have been eaten. When a plane tree on the sidewalk is lopped, one sees elegantly dressed women waiting to collect bundles of twigs for firewood. Yet the people carry themselves with a peculiar dignity which they perhaps learned under the German occupation. On the Metro they eye your foreign uniform with an air that seems to say, "We know you are well fed and have plenty of cigarettes. We know, you are the possessor of soap, and even of coffee. But let us pretend we are on an equal footing."

It is an interesting fact that there are almost no beggars—certainly far fewer than there were before the war. One is not even asked for cigarettes, though if one offers a cigarette spontaneously it is accepted with pathetic gratitude.

Almost as soon as I set foot in Paris I returned, as anyone would, to the quarters I had known best in the days before the war. Round Notre Dame it was almost the same as ever. The little bookstalls along the river bank were just the same, the print-sellers were even selling the same prints: the innumerable anglers were still catching nothing, the menders of mattresses were as busy as ever on the quays.

Further south, in the Latin Quarter, things were more changed. The various foreign colonies, even including the Arabs who used to do most of the navvy work of Paris, seemed all to have disappeared.

In the big Montparnasse cafés, instead of a cosmopolitan mob of artists, there sat middle-class French families thriftily sipping at glasses of fruit juice. The Panthéon had been spattered by machine-gun bullets. In the old quarter between the Boulevard Saint Michel and the Rue Monge I could at first find only one shop (an undertaker's) which was in exactly the same position as before.

Then, to my delight, I came upon a little bistro which I used to know and which had not changed hands. The proprietor welcomed me with open arms, refused to take more than half the cigarettes I offered him, and brought out a bottle of something that was very drinkable though it was not what its label declared it to be.

Across the street the tiny hotel where I used once to live[1] was boarded up and partly ruinous. It appeared empty. But as I came away, from behind the broken window pane of what used to be my own room, I saw two hungry-looking children peeping out at me, just like wild animals.[2]

1. Orwell lived in a small hotel in the rue du Pot de Fer, the eastern end of which is less than 200 metres west of the rue Monge at Monge Metro station.
2. This article, like others in the series, had sub-headings ('Streets Half Lit', 'Pale Babies', and 'The Little Bistro'). These are almost certainly the work of a sub-editor and have not been included here or elsewhere.

Vol. XVIII, p. 374

3049A. 'The True Pattern of H. G. Wells'

Manchester Evening News, 14 August 1946

According to his Payments Book, Orwell completed this obituary by 7 November 1945: see XVII, p. 476. He was paid £12 12s and, when *The Complete Works* was first published, it had not been traced. In *Notes and Queries*, Vol. 245 (September 2000), pp. 343–5, Professor Patrick Parrinder reported that the obituary was to be found in the Wells Collection, Rare Books Room, University of Illinois at Urbana-Champaign, and he kindly provided the editor with a copy. As the entry in the Payments Book shows, it was written by 7 November 1945; six months later, on 2 May 1946, the *Manchester Evening News* stated that Orwell was taking a rest from journalism for six months (XVIII, p. 257); the obituary was published within that period, three months after the announcement was made. The obituary is given half-a-dozen sub-headings but because these were probably the work of a sub-editor, not Orwell, they have been omitted here, as has been done for Orwell's other articles and reviews; typically the sub-editor has placed a sub-heading in the middle of a connected argument, something no author would do, and is probably responsible for splitting the essay into very short paragraphs (see, for example, the discussion of *Tono-Bungay*), contrary to Orwell's practice. Book titles have been italicised.

When a great man dies his career falls into perspective, and one is able to judge as one often cannot while he is still alive which parts of his achievement are the most significant and the likeliest to endure.

H. G. Wells was a man who preserved his energy and his intellectual curiosity up to the very last, and his tendency for many years had been to think of himself as a publicist and a philosopher rather than a mere artist. As a result his later activities have somewhat obscured the sheer literary brilliance of his earlier work.

Wells's originality and the special flavour of his books are partly traceable to the peculiarities of his upbringing. He was born in 1866 at Bromley, in Kent, the child of poor though not strictly working-class parents. His mother had been a housekeeper and his father was a gardener and professional cricketer who was afterwards the proprietor of a small shop.

This shop formed the background of Wells's earliest memories. He himself was apprenticed to a draper at 13, and underwent the miserable and ludicrous experiences which he afterwards described in *Kipps*. However, he was too gifted and too ambitious a boy to stay long in a job that he hated.

He had a genius for passing examinations and thanks to a series of scholarships he was soon able to escape into quite a different environment. For some years he studied at the Royal College of Science at South Kensington, then spent a short period as a teacher, and then, while still a very young man, began to make his living by writing for the magazines.[1]

Wells's two great sources of inspiration were on the one hand his memories of the friendly, comic, shabby-genteel, background of his boyhood, and on the other hand the scientific vision of the world which he had acquired at South Kensington.

The best of his scientific romances belong to his very early years. *The Time Machine* was his second published book, and *The Island of Dr. Moreau*, which future generations may well regard as his masterpiece, was his third. *The Invisible Man, The First Men in the Moon*, and *The War of the Worlds* had all been written before he was forty. A long series of brilliant short stories, "The Crystal Egg," "The Plattner Story," "In the Abyss," "The Man Who Made Diamonds," and many others, were also written at about this time.

It was by a sort of deviation from the scientific theme—a temporary lapse into magic—that he produced two rather unsuccessful fantasies, *The Sea Lady* and *The Wonderful Visit*.

It is often said that a creative writer has about fifteen years during which he is at the height of his powers, and Wells is a good illustration of this. Nearly all his best work was done between 1895 and 1910. During that period he was still near enough to his origins to produce such brilliant comedies of lower-middle-class life as *Kipps, The History of Mr Polly*, and—slightly less successful than the other two—*The Wheels of Chance*. The essential background of all of these is the same: The Kentish landscape, which Wells so deeply loved, and the draper's shop, which he did not love but knew only too well. He reached an even higher level in *Love and Mr. Lewisham*, where his two great themes—

lower-middle-class life, and scientific curiosity—are successfully brought together.

This book, which is moving as well as comic, centres round the science college where Wells had spent happy and formative years. And together with *Love and Mr. Lewisham* one can class certain of the short stories; for instance "A Slip under the Microscope"[2] and "Miss Winchelsea's Heart," stories which are among the best things of their length in the English language, though they have never had quite the praise they deserve.

From about 1905 onwards Wells began to produce books which were more definitely full-dress novels. He reached his peak as a novelist in *Tono-Bungay*, which was published in 1911.[3] Although it is full of obvious faults, *Tono-Bungay* is perhaps the most serious and sincere book that Wells ever wrote. It tells of a rather engaging little swindler who makes a vast fortune out of a worthless patent medicine and is finally ruined.

But there is more in it than that. Wells once again makes use of his boyhood memories, more successfully than ever, and his deep disgust with the planless, greedy society of the early twentieth century supplies a sort of driving force which can be felt on every page.

But in spite of the enormous number of novels that he produced, and in spite of his skill in writing dialogue and in reproducing certain kinds of atmosphere, Wells was not at his best in the "straight" novel. He had not quite enough patience or sympathy with his characters, and there were certain important classes of human being whom he was congenitally incapable of understanding.

The series of more ambitious novels—*Marriage, The New Machiavelli, The Research Magnificent, The Wife of Sir Isaac Harman* and others, which followed *Tono-Bungay*, must be written down as failures.

So must various novels written during and immediately after the last war, such as *Joan and Peter, Mr. Britling Sees It Through*, and *The Secret Places of the Heart*. In these novels Wells makes a grandiose effort to express his ideas about contemporary society, but on the whole they are unconvincing as well as shapeless. His sureness of touch deserted him when he had to describe people whose outlook and background were widely different from his own.

By the world at large, at any rate outside the English-speaking countries, Wells is probably thought of chiefly as the creator of Utopias. With his scientific training and his social non-conformity it was natural that he should attempt not only to construct imaginary worlds but to make detailed forecasts of the future.

Anticipations[4] and *A Modern Utopia* were his earliest efforts in this direction. So far as mechanical progress goes, Wells's predictions have often been brilliantly justified.

In *The World Set Free* [1914], for example, he made a sensationally accurate forecast of the atomic bomb. But when it came to predicting the direction in which human society would develop he was less successul. In most of his Utopias he errs by being too sane. He assumes that progress will be governed mainly by rational impulses, and he does not show much interest in the existing political structure and the concrete methods by which it might be changed. He never, indeed, had any patience with the detail of politics, and his brief membership of the Fabian Society merely led to a resounding quarrel. In some of his Utopias—*In the Days of the Comet*, for instance—he invokes a miracle or a cataclysm to bring the new society into being.

In others, such as *The Dream*, or *Men Like Gods*, it is simply placed in the far future or on some non-terrestrial plane, with no explanation of how it arose.

But there is one Utopia book which stands in a rather different class from the others. This is *The Sleeper Awakes*.[5] In this book Wells drops all traces of optimism and forecasts a highly organised totalitarian society based quite frankly on slave labour. In some ways it comes extremely close to what is actually happening, or appears to be happening, in the modern world, and it is in any case an astonishing feat of detailed imaginative construction. Wells himself, for some reason, never rated *The Sleeper Awakes* highly, and the extent to which it anticipates Aldous Huxley's *Brave New World* and other pessimistic Utopia books has not been generally recognised. Wells belonged to the generation which had won the battle for freedom of thought against Victorian obscurantism, and by temperament he was an optimist. Up to 1914 he probably believed—though with fairly frequent misgivings—that mankind was assured of a reasonable and orderly future. The war of 1914–18 shook his confidence, and from then onwards he became increasingly intent on preaching the need for world organisation.

This theme had often appeared in his earlier books, but his first full-length sermon on the text "unite or perish" was his *Outline of History*, the first version of which appeared in 1920.[6] However hasty, inaccurate and, in places, biased the *Outline of History* may be, it is still a remarkable book, one of the few attempts that have ever been made at writing universal history. It belongs in the same class as Winwood Reade's *Martyrdom of Man*,[7] a rather forgotten book, which Wells greatly admired.

Right up to his death Wells's output continued to be enormous, but it would be idle to pretend that the later books can compare with the earlier ones. Almost everything that he wrote after 1920 was a variation on the same theme—the need for world government and for a radical change in the intellectual habits of mankind—and though he continued to write novels the old magic was no longer in them.

No writer of our time, at any rate no English writer, has so deeply influenced his contemporaries as Wells. He was so big a figure, he has played so great a part in forming our picture of the world, that in agreeing or disagreeing with his ideas we are apt to forget his purely literary achievement. In his own eyes it was a secondary, almost unimportant, thing. He had faults of intellect and of character, but very few writers have ever had less literary vanity.

1. Wells won a scholarship to the Normal School of Science, later the Royal College of Science, South Kensington, London, in 1884. (A 'Normal School' was a Teacher-training college, named from the French, *école normale*.) He studied under T. H. Huxley and graduated from London University in zoology and geology. He then taught biology until 1893 when he published *A Text-book of Biology* in two volumes for the University Correspondence College Tutorial series. In the same year he published, with R. A. Gregory, *Honours Physiography*. Some of his early work was published in the *Science Schools Journal*.

2. Orwell dramatised 'A Slip under the Microscope' for the BBC's Indian Service, 6 October 1943; see XV, pp. 256–65.
3. *Tono-Bungay* was published in New York in 1908 and in England in 1909. Orwell omitted the hyphen.
4. *Anticipations of the Reaction of Mechanical and Scientific Progress upon Human life and Thought* (1902 for 1901).
5. Orwell regularly gave this title for *When the Sleeper Wakes: A Story of the Years to Come*, 1899.
6. Wells wrote this long book very rapidly. It was first published in twenty-four fortnightly parts, November 1919 to November 1920, with footnotes by other writers. It has been suggested that Wells made use of a manuscript which Florence Deeks submitted to Macmillan in Canada in July 1918. Her book was rejected and when the manuscript was returned to her, certain passages had been marked up. She believed her work had been plagiarised. See A. B. McKillop, *The Spinster & the Prophet: a Tale of H. G. Wells, Plagiarism and the History of the World* (2001), and its review by Allan Massie, *Daily Telegraph*, 10 February 2001. Orwell refers to the book several times, e.g. in 'Wells, Hitler and the World State', *837*, where he describes its 'principle villain' as 'the military adventurer, Napoleon' (p. 538).
7. *The Martyrdom of Man* was published in 1872 by William Winwood Reade (1838–75). Orwell reviewed it on 15 March 1946 (XVIII, pp. 1502). Reade was a nephew of the novelist Charles Reade.

Vol. XIX, p. 274

3351A. To Ivor Brown

20 February 1948   Handwritten

On 18 February 1948, an unsigned letter from Ivor Brown of *The Observer*, questioned Orwell about the review he had submitted of Kenneth Williamson's *The Atlantic Islands*. He had noted that high claims had been made for the book and that Eric Linklater[1] 'puts it very high'. Orwell took no line at all about the book but merely reported what Williamson said. Readers, publishers and authors 'like to see signs of enthusiasm and encouragement for good work, if it is good'. He himself had not read Williamson's book. He asked Orwell if he could 'give a bit more colour to your notice of it should you feel this is justified'.

Ward 3
Hairmyres Hosp.

Dear Ivor Brown,

I'm sorry, but it was an *awful* book. It had all the marks of an amateur's writing, everything jammed in indiscriminately, a sort of matey facetious manner that failed to come off, & a most irritating trick of giving everything its Faeroese name, which meant one had to look up the glossary every few lines. Its only merit was that it was informative about a little-known subject, which I think I indicated. Linklater's introduction didn't impress me as sincere. I thought of saying that the book was stodgy, or heavy going, or words to that effect, but didn't want to be unkind to an amateur.

I am not prepared to give praise on literary grounds to books of this type. One sinks one's standards below zero by pretending that they exist in a literary sense at all. This kind of book (eg.° another you have sent me, about caves in France[2]) are simply bits of topography, or travel diary set down by people who have no idea how to select or to write, & they get boosted because of local patriotism. If one is to review them, I do not see what we can do except to give an exposition.

Yours sincerely
George Orwell

Ivor Brown replied on 24 February saying he quite understood how Orwell felt about that type of book. The review appeared on 29 February 1948 (*3356*).

1. Eric Linklater (Robert Russell; 1899–1974), Scottish novelist (*Juan in America*, 1931), who wrote several war pamphlets (e.g., *The Highland Division*, 1942).
2. *My Caves* by Norbert Casteret, reviewed by Orwell, 14 March 1948 (*3361*).

3715A. The Best Novels of 1949: Some Personal Choices
The Observer, 1 January 1950

In addition to Orwell, the selections were made by John Betjeman, Cyril Connolly, Daphne du Maurier, Lionel Hale, Rosamond Lehmann, Alan Moorehead, William Sansom, Rebecca West, and Francis Wyndham. Only Rebecca West selected *Nineteen Eighty-Four*. This contribution was made over seven months after Orwell's last writing was published (*3625*) and less than a month before he died. The books are listed by Orwell in his reading for 1949 (*3727*) under August, March, and November respectively. *The Naked and the Dead* was also chosen by Connolly. Orwell wrote:

The Naked and the Dead, by Norman Mailer (Wingate). The only war novel of any distinction to appear hitherto. *The Oasis*, by Mary MacCarthy (Horizon[1]). An extremely well constructed short novel with an unfamiliar but interesting subject matter. *The Impossible Shore*, by Robert Kee (Eyre and Spottiswoode). Repportage° rather than a novel, but very convincing and in places moving.

1. The journal, *Horizon*, edited by Cyril Connolly.

3739. Purported Book Recommendations, 1952

Many Are Called by Edward Newhouse has on the front cover of its dust-jacket a recommendation by George Orwell. No evidence exists that Orwell was familiar with Newhouse's work. When commenting favourably in 'How Long is a Short Story' on 7 September 1944 (*2546*) on 'The superiority of contemporary American short-story writers', although Newhouse's first book of stories, *Anything Can Happen*, had been published in 1941 (the second, *The Iron Chain*, would not appear until 1946), he does not mention Newhouse. He mentions, in this context, Damon Runyon, Dorothy Parker, and, stepping back fifteen years, Ring Lardner. American authors he lists in his article as having written outstanding short stories are Edgar Allan Poe, Mark Twain ('The Man Who Corrupted Hadleyburg') and Jack London. Newhouse was born in Budapest in 1911, emigrated to the USA in 1923 and took American citizenship in 1929. He

565

served in the US Army Air Force, 1942–46. *Many Are Called* is a collection of forty-two stories, all but three of which were first published in *The New Yorker*, and was the first of his books of short stories to be published in England. His two earlier books of short stories had been published by Harcourt but this was published by William Sloane in 1951, well after Orwell's death. Gollancz published the book in October 1952. It is possible that Orwell had seen copies of Newhouse's stories in copies of *The New Yorker* (he reviewed *Lady Gregory's Journals* in that periodical on 19 April 1947, *3218*), or that Gollancz had arranged for some stories to be sent to Orwell. However, Orwell does not mention Newhouse in his detailed reading list for 1949. The style of the blurb seems more effusive than one would expect of Orwell and he disliked writing blurbs. 'George Orwell wrote:' is in large display type.

George Orwell wrote: "I am enchanted to come across important writing that also makes such good reading. Eloquence without cant, historic density without the burdens of detail, idiom unmarred by the fashionable yearning after foreheads villainous low—those are all achievements of the first order. The stories have a hard, brilliant clarity that we were accustomed, eighty years ago, to regard as French but have recently come to think of as transatlantic. Mark Twain had it, at his best."

3740. Additional Allusions

The following allusions, some requested by readers, would not readily fit the existing pagination. Because the paperback edition might have a wider readership than the hardback, perhaps these will be handy for some readers. Biblical references are to the King James version. Lineation is of the text lines (ignoring headings and footnotes). Some have been drawn for those contributed by the editor to Bartek Zborski's Polish translation of Orwell's essays. The four Penguins compiled from The Complete Works (Orwell in Spain, Orwell and Politics, Orwell's England, *and* Orwell and the Dispossessed, *published May 2000) contain additional notes. A few errors were introduced into Volume XI of the second edition and corrections to these are noted here.*

Volume IV: Keep the Aspidistra Flying

123/9–12: I considered but rejected the idea of adding what I can only guess was cut from the novel by Victor Gollancz's libel lawyer, Harold Rubinstein. Although I published what follows in *The Library* in 1991 (VI, 13, 137–9), no critic has suggested this passage should be restored—possibly none has noticed the suggestion. Orwell did not mention a cut and it would have required a significant change to the text so I forbore 'garbling' the text as we have it. However, the passage in the novel doesn't really make sense and therefore readers might like to consider this solution. The 'hero', Gordon Comstock, is attempting to seduce Rosemary. He quotes four lines of verse in late medieval French which seems to be from Villon (one of Orwell's and Gordon's pet authors—Gordon has a copy of Villon's poems on his mantelpiece, IV, 30–1) and, though he translates these for Rosemary, Orwell gives no translation for the reader (IV, 123). There is nothing about the lines which would explain why they should not be translated so it must be something about the poem as a whole that struck the libel lawyer who examined the book that it should not be given in full. In fact, the poem is not by Villon. Tracing its source was made easier by finding an edition which made an editorial comment on the significance of 'Ne pain ne voyant qu'aux fenestres' which Orwell mentions in another book, *Down and Out in Paris and London* (I, 121). Here Orwell writes of 'my copy of Villon's poems' and its editor's explanation of this line. The editorial note to which he refers appears in an edition of Villon edited by Pierre Jannet, published several times in the nineteenth century, and which contains 'Poésies attribuées à Villon'. One of the poems, a Rondel attributed to Villon, begins 'Une fois me dictes ouy' and contains the lines given in Orwell's novel. I have often thought that I should have taken my courage in both hands and included all these lines in my edition. Orwell quotes only stanza 2; this is the full text:

> Une fois me dictes ouy,
> En foy de noble et gentil femme;
> Je vous certife, ma Dame,
> Qu'oncques ne fuz tant resjouy.
>
> Veuillez le donc dire selon
> Que vous estes benigne et doulche,
> Car ce doulx mot n'est pas si long
> Qu'il vous face mal en la bouche.
>
> Soyez seure, si j'en jouy,
> Que ma lealle et craintive ame
> Gardera trop mieulx que nul ame
> Vostre honneur. Avez-vous ouy?
> Une fois me dictes ouy.

Did Orwell originally quote all three stanzas and did he translate them in *Keep the Aspidistra Flying*? Orwell seems inadvertently to have transposed 'le donc dire' as 'le dire donc'. The version quoted here is taken from *Oeuvres complètes de François Villon*, ed. Pierre Jannet (Paris, 1876), p. 134.

Volume VIII: Animal Farm

p. 23: In 1946, Dwight Macdonald wrote to Orwell asking him whether he was referring in *Animal Farm* only to the Soviet Union or making a larger statement about the philosophy of revolution. Orwell replied on 5 December 1946 (XVIII, 506–8) that he 'meant the moral [of *Animal Farm*] to be that revolutions only effect a radical improvement when the masses are alert and know how to chuck out their leaders as soon as the latter have done their job. The turning point of the story was supposed to be when the pigs kept the milk and apples for themselves' and he refers to the naval mutiny at Kronstadt in 1921. Shortly afterwards, he added four short speeches to his radio adaptation. These are they (with their speech numbers):

259. CLOVER: Do you think that is quite fair to appropriate the apples?
260. MOLLY: What, keep all the apples for themselves?
261. MURIEL: Aren't we to have any?
262. COW: I thought they were going to be shared equally.

Two live broadcasts were given on 14 and 15 January 1947 and a recording of the first performance was broadcast on 2 February. The BBC, in a mode to which in recent years we have become familiar, knew what was best for the author and us and scored out Orwell's addition, so it was never broadcast. These lines highlight what Orwell regarded as a 'key passage' of *Animal Farm* when he marked up p. 23, lines 5–16 of a copy which he gave to Geoffrey Gorer (see Bernard Crick, *George Orwell: A Life*, 1982, p. 490). I could have rectified this by adapting the radio script to the novel. I was chary of making so radical a change without authority but I did include this account, and the four speeches, in 'A Note on the Text' in the Penguin edition of the novel (1989, pp. xix–xx) and in the Penguin compilation, *Orwell and Politics* (2001, p. 233). However, my reluctance to make this change (and that noted above to *Keep the Aspidistra Flying*) has been a matter of regret to me.

Volume X

45, note 1, line 5: Guinever Buddicom died on 4 February 2002 at Bognor Regis the day after her 95th birthday.

51, *add to note 1*: Orwell's father was sixty when he was commissioned on 13 September 1917. He joined the 51st (Ranchi) Indian Labour Company at Marseilles and was reputedly the oldest Second Lieutenant in the British Army. In *The First Day of the Somme* (1917; 2001), Martin Middlebrook gives some account of Lt. Henry Webber. He joined up in 1914 at the age of 66 and served as a battalion transport officer for the 7th Lancashire Fusiliers. He was killed on 21 July near Mametz Wood; he was then 68.

207, note 2: The school at which Brenda Salkeld taught, St Felix School for Girls, Southwold, after being in existence for 105 years, was threatened with closure in the summer of 2002. However, within a week of this being announced, parents had raised £300,000 to save it (*Daily Telegraph*, 8 and 15 June 2002).

212, note 2: Dennis Collings died in March 2001.

441, note 2, George Garrett: 1896–1966; unemployed much of his life but worked on Liverpool docks from time to time; a seaman, an aspiring writer, and actor. Participated in the industrial troubles in Liverpool, 1921–22, and in the Hunger March of winter 1922, writing about both. See *The Collected George Garrett*, edited by Michael Murphy (1999).

485/6–7, 'I have married a wife': Luke, 14.20.

506, note 2: *add*: The following report appeared in the *Rangoon Gazette* for 22 March 1926 under the heading 'Rogue Elephant Shot': 'Major E. C. Kenny, subdivisional officer, Yamethin, when on tour in the Tatkon township on 16 March 1926, came across a rogue elephant feeding in a plantation grove at Dayouk-ku village 5 miles east of Tatkon and brought it down to the delight of the villagers. The elephant had killed a villager and caused great havoc in the plantations. It is not known whether or not this is the elephant proclaimed by the Bombay Burma Trading Corporation.' The similarities to 'Shooting an Elephant' will by apparent: the killing of a villager, ravaging plantations, the uncertainty as to whether the elephant belongs to a powerful trading company or not, and the little detail about the delight of the villagers. Kenny was not in trouble for his action, however. On 13 September 1926, the *Rangoon Gazette* announced he had been promoted Deputy Commissioner of the Pakokku District. Orwell was stationed at Moulmein when Kenny shot the elephant; he was transferred to Katha (the Kyauktada of *Burmese Days*) on 23 December 1926.

524/4 up: 'the worm who never turned': *3 Henry VI*, 2.2.17.

Volume XI

30/11 up: *in second edition change* establa *to* estaba
omit comma at end of line, after divisiòn
30/9 up: *in second edition change* Enclase *to* Enlase
32/25: *in second edition change* NKVA *to* NKVD
32/4: Bill Alexander was born in 1910 and died in 2000.
36/15: *for* rabid Trotskyists *read* confirmed Trotskyists
50, footnote 6: *omit* Not identified *and substitute this entry (run on from note 5 if necessary)*: 6. Ethel Macdonald (1909–1960), leading social activist in Scotland. During Spanish War she was the English-speaking announcer for CNT in Barcelona; arrested in purge of POUM and CNT, 1937, but escaped and helped others to escape, earning nickname of 'Spanish Pimpernel'.
164, footnote 1: *add date of death*: 1999 (*so* 1897–1999).
174 note 3, 186 note 5, and 305 note 31: *references re* Nin *should be to item* 382, n. 6, *not* 382, n. 5 on p. 60.
174 note 6: *add*: Antonov-Ovsëenko figures in Len Deighton's novel, *Funeral in Berlin* (1964) and in the film version starring Michael Caine as Harry Palmer. The character played in the film by Oscar Homolka, Colonel Stok, is said to have been with Antonov-Ovsëenko at the storming of the Winter Palace (end of chapter 16). Deighton provides a handy appendix (number 4) on the 'Soviet Security Systems' and that also mentions Antonov-Ovsëenko.
212, footnote 1: Robert Fyson suggests that Alec Henderson is a confusion by Orwell of Alec Brown and Philip Henderson. They are referred to

(correctly) next to each other in 'Inside the Whale', XII, 99 (last line of text).

305, note 36, line 1: *add dates of birth and death in brackets after* Montseny: (1905–1994).

312/2: *add superscript 2 for footnote reference after* will prevail" *and make new note:* 2. From Coventry Patmore, 'The Unknown Eros'.

314: *add to end of footnote 1:* He was the most prominent British intellectual to support anarchism before World War II and was closely associated with anarchism until he was knighted.

332, footnote 2: *omit first sentence – i.e.:* John Middleton Murry had . . . *to* . . . from Oxford University.

341, footnote 1: substitute *Revolt!, jointly edited by for Revolt* [no exclamation mark], edited by

341, footnote 5, line 2: *add after* 'vigorously for it.' *new sentence:* Supported World War II and advocated threatening USSR with Atomic Bomb at start of Cold War.

Volume XII

18, footnote 1, line 7: *add date of death to* Madge: 1996 (1912–1996)

21/4–5, 'the second-best bed [does not] invalidate[s] *Hamlet*': Shakespeare has been rebuked because, in his will, he left his wife their second-best bed. That does not mean that *Hamlet* is a worse play for that. However, the mention of this in the will, though a little puzzling, is not a sign that Shakespeare was mean or the marriage unhappy. In Elizabethan law, Shakespeare's wife would automatically receive the income from one-third of his estate. There was no need to mention the bed so it suggests it was something of special significance to the couple. Some scholars even suggest his wife asked for it to be specially mentioned.

29/19–27: *The History of the Fairchild Family: or the Child's Manual, being a collection of stories to show the importance and effects of a religious education* was written by Mrs Mary Sherwood (née Butt, 1775–1851), and published in 3 volumes, 1818–47. Among her other 'improving' books were *The History of Henry Milner* (4 vols, 1822–37) and *Little Henry and his Bearer Boosy* (1832). The last of these was written when she was living in India, married to her cousin, Henry Sherwood, an army officer. (A bearer was a personal servant.) She lived in India from 1805–16, where she ran schools, adopted orphans, and wrote and published several severely evangelical works; she also lost several babies. She adapted Bunyan's *The Pilgrim's Progress* for Indian readers as *The Indian Pilgrim* (1815). In all, she wrote more than 350 items. In her later years she mainly wrote anti-Roman Catholic works. In September 1932 Orwell asked Brenda Salkeld whether she had read *The Fairchild Family* (X, p. 268).

29/24–5, 'Let dogs delight' is by Isaac Watts (1674–1748), and is from one of his *Divine Songs for Children*, no. 16, 'Against Quarrelling'. Watts is the author of the hymns 'O God, our help in ages past' and 'When I survey the wondrous cross'.

30/last line, 'change of heart': From Auden, 'Sir, No Man's Enemy' (1930): 'New styles of architecture, a change of heart.'

34/24: *The Quarterly Review* was published from 1809 to 1922. It was one of the most important nineteenth-century journals. One of its reviewers was William Ewart Gladstone (1809–1898), four times Liberal Prime Minister. Orwell was fond of the journal and owned ten of the volumes published between 1811 and 1832.

48/21–2, 'the Elephant and Castle version of *Sweeney Todd*': Orwell is probably referring to the version of the melodrama, *Sweeney Todd, the Demon Barber of Fleet Street* performed at the Elephant and Castle Theatre. This may have been that written by Matt Wilkinson, 1870. The theatre was built in 1872 on the site of Newington Butts Theatre, built about 1576. The 1872 theatre was burnt down on 26 March 1878. A second theatre was built the following year. It was used as a music hall but in 1928 became a cinema.

50/16, Barham: Richard Harris Barham (1788–1845) was for a time a minor canon of St Paul's Cathedral. He was noted for his comic and grotesque treatments of medieval legend. *The Ingoldsby Legends*, published under the pen-name, Thomas Ingoldsby, was by far his most successful work. There were three series, 1840–47.

61/24–5, *St. Winifred's*: A novel, the full title of which is *St Winifred's: or the World of School* (1862), by Frederick William Farrar (1831–1903). Farrar was an assistant master then Master (1871–76) of Marlborough College. He left to become Rector of St Margaret's, Westminster Abbey (1876–95). His most famous book is *Eric, or Little by Little* (1858); he also wrote a *Life of Christ* (1874).

71/5 up: Sax Rohmer (= Arthur Henry Sarsfield Ward; 1883–1959) was a prolific author specialising in popular novels often with Chinese settings and characters. He is best known for *The Mystery of Dr Fu-Manchu* (1913) and also, perhaps, for *The Day the World Ended* (1930).

82/25–6, 'every day . . . becomes better and better': Emile Coué (1857–1926), formula of his faith-cures.

82/2–3 up, 'tenth possessor of a foolish face': Richard Savage, 'The Bastard' (1728), line 8 (which has 'transmitter' for 'possessor').

83/27–8, 'sorrows never come too late . . . flies': after lines in last stanza of Thomas Gray, 'Ode on a Distant Prospect of Eton College'.

84/2–3 up, 'mewling and puking in the nurse's arms': *As You Like It*, 2.7.14.

85, footnote 1: *add*: It is now acknowledged that this pun was made by Catherine Winkworth, a Manchester schoolgirl. It was first published in *Punch*, 18 May 1844.

92/11 up, Balaam's ass: Numbers, 22.22–35.

96/13 up, 'tragic sense of life': Miguel de Unamuno y Jugo (1864–1936), Spanish philosopher, *The Tragic Sense of Life in Men and Peoples* (1921; Spanish original, 1913).

98/5–6 up, 'It was an age of eagles and crumpets': this crux has been much better resolved by Dr Robert Fyson than in my note 28. He suggests it should be either 'scones and crumpets' or 'eagles and trumpets' and he points to T. S. Eliot's poem, 'A Cooking Egg' (*Poems*, 1920). The last five lines read (with a break between the first of these and the last four):

> Where are the eagles and the trumpets?
>   Buried beneath some snow-deep Alps.
> Over buttered scones and crumpets
>   Weeping, weeping multitudes
> Droop in a hundred A.B.C.'s.

The 'A.B.C.' was a chain of London teashops, the letters standing for Aerated Bread Company. The teashops no longer exist. (ABC was also, ironically, a process of making artificial manure from alum, blood, and clay dating from 1879.)

125/10–11, 'rendered unto Caesar the things that are God's': parody of 'Render to Caesar the things that are Caesar's, and to God the things that are God's', Mark, 12.17 (and Matthew, 22.21 [which . . . that] and Luke, 20.25 [which . . . which]).

129/1, 'Bohn's cribs': a series of literal translations of classical texts designed especially for schoolchildren.

151/1, 'with a misquotation from Shakespeare': Chamberlain's 'I believe it is peace for our time' on his return from Munich, 30 September 1938, and that he had brought peace with honour, echoed Disraeli in a speech to the House of Commons, 16 July 1878, following his attendance at the Berlin Congress on the Eastern Question: 'Lord Salisbury and myself have brought you back peace—but a peace I hope with honour'. Perhaps in the light of the outcome of the Munich Agreement, Shakespeare's 'Peace is to me a war' (*King John*, 3.1.113) was in Orwell's mind.

151/20–21, 'Shape without form . . . gesture without motion': T. S. Eliot, 'The Hollow Men' (1925), st. 2.

151/2–3 up, 'what have I done for thee, England, my England': W. E. Henley (1849–1903), 'For England's Sake' ('thee' for 'you').

189, note 14: *replace existing note with this*:

14. Possibly Richard Crossman (see *n. 7* above) or Cyril Connolly. Inez Holden suggested Christopher Hollis or a man called Carter, unknown to Orwell's friends. Whether or not Orwell's name was on a police file is unknown. In 1938–9 he felt sure he would end up in a concentration camp (see *443, 489, 527, and 528*). *Invasion 1940: The Nazi Invasion Plan for Britain by SS General Walter Schellenberg* (2000) does not include his name in the 'Special Search List GB' (*The Black Book*), though his publisher, Victor Gollancz, and Ruth Gollancz are listed (she being specifically associated in the list with the Left Book Club).

208/6 up: According to D. J. Taylor (whose biography of Orwell is due in 2003) the 'backward boy' was Bryan Morgan.

289/16–17: It *was* true that Chamberlain gave the vital vote. By 2002 it had become 'common knowledge', even being highlighted in the Channel Four television programme, *Churchill v Hitler: the Duel* (23 February 2002).

298/13: 'Stagolee': Stagolee (or Stackolee or Stagger Lee, two of many variants) was a legendary giant of Black folklore, although as Edward Cray, editor of *The Erotic Muse* (New York, 1969), notes in his introduction, it has 'passed from Negro provenience to general currency' (p. xxxii). He prints the music and seventeen stanzas, with a short introduction, on pp. 45–7. Stagolee made a compact with the Devil and, in exchange, was given a magic Stetson hat. When it is stolen, Stagolee kills the thief. He is arrested and his girl – 'None of that low-down trash' – hustles for him to raise bail money. However, he is executed in the electric chair and his girl is left 'Havin' the electric chair blues . . . for Stagolee'.

537/12, *Cavalry Quarterly*: this has proved difficult to trace. A *Cavalry Journal* was published from April 1920 to June 1966 at Fort Leavenworth, USA. It might have been mistakenly called a quarterly and it was published before 1920 and after 1966 under other names. The Library of Congress (but not the BL) catalogue has an entry for another *Cavalry Journal* (published quarterly) ed. by G. Gilbert Wood. The date given is simply '19–'. Wood (as Clarence Gilbert Wood) was editor of a journal called *Defenders of Our Empire*. The first issue (and perhaps the last?) of 104 pages was published in 1908. It is the sort of thing Orwell might have come across. A search of cavalry libraries revealed nothing.

539/15, a Rule of the Saints: one of Cromwell's attempts to provide a means of ruling England after he had disposed of the Long Parliament. In 1653, men 'fearing God and of approved integrity' were chosen by the army to assist in running the country. They were described as saints. They were unsuccessful and from 1654–56 Cromwell divided England into eleven districts each governed by a Major-General. Some were not too bad but their methods led to a permanent distaste in England for military rule. H. Bedford, *A Vindication of the Church of England* (1710), described the whole period, 1641–60, as 'when saints ruled England'.

Volume XIII

29/9, 'Youth's a stuff will not endure': *Twelfth Night*, 2.3.46.

111/15, 'the other-cheek school': 'whosoever shall smite thee on thy right cheek, turn to him the other also,' Matthew, 5.39.

213/15–16, 'all the ills that humanity is heir to': after 'the thousand natural shocks / That flesh is heir to,' *Hamlet*, 3.1.62–3.

260, note 1: *add*: Captain (Mrs) Lakshmi Sahgal, who was 88 in 2002, stood on behalf of the Communist Party in the Indian Presidential election of that year. She was head of INA's medical unit. She was captured by the Japanese at Singapore in 1942 and joined its forces in fighting the British in Burma. She was then taken prisoner by the British after the battle of Kohima in which the Japanese were routed. (*Daily Telegraph*, 15 June 2002)

328, note 4: *add*: Aung San's daughter, Suu Kyi, born shortly before his murder, led a long fight against the military government of Burma (Myanma). Her National League for Democracy won a landslide victory in

1990 but was not allowed to govern. She was awarded the Nobel Prize for Peace. She was virtually imprisoned for many years but released in May 2002.

426/9, 'the bread one casts on the waters sometimes fetches up in strange places': 'Cast thy bread upon the waters: for thou shalt find it after many days,' Ecclesiastes, 11.1.

499/19 up, 'Those who take the sword perish by the sword': Matthew, 26.52 ('Put up again thy sword into his place: for all they that take the sword shall perish with the sword).

509/15 up: *insert superscript* 8a *after* heart", *and at* 511: *add new footnote:* 8a. From Auden, 'Sir, No Man's Enemy' (1930): 'New styles of architecture, a change of heart'. Also referred to at last line of XII/30.

Volume XIV

279/2 up: Arthur Rackham (1867–1939), author and illustrator, especially of children's books. His drawings are held in many national collections, including those in Barcelona, Vienna, and Tate Britain, London.

291, line 3 of letter: *add superscript footnote reference* 2 *after* a while.
line 20: *make superscript reference* 2 *into reference* 3
add new footnote 2 *(and make existing footnote 2 into footnote 3):*
2. The reason is not known. Much later, on 28 August 1943, Ivor Brown wrote to Orwell asking him if he would like to go to Algiers and Sicily for *The Observer* (2255, XV/208). It may be that Orwell was having discussions about going abroad as early as January 1943. The North Africa campaign was then going well and on 14 January 1943 Churchill and Roosevelt were to meet at Casablanca.

301/13–14 up: passage quoted is from 'Alumnus Football' by Grantland Rice (1880–1954).

Volume XV

292/6 up, 'the mills of God': 'Though the mills of God grind slowly, yet they grind exceeding small', H. W. Longfellow (1807–1882), 'Retribution' (translation from the *Sinngedichte* of Friedrich von Logau).

301/7–8: *for* Ronald was killed in Spain fighting against Franco's forces. *substitute* Ronald Burghes, fought in Spain against Franco's forces; he died on 1 May 1997.

Volume XVI

40/13, Liberty's: Liberty & Co Ltd, was opened by Arthur Lasenby Liberty at 218a Regent Street, London, W1, in 1875 as East India House, because it specialised in selling soft coloured silks from the East. He later extended his premises (it now occupies 210–20) and sold a wider range of Oriental goods, especially Japanese work. Part of the building has a façade in Tudor style featuring timbers from two wooden warships, HMS *Hindustan* and HMS *Impregnable*. The firm had immense influence on fashion. Among its customers were leading figures of the Pre-Raphaelite movement. It won much publicity when its fabrics were chosen for Gilbert and Sullivan's *Patience* in 1881.

40/15, *An Unknown Country*: the correct line is *An Unknown Land*. (It was not corrected because the correct title is given in the index to refer to its review by Orwell, 24.12.1942, XIV, 254.) Orwell described it as 'founded ultimately on Bacon's *New Atlantis*'. It is a 'favourable Utopia' but fails, according to Orwell, because the author cannot describe a near-perfect society in which anyone would wish to live. Its author, Viscount Samuel (1870–1963) was born into a wealthy banking family but, influenced by the shameful conditions in which so many people lived, entered Parliament in 1902 as a Liberal. He held office in Asquith's Liberal Government for the first two years of World War I. He refused office under his successor, Lloyd George, because of what he regarded as the shameful way Asquith had been overthrown.

41/1–4: From a hymn of the sixteenth or seventeenth century, 'Jerusalem, my happy home'. In *The Methodist Hymn Book* (1933), the text reads 'precious stones' for 'chalcedony' (Hymn 655). *Hymns Ancient and Modern* (1916) has only five verses for the eleven in the Methodist book and the text reads very differently. One of the tunes to which it is sung, 'Diana', is a sixteenth-century air. Orwell also quoted it in 615, XII/150; see note 2 on p. 152.

41/5–9: From 'Holy, holy, holy, Lord God Almighty' by Bishop Reginald Heber (1783–1826). The texts of the hymns for this verse are the same in both hymnals quoted in the preceding note (36 and 160) and they have 'Who wert' for Orwell's 'That wast' in the last line.

90/7 up, *Handley Cross*, a hunting tale by Robert Smith Surtees, 1843; with John Leech's illustrations, 1854.

113/20 up: Henry Peter Brougham, 1st Baron Brougham and Vaux (1778–1868), Whig politician; Lord Chancellor, 1830–34. He championed popular education and was involved in the creation of the University of London.

210/10: for details of the Beveridge Report on Social Security, 1942, see XIV, 292–3, 351, 352.

236/6: *Un Chien Andalou* (Orwell had *Le* for *Un*) has been claimed as the first Surrealist film and was made by Luis Buñuel and Salvador Dali in 1929. Plate 143 of *Surrealism* by Patrick Waldberg (1978) illustrated a still from the film. Maurice Nadeau, in his *The History of Surrealism* (New York, 1965), lists five earlier such films from 1925, including Antonin Artaud's *La coquille et le clergyman* (1928). Buñuel and Dali also made *L'Age d'Or*, mentioned on p. 237.

239/1: James Branch Cabell (1879–1958), American novelist, many of his novels being set in a world of medieval myth (Poictesme), in which the hero strives for ideals which he realises are unattainable.

239/5: *Where the Rainbow Ends* was a very successful fairy play which ran for many Christmas seasons from 1911. It was written by Clifford Mills and John Ramsey (= Reginald Owen) and had music by Roger Quilter.

253/4: Wang Ching Wei is identified at 259/22.

277: add to n. 1: The V-1 was first called a P-Plane (Pilotless Plane), *Picture Post*, 1 June 1944.

334/26: *add superscript 2 after* Neill *and take in this footnote:*

2. Homer Tyrrell Lane (1876–1925), author of *Talking to Parents and Teachers* (1928). The 1949 edition had a preface by A. S. Neill. Alexander Sutherland Neill (1883–1973), Scottish educationalist who reacted against what he regarded as his own repressive education. He argued, and put into practice through his school, Summerhill, a libertarian education for children in which there was complete freedom for children to do what they liked, and no discipline. The titles of many of his books indicate his line of thought: *The Problem Child* (1926), *The Problem Parent* (1932), *The Dreadful School* (1937), *The Problem Teacher* (1939) and *The Problem Family* (1948). Among his other books are *Is Scotland Educated?* (1936) and *Summerhill: A Compilation* (1962).

349/26, 'John Thorndyke stories': These stories were written by R. Austin Freeman (1862–1943). They featured Dr Thorndyke, a pathologist-detective. For further details see, XX, 43, note 2.

349/27, 'Carrados stories': Max Carrados was the detective in some of the stories by Ernest Bramah Smith (1869?–1942), published under the shortened name, Max Bramah. Orwell briefly reviewed *The Wallet of Kai Lung* in 1936 (see *321*, X, 492 also note 2), and *The Secret of the League* more fully in 1940 (*655*, XII/212–3).

354/17 up: 'Carlyle, Creasey': Edward Creasy (no second 'e'), 1812–1878. He and Thomas Carlyle (1795–1881) saw the growth of German nationalism under Bismarck in the nineteenth century. Frederick the Great (1712–1786) was idolised by Carlyle, whose six-volume biography was published 1858–65.

428/1, 'B.B.C. . . . C.E.M.A.': see XVI, 388–9 for discussion and 391, note 6. C.E.M.A. (Council of the Encouragement of Music and the Arts) later became the Arts Council.

Volume XVII

63: *add to note 17*: The papers were released in October 1999; see Iain Sproat, 'In all innocence', *TLS*, 29 October 1999, pp. 14–15.

115, footnote 4: *add new last sentence*: Orwell refers to Landau in *Homage to Catalonia*, VI/161.

124, note 1: *Add date of death to* Anthony Powell: 2000 (1905–2000).

186/3 up: *add date of death for* Geoffrey Trease: 1998 (*so:* 1909–1998).

191, footnote 2: *add new sentence*: The essay was published in *Adelphi*, June 1936.

196/11 up: *add superscript footnote reference* 1a *after* Siberia *and add new note*: 1a. He was not exiled to Siberia but to Vologda, north of Moscow.

214/18: *add footnote reference* 2 *after* "Heptameron" *and add new note*: 2. The *Heptameron* is a collection of love stories attributed to Marguerite of Navarre (1492–1549). The title means 'seven days' (compare Boccaccio's *Decameron*).

240/11: *add footnote reference* 1 *after* "Hibbert Journal," *and add new note*: 1. *Hibbert Journal* (1902–70), quarterly devoted to religion, philosophy, sociology, and the arts.

243/9 up: *add footnote reference* 5 *after* Holiday." *and add note to p. 244*: 5. *Hindoo Holiday* is a memoir, not a novel.

244/17, Peter Blundell—"Mr. Podd of Borneo": Peter Blundell was an engineer and planter who worked chiefly in Borneo and Malaya. His real name was Frank Nestlé Butterworth. Most of his books are set in the East. *Mr Podd of Borneo* was published in 1919 and, according to its title-page, was 'The £250 Prize Humorous Novel'. He also wrote *Love Birds in the Coconuts* (1915), *Princess of the Yellow Moon* (1923), and *Star of the Incas* (1928).

257/6 up: *add footnote reference* 3a *after* to say it.' *and add new note on p. 260*: 3a. Attributed to Voltaire in S. G. Tallentyre, *The Friends of Voltaire* (1907).

265, footnote 4, line 2: Wales's *for* England's.

289, footnote 1 *at top of page, line 1: insert after* Oldag; *1905–77 and add at end of note:* He contributed anti-war cartoons to the anarchist press, some of which were collected in *The March of Death* (1943).

357/3 up: *add superscript reference* 1 *after* Sansom. *and add new note on p. 358*: 1. Philip Sansom (1916–1999), writer, editor, cartoonist, and public speaker (especially in Hyde Park). He was associated with *Freedom* and was involved in Syndicalism, the sex-reform movement, and campaigns against capital punishment and for those held in Franco's jails. He worked as a journalist on trade papers.

347–50, 'Good Bad Books'. Notes were requested for some of the authors mentioned. Notes on Leonard Merrick and on the introduction requested (by Graham Greene) can be found, with the introduction, at XVIII/216–19. There are notes on John Davys Beresford at XVI/115 in which Orwell tells him how much he admired *A Candidate for Truth* (1912), the second volume of the Jacob Stahl trilogy; Arthur Morris Binstead at XII/240; for Peter Blundell see 244/17 above; Richard Austin Freeman at XX/43; and Barry Eric Odell Pain (*not* Barrie), at XII/186. Of other authors, in the order mentioned, the following brief notes might be helpful.

Ernest Bramah Smith (1869?–1942) dropped 'Smith' as an author. His first novel, *The Wallet of Kai Lung*, was published in 1900. He created the blind detective, Max Carrados, for the first of the stories in which he featured in 1914. His most remarkable book, *The Secret of the League*, 1907, was written as a result of what became the Labour Party winning 29 seats in 1906 in a House of Commons even larger than that today. He forecasts what would happen with a Labour Party in power with a very big majority with chilling precision. Orwell briefly reviewed the book on 12 July 1940 (XII/ 212–13). The author of *Nineteen Eighty-Four* was puzzled that such a 'decent and kindly writer' as Bramah should envisage such a result which 'we should now describe as Fascist'.

Dr Nikola by **Guy Boothby** (1867–1905) was described by Orwell in a letter to Brenda Salkeld in September 1932 as 'a boy's sixpenny thriller but a first-rate one' (X/268).

Evariste Régis Huc (1813–1860) was a French missionary of the Vincentian Order in China. From 1844 to 1846, with a fellow missionary, Joseph Gabet, he made the journey described in *Travels in Tartary, Thibet, and China*. It was published under both their names in 1851 and translated into English by William Hazlitt (also 1851). He returned to Europe in 1852 and left the Vincentians the following year.

William Pett Ridge (1857–1936) was a prolific story writer publishing over sixty volumes. He also wrote four Cockney plays (1925) and two autobiographies (1923 and 1925).

Edith Nesbit (1858–1924) wrote a number of novels, including *The Incomplete Amorist* (1906), but is remembered for her books for children (some forty). *The Story of the Treasure Seekers* (1899) was the first of a trilogy. Her most justifiably famous book was *The Railway Children* (1906) based on events in her life when separated from her first husband, Hubert Bland, a political journalist, who was in prison. It was filmed in 1970. She and Bland were founder-members of the Fabian Society. Her *Ballads & Lyrics of Socialism* was published in 1908. After Bland died she married Thomas Tucker, a marine engineer.

George Birmingham (= James Owen Hannay; 1865–1950), a prolific novelist many of whose stories have Irish settings. He also wrote theological and devotional works and some travel books including *A Wayfarer in Hungary* (1925). In 1918 he published *A Padre in France*.

Arthur Morris Binstead (1861–1914), author and journalist. Orwell sometimes referred to him as William Binstead. He wrote under the pseudonym, 'Pitcher', for the *Sporting Times* (known from the colour of its newsprint as *The Pink 'Un*). His books include *Gals' Gossip* (1899) and *More Gals' Gossip* (1906).

William Wymark Jacobs (1863–1943), a prolific writer of humorous short stories, many with sea settings, for example, *Many Cargoes*, 1896. He wrote a number of plays and a famous story of the supernatural, *The Monkey's Paw*, dramatised in 1903; it had first appeared in *The Lady of the Barge and other stories* the previous year.

Walter Lionel George (1882–1926) wrote about twenty novels of which *Caliban* (1920) is the best known—or was. **Lord Northcliffe**, on whom it was based, was originally Alfred Harmsworth (1865–1922); he introduced popular newspaper journalism to Britain with the *Daily Mail* in 1896. He acquired *The Times* in 1908. His brother, Harold (1868–1940, Lord

Rothermere), took control of the *Daily Mail* when Northcliffe died. W. L. George also wrote non-fiction, including *Women of To-morrow* (1913), *Anatole France* (1915), *The Intelligence of Women* (1916), and *How to Invest Your Money* (1924).

Ernest Raymond (b. Argentières 1888; d. 1974), educated at Durham University and wrote many novels and some plays (e.g., *The Berg*, 1929, on the loss of the *Titanic*). Orwell reviewed his *A Song of the Tide* (16 November 1940, XII/285–6), described it as less successful than *We, the Accused* but still worth reading. *We, the Accused*, which Orwell thought 'a remarkable novel', was based on the Crippen murder case. Crippen murdered his wife in 1910 and fled to the USA with his mistress, Ethel Le Neve; they were apprehended by what is believed to be the first radio message to a ship leading to an arrest. Raymond was also the author of *The Damascus Gate* (1923).

May Sinclair (Mary Amelia St Clair Sinclair; 1863–1946) is more significant than to be judged as an author of 'good bad books'. She was largely self-educated, interested in the work of T. H. Green (see *A Defence of Idealism*, 1917), served in Belgium during the First World War (see *A Journal of Impressions in Belgium*, 1915), and wrote a pamphlet, *Feminism*, for the Suffragette movement (1912). Her study of the Brontës (*The Three Brontës*, 1912, and *The Three Sisters*, 1914) drew on her interest in psychoanalysis. These were published either side of *The Combined Maze* (1913). Unfortunately, in the 1920s she developed Parkinson's Disease. As *The Feminist Companion to Literature in English* (1990) puts it, 'Generally acknowledged in the 1920s as one of the most important writers of her day, the decline of her reputation is an enigma' (p. 987).

If Winter Comes (1921) by **Arthur Stuart Menteth Hutchinson** (1879–1971) was Hutchinson's most successful book but was not admired by Orwell; in 1936 he said it was a bad book (X/521). Orwell described its success as being due to its being 'about a man who was Good' (with a capital 'G'). Barry Pain parodied it in *If Summer Don't* (1922). Orwell reviewed Hutchinson's *He Looked for a City* on 16 November 1940 (XII/285–6), concluding, 'Anyone wanting a good cry might do worse than *He Looked for a City*.'

Vice Versa: A Lesson for Fathers (1882) by **F. Anstey** (= Thomas Anstey Guthrie; 1856–1934; the 'F' is decorative) comically describes the exchange of the bodies, but not the sensibilities, of a father and son. Mr Bultitude has to attend school and is beaten, as was his son, whilst the son stays at home and gets up to all sorts of mischief. Anstey specialised in fancy, comedy, and stories for children. *The Brass Bottle* (1900), in which a young architect acquires a bottle in which King Solomon had imprisoned a djinn, so enabling him to work magic, was also successful. He published much in *Punch* and also translated seven of Molière's plays (1931 and 1933).

King Solomon's Mines (1885) by **Sir Henry Rider Haggard** (also as Ryder; 1856–1925), author of many novels, mostly romances. Others which were successful include *Allan Quatermain* (1887), *She* (1887), and *Ayesha: the*

Return of She (1905). In 1910 his *Regeneration: on account of the social work of the Salvation Army* was published. He and Rudyard Kipling were friends.

Helen's Babies (1876) by the American author, **John Habberton** (1842–1921), is discussed by Orwell in 'Riding Down from Bangor' (22 November 1946, XVIII/493–97). It was incredibly popular and, as he says, pirated by more than twenty publishers in the British Empire alone. It has 'a sort of sweet innocence'. It tells of a young bachelor prevailed upon to look after two boys, aged five and three, whilst the parents go off on a fortnight's holiday'. He also wrote *Other People's Children*.

360/12 up: *insert between* Gollancz.' *and* Senhouse's:
Mabel Fierz saved the book, for it was she who took it to Moore.

386/18 up: *add footnote reference 2 after* thirteen, *and on 368 after line 14 add new note:* 2. Lawrence never worked in a coalmine.

476/2 up: *omit* Asterisk *and* dash; *substitute* The True Pattern of H. G. Wells *for* Not traced.

Volume XVIII

19, *add new footnote after footnote 1:*
1a. A turnip was a slang term for a large silver watch, popular in the nineteenth century.

114/3: *add new sentence after* 'page': Dr Christopher Pallis (alias Martin Grainger and Maurice Brinton) was later the leading figure in the Solidarity Group during the 1960s and 1970s.

202/2: *insert footnote reference 1a after* sauce," *and at 213/ after line 5 (i.e. after footnote 1): insert new footnote:*
1a. Attributed to Francesco Caracciolo, Duke of Brienza (1752–1799), Neopolitan admiral who, under Nelson, fought the French at Toulon in 1793. The number is usually given as sixty, not one hundred.

241, footnote 3: *add at end of note:* See also, *As You Like It*, 'like the toad, ugly and venomous, / Wears yet a precious jewel in his head' (2.1.13–14).

243, note 8: *add Meyer's date of death:* 2000.

252/7 up: *add superscript footnote reference 1 after* Mandel *and add new note:*
1. Georges Mandel, French Minister of Colonies who opposed capitulation of France in 1940. He was executed by the French Milice under Max Knipping on 6 July 1944. Knipping was executed in 1947.

259/16, 'Only the actions of the just ... in their dust': From James Shirley (1596–1666), 'The Contention of Ajax and Ulysses' (1659). The poem includes the famous lines, 'The glories of our blood and state, / Are shadows, not substantial things'.

267/14 up: Henryk Erlich (not Ehrlich) and Viktor Alter were Polish Jewish Socialist leaders. Their fate only came to light during the course of fierce Soviet protestations that they were not responsible for the massacre of Poles at Katyn, Starobielsk, Kozelsk, and Ostashkov. They claimed the Nazis had committed these atrocities and that this 'slanderous campaign hostile to the

Soviet Union' was 'taken up by the Polish Government [in London]' and 'fanned in every way by Polish official press'. As we now know, it was the Soviets who were guilty of this mass murder. In what is described as a '*Note*' to a very long account, *Keesing's Contemporary Archives* for 24 April to 1 May 1943 (page 5732) states that the two men were arrested when the Soviets invaded Eastern Poland at the time that the Germans were invading from the west. They were held in prison for about 18 months then tried for 'subversive activities' and sentenced to death, but that was commuted to ten years' imprisonment. A month after Germany attacked Russia on 22 June 1941, a Russo-Polish Agreement was signed and the men were released. However, they were re-arrested in December 1941, tried for conducting 'propaganda for an immediate peace with Germany', sentenced to death and executed. On the instructions of Vyacheslav Molotov (1890–1986), Soviet Foreign Minister, this information was passed by Maxim Litvinov (1876–1951), Soviet Ambassador to the USA, to William Green (1873–1952), President of the American Federation of Labor.

It is quite possible that the fates of Erlich and Alter suggested that meted out to Jones, Aaronson and Rutherford in *Nineteen Eighty-Four*. Certainly the Chestnut Tree café is based on Le Closerie des Lilas which Orwell frequented in Paris and where, earlier, Trotsky and Lenin had (like the 'traitors' in Orwell's novel) played chess in order to while away the time.

306/17, 'go to the ant': 'Go to the ant, thou sluggard; consider her ways, and be wise; / Which having no guide, overseer, or ruler / Provideth her meat in the summer, and gathereth her food in the harvest', Proverbs, 6.6–8.

319/13, 'the worm who never turned'; 'The smallest worm will turn, being trodden on', *3 Henry VI*, 2.2.17.

319/16, 19, 20: Eugene Aram; Austin Seven; Duggie: see X, 525, notes 1, 2, and 3.

419/21 up: The Tory Reform Committee ran from 1943–44. It issued a manifesto signed by 41 Conservative Party MPs. Its programme included the retention of compulsory military service after the war; close co-operation with the Dominions, USA, USSR, and China; a policy of full employment with an adequate minimum wage; provision of decent housing; development of education; a welfare service based on Lord Beveridge's report; comprehensive national health service; and encouragement of small traders; it rejected the antithesis between public and private enterprise.

431, note 2, *add*: The Archbishop's Commission for Evangelism was agreed at the Church Assembly of the Church of England in June 1943. The Commission was set up in January 1944 under the chairmanship of the Bishop of Rochester. The Archbishop at the time was Dr William Temple (1881–1944). He was succeeded by Dr Geoffrey Fisher (1887–1972). The Commission was to suggest ways of converting those who accepted the Christian ethic but who rejected the Christian Church. It was charged with examining the ways that the popular press and magazines, the BBC's programme *The Brains Trust*, films, and government propaganda influenced the public.

467: *add new note 3*: In the Anglican Church's *Book of Common Prayer*, 'The Litany, or General Supplication' is a sequence of requests and responses for priest and congregation. It is ordained that it should follow Morning Prayer on Sundays, Wednesdays, and Fridays, and at other times as directed, but this instruction is infrequently carried out in most parish churches nowadays. The requests that Orwell probably has in mind are: 'From lightning and tempest; from plague, pestilence, and famine; from battle and murder; and from sudden death', and 'In all time of our tribulation; in all time of our wealth; in the hour of death, and in the day of judgement'. The response to each is, 'Good Lord, deliver us'.

494/12–13: Artemus Ward (Charles Farrar Browne; 1834–67), American iconoclastic humorist. His best joke, in his own opinion, aimed at the leader of the Mormons, Brigham Young, was, 'The pretty girls in Utah mostly marry Young'.

505, *add new last sentence to footnote 1*: The verse appears in *The Second Jungle Book*, 'The Undertakers', as: 'In August was the Jackal born; / The Rains fell in September; / "Now such a fearful flood as this," / Says he, "I can't remember!"' '

Volume XIX

377/11 up, 'the twelfth': the 'Glorious Twelfth' of August – opening of the grouse-shooting season. Anthony Trollope writes of 'the Twelfth' in *The Duke's Children* (1880), ch. 35.

396/19 up: Feodor Chaliapin (1873–1938), great Russian operatic bass. He was one of the early stars of the gramophone. His most famous role was that of Boris in Moussorgsky's *Boris Godunov*.

369/19 up, 'the Russian Ballet': Orwell is referring to Sergey Diaghilev's Ballets Russes, which he formed in 1909 and which broke up after his death in 1929. With his outstanding dancer, Vaslav Nijinsky, he revolutionised ballet.

405/17 up, 'beasts that perish': 'Nevertheless man being in honour abideth not; he is like the beasts that perish', Psalms, 49.12.

464/16, 'casting motes out of other people's eyes': 'Judge not, that ye be not judged. / And why beholdest thou the mote that is in thy brother's eye, but considerest not the beam that is in thine own eye?', Matthew, 7.1, 3.

Volume XX

100, *add to line 4*: John Platts-Mills (1906–2001), unshakeable apologist for Stalin, he did not believe the Soviets committed atrocities even after Krushchev denounced Stalin in 1956. Expelled from the Labour Party, 1948. Included in Orwell's 'List', App. 9, XX, p. 253, after 'Padmore' but omitted from first edition of *Complete Works* because he was alive when it was published.

Summaries of letters found at University of Texas by Gordon Bowker

Mr Gordon Bowker, in the course of researching his new biography of George Orwell (due 2003), discovered some additional Orwell letters in the J. C. Trewin file at the Harry Ransom Humanities Center, University of Texas at Austin, and has kindly passed the following details to the editor. It is hoped that the full letters will be published at a later stage. They have been given their relevant volume, page, and item numbers here.

XVII, p. 244, *2717A*. To J. C. Trewin,[1] 13 August 1945, Typewritten: Suggests that Cedric Dover (though embittered about 'the colour question') would be 'a useful man man' to have on *The Observer*'s list of reviewers and writers re Asia and, in particular, India (see *2717*). Details about Orwell's submitting his review of 'the Sewell book' (see *2726*).

1. John Courtney Trewin (1908–1990), literary editor of *The Observer*, 1943–48. He was a fine drama critic and writer on the theatre.

XVII, p. 263, *2723A*. To J. C. Trewin, 17 August 1945, Typewritten: Would be on holiday 10–25 September. Was anxious to review 'the Dickens book'. Would it be available before he went away? (See *2739*.)

XIX, p. 34, *3165A*. To David Astor, 30 January 1947, Typewritten: Suggested Hugh Gordon Porteous and G. S. Fraser (spelt 'Frazer') as likely writers. Annotated by Astor for J. C. Trewin asking for his views on Orwell's suggestions. Orwell would speak to Julian Symons (? about undertaking something Orwell was too busy to do?).

XIX, p. 239, *3321A*. Dated only 'Friday' and to an unknown person (but perhaps David Astor), Typewritten. Says Ivor Brown (see *3315*, *n. 1*) had written complaining that material delivered on a Friday was too late. Orwell said he could easily turn in his 'stuff' on Thursdays – or Wednesdays or Tuesdays – if he received books in time. He had been given no notice of the change in scheduling. The letter is typewritten so could not have been sent between 31 October 1947 and 1 May 1948 when, owing to illness, all Orwell's letters were handwritten. It is placed here with Orwell's first letter to Brown.

XIX, p. 399, *3410A*. To J. C. Trewin, 5 June 1948, Handwritten: Will soon let Trewin have review of 'the Attlee book' (see *3419*). Could he review *The Dawn's Delay* by Hugh Kingsmill? No need to send a copy for he already had one (see *3425*).

XX, p. 176, *3702A*. Sonia Brownell for George Orwell, 14 October 1949, Handwritten: Mr Orwell was ill but, if he sent a copy of *1984*, Orwell would sign it. Sonia and Orwell had been married on 13 October (see *3702*). 'Groves' could be Reg Groves. He had preceded Orwell at the Westrope's bookshop, but they did not know each other well.

r

Editorial Note to the Second Edition

Publication of a reprint of this edition enables me to include twelve letters which came to light after the edition was published. Three are from Orwell to Daniel George (Bunting) and two from Lord David Cecil to W. J. Turner in connection with Orwell's *The English People* in the series *Britain in Pictures*. I am grateful to T. E. D. Klein (through the agency of Peter Cannon) for permission to publish the letters to Daniel George of 17 February and 28 December 1944; and to Messrs Maggs Bros. Ltd for permission to publish the letter to him of 10 April 1944. I am grateful to Denis Roy Bentham for supplying the two letters from Lord David Cecil and to Laura Cecil on behalf of the David Cecil Estate for permission to print them; they throw an interesting light on the publication of *The English People*. I am grateful to the Hon. David Astor for finding six letters that illuminate Orwell's relationship with *The Observer*, especially as a reviewer, and also a letter from Avril Dunn to David Astor and for making me photocopies of these. Seven letters are included in Appendix 15; that from Avril Dunn appears on XX/187; the others are incorporated in notes in the body of the text. Professor Patrick Parrinder kindly provided the text for Orwell's obituary of H. G. Wells. There is also a supposed recommendation by Orwell for a book published in 1952.

The edition includes a corrected Spanish text of item 374A, the report to the Tribunal for Espionage and High Treason in Valencia, and an improved translation. I am very grateful to Robert A. McNeil, Head of Hispanic Collections, Bodleian Library, Oxford, for providing these and for checking documents in Barcelona.

I have been enabled to correct typographical errors, amend mistakes, and provide some additional notes and dates of the deaths of those who have died since the edition was published. The extent and manner of additions has been restricted by the necessity of retaining the existing pagination to avoid re-indexing but some additional allusions are listed at the very end of Volume XX. I am deeply grateful to all those who wrote, and especially to Jeffrey Meyers, Nicolas Walter (1934–2000), Gordon Bowker, Bartek Zborski and Dr Robert Fyson, who went to considerable trouble to help me. Sharp-eyed readers for the Folio Society spotted a number of typographical errors. I am also grateful to the publishers, Secker & Warburg, for allowing these additions and corrections.

P. D.
20 June 2002